CHILTON'S

REPAIR MANUAL

CHRYSLER FRONT WHEEL DRIVE 1981–92

All U.S. and Canadian models of Chrysler/Dodge/Plymouth Acclaim, Aries, Caravelle, Daytona, Dynasty, E-Class, Executive Sedan, Imperial, Lancer, Laser, Lebaron, Monaco, New Yorker, Reliant, Shadow, Spirit, Stealth, Sundance, Town & Country, 400 and 600

Sr. Vice President	Ronald A. Hoxter
Publisher and Editor-In-Chief	Kerry A. Freeman, S.A.E.
Managing Editors	Peter M. Conti, Jr. □ W. Calvin Settle, Jr., S.A.E.
Assistant Managing Editor	Nick D'Andrea
Senior Editors	Richard J. Rivele, S.A.E. □ Ron Webb
Director of Manufacturing	Mike D'Imperio
Manager of Manufacturing	John F. Butler
Editor	Anthony Tortorici A.S.E., S.A.E.

CHILTON BOOK COMPANY

ONE OF THE DIVERSIFIED PUBLISHING COMPANIES,
A PART OF CAPITAL CITIES/ABC, INC.

SAFETY NOTICE

Proper service and repair procedures are vital to the safe, reliable operation of all motor vehicles, as well as the safety of those performing repairs. The book outlines procedures for servicing and repairing vehicles using safe effective methods. The procedures contain many NOTES, CAUTIONS and WARNINGS which should be followed along with standard safety procedures to eliminate the possibility of personal injury or improper service which could damage the vehicle or compromise its safety.

It is important to note that repair procedures and techniques, tools and parts for servicing motor vehicles, as well as the skill and experience of the individual performing the work vary widely. It is not possible to anticipate all of the conceivable ways or conditions under which vehicles may be serviced, or to provide cautions as to all of the possible hazards that may result. Standard and accepted safety precautions and equipment should be used during cutting, grinding, chiseling, prying, or any other process that can cause material removal or projectiles.

Some procedures require the use of tools specially designed for a specific purpose. Before substituting another tool or procedure, you must be completely satisfied that neither your personal safety, nor the performance of the vehicle will be endangered.

Although the information in this guide is based on industry sources and is as complete as possible at the time of publication, the possibility exists that the manufacturer made later changes which could not be included here. While striving for total accuracy, Chilton Book Company cannot assume responsibility for any errors, changes, or omissions that may occur in the compilation of this data.

PART NUMBERS

Part numbers listed in the reference are not recommendations by Chilton for any product by brand name. They are references that can be used with interchange manuals and aftermarket supplier catalogs to locate each brand supplier's discrete part number.

SPECIAL TOOLS

Special tools are recommended by the vehicle manufacturer to perform their specific job. Use has been kept to a minimum, but where absolutely necessary, they are referred to in the text by the part number of the tool manufacturer. These tools can be purchased, under the appropriate part number, from Miller Special Tools, Utica Tool Co., 32615 Park La., Garden City, MI 48135 or an equivalent tool can be purchased locally from a tool supplier or parts outlet. Before substituting any tool for the one recommended, read the SAFETY NOTICE at the top of this page.

ACKNOWLEDGEMENTS

Chilton Book Company expresses appreciation to Chrysler Corp., Detroit Michigan for their generous assistance.

Manufactured in the United States of America
1234567890   1098765432

Chilton's Repair Manual: Chrysler Front Wheel Drive 1981–92
ISBN 0-8019-8367-3 pbk.
Library of Congress Catalog Card No. 91-??????

CONTENTS

GENERAL INFORMATION and MAINTENANCE

ENGINE PERFORMANCE and TUNE-UP

ENGINE and ENGINE OVERHAUL

EMISSION CONTROLS

FUEL SYSTEM

CHASSIS ELECTRICAL

General Information and Maintenance

1

HOW TO USE THIS BOOK

Chilton's Repair Manual for Chrysler Front Wheel Drive cars is intended to help you learn more about the inner workings of your vehicle and save you money on its upkeep and operation.

The first two chapters will be the most used, since they contain maintenance and tune-up information and procedures. Studies have shown that a properly tuned and maintained car can get at least 10% better gas mileage than an out-of-tune car. The other chapters deal with some of the more complex systems of your car. Operating systems from engine through brakes are covered to the extent that the do-it-yourselfer becomes mechanically involved. It will give you detailed instructions to help you change your own oil, filters, brake pads and shoes, replace spark plugs, and do many more jobs that will save you money, give you personal satisfaction, and help you avoid expensive problems.

A secondary purpose of this manual is a reference for owners who want to understand their car and/or their mechanics better. In this case, no tools at all are required.

BEFORE REMOVING ANY BOLTS, READ THROUGH THE ENTIRE PROCEDURE AND REFER TO ALL THE NECESSARY ILLUSTRATIONS. This will give you the overall view of what tools and supplies will be required. There is nothing more frustrating than having to walk to the bus stop on Monday morning because you were short one bolt on Sunday afternoon. So read ahead and plan ahead. Each operation should be approached logically and all procedures thoroughly understood before attempting any work.

All chapters contain adjustments, maintenance, removal and installation procedures. When repair is not considered practical, we tell you how to remove the part and then how to install the new or rebuilt replacement. In this way, you at least save the labor costs. Backyard repair of such components as the alternator is just not practical.

Two basic mechanic's rules should be mentioned here. One, whenever the left side of the car or engine is referred to, it is meant to specify the driver's side of the car. Conversely, the right side of the car means the passenger's side. Secondly, most screws and bolt are removed by turning counterclockwise, and tightened by turning clockwise.

Safety is always the most important rule. Constantly be aware of the dangers involved in working on an automobile and take the proper precautions. (See the section "Servicing Your Vehicle Safely" and the SAFETY NOTICE on the acknowledgement page.)

Pay attention to the instructions provided. There are 3 common mistakes in mechanical work:

1. Incorrect order of assembly, disassembly or adjustment. When taking something apart or putting it together, doing things in the wrong order usually justs cost you extra time; however, it CAN break something. Read the entire procedure before beginning disassembly. Do everything in the order in which the instructions say you should do it, even if you can't immediately see a reason for it. When you're taking apart something that is very intricate (for example, a carburetor), you might want to draw a picture of how it looks when assembled at one point in order to make sure you get everything back in its proper position. (We will supply exploded view whenever possible). When making adjustments, especially tune-up adjustments, do them in order; often, one adjustment affects another, and you cannot expect even satisfactory results unless each adjustment is made only when it cannot be changed by any order.

2. Overtorquing (or undertorquing). While it is more common for over-torquing to cause damage, undertorquing can cause a fastener to vibrate loose causing serious damage. Especial-

ly when dealing with aluminum parts, pay attention to torque specifications and utilize a torque wrench in assembly. If a torque figure is not available, remember that if you are using the right tool to do the job, you will probably not have to strain yourself to get a fastener tight enough. The pitch of most threads is so slight that the tension you put on the wrench will be multiplied many, many times in actual force on what you are tightening. A good example of how critical torque is can be seen in the case of spark plug installation, especially where you are putting the plug into an aluminum cylinder head. Too little torque can fail to crush the gasket, causing leakage of combustion gases and consequent overheating of the plug and engine parts. Too much torque can damage the threads, or distort the plug which changes the spark gap.

There are many commercial products available for ensuring that fasteners won't come loose, even if they are not torqued just right (a very common brand is Loctite®). If you're worried about getting something together tight enough to hold, but loose enough to avoid mechanical damage during assembly, one of these products might offer substantial insurance. Read the label on the package and make sure the products is compatible with the materials, fluids, etc. involved before choosing one.

3. Crossthreading. This occurs when a part such as a bolt is screwed into a nut or casting at the wrong angle and forced. Cross threading is more likely to occur if access is difficult. It helps to clean and lubricate fasteners, and to start threading with the part to be installed going straight in. Then, start the bolt, spark plug, etc. with your fingers. If you encounter resistance, unscrew the part and start over again at a different angle until it can be inserted and turned several turns without much effort. Keep in mind that many parts, especially spark plugs, used tapered threads so that gentle turning will automatically bring the part you're treading to the proper angle if you don't force it or resist a change in angle. Don't put a wrench on the part until its's been turned a couple of turns by hand. If you suddenly encounter resistance, and the part has not seated fully, don't force it. Pull it back out and make sure it's clean and threading properly.

Always take your time and be patient; once you have some experience, working on your car will become an enjoyable hobby.

TOOLS AND EQUIPMENT

It would be impossible to catalog each and every tool that you may need to perform all the operations included in this manual. It would also not be wise for the amateur to rush out and buy an expensive set of tools on the theory that he may need one of them at some time. The best approach is to proceed slowly, gathering together a good quality set of those tools that are used most frequently. Don't be misled by the low cost of bargain tools. It is far better to spend a little more for quality, name brand tools. Forged wrenches, 6- or 12-point sockets and fine-tooth ratchets are by far preferable to their less expensive counterparts. As any good mechanic can tell you, there are few worse experiences than trying to work on a car or truck with bad tools. Your monetary savings will be far outweighed by frustration and mangled knuckles.

Begin accumulating those tools that are used most frequently; those associated with routine maintenance and tune-up. In addition to the normal assortment of screwdrivers and pairs of pliers, you should have the following tools for routine maintenance jobs:

1. SAE and Metric wrenches, sockets and combination open end/box end wrenches
2. Jackstands for support
3. Oil filter wrench
4. Oil filler spout or funnel
5. Grease gun for chassis lubrication
6. Hydrometer for checking the battery
7. A low flat pan for draining oil
8. Lots of rags for wiping up the inevitable mess.

In addition to the above items, there are several others that are not absolutely necessary, but are handy to have around. These include oil drying compound, a transmission funnel, and the usual supply of lubricants, antifreeze and fluids, although these can be purchased as needed. This is a basic list for routine maintenance, but only your personal needs can accurately determine your list of tools.

The next list of tools is for tune-ups. While the tools involved here are slightly more sophisticated, they need not be outrageously expensive. There are several inexpensive tach/dwell meters on the market that are every bit as good for the average mechanic as a $100.00 professional model. Just be sure that the one you buy shows at least 1,200–1,500 rpm on the tach scale, and that it works on 4, 6, and 8-cylinder engines. A basic list of tune-up equipment would include:

1. Tach/dwell meter.
2. Spark plug wrench.
3. Timing light (preferably a DC, power type light that works from the battery).
4. A set of flat feeler gauges.
5. A set of round wire spark plug gauges.

In addition to these basic tools, there are several other tools and gauges you may find useful. These include:

1. A compression gauge. The screw-in type takes more time to use, but eliminates the possibility of a faulty reading due to escaping pressure.

2. A manifold vacuum gauge.

3. A test light.

4. An induction meter. This is used for determining whether or not there is current in a wire. These are handy for use if a wire is broken somewhere in a wiring harness. As a final note, you will probably find a torque wrench necessary for all but the most basic work. The bar type models are perfectly adequate, although the newer click type are more precise.

Special Tools

NOTE: *Special tools are occasionally necessary to perform a specific job or are recommended to make a job easier. Their use has been kept to a minimum. When a special tool is indicated, it will be referred to by manufacturer's part number, and, where possible, an illustration of the tool will be provided so that an equivalent tool may be used.*

Some special tools are available commercially from major tool manufacturers. Others for your Chyrsler car can be purchased from your dealer or from Utica Tool Co. (see the copyright page for the complete address).

SERVICING YOUR VEHICLE SAFELY

It is virtually impossible to anticipate all of the hazards involved with maintenance and service but care and common sense will prevent most accidents. The rules of safety for mechanics range from "don't smoke around gasoline" to "use the proper tool for the job". The trick to avoiding injuries is to develop safe work habits and take every possible precaution. Two critical items are working at a sensible pace and visualizing what you will be doing and what will happen before you perform each step of an operation.

Do's

• Do keep a fire extinguisher and first aid kit within easy reach.

• Do wear safety glasses or goggles when cutting, drilling, grinding or prying. If you wear glasses for the sake of vision, they should be made of hardened "safety" glass that can serve also as protection. If they are not of hardened glass, you should wear safety goggles over your regular glasses.

• Do shield your eyes whenever you work

around the battery. Batteries contain sulphuric acid. In case of contact with the eyes or skin, flush the area with water or a mixture of water and baking soda and get medical attention immediately.

• Do use jackstands for any undercar service. The bumper jack which comes with the car is for raising the vehicle when the consequences of having it fall are minimal; jackstands are for making sure the vehicle stays raised until you want it to come down. Whenever your vehicle is raised, block the wheels remaining on the ground and set the parking brake.

• Do use adequate ventilation when working with any chemicals or hazardous materials.

• Do disconnect the negative battery cable when working on the electrical system. The secondary ignition system can contain up to 40,000 volts.

• Do follow manufacturer's directions whenever working with potentially hazardous materials. Both brake fluid and antifreeze are poisonous if taken internally.

• Do properly maintain your tools. Loose hammerheads, mushroomed punches and chisels, frayed or poorly grounded electrical cords, excessively worn screwdrivers, spread wrenches, cracked sockets, slipping ratchets, or faulty droplight sockets can cause accidents.

• Do use the proper size and type of tool for the job being done.

• Do, whenever possible, pull on a wrench handle rather than push on it, and adjust your stance to prevent a fall when a bolt suddenly breaks loose.

• Do be sure that adjustable wrenches are tightly closed on the nut or bolt and pulled so that the face is on the side of the fixed jaw.

• Do select a wrench or socket that fits the nut or bolt. The wrench or socket should sit straight, not cocked.

• Do strike squarely with a hammer; avoid glancing blows.

• Do set the parking brake and block the drive wheels if the work must be done with the engine running.

Don'ts

• Don't run an engine in a garage or anywhere else without proper ventilation — EVER! Carbon monoxide is poisonous; it takes a long time to leave the human body and you can build up a deadly supply of it in your system by simply breathing a little every day. You will not be bothered by a strong smell of exhaust and cannot smell carbon monoxide. You will not realize you are slowly poisoning yourself. Always use power vents, windows, fans or open the garage door.

• Don't work around moving parts while wearing a necktie or other loose clothing. Short sleeves are much safer than long, loose sleeves; hard-toed shoes with neoprene soles protect your toes and give a better grip on slippery surfaces. Jewelry such as watches, fancy belt buckles, beads or body adornment of any kind is not safe working around a truck. Long hair should be secured under a hat or cap.

• Don't use pockets for toolboxes. A fall or bump can drive a screwdriver deep into your body. Even a wiping cloth hanging from the back pocket can wrap around a spinning shaft or fan.

• Never attempt to pry out a part such as a freeze plug with a screwdriver. If the plug or other item suddenly comes loose, this, too, could drive the screwdriver into your body.

• Don't smoke when working around gasoline, cleaning solvent or other flammable material.

• Don't use gasoline to wash your hands; there are excellent soaps available. Gasoline may contain lead, and lead can enter the body through a cut, accumulating in the body until you are very ill. Gasoline also removes all the natural oils from the skin so that bone dry hands will absorb oil and grease.

• Don't use gasoline as a solvent, either. It is highly flammable. Use a non-volatile solvent intended for safe use in parts cleaning

• Don't service the air conditioning system unless you are equipped with the necessary tools and training. The refrigerant, R-12, when released into the air, will instantly freeze any surface it contacts, including your eyes. Although the refrigerant is normally non-toxic, R-12 becomes a deadly poisonous gas in the presence of an open flame. One good whiff of the vapors from burning refrigerant can be fatal. So, never smoke or have any other source of flame around when there may be leaking refrigerant gas.

MODEL IDENTIFICATION

NOTE: *For all Chrysler front wheel drive vehicles starting in 1989 model year refer to the "Model Chart" as necessary. Some vehicles may change body model codes from year to year, some similar name vehicles may have two different body model codes.*

Chrysler K cars include the Plymouth Reliant, Dodge Aries, Dodge 600 hardtop and convertible, and Chrysler LeBaron, Town & Country, and Limousine. The Reliant and Aries come in 2-door and 4-door sedan and station wagon

VEHICLE IDENTIFICATION CHART

Body	Vehicle Code	Vehicle Name	Body Style	Series
	C	LeBaron Landau	41	Premium
	D	Spirit	41	High
	D	Spirit LE	41	Premium
AA	D	Spirit ES	41	Performance/Image
	P	Acclaim	41	High
	P	Acclaim LE	41	Premium
	P	Acclaim LX	41	Performance/Image
	C	New Yorker Salon	41	High
AC	C	New Yorker Landau	41	Special
	D	Dynasty	41	High
	D	Dynasty LE	41	Premium
	V	Daytona	24	Low
AG	V	Daytona ES	24	High Special
	V	Daytona Shelby	24	Performance/Image
AJ	C	LeBaron	21, 27	High
	C	LeBaron	21, 27	Premium
AL	Z	Omni	44	Economy
	M	Horizon	44	Economy
AP	D	Shadow	24, 44	Low/High
	P	Sundance	24, 44	Low/High
AY	C	New Yorker 5th Avenue	41	Special
	C	Imperial	41	Premium

(Model chart)

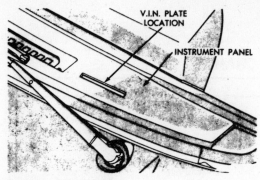

Location of V.I.N. plate

styles. The Chrysler K cars may be either hard-tops or convertibles.

The Chrysler E cars are the Plymouth Caravelle and Dodge 600 4-door sedans and the Chrysler New Yorker 4-door sedan and Turbo 4-door sedan. Model information is contained in digits 1–5 of the Vehicle Identification Number. See the chart below for a specific listing of the codes.

The P cars include the Plymouth Sundance and Dodge Shadow.

The Dodge Daytona and Chrysler Laser are G cars. The old style Chrysler Laser was produced only up until 1986. The new style Chrysler Laser was introduced in the 1990 model year.

The Dodge Lancer and LeBaron GTS are H cars.

The Dynasty and New Yorker are C body vehicles (1988).

The LeBaron coupe and convertible are J body vehicles (1987–88)

SERIAL NUMBER IDENTIFICATION

Vehicle

The vehicle serial number is located on a plate on the top left side of the instrument panel and is visible through the windshield. The VIN consists of 17 elements embossed on a gray colored plate.

Engine

All engine assemblies carry an engine identification number (EIN). The 135 cu. in. (2.2 Liter) engine identification number is located on the left rear face of the block directly under the head. The 156 cu. in. (2.6 Liter) identification number is located on the left side of the block between the core plug and the rear of the block on models through 1985. In 1986, the 2.6 liter Mitsubishi built engine was replaced by a 2.5 li-

ter powerplant developed jointly by Mitsubishi and Chrysler and manufactured in the U.S. The 2.5 liter engine's identification tag is located on the left side of the block between the core plug and the rear face of the block (the "rear" face is the end of the block nearer the radiator).

On the 3.0L and 3.3L engines, the EIN is located on the engine block directly under the cylinder head. On the Stealth and (1990–92) Laser vehicles, the engine model number is stamped at the front side on the top edge of the cylinder block. On the Dodge Monaco vehicle, the engine identification tag is attached to the right side of the cylinder block below the exhaust manifold.

In addition to the EIN, some engines have a serial number, which must be referred to when ordering engine replacement parts. The serial number on the 135 cu. in. (2.2 Liter) engine is located on the rear face of the block directly below the head. On the 156 cu. in. (2.6 Liter) engine it is located on the right front side of the engine block, adjacent to the exhaust manifold. On the 2.5 liter engine, it is located on the right rear (dash panel) side of the block, adjacent to and near the exhaust manifold stud.

Transaxle

The Transaxle Identification Number is stamped on a boss located on the upper part of the transaxle housing. Every transaxle also carries an assembly part number, which is also required for parts ordering purposes. On the A-412 manual transaxle, it is located on the top of the housing, between the timing window and the differential. On all other types of manual transaxles, this number is located on a metal tag attached to the front of the transaxle. On automatic models, it is stamped on a pad located just above the oil pan at the rear of the unit. On the Dodge Monaco vehicle, the transaxle identification tag is on the left (driver) side of the case just above the oil pan. These transaxles also have an additional number located on the upper edge of the bell housing.

ROUTINE MAINTENANCE

Air Cleaner
REMOVAL AND INSTALLATION

NOTE: *Refer to the necessary illustration of your engine for removal and installation of the air cleaner element use the following service procedures as guide for this repair.*

2.2 Liter Carbureted Engines

NOTE: *Make sure you perform the steps in exactly the sequence described below, or the*

VIN CODE CHART

Year	1981	1982	1983	1984
Position 1 Country of Origin	1—US	1—US	1—US	1—US 2—Canada 3—Mexico 4—Japan
2 Make	B—Dodge P—Plymouth	B—Dodge C—Chrysler P—Plymouth	B—Dodge C—Chrysler P—Plymouth	B—Dodge C—Chrysler P—Plymouth
3 Gen'l Vehicle Type	3—Pass. Car	3—Pass. Car	3—Pass. Car	3—Pass. Car
4 Passenger Safety System	B—Man. Seat Belts	B—Man. Seat Belts D—3000 lbs. GVW	B—Man. Seat Belts D—3000 lbs. GVW	B—Man. Seat Belts D—3000 lbs. GVW
5 Car Line	K—Aries & Reliant	C—Le Baron D—Aries P—Reliant V—400	C—Le Baron D—Aries E—600 D—Reliant T—New Yorker V—400	C—Le Baron D—Aries E—600 M—Horizon P—Reliant T—New Yorker/ E-Class V—600
6 Series	1—Economy 2—Low 3—High 5—Premium	1—Economy 2—Low 4—High 5—Premium 6—Special	1—Economy 2—Low 4—High 5—Premium 6—Special	1—Economy 2—Low 4—High 5—Premium 6—Special
7 Body Style	1—2 Dr. Sedan 4—2 + 2 Hatchback 5—2 Dr. Convertible 6—4 Dr. Sedan 8—4 Dr. Hatchback 9—4 Dr. Wagon	1—2 Dr. Sedan 2—2 Dr. Specialty Hardtop 4—2 + 2 Hatchback 5—2 Dr. Convertible 6—4 Dr. Sedan 8—4 Dr. Hatchback 9—4 Dr. Wagon	1—2 Dr. Sedan 2—2 Dr. Specialty Hardtop 3—2 Dr. Hardtop 4—2 Dr. Hatchback 5—2 Dr. Convertible 6—4 Dr. Sedan 8—4 Dr. Hatchback 9—4 Dr. Wagon	1—2 Dr. Sedan 2—2 Dr. Specialty Hardtop 3—2 Dr. Hardtop 4—2 Dr. Hatchback 5—2 Dr. Convertible 6—4 Dr. Sedan 8—4 Dr. Hatchback 9—4 Dr. Wagon
8 Engine	B—2.2L D—2.6L	B—2.2L C—2.2L Turbocharged D—2.6L	C—2.2L G—2.6L	C—2.2L D—2.2L EFI E—2.2L Turbocharged G—2.6L
9 Check Digit	The digit in position 9 is used for VIN verification. "1–9", "0", or "X"			
10 Model Year	B—'81	C—'82	D—'83	E—'84
11 Assembly Plant	C—Jefferson D—Belvidere F—Newark	C—Jefferson D—Belvidere F—Newark G—St. Louis	C—Jefferson D—Belvidere F—Newark G—St. Louis	C—Jefferson D—Belvidere F—Newark G—St. Louis X—Missouri
12–17 Sequence Number	These digits identify your particular car			

VIN CODE CHART (cont.)

1985	1986	1987	1988
1—US	1—US	1—US	1—US
2—Canada	2—Canada	2—Canada	2—Canada
3—Mexico	3—Mexico	3—Mexico	3—Mexico
4—Japan	4—Japan	4—Japan	4—Japan
B—Dodge	B—Dodge	B—Dodge	B—Dodge
C—Chrysler	C—Chrysler	C—Chrysler	C—Chrysler
P—Plymouth	P—Plymouth	P—Plymouth	P—Plymouth
3—Pass. Car	3—Pass. Car	3—Pass. Car	3—Pass. Car
			7—Truck
B—Man. Seat Belts	B—Man. Seat Belts	B—Man. Seat Belts	B—Man. Seat Belts
D—3000 lbs. GVW	D—3000 lbs. GVW	D—3000 lbs. GVW	D—3000 lbs. GVW
C—Le Baron/ET5	C—Le Baron	C—Le Baron	D—Dynasty
D—Aries	D—Aries	D—Aries	C—New Yorker Landau
E—600	E—600	E—600	J—Caravelle
T—New Yorker	T—New Yorker	T—New Yorker	E—600
P—Reliant	P—Reliant	X—Lancer	T—New Yorker Turbo
V—600	V—600	L—Caravelle (Canada)	V—Daytona
	A—V Daytona	M—Horizon	X—Lancer
	A—C Laser	P—Reliant	H—Le Baron GTS
	H—Le Baron GTS	J—Caravelle (U.S.)	J—Le Baron
		Z—Omni	P—Reliant
		A—V Daytona	D—Aries
		H—Le Baron GTS	C—Le Baron
		S—Sundance	S—Sundance
		S—Shadow	S—Shadow
		J—Le Baron	
1—Economy	1—Economy	1—Economy	1—Economy
2—Low	2—Low	2—Low	2—Low
4—High	4—High	3—Medium	3—Medium
5—Premium	5—Premium	4—High	4—High
6—Special	6—Special	5—Premium	5—Premium
		6—Special	6—Special
1—2 Dr. Sedan	1—2 Dr. Sedan	1—2 Dr. Sedan	1—2 Dr. Sedan
2—2 Dr. Specialty Hardtop	2—2 Dr. Specialty Hardtop	3—2 Dr. Hardtop	3—2 Dr. Hardtop
3—2 Dr. Hardtop	3—2 Dr. Hardtop	4—2 Dr. Hatchback	4—2 Dr. Hatchback
4—2 Dr. Hatchback	4—2 Dr. Hatchback	5—2 Dr. Convertible	5—2 Dr. Convertible
5—2 Dr. Convertible	5—2 Dr. Convertible	6—4 Dr. Sedan	6—4 Dr. Sedan
6—4 Dr. Sedan	6—4 Dr. Sedan	8—4 Dr. Hatchback	8—4 Dr. Hatchback
8—4 Dr. Hatchback	8—4 Dr. Hatchback	9—4 Dr. Wagon	9—4 Dr. Wagon
9—4 Dr. Wagon	9—4 Dr. Wagon		
C—2.2L	C—2.2L	C—2.2L	C—2.2L
D—2.2L EFI	D—2.2L EFI	D—2.2L EFI	D—2.2L EFI
E—2.2L Turbocharged	E—2.2L Turbo	E—2.2L Turbo	E—2.2L Turbo
G—2.6L	K—2.5L	K—2.5L	K—2.5L
			3—3.0L
F—'85	G—'86	H—1987	J—1988
C—Jefferson	A—Outer Drive	A—Outer Drive	A—Outer Drive
D—Belvidere	C—Jefferson	C—Jefferson	C—Jefferson
F—Newark	D—Belvidere	D—Belvidere	D—Belvidere
G—St. Louis 1	F—Newark	F—Newark	E—Modena
K—Pillette Road	G—St. Louis	G—St. Louis	F—Newark
N—Sterling	K—Pillette Road	K—Pillette Road	G—St. Louis
R—Windsor	N—Sterling	N—Sterling Heights	N—Sterling
T—Toluca	R—Windsor	R—Windsor	R—Windsor
W—Clairpointe	T—Toluca	T—Toluca	T—Toluca
X—St. Louis 2	X—St. Louis 2	X—St. Louis 2	W—Kenosha
			X—St. Louis 2

1989 V.I.N. CODE CHART

Position	Code Options			Interpretation
1	1 = United States	2 = Canada	3 = Mexico	Country of Origin
2	B = Dodge	C = Chrysler	P = Plymouth	Make
3	3 = Passenger		7 = Truck	Type of Vehicle

4	A = Airbag
	B = Manual Seat Belt
	C = Automatic Seat Belt
			X = Driver Airbag, Passenger
			   Manual Seat Belt
			Y = Driver Airbag, Passenger
			   Automatic Seat Belt
				Passenger Safety System

5	C = New Yorker Landau H = LeBaron GTS J = LeBaron H = Lancer	K = Aries P = Shadow C = Dynasty L = Horizon	K = Reliant P = Sundance G = Daytona L = Omni	Line
6	1 = Economy 2 = Low	3 = Medium 4 = High	5 = Premium 6 = Special	Series
7	1 = 2 Dr. Sedan 3 = 2 Dr. Hardtop 4 = 2 Dr. Hatchback	5 = 2 Dr. Convertible 6 = 4 Dr. Sedan	8 = 4 Dr. Hatchback 9 = 4 Dr. Wagon	Body Style
8	A = 2.2L Turbo II C = 2.2L	D = 2.2L E.F.I. E = 2.2L Turbo	K = 2.5L 3 = 3.0L	Engine
9*	(1 thru 9, 0 or X)			Check Digit
10	K = 1989			Model Year
11	A = Outer Drive C = Jefferson D = Belvidere F = Newark	G = St. Louis 1 N = Sterling Heights W = Kenosha	X = St. Louis 2 R = Windsor T = Toluca	Assembly Plant
12 thru 17	(6 Digits)			Sequence Number

*Digit in position 9 is used for V.I.N. verification.

1990 V.I.N. CODE CHART

Position	Code Options			Interpretation
1	1 = United States	2 = Canada	3 = Mexico	Country of Origin
2	B = Dodge	C = Chrysler	P = Plymouth	Make
3	3 = Passenger			Type of Vehicle

4	A = Airbag
	B = Manual Seat Belt
	C = Automatic Seat Belt
			X = Driver Airbag, Passenger
			   Manual Seat Belt
			Y = Driver Airbag, Passenger
			   Automatic Seat Belt
				Passenger Safety System

5	A = Chrysler LeBaron Landau C = Dynasty A = Spirit A = Acclaim C = New Yorker Landau	G = Daytona J = Chrysler LeBaron L = Omni L = Horizon	P = Shadow P = Sundance Y = New Yorker 5th Avenue/Imperial	Line
6	1 = Economy 2 = Low	4 = High 5 = Premium	6 = Special/Sport 7 = Performance Image	Series
7	1 = 2 Dr. Coupe 4 = 2 Dr. Hatchback	5 = 2 Dr. Convertible 6 = 4 Dr. Sedan	8 = 4 Dr. Hatchback	Body Style
8	C = 2.2L Turbo II D = 2.2L E.F.I.	J = 2.5L Turbo K = 2.5L E.F.I.	3 = 3.0L R = 3.3L	Engine
9*	(1 thru 9, 0 or X)			Check Digit
10	L = 1990			Model Year
11	A = Outer Drive D = Belvidere C = Jefferson F = Newark	G = St. Louis 1 H = Bramalea	N = Sterling Heights T = Toluca	Assembly Plant
12 thru 17	(6 Digits)			Sequence Number

*Digit in position 9 is used for V.I.N. verification.

VEHICLE IDENTIFICATION NUMBER DECODING CHART

POSITION	INTERPRETATION	CODE OPTIONS	
1	Country	1 = United States	2 = Canada
2	Make	E = Eagle	B = Dodge
3	Vehicle type	3 = Passenger car	
4	Other	C = Automatic seat belt Y = Driver air bag, passenger automatic seat belt	X = Driver air bag, passenger manual seat belt
5	Line	B = Dodge Monaco	B = Eagle Premier
6	Series	5 = Premium line	6 = Special/Sport
7	Body	6 = 4 Door Sedan	
8	Engine	U = 3.0 Liter	
9①	Check digit	(1 through 9, 0 Orx)	
10	Model year	M = 1991	
11	Assembly Plant	H = Bramelea	
12 through 17	Sequence number	(6 Digits)	

① Digit in Position 9 is used for V.I.N. Verification.

VEHICLE IDENTIFICATION NUMBER DECODING CHART

POSITION	INTERPRETATION	CODE OPTIONS		
1	Country of Origin	1 = United States	2 = Canada	3 = Mexico
2	Make	B = Dodge	C = Chrysler	P = Plymouth
3	Type of Vehicle	3 = Passenger Car		
4	Passenger Safety System	C = Automatic Seat Belt X = Driver Airbag/Passenger Manual Seat Belt Y = Driver Airbag/Passenger Automatic Seat Belt		
5	Line	A = Chrysler-LeBaron (4 door) A = Dodge-Spirit, Spirit LE, Spirit LS A = Plymouth-Acclaim, Acclaim LE, Acclaim LX C = Chrysler-New Yorker Salon C = Dodge-Dynasty, Dynasty LE (US) G = Dodge-Daytona, Daytona ES, Daytona Shelby J = Chrysler-LeBaron (2 door) N = Chrysler-Dynasty, Dynasty LE (Canada) P = Dodge-Shadow America, Shadow, Shadow ES P = Plymouth-Sundance America, Sundance, Sundance RS Y = Chrysler-Fifth Avenue, Chrysler Imperial		
6	Series	1 = Economy Line 2 = Low Line 4 = High Line 5 = Premium Line 6 = Sport/Special 7 = Perform/Image		
7	Body Style	1 = 2 Door Coupe 4 = 2 Door Hatchback 5 = Convertible 6 = 4 Door Sedan 8 = 4 Door Hatchback		
8	Engine	A = 2.2L Turbo III D = 2.2L EFI J = 2.5L Turbo K = 2.5L EFI L = 3.8L EFI R = 3.3L EFI 3 = 3.0L MPI		
9	Model Year	M = 1991		
10	Assembly Plant	D = Belvidere F = Newark G = St. Louis I N = Sterling Heights T = Toluca-Mexico		
12 through 17 = Vehicle Build Sequence				

VEHICLE IDENTIFICATION NUMBER DECODING CHART

POSITION	INTERPRETATION	CODE OPTIONS		
1	Country of Origin	1 = United States	2 = Canada	3 = Mexico
2	Make	B = Dodge	C = Chrysler	P = Plymouth
3	Type of Vehicle	3 = Passenger Car		
4	Passenger Safety System	C = Automatic Seat Belt X = Driver Airbag/Passenger Manual Seat Belt Y = Driver Airbag/Passenger Automatic Seat Belt		
5	Line	A = Chrysler-LeBaron (4 door) A = Dodge-Spirit, Spirit LE, Spirit LS A = Plymouth-Acclaim, Acclaim LE, Acclaim LX C = Chrysler-New Yorker Salon C = Dodge-Dynasty, Dynasty LE (US) G = Dodge-Daytona, Daytona ES, Daytona Shelby J = Chrysler-LeBaron (2 door) N = Chrysler-Dynasty, Dynasty LE (Canada) P = Dodge-Shadow America, Shadow, Shadow ES P = Plymouth-Sundance America, Sundance, Sundance RS Y = Chrysler-Fifth Avenue, Chrysler Imperial		
6	Series	1 = Economy Line 2 = Low Line 4 = High Line 5 = Premium Line 6 = Sport/Special 7 = Perform/Image		
7	Body Style	1 = 2 Door Coupe 4 = 2 Door Hatchback 5 = Convertible 6 = 4 Door Sedan 8 = 4 Door Hatchback		
8	Engine	A = 2.2L Turbo III D = 2.2L EFI J = 2.5L Turbo K = 2.5L EFI L = 3.8L EFI R = 3.3L EFI 3 = 3.0L MPI		
9	Model Year	M = 1991		
10	Assembly Plant	D = Belvidere F = Newark G = St. Louis I N = Sterling Heights T = Toluca-Mexico		

12 through 17 = Vehicle Build Sequence

VEHICLE IDENTIFICATION NUMBER DECODING CHART

POSITION	INTERPRETATION	CODE OPTIONS	
1	Country	1 = United States	2 = Canada
2	Make	E = Eagle	B = Dodge
3	Vehicle type	3 = Passenger car	
4	Other	C = Automatic seat belt Y = Driver air bag, passenger automatic seat belt	X = Driver air bag, passenger manual seat belt
5	Line	B = Dodge Monaco	B = Eagle Premier
6	Series	5 = Premium line	6 = Special/Sport
7	Body	6 = 4 Door Sedan	
8	Engine	U = 3.0 Liter	
9 ①	Check digit	(1 through 9, 0 Orx)	
10	Model year	M = 1991	
11	Assembly Plant	H = Bramelea	
12 through 17	Sequence number	(6 Digits)	

① Digit in Position 9 is used for V.I.N. Verification.

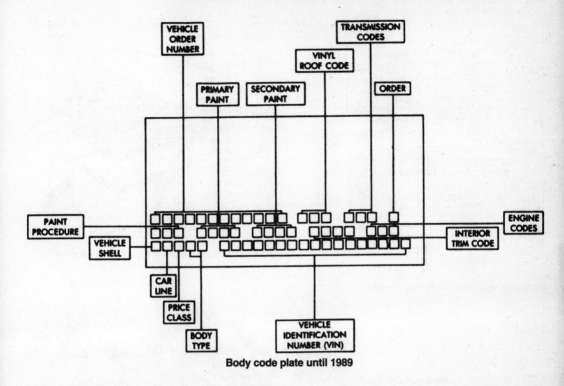

Body code plate until 1989

air cleaner may leak, causing accelerated engine wear.

On the 2.2 liter carbureted engine, replace the air cleaner element by removing the three wing nuts retaining the air cleaner-crossover cover to the carburetor and bracket. Lift the cover, pull the element out, and replace it, making sure you install it with the screen upward. Position the cover on top, aligning the three clips and making sure the element seals all around. Let the three studs stick upward through the whole for each in the cover. Then, install both of the plastic wing nuts onto the two studs on the carburetor and tighten each just finger tight (14 inch lbs.). After those nuts

have been properly torqued, install the other wingnut — the one that fastens the air cleaner to the support bracket — and tighten it in a similar manner. Finally, close the three hold-down clips.

1981–86 2.2 Liter Electronic Fuel Injection Engine

To remove the air cleaner, remove the clamp fastening the air hose at the throttle body and unclip the five clips that fasten the top of the air cleaner to the lower housing. Pull the air hose off the throttle body and then lift the cover and

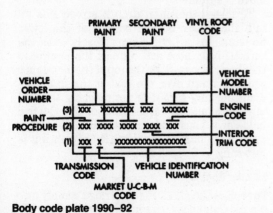

Body code plate 1990–92

Location of the transaxle identification number (T.I.N.) on all transaxles, and the assembly part number for automatic transaxles

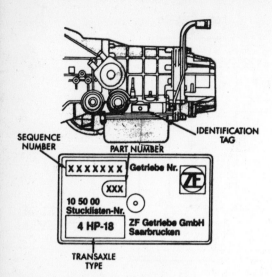

SEQUENCE NUMBER

PART NUMBER

IDENTIFICATION TAG

TRANSAXLE TYPE

Transaxle tag location—Dodge Monaco

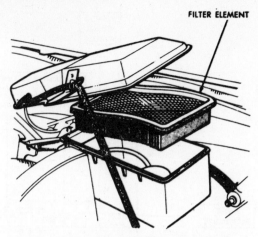

FILTER ELEMENT

Air cleaner installation—2.2 carbureted engine

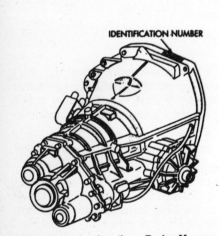

IDENTIFICATION NUMBER

Additional number location—Dodge Monaco

FILTER ELEMENT

2.6L engine air cleaner filter

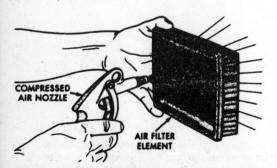

COMPRESSED AIR NOZZLE

AIR FILTER ELEMENT

Cleaning air filter element

hose off the bottom of the air cleaner. Now remove the filter.

To install the filter, drop it screen side up into the plastic bottom section of the lower housing. Install the clamp loosely onto the throttle body hose and connect the hose onto the throttle body. Slide the top of the air cleaner squarely down over the seal of the filter element, making sure it is not pinching the seal anywhere but lies flat all around. Clip the five hold-down clips and then tighten the clamp around the hose at the throttle body until it is just snug — 25 inch lbs.

2.6 Liter Engine

To replace the air cleaner cartridge, simply unclip the four clips fastening the top in place, lift

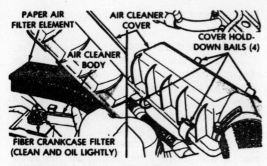

Air cleaner assembly—3.0L engine

the top off the lower housing (the intake hose is flexible enough to permit this) and remove the filter. Install in reverse order, making sure all parts are positioned correctly to prevent leaks. Clean the inside of the air cleaner housing before installing the air filter.

2.2 Liter, 2.5 Liter and Most Late Model EFI Engines

When changing the filter element in this air cleaner, the body of the unit remains mounted on the intake manifold. Only the top cover need be removed (refer to the necessary illustration) unless the crankcase ventilation filter must be

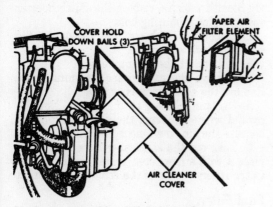

Air cleaner assembly—2.5L turbo engine

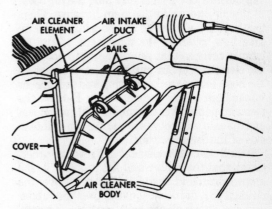

Air cleaner assembly—16 valve engine

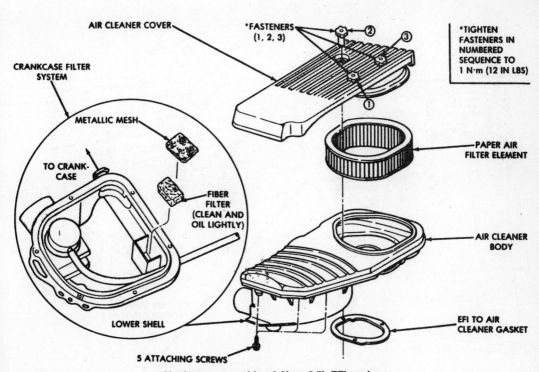

Air cleaner assembly—2.2L or 2.5L EFI engines

serviced. To replace the air cleaner, remove the three attaching thumbscrews and remove the air cleaner top cover. Then, grab the paper element at two locations on the inside diameter to lift it out of the housing.

Install in reverse order, turning the element so its flat sides line up with those in the housing. Be careful to tighten the three fasteners for the top cover in the numbered order shown in the illustration. They need not be extremely tight (recommended torque is only 12 inch lbs.).

2.2 Liter Turbocharged Engines

To remove the air cleaner element, first unclip the hold-down bails attaching the top cover of the air cleaner to the main housing. Then, gently pull the cover off the housing. If the intake hose restricts the movement of the air cleaner cover so that you cannot gain access to the element without putting a lot of stress on the hose, loosen the hose clamp and pull the air intake hose off the housing cover. Remove the element, noting that the rubber seal goes in last and fits into the groove around the top or intake side of the lower housing.

Install the new element in reverse order. Check that the rubber seal fits properly in the groove all around. Install the top cover over the element so it fits down squarely over the rubber seal and attach all the bails securely. If necessary, reconnect the intake hose and tighten the clamp securely.

1990–92 Laser and Stealth (Non-Turbocharged Engine)

1. Disconnect the air-flow sensor connector.
2. Remove the air intake hose. Unclamp the air cleaner cover.
3. Push the air intake hose backward and remove the air cleaner cover. Note be careful when removing the air cleaner cover, because the air-flow sensor is attached.
4. Take out the air cleaner element and replace it with a new filter. Install the new filter in the reverse order of the removal procedure.

1990–92 Laser and Stealth (Turbocharged Engine)

1. Disconnect the air-flow sensor connector. On Stealth vehicles, remove the clutch booster vacuum pipe mounting bolt.
2. Disconnect the boost hose. Disconnect the solenoid valve with hoses.
3. Disconnect the air intake hose.
4. Remove the air cleaner retaining bolts. Remove the air cleaner assembly.
5. Unclamp the air cleaner cover. Note be careful when removing the air cleaner cover, because the air-flow sensor is attached.
6. Take out the air cleaner element and replace it with a new filter. Install the new filter in the reverse order of the removal procedure.

Fuel Filter

CAUTION: *Never smoke when working around gasoline! Avoid all sources of sparks*

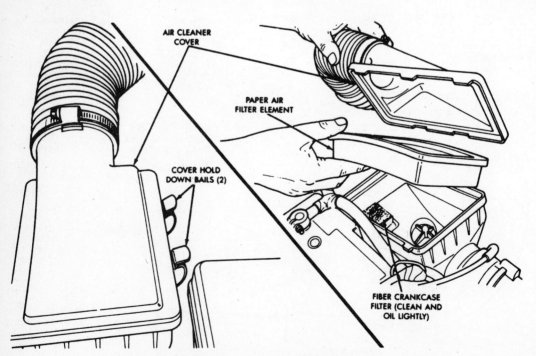

AIR CLEANER COVER

PAPER AIR FILTER ELEMENT

COVER HOLD DOWN BAILS (2)

FIBER CRANKCASE FILTER (CLEAN AND OIL LIGHTLY)

Air cleaner assembly—3.3L or 3.8L engines

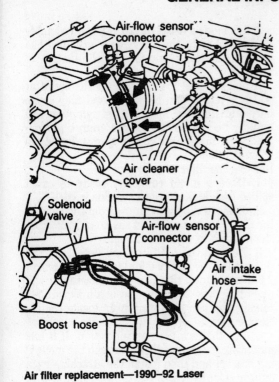

Air filter replacement—1990–92 Laser

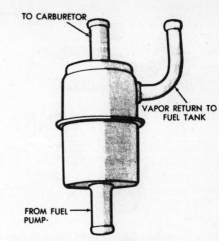

Fuel filter vapor separator 2.2L engine

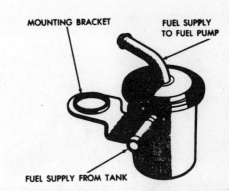

Fuel filter 2.6L engine

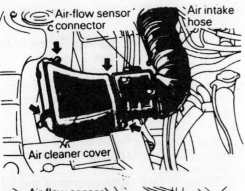

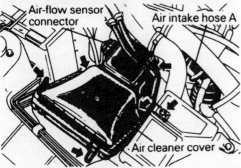

Air filter replacement—Stealth

or ignition. *Gasoline vapors are EXTREMELY volatile!*

REMOVAL AND INSTALLATION

Carbureted Engines

There are two fuel filters in the present system. One is part of the gauge unit assembly located inside the fuel tank on the suction end of the tube. This filter normally does not need servicing, but may be replaced or cleaned if a very large amount of extremely coarse material gets into the tank and clogs it.

The 2.2 liter engine usually uses a disposable filter-vapor separator that is located on the front side of the engine block between the fuel pump and carburetor. On some applications, this filter has not only inlet and outlet connections, but a third connection designed to permit fuel to return to the tank so that vapor that accumulates in hot weather will not interfere with carburetion.

The 2.6 liter engine uses a disposable, canister type filter in most applications. This type filter has only two connections.

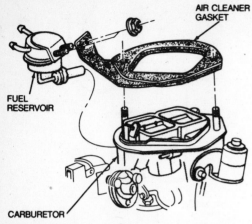

The fuel reservoir type filter used on some models

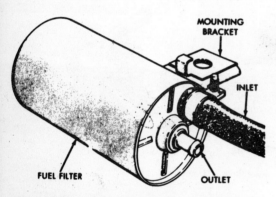

The fuel filter used on fuel injected models through the 1987 model year

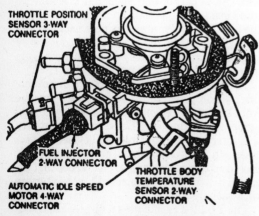

Fuel injector harness location—2.2L and 2.5L non-turbocharged engines

A few models use a filter-reservoir assembly that attaches to the air cleaner and also has three connections, one for the elimination of vapor.

A plugged fuel filter can limit the speed at which a vehicle can be driven and may cause hard starting. The most critical symptom will usually be suddenly reduced engine performance at maximum engine power levels, as when passing.

Remove the filter as follows:

1. Have a metal container ready to catch spilled fuel. Make sure the engine is cool.

2. Remove the hose clamps from each end of the filter. Then, disconnect the hoses, collecting the fuel in the metal container.

3. Remove the old filter and hoses. On the non-return (two connection) type filter used on 2.6 liter engines, this requires unfastening the mounting bracket. On the reservoir type filter, remove the two mounting nuts inside the air cleaner.

4. Put the new filter into position. If it has mounting studs, pass them through the mounting bracket and then install the attaching nuts snugly. Connect the hoses, and install and tighten the hose clamps (if the hoses are hard to force onto the nipples, you can wet them inside just very slightly). Make sure the clamps are located a short distance away from the ends of the hoses and on the inside of the nipples located on the ends of the filter connections.

5. Start the engine and check for leaks.

Fuel Injected Engines (Except Monaco, 1990–92 Laser and Stealth)

CAUTION: *Fuel injected engines use high pressure in their operation. This pressure is maintained through the action of check valves even when the engine is off. Therefore, you must be sure to work on the fuel carrying parts of injected cars only when the engine has cooled off and only after you have properly bled the pressurized fuel from the system. Failure to do this could readily cause a fire or injury.*

1. Relieve fuel system pressure as follows for vehicles built up till 1988 model year:

a. Loosen the fuel tank cap to release any accumulated air pressure that may be there. Then, disconnect the electrical connector at the single fuel injector on the throttle body on cars with throttle body injection. On cars with multi-point injection, disconnect the electrical connector on the injector closest to the battery.

b. Use a jumper wire to ground one of the injector terminals for whichever injector you've disconnected.

c. Connect one end of a jumper wire to the

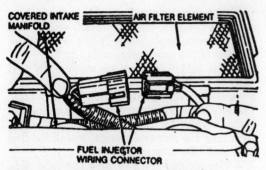

Fuel injector harness location—3.0L engine

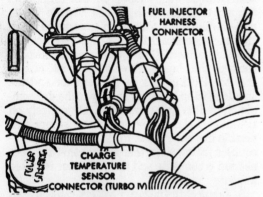

Fuel injector harness location—turbocharged engine, except 2.2L DOHC. The connector may vary between vehicles

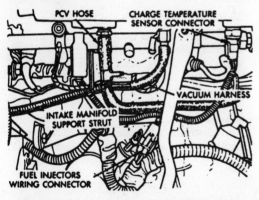

Fuel injector harness location—2.2L DOHC engine

other injector terminal. Then, just touch the other end of the second jumper to the battery positive post for nearly 10 seconds. *Make sure you do not maintain this connection for more than the maximum of 10 seconds or the injector could be damaged.*

2. Relieve fuel system pressure as follows for vehicles built from 1989–92 model year:

    a. Loosen the fuel filler cap to release fuel tank pressure.

    b. Locate and disconnect the fuel injector harness connector.

    c. Connect a jumper wire from terminal No. 1 of the appropriate connector to ground.

    d. Being careful not to allow contact between the jumper leads, connect a jumper wire to terminal No. 2 of the connector and touch the other end of the jumper to the positive battery post for no longer than 5 seconds. This will relieve fuel pressure.

3. Remove the retaining screw that mounts the filter to its retaining bracket so you can reach the hose clamps.

4. Then, loosen the clamps for both the inlet and outlet lines. Quickly wrap a shop towel around these connections to collect escaping fuel safely. Then, dispose of this towel in such a way as to protect it from heat the the chance of fire.

5. Note the routing of the hoses. The high pressure hose from the tank and pump goes to the inlet connection, which is always located toward the outer edge of the filter. The outlet hose to the engine is labeled on some filters and is always at the center. Pull the hoses off the connections on the filter. Replace the filter, draining fuel into a metal container and disposing of it safely. Inspect the hoses and clamps and replace defective parts as necessary.

NOTE: *Chrysler uses and recommends hoses that meet their specifications and are labeled "EFM/EFI18519". Make sure you use either this type of hose or an equivalent, high pressure — up to 55 psi (379kpa) type of fuel hose available in the automotive aftermarket. Be sure not to use ordinary rubber fuel hose, as this is not tough enough for high pressure use and may not be able to resist the destruction caused by certain types of contamination. Also, if hose clamps require replacement, note that the original equipment clamps have rolled edges to keep the edge of the band from cutting into this hose, due to the necessary use of high clamping forces with a high pressure fuel system. Make sure that you use either an original equipment clamp or a similar type of clamp available in the aftermarket.*

To install:

6. Reconnect the hoses, using the proper routing noted as you disconnected them. You may want to very slightly wet the inside diameter of the hoses to make it easier to install them onto the filter connections. Install them as far as possible, until they are well over the bulges at the ends of the connectors. Install the clamps so they are a short distance away from the ends of the hoses but well over the bulged areas at the ends of the filter connections. Tighten both clamps securely. If you have an inch lb. torque wrench torque them to 10 inch lbs.

7. Remount the filter on the bracket snugly with the screw. Start the engine and check for

leaks, tightening the hose clamps, replacing parts, or forcing the hoses farther onto the connectors, if necessary.

Dodge Monaco

CAUTION: *Always wear eye protection when servicing the fuel system. Do not smoke or allow open flame near the fuel system or components during fuel system service.*

1. Relieve the fuel pressure as follows:

   a. Loosen the fuel filler cap to release fuel tank pressure.

   b. Disconnect the fuel pump harness connector located in the rear of the vehicle near the fuel tank.

   c. Start the vehicle and allow it to run until it stalls from lack of fuel. Turn the key to the **OFF** position.

   d. Disconnect the negative battery cable, then reconnect the fuel pump connector.

   e. Wrap shop towels around the fitting that is being disconnected to absorb residual fuel in the lines.

2. The filter is located on the frame rail near the rear of the vehicle. Depress, or squeeze the retainer tabs together and slowly pull the connectors from the fuel filter. Note the retainer tabs stay on the fuel filter nipples.

3. Remove the screw holding the fuel filter in place and remove the filter.

To install:

4. Carefully remove the retainers from the fuel filter nipples with a thin straight blade tool. Insert the tool between the filter nipple and the wedge portion of the retainer that seats against the shoulder of the nipple. Press the wedge back and slip the wedge over the nipple shoulder. Repeat this on the other side of the retainer and then pull the retainer off the nipple.

5. Push the retainers back into the fuel line quick-connect fittings. Ensure that the locking ears and the shoulder (stop bead) on the fuel tube are completely visible in the windows on the side of the quick-connect fitting.

6. The fuel filter may be marked **IN** and **OUT** at the nipple ends. The side marked **IN** is connected to the fuel line from the fuel tank. The side of the filter marked **OUT** is connected to the fuel line that runs to the engine. After determining the proper direction, install the fuel filter with the attaching screw.

7. Use a clean cloth to wipe the tube ends clean and lightly lubricate the fuel tube ends with clean 30 weight motor oil. The connectors contain O-rings which do not have to be replaced when the fittings are disconnected. Push the quick-connect fitting over the fuel tube until a click is heard. If the quick-connect fitting is the type that has windows on the side, ensure that the locking ears on the retainer and the shoulder (stop bead) on the fuel tube are completely visible in the windows. Do not rely on the audible click to confirm that a secure connection has been made. Pull back on the quick-connect fitting to further ensure that the connection is complete and the connector is locked in place.

8. Connect the negative battery cable, install the fuel filler cap, turn the key to the **ON** position to pressurize the fuel system and check for leaks.

1990–92 Laser And Stealth

CAUTION: *Always wear eye protection when servicing the fuel system. Do not smoke or allow open flame near the fuel system or components during fuel system service.*

1. Relieve the fuel pressure as follows:

   a. Loosen the fuel filler cap to release fuel tank pressure.

   b. Disconnect the fuel pump harness connector located at the rear of the fuel tank. On

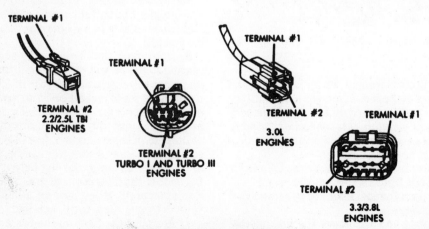

Injector harness connections

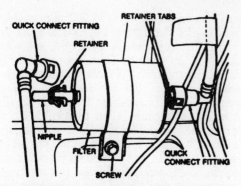

Fuel filter with special fittings—Dodge Monaco

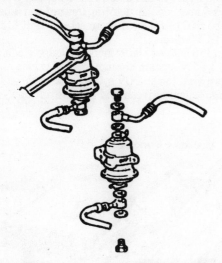

Removing fuel filter—1990–92 Laser and Stealth

Stealth remove the fuel system access cover in the luggage compartment.

c. Start the vehicle and allow it to run until it stalls from lack of fuel. Turn the key to the **OFF** position.

d. Disconnect the negative battery cable, then reconnect the fuel pump connector.

e. Wrap shop towels around the fitting that is being disconnected to absorb residual fuel in the lines.

2. The filter is located in the engine compartment, mounted either on the firewall or inner fender panel.

3. Where applicable, remove the air cleaner assembly, battery and tray.

4. Hold the fuel filter nut securely with a backup wrench. Cover the hoses with shop towels and remove the eye bolt. Discard the gaskets.

5. On Stealth, the high pressure hose connection is accomplished with another eye bolt connection; first separate the flare nut connection at the line, then repeat Step 4. Otherwise,

separate the flare nut connection at the filter. Discard the gaskets.

6. Remove the mounting bolts and remove the fuel filter from the vehicle.

To install:

7. If equipped with the flare fitting, install a new O-ring and tighten the fitting by hand before installing the filter to the vehicle.

8. Install the filter only finger-tight to its bracket temporarily.

9. Install new O-rings and connect the high pressure hose and eye bolt, then the main pipe and eye bolt. Tighten the eye bolts to 22 ft. lbs. All connection must be tight at this point of the service procedure.

10. Tighten the mounting bolts fully.

11. Install the air cleaner assembly, battery and tray, if removed.

12. Connect the negative battery cable, install the fuel filler cap, turn the key to the **ON** position to pressurize the fuel system and check for leaks.

PCV Valve

NOTE: *Due to the year coverage and the may engines used in this repair manual always refer to the owner's manual of your vehicle for the correct mileage interval for replacement of a component. Refer to the necessary illustration for the location of the PCV vavle for your vehicle.*

Regardless of PCV valve or system performance, the valve itself should be replaced at specified intervals. At this time, you should inspect the hoses for clogging and spray a small amount of a safe cleaning solvent designed for this purpose through the hoses to remove any accumulated sludge or varnish.

If the car has the PCV module used on carbu-

Servicing the PCV valve—2.2 liter engine shown

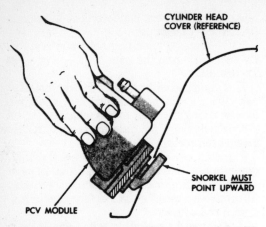

Removing or installing the PCV module on the 2.2 liter engine

reted 2.2L engines and has 50,000 miles on it or a multiple of that figure, the module must be cleaned. First, remove the PCV valve and vent hose from the module. Then, depress the retaining clip and turn the module counterclockwise to remove it. Use kerosene or a similar cleaning solvent (not gasoline!) to flush the filter inside the module. Allow to dry. Then, invert the module and fill it with SAE 30 engine oil. Turn it right side up and permit the oil to drain through the vent located on top of the air cleaner. Then, carefully depress the retaining clip, insert the module and turn it clockwise until it reaches its normal position to install it. Do not force the module in or to turn. Note that the snorkel must end up pointing upward and must not be free to rotate. Reconnect the vent hose and PCV valve.

On 1987–88 and later models (Dodge Monaco uses a CCV system similar to PCV valve), the air drawn into the PCV system passes through a foam or metal mesh and foam filtration sys-

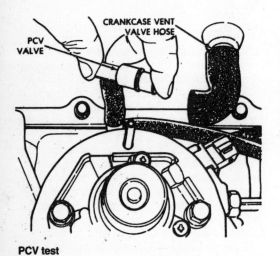

PCV test

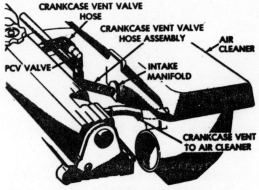

PCV system—2.2L and 2.5L engines

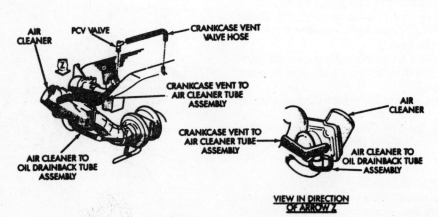

VIEW IN DIRECTION OF ARROW Z

PCV system—Turbo I engines

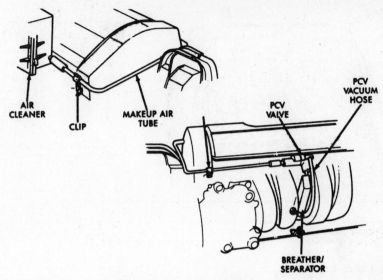

PCV system—Turbo III engines

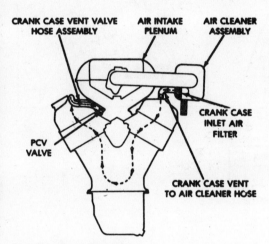

PCV system—3.0L engine

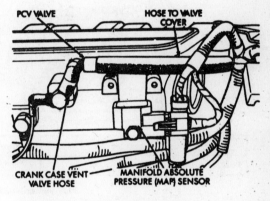

PCV system—3.3L and 3.8L engines

tem. At the maintenance interval when PCV valve replacement is required, you should remove this element (or these elements) and replace it (or them). These elements are typically located in a corner of the air cleaner housing where you can see them as soon as the air filter element has been removed. If they become clogged before the normal service interval, they may be cleaned in a solvent such as kerosene and then coated with engine oil. When the car has reached the normal maintenance interval for the PCV system, these filters should be replaced.

Evaporative Canister Filter

SERVICING

The function of the Evaporative Control System is to prevent gasoline vapors from the fuel tank from escaping into the atmosphere. Periodic maintenance is required only on 1981–82 models (on all other vehicles a sealed, maintenance free, charcoal canister is used). The fiberglass filter on the bottom of the canister must be replaced on these models, but only if the vehicle is driven under dusty conditions.

REMOVAL AND INSTALLATION

To replace the filter, note locations of the hoses going to the canister, and then disconnect them. Unclamp the canister, pull the filter out as shown, and replace it in reverse order.

Battery

NOTE: *After battery and or clamps/ terminals are service, DO NOT hammer on the battery clamps to install them as this may* **crack the battery case or damage the** *terminals.*

<1.8L Engine>

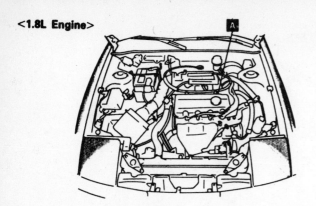

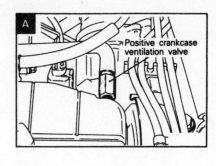

Positive crankcase ventilation valve

Name	Symbol
Positive crankcase ventilation valve	A

<2.0L DOHC Engine>

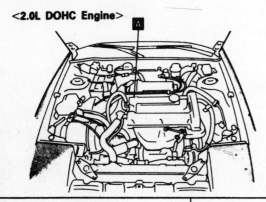

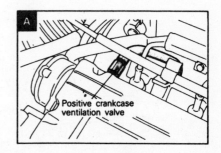

Positive crankcase ventilation valve

Name	Symbol
Positive crankcase ventilation valve	A

PCV system—1990–92 Laser

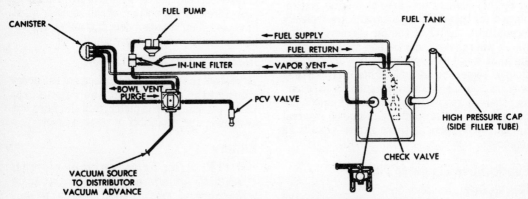

Evaporation control system—2.6L engine

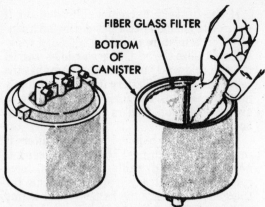

FIBER GLASS FILTER

BOTTOM OF CANISTER

Replacing evaporative canister filter (1981–82 models)

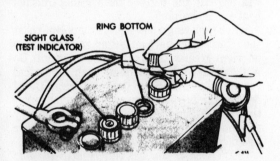

SIGHT GLASS (TEST INDICATOR)

RING BOTTOM

Check the fluid level—standard battery

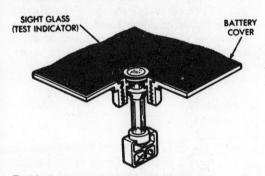

SIGHT GLASS (TEST INDICATOR)

BATTERY COVER

Test indicator—maintenance free battery

Two types of batteries are used, Standard and Maintenance Free. Both batteries are equipped with a Test Charge Indicator. This indicator is a built-in hydrometer, which replaces one of the battery filler caps in the Standard battery and is permanently installed in the cover on the Maintenance Free battery.

Visual inspection of the indicator sight glass will aid in determining battery condition. The indicator shows green if the battery is above 76–80 percent of being fully charged, and dark if it needs charging. A light yellow means the battery requires water or may need replacing.

For standard batteries, check the fluid level

in each cell every month (more often in hot weather or on long trips). If the water is low, fill it to the bottom of the filler well with distilled water.

Loose, dirty, or corroded battery terminals are a frequent cause of "no-start"conditions. Every 12 months or as necessary, remove the battery terminals and clean them, giving them a light coating of petroleum jelly when you are finished. This will help to retard corrosion.

NOTE: *Never disconnect the battery with the engine running or with the ignition turned ON. Severe and expensive damage to the on-board computers will result. With the ignition off and the key removed for safety, always*

Special pullers are available to remove the cable clamps

Clean the battery posts with a wire brush, or the special tool shown

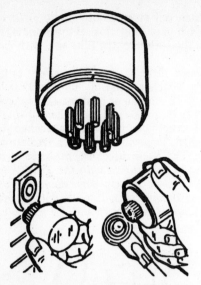

Special tools are also available for cleaning the posts and clamps on side terminal batteries

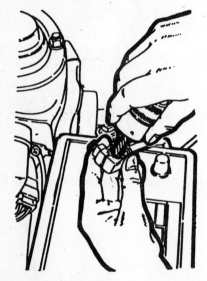

Clean the inside of the clamps with a wire brush, or the special tool

disconnect the negative (−) cable first and connect it last.

Check the battery cables for signs of wear or chafing and replace any cable or terminal that looks marginal. Battery terminals can be easily cleaned; inexpensive cleaning tools are an excellent investment that will pay for themselves many times over. They can usually be purchased from any well-equipped auto store or parts department. The accumulated white powder and corrosion can be cleaned from the top of the battery with an old toothbrush and a solution of baking soda.

If the battery becomes corroded, or if electrolyte should splash out during additions of water, a mixture of baking soda and water will neutralize the acid. This should be washed off with cold water after making sure that the cell caps are tight. Battery fluid is particularly nasty to painted surfaces; work carefully to avoid spillage on fenders and other painted bodywork.

If a charging is required while the battery is in the car, disconnect the battery cables, negative (ground) cable first. If you have removed the battery from the vehicle for charging, make sure the battery is not sitting on bare earth or concrete while being charged. A block of wood or a small stack of newspapers will prevent the battery from losing internal heat while charging.

When replacing a battery, it is important that the replacement have an output rating equal to or when greater than original equipment. Do not confuse physical size with electrical capacity. A stronger battery (capable of delivering more power) need not be much larger that the original. A physically larger battery may not fit in the car and may actually deliver less power than the original.

CAUTION: *If you get battery acid in your eyes or on your skin, rinse it off immediately with lots of water and see a physician. The gases formed inside the battery cells are highly explosive. Never check the level of the electrolyte in the presence of flame or when smoking. Never charge a battery in an unventilated area. Never smoke around a battery being charged.*

Drive Belts

INSPECTION

Check the drive belts every 15,000 miles or once a year, for evidence of wear such as cracking, fraying, and incorrect tension. Determine the belt tension at a point half-way between the pulleys by pressing on the belt with moderate thumb pressure. The belt should deflect about ¼–½ in. (6–13mm) at this point. Note that "deflection"is not play, but the ability of the belt, under actual tension, to stretch slightly and give.

Although it is generally easier on the component to have the belt too loose than too tight, a very loose belt may place a high impact load on a bearing due to the whipping or snapping action of the belt. A belt that is slightly loose may slip, especially when component loads are high. This slippage may be hard to identify. For example, the generator belt may run okay during the day, and then slip at night when headlights are turned on. Slipping belts wear quickly not

HOW TO SPOT WORN V-BELTS

V-Belts are vital to efficient engine operation—they drive the fan, water pump and other accessories. They require little maintenance (occasional tightening) but they will not last forever. Slipping or failure of the V-belt will lead to overheating. If your V-belt looks like any of these, it should be replaced.

Cracking or weathering

This belt has deep cracks, which cause it to flex. Too much flexing leads to heat build-up and premature failure. These cracks can be caused by using the belt on a pulley that is too small. Notched belts are available for small diameter pulleys.

Softening (grease and oil)

Oil and grease on a belt can cause the belt's rubber compounds to soften and separate from the reinforcing cords that hold the belt together. The belt will first slip, then finally fail altogether.

Glazing

Glazing is caused by a belt that is slipping. A slipping belt can cause a run-down battery, erratic power steering, overheating or poor accessory performance. The more the belt slips, the more glazing will be built up on the surface of the belt. The more the belt is glazed, the more it will slip. If the glazing is light, tighten the belt.

Worn cover

The cover of this belt is worn off and is peeling away. The reinforcing cords will begin to wear and the belt will shortly break. When the belt cover wears in spots or has a rough jagged appearance, check the pulley grooves for roughness.

Separation

This belt is on the verge of breaking and leaving you stranded. The layers of the belt are separating and the reinforcing cords are exposed. It's just a matter of time before it breaks completely.

only due to the direct effect of slippage but also because of the heat the slippage generates. Extreme slippage may even cause a belt to burn. A very smooth, glazed appearance on the belt's sides, as opposed to the obvious pattern of a fabric cover, indicates that the belt has been slipping.

ADJUSTMENT/INSTALLATION

WARNING: *Be careful not to overtighten the drive belts, as this will damage the driven component's bearings.*

Except Alternator/Water Pump Drive Belt (1981-88 model year)

If the deflection is found to be too much or too little, loosen the accessory's slotted adjusting bracket bolt. If the hinge bolt is very tight, it too may have to be loosened. Use a wooden hammer handle or a broomstick to lever the accessory closer to or farther away from the engine to provide the correct tension. Do not use a metal prybar, which may damage the component by springing the housing. When the belt tension seems correct, tighten the bolts and then recheck the adjustment, in case the component has moved slightly.

Alternator/Water Pump Drive Belt (1981-88 model year)

On most of the engines covered in this guide, the alternator/water pump drive belt is tensioned by a more sophisticated screw type tensioner which makes precise tension adjustment

much easier. If the belt deflection is found to be incorrect, first loosen the locknut located on the locking screw or the lockbolt. On all but 1988 models, this is located in a slotted portion of the outboard alternator mounting bracket. On 1988 models, loosen the T-bolt located in the center of the disc shaped portion of the outboard alternator bracket. Then, on all models, tighten or loosen the tensioning bolt located outboard of the alternator. This bolt is tightened (turned clockwise) to increase belt tension and loosened to decrease it. When the belt tension is correct, tighten the lockbolt.

If a belt must be replaced, the driven unit must be loosened and moved to its extreme loosest position, generally by moving it toward the center of the motor. After removing the old belt, check the pulleys for dirt or built-up material which could affect belt contact. Carefully install the new belt, remembering that it is new and unused — it may appear to be just a little too small to fit over the pulley flanges. Fit the belt over the largest pulley (usually the crankshaft pulley at the bottom center of the motor) first, then work on the smaller one(s). Gentle pressure in the direction of rotation is helpful. Some belts run around a third or idler pulley, which acts as an additional pivot in the belt's path. It may be possible to loosen the idler pulley as well as the main component, making your job much easier. Depending on which belt(s) you are changing, it may be necessary to loosen or remove other interfering belts to get at the one(s) you want.

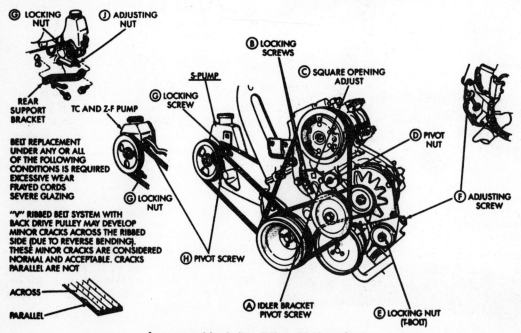

Accessory drive belts—2.2L and 2.5L engines

When buying replacement belts, remember that the fit is critical according to the length of the belt ("diameter"), the width of the belt, the depth of the belt and the angle or profile of the V shape or the ribs. The belt shape should exactly match the shape of the pulley; belts that are not an exact match can cause noise, slippage and premature failure.

After the new belt is installed, draw tension on it by moving the driven unit away from the motor and tighten its mounting bolts. This is sometimes a three or four-handed job; you may find an assistant helpful. Make sure that all the bolts you loosened get retightened and that any other loosened belts also have the correct tension. A new belt can be expected to stretch a bit after installation so be prepared to re-adjust your new belt, if needed, within the first two hundred miles of use.

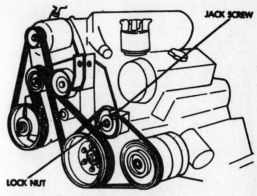

Accessory drive belts—3.0L engine

2.2L/2.5L Engine A/C Compressor Belt 1989–92 model year

1. Loosen the idler bracket pivot screw A and locking screws B to remove and install belt and or belt tension.
2. Adjust belt tension by applying torque to square hole C on idler bracket. Adjust tension to specifications given in "Belt Tension Chart".
3. Tighten in order, first locking screws B then pivot screw A to 40 ft. lbs.

2.2/2.5L Engine Power Steering Pump Belt ZF and TC Types (1989–92 model year)

1. Loosen locking nut and locking screw G and pivot nut H.
2. Loosen adjusting screw J to release belt tension. Tighten adjusting nut J to adjust bel;t tension to specification.
3. Tighten locking nut G and screw H to 40 ft. lbs. Tighten lockikng screw to 20 ft. lbs.

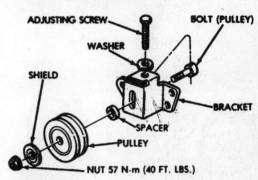

A/C belt idler

2.2/2.5L Engine Power Steering Pump Belt S Type (1989–92 model year)

1. From on top of the vehicle loosen locking screw G. From under the vehicle loosen the pivot screw and pivot nut H.
2. After installing a new belt adjust belt tension with ½ in. breaker bar installed in adjusting bracket. See tension specification in Chart.
3. Tighten locking screw G to 40 ft. lbs. Tighten pivot screw H and pivot nut nut to 40 ft. lbs.

2.2/2.5L Engine Alternator Belt (1989–92 model year)

1. Loosen T-bolt locking nut E and adjusting screw F to remove and install belt and or adjust belt.
2. Tighten adjusting screw F to adjust belt

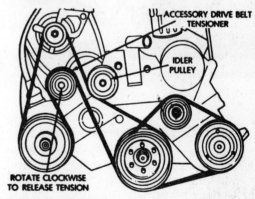

Release belt tensioner

tension to specification shown in Belt Tension Chart.
3. Tighten T-bolt locking nut E to 40 ft. lbs.

3.0L Engine A/C Comnpressor Belt

1. To remove and install this drive belt, first loosen the idler pulley lock nut, then turn the adjusting screw to raise or lower the idler pulley.
2. To adjust this belt, loosen the idler pulley nut and adjust belt tension by tightening adjusting screw. Tighten pulley nut to 40 ft. lbs. after adjustment.

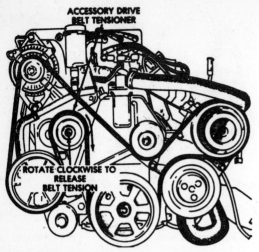

Accessory drive belts—3.3/3.8L engines

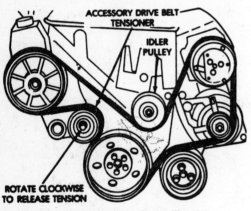

Accessory drive belts—2.2L Turbo III

3.0L Engine Alternator/Power Steering Pump Belt

This belt is provided with a dynamic tensioner to maintain proper belt tension. To remove or install this belt, release tension by rotating the tension clockwise.

3.3L/3.8L And Turbo III Engine Accessory Drive Belt

This belt is provided with a dynamic tensioner to maintain proper belt tension. To remove or install this belt, remove the right front splash shield and release tension by rotating the tension clockwise.

Hoses

REMOVAL AND INSTALLATION

CAUTION: *When draining the coolant, keep in mind that cats and dogs are attracted by the ethylene glycol antifreeze, and are quite likely to drink any that is left in an uncovered* container *or in puddles on the ground. This will prove fatal in sufficient quantity. Always drain the coolant into a sealable container. Coolant should be reused unless it is contaminated or several years old.*

All Models

CAUTION: *Do not perform this procedure on a hot or warm engine. Otherwise, serious injury could result.*

1. Drain the cooling system through the bottom of the radiator (the block need not be drained to replace the hoses.

2. Remove the top hose from the radiator neck and the thermostat housing.

3. Remove the bottom hose from the water pump and the bottom of the radiator.

4. Remove the heater hoses from the core connections near the firewall and the nipples on the cylinder head and thermostat housing. Remove any bypass hoses from the thermostat housing and intake manifold.

5. Check the hoses for damage. Hoses that are brittle, cracked, or extremely soft and pliable require replacement. Replace them as necessary.

6. Inspect the clamps for corrosion, fatigue (causing them to lose their springiness), or, in the case of aircraft type clamps, stripped threads. Replace any clamps that are questionable.

7. Installation is the reverse of removal. Refill and bleed the cooling system.

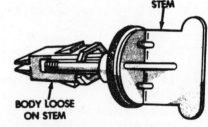

Draincock assembly

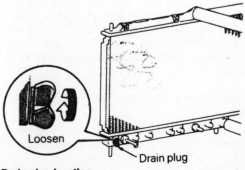

Drain plug location

HOW TO SPOT BAD HOSES

Both the upper and lower radiator hoses are called upon to perform difficult jobs in an inhospitable environment. They are subject to nearly 18 psi at under hood temperatures often over 280°F., and must circulate nearly 7500 gallons of coolant an hour—3 good reasons to have good hoses.

A good test for any hose is to feel it for soft or spongy spots. Frequently these will appear as swollen areas of the hose. The most likely cause is oil soaking. This hose could burst at any time, when hot or under pressure.

Swollen hose

Cracked hoses can usually be seen but feel the hoses to be sure they have not hardened; a prime cause of cracking. This hose has cracked down to the reinforcing cords and could split at any of the cracks.

Cracked hose

Weakened clamps frequently are the cause of hose and cooling system failure. The connection between the pipe and hose has deteriorated enough to allow coolant to escape when the engine is hot.

Frayed hose end (due to weak clamp)

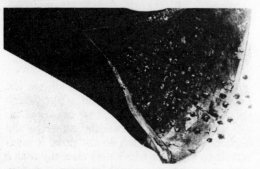

Debris, rust and scale in the cooling system can cause the inside of a hose to weaken. This can usually be felt on the outside of the hose as soft or thinner areas.

Debris in cooling system

Air Conditioning

SAFETY WARNINGS

The refrigerant used in the air conditioning system will freeze any surface, including your eyes, that it contacts. In addition, the refrigerant decomposes into a poisonous gas in the presence of flame. Further, the refrigerant normally produces high pressure in the system, especially when it is running.

For these reasons, any discharging or recharging of the air conditioning system should be left to a professional. Do not, under any circumstances, attempt to loosen or tighten any fittings or perform any work other than that outlined here.

SYSTEM INSPECTION

Checking for Oil Leaks

Refrigerant leaks show up as oily areas on the various components because the compressor oil is transported around the entire system along with the refrigerant. Look for oil spots on all the hoses and lines, and especially on the hose and tubing connections. If there are oily deposits, the system may have a leak, and you should have it checked by a qualified repairman.

NOTE: *A small area of oil on the front of the compressor is normal and no cause for alarm.*

REFRIGERANT LEVEL CHECKS

The first order of business when checking the sight glass is to find it. It will be in the head of the receiver/drier. In some cases, it may be covered by a small rubber plug designed to keep it clean (some vehicles may not have sight glass). Once you've found it, remove the cover, if necessary, wipe it clean and proceed as follows:
1. With the engine and the air conditioning

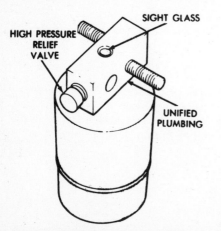

The refrigerant sight glass on air conditioned vehicles is located in the top of the receiver-drier

system running, look for the flow of refrigerant through the sight glass. If the air conditioner is working properly, you'll be able to see a continuous flow of clear refrigerant through the sight glass, with perhaps an occasional bubble at very high outside temperatures.

2. Cycle the air conditioner ON and OFF to make sure what you are seeing is a pure stream of liquid refrigerant. Since the refrigerant is clear, it is possible to mistake a completely discharged system for one that is fully charged. Turn the system OFF and watch the sight glass. If there is refrigerant in the system, you'll see bubbles during the OFF cycle. Also, the lines going into and out of the compressor will be at radically different temperatures (be careful about touching the line going forward to the condenser, which is in front of the radiator, as it will be very hot). If the bubbles disappear just after you start the compressor, there are no bubbles when the system is running, and the air flow from the unit in the car is cold, everything is O.K.

3. If you observe bubbles in the sight glass while the system is operating, the system is low on refrigerant. You may want to charge it yourself, as described later. Otherwise, have it checked by a professional.

4. If all you can see in the sight glass is oil streaks, this is an indication of trouble. This is true because there is no liquid refrigerant in the system (otherwise, the oil would mix with the refrigerant and would be invisible). Most of the time, if you see oil in the sight glass, it will appear as a series of streaks, although occasionally it may be a solid stream of oil. In either case, it means that part of the charge of refrigerant has been lost.

DISCHARGING AND RECHARGING THE SYSTEM

NOTE: *Have the air conditioning system discharged and recharged at an approved facility equipped with a refrigerant recovery system. Do not perform this procedure yourself, since the refrigerant in your vehicle has been shown to damage the ozone layer when released into the atmosphere. In addition, improper charging techniques can result in an explosion and severe frostbite or death.*

Windshield Wipers

For maximum effectiveness and longest element life, the windshield and wiper blades should be kept clean. Dirt, tree sap, road tar and so on will cause streaking, smearing and blade deterioration if left on the glass. It is advisable to wash the windshield carefully with a commercial glass cleaner at least once a month.

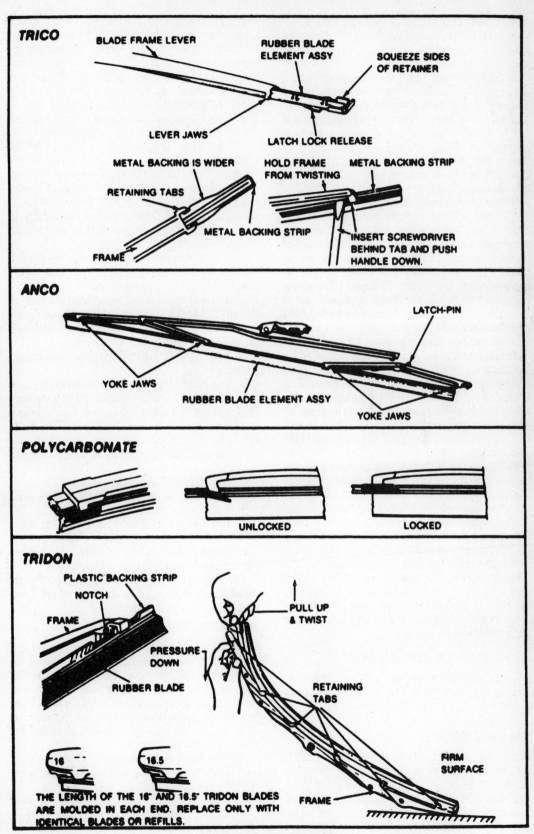

TRICO

BLADE FRAME LEVER

RUBBER BLADE ELEMENT ASSY

SQUEEZE SIDES OF RETAINER

LEVER JAWS

LATCH LOCK RELEASE

METAL BACKING IS WIDER

HOLD FRAME FROM TWISTING

METAL BACKING STRIP

RETAINING TABS

METAL BACKING STRIP

FRAME

INSERT SCREWDRIVER BEHIND TAB AND PUSH HANDLE DOWN.

ANCO

LATCH-PIN

YOKE JAWS

RUBBER BLADE ELEMENT ASSY

YOKE JAWS

POLYCARBONATE

UNLOCKED

LOCKED

TRIDON

PLASTIC BACKING STRIP

NOTCH

FRAME

PULL UP & TWIST

PRESSURE DOWN

RUBBER BLADE

RETAINING TABS

16

16.5

FIRM SURFACE

FRAME

THE LENGTH OF THE 16" AND 16.5" TRIDON BLADES ARE MOLDED IN EACH END. REPLACE ONLY WITH IDENTICAL BLADES OR REFILLS.

Popular styles of wiper refills

Wipe off the rubber blades with the wet rag afterwards. Do not attempt to move the wipers by hand; damage to the motor and drive mechanism will result.

If the blades are found to be cracked, broken or torn, they should be replaced immediately. Replacement intervals will vary with usage, although ozone deterioration usually limits blade life to about one year. If the wiper pattern is smeared or streaked, or if the blade chatters across the glass, the elements should be replaced. It is easiest and most sensible to replace the elements in pairs.

There are basically three different types of refills, which differ in their method of replacement. One type has two release buttons, approximately ⅓ of the way up from the ends of the blade frame. Pushing the buttons down releases a lock and allows the rubber filler to be removed from the frame. The new filler slides back into the frame and locks in place.

The second type of refill has two metal tabs which are unlocked by squeezing them together. The rubber filler can then be withdrawn from the frame jaws. A new refill is installed by inserting the refill into the front frame jaws and sliding it rearward to engage the remaining frame jaws. There are usually four jaws. Be certain when installing that the refill is engaged in all of them. At the end of its travel, the tabs will lock into place on the front jaws of the wiper blade frame.

The third type is a refill made from polycarbonate. The refill has a simple locking device at one end which flexes downward out of the groove into which the jaws of the holder fit, allowing easy release. By sliding the new refill through all the jaws and pushing through the slight resistance when it reaches the end of its travel, the refill will lock into position.

Regardless of the type of refill used, make sure that all of the frame jaws are engaged as the refill is pushed into place and locked. The metal blade holder and frame will scratch the glass if allowed to touch it.

ARM AND BLADE REPLACEMENT

A detailed description and procedures for replacing the wiper arm and blade is found in Chapter 6.

Tires and Wheels

Inspect the tires regularly for wear and damage. Remove stones or other foreign particles which may be lodged in the tread. If tread wear is excessive or irregular it could be a sign of front end problems, or simply improper inflation. The inflation should be checked at least once per month and adjusted if necessary. The tires must be cold (driven less than one mile) or an inaccurate reading will result. Do not forget to check the spare. The correct inflation pressure for your vehicle can be found on a decal mounted to the car. Depending upon model and year, the decal can be located at the driver's door, the passenger's door or the glove box. If you cannot find the decal a local automobile tire dealer can furnish you with information.

Inspect tires for uneven wear that might indicate the need for front end alignment or tire rotation. Tires should be replaced when a tread wear indicator appears as a solid band across the tread. When you buy new tires, give some thought to the following points, especially if you are switching to larger tires or to another profile series (50, 60, 70, 78):

1. The wheels must be the correct width for the tire. Tire dealers have charts of tire and rim compatibility. A mismatch can cause sloppy handling and rapid tread wear. The old rule of thumb is that the tread width should match the rim width (inside bead to inside bead) within 1 in. (25mm). For radial tires, the rim width should be 80% or less of the tire (not tread) width.

2. The height (mounted diameter) of the new tires can greatly change speedometer accuracy, engine speed at a given road speed, fuel mileage, acceleration, and ground clearance. Tire makers furnish full measurement specifications. Speedometer drive gears may be available from dealers for correction.

NOTE: *Dimensions of tires marked the same size may vary significantly, even among tires from the same maker.*

3. The spare tire should be usable, at least for low speed operation, with the new tires.

4. There shouldn't be any body interference when loaded, on bumps, or in turning.

The only sure way to avoid problems with these points is to stick to tire and wheel sizes available as factory options.

TIRE ROTATION

Tires should be rotated periodically to get the maximum tread life available. A good time to do this is when changing over from regular tires to snow tires, or about once per year. If front end problems are suspected have them corrected before rotating the tires. Torque the lug nuts to 80 ft. lbs. on 1981–82 vehicles and 95 ft. lbs. on 1983–92 vehicles.

NOTE: *Mark the wheel position or direction of rotation on radial, or studded snow tires before removing them.*

CAUTION: *Avoid overtightening the lug nuts to prevent damage to the brake disc or drum. Alloy wheels can also be cracked by overtightening. Use of a torque wrench is*

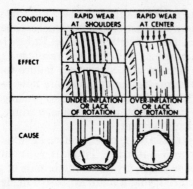

Tire wear

Tread Wear Indicator

Tread wear indicators are built into tires to assist you in determining when your tires should be replaced. When the indicators appear in 2 or more adjacent grooves, the tire should be replaced

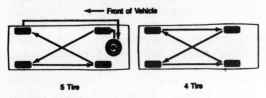

Standard tread rotation pattern

highly recommended. Tighten the lug nuts in a criss-cross sequence shown to the figures quoted in the paragraph above.

TIRE DESIGN

Most automotive experts are in agreement that radial tires are better all-around performers, giving prolonged wear and better handling. An added benefit which you should consider when purchasing tires is that radials have less rolling resistance and can give up to a 10% increase in fuel economy over a bias-ply tire.

Tires of different construction should never be mixed. Always replace tires in sets of four or five when switching tire types and never substitute a belted tire for a bias-ply, a radial for a belted tire, etc. An occasional pressure check and periodic rotation could make your tires last much longer than a neglected set and maintain the safety margin which was designed into them.

TIRE INFLATION

Always keep the pressure of the tires within the range specified on the side of the tire. If storing the tires, keep the tires at the proper inflation pressure if they are mounted on wheels. Keep them in a cool dry place. If the tires are stored in the garage or basement, do not let them stand on a concrete floor; lay them down on a strip of wood or equivalent.

CARE OF SPECIAL WHEELS

Normal appearance maintenance of aluminum wheels includes frequent washing and waxing. However, you *must be careful to avoid the use of abrasive cleaners*. Failure to heed this warning will cause the protective coating to be damaged.

The special coating may also be abraded by repeated washing of the car in an automatic car wash using certain types of brushes. Once the finish abrades, it will provide less protection; then, even normal exposure to either caustic cleaners or road salt will cause the process to continue. If the wheel reaches this point it will require refinishing.

FLUIDS AND LUBRICANTS

Fuel and Engine Oil Recommendations

Chrysler Corporation recommends the use of a high quality, heavy duty detergent oil with the proper viscosity for prevailing conditions. Oils labeled "For Service SG/CC" on the top of the can are satisfactory for use in all engines; however, a higher quality oil, labeled "For Service SG/CD" is preferred for use in turbocharged engines.

It's important to recognize the distinctions between these oil types and the additional

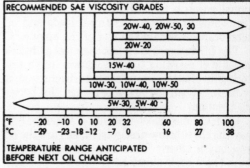

Oil viscosity recommendations for 1981–87 models

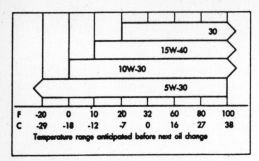

						30		
				15W-40				
		10W-30						
			5W-30					

F	-20	0	10	20	32	60	80	100
C	-29	-18	-12	-7	0	16	27	38

Temperature range anticipated before next oil change

Oil viscosity recommendations for 1988 models

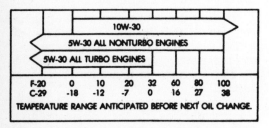

		10W-30						
	5W-30 ALL NONTURBO ENGINES							
5W-30 ALL TURBO ENGINES								

F-20	0	10	20	32	60	80	100
C-29	-18	-12	-7	0	16	27	38

TEMPERATURE RANGE ANTICIPATED BEFORE NEXT OIL CHANGE.

Oil viscosity recommendations for 1989–92 models

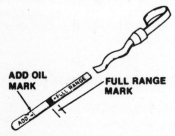

ADD OIL MARK

FULL RANGE MARK

Add oil when the level is at or very close to the "Add oil" mark. One quart will bring it into the "Full Range" as marked

stresses put on oil used in turbocharged engines. Since the turbocharger bearings receive heat conducted directly from the unit's turbine, which may reach a cherry-red heat, oil passing through these bearings may reach temperatures high enough to cause chemical breakdown. This problem is especially severe right when the engine is shut down. Also, the additional power a turbocharged engine produces translates to higher mechanical loads and oil temperatures within the rest of the engine.

The CD designated oil has chemical additives capable of resisting this breakdown and countering its effects. If your car is turbocharged, it will almost surely pay you to use the better designation.

Oil must also meet viscosity standards. Follow the chart below precisely. Make sure the oil you buy is clearly labeled so as to confirm to both these basic standards.

A prime requirement is the use of unleaded

fuel only. All the vehicles covered in this manual require the use of unleaded fuel exclusively, to protect the catalytic converter. Failure to follow this recommendation will result in failure of the catalyst and consequent failure to pass the emission test many states are now requiring. The use of unleaded fuel also prolongs the life of spark plugs, the engine as a whole, and the exhaust system.

Fuels of the same octane rating have varying anti-knock qualities. Thus, if your engine knocks or pings, try switching brands of gasoline before trying a more expensive higher octane fuel. Fuel should be selected for the brand and octane which performs without pinging.

Your engine's fuel requirements can change with time, due to carbon buildup which changes the compression ratio. If switching brands or grades of gas doesn't work, check the ignition timing. If it is necessary to retard timing from specifications, don't change it more than about 4°. Retarded timing will reduce power output and fuel mileage and increase engine temperature.

Basic engine octane requirements, to be used in your initial choice of fuel, are 87 octane, unleaded. This rating is an average of Research and Motor methods of determination (R plus M/2). For increased vehicle performance and gas mileage, turbocharged engines, use a premium unleaded fuel — that is, one with a rating of 91 octane. More octane results in better performance and economy in these engines because the ignition system will compensate for their characteristics by advancing the timing.

Gasohol consisting of 10% ethanol and gasoline may be used in your car, but gasolines containing methanol (wood alcohol) are not ap-

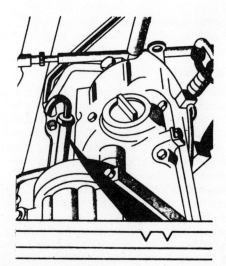

Oil level indicator dipstick

proved. They can damage fuel system parts and cause operating problems.

Engine

OIL LEVEL CHECK

The engine oil level is checked with the dipstick, which is located on the radiator side of the engine. The oil should be checked either before the engine is started or 10 minutes after it has been shut off. This gives the oil time to drain back to the oil pan and prevents an inaccurate oil level reading. Remove the dipstick from the tube, wipe it clean, and insert it back into the tube. Remove it again and observe the oil level. It should be maintained within the indicated range on the dipstick, that is from the maximum level to one quart low.

NOTE: *Do not overfill the crankcase. This will cause oil aeration and loss of oil pressure.*

Be sure to use only oil with an SG rating.

OIL AND FILTER CHANGE

CAUTION: *The EPA warns that prolonged contact with used engine oil may cause a number of skin disorders, including cancer! You should make every effort to minimize your exposure to used engine oil. Protective gloves should be worn when changing the oil. Wash your hands and any other exposed skin areas as soon as possible after exposure to used engine oil. Soap and water, or waterless hand cleaner should be used.*

NOTE: *The manufacturer recommends that the oil filter be changed at every other oil change, after the initial change. This can prove to be effective maintenance, especially if the change interval is carefully adapted to the driving conditions. However, Chilton's philosophy is that changing the filter at every oil change is excellent insurance against filter clogging and the consequent drastically increased wear this will cause. Further, replacing the filter removes a substantial amount of dirty oil whose additives are depleted — an amount that otherwise remains in the system. We recommend, therefore, that the engine oil and oil filter should be changed at the same time, at the intervals recommended on the Maintenance Intervals Chart.*

1. Run the engine until it reaches normal operating temperature.
2. Shut it off, firmly apply the parking brake, and block the wheels.
3. Raise and support the front end on jackstands.
4. Place a drip pan beneath the oil pan and remove the drain plug.

CAUTION: *The oil could be very hot! Protect yourself by using rubber gloves if necessary.*
5. Allow the engine to drain thoroughly.
6. While the oil is draining, replace the filter as described below.
7. When the oil has completely drained, wipe the threads of the plug clean and install it. Tighten it snugly.

NOTE: *The threads in the oil pan are easily stripped! Do not overtighten the plug!*
8. Fill the crankcase with the proper amount of oil shown in the Capacities Chart in this section.
9. Start the engine and check for leaks.

Replacing The Oil Filter

1. Place the drip pan beneath the oil filter.
2. Using an oil filter wrench, turn the filter counterclockwise to remove it.

CAUTION: *The oil could be very hot! Protect yourself by using rubber gloves if necessary.*
3. Wipe the contact surface of the new filter clean and coat the entire inner surface of the rubber gasket with clean engine oil.
4. Wipe the mating surface of the adapter on the block with a clean rag or paper towel.
5. Refer to the instructions on the filter or filter box to determine how tight to make the filter. It will say to turn the filter a certain distance past the point where its gasket touches the block about 1 full turn.
6. Screw the new filter into position on the block until the gasket just touches the block sealing surface. Then hand-turn the filter the additional distance specified on the installation instructions *and no farther.*

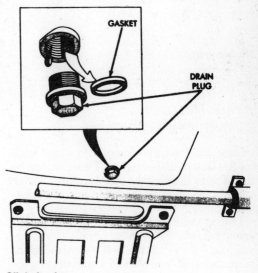

Oil drain plug

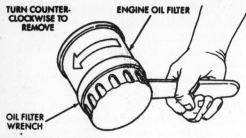

TURN COUNTER-CLOCKWISE TO REMOVE

ENGINE OIL FILTER

OIL FILTER WRENCH

Remove the oil filter

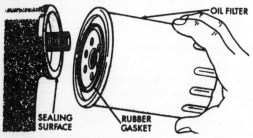

OIL FILTER

SEALING SURFACE

RUBBER GASKET

Install the oil filter

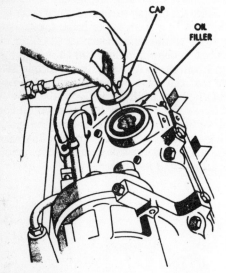

CAP

OIL FILLER

Crankcase fill

Manual Transaxle

FLUID RECOMMENDATIONS

Some early vehicles may be equipped with the A-412 manual transaxle. This unit can be identified by locating the position of the starter which is found on the radiator side of the engine compartment. If it becomes necessary to add fluid to this unit, SAE 80W-90 gear lube is recommended.

If your vehicle has the A-460 or A-465 manual transaxle (4- and 5-speed transaxles respectively), the starter will be next to the firewall.

When it becomes necessary to add fluid to this unit, Dexron®II is recommended. On the A-520 and A-555 manual transaxles used in 1987–88 models, add SAE 5W-30 SG or SG/CC or the equivalent. On all 1989–92 FWD vehicles except 1990–92 Laser and Stealth with manual transaxle, Chrysler Motors recommends Mopar® engine oil, SG or SG/CD SAE 5W-30 or equivalent. On 1990–92 Laser and Stealth use Mopar Hypoid gear oil or equivalent API classification GL-4 or higher.

LEVEL CHECK

The manual transmission fluid level is checked by removing the filler plug. This plug is located on the left side of the unit – at what would normally be the rear of the unit on a front engine, rear drive car, or the side opposite the clutch housing.

1. If you have the right size solid wrench, use that rather than an adjustable one. If you use an adjustable wrench, fit it very snugly and make sure the movable jaw is on the side toward which you are turning (that is, on the right side, if the wrench handle is below the plug). The 1986 and later cars use a filler plug with a finger grip. Just grab the plug with your fingers rather than using a wrench. Loosen the plug and remove it.

2. If a little fluid runs out, the level is, of course, okay. If not, feel for the presence of fluid by sticking your finger or a clean object into the hole. The level must be within $\frac{3}{16}$ in. (5mm) of the bottom of the hole. If necessary, add fluid with a clean syringe. Wipe off the threads, replace the filler plug, and tighten it just snug.

DRAIN AND REFILL

NOTE: *On most vehicles the manual transaxle does not require periodic maintenance refer to the vehicle owner's manual maintenance schedules. The oil should be changed only when water contamination is suspected. The 1990–92 Laser and Stealth vehicles have a drain plug remove drain plug to drain fluid if necessary.*

1. The unit has no drain plug. To drain the fluid, you will need a tube of RTV sealant and a supply of clean rags. Place a drain pan under the cover at the rear of the unit (the side away from the engine and clutch).

2. Remove the bolts or studs. Gently pull the cover away from the transaxle and remove it to allow the fluid to drain.

3. Clean the magnet and the inside surface of the cover. Make sure to remove all old sealant. Then, use the tube of sealant to form a new gasket on the inside of the cover, as shown in the illustration.

4. Install the cover mounting bolts and

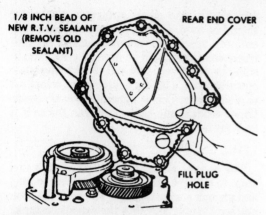

Forming a bead of sealer on the manual transaxle rear cover

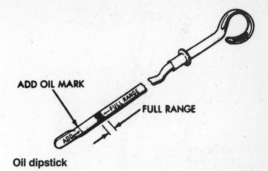

Oil dipstick

torque them to 21 ft. lbs. on the A-460/465/525 models and to 40 ft. lbs. on the A-520 and A-555 manual transaxles used in 1987-88 models. Refill the unit with the approved fluid until it appears at the filler plug and install and tighten the plug.

Automatic Transaxle

FLUID RECOMMENDATIONS

ATF bearing the designation "Dexron®II" should be used for all automatic transaxles up through 1986. For 1987-92 models, Chrysler recommends the use of Mopar ATF fluid type 7176 "...for optimum transmission performance." Dexron®II may be used if the Chrysler fluid is not available.

The Dodge Monaco with ZF-4 transaxle requires Mopar Mercon® automatic transmission fluid

LEVEL CHECK

On 1983 and earlier models, the automatic transaxle fluid level must be checked when the transmission is at normal operating temperature. Otherwise, the fluid will not have expanded enough to give an accurate reading. Drive the car at least 10 miles to ensure the transmission has warmed up.

On 1984 and later models, the fluid can be checked after a short drive (3-4 miles), at which time it is considered to be "Warm" or after 15 miles or more of operation, at which time it will have reached about 180°F (82°C) and is considered to the "Hot". If the fluid is warm, it will be comfortable to grab the wet end of the dipstick just after pulling it out (just be sure not to check the level if the dipstick feels cold). If the fluid is hot, you will not be able to hold the wet end of the dipstick comfortably. *Be careful in checking it to pinch it very briefly so you will not*

be burned. Once temperature is determined, fluid level is checked in the following manner:

1. With the parking brake engaged and the engine idling shift the transmission through the shift pattern and return it to the Park position. Make sure the transmission runs for at least 60 seconds before attempting to check fluid level.

2. Remove the dipstick. The fluid level should be between the ADD and FULL marks. On the models with two fluid level ranges, just read the "Warm" or "Hot" section of the stick, as appropriate. Add fluid (with a funnel, if necessary), right through the dipstick tube, until the level reaches the "FULL" mark, but never until it goes above it. Note that it is *vitally* important not to overfill the transmission. This is because overfilling will cause the moving parts to aerate or foam the oil so that shifting characteristics will change and the transmission may be damaged due to poor lubrication.

DRAIN AND REFILL

On most vehicles (except Dodge Monaco, 1990–92 Laser ansd Stealth 30,000 miles or 30 months change intervals) the automatic transaxle does not require periodic maintenance unless the vehicle is subjected to severe service conditions refer to the vehicle owner's manual maintenance schedules. Refer to Chapter 7 for the necessary service procedure.

PAN AND FILTER SERVICE

Refer to Chapter 7 for the necessary service procedures.

DIFFERENTIAL FLUID CHECK AUTOMATIC TRANSAXLE

1981–82 Models

Under normal operating conditions, lubricant changes are not required for this unit. However, fluid level checks are required every 7500 miles or 12 months whichever comes first. The fluid level should be within ⅜ in. (10mm) of the bottom of the fill plug.

NOTE: *A rod with a U-bend at the end can be*

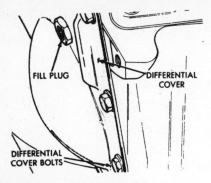

FILL PLUG

DIFFERENTIAL COVER

DIFFERENTIAL COVER BOLTS

Differential (cover) fill plug location

made to check the fluid level. If it becomes necessary to add or replace the fluid use only Dexron®II automatic transmission fluid.

Rear Drive Axle

FLUID RECOMMENDATIONS

The rear axle lubricant for vehicles equipped with AWD should be API classification GL-5 or higher.

LEVEL CHECK

On vehicles equipped with AWD, remove the filler plug and inspect the oil level at the bottom of the filler hole. If the oil level is slightly below the filler hole, it is in satisfactory condition.

DRAIN AND REFILL

On vehicles equipped with AWD, remove the drain plug and drain out the oil. Put the oil plug back in place and then pour new oil in through the filler hole.

Cooling System

FLUID RECOMMENDATIONS

The cooling system was filled at the factory with a high quality coolant solution that is good for year around operation and protects the system from freezing. If coolant is needed, a 50/50

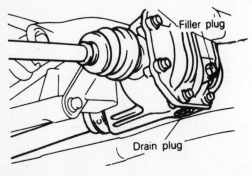

Filler plug

Drain plug

Rear axle assembly

mix of ethylene glycol antifreeze and water should be used. Alcohol or methanol base coolants are specifically not recommended. Antifreeze solution should be used all year, even in summer, to prevent rust and to take advantage of the solution's higher boiling point compared to plain water. This is imperative on air conditioned models; the heater core can freeze if it isn't protected.

LEVEL CHECK

The coolant should be checked at each fuel stop, to prevent the possibility of overheating and serious engine damage. To check the coolant level simply look into the expansion tank.

CAUTION: *The radiator coolant is under pressure when hot. To avoid the danger of physical injury, coolant should be checked or replenished only when cool. To remove the cap, slowly rotate it counterclockwise to the stop, but do not press down. Wait until all pressure is released (indicated when the hissing sound stops) then press down on the cap while continuing to rotate it counterclockwise. Wear a glove or use a thick rag for protection.*

WARNING: *Never add large quantities of cold coolant to a hot engine. A cracked engine block may result. If it is absolutely necessary to add coolant to a hot engine, do so only with the engine idling and add only small quantities at a time.*

Simply add coolant mixture to the tank until the upper level line is reached. If the system shows signs of overheating and, possibly, a small leak, you may want to check the level in the radiator *when the engine is cold.* If the radiator is not full, replace the cap, as it has lost the ability to retain vacuum or is of improper design for a coolant overflow tank type of system, such as that used on your car.

Each year, the cooling system should be serviced as follows:

1. Wash the radiator cap and filler neck with clean water.

2. Check the coolant for proper level and freeze protection.

3. Have the system pressure tested. If a replacement cap is installed, be sure that it conforms to the original specifications.

4. Tighten the hose clamps and inspect all hoses. Replace hoses that are swollen, cracked or otherwise deteriorated.

5. Clean the frontal area of the radiator core and the air conditioning condenser, if so equipped.

DRAIN AND REFILL

Every 2 years, the system should be serviced as follows:

1. Run the engine with the cap removed and the heater on until operating temperature is reached (indicated by heat in the upper radiator hose).

2. With the engine stopped, open the radiator drain cock located at the bottom of the radiator, and (to speed the draining) the engine block drains, if any (most of the cars covered in this manual do not have block drains).

3. Completely drain the coolant, and close the drain cocks.

4. Add sufficient clean water to fill the system. Run the engine and drain and refill the system as often as necessary until the drain water is nearly colorless.

5. Add sufficient ethylene glycol coolant to provide the required freezing and corrosion protection (at least a 50% solution of antifreeze and water). Fill the radiator to the cold level. Run the engine with the cap removed until normal operating temperature is reached.

6. Check the hot level.

7. Install the cap.

FLUSHING AND CLEANING THE SYSTEM

A well maintained system should never require aggressive flushing or cleaning. However, you may find that you (or a previous owner) has neglected to change the antifreeze often enough to fully protect the system. It may have obviously accumulated rust inside, or you there may be visible clogging of the radiator tubes.

There are two basic means of rectifying this situation for the do-it-yourselfer. One is to purchase a kit designed to allow you to reverse-flush the system with the pressure available from a garden hose. This kit comes with special fittings which allow you to force water downward inside the engine block and upward (or in reverse of normal flow) in the radiator. It will have complete instructions.

The other means is to purchase a chemical cleaner. The cleaner is installed after the system is flushed and filled with fresh water and cleans the system as you drive a short distance or idle the engine hot. In all cases, the cleaner must be flushed completely from the system after use. In some cases, it may be necessary to follow up with use of a neutralizer. Make sure to follow the instructions very carefully. These cleaners are quite potent, chemically, and work very well; because of that fact, you must be careful to flush and, if necessary, neutralize the effect of the cleaner to keep it from damaging your cooling system.

If the radiator is severely clogged, it may be necessary to have the tubes rodded out by a professional radiator repair shop. In this case, the radiator must be removed and taken to the shop for this highly specialized work. You can

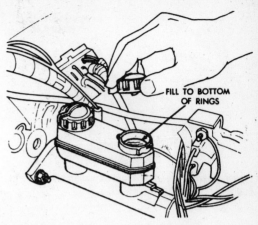

Checking the master cylinder fluid level

save money on the job by removing and replacing the radiator yourself, as described in Chapter 3.

Master Cylinder

FLUID RECOMMENDATIONS

Use *only* brake fluid conforming to Federal DOT 3 specifications.

LEVEL CHECK

Once every 7500 miles or 6 months check the brake fluid level in the master cylinder. The master cylinder is mounted either on the firewall or the brake booster, and is divided into two reservoirs. The fluid must be maintained at the bottom of the split ring.

NOTE: *On vehicles with anti-lock brake system, depressurize the system BEFORE, inspecting the fluid level. Turn OFF the ignition and remove the key. Pump the brake pedal at least 50 times to relieve the pressure in the brake system.*

Remove the two master cylinder caps and fill to the bottom of the split rings using DOT 3 brake fluid. If the brake fluid level is chronically low there may be a leak in the system which should be investigated immediately.

NOTE: *Brake fluid absorbs moisture from the air, which reduces its effectiveness and causes corrosion. Never leave the brake fluid can or master cylinder uncovered any longer than necessary. Brake fluid also damages paint. If any is spilled, it should be washed off immediately with clear, cold water.*

Power Steering Pump

FLUID RECOMMENDATIONS

Use power steering fluid, Part No. 2084329 on 1981–83 models, and Part No. 4318055 on later models, or its equivalent.

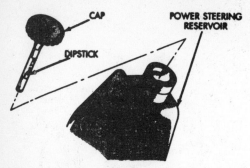

Power steering reservoir dipstick assembly—2.2/2.5L engines

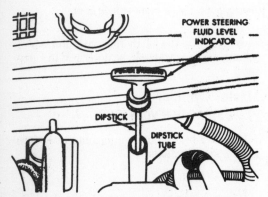

Power steering reservoir dipstick assembly—3.0L engine

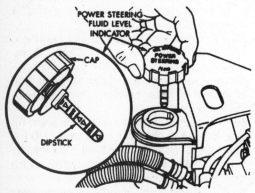

Power steering reservoir dipstick assembly—3.3/3.8L engines

LEVEL CHECK

Maintain the proper fluid level as indicated on the cap of the reservoir. Check the level with the engine off and at normal ambient temperature (overnight cold). The dipstick should indicate FULL COLD. If the reservoir needs fluid refill with the approved fluid.

Manual Steering Gear

FLUID RECOMMENDATIONS

The approved lubricant for the steering gear is API GL-5. However, the rack and pinion manual steering units used on this car are permanently sealed. The lubricant is replenished only in connection with a major rebuild of the unit not covered by this manual.

LEVEL CHECK

The manual steering gear is permanently lubricated at the factory and periodic replenishment of lubricant is not needed. However, you should inspect the two rubber boots that seal between the housing and the tie rod ends when checking the engine oil and other fluid levels. Make sure there is no leakage and that the boots are intact. Have the boots replaced if necessary. Check also for leakage where the steering shaft passes into the gearbox.

Chassis Greasing

Chassis greasing can be performed with a pressurized grease gun or it can be performed at home using a hand-operated grease gun. Wipe the fittings clean before greasing, in order to prevent the possibility of forcing any dirt into the component.

Ball joint and steering linkages are semi-permanently lubricated at the factory with a special grease. They should be regreased every 30,000 miles or 3 years whichever comes first. When regreasing is necessary, use only special long life chassis grease such as Multi-Mileage lubricant Part No. 2525035 or its equivalent.

Body Lubrication

Body hinges and latches should be lubricated, as necessary, to maintain smooth operation of doors and the front and rear hoods. Wipe all parts with a clean rag prior to lubrication. *Pay particular attention to the smooth operation of hood latch components as failure to operate can produce an extreme safety hazard — inspect and lubricate these with great care. If any problems appear, have them corrected immediately.* Lubricate each part with the grease specified below:

- Door hinges — Engine oil.
- Door latches, rotors, and strikers — Wheel bearing grease.
- Hood latch, release mechanism, and safety catch — apply sparingly to all contact areas — Multipurpose lubricant NLGI Grade 2.
- Hood hinges and counterbalance springs — Mopar Multi-mileage Lubricant 4318062 or equivalent.

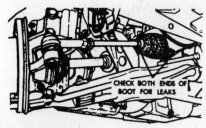

Inspect steering linkage

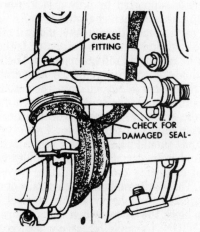

Tie rod seal and grease fitting

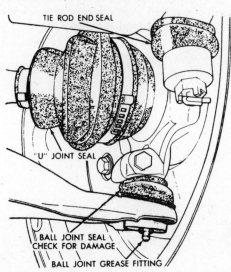

Front suspension ball joint seal and grease fitting

- Seat regulator and track adjusters — Mopar Spray White Lube 4318066 or equivalent.
- Tailgate — all pivot and slide contact surfaces on hinges, quick release pins, and release handles — Spray White Lube.
- Tailgate check arms — Engine oil.

Wheel Bearings

Your Chrysler front wheel drive vehicle is equipped with permanently sealed front wheel bearings. There is no periodic adjustment for these units.

The rear wheel bearings should be inspected whenever the drums are removed to inspect or service the brakes, or at least every 22,500 miles. For lubrication procedures of these bearings refer to Chapter 7.

TRAILER TOWING

NOTE: *Trailer towing on 1990–92 Laser, Stealth and some other models such as convertible models is not recommended by the manufacturer.*

Trailer towing is best performed by vehicles equipped with special towing packages to improve engine and transmission cooling and to help the suspension system carry the extra weight. However, towing is permitted without these special systems, provided the road conditions are normal (both ascending and descending steep hills must be avoided) and the temperatures are moderate (extreme heat must also be avoided). The sole exception is that towing is *strictly prohibited with a turbocharged engine.* This is because of the tremendous ability of the turbocharged engine to produce high power output, which, in the absence of towing a trailer, can usually be sustained for only very short periods.

The Maximum loads depend on the engine and transmission in use. They are:

- 2.2L manual transmission — 1,000 lbs. (454kg)
- 2.2L automatic transmission — 1,500 lbs. (680kg)
- 2.5L manual transmission — 1,000 lbs. (454kg)
- 2.5L automatic transmission — 2,000 lbs. (907kg)
- 2.6L Mitsubishi engine — 2,000 lbs. (907kg)

The trailer tongue load must not cause the total weight permitted for your car to be exceeded. Note also that, if the trailer weighs more than 1,000 lbs. (454kg) it must not be towed without its own brakes, as the capacity of the vehicle's brakes will be substantially exceeded.

Check the automatic transmission fluid level and color. Make sure the fluid level is correct. If the fluid is burnt, replace the fluid and filter. Should the temperature gauge rise above the normal indication while driving on the highway, reduce your speed. If the engine begins to get hot in traffic, put the (automatic) transmission in neutral and allow the engine to idle and normal idle speed.

PUSHING AND TOWING

On 1990–92 Laser, Stealth and Dodge Monaco, always use a flat bed tow truck to tow these vehicles. Many Chrysler vehicles are equipped with air dams, spoilers or ground effect skirting in these cases the use of a wheel lift or flat bed type towing equipment is recommended. Refer to the vehicle owner's manual for any additional information as necessary.

Most older vehicles can be towed from either the front or rear. If the vehicle is towed from the front for an extended distance make sure the parking brake is completely released.

Manual transmission vehicles may be towed on the front wheels at speeds up to 35 mph, for a distance not to exceed 15 miles, provided the transmission is in neutral and the driveline has not been damaged. The steering wheel must be clamped in a straight ahead position.

WARNING: *Do not use the steering column lock to secure front wheel position for towing.*

Automatic transmission vehicles may be towed on the front wheels at speeds not to exceed 25 mph for a period of 15 miles.

WARNING: *If this requirement cannot be met, the front wheels must be placed on a dolly.*

JUMP STARTING

See page 43.

JACKING

The standard jack utilizes special receptacles located at the body sills to accept the scissors jack supplied with the vehicle for emergency road service. The jack supplied with the car should never be used for any service operation other than tire changing. Never get under the car while it is supported by only a jack. Always block the wheels when changing tires.

The service operations in this manual often require that one end or the other, or both, of the car be raised and safely supported. The ideal method, of course, would be a hydraulic hoist. Since this is beyond both the resource and requirement of the do-it-yourselfer, a small hydraulic, screw or scissors jack will suffice for the procedures in this guide. Two sturdy jackstands should be acquired if you intend to work under the car at any time. An alternate method of raising the car would be drive-on ramps. These are available commercially or can be fabricated from heavy boards or steel. Be sure to block the wheels when using ramps.

CAUTION: *Concrete blocks are not recommended for supporting the car. They are likely to crumble if the load is not evenly distributed. Boxes and milk crates of any description must not be used to support the car!*

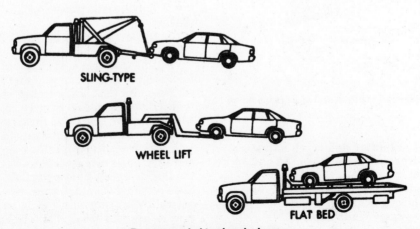

SLING-TYPE

WHEEL LIFT

FLAT BED

Recommended towing devices

JUMP STARTING A DEAD BATTERY

The chemical reaction in a battery produces explosive hydrogen gas. This is the safe way to jump start a dead battery, reducing the chances of an accidental spark that could cause an explosion.

Jump Starting Precautions

1. Be sure both batteries are of the same voltage.
2. Be sure both batteries are of the same polarity (have the same grounded terminal).
3. Be sure the vehicles are not touching.
4. Be sure the vent cap holes are not obstructed.
5. Do not smoke or allow sparks around the battery.
6. In cold weather, check for frozen electrolyte in the battery.
7. Do not allow electrolyte on your skin or clothing.
8. Be sure the electrolyte is not frozen.

Jump Starting Procedure

1. Determine voltages of the two batteries; they must be the same.
2. Bring the starting vehicle close (they must not touch) so that the batteries can be reached easily.
3. Turn off all accessories and both engines. Put both cars in Neutral or Park and set the handbrake.
4. Cover the cell caps with a rag—do not cover terminals.
5. If the terminals on the run-down battery are heavily corroded, clean them.
6. Identify the positive and negative posts on both batteries and connect the cables in the order shown.
7. Start the engine of the starting vehicle and run it at fast idle. Try to start the car with the dead battery. Crank it for no more than 10 seconds at a time and let it cool off for 20 seconds in between tries.
8. If it doesn't start in 3 tries, there is something else wrong.
9. Disconnect the cables in the reverse order.
10. Replace the cell covers and dispose of the rags.

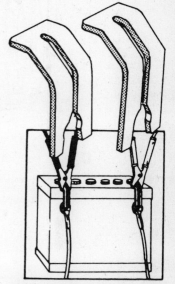

Side terminal batteries occasionally pose a problem when connecting jumper cables. There frequently isn't enough room to clamp the cables without touching sheet metal. Side terminal adaptors are available to alleviate this problem and should be removed after use.

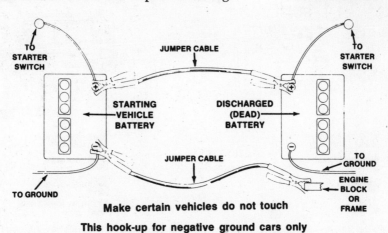

TO STARTER SWITCH

JUMPER CABLE

TO STARTER SWITCH

STARTING VEHICLE BATTERY

DISCHARGED (DEAD) BATTERY

JUMPER CABLE

TO GROUND

ENGINE BLOCK OR FRAME

TO GROUND

Make certain vehicles do not touch

This hook-up for negative ground cars only

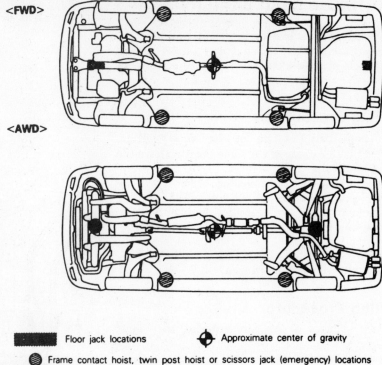

Floor jack locations

Approximate center of gravity

Frame contact hoist, twin post hoist or scissors jack (emergency) locations

Hoisting and jacking points—1990–92 Laser and Stealth

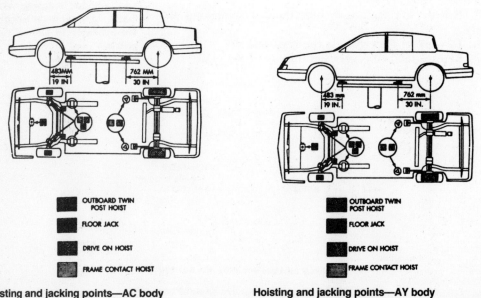

OUTBOARD TWIN POST HOIST

FLOOR JACK

DRIVE ON HOIST

FRAME CONTACT HOIST

OUTBOARD TWIN POST HOIST

FLOOR JACK

DRIVE ON HOIST

FRAME CONTACT HOIST

Hoisting and jacking points—AC body

Hoisting and jacking points—AY body

MAINTENANCE INTERVALS CHART 1981–87
Chrysler Front Wheel Drive Cars

Operation	Mileage Interval (in thousands)
Engine Oil/Filter Change (without Turbocharger)	7.5 (12 months)①
Engine Oil/Filter Change (with Turbocharger)	7.5 (6 months)
Carburetor Air Filter (2.6L engine)	30
Apply Solvent to Choke/Fast Idle Cam (Carb. only)	30
Replace Spark Plugs (with Cat. Conv.)	30
Replace Spark Plugs (without Cat. Conv.)	15
Adjust Valve Lash (2.6L Engine)	15
Adjust/Inspect Drive Belts	15
Drain and Flush Cooling System	30 (24 months)②
Inspect Brake Hoses	7.5 (12 months, 6 months on Turbos)
Inspect Front and Rear Brake Linings	22.5
Inspect Rear Wheel Bearings	22.5
Lubricate Tie Rod Ends and Steering Linkage	48 (3 years)
Lubricate Ball Joints (1981–83 only)	48 (3 years)
Check Auto Transaxle Differential Fluid Level (1981–83 only)	7.5 (12 months)

① In severe service, change at 3000 miles, 3 months. This includes stop and go driving in extreme cold, driving in dusty conditions, extensive idling, operating at sustained high speeds with temperatures above 90°F.
② Original factory fill may be used for 52,500 miles and 36 months.

MAINTENANCE INTERVALS CHART 1988
Chrysler Front Wheel Drive Cars

Operation	Mileage Interval (in thousands)
Change Engine Oil and Filter①	7.5 (12 months)
Inspect/Adjust Drive Belts	15
Replace Spark Plugs	30
Replace Engine Air Filter	30
Replace Oxygen Sensor	52.5
Replace EGR Valve and Tube and Clean Passage	52.5 (60 months)
Replace PCV Filter	30
Replace PCV Valve	60 (60 months)
Replace Vacuum Operated Emission Controls	52.5 (60 months)
Adjust Idle Mixture (with Propane)	52.5
Check/Adjust Ignition Timing	60
Replace Ign. Wires, Cap, and Rotor	60
Flush/Replace Coolant	52.5 (36 months)②
Replace Alternator Brushes	75
Inspect Brake Hoses	7.5 (12 months non-turbo, 6 months turbo)
Inspect Brake Linings Front and Rear	22.5
Inspect Rear Wheel Bearings	82.5 (then every 30,000 miles)
Lubricate Tie Rod Ends and Steering Linkage	90 (36 months)

① At this time, inspect driveshaft boots for leaks and replace as necessary.
② After first change, replace at 24 months/30,000 miles. Check hoses, cap, clamps, and coolant for cleanliness every 12 months.

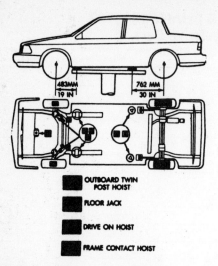

Hoisting and jacking points—AA body

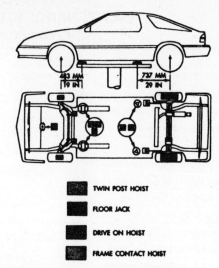

Hoisting and jacking points—AG body

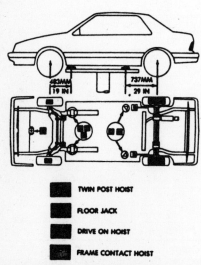

Hoisting and jacking points—AP body

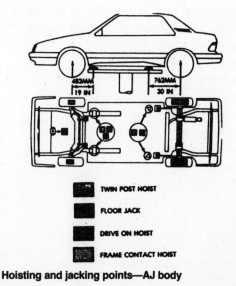

Hoisting and jacking points—AJ body

LUBRICATION AND MAINTENANCE SCHEDULES
1988–92 Chrysler Front Wheel Drive Cars

SCHEDULED MAINTENANCE FOR CONTROL AND VEHICLE PERFORMANCE. Inspection and service should be performed when malfunction is suspected.

SERVICE—Kilometers × 1000	12	24	36	48	60	72
—Miles × 1000	7.5	15	22.5	30	37.5	45
CHANGE ENGINE OIL NON-TURBO 12 Months	X	X	X	X	X	X
TURBO 6 Months**	X	X	X	X	X	X
REPLACE ENGINE OIL FILTER*	X		X		X	
INSPECT ENGINE AIR FILTER		X		X		X
REPLACE SPARK PLUGS Mileage Only				X		
INSPECT DRIVE BELTS Service as Required			X	X		X

*If mileage is less than 12,000 km (7,500 miles) change filter at every oil change
**4,800 km (3,000 miles) or 3 months if SG service engine oil is used.

GENERAL MAINTENANCE

	12	24	36	48	60	72
INSPECT BAKE LININGS All Wheels-Service as Required			X			X
GREASE TIE ROD ENDS at 3 Years or				X		
GREASE BALL JOINTS at 3 Years or				X		
INSPECT DRIVE SHAFT BOOTS for Leaks	X	X	X	X	X	X
INSPECT BRAKE HOSES at Every Oil Change and Whenever Brakes Are Serviced						
INSPECT COOLING SYSTEM Every 12 Months						
FLUSH AND WINTERIZE COOLING SYSTEM Every 36 Months or 83,000 km (52,000 miles)						
INSPECT AND LUBRICATE REAR WHEEL BEARINGS			X			X

SEVERE SERVICE MAINTENANCE Driving in Stop/Go Conditions, Long Idling Periods, Frequent Short Trips, Operating at Sustained High Speeds in Temperatures Above 32°C (90°F).

Kilometers × 1000	4.8	9.6	14	19	24	29	34	38	43	48	53	58	62	67	72	77
Mileage × 1000	3	6	9	12	15	18	21	24	27	30	33	36	39	42	45	48
CHANGE OIL***—6 Months	X	X	X	X	X	X	X	X	X	X	X	X	X	X	X	X
REPLACE OIL FILTER	X		X		X		X		X		X		X		X	
REPLACE AIR FILTER Inspect and Replace if Required					X					X					X	
INSPECT BALL JOINTS	X	X	X	X	X	X	X	X	X	X	X	X	X	X	X	X
INSPECT CV JOINTS	X	X	X	X	X	X	X	X	X	X	X	X	X	X	X	X
CHANGE TRANS FLUID Adjust Bands at Time of Fluid and Filter Change					X					X					X	
LUBRICATE THE ROD ENDS Every 18 Months or Mileage Specified					X					X					X	
INSPECT BRAKE LININGS All Wheels—Replace as Necessary		X				X			X			X			X	

***3 months if SG service engine oil is used.

LUBRICATION AND MAINTENANCE SCHEDULES
1990–92 Laser

No.	Emission Control System Maintenance	Service Intervals	Kilometers in Thousands 24	48	72	80	96
			Mileage in Thousands 15	30	45	50	60
1	Check Fuel System (Tank, Line and Connections and Fuel Filler Cap) for Leaks Every 5 Years		or			X	
2	Check Fuel Every 2 Years for Leaks or Damage		or	X			X
3	Replace Air Cleaner Element		at	X			X
4	Replace Spark Plugs		at	X			X

GENERAL MAINTENANCE SERVICE FOR PROPER VEHICLE PERFORMANCE

No.	General Maintenance		Service Intervals	Kilometers in Thousands 24	48	72	80	96
				Mileage in Thousands 15	30	45	50	60
5	Timing Belt (Including the Balancer Belt)		Replace	at				X
6	Drive Belt (for Water Pump and Alternator)		Inspect for tension	at	X			X
7	Engine Oil	Non-Turbo	Change Every Year	or	Every 12,000 km (7,5000 miles)			
		Turbo	Change Every 6 Months		Every 8,000 km (5,000 miles)			
8	Engine Oil Filter	Non-Turbo	Chang Every Year	or	X X X			X
		Turbo	Change Every Year		Every 16,000 km (10,000 miles)			
9	Manual Transaxle Oil		Inspect Oil Level	at	X			X
10	Automatic Transaxle Fluid		Inspect Fluid Level Every Year	or	X X X			X
			Change Fluid	at	X			X
11	Engine Coolant		Replace Every 2 Years	or	X			X
12	Disc Brake Pads		Inspect for Wear Every Year	or	X X X			X
13	Brake Hoses		Check for Deterioration or Leaks Every Year	or	X X X			X
14	Ball Joint and Steering Linkage Seals		Inspect for Grease Leaks and Damage Every 2 Years	or	X			X
15	Drive Shaft Boots		Inspect for Grease Leaks and Damage Every Year	or	X X X			X
16	Rear Axle <AWD>	With LSD	Change Oil		X			X
		Without LSD	Inspect Oil Level		X			X
17	Exhaust System (Connection Portion of Muffler, Pipings and Converter Heat Shields)		Check and Service as Required Every 2 Years	or	X			X

NOTE: LSD—Limited-slip differential

LUBRICATION AND MAINTENANCE SCHEDULES
1990–92 Laser

SCHEDULED MAINTENANCE UNDER SEVERE USAGE CONDITIONS
The maintenance items should be performed according to the following table.

Maintenance Item	Service to be Performed	12 (7.5)	24 (15)	36 (22.5)	48 (30)	60 (37.5)	72 (45)	80 (50)	84 (52.5)	96 (60)	A	B	C	D	E	F	G
		Mileage Intervals Kilometers in Thousands (Miles in Thousands)									**Severe Usage Conditions**						
Air Cleaner Element	Replace	More Frequently									X				X		
Spark Plugs	Replace	X		X		X			X		X	X	X				
Engine Oil	Change Every 3 Months or	Every 4,800 km (3,000 miles)									X	X	X	X			X
Engine Oil Filter	Replace Every 6 Months or	Every 9,600 km (6,000 miles)									X	X	X	X			X
Disc Brake Pads	Inspect for Wear	More Frequently									X					X	

Severe usage conditions
  A—Driving in dusty conditions
  B—Trailer towing or police, taxi, or commercial type operation
  C—Extensive idling
  D—Short trip operation at freezing temperatures (engine not thoroughly warmed up)
  E—Driving in sandy areas
  F—Driving in salty areas
  G—More than 50% operation in heavy city traffic during hot weather above 32°C (90°F)

LUBRICATION AND MAINTENANCE SCHEDULES
1991–92 Laser

SCHEDULED MAINTENANCE UNDER SEVERE USAGE CONDITIONS
The maintenance items should be performed according to the following table.

Maintenance Item	Service to be Performed	12 (7.5)	24 (15)	36 (22.5)	48 (30)	60 (37.5)	72 (45)	80 (50)	84 (52.5)	96 (60)	A	B	C	D	E	F	G
		Mileage Intervals Kilometers in Thousands (Miles in Thousands)									**Severe Usage Conditions**						
Air Cleaner Element	Replace	More Frequently									X				X		
Spark Plugs	Replace	X		X		X			X		X	X	X				
Engine Oil	Change Every 3 Months or	Every 4,800 km (3,000 miles)									X	X	X	X			X
Engine Oil Filter	Replace Every 6 Months or	Every 9,600 km (6,000 miles)									X	X	X	X			X
Disc Brake Pads	Inspect for Wear	More Frequently									X					X	

Severe usage conditions
  A—Driving in dusty conditions
  B—Trailer towing or police, taxi, or commercial type operation
  C—Extensive idling
  D—Short trip operation at freezing temperatures (engine not thoroughly warmed up)
  E—Driving in sandy areas
  F—Driving in salty areas
  G—More than 50% operation in heavy city traffic during hot weather above 32°C (90°F)

LUBRICATION AND MAINTENANCE SCHEDULES
1991–92 Stealth

No.	Emission Control System Maintenance	Service Intervals		Kilometers in Thousands — 24	48	72	80	96
				Mileage in Thousands — 15	30	45	50	60
1	Check Fuel System (Tank, Line and Connections and Fuel Filler Cap) for Leaks Every 5 Years			or			X	
2	Check Fuel Hoses for Leaks or Damage Every 2 Years			or	X			X
3	Replace Air Cleaner Element		at		X			X
4	Replace Spark Plugs	at	SOHC			X		X
			DOHC					X

GENERAL MAINTENANCE SERVICE FOR PROPER VEHICLE PERFORMANCE

No.	General Maintenance		Service Intervals		Kilometers in Thousands — 24	48	72	80	96
					Mileage in Thousands — 15	30	45	50	60
5	Timing Belt		Replace	at					X
6	Drive Belt (for Alternator)		Inspect for tension	at		X			X
7	Engine Oil	Non-Turbo	Change Every Year	or	Every 12,000 km (7,5000 miles)				
		Turbo	Change Every 6 Months		Every 8,000 km (5,000 miles)				
8	Engine Oil Filter	Non-Turbo	Change Every Year	or	X	X	X		X
		Turbo	Change Every Year		Every 16,000 km (10,000 miles)				
9	Manual Transaxle Oil		Inspect Oil Level	at		X			X
10	Automatic Transaxle Fluid		Inspect Fluid Level Every Year	or	X	X	X		X
			Change Fluid	at		X			X
11	Engine Coolant		Replace Every 2 Years	or		X			X
12	Disc Brake Pads		Inspect for Wear Every Year	or	X	X	X		X
13	Brake Hoses		Check for Deterioration or Leaks Every Year	or	X	X	X		X
14	Ball Joint and Steering Linkage Seals		Inspect for Grease Leaks and Damage Every 2 Years	or		X			X
15	Drive Shaft Boots		Inspect for Grease Leaks and Damage Every Year	or	X	X	X		X
16	Rear Axle <AWD>	With LSD	Change Oil			X			X
		Without LSD	Inspect Oil Level			X			X
17	Exhaust System (Connection Portion of Muffler, Pipings and Converter Heat Shields)		Check and Service as Required Every 2 Years	or		X			X

NOTE: LSD—Limited-slip differential

CAPACITIES
Acclaim, Aries, Caravelle, Daytona, Dynasty, E-Class Executive Sedan, Imperial, Lancer, Laser (1984–86) Le Baron, New Yorker Reliant, Shadow, Spirit, Sundance Town & Country, 400 and 600

Year	Engine Displacement liter (cc)	Engine Crankcase with Filter	Transmission (pts.)			Transfer case (pts.)	Drive Axle		Fuel Tank (gal.)	Cooling System (qts.)
			4-Spd	5-Spd	Auto.		Front (pts.)	Rear (pts.)		
1981	2.2L	4	4	—	15	—	2	—	13	7
	2.6L	5	4	—	17	—	2	—	13	8½
1982	2.2L	4	4	—	15	—	2	—	13	7
	2.6L	5	4	—	15	—	2	—	13	8½
1983	2.2L	4	4	4½	18	—	①	—	13②	9
	2.6L	5	4	4½	18	—	①	—	13②	9
1984	2.2L	4	4	4½	18	—	①	—	14	9
	2.6L	5	4	4½	18	—	①	—	14	9
1985	2.2L	4③	4	5	18	—	①	—	14	9
	2.6L	5	4	5	18	—	①	—	14	9
1986	2.2L	4③	5	5	18	—	①	—	14	9
	2.5L	5	5	5	18	—	①	—	14	9
1987	2.2L	4③	5	5	18	—	①	—	14	9
	2.5L	4	5	5	18	—	①	—	14	9
1988	2.2L	4	5	5	18	—	①	—	14④	9
	2.5L	4	5	5	18	—	①	—	14④	9
1989	2.2L	4.5	—	5	18	—	①	—	14⑤	9
	2.5L	4.5	—	5	18	—	①	—	14⑤	9
	3.0L	4.5	—	5	18	—	①	—	14⑤	9
1990	2.2L	4.5	—	5	18	—	①	—	14⑤	9
	2.5L	4.5	—	5	18	—	①	—	14⑤	9
	3.0L	4.5	—	5	18	—	①	—	14⑤	9
	3.3L	4.5	—	5	18	—	①	—	14⑤	9
1991	2.2L	4.5	—	5	18	—	①	—	14⑤	9
	2.5L	4.5	—	5	18	—	①	—	14⑤	9
	3.0L	4.5	—	5	18	—	①	—	14⑤	9
	3.3L	4.5	—	5	18	—	①	—	14⑤	9
	3.8L	4.5	—	5	18	—	①	—	14⑤	9
1992	2.2L	4.5	—	5	18	—	①	—	14⑤	9
	2.5L	4.5	—	5	18	—	①	—	14⑤	9
	3.0L	4.5	—	5	18	—	①	—	14⑤	9
	3.3L	4.5	—	5	18	—	①	—	14⑤	9
	3.8L	4.5	—	5	18	—	①	—	14⑤	9

① The differential is combined with the transaxle assembly 1983 and later models.
② Model with EFI-14 gallons
③ 2.2L Turbo Engine—5 quarts
④ LeBaron and LeBaron GTS—16 gallons
⑤ AA, AC or AY Body—16 gallons

CAPACITIES
1990–92 Plymouth Laser

Year	Engine Displacement liter (cc)	Engine Crankcase with Filter	Transmission (pts.)			Transfer case (pts.)	Drive Axle		Fuel Tank (gal.)	Cooling System (qts.)
			4-Spd	5-Spd	Auto.		Front (pts.)	Rear (pts.)		
1990	1.8L	4	—	4	12	—	—	—	16	6½
	2.0L	4½	—	4①	13	—	—	—	16	7½
1991	1.8L	4	—	4	12	—	—	—	16	6½
	2.0L	4½	—	4①	13	—	—	—	16	7½
1992	1.8L	4	—	4	12	—	—	—	16	6½
	2.0L	4½	—	4①	13	2②	—	2②	16	7½

① FWD and AWD Turbocharged engine 5 pts.
② If equipped with all wheel drive (AWD).

CAPACITIES
1991–92 Dodge Stealth

Year	Engine Displacement liter (cc)	Engine Crankcase with Filter	Transmission (pts.)			Transfer case (pts.)	Drive Axle		Fuel Tank (gal.)	Cooling System (qts.)
			4-Spd	5-Spd	Auto.		Front (pts.)	Rear (pts.)		
1991	3.0L	4.2	—	5	16	1①	—	2①	20	8½
1992	3.0L	4.2	—	5	16	1①	—	2①	20	8½

① If equipped with all wheel drive (AWD)

CAPACITIES
1990–92 Dodge Monaco

Year	Engine Displacement liter (cc)	Engine Crankcase with Filter	Transmission (pts.)			Transfer case (pts.)	Drive Axle		Fuel Tank (gal.)	Cooling System (qts.)
			4-Spd	5-Spd	Auto.		Front (pts.)	Rear (pts.)		
1990	3.0L	6.5	—	—	15	—	—	1	17	9½
1991	3.0L	6.5	—	—	15	—	—	1	17	9½
1992	3.0L	6.5	—	—	15	—	—	1	17	9½

Engine Performance and Tune-Up

2

TUNE-UP SPECIFICATIONS CHART

See page 54.

TUNE-UP PROCEDURES

Neither tune-up or troubleshooting can be considered independently since each has a direct relationship with the other.

It is advisable to follow a definite and thorough tune-up procedure.

Tune-up consists of three separate steps: Analysis, the process of determining whether normal wear is responsible for performance loss, and whether parts require replacement or service and adjustment.

The manufacturer's recommended interval for tune-ups is every 30,000 miles. This interval should be shortened if the car is subjected to severe operating conditions such as trailer pulling or stop and start driving, or if starting and running problems are noticed. It is assumed that the routine maintenance described in Chapter 1 has been kept up, as this will have an effect on the results of the tune-up. All the applicable tune-up steps should be followed, as each adjustment complements the effects of the others. If the tune-up (emission control) sticker in the engine compartment disagrees with the information presented in the "Tune-up Specifications" chart in this chapter, the sticker figures must be followed. The sticker information reflects running changes made by the manufacturer during production.

Troubleshooting is a logical sequence of procedures designed to locate a particular case of trouble.

It is advisable to read the entire section before beginning a tune-up, although those who are more familiar with tune-up procedures may wish to go directly to the instructions.

Spark Plugs

A typical spark plug consists of a metal shell surrounding a ceramic insulator. A metal electrode extends downward through the center of the insulator and protrudes a small distance. Located at the end of the plug and attached to the side of the outer metal shell is the side electrode. The side electrode bends in at a 90° angle so that its tip is even with, and parallel to, the tip of the center electrode. The distance between these two electrodes, measured in thousandths of an inch or milimeters, is called the spark plug gap. The spark plug in no way produces a spark but merely provides a gap across which the current can arc. The coil produces anywhere from 20,000 to 40,000 volts which travels to the distributor where it is distributed through the spark plug wires to the spark plugs. The current passes along the center electrode and jumps the gap to the side electrode, and, in do doing, ignites the air/fuel mixture in the combustion chamber.

SPARK PLUG HEAT RANGE

Spark plug heat range is the ability of the plug to dissipate heat. The longer the insulator (or the farther it extends into the engine), the hotter the plug will operate; the shorter the insulator the cooler it will operate. A plug that absorbs little heat and remains too cool will quickly accumulate deposits of oil and carbon since it is not hot enough to burn them off. This leads to plug fouling and consequently to misfiring. A plug that absorbs too much heat will have no deposits, but, due to the excessive heat, the electrodes will burn away quickly and in some instances, preignition may result. Preignition takes place when plug tips get so hot that they glow sufficiently to ignite the fuel/air mixture before the actual spark occurs. This early ignition will usually cause a pinging during low speeds and heavy loads.

GASOLINE ENGINE TUNE-UP SPECIFICATIONS

Year	Engine Displacement Liters (cc)	Spark Plugs Gap (in.)	Ignition Timing (deg.)		Fuel Pump (psi)	Idle Speed (rpm)		Valve Clearance	
			MT	AT		MT	AT	In.	Ex.
1981	2.2L	0.035	10B	10B	4–6	900	900	NA	NA
	2.6L	0.035	—	7B	4–6	—	800	0.006	0.010
1982	2.2L	0.035	12B	12B	4–6	900	900	NA	NA
	2.6L	0.035	—	7B	4–6	—	800	0.006	0.010
1983	2.2L	0.035	10B	10B	4–6	775	900	NA	NA
	2.6L	0.035	7B	7B	4–6	800	800	0.006	0.010
1984	2.2L	0.035	10B	10B	4–6①	800	900	NA	NA
	2.6L	0.035	—	7B	4–6	—	800	0.006	0.010
1985	2.2L	0.035	10B	10B	4–6①	800	900	NA	NA
	2.6L	0.035	7B	7B	4–6	800	800	0.006	0.010
1986	2.2L	0.035	②	②	4–6①	②	②	NA	NA
	2.5L	0.035	②	②	14.5	②	②	NA	NA
1987	2.2L	0.035	10B	10B	4–6①	900	900	NA	NA
	2.5L	0.035	10B	10B	14.5	900	900	NA	NA
1988	2.2L	0.035	12B	12B	14.5③	850	850	NA	NA
	2.5L	0.035	12B	12B	14.5	850	850	NA	NA
1989	2.2L	0.035	12B	12B	14.5③	850	850	NA	NA
	2.5L	0.035	12B	12B	14.5③	850	850	NA	NA
	3.0L	0.040	—	12B	48	—	700	NA	NA
1990	1.8L⑦	0.040	5B	5B	48	850	650	NA	NA
	2.0L⑦	0.040	5B	5B	48	850	650	NA	NA
	2.2L	0.035	12B	12B	14.5③	900	850	NA	NA
	2.5L	0.035	12B	12B	14.5③	900	850	NA	NA
	3.0L	0.040	—	12B	48	—	700	NA	NA
	3.0L④	0.035	②	②	30	②	②	NA	NA
	3.3L	0.050	—	12B	43–53	—	750	NA	NA
1991	1.8L⑦	0.040	5B	5B	48	850	650	NA	NA
	2.0L⑦	0.040	5B	5B	48	850	650	NA	NA
	2.2L	0.035	12B	12B	39⑥	850	850	NA	NA
	2.5L	0.035	12B	12B	39③⑥	850	850	NA	NA
	3.0L	0.040	—	12B	48	—	700	NA	NA
	3.0L④	0.035	②	②	30	②	②	NA	NA
	3.0L⑤	0.040	5B	5B	48	700	700	NA	NA
	3.3L	0.050	—	12B	43–53	—	750	NA	NA
	3.8L	0.050	—	12B	43–53	—	750	NA	NA
1992	1.8L⑦	0.040	5B	5B	48	850	650	NA	NA
	2.0L⑦	0.040	5B	5B	48	850	650	NA	NA
	2.2L	0.035	12B	12B	39⑥	850	850	NA	NA
	2.5L	0.035	12B	12B	39③⑥	850	850	NA	NA
	3.0L	0.040	—	12B	48	—	700	NA	NA
	3.0L④	0.035	②	②	30	②	②	NA	NA
	3.0L⑤	0.040	5B	5B	48	700	700	NA	NA
	3.3L	0.050	—	12B	43–53	—	750	NA	NA
	3.8L	0.050	—	12B	43–53	—	750	NA	NA

NA—Not adjustable
① EFI Type Fuel System—Fuel Pressure 55 psi
② Refer to engine compartment sticker
③ Turbocharged engine—Fuel pressure 55 psi
④ Engine application is 1990–92 Dodge Monaco
⑤ Engine application is 1991–92 Dodge Stealth
⑥ Early 1991 Shadow convertible: 14.5 psi
⑦ Engine application is 1990–92 Laser

The general rule of thumb for choosing the correct heat range when picking a spark plug is: if most of your driving is long distance, high speed travel, use a colder plug; if most of your driving is stop and go, use a hotter plug. Original equipment plugs are compromise plugs, but most people never have occasion to change their plugs from the factory-recommended heat range.

Some later model vehicles may use Platinum tip type spark plugs. Use care not to damage the Platinum tip. The Platinum type spark plugs can usually be indentify with 5 blue lines around the the spark plug porcelain insulator.

REMOVAL AND INSTALLATION

Rough idle, hard starting, frequent engine miss at high speeds and physical deterioration gap are all indications that the plugs should be replaced.

The electrode end of a spark plug is a good indicator of the internal condition of your car's engine. If a spark plug is fouled, causing the engine to misfire, the problem will have to be found and corrected. Often, "reading" the plugs will lead you to the cause of the problem. Spark plug conditions and probable causes are listed in the color section.

NOTE: *A small amount of light tan or rust red colored deposits at the electrode end of the plug is normal. These plugs need not be renewed unless they are severely worn.*

1. Before removing the spark plugs, number the plug wires so that the correct wire goes on

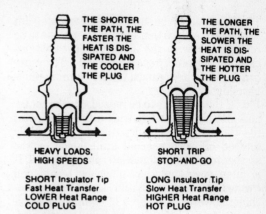
Spark plug heat range

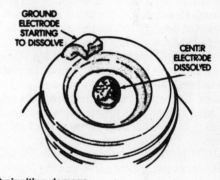
Preignition damage

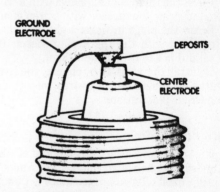
Electrode gap bridging

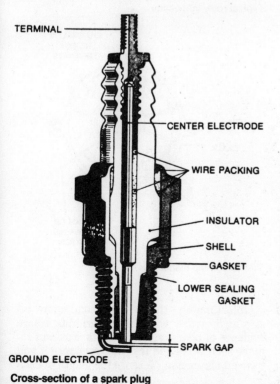
Cross-section of a spark plug

the plug when replaced. This can be done with pieces of adhesive tape.

2. Next, clean the area around the plugs by brushing or blowing with compressed air.

3. Disconnect the plug wires by twisting and pulling on the rubber cap, not on the wire.

4. Remove each plug with a rubber-insert spark plug socket. Make sure that the socket is all the way down on the plug to prevent it from slipping and cracking the porcelain insulator.

5. After removing each plug, evaluate its condition. A spark plug's useful life is approximately 30,000 miles with electronic ignition.

Thus, it would make sense to replace a plug if it has been in service that long. If the plug is to be replaced, refer to the Tune-up Specifications chart for the proper spark plug type. The numbers indicate heat range; hotter running plugs have higher numbers.

6. If the plugs are to be reused, file the center and side electrodes flat with a fine, flat point file. Heavy or baked on deposits can be carefully scraped off with a small knife blade or the scraper tool on a combination spark plug tool. It is often suggested that plugs be tested and cleaned on a service station sandblasting machine; however, this piece of equipment is becoming rare. Check the gap between the electrodes with a round wire spark plug gapping gauge. Do not use a flat feeler gauge; it will give an inaccurate reading. if the gap is not as specified, use the bending tool on the spark plug gap gauge to bend the outside electrode. Be careful not to bend the electrode too far or too often, because excessive bending may cause the electrode to break off and fall into the combustion chamber. This would require removing the cylinder head to reach the broken piece and could also result in cylinder wall, piston ring, or valve damage.

CAUTION: *Never bend the center electrode of the spark plug. This will break the insulator and render the plug useless.*

7. Clean the threads of old plugs with a wire brush. Lubricate the threads with a drop of oil.

8. Screw the plugs in finger tight, and then tighten them with the spark plug socket. Be very careful not to overtighten them.

9. Reinstall the wires. If, by chance, you have forgotten to number the plug wires, refer to the Firing Order illustrations.

Spark Plug Wires

The plug wires carry a very tiny amount of current under extremely high voltage. The conductors inside must offer some resistance to flow of current, or operation of a radio in the car or even nearby would be impossible. For these reasons, these wires deteriorate steadily and often produce puzzling and unexpected lapses in performance. The most typical evidence of wire problems is the sudden failure of the car to start on a damp morning.

The wires should be inspected frequently for full seating at the plugs and distributor cap towers. Before inspection, wipe the wires carefully with a cloth slightly moistened with a nonflammable solvent so it will be easier to see cracks or other damage. The insulation and all rubber boots should be flexible and free of cracks. Replace the wires as a set as soon as any such problems develop.

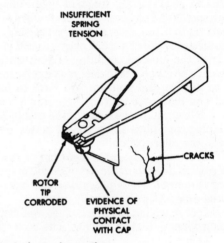

Removing the plug wires from the cap on late model cars

Typical rotor inspection

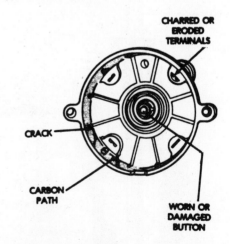

Distributor cap inspection

Unfortunately, the invisible conductors inside high quality wires can deteriorate before evidence of poor insulation exists. You can remove such wires and test the resistance if you have an ohmmeter. Measure the length of each wire with a ruler and then multiply the length by the figures given, in order to measure total resistance. Resistance must be 250–600Ω per inch (25mm) or 3,000–7200Ω per foot (305mm). If you wish to check the cap at the same time, you can run your test between the spark plug end of the plug wire and the contact at the center of the inside of the cap.

If you do not have an ohmmeter, you may want to take you car to a mechanic or diagnostic center with an oscilloscope type of diagnosis system. This unit will read the curve of ignition voltage and uncover problems with wires, or any other component, easily. You may also want to refer to the color section on spark plug analysis, as looking at the plugs may help you to identify wire problems.

To replace the wires, note first that on most of the models covered by this book, original equipment Chrysler wires cannot be pulled out of the distributor cap. Remove the cap and release each wire from INSIDE by pinching the locking jaws together with a pair of needle-nose pliers. Always replace the wires (match old wire to new wire for correct length) one at a time in order to avoid having to study and follow the firing order diagrams.

FIRING ORDERS

NOTE: *To avoid confusion, remove and tag and wires one at a time, for replacement.*

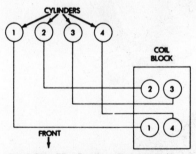

Spark Plug Wire Routing—Turbo III Engine

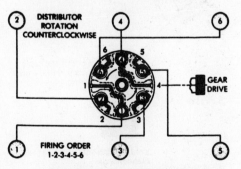

Spark Plug Wire Routing—3.0L Engine

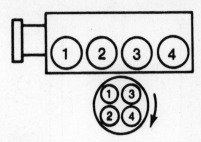

2.2L and 2.5L
Firing order: 1-3-4-2
Distributor rotation clockwise

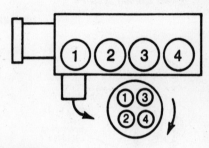

2.6L engine
Firing order: 1-3-4-2
Distribution rotation: clockwise

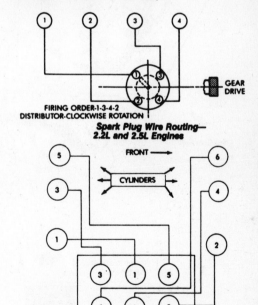

FIRING ORDER-1-3-4-2
DISTRIBUTOR-CLOCKWISE ROTATION
Spark Plug Wire Routing—
2.2L and 2.5L Engines

Spark Plug Wire Routing— 3.3L and 3.8L Engines

Chrysler front wheel drive cars

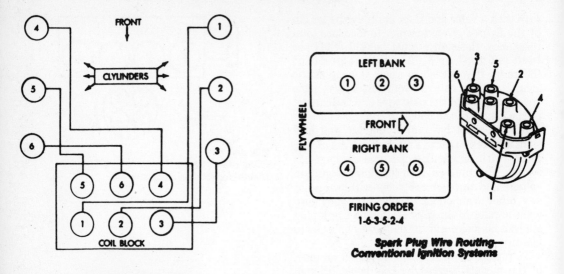

*Spark Plug Wire Routing—
Direct Ignition Systems*

*Spark Plug Wire Routing—
Conventional Ignition Systems*

FIRING ORDER
1-6-3-5-2-4

1990–92 Dodge Monaco

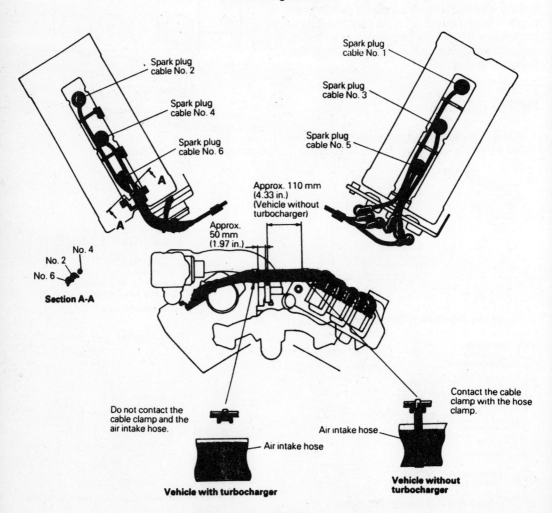

Spark plug cable No. 2

Spark plug cable No. 4

Spark plug cable No. 6

Spark plug cable No. 1

Spark plug cable No. 3

Spark plug cable No. 5

Approx. 110 mm (4.33 in.) (Vehicle without turbocharger)

Approx. 50 mm (1.97 in.)

No. 4
No. 2
No. 6

Section A-A

Do not contact the cable clamp and the air intake hose.

Air intake hose

Contact the cable clamp with the hose clamp.

Air intake hose

Vehicle with turbocharger

Vehicle without turbocharger

Spark plug wire routing—1991–92 Stealth

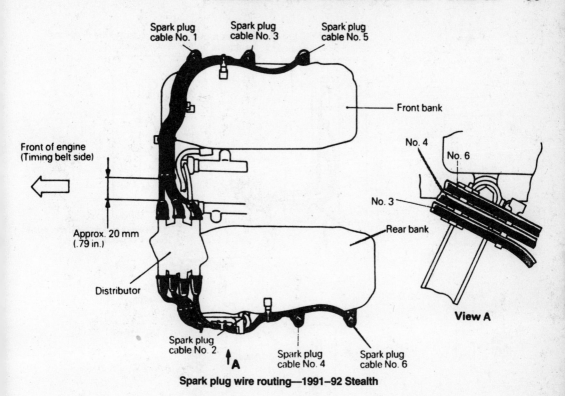

Spark plug wire routing—1991–92 Stealth

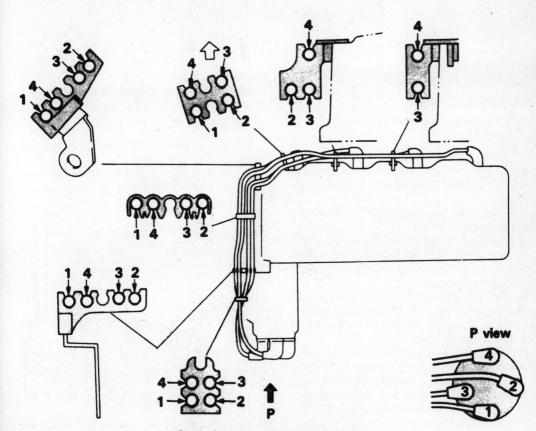

Spark plug wire routing—1990–92 Laser

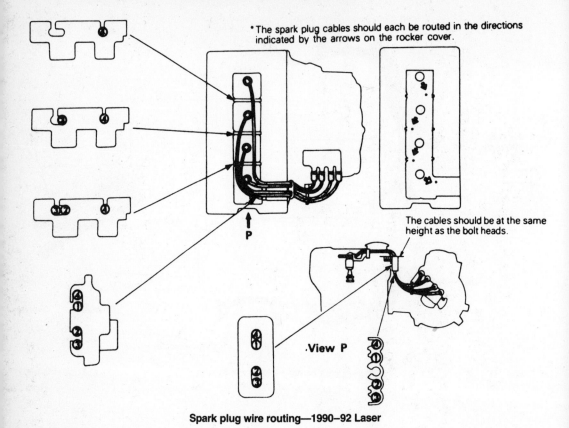

* The spark plug cables should each be routed in the directions indicated by the arrows on the rocker cover.

The cables should be at the same height as the bolt heads.

·View P

P

Spark plug wire routing—1990–92 Laser

ELECTRONIC IGNITION

PARTS REPLACEMENT

Hall-Effect Pickup Assembly Replacement

2.2L AND 2.5L ENGINES

1. Remove the distributor splash shield mounting screws (2) along with the pickup lead connector retainer screw and remove the splash shield.

2. Loosen the two distributor cap retaining screws. Remove the cap.

3. Pull the rotor up off the distributor shaft.

4. Remove the two clips retaining the hall-effect pickup assembly to the distributor body on 1985 and earlier models.

5. Pull the hall-effect pickup lead multi-prong connector out of its retaining clip and disconnect it. Then, lift the unit out of the top of the distributor body.

6. Install the new pickup in reverse order. Make sure the multi-prong connector is securely plugged in and then securely mounted in its retaining clip. Make sure, too, that the pickup retaining clips, if used, are installed securely. On 1986 and later models, make sure the pickup wires are routed properly through the hole in the distributor body so they will not be pinched and damaged when the distributor cap is reinstalled.

2.6L Engine

1. Unscrew the two phillips type retaining screws and remove the cap.

2. Unscrew the two similar screws retaining the rotor and remove it.

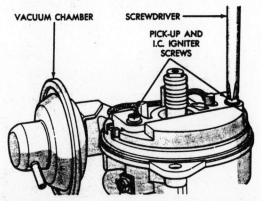

VACUUM CHAMBER   SCREWDRIVER

PICK-UP AND
I.C. IGNITER
SCREWS

Removing the pickup and igniter—2.6L engine distributor

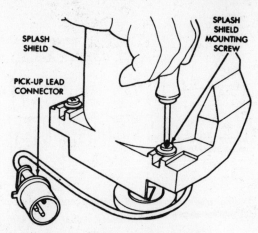

Pickup lead connector and splash shield

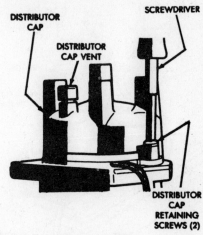

Distributor cap retaining screws

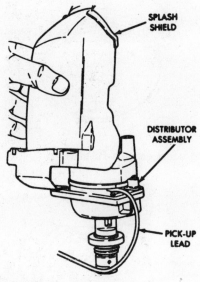

Splash shield

3. *Using a box or socket wrench for maximum torque,* remove the governor assembly retaining bolt from the upper end of the distributor shaft. Then, slide the governor assembly upward and off the shaft. Make sure to keep governor springs either in place or in order for proper installation in the same positions (they are not interchangeable).

4. Remove the wire retaining screw from the retaining clamp on the side of the distributor.

5. Remove the pickup/igniter mounting screws from the clip on the side of the distributor. Unplug the pickup/wiring connector from the harness. Then, remove both the pickup coil and igniter, keeping them together. Pull the wiring conduit out of the side of the distributor.

6. If you are replacing the breaker assembly or pole piece underneath, remove the two retaining screws and remove it.

7. Installation is the reverse of removal procedure.

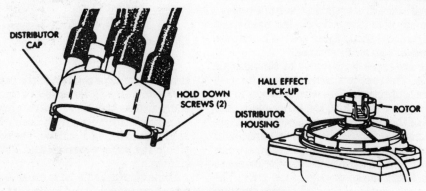

Distributor cap and housing assembly

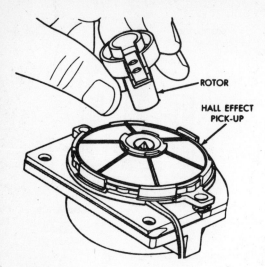

Ignition rotor

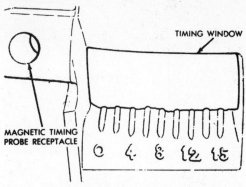

Timing mark location all manual and automatic transaxles except A-412

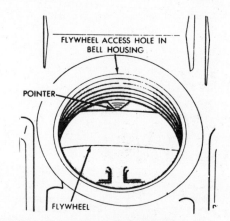

Timing mark location A-412 transaxle

IGNITION TIMING

Except 1990–92 Laser and Stealth

Timing should be checked at each tune-up. Timing isn't likely to change very much with electronic ignition. Always refer to Emission Control Sticker (tune-up sticker) in the engine compartment as a specification guide. The sticker information reflects running changes made by the manufacturer during production of the vehicle.

On Chrysler front wheel driver cars equipped 3.3L/3.8L Turbo III model vehicles, equipped with DIS (direct ignition system) ignition timing is not adjustable.

On 1990–92 Dodge Monaco equipped with 3.0L engine ignition timing is not adjustable.

On all 2.2 and 2.5L engines, the timing marks are located on the flywheel with the pointer on an access hole in the transaxle, or on the edge of the access hole with a line on the flywheel. On 2.6L and 3.0L engines, the timing marks are on a special bracket mounted on the front of the block and there is a notch in the front pulley.

A stroboscopic (dynamic) timing light must be used, because static lights are too inaccurate for emission controlled engines.

There are three basic types of timing light available. The first is a simple neon bulb with two wire connections. One wire connects to the spark plug terminal and the other plugs into the end of the spark plug wire for the No. 1 cylinder, thus connecting the light in series with the spark plug. This type of light is pretty dim and must be held close to the timing marks to be seen. It has the advantage of low price. The second type operates from the car's battery;

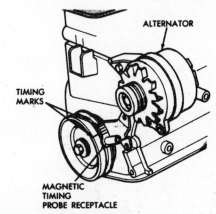

Timing marks 2.6L engine

two alligator clips connect to the battery terminals, while an adapter enables a third clip to be connected to the No. 1 spark plug and wire. This type provides a bright flash which can be seen even in bright sunshine. The third type replaced the battery current with 110 volt house current.

Some timing lights have other features built into them, such as dwell meters or tachometers.

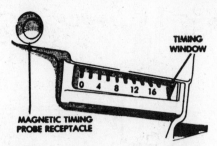

Timing scale—2.2L, 2.5L and Turbo engines

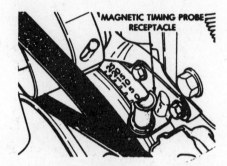

Timing scale—3.0L engine

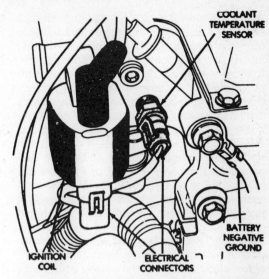

Coolant temperature sensor—2.2L, 2.5L and Turbo engines

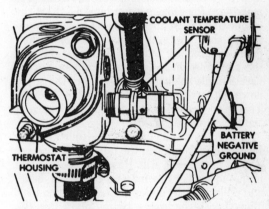

Coolant temperature sensor—Early 1991–92 AP body style convertible models

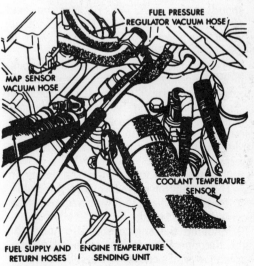

Coolant temperature sensor—3.0L engine

These are nice, in that they reduce the tangle of wires under the hood when you're working, but may duplicate the functions of tools you already have. One worthwhile feature, which is becoming more of a necessity with higher voltage ignition systems, is an inductive pickup. The inductive pickup clamps around the No. 1 spark plug wire, sensing the surges of high voltage electricity as they are sent to the plug. The advantage is that no mechanical connection is inserted between the wire and the plug, which eliminates false signals to the timing light. A timing light with an inductive pickup should be used on electronic ignition systems.

NOTE: *For vehicles with both Throttle Body and Multi-Point injection, refer to Chapter 5 for additional information.*

To check and adjust the timing:

1. Warm the engine to normal operating temperature. Shut off the engine and connect the timing light to the No. 1 spark plug. Do not under any circumstances pierce a wire to hook up a light.

2. Clean off the timing marks and mark the pulley or damper notch and the timing scale with white chalk or paint. The timing notch on the damper or pulley can be elusive. Bump the engine around with the starter or turn the crankshaft with a wrench on the front pulley bolt to get it to an accessible position.

NOTE: *The 2.2 and 2.5 Liter engines have their timing marks on the flywheel and bell housing.*

3. Disconnect and plug the vacuum advance hose at the distributor or, at the spark advance computer vacuum transducer on (carbureted) models that have one in all years through 1987, to prevent any distributor advance. The computer is located in the air intake on the driver's side fender well, with the vacuum transducer's diaphragm clearly in view on top. The vacuum line is the rubber hose connected to the metal cone-shaped canister on the side of the distributor or the top/center of the transducer diaphragm. A short screw, pencil, or a golf tee can be used to plug the hose. On 1986 models equipped with a carburetor switch, connect a jumper wire between the carburetor switch and ground. On 1987 2.2 and 2.5L engines with Electronic Fuel Injection, and all 1988 and later models, disconnect the coolant temperature sensor electrical lead at the sensor, which is located on the thermostat housing.

4. Make sure the idle screw rests against its stop. If necessary, open and close the throttle to make sure the linkage is not binding. Start the engine and adjust the idle speed to that specified in the "Tune-up Specifications" chart. Some cars require that the timing be set with the transmission in Neutral. You can disconnect the idle solenoid, if any, to get the speed down. Otherwise, adjust the idle speed screw. This is to prevent any centrifugal advance of timing in the distributor.

5. Aim the timing light at the timing marks. Be careful not to touch the fan, which may appear to be standing still. Keep your clothes and hair, and the light's wire clear of the fan, belts, and pulleys. If the pulley or damper notch isn't aligned with the proper timing mark (see the Tune-up Specifications chart), the timing will have to be adjusted.

NOTE: *TDC or Top Dead Center corresponds to 0°, B, or BTDC, or Before Top Dead Center, may be shown as BEFORE; A, or ATDC, or After Top Dead Center, may be shown as AFTER.*

6. Loosen the distributor base clamp locknut. You can buy special wrenches which will make this task easy. Turn the distributor slowly to adjust the timing, holding it by the body and not the cap. Turn the distributor in the direction of rotor rotation (found in the Firing Order illustrations) to retard, and against the direction to advance.

7. Tighten the locknut. Check the timing, in case the distributor moved as you tightened it.

8. Reconnect the distributor vacuum hose. Correct the idle speed.

9. Shut off the engine and disconnect the light. Reconnect the coolant temperature sensor connector, if necessary. On 1988 and later models, some fault codes may be set. They can

Insert paper clip as shown—timing procedure Step 1

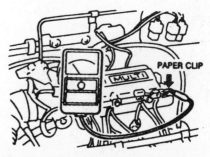

Tachometer hookup using paper clip adapter—timing procedure Step 2

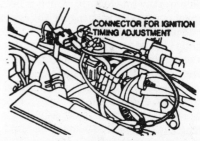

Since timing is controlled by the computer, this test lead must be grounded to override the settings so adjustment can be made—timing procedure step

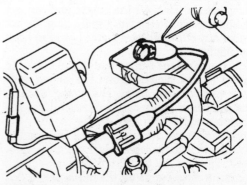

1990–92 Laser timing connector location

1991–92 Stealth timing connector location

be cleared immediately only with a special test instrument. However, as the ignition is turned ON and OFF 50–100 times (some later model years may take less re-starts to clear codes) in normal use, they will automatically be cleared by the system.

1990–92 Laser and Stealth

1. Start the engine, set the parking brake and run the engine until at normal operating temperature. Keep all lights and accessories OFF and the front wheels straight ahead. Place the transaxle in **P** for automatic transaxle or Neutral for manual transaxle.

2. Locate the wire connector on the ignition coil connector. Insert a paper clip behind the TACH terminal connector to act as a tachometer adapter. Connect a tachometer to the paper clip. If not at specification, set the idle speed at the correct level. This setting is fixed at the factory and normally does not need adjusting.

3. Turn the engine OFF. Remove the waterproof cover from the ignition timing adjusting connector. This connector is located on the firewall just behind the battery on Laser and Stealth. Connect a jumper wire from this terminal to a good ground.

4. Connect a conventional power timing light to the No. 1 cylinder spark plug wire. Start the engine and run at idle.

5. Aim the timing light at the timing scale located near the crankshaft pulley.

6. Loosen the distributor or crank angle sensor hold-down nut just enough so the housing can be rotated.

7. Turn the housing in the proper direction until the specified timing is reached. Tighten the hold-down nut and recheck the timing. Turn the engine OFF.

8. Remove the jumper wire from the ignition timing adjusting terminal and install the waterproof cover.

9. Start the engine and check the actual timing (the timing without the terminal ground-

ed). This reading should be 5° more than the basic timing. This value may increase according to altitude. As long as the basic timing is correct, the engine is timed correctly. Also, actual timing may fluctuate because of slight variation accomplished by the ECU. The basic timing, though, should remain steady.

10. Turn the engine OFF and disconnect the timing apparatus and tachometer.

VALVE LASH

If the valve clearance is too large, part of the lift of the camshaft will be used in removing the excessive clearance. Consequently, the valve will not be opening as far as it should. This condition has two effects: the valve train components will emit a tapping sound as they take up the excessive clearance and the engine will perform poorly because the valves don't open fully and allow the proper amount of gases to flow into and out of the engine.

If the valve clearance is too small, the intake valve and the exhaust valves will open too far and they will not fully seat on the cylinder head when they close. When a valve seats itself on the cylinder head, it does two things: it seals the combustion chamber so that none of the gases in the cylinder escape and it cools itself by transferring some of the heat it absorbs from the combustion in the cylinder to the cylinder head and to the engine's cooling system. If the valve clearance is too small, the engine will run poorly because of the gases escaping from the combustion chamber. The valves will also become overheated and will warp, since they cannot transfer heat unless they are touching the valve seat in the cylinder head.

NOTE: *While all valve adjustments must be made as accurately as possible, it is better to have the valve adjustment slightly loose than*

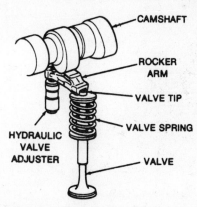

Hydraulic valve adjuster used on 2.2L engine

slightly tight as a burned valve may result from overly tight adjustments.

2.2L and 2.5L Engines

The 2.2L and 2.5L engines use hydraulic lash adjusters. No periodic adjustment or checking is necessary.

2.6L Engine

The 2.6L engine has a jet valve located beside the intake of each cylinder.

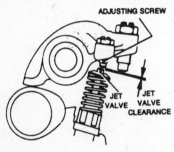

Adjusting the jet valve on 2.6L engines

Adjusting the valve lash on 2.6L engines

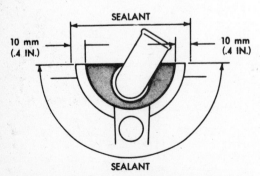

Applying sealant on the 2.6 liter valve cover

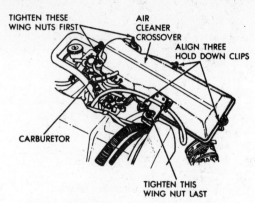

Air cleaner assembly

NOTE: *When adjusting valve clearances, the jet valve must be adjusted before the intake valve.*

1. Start the engine and allow it to reach normal operating temperature.

2. Stop the engine and remove the air cleaner and its hoses. Remove any other cables, hoses, wires, etc., which are attached to the valve cover, and remove the valve cover.

3. Disconnect the high tension coil-to-distributor wire at the coil.

4. Watch the rocker arms for No. 1 cylinder and rotate the crankshaft until the exhaust valve is closing and the intake valve has just started to open. At this point, no. 4 cylinder will be at Top Dead Center (TDC) commencing its firing stroke.

5. Loosen the locknut on cylinder no. 4 intake valve adjusting screw 2 or more turns.

6. Loosen the locknut on the jet valve adjusting screw.

7. Turn the jet valve adjusting screw counterclockwise and insert a 0.006 in. (0.15mm) feeler gauge between the jet valve stem and the adjusting screw.

8. Tighten the adjusting screw until it touches the feeler gauge.

NOTE: *Take care not to press on the valve while adjusting because the jet valve spring is very weak.*

If the adjusting screw is tight, special care must be taken to avoid pressing down on the jet valve when adjusting the clearance or a false reading will result.

9. Tighten the locknut securely while holding the rocker arm adjusting screw with a screwdriver to prevent it from turning.

10. Make sure that a 0.006 in. (0.15mm) feeler gauge can be easily inserted between the jet valve and the rocker arm.

11. Adjust no. 4 cylinder's intake valve to 0.006 in. (0.15mm) and its exhaust valve to 0.010 in.(0.25mm). Tighten the adjusting screw locknuts and recheck each clearance.

12. Perform step 4 in conjunction with the chart below to set up the remaining three cylinders for valve adjustments (use same intake and exhaust clearance specifications).

13. Replace the valve cover and all other components. Apply sealer to the top surface of the semi-circular packing. Run the engine and check for oil leaks at the valve cover.

IDLE SPEED AND MIXTURE ADJUSTMENT

NOTE: *Always refer to Emission Control Sticker (tune-up sticker) in the engine compartment as a specification guide. The sticker information reflects running changes made by the manufacturer during production of the vehicle.*

IDLE SPEED

Carbureted vehicles use the Holley 5220/6250/6520 Series carburetors. Idle speed is adjusted on the top of the idle stop solenoid. Fuel injected cars, whether equipped with Throttle Body or Multi-Point injection use an Automatic Idle Speed motor. This is a throttle bypass system that is computer controlled, and DOES NOT require periodic adjustment (refer to Chapter 5 for additional information). To adjust the idle speed on carbureted vehicles, follow the appropriate procedure below.

2.2L and 2.5L Carbureted Engines

1. Make sure the ignition timing is sect correctly. Set the parking brake securely and put the transaxle in Neutral (manual) or Park (automatic). Turn off all lights and accessories. Connect a tachometer to the engine. Then, start it and allow it to run on the bottom step of the fast idle cam until it has reached operating temperature. Open the throttle so the engine will run at normal idle speed.

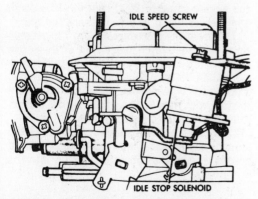

Adjust the idle speed on carbureted cars with the idle speed screw, located on top of the idle stop solenoid

2. Unplug the radiator fan electrical connector and jumper the connector to ground to make the fan run continuously.

3. Pull the PCV valve out of the crankcase vent module.

4. Disconnect the oxygen feedback system test connector located on the left fender shield. Also disconnect the wiring from the kicker vacuum solenoid – the connector is also located on the left fender shield.

5. Turn the idle speed screw on top of the solenoid kicker to obtain the correct idle speed, as shown in the Tune-Up Specifications chart.

6. Reconnect the two disconnect connectors and install the PCV valve back into the vent module.

7. Increase rpm to about 2500 for 15 seconds and then return it to idle speed. Even though idle speed might be different now, you need not reset it. Disconnect the jumper wire and reconnect the fan motor connector. Turn off the engine.

2.6L Mitsubishi Engines

1. Make sure the ignition timing is set correctly. Set the parking brake securely and put the transaxle in Neutral (manual) or Park (automatic). Turn off all lights and accessories. Connect a tachometer to the engine. Then, start it and allow it to run on the bottom step of the fast idle cam until it has reached operating temperature. Open the throttle so the engine will run at normal idle speed.

2. Unplug the radiator fan electrical connector. On 1983 and earlier models, allow the engine to idle for 1 minute to stabilize rpm.

3. On 1984 models, turn the engine off and then disconnect the negative battery cable for 3 seconds and reconnect it. Disconnect the engine harness lead from the O$_2$ sensor connector at the bullet connector. Avoid pulling on the sensor wire when doing this.

4. On 1983–85 models, open the throttle and allow the engine to run at 2500 rpm for 10 seconds. Then, return the engine to normal idle speed.

5. Wait two minutes.

6. Read the idle speed on the tach. If the rpm is not correct, and if the car has electronic feedback control, disconnect the idle switch connector. Now, if the rpm is not correct, turn the idle speed screw, accessible through the bracket on the carburetor body, to get the correct idle rpm.

7. If the car has air conditioning, set the temperature control level to the coldest position and turn the air conditioner on. Then, set the idle-up speed screw to obtain 900 rpm with the compressor running.

8. Turn off the engine, reconnect the fan,

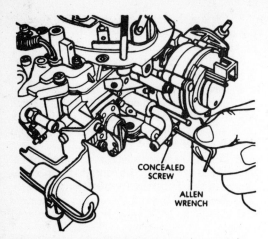

Adjusting propane enrichment rpm—carbureted engine idle mixture adjustment

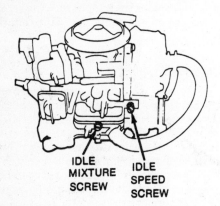

Location of idle speed and mixture adjusting screws on 2.6L engines

disconnect the tachometer, and reconnect the idle switch connector.

IDLE MIXTURE

Chrysler recommends the use of propane enrichment procedure to adjust the mixture. The equipment needed for this procedure is not readily available to the general public. The procedure is included here for reference purposes:

1. Remove the concealment plug located under the choke housing.

2. Set the parking brake and make sure a manual transaxle is in Neutral and an automatic one is in Park.

3. Connect a tachometer to the engine. Then, start it and allow it to run on the bottom step of the fast idle cam until it has reached operating temperature. Open the throttle so the engine will run at normal idle speed.

2. Unplug the radiator fan electrical connector and install a jumper wire so the fan runs continuously.

3. Pull the PCV valve out of the crankcase vent module so it will draw underhood air.

4. Disconnect the oxygen feedback system test connector located on the left fender shield.

5. Disconnect the vacuum harness from the CVSCC valve and plug both hoses. On the 2.2L engine only, disconnect the wiring from the single solenoid kicker vacuum control solenoid, which is located on the left fender shield.

6. Disconnect the vacuum hose which leads to the heated air sensor at the three-way connector and install the supply hose from the propane bottle where it was connected. Make sure the propane valves are fully closed and that the bottle is in a safe and secure position that will maintain it upright.

7. Open the propane main valve. Leaving the air cleaner in place, slowly and very steadily open the propane metering valve while you watch the tach, until maximum rpm is reached. You will note that there will be an optimum mixture, after which further addition of propane will cause the engine rpm to begin falling. Note what this rpm is and carefully adjust the propane valve to produce this exact rpm.

8. Adjust the idle speed screw on top of the solenoid kicker (without changing the propane setting) so that the tach reads the propane enrichment rpm shown on the engine compartment sticker.

9. Increase the engine speed to 2500 rpm for 15 seconds and then return it to idle. Read the rpm and, if it has changed, readjust the idle speed to give the specified rpm.

10. Turn off the propane system main valve and allow the engine speed to stabilize. With the air cleaner in place, slowly adjust the mixture screw to achieve the specified idle set rpm with an Allen wrench. Work very slowly and pause after slight adjustment increments to allow the engine rpm to stabilize. Again, increase the engine speed to 2500 rpm for 15 seconds and then return it to idle. Recheck the rpm.

11. Repeat the procedure of Step 7 to get optimum propane enrichement rpm at these new basic settings. Reread the tach. If this rpm is more than 25 rpm either side of the specified propane enrichment rpm, repeat the procedure starting with Step 7. The adjustment is correct when the test in this step is passed.

12. Turn off both propane valves, remove the propane supply hose, and reinstall the vacuum hose. Reinstall the concealment plug into the carburetor.

Virgil Parker
1994

ENGINE ELECTRICAL

Ignition Coil

TESTING

Except Direct Ignition Systems

Remove coil wire from the distributor cap. Hold the end of the cable about ¼ in. (6mm) away from a good engine ground. Crank the engine and look for a spark at coil wire end (secondary cable). If there is a spark at coil wire (secondary cable) it must be constant. If it is, have a helper continue to crank engine and while slowly moving coil wire (secondary cable) away from the ground, look for arcing at the coil tower. If arcing occurs replace coil assembly. If spark is not constant or there is no spark more complex diagnostic testing must be preform on the vehicle.

Every time an ignition coil assembly is replaced because of a burned tower, carbon tracking, arcing at the tower, or damage to the nipple or boot on the coil end of the coil wire (secondary cable), replace the cable (coil wire). Any arcing at the tower will carbonize the nipple so that placing it on a new coil assembly will invariably cause another coil failure.

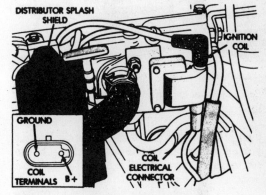

Coil terminals 2.2L and 2.5L engines

If coil wire shows any signs of damage, the coil wire (secondary cable) should be replaced since carbon tracking on an old cable can cause arcing and ruin a new coil assembly.

NOTE: *To perform this test of the coil, on vehicles from 1981–87, you have to make up several jumper wires. You'll need two simple wires several feet long with alligator clips on the ends. A third wire must incorporate a capacitor of 0.33 MicroFarad capacitance. The materials and components needed to make up such jumpers should be available at a reasonable price in a local electronics store.*

1. Turn the ignition key off. Disconnect the negative battery cable. Then, carefully remove the retaining nuts and disconnect the two coil primary leads. Wrap the positive (+) lead in electrician's tape or otherwise ensure that it cannot accidentally ground during the test.

2. Run a jumper wire from the battery positive (+) terminal directly to the coil positive (+) terminal. Run the jumper wire incorporating the capacitor from the coil negative terminal to a good ground. Reconnect the battery negative cable and turn on the ignition switch. Fasten one end of the remaining standard

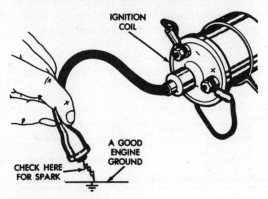

Checking for spark

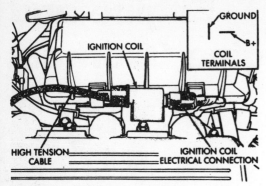

Coil terminals 3.0L engine

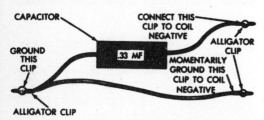

Special jumper to ground coil negative

jumper wire in a position where the clip cannot ground. Then connect the other end of it to the coil negative terminal. Turn on the ignition key.

3. Unclip the coil high tension lead from inside the distributor cap and pull it out. Hold the distributor end of the lead ¼ in. (6mm) from a good ground. Ground the standard jumper wire coming from the coil negative terminal.

4. Break the ground in the standard lead coming from the coil negative as you watch for spark. The coil should produce a hot, blue-white spark. Repeat the test looking at the coil tower. If sparks are visible there, replace the ignition wires if the rubber boots are deteriorated, or the coil, if the tower is burned and tracked.

5. If the coil tower and wire boots are okay, and this test fails to produce a spark, replace the coil.

On 1987–89 cars, you can confirm the problem with the coil using an ohmmeter. Turn off the ignition switch, and disconnect the negative battery cable. With the coil primary wires still disconnected, test the resistance between positive and negative primary terminals of the coil. It must be 1.35–1.55Ω. For secondary resistance, first determine whether the coil is a Chrysler Prestolite, Chrysler Essex, or Diamond brand coil by wiping off the coil and looking for appropriate lettering. Then, pull the high tension lead out of the coil tower and run the ohmmeter lead between the coil negative primary terminal and the brass connector down inside the tower. Resistance ranges must be as follows:

- Chrysler Prestolite – 9,400–11,700Ω
- Chrysler Essex – 9,000–12,200Ω
- Diamond – 15,000–19,000Ω

For 1990–92 vehicles follow the same service procedure but refer to the necessary specifications chart for the correct range.

If the coil tests okay, you must be sure to turn off the ignition switch and have the battery negative cable disconnected before reconnecting the primary leads.

REMOVAL AND INSTALLATION

All Vehicles

1. Disconnect the negative battery cable.
2. Remove the coil to distributor ignition cable (coil wire).
3. Disconnect the wiring harness connector from the coil assembly. On other type of coil assembly remove the nuts and lock washers holding wire terminals in place.
4. Remove the screws holding the ignition coil to the coil bracket or loosen the clamp and remove the coil assembly.
5. Installation is the reverse of the removal procedure. Continue pushing on cable and nipple until cable is properly seated in cap tower. Snap should be heard as terminal goes into place.

Distributor

REMOVAL AND INSTALLATION

1. Disconnect the negative battery cable. Disconnect the distributor pickup lead wire at the harness connector. Remove the two retaining screws and remove the distributor splash shield.
2. Remove the two distributor cap retaining screws and then remove the distributor cap.

IGNITION COIL						
Coil	Chrysler Prestolite	Chrysler Essex	(Epoxy) Diamond	(Oil Filled) Diamond	(3.3L) Diamond	(3.3L) Marshall
Primary Resistance @ 21°C–27°C (70°–80°F)	1.34 to 1.55	1.34 to 1.55	.97 to 1.18	1.34 to 1.55	0.52 to 0.63	0.53 to 0.65
Secondary Resistance @ 21°C–27°C (70°–80°F)	9,400 to 11,700	9,000 to 12,200	11,000 to 15,300	15,000 to 19,000	11,500 to 15,500	7,000 to 9,000

Ignition Coil Chart 1990

Coil	Primary Resistance 21°C–27°C (70°F–80°F)	Secondary Resistance 21°C–27°C (70°F–80°F)
(Epoxy) 4 Cylinder—Diamond	0.97–1.18 ohms	11,300–15,300 ohms
(Epoxy) 4 Cylinder—Toyodenso	0.95–1.20 ohms	11,300–13,300 ohms
(Epoxy) 3.0L—Diamond	0.97–1.18 ohms	11,000–15,300 ohms
Turbo III—Diamond	0.52–0.63 ohms	11,600–15,800 ohms
3.3L/3.8L—Diamond	0.52–0.63 ohms	11,600–15,800 ohms
3.3L/3.8L—Toyodenso	0.51–0.61 ohms	11,500–13,500 ohms
4 Cylinder (Oil Filled) Prestolite	1.34–1.55 ohms	9,400–11,700 ohms
4 Cylinder (Oil Filled) Essex	1.34–1.55 ohms	9,000–12,200 ohms
4 Cylinder (Oil Filled) Diamond	1.34–1.55 ohms	15,000–19,000

Ignition Coil Chart 1991–92

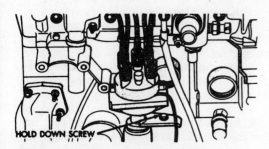

Distributor hold down—2.2L, 2.5L and turbo engines

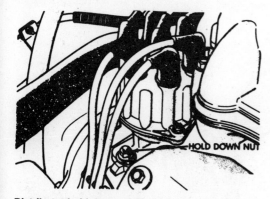

Distributor hold down—3.0L engine

3. Rotate the engine crankshaft (in the direction of normal rotation) until No. 1 cylinder is at TDC on compression stroke. At this point, the timing marks will line up at TDC and, *at the same time* the rotor will point to the high tension wire terminal for No. 1. cylinder in the cap.

If the rotor does not line up properly, turn the engine crankshaft another 360°. Make a mark on the block where the rotor points for installation reference. Also mark the relationship between the body of the distributor and the block so you can install the distributor with the ignition timing nearly correct.

4. Remove the distributor holddown bolt.

5. Carefully lift the distributor from the engine. The shaft will rotate slightly as the distributor is removed because of the curvature in the teeth of the drive gear. Note the angle at which the rotor sits as the shaft stops rotating and mark it.

6. Installation is the reverse of removal. When installing the distributor, start inserting it with the rotor lined up with the second mark you made. If the distributor drive gear does not immediately engage with the accessory shaft, turn the rotor back and forth very slighty, keeping it as nearly aligned with the second mark as possible, until it engages easily, making it easy to slide the distributor into the block. Then, when the distributor seats on the block, verify that the first mark and the rotor tip are lined up. Make sure the distributor seats so the gasket at its base will seal.

7. Adjust the ignition timing, as described in Chapter 2.

NOTE: *The following procedure is to be used if the engine was cranked with the distributor removed.*

1. If the engine has been cranked over while the distributor was out of the engine, rotate the

crankshaft until the number one piston is at TDC on the compression stroke. This will be indicated by the 0 mark on the flywheel or crank pulley aligning with the pointer on the clutch housing or engine front cover. Now, you must verify that No. 1 cylinder is at Top Dead Center firing position, and not at the top of the exhaust stroke. Do this in one of two ways:

a. Remove the valve cover and check the positions of No. 1 valve springs and rockers. The valves should be closed (with springs up all the way) and the rockers should be in contact with the base circles of the cams, rather than the cam lobes. If the cam is actuating the valves, rotate the engine another 360° until the timing marks are again at Top Dead Center.

b. Remove the No. 1 Cylinder spark plug and put your finger over the spark plug hole as you crank the engine toward Top Dead Center. If the engine is approaching the firing position, you will feel air being forcibly expelled from the cylinder because the valves will be closed, sealing off the cylinder. If the engine is approaching Top Dead Center of the exhaust stroke, air will not be forcibly expelled. If this latter situation is the case, turn the engine another 360°, and feel for air pressure.

Once the engine is at TDC No. 1 firing position:

2. Position the rotor just ahead of the #1 terminal of the cap, at the second mark made earlier, and lower the distributor into the engine. With the distributor fully seated, the rotor should be directly under the #1 terminal in the cap.

3. If the engine was not disturbed while the distributor was out, lower the distributor into the engine, engaging the gears by rocking the shaft back and forth, if necessary, and making sure that the gasket is properly seated in the block. The rotor should line up with the mark made before removal.

4. Tighten the holddown bolt and connect the wires.

5. Check and, if necessary, adjust the ignition timing.

Ignition Computer/Power Module 1981–87

REMOVAL AND INSTALLATION

NOTE: *The grease located in the 10 or 14 way connector cavity in the computer is necessary to prevent moisture from corroding the terminals. Not only should this grease be left in place, but if the layer is less than ⅛ in. (3mm) thick, spread Mopar Multi-purpose grease Part No. 2932524 or an equivalent available in the aftermarket in an even layer over the end of each connector plug before reconnecting them.*

1. Disconnect the negative battery cable. Then, disconnect the 10 and 14-way dual connectors.

2. Disconnect the outside air duct at the computer housing. Disconnect the vacuum line at the vacuum transducer on top of the housing.

3. Remove the 3 mounting screws that fasten the computer to the inside of the left front fender and remove it.

4. Installation is the reverse of removal procedure.

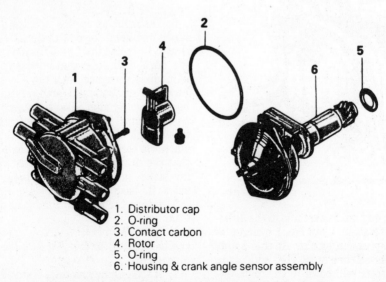

1. Distributor cap
2. O-ring
3. Contact carbon
4. Rotor
5. O-ring
6. Housing & crank angle sensor assembly

Exploded view of distributor assembly—1991–92 Stealth

Single Module Engine Controller 1988–89
Single Board Engine Controller 1989–92

REMOVAL AND INSTALLATION

NOTE: *The grease located in the 14 way connector cavity in the computer is necessary to prevent moisture from corroding the terminals. Not only should this grease be left in place, but if the layer is less than ⅛ in. (3mm) thick, spread Mopar Multi-purpose grease Part No. 2932524 or an equivalent available in the aftermarket in an even layer over the end of each connector plug before reconnecting them.*

1. Disconnect both battery cables (negative first). If necessary remove the battery from the vehicle.

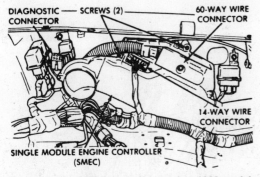

Removing the SMEC controller used on 1988 models

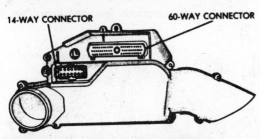

Single module engine controller (SMEC)

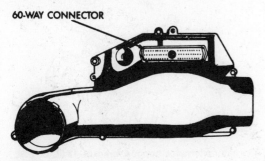

Single board engine controller (SBEC)

2. Disconnect the air cleaner duct at the engine controller.
3. Remove the 2 module mounting screws.
4. Move the unit out slightly for access and then disconnect both the 14 and 60-way wiring connectors or 60-way connector. Remove the engine controller from the engine compartment.
5. Install the module in reverse order, making sure to connect the electrical connectors before attempting to mount it. Start engine and check for proper operation.

Alternator

ALTERNATOR PRECAUTIONS

Several precautions must be observed with alternator equipped vehicles to avoid damaging the unit. They are as follows:

1. If the battery is removed for any reason, make sure that it is reconnected with the correct polarity. Reversing the battery connections may result in damage to the one-way rectifiers.
2. When utilizing a booster battery as a starting aid, always connect it as follows: positive to positive, and negative (booster battery) to a good ground on the engine of the car being started.
3. Never use a fast charger as a booster to start cars with alternating current (AC) circuits.
4. When servicing the battery with a fast charger, always disconnect the car battery cables.
5. Never attempt to polarize an alternator.
6. Avoid long soldering times when replacing diodes or transistors. Prolonged heat is damaging to alternators.
7. Do not use test lamps of more than 12 volts (V) for checking diode continuity.
8. Do not short across or ground any of the terminals on the alternator.
9. The polarity of the battery, alternator, and regulator must be matched and considered before making any electrical connections within the system.
10. Never separate the alternator on an open circuit. Make sure that all connections within the circuit are clean and tight.
11. Disconnect the battery terminals when performing any service on the electrical system. This will eliminate the possibility of accidental reversal of polarity.
12. Disconnect the battery ground cable if arc welding is to be done on any part of the car.

REMOVAL AND INSTALLATION

NOTE: *On some vehicles the A/C compressor (without disconnecting the A/C refrigerant lines-position compressor out of the way)*

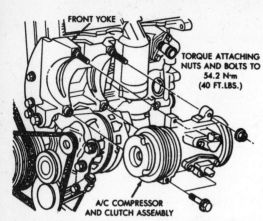

A/C compressor removal and installation—2.2L and 2.5L engine

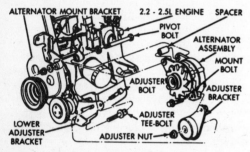

Remove or install all necessary mounting bolts

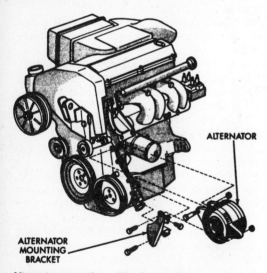

Alternator mounting—16 valve engine

4. Remove all necessary drive belts, brackets and any necessary component to gain access to alternator assembly.

5. Remove the adjusting bolt or bolt and nut and the pivot bolt.

6. Remove the alternator.

7. Installation is the reverse of removal procedure. Adjust the belt tension to allow ½ in. (13mm) of play on the longest run.

Regulator

REMOVAL AND INSTALLATION

NOTE: *The alternator on the 2.6 liter engine, 1990–92 Laser and Stealth has an integral regulator. No adjustments are possible. The voltage of many late model and all 1988 and later alternators is regulator via the Power Module or SMEC controller. Other al-*

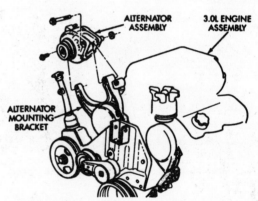

Remove or install alternator mounting bolts—3.0L engine

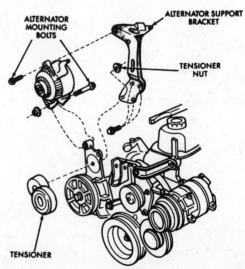

Alternator/alternator support bracket—3.3L or 3.8L engine

must be removed to gain access in order to remove the alternator.

1. Disconnect the negative battery terminal.

2. Disconnect the wiring and label it for easy reinstallation.

3. Loosen the alternator adjusting bracket bolt, or adjusting nut and bolt.

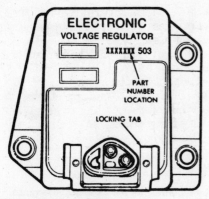

Electronic voltage regulator

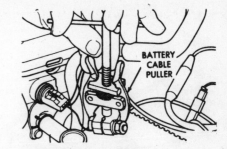

Disconnecting the battery cables

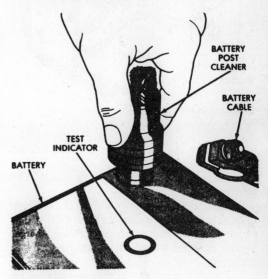

Cleaning battery post

ternators used with the 2.2L and 2.5L engines may incorporate a separate regulator.

1. Disconnect the negative battery terminal.

2. Remove the electrical connection.

3. Remove the mounting bolts and remove the regulator.

4. This regulator is not adjustable and must be replaced as a unit if found to be defective.

5. Installation is the reverse of removal.

Battery

REMOVAL AND INSTALLATION

CAUTION: *Batteries often develop acid leaks! In all battery handling, you should wear thick (not medical or household) rubber gloves. Failure to do this could result in acid burns!*

1. Make *sure* that the ignition switch is off.

2. Disconnect both of the battery cables, negative (–) first, as follows:

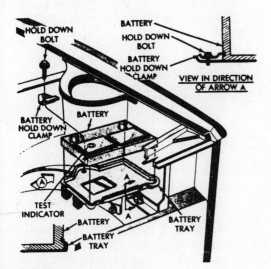

The battery mounting system

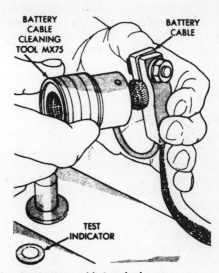

Cleaning battery cable terminal

a. Loosen the nuts which secure the cable ends to the battery terminals.

b. Lift the battery cables from the terminals with a twisting motion. If there is a battery cable puller available, make use of it.

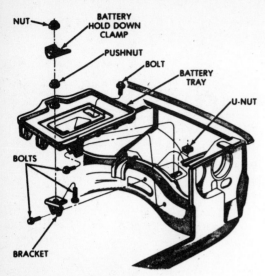

Exploded view battery tray

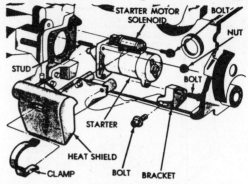

Starter mounting for the 2.2 and 2.5L engines

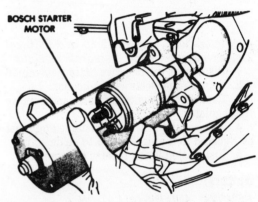

Remove or install starter motor—Bosch starter

3. Remove its bolt and remove the battery holddown clamp.

4. Carefully lift the battery out of the vehicle.

5. Clean the battery tray with a mild solution of baking soda and water, using a stiff, bristle brush. If the battery is to be reinstalled, clean it as well, and then wipe it with a rag dampened in ammonia.

6. Install the battery in reverse order of removal procedure, tightening the clamp bolt.

7. Install the battery cables so that the tops of the clamps are flush with the terminals and torque the nuts evenly. Coat the terminals with a petroleum grease or equivalent.

Starter

REMOVAL AND INSTALLATION

1. Disconnect the negative battery terminal. Raise and safely support the vehicle as necessary. Remove the engine undercovers if so equipped.

2. Remove the bolts attaching the starter to the flywheel housing and the rear bracket to the engine or transaxle.

3. On early model 2.2 liter engine loosen the air pump tube at the exhaust manifold and move the tube bracket away from the starter.

4. Remove the heat shield and its clamp if so equipped.

5. Remove the electrical connections from the starter.

6. Disconnect the speedometer cable from the transaxle if necessary to gain clearance to remove the starter assembly. Remove the starter.

7. Installation is the reverse of removal procedure. Make sure all electrical connections are tight. Reconnect the battery and check for proper operation.

SOLENOID REPLACEMENT

1. Remove the starter as previously outlined.

2. Disconnect the field coil wire from the solenoid by removing the nut and pulling the connector off.

3. Remove the solenoid mounting screws.

4. Remove the solenoid by working the plunger stem off the shift fork.

5. Installation is the reverse of removal.

ENGINE MECHANICAL

Description

A 135 cu. in. (2.2 Liter) four cylinder engine is standard. A 156 cu. in. (2.6 Liter) engine, manufactured by Mitsubishi, is optional on 1982–86 models. A 153 cu. in. 2.5 L Chrysler built engine is optional on 1987–88 models. It is based on the 2.2 L engine, achieving its increased size through a longer stroke (4.09 vs.

ALTERNATOR AND REGULATOR SPECIFICATIONS

| Year | Alternator | | | Regulator | |
	Manufacturer	Rating	Minimum Output (amps)	Type	Volts @ 80°F
1981–83	Chrysler	65	62	Chrysler	13.9–14.6
	Chrysler	60	57	Chrysler	13.9–14.6
	Mitsubishi	—	74	Integral	
1984	Chrysler	78	56	Chrysler	13.9–14.6
	Bosch	60	45	Chrysler	13.9–14.6
	Bosch	90	89	Integral	
	Mitsubishi	75	74	Integral	
1985	Chrysler	60	45	Chrysler	13.9–14.6
	Bosch	65	50	Chrysler	13.9–14.6
	Bosch	90	89	Integral	
	Mitsubishi	75	74	Integral	
	Chrysler	40/90	96	In Engine Electronics	
	Bosch	40/90	87	In Engine Electronics	
1986	Chrysler	78	56	Chrysler	13.9–14.6
	Chrysler	60	45	Chrysler	13.9–14.6
	Bosch	65	50	Chrysler	13.9–14.6
	Chrysler	40/90	87	In Engine Electronics	
	Bosch	40/90	80	In Engine Electronics	
	Bosch	40/100	87	In Engine Electronics	
1987	Chrysler	78	56	Chrysler	13.9–14.6
	Chrysler	78	56	In Engine Electronics	
	Bosch	40/90	87	In Engine Electronics	
	Bosch	40/90	80	In Engine Electronics	
	Chrysler	50/120	98	In Engine Electronics	
1988	Bosch	35/75	30	In Engine Electronics	
	Bosch	40/90	40	In Engine Electronics	
	Chrysler	40/90	87	In Engine Electronics	
	Chrysler	50/120	98	In Engine Electronics	

Virgil Parker

ALTERNATOR SPECIFICATION CHART—1989–90

| SPECIFICATIONS | | | | |
Type	Part Number	Pulley Grooves	Engine Usage	Minimum Output*
Denso 75 HS	4557301	4	2.2–2.5L	68 AMP
Denso 90 HS	5234031	4	2.2–2.5L	87 AMP
Denso 90 HS	5234029	5	3.0L	87 AMP
Denso 90 HS	5234032	6	3.3L	87 AMP
Denso 120 HS	5234208	4	2.2–2.5L	98 AMP
Denso 120 HS	5234260	5	3.0L	98 AMP
Denso 120 HS	5234231	6	2.2–2.5L	98 AMP
Bosch 90 RS	5234208	4	2.2–2.5L	75 AMP

*Alternator Full Fielded at 1250 Engine RPM

ALTERNATOR SPECIFICATION CHART—1991

Type	**Case I.D. Tag Number	Pulley Grooves	Engine Usage	*Minimum Output
Bosch 90 HS	4557431	4	2.2L–2.5L	84 AMP
Bosch 90 HS	4557432	6	3.0L	86 AMP
Bosch 90 RS	5234231	4	2.2L–2.5L	88 AMP
Denso 75 HS	4557301	4	2.2L–2.5L	68 AMP
Denso 90 HS	5234031	4	2.2L–2.5L	86 AMP
Denso 90 HS	5234032	6	3.0L–3.3L–3.8L	90 AMP
Denso 120 HS	5234033	6	3.0L–3.3L–3.8L	102 AMP

*With Alternator Full Fielded at 1250 RPM
**Case I.D. Tag Number is Located on Bottom of Alternator Case

STARTER SPECIFICATIONS

Year	Part No.	Application	Cranking Amps	No-Load Test Volts	No-Load Test Amps	No-Load Test RPM
1981–83	5213045	2.2—All	120–160	11	47	6600
1984–85	5213045	2.2 Non-Turbo (Bosch)	120–160	11	47	6600
	5213645	2.2 Non-Turbo (Nippondenso)	120–160	11	47	6600
	5213645	2.2 Non-Turbo (Nippondenso)	120–160	11	47	6600
	5213450	2.2 Turbo	120–160	11	47	6600
	5213235	2.6—All	150–210	11	85	3700
1986	5226442	2.2 Non-Turbo (Bosch)	120–160	11	47	6600
	5226742	2.2 Non-Turbo (Nippondenso)	120–160	11	47	6600
	5226441	2.2 Turbo	120–160	11	47	6600
	5226444	2.6—All	150–210	11	85	3700
1987	5226442	2.2 Non-Turbo (Bosch)	150–210	11	47	6600
	5226441	2.2 Turbo (Bosch)	150–210	11	47	6600
	5226844	2.2 EFI (Bosch)	160–220	11	85	3700
	5226842	2.2 Turbo (Bosch)	150–210	11	75	4020
	5227282	2.2 Non-Turbo (Nippondenso)	150–210	11	82	3625
	5227282	2.2 Turbo (Nippondenso)	150–210	11	82	3625
	5227282	2.5—All	150–210	11	82	3625
1988	5227282	2.2—All	150–220	11	82	3625
	5227282	2.5 (Nippondenso)	150–220	11	82	3625
	5227282	2.2 (Bosch)	150–220	11	85	3700
1989	5227248	3.0L (Nippondenso)	150–220	11	74	3980
	5227548	3.0L (Bosch)	150–220	11	69	3447
	5233006	2.2/2.5L (Bosch)	150–220	11	69	3447
1990–91	5234648	3.0L (Nippondenso)	150–220	11	74	3980
	5234509	3.3/3.8L (Nippondenso)	150–220	11	74	3980
	5227548	3.0L (Bosch)	150–220	11	69	3447
	5233006	2.2/2.5L (Bosch)	150–220	11	69	3447

NOTE: Part numbers may be changed by manufacturer at any time, always refer to updated parts manual.

3.62). Also optional on some recent models is a turbocharged version of the 2.2, employing dished pistons which lower the compression ratio to 8.5:1.

The 2.6 Liter optional engine is also a four cylinder overhead camshaft power plant with a cast iron block, aluminum head and a silent shaft system. The countershafts (silent shafts) are incorporated in the cylinder block to reduce noise and vibration. Its most distinguishing feature is a jet valve located beside the intake valve of each cylinder. This valve works off the intake valve rocker arm and injects a swirl of air into the combustion chamber to promote more complete combustion.

The 2.5 Liter engine is basically similar to the 2.2, although a different block casting must be used to accomodate the longer stroke. Even though many basic components and dimensions are shared, the 2.5L (and 2.2L Turbo III) incorporates one very radical change: a balance shaft system to minimize vibration. These two, counter-rotating shafts are located in a special housing mounted to the underside of the block and under the crankshaft, within the oil pan. The shafts are interconnected by gears and driven (from the crankshaft) through a roller chain to keep them in time.

A 3.0L engine used on 1990–92 Dodge Monaco is a V-type lightweight, overhead valve engine. The cylinder head has hemispherical combustion chambers with raised intake manifold ports and large valves which optimize power and efficiency.

Engine Overhaul Tips

Most engine overhaul procedures are fairly standard. In addition to specific parts replacement procedures and complete specifications for your individual engine, this chapter also is a guide to accept rebuilding procedures. Competent and accurate machine shop services will ensure maximum performance, reliability and engine life.

In most instances it is more profitable for the do-it-yourself mechanic to remove, clean and inspect the component, buy the necessary parts and deliver these to a shop for actual machine work.

Aluminum has become extremely popular for use in engines, due to its low weight. Observe the following precautions when handling aluminum parts:

• Never hot tank aluminum parts (the caustic hot tank solution will eat the aluminum.

• Remove all aluminum parts (identification tag, etc.) from engine parts prior to the tanking.

• Always coat threads lightly with engine oil or anti-seize compounds before installation, to prevent seizure.

• Never overtorque bolts or spark plugs especially in aluminum threads.

Stripped threads in any component can be repaired using any of several commercial repair kits (Heli-Coil®, Microdot®, Keenserts®, etc.).

When assembling the engine, any parts that will be frictional contact must be prelubed to provide lubrication at initial start-up. Any product specifically formulated for this purpose can be used, but engine oil is not recommended as a prelube, as it will not be retained on the wearing surfaces in sufficient quantities to provide adequate lubrication for new parts.

When semi-permanent (locked, but removable) installation of bolts or nuts is desired, threads should be cleaned and coated with Loctite® or other similar, commercial nonhardening sealant.

Engine
REMOVAL AND INSTALLATION

CAUTION: *When draining the coolant, keep in mind that cats and dogs are attracted by the ethylene glycol antifreeze, and are quite likely to drink any that is left in an uncovered container or in puddles on the ground. This will prove fatal in sufficient quantity. Always drain the coolant into a sealable container. Coolant should be reused unless it is contaminated or several years old.*

The EPA warns that prolonged contact with used engine oil may cause a number of skin disorders, including cancer! You should make every effort to minimize your exposure to used engine oil. Protective gloves should be worn when changing the oil. Wash your hands and any other exposed skin areas as soon as possible after exposure to used engine oil. Soap and water, or waterless hand cleaner should be used.

2.2L, 2.5L AND 2.6L Engines

NOTE: *The following procedure can be used on all years and models. Slight variations may occur due to extra connections, etc., but the basic procedure should cover all years and models.*

1. Disconnect the negative battery cable and all engine ground straps. Relieve the fuel pressure as necessary.
2. Mark the hood hinge outline on the hood and remove the hood.
3. Drain the cooling system and oil pan. Remove the radiator hoses, fan assembly, radiator and intercooler, if equipped.
4. Remove the air cleaner, duct hoses and oil filter.

GENERAL ENGINE SPECIFICATIONS

Year	Engine Displacement Liters (cc)	Fuel System Type	Net Horsepower @ rpm	Net Torque @ rpm (ft. lbs.)	Bore × Stroke (in.)	Oil Compression Ratio	Pressure @ rpm
1981	2.2L	2 bbl	84 @ 4800	111 @ 2800	3.44 × 3.62	8.5:1	50
	2.6L	2 bbl	92 @ 4500	131 @ 2500	3.59 × 3.86	8.2:1	57
1982	2.2L	2 bbl	84 @ 4800	111 @ 2800	3.44 × 3.62	8.5:1	50
	2.6L	2 bbl	92 @ 4500	131 @ 2500	3.59 × 3.86	8.2:1	57
1983	2.2L	2 bbl	94 @ 4800	158 @ 2800	3.44 × 3.62	9.0:1	50
	2.6L	2 bbl	93 @ 4500	179 @ 2500	3.59 × 3.86	8.2:1	56
1984	2.2L	2 bbl	96 @ 5200	119 @ 3200	3.44 × 3.62	9.0:1	50
	2.2L	EFI	99 @ 5600	121 @ 3200	3.44 × 3.62	8.0:1	50
	2.2L	EFI Turbo	142 @ 5600	160 @ 3600	3.44 × 3.62	8.1:1	50
	2.6L	2 bbl	101 @ 4800	140 @ 2800	3.59 × 3.86	8.7:1	85
1985	2.2L	2 bbl	96 @ 5200	119 @ 3200	3.44 × 3.62	9.0:1	50
	2.2L	EFI	99 @ 5600	121 @ 3200	3.44 × 3.62	9.0:1	50
	2.2L	EFI Turbo	146 @ 5200	168 @ 3600	3.44 × 3.62	8.1:1	50
	2.6L	2 bbl	101 @ 4800	140 @ 2800	3.59 × 3.86	8.7:1	85
1986	2.2L	2 bbl	96 @ 5200	119 @ 3200	3.44 × 3.62	9.5:1	50
	2.2L	EFI	99 @ 5600	121 @ 3200	3.44 × 3.62	9.5:1	50
	2.2L	EFI Turbo	146 @ 5200	170 @ 3600	3.44 × 3.62	8.5:1	50
	2.5L	EFI	100 @ 4800	133 @ 2800	3.44 × 4.09	9.0:1	50
1987	2.2L	2 bbl	96 @ 5200	119 @ 3200	3.44 × 3.62	9.5:1	50
	2.2L	EFI	99 @ 5600	121 @ 3200	3.44 × 3.62	9.5:1	50
	2.2L	EFI Turbo	146 @ 5200	170 @ 3600	3.44 × 3.62	8.0:1	50
	2.5L	EFI	100 @ 4800	133 @ 2800	3.44 × 4.09	9.0:1	80
1988	2.2L	EFI	97 @ 5200	122 @ 3200	3.44 × 3.62	9.5:1	52
	2.2L	EFI Turbo	146 @ 5200	171 @ 3600	3.44 × 3.62	8.1:1	52
	2.5L	EFI	100 @ 4800	136 @ 2800	3.44 × 4.09	9.0:1	52
1989	2.2L	Turbo	174 @ 5200	170 @ 3600	3.44 × 3.62	8.1:1	50
	2.2L	EFI	99 @ 5600	121 @ 3200	3.44 × 3.62	9.5:1	50
	2.5L	EFI	100 @ 4800	135 @ 2800	3.44 × 4.09	8.9:1	50
	2.5L	Turbo	150 @ 4800	180 @ 2000	3.44 × 4.09	7.8:1	50
	3.0L	EFI	141 @ 5000	171 @ 2000	3.59 × 2.99	8.6:1	50
1990	1.8L	MPI	92 @ 5000	105 @ 3500	3.17 × 3.39	9.0:1	41
	2.0L	MPI	135 @ 6000	125 @ 5000	3.35 × 3.47	9.0:1	41
	2.0L	Turbo	190 @ 6000	203 @ 3000	3.35 × 3.47	7.8:1	41
	2.2L	Turbo	174 @ 5200	210 @ 2400	3.44 × 3.62	8.0:1	50
	2.2L	EFI	99 @ 4800	122 @ 3200	3.44 × 3.62	9.5:1	50
	2.5L	EFI	100 @ 4800	135 @ 2800	3.44 × 4.09	8.9:1	50
	2.5L	Turbo	150 @ 4800	180 @ 2000	3.44 × 4.09	7.8:1	50
	3.0L	EFI	141 @ 5000	171 @ 2800	3.59 × 2.99	8.9:1	50
	3.0L	MPI	150 @ 5000	171 @ 3750	3.66 × 2.87	9.3:1	60
1991	1.8L	MPI	92 @ 5000	105 @ 3500	3.17 × 3.39	9.0:1	40
	2.0L	MPI	135 @ 6000	125 @ 5000	3.35 × 3.47	9.0:1	40
	2.0L	Turbo	190 @ 6000	203 @ 3000	3.35 × 3.47	7.8:1	40
	2.2L	EFI	99 @ 4800	122 @ 3200	3.44 × 3.62	9.5:1	50
	2.5L	EFI	100 @ 4800	135 @ 2800	3.44 × 4.09	8.9:1	50
	2.5L	Turbo	150 @ 4800	180 @ 2000	3.44 × 4.09	7.8:1	50
	3.0L	EFI	141 @ 5000	170 @ 2800	3.59 × 2.99	8.9:1	50
	3.0L ①	MPI	150 @ 5000	171 @ 3750	3.66 × 2.87	9.3:1	60

GENERAL ENGINE SPECIFICATIONS

Year	Engine Displacement Liters (cc)	Fuel System Type	Net Horsepower @ rpm	Net Torque @ rpm (ft. lbs.)	Bore × Stroke (in.)	Oil Compression Ratio	Pressure @ rpm
	3.0L②	MPI	164 @ 5500	185 @ 4000	3.58 × 2.99	8.9:1	50
	3.0L③	MPI	222 @ 6000	201 @ 4500	3.58 × 2.99	10.0:1	50
	3.0L④	Turbo	300 @ 6000	307 @ 2500	3.58 × 2.99	8.0:1	50
	3.3L	EFI	183 @ 3600	183 @ 3600	3.66 × 3.19	8.9:1	50
	3.8L	EFI	150 @ 4400	203 @ 3200	3.78 × 3.42	9.0:1	50
1992	1.8L	MPI	92 @ 5000	105 @ 3500	3.17 × 3.39	9.0:1	40
	2.0L	MPI	135 @ 6000	125 @ 5000	3.35 × 3.47	9.0:1	40
	2.0L	Turbo	190 @ 6000	203 @ 3000	3.35 × 3.47	7.8:1	40
	2.2L	EFI	99 @ 4800	122 @ 3200	3.44 × 3.62	9.5:1	50
	2.5L	EFI	100 @ 4800	135 @ 2800	3.44 × 4.09	8.9:1	50
	2.5L	Turbo	150 @ 4800	180 @ 2000	3.44 × 4.09	7.8:1	50
	3.0L	EFI	141 @ 5000	170 @ 2800	3.59 × 2.99	8.9:1	50
	3.0L①	MPI	150 @ 5000	171 @ 3750	3.66 × 2.87	9.3:1	60
	3.0L②	MPI	164 @ 5500	185 @ 4000	3.58 × 2.99	8.9:1	50
	3.0L③	MPI	222 @ 6000	201 @ 4500	3.58 × 2.99	10.0:1	50
	3.0L④	Turbo	300 @ 6000	307 @ 2500	3.58 × 2.99	8.0:1	50
	3.3L	EFI	183 @ 3600	183 @ 3600	3.66 × 3.19	8.9:1	50
	3.8L	EFI	150 @ 4400	203 @ 3200	3.78 × 3.42	9.0:1	50

MPI—Multiport fuel injection
EFI—Electronic fuel injection
① 1990–92 Dodge Monaco application
② 1991–92 Dodge Stealth application—
Single overhead cam design
③ 1991–92 Dodge Stealth application—
Double overhead cam design
④ 1991–92 Dodge Stealth application—
Double overhead cam design with turbo.
NOTE: Horsepower and torque are SAE net figures. They are measured at the rear of the transmission with all accessories installed and operating. Since the figures vary when a given engine is installed in different models, some are representative rather than exact.

5. Unbolt the air conditioning compressor from its mount, if equipped and position it aside.

6. Remove the power steering pump mounting bolts and position the pump aside, without disconnecting any fluid lines.

7. Label and disconnect all electrical connectors from the engine, alternator and fuel system.

8. Disconnect and plug the fuel lines and heater hoses.

9. Disconnect the throttle and or carburetor linkage.

10. Remove the alternator.

11. Raise the vehicle and support safely.

12. Disconnect the exhaust pipe from the manifold. Remove the right inner fender shield.

13. If equipped with a manual transaxle, remove the transaxle.

14. If equipped with an automatic transaxle, perform the following procedures:

a. Remove the lower cover from the transaxle case.

b. Remove the starter and set it aside.

c. Matchmark the flexplate to the torque converter for installation purposes.

d. Remove the torque converter bolts. Separate the converter from the flexplate. Remove the lower bellhousing bolts.

15. Lower the vehicle and support the transaxle, if still in the vehicle, with a floor jack or equivalent. Attach an engine lifting device to the engine.

16. Remove the remaining bellhousing bolts.
NOTE: *If removing the insulator-to-rail screws, first mark the position of the insulator on the side rail to insure proper alignment during reinstallation.*

VALVE SPECIFICATIONS

Year	Engine Displacement Liters (cc)	Seat Angle (deg.)	Face Angle (deg.)	Spring Test Pressure (lbs. @ in.)	Spring Installed Height (in.)	Stem-to-Guide Clearance (in.)		Stem Diameter (in.)	
						Intake	Exhaust	Intake	Exhaust
1981	2.2L	45	45.5	175 @ 1.22	1.65	0.001–0.003	0.002–0.004	0.312–0.313	0.311–0.312
	2.6L	43.75	45.25	34.1 @ 1.18	1.59	0.001–0.002	0.002–0.003	0.315	0.315
1982	2.2L	45	45.5	175 @ 1.22	1.65	0.001–0.003	0.002–0.004	0.312–0.313	0.311–0.312
	2.6L	43.75	45.22	34.1 @ 1.18	1.59	0.001–0.002	0.002–0.003	0.315	0.315
1983	2.2L	45	45	175 @ 1.22	1.65	0.0009–0.0026	0.0030–0.0047	0.3124	0.3103
	2.6L	45	45	61 @ 1.59	1.59	0.0012–0.0024	0.0020–0.0035	0.315	0.315
1984	2.2L	45	45	175 @ 1.22	1.65	0.0009–0.0026	0.0030–0.0047	0.3124	0.3103
	2.6L	45	45	61 @ 1.59	1.59	0.0012–0.0024	0.0020–0.0035	0.315	0.315
1985	2.2L	45	45	150 @ 1.22	1.65	0.0009–0.0026	0.0030–0.0047	0.3124	0.3103
	2.2L Turbo	45	45	175 @ 1.22	1.65	0.0009–0.0026	0.0030–0.0047	0.3124	0.3103
	2.6L	45	45	61 @ 1.59	1.59	0.0012–0.0024	0.0020–0.0035	0.315	0.315
1986	2.2L	45	45	150 @ 1.22	1.65	0.0009–0.0026	0.0030–0.0047	0.3124	0.3103
	2.2L Turbo	45	45	175 @ 1.22	1.65	0.0009–0.0026	0.0030–0.0047	0.3124	0.3103
	2.5L	45	45	150 @ 1.22	1.65	0.0009–0.0026	0.0030–0.0047	0.3124	0.3103
1987	2.2L	45	45	150 @ 1.22	1.65	0.0009–0.0026	0.0030–0.0047	0.3124	0.3103
	2.2L Turbo	45	45	175 @ 1.22	1.65	0.0009–0.0026	0.0030–0.0047	0.3124	0.3103
	2.5L	45	45	150 @ 1.22	1.65	0.0009–0.0026	0.0030–0.0047	0.3124	0.3103
1988	2.2L	45	45	202 @ 1.22	1.65	0.0009–0.0026	0.0030–0.0047	0.3124	0.3103
	2.2L Turbo	45	45	202 @ 1.22	1.65	0.0009–0.0026	0.0030–0.0047	0.3124	0.3103
	2.5L	45	45	202 @ 1.22	1.65	0.0009–0.0026	0.0030–0.0047	0.3124	0.3103
1989	2.2L	45	45	114	1.65	0.001–0.003	0.0030–0.0047	0.3124	0.3103
	2.5L	45	45	114	1.65	0.001–0.003	0.0030–0.0047	0.3124	0.3103
	3.0L	44.5	45.5	180	1.59	0.001–0.002	0.0020–0.0030	0.3130–0.3140	0.3120–0.3130
1990	1.8L	44	45	62	1.93	0.0012–0.0024	0.0020–0.0035	0.310	0.310
	2.0L	44	45	66	1.92	0.0008–0.0019	0.0020–0.0033	0.2585–0.2591	0.2571–0.2579
	2.0L Turbo	44	45	66	1.92	0.008–0.0019	0.0020–0.0033	0.2585–0.2591	0.2571–0.2579

VALVE SPECIFICATIONS

Year	Engine Displacement Liters (cc)	Seat Angle (deg.)	Face Angle (deg.)	Spring Test Pressure (lbs. @ in.)	Spring Installed Height (in.)	Stem-to-Guide Clearance (in.)		Stem Diameter (in.)	
						Intake	Exhaust	Intake	Exhaust
	2.2L	45	45	114	1.65	0.001–0.003	0.0030–0.0047	0.3124	0.3103
	2.5L	45	45	114	1.65	0.001–0.003	0.0030–0.0047	0.3124	0.3103
	3.0L	44.5	45.5	180	1.59	0.001–0.002	0.0020–0.0030	0.3130–0.3140	0.3120–0.3130
	3.0L①	45	45	155	1.813	NA	NA	0.315	0.315
1991	1.8L	44	45	62	1.93	0.0012–0.0024	0.0020–0.0035	0.310	0.310
	2.0L	44	45	66	1.92	0.0008–0.0019	0.0020–0.0033	0.2585–0.2591	0.2571–0.2579
	2.0L Turbo	44	45	66	1.92	0.0008–0.0019	0.0020–0.0033	0.2585–0.2591	0.2571–0.2579
	2.2L	45	45	114	1.65	0.001–0.003	0.0030–0.0047	0.3124	0.3103
	2.5L	45	45	114	1.65	0.001–0.003	0.0030–0.0047	0.3124	0.3103
	3.0L	44.5	45.5	180	1.59	0.001–0.002	0.0020–0.0030	0.3130–0.3140	0.3120–0.3130
	3.0L①	45	45	155	1.813	NA	NA	0.315	0.315
	3.0L②	44	45	74	1.63	0.0012–0.0039	0.0020–0.0059	0.314	0.314
	3.0L③	44	45	62	1.53	0.0008–0.0039	0.0020–0.0047	0.260	0.260
	3.3L	45	44.5	60	1.56	0.001–0.003	0.002–0.016	0.312–0.313	0.311–0.312
	3.8L	45	44.5	60	1.56	0.001–0.003	0.002–0.016	0.312–0.313	0.311–0.312
1992	1.8L	44	45	62	1.93	0.0012–0.0024	0.0020–0.0035	0.310	0.310
	2.0L	44	45	66	1.92	0.0008–0.0019	0.0020–0.0033	0.2585–0.2591	0.2571–0.2579
	2.0L Turbo	44	45	66	1.92	0.0008–0.0019	0.0020–0.0033	0.2585–0.2591	0.2571–0.2579
	2.2L	45	45	114	1.65	0.001–0.003	0.0030–0.0047	0.3124	0.3103
	2.5L	45	45	114	1.65	0.001–0.003	0.0030–0.0047	0.3124	0.3103
	3.0L	44.5	45.5	180	1.59	0.001–0.002	0.0020–0.0030	0.3130–0.3140	0.3120–0.3130
	3.0L①	45	45	155	1.813	NA	NA	0.315	0.315
	3.0L②	44	45	74	1.63	0.0012–0.0039	0.0020–0.0059	0.314	0.314
	3.0L③	44	45	62	1.53	0.0008–0.0039	0.0020–0.0047	0.260	0.260
	3.3L	45	44.5	60	1.56	0.001–0.003	0.002–0.016	0.312–0.313	0.311–0.312
	3.8L	45	44.5	60	1.56	0.001–0.003	0.002–0.016	0.312–0.313	0.311–0.312

NA—Not Available
① 1990–92 Dodge Monaco Application
② 1991–92 Dodge Stealth Application—
   Single overhead cam design
③ 1991–92 Dodge Stealth Application—
   Double overhead cam design

CRANKSHAFT AND CONNECTING ROD SPECIFICATIONS

All measurements are given in inches.

Year	Engine Displacement Liters (cc)	Crankshaft				Connecting Rod		
		Main Brg. Journal Dia.	Main Brg. Oil Clearance	Shaft End-play	Thrust on No.	Journal Diameter	Oil Clearance	Side Clearance
1981	2.2L	2.362–2.363	0.0004–0.0026	0.002–0.007	3	1.968–1.969	0.0004–0.0026	0.005–0.013
	2.6L	2.362	0.0008–0.0028	0.002–0.007	3	2.086	0.0008–0.0028	0.004–0.010
1982	2.2L	2.362–2.363	0.0004–0.0026	0.002–0.007	3	1.968–1.969	0.0004–0.0026	0.005–0.013
	2.6L	2.362	0.0008–0.0028	0.002–0.007	3	2.086	0.0004–0.0026	0.005–0.013
1983	2.2L	2.362–2.363	0.0003–0.0031	0.002–0.007	3	1.968–1.969	0.0008–0.0034	0.005–0.013
	2.2L Turbo	2.362–2.363	0.0004–0.0023	0.002–0.007	3	1.968–1.969	0.0008–0.0031	0.005–0.013
	2.6L	2.3622	0.0008–0.0028	0.002–0.007	3	2.086	0.0008–0.0028	0.004–0.010
1984	2.2L	2.362–2.363	0.0003–0.0031	0.002–0.007	3	1.968–1.969	0.0008–0.0034	0.005–0.013
	2.2L Turbo	2.362–2.363	0.0004–0.0023	0.002–0.007	3	1.968–1.969	0.0008–0.0031	0.005–0.013
	2.6L	2.362	0.0008–0.0028	0.002–0.007	3	2.086	0.0008–0.0028	0.004–0.010
1985	2.2L	2.362–2.363	0.0003–0.0031	0.002–0.007	3	1.968–1.969	0.0008–0.0034	0.005–0.013
	2.6L Turbo	2.362–2.363	0.0004–0.0023	0.002–0.007	3	1.968–1.969	0.0008–0.0031	0.005–0.013
	2.6L	2.362	0.0008–0.0028	0.002–0.007	3	2.086	0.0008–0.0028	0.004–0.010
1986	2.2L	2.362–2.363	0.0003–0.0031	0.002–0.007	3	1.968–1.969	0.0008–0.0034	0.005–0.013
	2.2L Turbo	2.362	0.0004–0.0023	0.002–0.007	3	1.968–1.969	0.0008–0.0031	0.005–0.013
	2.5L	2.362–2.363	0.0003–0.0031	0.002–0.007	3	1.968–1.969	0.0008–0.0034	0.005–0.013
1987	2.2L	2.362–2.363	0.0003–0.0031	0.002–0.007	3	1.968–1.969	0.0008–0.0034	0.005–0.013
	2.2L Turbo	2.362	0.0004–0.0023	0.002–0.007	3	1.968–1.969	0.0008–0.0031	0.005–0.013
	2.5L	2.362–2.363	0.0003–0.0031	0.002–0.007	3	1.968–1.969	0.0008–0.0034	0.005–0.013
1988	2.2L	2.362–2.363	0.0004–0.0028	0.002–0.007	3	1.968–1.969	0.0008–0.0034	0.005–0.013
	2.2L Turbo	2.362–2.363	0.0004–0.0028	0.002–0.007	3	1.968–1.969	0.0008–0.0031	0.005–0.013
	2.5L	2.362–2.363	0.0004–0.0028	0.002–0.007	3	1.968–1.969	0.0008–0.0034	0.005–0.013
1989	2.2L	2.362–2.363	0.0004–0.0040	0.002–0.014	3	1.968–1.969	0.0008–0.0040	0.005–0.013
	2.5L	2.362–2.363	0.0004–0.0040	0.002–0.014	3	1.968–1.969	0.0008–0.0040	0.005–0.013
	3.0L	2.361–2.362	0.0006–0.0020	0.002–0.010	3	1.968–1.969	0.0008–0.0028	0.004–0.010
1990	1.8L	2.240	0.0008–0.0020	0.0020–0.0070	3	1.770	0.0008–0.0020	0.0039–0.0098

CRANKSHAFT AND CONNECTING ROD SPECIFICATIONS

All measurements are given in inches.

Year	Engine Displacement Liters (cc)	Crankshaft				Connecting Rod		
		Main Brg. Journal Dia.	Main Brg. Oil Clearance	Shaft End-play	Thrust on No.	Journal Diameter	Oil Clearance	Side Clearance
	2.0L	2.243–2.244	0.0008–0.0020	0.0020–0.0070	3	1.770–1.771	0.0008–0.0020	0.0040–0.0098
	2.2L	2.362–2.363	0.0004–0.0040	0.002–0.014	3	1.968–1.969	0.0008–0.0040	0.005–0.013
	2.5L	2.362–2.363	0.0004–0.0040	0.002–0.014	3	1.968–1.969	0.0008–0.0040	0.005–0.013
	3.0L	2.361–2.362	0.0006–0.0020	0.002–0.010	3	1.968–1.969	0.0008–0.0028	0.004–0.010
	3.0L ①	2.757–2.758	0.0015–0.0035	0.002–0.007	1	2.361	0.0008–0.0030	0.008–0.015
1991	1.8L	2.240	0.0008–0.0020	0.0020–0.0070	3	1.770	0.0008–0.0020	0.0039–0.0098
	2.0L	2.243–2.244	0.0008–0.0020	0.0020–0.0070	3	1.770–1.771	0.0008–0.0020	0.0040–0.0098
	2.2L	2.362–2.363	0.0004–0.0040	0.002–0.014	3	1.968–1.969	0.0008–0.0034	0.005–0.013
	2.5L	2.362–2.363	0.0004–0.0040	0.002–0.014	3	1.968–1.969	0.0008–0.0034	0.005–0.013
	3.0L	2.361–2.363	0.0006–0.0020	0.002–0.010	3	1.968–1.969	0.0008–0.0028	0.004–0.010
	3.0L ①	2.757–2.758	0.0015–0.0035	0.002–0.007	1	2.361	0.0008–0.0030	0.008–0.015
	3.0L ②	2.358	0.0008–0.0019	0.0020–0.0098	3	1.965	0.0006–0.0018	0.0040–0.0098
	3.0L ③	2.358	0.0007–0.0017	0.0020–0.0098	3	1.965	0.0006–0.0018	0.0040–0.0098
	3.3L	2.519	0.0007–0.0022	0.003–0.009	2	2.283	0.0008–0.0030	0.005–0.015
	3.8L	2.519	0.0007–0.0022	0.003–0.009	2	2.283	0.0008–0.0030	0.005–0.015
1992	1.8L	2.240	0.0008–0.0020	0.0020–0.0070	3	1.770	0.0008–0.0020	0.0039–0.0098
	2.0L	2.243–2.244	0.0008–0.0020	0.0020–0.0070	3	1.770–1.771	0.0008–0.0020	0.0040–0.0098
	2.2L	2.362–2.363	0.0004–0.0040	0.002–0.014	3	1.968–1.969	0.0008–0.0034	0.005–0.013
	2.5L	2.362–2.363	0.0004–0.0040	0.002–0.014	3	1.968–1.969	0.0008–0.0034	0.005–0.013
	3.0L	2.361–2.363	0.0006–0.0020	0.002–0.010	3	1.968–1.969	0.0008–0.0028	0.004–0.010
	3.0L ①	2.757–2.758	0.0015–0.0035	0.002–0.007	1	2.361	0.0008–0.0030	0.008–0.015
	3.0L ②	2.358	0.0008–0.0019	0.0020–0.0098	3	1.965	0.0006–0.0018	0.0040–0.0098
	3.0L ③	2.358	0.0007–0.0017	0.0020–0.0098	3	1.965	0.0006–0.0018	0.0040–0.0098
	3.3L	2.519	0.0007–0.0022	0.003–0.009	2	2.283	0.0008–0.0030	0.005–0.015
	3.8L	2.519	0.0007–0.0022	0.003–0.009	2	2.283	0.0008–0.0030	0.005–0.015

① 1990–92 Dodge Monaco Application
② 1991–92 Dodge Stealth Application—Single Overhead Cam Design
③ 1991–92 Dodge Stealth Application—Double Overhead Cam Design

CAMSHAFT SPECIFICATIONS

All measurements given in inches.

Year	Engine Displacement Liters (cc)	Journal Diameter					Elevation		Bearing Clearance	Camshaft End Play
		1	2	3	4	5	In.	Ex.		
1981	2.2L	1.375–1.376	1.375–1.376	1.375–1.376	1.372–1.376	1.375–1.376	0.430	0.430	0.010 Max	0.006
1982	2.2L	1.375–1.376	1.375–1.376	1.375–1.376	1.372–1.376	1.375–1.376	0.430	0.430	0.010 Max	0.006
1983	2.2L	1.375–1.376	1.375–1.376	1.375–1.376	1.375–1.376	1.375–1.376	0.430	0.430	0.010 Max	0.006
1984	2.2L	1.375–1.376	1.375–1.376	1.375–1.376	1.375–1.376	1.375–1.376	0.430	0.430	0.010 Max	0.006
1985	2.2L	1.375–1.376	1.375–1.376	1.375–1.376	1.375–1.376	1.375–1.376	0.430	0.430	0.010 Max	0.006
1986	2.2L	1.375–1.376	1.375–1.376	1.375–1.376	1.375–1.376	1.375–1.376	0.430	0.430	0.010 Max	0.006
	2.5L	1.375–1.376	1.375–1.376	1.375–1.376	1.375–1.376	1.375–1.376	0.430	0.430	0.010 Max	0.006
1987	2.2L	1.375–1.376	1.375–1.376	1.375–1.376	1.375–1.376	1.375–1.376	0.430	0.430	0.010 Max	0.006
	2.5L	1.375–1.376	1.375–1.376	1.375–1.376	1.375–1.376	1.375–1.376	0.430	0.430	0.010 Max	0.006
1988	2.2L	1.375–1.376	1.375–1.376	1.375–1.376	1.375–1.376	1.375–1.376	NA	NA	—	0.005–0.020
	2.5L	1.375–1.376	1.375–1.376	1.375–1.376	1.375–1.376	1.375–1.376	NA	NA	—	0.005–0.020
1989	2.2L	1.375–1.376	1.375–1.376	1.375–1.376	1.375–1.376	1.375–1.376	NA	NA	—	0.005–0.020
	2.5L	1.375–1.376	1.375–1.376	1.375–1.376	1.375–1.376	1.375–1.376	NA	NA	—	0.005–0.020
	3.0L	NA	NA	NA	NA	NA	①	①	—	NA
1990	1.8L	1.3360–1.3366	1.3360–1.3366	1.3360–1.3366	1.3360–1.3366	1.336–1.337	1.4138	1.4138	0.0020–0.0035	0.004–0.008
	2.0L	1.0217–1.0224	1.0217–1.0224	1.0217–1.0224	1.0217–1.0224	1.020②	1.3974	1.3858	0.0020–0.0035	0.004–0.008
	2.2L	1.375–1.376	1.375–1.376	1.375–1.376	1.375–1.376	1.375–1.376	NA	NA	—	0.005–0.020
	2.5L	1.375–1.376	1.375–1.376	1.375–1.376	1.375–1.376	1.375–1.376	NA	NA	—	0.005–0.020
	3.0L	NA	NA	NA	NA	NA	①	①	—	NA
	3.0L③	NA	NA	NA	NA	NA	NA	NA	NA	0.003–0.0055
1991	1.8L	1.3360–1.3366	1.3360–1.3366	1.3360–1.3366	1.3360–1.3366	1.336–1.337	1.4138	1.4138	0.0020–0.0035	0.004–0.008
	2.0L	1.0217–1.0224	1.0217–1.0224	1.0217–1.0224	1.0217–1.0224	1.020②	1.3974	1.3858	0.0020–0.0035	0.004–0.008
	2.2L	1.375–1.376	1.375–1.376	1.375–1.376	1.375–1.376	1.375–1.376	NA	NA	—	0.005–0.020
	2.5L	1.375–1.376	1.375–1.376	1.375–1.376	1.375–1.376	1.375–1.376	NA	NA	—	0.005–0.020
	3.0L	NA	NA	NA	NA	NA	①	①	—	NA
	3.0L③	NA	NA	NA	NA	NA	NA	NA	NA	0.003–0.0055
	3.0L④	1.34	1.34	1.34	1.34	—	1.6430–1.6440	1.6430–1.6440	0.0020–0.0035	0.004–0.008
	3.0L⑤	1.02	1.02	1.02	1.02	1.02	1.3776–1.3972	1.3661–1.3858	0.0020–0.0035	0.004–0.008

CAMSHAFT SPECIFICATIONS

All measurements given in inches.

Year	Engine Displacement Liters (cc)	Journal Diameter					Elevation		Bearing Clearance	Camshaft End Play
		1	2	3	4	5	In.	Ex.		
	3.3L	1.997–1.999	1.980–1.982	1.965–1.967	1.949–1.952	—	0.400	0.400	0.001–0.005	0.005–0.012
	3.8L	1.997–1.999	1.980–1.982	1.965–1.967	1.949–1.952	—	0.400	0.400	0.001–0.005	0.005–0.012
1992	1.8L	1.3360–1.3366	1.3360–1.3366	1.3360–1.3366	1.3360–1.3366	1.336–1.337	1.4138	1.4138	0.0020–0.0035	0.004–0.008
	2.0L	1.0217 1.0224	1.0217 1.0224	1.0217–1.0224	1.0217–1.0224	1.020②	1.3974	1.3858	0.0020–0.0035	0.004–0.008
	2.2L	1.375–1.376	1.375–1.376	1.375–1.376	1.375–1.376	1.375–1.376	NA	NA	—	0.005–0.020
	2.5L	1.375–1.376	1.375–1.376	1.375–1.376	1.375–1.376	1.375–1.376	NA	NA	—	0.005–0.020
	3.0L	NA	NA	NA	NA	NA	①	①	—	NA
	3.0L③	NA	NA	NA	NA	NA	NA	NA	NA	0.003–0.0055
	3.0L④	1.34	1.34	1.34	1.34	—	1.6430–1.6440	1.6430–1.6440	0.0020–0.0035	0.004–0.008
	3.0L⑤	1.02	1.02	1.02	1.02	1.02	1.3776–1.3972	1.3661–1.3858	0.0020–0.0035	0.004–0.008
	3.3L	1.997–1.999	1.980–1.982	1.965–1.967	1.949–1.952	—	0.400	0.400	0.001–0.005	0.005–0.012
	3.8L	1.997–1.999	1.980–1.982	1.965–1.967	1.949–1.952	—	0.400	0.400	0.001–0.005	0.005–0.012

NA—Not Available
① Height of Cam Lobe: 1.604–1.624 in.
② Six journals are used. All are 1.020 diameter
   Bearing caps Nos. 2–5 are the same shape. "L" or "R" is stamped on No. 1 bearing cap. L = intake side, R = exhaust side. Bearing caps should be reinstalled at their original locations.
③ 1990–92 Dodge Monaco Application
④ 1991–92 Dodge Stealth Application—Single Overhead Cam Design
⑤ 1991-92 Dodge Stealth Application—Double Overhead Cam Design

PISTON AND RING SPECIFICATIONS

All measurements are given in inches.

Year	Engine Displacement Liters (cc)	Piston Clearance	Ring Gap			Ring Side Clearance		
			Top Compression	Bottom Compression	Oil Control	Top Compression	Bottom Compression	Oil Control
1981	2.2L	0.0005–0.0240	0.011–0.021	0.011–0.021	0.015–0.055	0.0015–0.0031	0.0015–0.0037	Snug
	2.6L	0.0005–0.0240	0.011–0.018	0.011–0.018	0.008–0.035	0.0024–0.0039	0.0008–0.0024	Snug
1982	2.2L	0.0005–0.0240	0.011–0.021	0.011–0.021	0.015–0.055	0.0015–0.0031	0.0015–0.0037	Snug
	2.6L	0.0005–0.0240	0.011–0.018	0.011–0.018	0.008–0.035	0.0024–0.0039	0.0008–0.0024	Snug
1983	2.2L	0.0005	0.011–0.021	0.011–0.021	0.015–0.055	0.0015–0.0031	0.0015–0.0037	Snug
	2.6L	0.0008–0.0016	0.010–0.018	0.010–0.018	0.008–0.035	0.0024–0.0039	0.0008–0.0024	Snug
1984	2.2L	0.0005	0.011–0.021	0.011–0.021	0.015–0.055	0.0015–0.0031	0.0015–0.0037	Snug

PISTON AND RING SPECIFICATIONS

All measurements are given in inches.

Year	Engine Displacement Liters (cc)	Piston Clearance	Ring Gap			Ring Side Clearance		
			Top Compression	Bottom Compression	Oil Control	Top Compression	Bottom Compression	Oil Control
	2.6L	0.0008–0.0016	0.010–0.018	0.010–0.018	0.008–0.035	0.0024–0.0039	0.0008–0.0024	Snug
1985	2.2L	0.0005	0.011–0.021	0.011–0.021	0.015–0.055	0.0015–0.0031	0.0015–0.0031	Snug
	2.6L	0.0008–0.0016	0.010–0.018	0.010–0.018	0.008–0.035	0.0024–0.0039	0.0008–0.0024	Snug
1986	2.2L	0.0005–0.0015	0.011–0.021	0.011–0.021	0.015–0.055	0.0015–0.0031	0.0015–0.0037	0.008
	2.2L Turbo	0.0015–0.0025	0.010–0.020	0.009–0.019	0.015–0.055	0.0015–0.0031	0.0015–0.0037	0.008
	2.5L	0.0015–0.0015	0.011–0.021	0.011–0.021	0.015–0.055	0.0015–0.0031	0.0015–0.0037	0.008
1987	2.2L	0.0005–0.0015	0.011–0.021	0.011–0.021	0.015–0.055	0.0015–0.0031	0.0015–0.0037	0.008
	2.2L Turbo	0.0015–0.0026	0.010–0.020	0.009–0.019	0.015–0.055	0.0015–0.0031	0.0015–0.0037	0.008
	2.5L	0.0005–0.0015	0.011–0.021	0.011–0.021	0.015–0.055	0.0015–0.0031	0.0015–0.0037	0.008
1988	2.2L	0.0005–0.0015	0.011–0.021	0.011–0.021	0.015–0.055	0.0015–0.0031	0.0015–0.0037	0.008
	2.2L Turbo	0.0015–0.0026	0.010–0.020	0.009–0.019	0.015–0.055	0.0015–0.0031	0.0015–0.0037	0.008
	2.5L	0.0005–0.0015	0.011–0.021	0.011–0.021	0.015–0.055	0.0015–0.0031	0.0015–0.0037	0.008
1989	2.2L Turbo	0.0005–0.0027	0.010–0.039	0.009–0.037	0.015–0.074	0.0016–0.0030	0.0016–0.0035	0.0002–0.0080
	2.2L	0.0005–0.0027	0.010–0.039	0.011–0.039	0.015–0.074	0.0015–0.0040	0.0015–0.0040	0.0002–0.0080
	2.5L Turbo	0.0006–0.0030	0.010–0.039	0.009–0.037	0.015–0.074	0.0016–0.0030	0.0016–0.0035	0.0002–0.0080
	2.5L	0.0010–0.0027	0.010–0.039	0.011–0.039	0.015–0.074	0.0015–0.0040	0.0015–0.0040	0.0002–0.0080
	3.0L	0.0008–0.0015	0.012–0.018	0.010–0.016	0.012–0.035	0.0020–0.0035	0.0008–0.0020	NA
1990	1.8L	0.0004–0.0012	0.0118–0.0177	0.0079–0.0138	0.0080–0.0280	0.0018–0.0033	0.0008–0.0024	NA
	2.0L	0.0008–0.0016	0.0098–0.0177	0.0138–0.0197	0.0079–0.0276	0.0012–0.0028	0.0012–0.0028	NA
	2.0L Turbo	0.0012–0.0020	0.0098–0.0177	0.0138–0.0197	0.0079–0.0276	0.0012–0.0028	0.0012–0.0028	NA
	2.2L Turbo	0.0005–0.0027	0.010–0.039	0.009–0.037	0.015–0.074	0.0016–0.0030	0.0016–0.0035	0.0002–0.0080
	2.2L	0.0005–0.0027	0.010–0.039	0.011–0.039	0.015–0.074	0.0015–0.0040	0.0015–0.0040	0.0002–0.0080
	2.5L Turbo	0.0006–0.0030	0.010–0.039	0.009–0.037	0.015–0.074	0.0016–0.0030	0.0016–0.0035	0.0002–0.0080
	2.5L	0.0010–0.0027	0.010–0.039	0.011–0.039	0.015–0.074	0.0015–0.0040	0.0015–0.0040	0.0002–0.0080
	3.0L	0.0012–0.0020	0.012–0.018	0.010–0.016	0.012–0.035	0.0020–0.0035	0.0008–0.0020	NA
	3.0L①	0.0013–0.0021	0.0160–0.022	0.016–0.022	NA	0.0010–0.0020	0.0010–0.0020	0.0015–0.0035

PISTON AND RING SPECIFICATIONS

All measurements are given in inches.

Year	Engine Displacement Liters (cc)	Piston Clearance	Ring Gap			Ring Side Clearance		
			Top Compression	Bottom Compression	Oil Control	Top Compression	Bottom Compression	Oil Control
1991	1.8L	0.0004–0.0012	0.0118–0.0177	0.0079–0.0138	0.0080–0.0280	0.0018–0.0033	0.0008–0.0024	NA
	2.0L	0.0008–0.0016	0.0098–0.0177	0.0138–0.0197	0.0079–0.0276	0.0012–0.0028	0.0012–0.0028	NA
	2.0L Turbo	0.0012–0.0020	0.0098–0.0177	0.0138–0.0197	0.0079–0.0276	0.0012–0.0028	0.0012–0.0028	NA
	2.2L	0.0005–0.0027	0.010–0.039	0.011–0.039	0.015–0.074	0.0015–0.0040	0.0015–0.0040	0.0002–0.0080
	2.5L Turbo	0.0006–0.0030	0.010–0.039	0.009–0.037	0.015–0.074	0.0016–0.0030	0.0016–0.0035	0.0002–0.0080
	2.5L	0.0010–0.0027	0.010–0.039	0.011–0.039	0.015–0.074	0.0015–0.0040	0.0015–0.0040	0.0002–0.0080
	3.0L	0.0012–0.0020	0.012–0.018	0.010–0.016	0.012–0.035	0.0020–0.0035	0.0008–0.0020	NA
	3.0L①	0.0013–0.0021	0.0160–0.0220	0.0160–0.0220	NA	0.0010–0.0020	0.0010–0.0020	0.0015–0.0035
	3.0L②	0.0012–0.0020	0.0118–0.0177	0.0098–0.0157	0.0118–0.0154	0.0020–0.0035	0.0008–0.0024	NA
	3.0L③	0.0012–0.0020	0.0118–0.0177	0.0177–0.0236	0.0079–0.0236	0.0012–0.0028	0.0008–0.0024	NA
	3.3L	0.0009–0.0022	0.0012–0.0022	0.0012–0.0022	0.0010–0.0040	0.0012–0.0037	0.0012–0.0037	0.0005–0.0089
	3.8L	0.0009–0.0022	0.0012–0.0022	0.0012–0.0022	0.0010–0.0040	0.0012–0.0037	0.0012–0.0037	0.0005–0.0089
1992	1.8L	0.0004–0.0012	0.0118–0.0177	0.0079–0.0138	0.0080–0.0280	0.0018–0.0033	0.0008–0.0024	NA
	2.0L	0.0008–0.0016	0.0098–0.0177	0.0138–0.0197	0.0079–0.0276	0.0012–0.0028	0.0012–0.0028	NA
	2.0L Turbo	0.0012–0.0020	0.0098–0.0177	0.0138–0.0197	0.0079–0.0276	0.0012–0.0028	0.0012–0.0028	NA
	2.2L	0.0005–0.0027	0.010–0.039	0.011–0.039	0.015–0.074	0.0015–0.0040	0.0015–0.0040	0.0002–0.0080
	2.5L Turbo	0.0006–0.0030	0.010–0.039	0.009–0.037	0.015–0.074	0.0016–0.0030	0.0016–0.0035	0.0002–0.0080
	2.5L	0.0010–0.0027	0.010–0.039	0.011–0.039	0.015–0.074	0.0015–0.0040	0.0015–0.0040	0.0002–0.0080
	3.0L	0.0012–0.0020	0.012–0.018	0.010–0.016	0.012–0.035	0.0020–0.0035	0.0008–0.0020	NA
	3.0L①	0.0013–0.0021	0.0160–0.0220	0.016–0.022	NA	0.0010–0.0020	0.0010–0.0020	0.0015–0.0035
	3.0L②	0.0012–0.0020	0.0118–0.0177	0.0098–0.0157	0.0118–0.0154	0.0020–0.0035	0.0008–0.0024	NA
	3.0L③	0.0012–0.0020	0.0118–0.0177	0.0177–0.0236	0.0079–0.0236	0.0012–0.0028	0.0008–0.0024	NA
	3.3L	0.0009–0.0022	0.0012–0.0022	0.0012–0.0022	0.0010–0.0040	0.0012–0.0037	0.0012–0.0037	0.0005–0.0089
	3.8L	0.0009–0.0022	0.0012–0.0022	0.0012–0.0022	0.0010–0.0040	0.0012–0.0037	0.0012–0.0037	0.0005–0.0089

NA—Not Available
① 1990–92 Dodge Monaco Application
② 1991–92 Dodge Stealth Application—Single Overhead Cam Design
③ 1991–92 Dodge Stealth Application—Double Overhead Cam Design

TORQUE SPECIFICATIONS
Acclaim, Aries, Caravelle, Daytona, Dynasty, E-Class, Executive Sedan, Imperial, Lancer, Laser (1984–86) LeBaron, New Yorker, Reliant, Shadow, Spirit, Sundance, Town & Country, 400 and 600 Models

All readings in ft. lbs.

Year	Engine Displacement Liters	Cylinder Head Bolts	Main Bearing Bolts	Rod Bearing Bolts	Crankshaft Damper Bolts	Flywheel Bolts	Manifold	
							Intake	Exhaust
1981	2.2L	45①	40②	30②	50	NA	17	17
	2.6L	69③	34	58	87	97	13	13
1982	2.2L	45①	40②	30②	50	65	200④	200④
	2.6L	69③	34	58	87	—	150④	150④
1983	2.2L	45①	40②	30②	50	65	200④	200④
	2.6L	69③	34	58	87	—	150④	150④
1984	2.2L	45①	40②	30②	50	65	200④	200④
	2.6L	69③	34	58	87	—	150④	150④
1985	2.2L	45①	40②	30②	50	65	200④	200④
	2.6L	69③	34	58	87	—	150④	150④
1986	2.2L	65⑤	40②	30②	50	70	200④	200④
	2.5L	65⑤	40②	30②	50	70	200④	200④
1987	2.2L	65⑤	40②	30②	50	70	200④	200④
	2.5L	65⑤	40②	30②	50	70	200④	200④
1988	2.2L	65⑤	40②	30②	50	70	200④	200④
	2.5L	65⑤	40②	30②	50	70	200④	200④
1989	2.2L	⑥	30⑦	40⑦	10	70	17	17
	2.5L	⑥	30⑦	40⑦	10	70	17	17
	3.0L	70	60	38	110	70	17	17
1990	2.2L	⑥	30⑦	40⑦	10	70	17	17
	2.5L	⑥	30⑦	40⑦	10	70	17	17
	3.0L	70	60	38	110	70	17	17
1991	2.2L	⑥	30⑦	40⑦	10	70	17	17
	2.5L	⑥	30⑦	40⑦	10	70	17	17
	3.0L	70	60	38	110	70	17	17
	2.2L Turbo	⑥	⑧	45–50	10	70	17	17
	3.3L	⑨	30⑦	40⑦	40	70	17	17
	3.8L	⑨	30⑦	40⑦	40	70	17	17
1992	2.2L	⑥	30⑦	40⑦	10	70	17	17
	2.5L	⑥	30⑦	40⑦	10	70	17	17
	3.0L	70	60	38	110	70	17	17
	2.2L Turbo	⑥	⑧	45–50	10	70	17	17
	3.3L	⑨	30⑦	40⑦	40	70	17	17
	3.8L	⑨	30⑦	40⑦	40	70	17	17

① Torque Sequence 30–45–45 plus ¼ turn
② Plus ¼ turn
③ Cold engine; Hot engine 76 ft. lbs.
④ Readings in inch pounds
⑤ Torque Sequence—45–65–65 plus ¼ turn
⑥ Sequence: 45, 65, 65 plus ¼ turn
⑦ Plus ¼ turn
⑧ Sequence: 32, 43, 76
⑨ Sequence: 45, 65, 65, plus ¼ turn
   Torque the small bolt in the rear of the head to 25 ft. lbs. last

TORQUE SPECIFICATIONS
1990–92 Laser and Stealth
All readings in ft. lbs.

Year	Engine Displacement Liters	Cylinder Head Bolts	Main Bearing Bolts	Rod Bearing Bolts	Crankshaft Damper Bolts	Flywheel Bolts	Manifold		Spark Plugs
							Intake	Exhaust	
1990	1.8L	51–54	37–39	24–25	80–94	94–101	13–18	18–22	15–21①
	2.0L	65–72	47–51	36–38	80–94	94–101	18–22	18–22	15–21①
	2.0L (Turbo)	65–72	47–51	36–38	80–94	94–101	18–22	18–22	15–21①
1991	1.8L	51–54	37–39	24–25	80–94	94–101	13–18	18–22	15–21①
	2.0L	65–72	47–51	36–38	80–94	94–101	18–22	18–22	15–21①
	2.0L (Turbo)	65–72	47–51	36–38	80–94	94–101	18–22	18–22	15–21①
	3.0L③	76–83	58	38	108–116	55	13	13	18①
	3.0L④	76–83	58	38	130–137	55	14	33	18①
	3.0L⑤	87–94	58	38	130–137	55	9–11	22②	18①
1992	1.8L	51–54	37–39	24–25	80–94	94–101	13–18	18–22	15–21①
	2.0L	65–72	47–51	36–38	80–94	94–101	18–22	18–22	15–21①
	2.0L (Turbo)	65–72	47–51	36–38	80–94	94–101	18–22	18–22	15–21①
	3.0L③	76–83	58	38	108–116	55	13	13	18①
	3.0L④	76–83	58	38	130–137	55	14	33	18①
	3.0L⑤	87–94	58	38	130–137	55	9–11	22②	18①

① Spark plugs used in aluminum heads should always have lubricated threads
② See text for special sequence
③ Single Overhead Cam design
④ Double Overhead Cam design
⑤ Double Overhead Cam design with turbo

TORQUE SPECIFICATIONS
1990–92 Dodge Monaco
All readings in ft. lbs.

Year	Engine Displacement Liters	Cylinder Head Bolts	Main Bearing Bolts	Rod Bearing Bolts	Crankshaft Damper Bolts	Flywheel Bolts	Manifold		Spark Plugs
							Intake	Exhaust	
1990	3.0L	①	②	35	125	48–54	11	13	11
1991	3.0L	①	②	35	125	48–54	11	13	11
1992	3.0L	①	②	35	125	48–54	11	13	11

① See text
② Tighten in 2 steps, in sequence:
1st—20 ft. lbs.
2nd—Angular torque 75 degrees

17. Remove the front engine mount nut/bolt and the left insulator through bolt or the insulator bracket to transaxle bolts.

18. Lift the engine from the vehicle and remove.

To install:

19. Lower the engine into the engine compartment. Make sure the lifting device is supporting the full weight of the engine and loosely install all of the mounting bolts until all are threaded. Then tighten all bolts.

20. Remove the lifting device.

21. Raise the vehicle and support safely.

22. If equipped with a manual transaxle, install the transaxle.

23. If equipped with an automatic transaxle, install the torque converter bolts and torque to 55 ft. lbs. (75 Nm). Install the torque converter inspection plate and starter.

24. Connect the exhaust pipe. Lower the vehicle.

25. Install the alternator, power steering pump and air conditioning compressor, if equipped.

26. Connect the fuel lines and heater hoses.

27. Connect the throttle and or carburetor linkage.

28. Connect all remaining electrical connectors.

29. Install the air cleaner assembly and oil filter.

30. Install the radiator, fan assembly, hoses and intercooler, if equipped.

31. Fill the engine with the proper amount of engine oil. Connect the negative battery cable.

32. Refill the cooling system. Start the engine, allow it to reach normal operating temperature. Check for leaks.

33. Check the ignition timing and adjust if necessary.

34. Install the hood. Roadtest the vehicle for proper operation.

3.0L, 3.3L And 3.8L Engines

1. Disconnect the negative battery cable. Relieve the fuel pressure.

2. Matchmark the hinge-to-hood position and remove the hood.

3. Drain the cooling system. Disconnect and label all engine electrical connections.

4. Remove the coolant hoses from the radiator and engine. Remove the radiator and cooling fan assembly.

5. Remove the air cleaner assembly. Disconnect the fuel lines from the engine. Disconnect the accelerator cable from the throttle body.

6. Raise the vehicle and support safely. Drain the engine oil.

7. Remove the air conditioning compressor mounting bolts, the drive belts and position the compressor aside. Disconnect the exhaust pipe from the exhaust manifold.

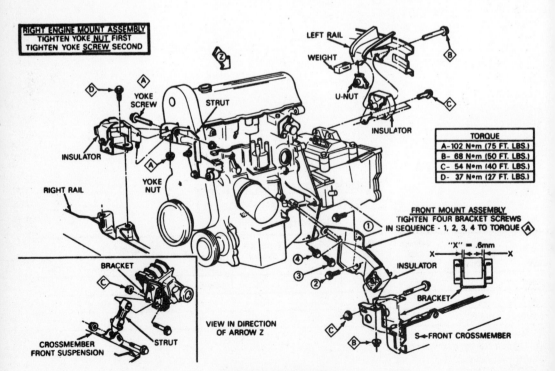

Typical engine mounting

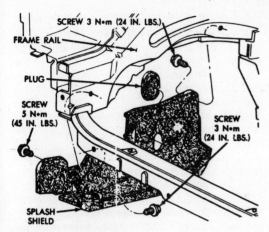

Right inner splash shield

8. Remove the transaxle inspection cover, matchmark the converter to the flexplate, and remove the torque converter bolts.

9. Remove the power steering pump mounting bolts and set the pump aside, upright, with the fluid lines attached.

10. Remove the lower bellhousing bolts. Disconnect and label the starter motor wiring and remove the starter motor from the engine.

11. Lower the vehicle. Disconnect and label all electrical connectors from the engine, alternator and fuel injection system, vacuum hoses, and engine ground straps.

12. Support the transaxle with a floor jack or equivalent. Attach an engine lifting device to the engine.

13. Remove the upper transaxle-to-engine bolts.

14. To separate the engine mounts from the insulators, mark the right insulator-to-right frame support and remove the mounting bolts. Remove the front engine mount through bolt. Remove the left insulator through bolt from inside the wheel housing. Remove the insulator bracket-to-transaxle bolts.

15. Lift and remove the engine from the vehicle.

To install:

16. Lower the engine into the engine compartment. Align the engine mounts and install the bolts; do not tighten the bolts until all bolts have been installed. Torque the through bolts to 75 ft. lbs. (102 Nm).

17. Install the upper transaxle-to-engine mounting bolts and torque to 75 ft. lbs. (102 Nm). Remove the engine lifting fixture from the engine.

18. Raise the vehicle and support safely.

19. Align the converter marks, and install the torque converter bolts. Install the transaxle inspection cover.

20. Connect the exhaust pipe to the exhaust manifold. Install the starter motor and connect the wiring.

21. Install the power steering pump and air conditioning compressor. Adjust the drive belt tension, if necessary.

22. Lower the vehicle. Reconnect all vacuum hoses and electrical connections to the engine.

23. Connect the fuel lines and accelerator cable.

24. Install the radiator and fan assembly. Connect the fan motor wiring. Connect the radiator hoses and refill the cooling system.

25. Refill the engine with the proper oil to the correct level.

26. Connect the engine ground straps. Install the hood and align the matchmarks. Connect the battery.

27. Start and run the engine until it reaches normal operating temperatures and check for leaks. Adjust the transaxle linkage, if necessary.

28. Roadtest the vehicle for proper operation.

1990–92 Dodge Monaco

NOTE: *Disconnecting the negative battery cable on some vehicles may interfere with the functions of the on-board computer systems and may require the computer to undergo a relearning process, once the negative battery cable is reconnected.*

1. Disconnect the negative battery cable. Matchmark the hood to the hinges and remove the hood.

2. Disconnect the coil wire all vacuum hoses and fuel lines.

3. Disconnect the lower radiator hose and drain the coolant. Remove the air cleaner.

4. Remove the grille. Remove the screws retaining the front facia panel and radiator support and remove the panel and support.

5. Remove the radiator and cooling fan. If equipped with air conditioning, safely discharge the air conditioning system and remove the condenser and the radiator as an assembly.

6. Disconnect the electrical leads to the unit ECU or SBEC.

7. Remove the accelerator cable from the brackets on the valve cover.

8. Remove the bolts that attach the exhaust head pipes to the exhaust manifold. Remove the heater hoses and on automatic transaxle equipped vehicles, remove the cooler lines.

9. Raise the vehicle and safely support. Remove the underbody splash shield.

10. Remove the power steering pump mounting bolts and support the pump to the side. Remove the header pipe to converter bolts and remove the converter.

11. If equipped with automatic transaxle, dis-

connect the shifter linkages. On manual transaxle vehicles, disconnect the clutch cable at the transaxle.

12. Remove the wheel assemblies and remove the front stabilizer bar. Remove the brake calipers and support aside. Disconnect the tie rod ends from the steering knuckle. Remove the halfshaft retaining pin and remove the halfshaft assembly. Remove the strut-to-steering knuckle bolts.

13. Loosen the upper strut mounting bolts and swing the axle/strut assembly aside. Support the axles safely.

14. Disconnect the speedometer cable. Disconnect the vapor canister and remove it.

15. Loosen the bolts attaching the transmission support to the engine cradle. Remove the bolts attaching the left and right halves of the crossmember to the transaxle. Lower the vehicle.

16. Attach a suitable lifting device to the engine lifting eyes and lift the engine slightly. Remove the engine support bolts and remove the engine/transaxle assembly. Lift the engine out at an angle, make sure the transaxle clears the engine compartment. Separate the engine from the transaxle.

To install:

17. Position the engine/transaxle assembly in the vehicle and align the engine mounts with the engine cradle.

18. Install the engine mount bolts and remove the lifting device. Install the left and right sections of the crossmember.

19. Position and install the halfshafts to the transaxle, use new retaining pins. Install the shock absorber to steering knuckle bolts and attach the tie rod ends. Attach the front stabilizer bar.

20. Install the brake calipers and install the front wheels.

21. Install the converter to the header pipe. Install the power steering pump and adjust the belt tension. Connect the shift linkage and throttle cables.

22. Reconnect all electrical and vacuum leads. Install the canister and the air cleaner assemblies. Reconnect the fuel lines and coolant hoses.

23. Install the radiator and fan assemblies. Attach the front facia and support assembly. Install the grille.

24. Install the hood.

25. Check and fill all fluid levels properly.

26. Connect the negative battery cable and road test the vehicle.

1990–92 Laser and Dodge Stealth

NOTE: *Disconnecting the negative battery cable on some vehicles may interfere with the functions of the on board computer systems and may require the computer to undergo a relearning process, once the negative battery cable is reconnected.*

1. Relieve fuel system pressure.

2. Disconnect the negative battery cable.

3. Matchmark the hood and hinges and remove the hood assembly. Remove the air cleaner assembly and all adjoining air intake duct work.

4. Drain the engine coolant and remove the radiator assembly and intercooler.

5. Remove the transaxle.

6. Disconnect and tag for assembly reference the connections for the accelerator cable, heater hoses, brake vacuum hose, connection for vacuum hoses, high pressure fuel line, fuel return line, oxygen sensor connection, coolant temperature gauge connection, coolant temperature sensor connector, connection for thermo switch sensor, if equipped with automatic transaxle, the connection for the idle speed control, the motor position sensor connector, the throttle position sensor connector, the EGR temperature sensor connection (California vehicles), the fuel injector connectors, the power transistor connector, the ignition coil connector, the condenser and noise filter connector, the distributor and control harness, the connections for the alternator and oil pressure switch wires.

7. Remove the air conditioner drive belt and the air conditioning compressor. Leave the hoses attached. Do not discharge the system. Wire the compressor aside.

8. Remove the power steering pump and wire aside.

9. Remove the exhaust manifold to head pipe nuts. Discard the gasket.

10. Attach a hoist to the engine and take up the engine weight. Remove the engine mount bracket. Remove any torque control brackets (roll stoppers). Note that some engine mount pieces have arrows on them for proper assembly. Double check that all cables, hoses, harness connectors, etc., are disconnected from the engine. Lift the engine slowly from the engine compartment.

To install:

11. Install the engine and secure all control brackets.

12. Install the exhaust pipe, power steering pump and air conditioning compressor.

13. Checking the tags installed at removal, reconnect all electrical and vacuum connections.

14. Install the transaxle.

15. Install the radiator assembly and intercooler.

16. Install the air cleaner assembly.

17. Fill the engine with the proper amount of

engine oil. Connect the negative battery cable.

18. Refill the cooling system. Start the engine, allow it to reach normal operating temperature. Check for leaks.

19. Check the ignition timing and adjust if necessary.

20. Install the hood.

21. Road test the vehicle and check all functions for proper operation.

Rocker Arm (Valve) Cover

REMOVAL AND INSTALLATION

4-Cylinder Engines

NOTE: *On the 1990–92 Laser vehicle use this procedure as a guide — modify service steps as necessary.*

1. Disconnect the negative battery cable. On carbureted engines, disconnect the PCV line from the module, depress the retaining clip, and turn the module counterclockwise to unlock it from the valve cover. Then, remove it.

2. Remove/disconnect any other lines or hoses that run across the cover assembly.

3. Loosen the 10 cover installation bolts and remove them. Gently rock the cover to free it from the gasket or sealer and remove it.

4. On 1986 and later models with TBI, remove the air/oil separating curtain located on top of the head just under the valve cover, if so equipped. Be careful to keep the rubber bumpers located at the top of the curtain in place.

5. Replace the two end seals, forcing the locating tabs into the matching holes in the cover.

6. To install, first, if the engine has the air/oil separating curtain, install it as described below (otherwise, proceed to the next step):

  a. Position the curtain manifold side first with the upper surface contacting the cylinder head and the cutouts over the cam towers. The cutouts must face the manifold.

  b. Press the distributor side of the curtain into position below the cylinder head rail.

  c. Make sure both rubber bumpers are in place at the top.

7. On 1981–87 engines, form a gasket on the sealing surface of the head. It is necessary to

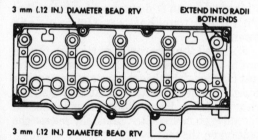

3 mm (.12 IN.) DIAMETER BEAD RTV EXTEND INTO RADII BOTH ENDS

3 mm (.12 IN.) DIAMETER BEAD RTV

Applying RTV sealer to the cylinder head to seal the cam cover

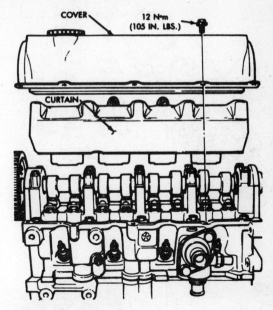

COVER   12 N•m (105 IN. LBS.)

CURTAIN

Rocker cover and curtain

use an RTV silicone aerobic gasket material (Chrysler Part No. 4318025 or equivalent).

8. On 1988 and later engines, install the gasket onto the cam cover (on normally aspirated engines with Throttle Body Injection, fasten the gasket in place by forcing the tabs through the holes in the cover).

9. Install the reinforcements over both sides if so equipped. Install the mounting bolts and torque them alternately and evenly to 105 inch lbs.

6-Cylinder Engines

NOTE: *On the 1991–92 Dodge Stealth vehicle use this procedure as a guide — modify service steps as necessary. On some models, the right and left hand cylinder rocker (valve) cover gaskets may not interchangeable — match up the old gaskets before installation.*

1. Disconnect the negative battery cable.

2. Remove the air cleaner assembly and mark and reposition the spark plug wires.

3. Remove all vacuum connections as necessary.

4. Remove the rocker cover screws and remove the cover.

To install:

5. Clean cylinder head and cover mating surfaces. Install a NEW gasket.

6. Apply a $\frac{1}{16}$ in. (1.6mm) bead of RTV $\frac{3}{8}$ in. (9.5mm) long in 4 cover ends on rocker cover.

7. Install cover and torque the retaining bolt/washers to 88 inch lbs. (9 ft. lbs. on 1990–92 Dodge Monaco) Start engine and check for leaks.

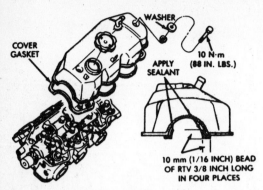

Rocker cover typical 6-cylinder

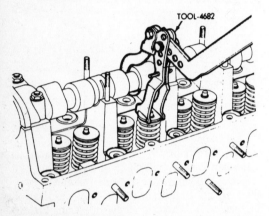

Depressing a valve with the special tool in order to remove its rocker lever

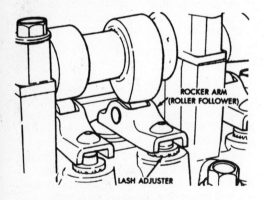

Rocker arm and lash adjuster

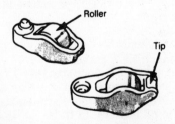

Inspect roller (rocker arm) at these points for damage or wear

Rocker Shafts

REMOVAL AND INSTALLATION

Some engines covered by this manual have rocker shafts (rocker shaft and arm assemblies). Refer to "Camshaft and Bearings Removal and Installation" later in this chapter for rocker arm and shaft removal procedures for the applicable engine.

Always keep all parts in order for correct installation. Torque the rocker shaft retaining bolts gradually (in sequence — if no sequence is given start from the the center and work outward) and evenly to the proper specification. On some engines allow tappet bleed down time (about 20 minutes) after installation before starting the engine.

Rocker Arms

REMOVAL AND INSTALLATION

The rocker arms may be removed very easily after camshaft removal. In case they are to be removed as a group for inspection or to proceed further with disassembly, mark each as to location for installation in the same position.

If the rockers are to be removed in order to gain access to a valve or lifter (camshaft installed), you will need a special tool designed to hook over the camshaft and depress the applicable valve. Use Chrysler Tool No. 4682 or an equivalent tool purchased in the aftermarket. To remove a rocker:

1. Remove the valve cover. Mark the rocker as to its location, unless you expect to remove only one, or one at a time.

2. Turn the engine over, using a wrench on the crankshaft pulley, until the cam that actuates the rocker you want to remove it pointing straight up.

3. Install the tool so that the jaws on its fulcrum fit on either side of the valve cap. Then, clip the hook at its forward end over the adjacent thin section of the camshaft (a part not incorporating either a cam or a bearing journal).

4. Lift the rocker gently at the lash adjuster end (the end opposite the tool). Pull downward gently on the outer end of the tool lever just until the rocker can be disengaged from the lifter. **Pull it out from between the valve and camshaft.**

5. Install the new rocker or reinstall the old one in reverse order. That is, depress the valve just far enough to slide the lever in between the top of the valve stem and the camshaft and still clear the lifter. When the rocker is located on the valve stem and lifter, gradually release the tension on the tool.

6. Repeat the procedure until all the necessary rockers have been replaced.

7. Check and make sure the locks on the the valve springs are in the proper location. Install the valve cover.

NOTE: *Visually check the roller on the rocker arm and replace if dent, damage or seizure is evident. Check the roller for smooth rotation, replace if its binds or there is an excessive play. Check the valve contact surface for possible damage when performing this repair.*

Thermostat

REMOVAL AND INSTALLATION

The thermostat on the 2.2 and 2.5 Liter engines is located in the thermostat housing on the cylinder head. 2.6 Liter engines have the thermostat housing near the intake manifold. Refer to the necessary illustrations for thermostat locations on other engines.

1. Drain the cooling system to a level below the thermostat.

CAUTION: *When draining the coolant, keep in mind that cats and dogs are attracted by the ethylene glycol antifreeze, and are quite likely to drink any that is left in an uncovered container or in puddles on the ground. This will prove fatal in sufficient quantity. Always drain the coolant into a sealable container. Coolant should be reused unless it is contaminated or several years old.*

2. Remove the hose clamp and then disconnect the hose from the thermostat housing.

3. Remove the two mounting bolts and then remove the thermostat housing.

4. Remove the thermostat and discard the gasket. Clean both gasket surfaces thoroughly.

To install:

5. Dip the new gasket in water and then install it. Position the thermostat in the water box, making sure it is properly seated by centering it in the water box, on top of the gasket. Install the housing and install the two bolts. Tighten thermostat housing retaining bolts gradually and evenly.

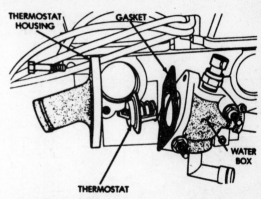

Thermostat, housing and water box—Turbo III

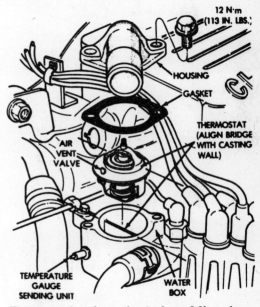

Thermostat, housing and water box—3.0L engine

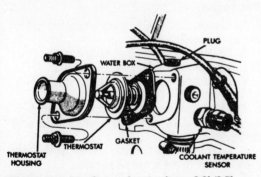

Thermostat, housing and water box—2.2L/2.5L engine

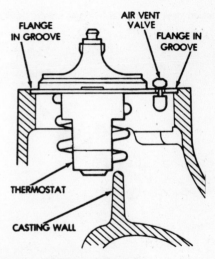

Thermostat installed—3.0L engine

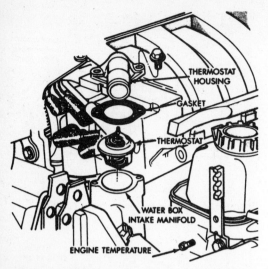

Thermostat, housing and water box—3.3L/3.8L engine

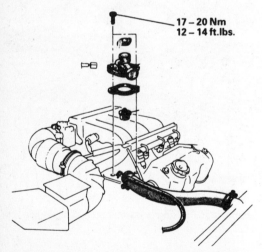

17 – 20 Nm
12 – 14 ft.lbs.

Exploded view thermostat—Dodge Stealth SOHC

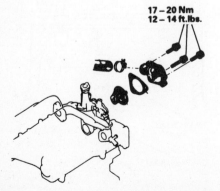

17 – 20 Nm
12 – 14 ft.lbs.

Exploded view thermostat—Dodge Stealth DOHC

6. Reconnect the hose and install and tighten the hose clamp.

7. Refill the cooling system, start the engine, and check for leaks. After the engine has reached operating temperature, allow it to cool. Then, recheck coolant level in the radiator, refilling as necessary.

Cooling System Bleeding

To bleed air from the 2.2L and 2.5L engines, remove the plug or sensor on the top of the thermostat housing. Fill the radiator with coolant until the coolant comes out the hole. Install the plug and continue to fill the radiator. This will vent all trapped air from the engine.

The thermostat in the 3.0L engine Chrysler front wheel drive vehicles, 1990–92 Laser and Dodge Stealth are equipped with a small air vent valve that allows trapped air to bleed from the system during refilling. This valve negates the need for cooling system bleeding in those engines.

On the 1990–92 Dodge Monaco the air bleed is on the thermostat housing. Remove the plug and fill the radiator with coolant until the coolant comes out the hole. Install the plug and continue to fill the radiator. This will vent all trapped air from the engine.

On the 3.3L and 3.8L engines remove the engine temperature sensor. Fill the radiator with coolant until the coolant comes out the hole. This will vent all trapped air from the engine.

Intake Manifold

REMOVAL AND INSTALLATION

CAUTION: *When draining the coolant, keep in mind that cats and dogs are attracted by the ethylene glycol antifreeze, and are quite likely to drink any that is left in an uncovered container or in puddles on the ground. This will prove fatal in sufficient quantity. Always drain the coolant into a sealable container. Coolant should be reused unless it is contaminated or several years old.*

2.6L Engine

1. Disconnect the battery negative cable. Drain the cooling system.

2. Disconnect the coolant hose running from the water pump to the intake manifold.

3. Disconnect the carburetor air intake hose and move it out of the way.

4. Label and then disconnect all vacuum hoses connected to the intake manifold and carburetor.

5. Disconnect the throttle linkage at the carburetor and move it out of the way.

6. Disconnect the inlet line at the fuel filter, collecting gasoline that spills out in a metal cup.

Then, remove the fuel filter and pump and move them to one side.

7. Remove the mounting nuts and accompanying washers from the manifold attaching studs, and remove the manifold from the engine.

To install:

8. Clean all gasket surfaces and install the intake manifold using new gaskets. Torque the bolts in three stages to the specified torque.

9. Reinstall the fuel pump and fuel filter. Connect the inlet line and clamp it securely.

10. Reconnect the throttle linkage to the carburetor and adjust it to eliminate excessive play.

11. Reconnect all the vacuum hoses to the intake manifold and carburetor, according to labels made earlier.

12. Connect the carburetor air intake hose to the carburetor and clamp it securely.

13. Connect the coolant hose running from the water pump to the intake manifold.

14. Refill the cooling system with 50/50 ethylene glycol and water mix. Connect the battery. Start the engine, and operate it, checking for leaks. After the engine reaches operating temperature, shut it off. When it has cooled, refill the cooling system.

2.2L Turbo III Engine

1. Disconnect the negative battery cable. Relieve the fuel system pressure. Drain the cooling system.

2. Remove the fresh air duct from the air filter housing. Remove the inlet hose from the intercooler.

3. Remove the radiator hose from the thermostat housing.

4. Remove the DIS ignition coil from the intake manifold.

5. Disconnect the throttle and speed control cables from the throttle body.

6. Disconnect the intercooler-to-throttle body outlet hose. Disconnect the vacuum hoses from the throttle body and carefully remove the harness.

7. Disconnect the AIS motor and TPS wiring connectors.

8. Remove the PCV breather/separator box and vacuum harness assembly. Remove the brake booster hose, vacuum vapor harness and fuel pressure regulator from the intake manifold.

9. Disconnect the fuel injector wiring harness and charge temperature sensor.

10. Wrap shop towels around the fittings and disconnect the fuel supply and return fuel lines.

11. Remove the intake manifold retaining bolts and remove the manifold from the cylinder head.

To install:

12. Inspect the manifold for damage of any kind. Thoroughly clean and dry the mating surfaces.

13. Install the new gasket and manifold to the cylinder head. Starting at the center and working outwards, torque the bolts gradually and evenly to 17 ft. lbs. (23 Nm).

14. Lubricate the quick connect fuel fittings with oil and connect to the chassis tubes. Ensure they are locked by pulling on them.

15. Install the PCV breather/separator box and vacuum harness assembly. Connect the brake booster hose, vacuum vapor harness and fuel pressure regulator to the intake manifold.

16. Connect the fuel injector wiring harness and charge temperature sensor. Connect the AIS motor and TPS wiring connectors.

17. Connect the vacuum hoses from the throttle body and carefully remove the harness. Connect the intercooler-to-throttle body outlet hose.

18. Connect the throttle and speed control cables from the throttle body.

19. Install the DIS ignition coil to the intake manifold.

20. Connect the radiator hose to the thermostat housing.

21. Install the inlet hose to the intercooler. Install the fresh air duct to the air filter housing.

22. Refill and bleed the cooling system. Connect the negative battery cable. Start the engine and check for leaks.

3.0L Engine

1. Disconnect the negative battery cable. Relieve the fuel system pressure.

2. Drain the cooling system.

3. Remove the throttle body to air cleaner hose.

4. Remove the throttle body and transaxle kickdown linkage.

5. Remove the AIS motor and TPS wiring connectors from the throttle body.

6. Remove and label the vacuum hose harness from the throttle body.

7. From the air intake plenum, remove the PCV and brake booster hoses and the EGR tube flange.

8. Disconnect and label the charge and temperature sensor wiring at the intake manifold.

9. Remove the vacuum connections from the air intake plenum vacuum connector.

10. Remove the fuel hoses from the fuel rail.

11. Remove the air intake plenum mounting bolts and remove the plenum.

12. Remove the vacuum hoses from the fuel rail and pressure regulator.

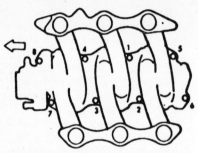

Intake manifold bolt torque sequence—3.0L engine

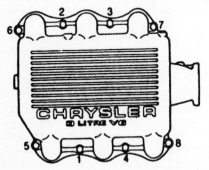

Air intake plenum bolt torque sequence—3.0L engine

13. Disconnect the fuel injector wiring harness from the engine wiring harness.

14. Remove the fuel pressure regulator mounting bolts and remove the regulator from the fuel rail.

15. Remove the fuel rail mounting bolts and remove the fuel rail from the intake manifold.

16. Separate the radiator hose from the thermostat housing and heater hoses from the heater pipe.

17. Remove the intake manifold mounting bolts and remove the manifold from the engine.

18. Clean the gasket mounting surfaces on the engine and intake manifold.

To install:

19. Using new gaskets, position the intake manifold on the engine and install the mounting nuts and washers.

20. Torque the mounting nuts gradually and evenly, in sequence, to 15 ft. lbs. (20 Nm).

21. Make sure the injector holes are clean. Lubricate the injector O-rings with a drop of clean engine oil and install the injector assembly onto the engine.

22. Install and torque the fuel rail mounting bolts to 10 ft. lbs. (14 Nm).

23. Install the fuel pressure regulator onto the fuel rail.

24. Install the fuel supply and return tube and the vacuum crossover hold-down bolt.

25. Connect the fuel injection wiring harness to the engine wiring harness.

26. Connect the vacuum harness to the fuel pressure regulator and fuel rail assembly.

27. Remove the cover from the lower intake manifold and clean the mating surface.

28. Place the intake plenum gasket with the beaded sealant side up, on the intake manifold. Install the air intake plenum and torque the mounting bolts gradually and evenly, in sequence, to 10 ft. lbs. (14 Nm).

29. Connect or install all remaining items that were disconnected or removed during the removal procedure.

30. Refill the cooling system. Connect the negative battery cable and check for leaks using the DRB II special tool or equivalent to activate the fuel pump.

3.3L And 3.8L Engines

1. Disconnect the negative battery cable. Relieve the fuel pressure. Drain the cooling system.

2. Remove the air cleaner to throttle body hose assembly.

3. Disconnect the throttle cable and remove the wiring harness from the bracket.

4. Remove AIS motor and TPS wiring connectors from the throttle body.

5. Remove the vacuum hose harness from the throttle body.

6. Remove the PCV and brake booster hoses from the air intake plenum.

7. Disconnect the charge temperature sensor electrical connector. Remove the vacuum harness connectors from the intake plenum.

8. Remove the cylinder head to the intake plenum strut.

9. Disconnect the MAP sensor and oxygen sensor connectors. Remove the engine mounted ground strap.

10. Remove the fuel hoses from the fuel rail and plug them.

11. Remove the DIS coils and the alternator bracket to intake manifold bolt.

12. Remove the upper intake manifold attaching bolts and remove the upper manifold.

13. Remove the vacuum harness connector from the fuel pressure regulator.

14. Remove the fuel tube retainer bracket screw and fuel rail attaching bolts. Spread the retainer bracket to allow for clearance when removing the fuel tube.

15. Remove the fuel rail injector wiring clip from the alternator bracket.

16. Disconnect the cam sensor, coolant temperature sensor and engine temperature sensor.

17. Remove the fuel rail.

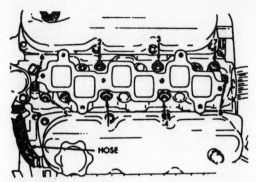

Intake manifold bolt torque sequence—3.3L/3.8L engine

18. Remove the upper radiator hose, bypass hose and rear intake manifold hose.

19. Remove the intake manifold bolts and remove the manifold from the engine.

20. Remove the intake manifold seal retaining screws and remove the manifold gasket.

21. Clean out clogged end water passages and fuel runners.

To install:

22. Clean and dry all gasket mating surfaces.

23. Place a drop of silicone sealer onto each of the 4 manifold-to-cylinder head gasket corners.

CAUTION: *The intake manifold gasket is composed of very thin and sharp metal. Handle this gasket with care or damage to the gasket or personal injury could result.*

24. Install the intake manifold gasket and torque the end retainers to 10 ft. lbs. (12 Nm).

25. Install the intake manifold and torque the bolts in sequence to 10 inch lbs. Repeat the sequence increasing the torque to 17 ft. lbs. (23 Nm) and recheck each bolt for 17 ft. lbs. of torque. After the bolts are torqued, inspect the seals to ensure that they have not become dislodged.

26. Lubricate the injector O-rings with clean oil and position the fuel rail in place. Install the rail mounting bolts.

27. Connect the cam sensor, coolant temperature sensor and engine temperature sensor.

28. Install the fuel rail injector wiring clip to the alternator bracket.

29. Install the fuel rail attaching bolts and fuel tube retainer bracket screw.

30. Install the vacuum harness to the pressure regulator.

31. Install the upper intake manifold with a new gasket. Install the bolts only finger-tight. Install the alternator bracket to intake manifold bolt and the cylinder head to intake manifold strut and bolts. Torque the intake manifold mounting bolts to 21 ft. lbs. (28 Nm) starting from the middle and working outward. Torque the bracket and strut bolts to 40 ft. lbs. (54 Nm).

32. Install or connect all items that were removed or disconnected from the intake manifold and throttle body.

33. Connect the fuel hoses to the rail. Push the fittings in until they click in place.

34. Install the air cleaner assembly.

35. Connect the negative battery cable and check for leaks using the DRB II to activate the fuel pump.

1990–92 Dodge Monaco 3.0L Engine

1. Relieve the fuel system pressure.

2. Disconnect the negative battery cable.

3. Remove the engine cover retaining bolts and remove the cover.

4. Remove the air inlet cover from the throttle body.

5. Disconnect the transaxle kickdown cable, accelerator cable and cruise control cable from the throttle body. Remove the vacuum hoses from the intake manifold.

6. Remove the electrical connector from the throttle position sensor. Disconnect and tag the electrical connectors from the fuel injectors and lay the harness aside.

7. Remove the EGR tube. Remove the wire from the air temperature sensor.

8. Remove the fuel lines from the injector rails.

9. Remove the 4 bolts retaining the intake manifold and remove the manifold. Remove the O-rings from the cylinder heads and discard them.

NOTE: *When the intake manifold has been removed the O-rings in the cylinder heads must be replaced.*

10. Clean all gasket mating surfaces.

To install:

11. Use new O-rings and install the intake manifold. Torque the retaining bolts to 11 ft. lbs. (15 Nm) in an "X" pattern.

12. Install the fuel lines to the fuel rail assembly. Connect the electrical connectors to the fuel injectors. Connect all of the electrical connectors and vacuum hoses removed.

13. Connect the EGR tube. Connect the transaxle kickdown cable, accelerator and cruise control cables. Connect the negative battery cable.

14. Install the air inlet to the throttle body. Install the engine cover.

15. Connect the negative battery cable.

16. Run the engine and check for leaks.

1990–92 Laser And Dodge Stealth

EXCEPT 3.0L ENGINE

1. Relieve the fuel system pressure.

2. Disconnect battery negative cable and drain the cooling system.

3. Disconnect the accelerator cable, breather hose and air intake hose.

4. Disconnect the upper radiator hose, heater hose and water bypass hose.

5. Remove all vacuum hoses and pipes as necessary, including the brake booster vacuum line.

6. Disconnect the high pressure fuel line, fuel return hose and throttle control cable brackets.

7. Remove and tag all electrical connectors that may interfere with the removal procedure, including spark plug wires.

8. Remove the fuel rail, fuel injectors, pressure regulator and insulators.

9. Remove the throttle body stay bracket.

10. If the thermostat housing is preventing removal of the intake manifold, remove it.

11. Remove the intake manifold mounting bolts and remove the intake manifold assembly. Disassemble on a work bench.

To install:

12. Assemble the intake manifold assembly using all new gaskets. Torque air intake plenum bolts to 11–14 ft. lbs. (15–19 Nm).

13. Clean all gasket material from the cylinder head intake mounting surface and intake manifold assembly. Check both surfaces for cracks or other damage. Check the intake manifold water passages and jet air passages for clogging. Clean if necessary.

14. Install a new intake manifold gasket to the head and install the manifold. Torque the manifold in a criss-cross pattern, starting from the inside and working outwards to 11–14 ft. lbs. (15–19 Nm).

15. Install the thermostat housing.

16. Install the intake manifold brace bracket, distributor and throttle body stay bracket.

17. Connect or install all hoses, cables and electrical connectors that were removed or disconnected during the removal procedure.

18. Fill the system with coolant.

19. Connect the negative battery cable, run the vehicle until the thermostat opens, fill the radiator completely.

20. Check and adjust the idle speed and ignition timing.

21. Once the vehicle has cooled, recheck the coolant level.

3.0L ENGINE

1. Relieve the fuel system pressure.

2. Disconnect battery negative cable and drain the cooling system.

3. Remove the air intake hose(s).

4. Disconnect the throttle control cables from the throttle body.

5. Matchmark and disconnect the vacuum hoses including the brake booster hose.

6. Disconnect all harness connectors.

7. Disconnect EGR components on California vehicles.

8. Remove the plenum retaining bracket.

9. Remove the plenum retaining nuts and bolts and remove the air intake plenum. Discard the gasket.

10. Disconnect the high pressure and return fuel hoses.

11. Matchmark and disconnect the vacuum hoses.

12. Disconnect the harness connector.

13. Remove the fuel rail with the injectors attached.

14. On SOHC engines, disconnect the water hoses. On DOHC engines, remove the timing belt upper cover.

15. Remove the intake manifold mounting nuts; turbocharged engines have cone disc springs under some of the nuts which should be removed. Remove the intake manifold and discard the gaskets.

To install:

16. Check all items for cracks, clogging and warpage. Maximum warpage is 0.008 in. (0.2mm). Replace all questionable parts.

17. Thoroughly clean and dry the mating surfaces of the heads, intake manifold and air intake plenum.

18. Install new intake manifold gaskets to the heads with the adhesive side facing up.

19. Place the manifold on the heads install the cone disc springs and/or the lock washers.

20. Lubricate the studs lightly with oil, then install the nuts following this procedure:

   a. Tighten the nuts on the front bank to 26–43 inch lbs. (3–5 Nm).

   b. Tighten the nuts on the rear bank to 9–11 ft. lbs. (12–15 Nm).

   c. Tighten the nuts on the front bank to 9–11 ft. lbs. (12–15 Nm).

   d. Repeat Steps B and C.

   e. On non-turbocharged engines only, tighten the nuts to a final torque of 13–14 ft. lbs. (18–19 Nm).

21. On SOHC engines, connect the water hoses. On DOHC engines, install the timing belt upper cover.

22. Install the fuel rail assembly.

23. Connect the harness connector and vacuum hoses.

24. Replace the O-ring and connect the fuel hoses.

25. Install a new intake air plenum gasket and install the plenum. Tighten the retaining nuts and bolts evenly and gradually to 13 ft. lbs. (18 Nm).

26. Install the retaining bracket.

27. Connect EGR components on California vehicles.

28. Connect the harness connectors and vacuum hoses.
29. Connect and adjust the throttle cables.
30. Install the air intake hose(s).
31. Fill the system with coolant.
32. Connect the negative battery cable, run the vehicle until the thermostat opens, fill the radiator completely.
33. Check and adjust the idle speed and ignition timing.
34. Once the vehicle has cooled, recheck the coolant level.

Exhaust Manifold

REMOVAL AND INSTALLATION

CAUTION: *When draining the coolant, keep in mind that cats and dogs are attracted by the ethylene glycol antifreeze, and are quite likely to drink any that is left in an uncovered container or in puddles on the ground. This will prove fatal in sufficient quantity. Always drain the coolant into a sealable container. Coolant should be reused unless it is contaminated or several years old.*

2.6L Engine

1. Remove air cleaner.
2. Remove the heat shield from the exhaust manifold. Remove the EGR lines and reed valve, if equipped.
3. Unbolt the exhaust flange connection.
4. Remove the nuts holding manifold to the cylinder head.
5. Remove the manifold.
6. Installation is the reverse of removal. Tighten flange connection bolts to 11–18 ft. lbs. Tighten manifold bolts to 11–14 ft. lbs.

2.2L Turbo III Engine

1. Disconnect the negative battery cable.
2. Remove the turbocharger assembly.
3. Remove the coolant tube from the cylinder head.
4. Remove the exhaust manifold retaining nuts and remove the manifold.
5. Clean the gasket mounting surfaces. Inspect the manifolds for cracks, flatness and/or damage.

To install:
6. Install a new exhaust manifold gasket. Do not use sealer of any kind.
7. Position the manifold on the studs and install the retaining nuts. Starting at the center and working outwards, torque the nuts gradually and evenly to 17 ft. lbs. (23 Nm).
8. Using a new gasket, connect the coolant tube to the cylinder head.
9. Install the turbocharger assembly.

10 Start the engine and check for exhaust leaks.

3.0L Engine

1. Disconnect the negative battery cable. Raise the vehicle and safely support.
2. Disconnect the exhaust pipe from the rear exhaust manifold, at the articulated joint.
3. Disconnect the EGR tube from the rear manifold and disconnect the oxygen sensor wire.
4. Remove the crossover pipe to manifold bolts.
5. Remove the rear manifold to cylinder head nuts and the manifold.
6. Lower the vehicle and remove the heat shield from the manifold.
7. Remove the front manifold to cylinder head nuts and remove the manifold.
8. Clean the gasket mounting surfaces. Inspect the manifolds for cracks, flatness and/or damage.

To install:
9. When installing, the numbers 1–3–5 on the gaskets are used with the rear cylinders and 2–4–6 are on the gasket for the front cylinders. Torque the manifold to cylinder head nuts to 14 ft. lbs. (19 Nm).
10. Install the crossover pipe to the manifold.
11. Connect the EGR tube and oxygen sensor wire.
12. Connect the exhaust pipe to the rear exhaust manifold, at the articulated joint.
13. Connect the negative battery cable and check the manifolds for leaks.

3.3L And 3.8 Engines

1. Disconnect the negative battery cable.
2. If removing the rear manifold, raise the vehicle and support safely. Disconnect the exhaust pipe at the articulated joint from the rear exhaust manifold.
3. Separate the EGR tube from the rear manifold and disconnect the oxygen sensor wire.
4. Remove the alternator/power steering support strut.
5. Remove the bolts attaching the crossover pipe to the manifold.
6. Remove the bolts attaching the manifold to the head and remove the manifold.
7. If removing the front manifold, remove the heat shield, bolts attaching the crossover pipe to the manifold and the nuts attaching the manifold to the head.
8. Remove the manifold from the engine.
9. The installation is the reverse of the removal procedure. Torque all exhaust manifold attaching bolts to 17 ft. lbs. (23 Nm).

10. Start the engine and check for exhaust leaks.

1990–92 Dodge Monaco 3.0L Engine

1. Disconnect the negative battery cable.
2. Disconnect the EGR tube from the right side manifold.
3. Raise the vehicle and support safely.
4. Remove the nuts retaining the header pipe to the manifolds.
5. On the right manifold, remove the nuts securing the dipstick tube to the manifold. On the left manifold, remove the starter heat shield and the heat stove.
6. Lower the vehicle.
7. Remove the manifold mounting nuts and remove the manifolds.
8. The installation is the reverse of the removal procedure. Tighten the nuts to 13 ft. lbs. (18 Nm).
9. Connect the negative battery cable and check for exhaust leaks.

1990–92 Laser and Dodge Stealth

NON-TURBOCHARGED ENGINES

1. Disconnect battery negative cable.
2. Raise the vehicle and support safely.
3. Remove the exhaust pipe to exhaust manifold nuts and separate exhaust pipe. Discard gasket.
4. Lower the vehicle.
5. Remove electric cooling fan assembly if necessary. If removing the front manifold on 3.0L engine, remove the dipstick tube. If removing the front manifold from 3.0L DOHC engine, remove the alternator.
6. Disconnect necessary EGR components.
7. Remove outer exhaust manifold heat shield, engine hanger and remove the oxygen sensor.
8. Remove the exhaust manifold mounting bolts, the inner heat shield and remove the exhaust manifold.
To install:
8. Clean all gasket material from the mating surfaces and check the manifold for damage.
9. Install a new gasket and install the manifold. Tighten the nuts to in a criss-cross pattern to:
   SOHC engines – 11–14 ft. lbs. (15–20 Nm).
   2.0L engines – 18–22 ft. lbs. (25–30 Nm).
   3.0L DOHC engine – 33 ft. lbs. (45 Nm).
10. Install the heat shields.
11. Connect EGR components.
12. Install the electric cooling fan assembly, dipstick tube or alternator.
13. Install a new gasket and connect the exhaust pipe.
14. Connect the negative battery cable and check for exhaust leaks.

2.0L TURBOCHARGED ENGINE

1. Disconnect the battery negative cable. Drain the cooling system.
2. Remove the condenser cooling fan and power steering pump and bracket as required.
3. Raise the vehicle and support safely.
4. Remove the exhaust pipe to turbocharger nuts and separate the exhaust pipe. Discard the gasket.
5. Lower vehicle. Remove air intake and vacuum hose connections.
6. Remove the upper exhaust manifold and turbocharger heat shields. Remove the exhaust manifold to turbocharger attaching bolts and nut.
7. Remove the engine hanger, water and oil lines from the turbo.
8. Remove the exhaust manifold mounting nuts. Remove the exhaust manifold and gasket.
To install:
9. Clean all gasket material from the mating surfaces and check the manifold for damage.
10. Install new gaskets and install the manifold. Tighten the manifold to head nuts in a criss-cross pattern to 18–22 ft. lbs. Tighten the manifold to turbo nut and bolts to 40–47 ft. lbs. (55–65 Nm).
11. Install the engine hanger, water and oil lines to the turbocharger.
12. Install the heat shields.
13. Install the new gasket and connect the exhaust pipe.
14. Install the condenser cooling fan and power steering pump.
15. Fill the cooling system.
16. Connect the negative battery cable and check for exhaust leaks.

3.0L TURBOCHARGED ENGINE

1. Disconnect the negative battery cable.
2. Drain the engine coolant.
3. Disconnect the exhaust pipe from the turbocharger and remove the turbocharger assembly.
4. Remove the heat shield.
5. Remove the mounting nuts and remove the exhaust manifold. Note that cone disc springs are installed at all lower mounting points.
To install:
6. Clean all gasket material from the mating surfaces and check the manifold for damage.
7. Install new gaskets and install the manifold. Make sure all cone disc springs are in their original locations with the grooved side facing the nut. Tighten the manifold nuts using the following procedure:
   a. Tighten all but the outer 2 nuts to 22 ft. lbs. (30 Nm).

b. Tighten the outer 2 nuts to 34–38 ft. lbs. (47–53 Nm).

c. Loosen the outer 2 nuts, then torque them to 22 ft. lbs. (30 Nm).

8. Install the heat shield.

9. Install the turbocharger assembly.

10. Fill the cooling system.

11. Connect the negative battery cable and check for exhaust leaks.

Intake/Exhaust Manifold

REMOVAL AND INSTALLATION

CAUTION: *When draining the coolant, keep in mind that cats and dogs are attracted by the ethylene glycol antifreeze, and are quite likely to drink any that is left in an uncovered container or in puddles on the ground. This will prove fatal in sufficient quantity. Always drain the coolant into a sealable container. Coolant should be reused unless it is contaminated or several years old.*

1981–88 2.2L Normally Aspirated and 2.5L Engines

NOTE: *These engines use a combined intake/exhaust manifold gasket. Therefore, the manifolds must always be removed and replaced together.*

1. Disconnect the negative battery cable. Drain the cooling system.

2. Remove the air cleaner and hoses.

3. If the engine is fuel injected, depressurize the fuel system, as described in Chapter 1. Remove all wiring and any hoses connected to the carburetor or injection throttle body and the manifold.

4. Disconnect the accelerator linkage.

5. Loosen the power steering pump mounting bolts and remove the belt. Disconnect the power brake vacuum hose at the manifold.

6. On Canadian cars only: Remove the coupling hose connecting the diverter valve and the exhaust manifold air injection tube.

7. Disconnect the water hose from the water crossover.

8. Raise the vehicle and support it securely. Disconnect the exhaust pipe at the manifold.

9. Remove the power steering pump, leaving lines connected, and hang it to one side so the hoses are not stressed.

10. Remove the intake manifold support bracket.

11. Remove the intake manifold-to-head bolts.

12. Lower the vehicle to the floor. Remove the intake manifold.

13. Remove the exhaust manifold retaining nuts and remove the exhaust manifold.

To install:

14. Clean all gasket surfaces and reposition the intake and exhaust manifolds using new gaskets. A composition gasket is installed as-is; a steel gasket must be coated with a sealer such as Chrysler Part No. 3419115 or equivalent.

15. Put the exhaust manifold into position and install the retaining nuts just finger-tight. Put the intake manifold into position and install all accessible bolts. Raise the car and support it securely.

16. Install all the manifold-to-head bolts finger-tight. Install the intake manifold support bracket. Install the power steering pump, bolting it into position with bolts just finger-tight. Connect the exhaust pipe at the manifold, using a new seal, and torque the bolts and nuts to 250 inch lbs.

17. Lower the car to the floor. Torque the manifold nuts and bolts in three stages, starting at the center and progressing outward, to the specified torque.

18. Connect the power brake vacuum hose to the manifold. Connect the water hose to the water crossover.

19. On Canadian cars only: Install the coupling hose connecting the diverter valve and the exhaust manifold air injection tube.

20. Install the power steering pump belt and adjust tension.

21. Connect the accelerator linkage. Install the air cleaner and hoses.

22. Install all wiring and any hoses disconnected from the carburetor or injection throttle body and the manifold. Refill the cooling system, reconnect the battery, start the engine and run it to check for leaks. Refill the cooling system after the engine has reached operating temperature (air has been bled out) and it has cooled off again.

1989–92 2.2L AND 2.5L Engines

Without Turbocharger

NOTE: *On some vehicles, some of the manifold attaching bolts are not accessible or too heavily sealed from the factory and cannot be removed on the vehicle. Head removal would be necessary in these situations.*

1. Disconnect the negative battery cable.

2. Relieve the fuel system pressure.

3. Drain the cooling system.

4. Remove the air cleaner and disconnect all vacuum lines, electrical wiring and fuel lines from the throttle body.

5. Disconnect the throttle linkage.

6. Loosen the power steering pump and remove the drive belt.

7. Remove the power brake vacuum hose from the intake manifold.

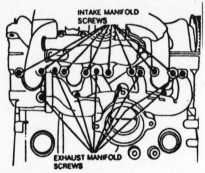

Combination manifold attaching nuts and bolts—2.2L and 2.5 non-turbocharged engines

8. Remove the water hoses from the water crossover.

9. Raise and safely support the vehicle. Disconnect the exhaust pipe from the exhaust manifold.

10. Remove the power steering pump from its mounting bracket and set it aside.

11. Remove the intake manifold support bracket, if equipped.

12. Remove the EGR tube, if equipped.

13. Remove the intake manifold bolts.

14. Lower the vehicle.

15. Remove the intake manifold.

16. Remove the exhaust manifold nuts.

17. Remove the exhaust manifold.

To install:

18. Install a new combination manifold gasket.

19. Install the manifold assembly. Starting from the middle and working outwards, install the mounting nuts and torque to 13 ft. lbs. (18 Nm). Install the heat cowl to the exhaust manifold.

20. Install the intake manifold. Starting from the middle and working outward, torque the bolts to 17 ft. lbs. (23 Nm.).

21. Install the EGR tube, if removed.

22. Install the intake support bracket, if equipped.

23. Install the power steering pump.

24. Raise the vehicle and support safely. Install the exhaust pipe to the exhaust manifold.

25. Install the water hoses to the water crossover.

26. Install the power brake vacuum hose to the intake manifold.

27. Connect the throttle linkage.

28. Install all vacuum lines, electrical wiring and fuel lines the throttle body.

29. Install the air cleaner assembly.

30. Refill the cooling system.

31. Connect the negative battery cable and check the manifolds for leaks.

With Turbocharger

NOTE: *On some vehicles, some of the manifold attaching bolts are not accessible or too heavily sealed from the factory and cannot be removed on the vehicle. Head removal would be necessary in these situations.*

1. Disconnect the negative battery cable. Drain the cooling system. Raise and safely support the vehicle.

2. Disconnect the exhaust pipe at the articulated joint. Disconnect the oxygen sensor at the electrical connection.

3. Remove the turbocharger to engine support bracket.

4. Loosen the oil drain back tube connector hose clamps. Move the tube down on the engine block fitting.

5. Disconnect the turbocharger coolant inlet tube from the engine block and disconnect the tube support bracket.

6. Remove the air cleaner assembly, including the throttle body adaptor, hose and air cleaner box with support bracket.

7. Disconnect the accelerator linkage, throttle body electrical connector and vacuum hoses.

8. Relocate the fuel rail assembly. Remove the bracket to intake manifold screws and the bracket to heat shield clips. Lift and secure the fuel rail with injectors, wiring harness and fuel lines intact, up and aside.

9. Disconnect the turbocharger oil feed line at the oil sending unit tee fitting.

10. Disconnect the upper radiator hose from the thermostat housing.

11. Remove the cylinder head, manifolds and turbocharger as an assembly.

12. With the assembly on a workbench, loosen the upper turbocharger discharge hose end clamp.

NOTE: *Do not disturb the center deswirler retaining clamp.*

13. Remove the throttle body to intake manifold screws and throttle body assembly. Disconnect the turbocharger coolant return tube from the water box. Disconnect the retaining bracket on the cylinder head.

14. Remove the heat shield to intake manifold screws and the heat shield.

15. Remove the turbocharger to exhaust manifold nuts and the turbocharger assembly.

16. Remove the intake manifold bolts and the intake manifold.

17. Remove the exhaust manifold nuts and the exhaust manifold.

To install:

18. Place a new 2-sided Grafoil type intake/exhaust manifold gasket; do not use sealant.

19. Position the exhaust manifold on the cylinder head. Apply anti-seize compound to

threads, install and torque the retaining nuts, starting at center and progressing outward in both directions, to 17 ft. lbs. (23 Nm). Repeat this procedure until all nuts are at 17 ft. lbs. (23 Nm).

20. Position the intake manifold on the cylinder head. Install and torque the retaining screws, starting at center and progressing outward in both directions, to 19 ft. lbs. (26 Nm). Repeat this procedure until all screws are at 19 ft. lbs. (26 Nm).

21. Connect the turbocharger outlet to the intake manifold inlet tube. Position the turbocharger on the exhaust manifold. Apply anti-seize compound to threads and torque the nuts to 30 ft. lbs. (41 Nm). Torque the connector tube clamps to 30 inch lbs. (41 Nm).

22. Install the tube support bracket to the cylinder head.

23. Install the heat shield on the intake manifold. Torque the screws to 105 inch lbs. (12 Nm).

24. Install the throttle body air horn into the turbocharger inlet tube. Install and torque the throttle body to intake manifold screws to 21 ft. lbs. (28 Nm). Torque the tube clamp to 30 inch lbs.

25. Install the cylinder head/manifolds/turbocharger assembly on the engine.

26. Reconnect the turbocharger oil feed line to the oil sending unit tee fitting and bearing housing, if disconnected. Torque the tube nuts to 10 ft. lbs. (14 Nm).

27. Install the air cleaner assembly. Connect the vacuum lines and accelerator cables.

28. Reposition the fuel rail. Install and torque the bracket screws to 21 ft. lbs. (28 Nm). Install the air shield to bracket clips.

29. Connect the turbocharger inlet coolant tube to the engine block. Torque the tube nut to 30 ft. lbs. (41 Nm). Install the tube support bracket.

30. Install the turbocharger housing-to-engine block support bracket and the screws hand tight. Torque the block screw 1st to 40 ft. lbs. (54 Nm). Torque the screw to the turbocharger housing to 20 ft. lbs. (27 Nm).

31. Reposition the drain back hose connector and tighten the hose clamps. Reconnect the exhaust pipe.

32. Connect the upper radiator hose to the thermostat housing.

33. Refill the cooling system.

34. Connect the negative battery cable and check the manifolds for leaks.

Turbocharger

REMOVAL AND INSTALLATION

CAUTION: *When draining the coolant, keep in mind that cats and dogs are attracted by the ethylene glycol antifreeze, and are quite likely to drink any that is left in an uncovered container or in puddles on the ground. This will prove fatal in sufficient quantity. Always drain the coolant into a sealable container. Coolant should be reused unless it is contaminated or several years old.*

Many turbocharger failures are due to oil supply problems. Heat soak after hot shutdown can cause the engine oil in the turbocharger and oil lines to "coke." Often the oil feed lines will become partially or completely blocked with hardened particles of carbon, blocking oil flow. Check the oil feed pipe and oil return line for clogging. Clean these tubes well. Always use new gaskets above and below the oil feed eye-bolt fitting. Do not allow particles of dirt or old gasket material to enter the oil passage hole and that no portion of the new gasket blocks the passage.

1984–85 Vehicles

1. Disconnect the battery and drain coolant.

2. From under the car:

a. Disconnect the exhaust pipe at the articulated joint and disconnect the O_2 sensor electrical connections.

b. Remove the turbocharger-to-block support bracket.

c. Loosen the clamps for the oil drain-back tube and then move the tube downward onto the block fitting so it no longer connects with the turbocharger.

d. Disconnect the turbocharger coolant supply tube at the block outlet below the power steering pump bracket and at the tube support bracket.

3. Disconnect and remove the air cleaner complete with the throttle body adaptor, hose, and air cleaner box and support bracket.

4. Loosen the throttle body to turbocharger inlet hose clamps. Then, remove the three throttle body-to-intake manifold attaching screws and remove the throttle body.

5. Loosen the turbocharger discharge hose end clamps, leaving the center band in place to retain the de-swirler.

6. Pull the fuel rail out of the way after removing the hose retaining bracket screw, four bracket screws from the intake manifold, and two bracket-to-heat shield retaining clips. The rail, injectors, wiring harness, and fuel lines will be moved as an assembly.

7. Disconnect the oil feed line at the turbocharger bearing housing.

8. Remove the three screws attaching the heat shield to the intake manifold and remove the shield.

9. Disconnect the coolant return tube and hose assembly at the turbocharger and water box. Remove the tube support bracket from the cylinder head and remove the assembly.

10. Remove the four nuts attaching the turbocharger to the exhaust manifold. Then, remove the turbocharger by lifting it off the exhaust manifold studs, tilting it downward toward the passenger side of the car, and then pulling it up and out of the car, and out of the engine compartment.

a. When repositioning the turbo on the mounting studs, make sure the discharge tube goes in position so it's properly connected to both the intake manifold and turbocharger. Apply an anti-seize compound such as Loctite® 771-64 or equivalent to the threads. Torque the nuts to 30 ft. lbs.

b. Observe the following torques:

- Oil feed line nuts: 125 inch lbs.
- Coolant tube nuts: 30 ft. lbs.
- Fuel rail bracket-to-intake manifold retaining screws: 250 inch lbs.
- Discharge tube hose clamp: 35 inch lbs.
- Throttle body-to-intake manifold screws: 250 inch lbs.
- Throttle body hose clamps: 35 inch lbs.
- Hose adapter-to-throttle body screws: 55 inch lbs.
- Air cleaner box support bracket screws: 40 ft. lbs.
- Coolant tube nut-to-block connector: 30 ft. lbs.

c. When installing the turbocharger-to-block support bracket, first install screws finger tight. Tighten the block screw first (to 40 ft. lbs.), and then tighten the screw going into the turbocharger housing (to 20 ft. lbs.). Tighten the articulated ball joint shoulder bolts to 250 inch lbs.

d. Make sure to fill the cooling system back up before starting the engine, recheck the level after the coolant begins circulating through the radiator, and check for leaks after you install the pressure cap. Check the turbocharger carefully for any oil leaks and correct if necessary.

1986 And Later Vehicles
Except 1990–92 Laser and Dodge Stealth

1. Disconnect the battery and drain the cooling system. Disconnect the air cleaner hoses and remove the air cleaner assembly.

2. Separate the throttle body from the intake manifold. Disconnect the PCV valve, vacuum vapor harness, power brake vacuum hose and accelerator linkage. On the Turbo II models only, disconnect the charge temperature sensor.

3. Refer to Chapter 5 under Fuel Injector Removal and Installation and remove the fuel rail.

4. Refer to the engine removal procedure earlier in this chapter and remove the front engine mount through bolt. Rotate the top of the engine mount forward and away from the firewall.

5. Unfasten the coolant line where it runs along the water box and turbo housing. Disconnect it at the turbocharger housing; remove the fitting from the turbocharger as well.

6. Disconnect the oil feed line at the turbo housing.

7. Remove the waste gate rod-to-gate retaining clip.

8. Remove the two upper and one lower (driver's side) nuts that retain the turbocharger to the manifold. Disconnect the oxygen sensor electrical lead and vacuum lines.

9. Raise the car and support it securely. Remove the right front wheel and tire for access.

10. Remove the right side driveshaft as described in Chapter 7.

11. Remove the turbocharger-to-block support bracket. Then, separate the oil drainback tube fitting from the turbo housing and remove the fitting and associated hose.

12. Remove the one remaining nut retaining the turbo to the manifold.

13. Disconnect the articulated exhaust pipe joint at the turbocharger turbine housing outlet.

14. Remove the lower coolant line and the inlet fitting through which coolant passes into the housing.

15. Lift the turbo off the manifold mounting studs and lower it down and out of the vehicle.

16. If you need to remove the intake manifold, now remove the 8 bolts and washers and remove it. The same basic procedure can be followed to remove the exhaust manifold.

To install:

17. Clean the manifold surfaces of all gasket materials. Inspect gasket surfaces for flatness--warping must not exceed 0.006 in. (0.152mm) per foot. Inspect the manifolds for cracks or distortion and replace as necessary.

18. Install a new two-sided grafoil or equivalent type gasket onto the block without sealer; then install the intake manifold. Put the intake manifold into position and install the bolts. Start torquing at the center and torque outward, tightening to 200 inch lbs. When all the bolts are torqued, repeat the process, torquing an additional 200 inch lbs. Repeat this process until the specified torque is reached.

19. Install the exhaust manifold the same way.

20. Position the turbocharger onto the exhaust manifold. Apply an anti-seize compound such as Loctite 771-64® or equivalent to the

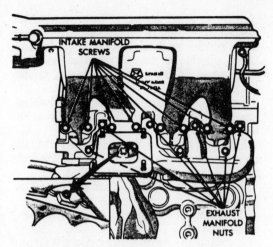

Turbo I and Turbo II intake/exhaust manifolds

threads and install one lower retaining nut on the passenger side, torquing to 40 ft. lbs.

21. Apply a thread sealant to the lower coolant inlet line fitting and install the fitting into the turbocharger housing. Connect the lower coolant line.

22. Install a new gasket and install the oil drain-back tube fitting into the turbocharger housing. Connect the coolant line to the fitting.

23. Install the turbocharger-to-block support bracket and install the attaching screws finger tight. First, torque the block screw to 40 ft. lbs. and then torque the screw attaching the bracket to the turbocharger housing to 20 ft. lbs.

24. Reposition the exhaust pipe and connect it to the turbo housing outlet. Torque the attaching bolts to 250 inch lbs. of torque.

25. Install the right side driveshaft. Lower the car to the ground.

26. Install the remaining three turbocharger-to-intake manifold nuts, torquing them to 40 ft. lbs.

27. Perform the remaining steps of the procedure in reverse order. Bear these points in mind:

   a. The oil feed line to the turbo bearing housing is torqued to 125 inch lbs.

   b. Apply thread sealer to turbo coolant line fittings and torque them to 30 ft. lbs.

   c. In reassembling the front engine mount, align the mount in the crossmember bracket, install the bolt, and torque it to 40 ft. lbs.

1990–92 Laser and Dodge Stealth

2.0L ENGINE

1. Disconnect the negative battery cable.

2. Drain the engine oil, cooling system and remove the radiator. On vehicles with air condi-

tioning, remove the condenser fan assembly with the radiator.

3. Disconnect the oxygen sensor connector and remove the sensor.

4. Remove the oil dipstick and tube.

5. Remove the air intake bellows hose, the wastegate vacuum hose, the connections for the air outlet hose, and the upper and lower heat shields.

6. Unbolt the power steering pump and bracket assembly and leaving the hoses connected, wire it aside.

7. Remove the self-locking exhaust manifold nuts, the triangular engine hanger bracket, the eyebolt and gaskets that connect the oil feed line to the turbo center section, and the water cooling lines. The water line under the turbo has a threaded connection.

8. Remove the exhaust pipe nuts and gasket and lift off the exhaust manifold. Discard the gasket.

9. Remove the 2 through bolts and 2 nuts that hold the exhaust manifold to the turbocharger.

10. Remove the 2 capscrews from the oil return line (under the turbo). Discard the gasket. Separate the turbo from the exhaust manifold. The 2 water pipes and oil feed line can still be attached.

11. Visually check the turbine wheel (hot side) and compressor wheel (cold side) for cracking or other damage. Check whether the turbine wheel and the compressor wheel can be easily turned by hand. Check for oil leakage. Check whether or not the wastegate valve remains open. If any problem is found, replace the part.

12. The wastegate can be checked with a pressure tester. Apply approximately 9 psi to the actuator and make sure the rod moves. Do not apply more than 10.3 psi or the diaphragm in the wastegate may be damaged. Do not attempt to adjust the wastegate valve.

To install:

13. Prime the oil return line with clean engine oil. Replace all locking nuts. Before installing the threaded connection for the water inlet pipe, apply light oil to the inner surface of the pipe flange. Assemble the turbocharger and exhaust manifold.

14. Install the exhaust manifold using a new gasket.

15. Connect the water cooling lines, oil feed line, and engine hanger.

16. If removed, install the power steering pump and bracket.

17. Install the heat shields, air outlet hose, wastegate hose and air intake bellows.

18. Install the oil dipstick tube and dipstick. Install the oxygen sensor.

19. Install the radiator assembly.

20. Fill the engine with oil, fill the cooling system and reconnect the negative battery cable.

3.0L ENGINE

Right Side (Front) Turbocharger

1. Disconnect the negative battery cable.
2. Remove the radiator.
3. Remove the right side transaxle bracket.
4. Remove the front exhaust pipe.
5. Carefully matchmark, diagram or photograph all air intake hoses and pipes along the front of the engine. It is imperative that all of these pieces are installed in the exact same positions when assembling. Remove the hoses and pipes and keep covered in a clean area.
6. Remove the alternator.
7. Remove the oil dipstick tube.
8. Remove the turbocharger heat protector.
9. Remove the water feed pipes.
10. Remove the oxygen sensor.
11. Remove the oil return line.
12. Remove the exhaust extension fitting and bracket.
13. Remove all air conditioning components preventing removal of the turbocharger.
14. Remove the oil feed tube.
15. Remove the turbocharger to exhaust manifold bolts and remove the turbocharger assembly.

To install:

16. Visually check the turbine wheel (hot side) and compressor wheel (cold side) for cracking or other damage. Check whether the turbine wheel and the compressor wheel can be easily turned by hand. Check for oil leakage. Check whether or not the wastegate valve remains open. If any problem is found, replace the part.

17. Clean all mating surfaces. Pour clean engine oil through the oil pipe feed hole in the turbocharger.

18. Install a new gasket and ring a install the turbocharger to the manifold. Torque the bolts to 40–47 ft. lbs. (55–65 Nm).

19. Replace the eye-bolt rings and install the oil feed pipe.

20. Install the removed air conditioning components.

21. Install the exhaust extension fitting and bracket with a new gasket. Torque the nuts to 40–47 ft. lbs. (55–65 Nm).

22. Install the oil return line with new gaskets.

23. Install the oxygen sensor.

24. Replace the eye-bolt rings and install the water feed pipes.

25. Install the turbocharger heat protector.

26. Install the dipstick tube.

27. Install the alternator.

28. Install all air intake hoses and pipes along the front of the engine. Make sure all are in their proper positions.

29. Install a new gasket and connect the front exhaust pipe.

30. Install the right side transaxle bracket.

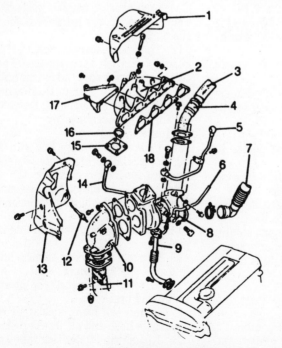

1. Upper heat shield
2. Exhaust manifold
3. Air hose connector
4. Air inlet fitting
5. Oil feed pipe
6. Water line
7. Connection-air intake
8. Turbocharger assembly
9. Oil drainback line
10. Exhaust fitting
11. Exhaust pipe
12. Oxygen sensor
13. Lower heat shield
14. Water line
15. Gasket
16. Ring
17. Brace/bracket
18. Manifold gasket

Turbocharger installation—2.0L engine

31. Install the radiator.
32. Fill the system with coolant.
33. Connect the negative battery cable and check for exhaust leaks.

Left Side (Rear) Turbocharger

1. Remove the battery.
2. Drain the coolant.
3. Remove the front exhaust pipe.
4. Disconnect the accelerator cable from the throttle body.
5. Remove the intake air hose, the air pipe across the top of the engine and its heat shield.
6. Remove the clutch booster vacuum hose and disconnect the accelerator cable from the pedal.
7. Remove the air intake hoses coming from the air cleaner box.
8. Remove the oxygen sensor and the turbocharger heat protector.
9. Remove the EGR pipe if equipped.
10. Remove the oil feed pipe.
11. Remove the EGR valve if equipped.
12. Remove the water feed pipes.
13. Remove the exhaust extension fitting and bracket.
14. Remove the inner heat protector.
15. Remove the oil return tube.
16. Remove the turbocharger to exhaust manifold nuts and remove the turbocharger assembly.

To install:

17. Visually check the turbine wheel (hot side) and compressor wheel (cold side) for cracking or other damage. Check whether the turbine wheel and the compressor wheel can be easily turned by hand. Check for oil leakage. Check whether or not the wastegate valve remains open. If any problem is found, replace the part.
18. Clean all mating surfaces. Pour clean engine oil through the oil pipe feed hole in the turbocharger.
19. Install a new gasket and ring a install the turbocharger to the manifold. Torque the nuts to 40–47 ft. lbs. (55–65 Nm).
20. Install the oil return line with new gaskets.
21. Install the inner heat protector.
22. Install the exhaust extension fitting and bracket with a new gasket. Torque the nuts to 40–47 ft. lbs. (55–65 Nm).
23. Replace the eye-bolt rings and install the water feed pipes.
24. Install the EGR valve if equipped.
25. Replace the eye-bolt rings and install the oil feed pipe.
26. Install the EGR pipe if equipped.
27. Install the turbocharger heat protector and oxygen sensor.

28. Install the air intake hoses coming from the air cleaner box. Make sure the triangular aligning marks are engaged.
29. Connect the accelerator cable to from the pedal and install the clutch booster vacuum hose.
30. Install the heat shield, the air pipe across the top of the engine and the air intake hose.
31. Connect the accelerator cable to the throttle body.
32. Install a new gasket and connect the front exhaust pipe.
33. Fill the system with coolant.
34. Install the battery.
35. Connect the negative battery cable and check for exhaust leaks.

Radiator

REMOVAL AND INSTALLATION

CAUTION: *When draining the coolant, keep in mind that cats and dogs are attracted by the ethylene glycol antifreeze, and are quite likely to drink any that is left in an uncovered container or in puddles on the ground. This will prove fatal in sufficient quantity. Always drain the coolant into a sealable container. Coolant should be reused unless it is contaminated or several years old.*

1. Disconnect the negative battery cable.
2. Drain the coolant.
3. Remove the upper hose and coolant reserve tank hose from the radiator.
4. Remove the electric cooling fan.
5. Raise the vehicle and support safely. Remove the lower hose from the radiator.
6. Disconnect the automatic transaxle cooler hoses, if equipped, and plug them. Lower the vehicle.
7. Remove the mounting brackets and carefully lift the radiator out of the engine compartment.

To install:

8. Lower the radiator into position.
9. Install the mounting brackets.
10. Raise the vehicle, if necessary, and support safely. Connect the automatic transaxle cooler lines, if equipped.
11. Lower the vehicle and connect the lower hose.
12. Install the electric cooling fan.
13. Connect the upper hose and coolant reserve tank hose.
14. Fill the system with coolant.
15. Connect the negative battery cable, run the vehicle until the thermostat opens, fill the radiator completely and check the automatic transaxle fluid level, if equipped.
16. Once the vehicle has cooled, recheck the coolant level.

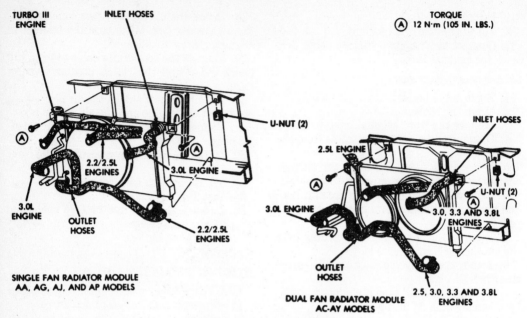

Radiator assembly—all models

A/C Condenser

REMOVAL AND INSTALLATION

CAUTION: *The air conditioning system in filled with refrigerant under high pressure. The refrigerant must be discharged and recovered at an approved facility by qualified personnel before you can safely work on any of the components.*

1. Have the air conditioning refrigerant discharged and recovered by a professional (See Chapter 1). Remove the radiator assembly as described above.

2. Remove the refrigerant line attaching nut and separate the lines at the condenser sealing plate. Immediately cap the ends with a plastic cap designed for this purpose or with plastic sheeting and tape.

3. Remove the two mounting bolts located near the top of the condenser. These attach the condenser to the radiator core support.

4. Lift the condenser out of the engine compartment, being careful not to damage fins or piping.

5. Install the condenser in reverse order. Replace all gaskets and O-rings. O-rings must be coated with refrigerant oil drawn from an unopened container prior to installation.

6. If the condenser used is a new one, make sure to have oil added to the system to replace that which was removed with the old condenser. This requires specialized service knowledge. Have the air conditioning system evacuated and recharged at an approved facility.

Water Pump

REMOVAL AND INSTALLATION

CAUTION: *When draining the coolant, keep in mind that cats and dogs are attracted by the ethylene glycol antifreeze, and are quite likely to drink any that is left in an uncovered container or in puddles on the ground. This will prove fatal in sufficient quantity. Always drain the coolant into a sealable container. Coolant should be reused unless it is contaminated or several years old.*

2.2, 2.5L And Turbo III Engines

1. Disconnect the battery negative cable. Drain the cooling system.

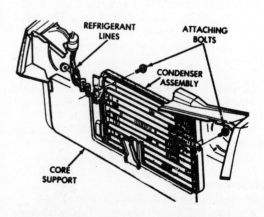

A/C condenser removal and installation typical

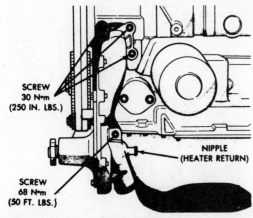

Replacing 2.2 and 2.5L water pump

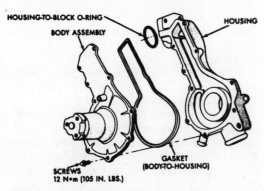

Water pump assembly—2.2L/2.5L engines

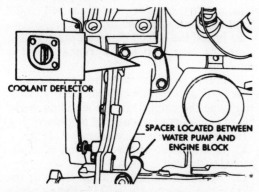

Coolant deflector—Turbo III

2. Remove the upper radiator hose.

3. Remove the alternator.

NOTE: *Do not disconnect the air conditioner compressor lines in the next step. The compressor can be moved far enough out of the way to remove the water pump without disturbing the refrigerant-filled lines.*

4. Unbolt the air conditioning compressor brackets from the water pump and secure the compressor out of the way. Support the compressor so it will not put stress on the lines.

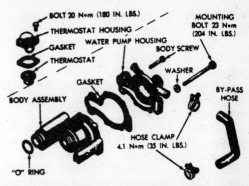

Thermostat Housing and Water Pump—2.6L engine

5. Disconnect the bypass hose, heater return hose, and lower radiator hose.

6. Unbolt and remove the water pump assembly. On the Turbo III engine, there is a spacer between the water pump and engine block on the lower screw. Disassemble the pump as follows:

a. Remove the three bolts fastening the drive pulley to the water pump.

b. Remove the 9 bolts fastening the water pump body to the housing. Then, use a chisel to gently break the bond between the pump and housing.

c. Clean the gasket surfaces on the pump body and housing. Remove the O-ring gasket and discard it. Clean the O-ring groove.

d. Apply RTV sealer to the sealing surface of the water pump body. The bead should be ⅛ in. (3mm) in diameter and should encircle all bolt holes. Assemble the pump body to the housing, install the 9 bolts, and torque them to 105 inch lbs. Make sure the gasketing material has set (as per package instructions) before actually filling the system.

e. Position a new O-ring in the O-ring groove. Then, put the pulley on the pump, install the 3 attaching bolts, and torque them to 250 inch lbs.

7. Installation is the reverse of removal. Torque the top 3 water pump bolts to 250 inch lbs. and the lower bolt to 50 ft. lbs. On the Turbo III engine install the coolant deflector into the block before installing the water pump on engine. Install spacer between the pump and block for Turbo III engine only before torquing pump to specifications. Make sure to refill the system (make sure that the thermostat is open) with 50/50 antifreeze/water mix. Recheck coolant level after vehicle has cooled.

2.6L Engine

1. Disconnect the negative battery cable. Drain the cooling system.

2. Disconnect the radiator hose, bypass hose, and heater hose at the pump.

3. Remove the two mounting bolts and remove the drive pulley shield.

4. Remove the lock screw and the two pivot screws. Then, separate the pump from the drive belt and remove it.

5. Remove the bolts attaching the water pump housing to the pump body and separate the pump from the body.

6. Discard the gasket and clean the gasket surfaces. Remove the O-ring, replace it, and clean the O-ring groove.

7. Install a new gasket on the pump body, put the new pump into position onto it, and then install the bolts, torquing them to 80 inch lbs. Put a new O-ring into the O-ring groove.

8. Position the pump on the engine, connect the drive belt, and install the pivot and locking screws loosely. Tension the drive belt and then final-tighten all three mounting bolts.

9. The remaining steps are the reverse of the removal procedure. Make sure to refill the system (make sure that the thermostat is open) with 50/50 antifreeze/water mix. Recheck coolant level after vehicle has cooled.

3.0L Engine

1. Disconnect the negative battery cable.

2. Drain the cooling system.

3. Remove the timing cover. If the same timing belt will be reused, mark the direction of the timing belt's rotation, for installation in the same direction. Make sure the engine is positioned so the No. 1 cylinder is at the TDC of its compression stroke and the sprockets timing marks are aligned with the engine's timing mark indicators.

4. Loosen the timing belt tensioner bolt and remove the belt. Position the tensioner as far away from the center of the engine as possible and tighten the bolt. Remove the water pump mounting bolts, separate the pump from the

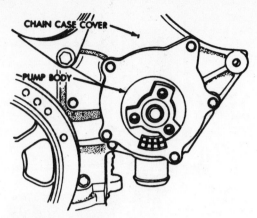

Water pump—3.3L/3.8L engines

water inlet pipe and remove the pump from the engine.

To install:

5. Install the pump with a new gasket to the engine. Torque the water pump mounting bolts to 20 ft. lbs. (27 Nm).

6. If not already done, position both camshafts so the marks line up with those on the alternator bracket (rear bank) and inner timing cover (front bank). Rotate the crankshaft so the timing mark aligns with the mark on the oil pump.

7. Install the timing belt on the crankshaft sprocket and while keeping the belt tight on the tension side (right side), install the belt on the front camshaft sprocket.

8. Install the belt on the water pump pulley, then the rear camshaft sprocket and the tensioner.

9. Rotate the front camshaft counterclockwise to tension the belt between the front camshaft and the crankshaft. If the timing marks became misaligned, repeat the procedure.

10. Install the crankshaft sprocket flange.

11. Loosen the tensioner bolt and allow the spring to tension the belt.

12. Turn the crankshaft 2 full turns in the clockwise direction only until the timing marks align again. Now that the belt is properly tensioned, torque the tensioner lock bolt to 21 ft. lbs. (29 Nm).

13. Refill the cooling system. This system uses a self-bleeding thermostat, so there is no need to bleed the system. Connect the negative battery cable and road test the vehicle.

3.3L And 3.8L Engines

1. Disconnect the negative battery cable.

2. Drain the cooling system.

3. Remove the serpentine belt.

4. Raise the vehicle and support safely. Re-

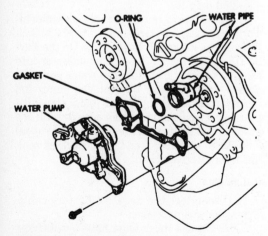

Water pump—3.0L engines

move the right front tire and wheel assembly and lower fender shield.

5. Remove the water pump pulley.

6. Remove the 5 mounting screws and remove the pump from the engine.

7. Discard the O-ring.

To install:

8. Using a new O-ring, install the pump to the engine. Torque the mounting bolts to 21 ft. lbs. (30 Nm).

9. Install the water pump pulley.

10. Install the fender shield and tire and wheel assembly. Lower the vehicle.

11. Install the serpentine belt.

12. Remove the engine temperature sending unit. Fill the radiator with coolant until the coolant comes out the sending unit hole. Install the sending unit and continue to fill the radiator.

13. Connect the negative battery cable, run the vehicle until the thermostat opens, fill the radiator completely and check for leaks.

14. Once the vehicle has cooled, recheck the coolant level.

1990–92 Dodge Monaco 3.0L Engine

1. Disconnect the negative battery cable.

2. Drain the cooling system.

3. Remove the spark plug wire holder from the top of the thermostat housing. Remove the nuts holding the engine damper to the engine.

4. Remove the accessory drive belt. Remove the upper and lower radiator hoses from the radiator.

5. Disconnect the electrical lead to the coolant temperature sensor.

6. At the back of the water pump, disconnect the hoses to the cylinder heads and the heater hoses.

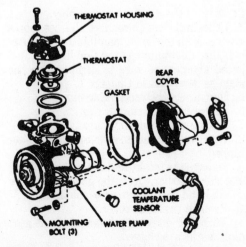

Water pump and thermostat assembly—Dodge Monaco 3.0L engine

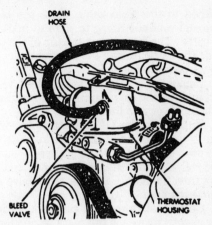

Cooling system bleed valve—Dodge Monaco 3.0L engine

7. Remove the water pump mounting bolts and remove the water pump.

To install:

8. Position the water pump to the block and tighten the mounting bolts to 13 ft. lbs.

9. Connect all of the hoses to the water pump, making sure they are not kinked. Connect the electrical lead to the coolant temperature sensor.

10. Install the accessory drive belt and the engine damper. Adjust the drive belt tension.

11. Install the spark plug wire holder to the thermostat housing.

12. Fill the cooling system.

13. Connect the negative battery cable. Start the engine and bleed the cooling system. Check for leaks.

COOLING SYSTEM BLEEDING
1990–92 DODGE MONACO 3.0L ENGINE

NOTE: *This procedure should be followed after any cooling system component has been replaced or removed and installed. It is essential that coolant does not contact the accessory drive belt or pulleys. Chemicals deteriorate the synthetic materials in the belt. Always protect the the serpentine belt and pulleys with clean shop towels. When installing the drain hose to the air bleed valve on the thermostat housing, route the hose away from the belt, pulleys and cooling fan.*

1. Attach one end of a 4 ft. (122cm) long ¼ in. (6mm) hose to the air bleed on the thermostat housing. Route the hose away from the drive belt and pulleys. Place the other end of the hose in a clean container. The purpose of this hose is to keep coolant away from the belt and pulleys.

2. Open the bleed valve.

3. Slowly fill the coolant pressure bottle until a steady stream of coolant flows from the hose

attached to the bleed valve. Close the bleed valve and continue filling to the full mark on the bottle. The full mark is the top of the post inside the bottle. Install the cap tightly on the coolant pressure bottle.

4. Remove the hose from the bleed valve, start and run the engine until the upper radiator hose is warm to the touch.

5. Turn the engine **OFF**. Reattach the drain hose to the bleed valve. Be sure to route the hose away from the belt and pulleys. Open the bleed valve until a steady stream of coolant flows from the hose. Close the bleed valve and remove the hose.

6. Check that the coolant pressure bottle is at or slightly above the full mark, at the top of the post inside the coolant pressure bottle. The full mark on the coolant pressure bottle is the correct coolant level for a cold engine. A hot engine will normally have a coolant level higher than the full mark.

1990–92 Laser And Dodge Stealth

1. Disconnect the negative battery cable.
2. Drain the cooling system.
3. Remove the engine undercover.
4. Remove the timing belt.
5. Disconnect the hoses from the pump, if equipped. Remove the alternator bracket.
6. Remove the water pump, gasket and O-ring where the water inlet pipe joins the pump.
To install:
7. Thoroughly clean and dry both gasket surfaces of the water pump and block.
8. Install a new O-ring into the groove on the front end of the water inlet pipe. Do not apply oils or grease to the O-ring. Wet with water only.
9. Install the gasket and pump assembly and tighten the bolts. Note the marks on the bolt heads. Those marked **4** should be torqued to 9–11 ft. lbs. Those bolts marked **7** should be torqued from 14–20 ft. lbs.
10. Connect the hoses to the pump.
11. Reinstall the timing belt and related parts.
12. Install the engine undercover.
13. Fill the system with coolant.
14. Connect the negative battery cable, run the vehicle until the thermostat opens and fill the radiator completely.
15. Once the vehicle has cooled, recheck the coolant level.

COOLING SYSTEM BLEEDING
1990–92 LASER AND DODGE STEALTH

All vehicles are equipped with a self-bleeding thermostat. Slowly fill the cooling system in the conventional manner; air will vent through the jiggle valve in the thermostat. Run the vehicle until the thermostat has opened and continue filling the radiator. Recheck the coolant level after the vehicle has cooled.

Cylinder Head
REMOVAL AND INSTALLATION

CAUTION: *When draining the coolant, keep in mind that cats and dogs are attracted by the ethylene glycol antifreeze, and are quite likely to drink any that is left in an uncovered container or in puddles on the ground. This will prove fatal in sufficient quantity. Always drain the coolant into a sealable container. Coolant should be reused unless it is contaminated or several years old.*

The EPA warns that prolonged contact with used engine oil may cause a number of skin disorders, including cancer! You should make every effort to minimize your exposure to used engine oil. Protective gloves should be worn when changing the oil. Wash your hands and any other exposed skin areas as soon as possible after exposure to used engine oil. Soap and water, or waterless hand cleaner should be used.

NOTE: *REVIEW ENTIRE PROCEDURE BEFORE STARTING THIS REPAIR. MAKE SURE TO LOCATE THE CORRECT YEAR, ENGINE AND MODEL SERVICE PROCEDURE FOR YOUR VEHICLE.*

1981–88 2.2L, 2.5L And Turbo Engines

1. Disconnect the negative battery terminal. Make sure the engine is cold.
2. Drain the cooling system. If the dipstick bracket attaches to the thermostat housing, disconnect the it from the thermostat housing and rotate the dipstick bracket away from the mounting stud to disconnect it without bending it.
3. Remove the air cleaner assembly.
4. Label and then disconnect all lines, hoses and wires from the head, manifold and carburetor. Before disconnecting the fuel lines on fuel injected engines, be sure to depressurize the system as described in Chapter 1.
5. Disconnect the accelerator linkage.
6. Remove the distributor cap.
7. Disconnect the exhaust pipe.
8. Remove the carburetor on engines so-equipped.
9. Remove the intake and exhaust manifolds as described earlier. On turbo engines, remove the turbo and then remove the manifolds.
10. Remove the front cover.
11. Turn the engine by hand until all gear timing marks are aligned.
12. Loosen the drive belt tensioner and slip the timing belt off the sprockets.

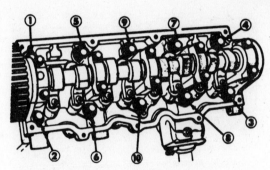

Cylinder head bolt removal sequence—2.2L and 2.5L engines

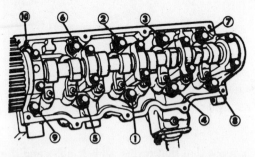

Cylilnder head bolt torque sequence—2.2L and 2.5L engines

13. If equipped with air conditioning, remove the compressor from the mounting brackets and support it out of the way with wires. Remove the mounting bracket from the head. Then, if the engine is equipped with the solid mount attached to block and head:

a. Remove the alternator pivot bolt and remove the alternator.

b. Remove the A/C belt idler.

c. If the car has a turbo, remove the right engine mount yoke bolt, which secures the isolator support bracket to the engine mount bracket.

d. Now, remove all 5 side mounting bolts – those facing the radiator.

e. Remove the front mounting nut and bolt (both face the fender well). Coolant will leak from the bolthole.

f. Now, rotate the bracket away from the engine and slide it on the stud until it is free.

g. Now, reinstall the front mounting bolt into the hole to stop the leakage of coolant.

14. Remove the valve cover, gaskets and seals as described above.

15. Remove head bolts in the order shown.

16. Lift off the head and discard the gasket.

17. Inspect the cylinder head and block surfaces with a straightedge and feeler gauge to make sure it is flat within 0.004 in. (0.10mm). If not, the cylinder head or block deck must be machined. Clean both gasket surfaces thoroughly.

To install:

18. Make certain all gasket surfaces are thoroughly cleaned and are free of deep nicks or scratches. Always use new gaskets and seals. Never reuse a gasket or seal, even if it looks good.

19. Position the head on the block, and then insert bolts 8 and 10 (see illustration) to align the head, gasket and block.

NOTE: *With the 1986 model year, the 10mm bolts have been replaced with 11mm bolts marked "11" on the head. Tighten bolts in the order shown to specifications. This is a four step procedure.*

On 1981–86 models: first torque the bolts in the order shown to 30 ft. lbs.; then, torque them in the order shown to 45 ft. lbs.; again, in the order shown, torque them to 45 ft. lbs; then, turn each bolt ¼ turn tighter, again in the order shown.

On 1986–88 models: first torque the bolts in the order shown to 45 ft. lbs.; then, torque them in the order shown to 65 ft. lbs.; again, in the order shown, torque them to 65 ft. lbs; then, turn each bolt ¼ turn tighter, again in the order shown.

Note that on the 1986–88 models using the 11mm bolts, torque must reach 90 ft. lbs.; otherwise, replace the bolt.

20. Install the valve cover, gaskets and seals as described above.

21. If the car is equipped with air conditioning:

a. Remove the front mounting bolt for the compressor installed to stop coolant leakage.

b. Install the A/C compressor bracket by rotating it into place in reverse of the removal procedure. Install the front mounting nut and bolt and all 5 side mounting bolts.

c. On turbo cars the right engine mount yoke bolt was removed. Reinstall it to secure the isolator support bracket to the engine mounting bracket. Torque it to 75 ft. lbs.

d. Install the A/C belt idler.

e. Install the alternator, including the alternator pivot bolt.

22. Make sure all timing marks are aligned. Install the timing belt and tension it as described later. The drive belt is correctly tensioned when it can be twisted 90 degrees with the thumb and index finger midway between the camshaft and the intermediate shaft. Check to make sure tension is correct.

23. Install the front cover. Install the intake and exhaust manifolds (with turbo, if so equipped), as described below in this chapter. Reconnect the exhaust pipe, using a new seal, and torque the nuts/bolts to 250 inch lbs.

24. Install the distributor cap. Connect the accelerator linkage.

25. Reconnect all electrical wiring, fuel and vacuum hoses, and other wiring.

26. Install the air cleaner and reconnect all air and vacuum hoses.

27. Fill the cooling system. Reconnect the battery negative cable. Start the engine and run it until it reaches operating temperature, checking for leaks. After the engine has cooled, refill the cooling system.

2.6L Engine

NOTE: *Do not perform this operation on a warm engine. Remove the head bolts in the sequence shown in several steps. Loosen the head bolts evenly, not one at a time. Do not attempt to slide the cylinder head off the block, as it is located with dowel pins. Lift the head straight up and off the block.*

1. Disconnect the battery. Remove the air cleaner and duct. Remove the PCV hose. Remove the water pump pulley cover and remove the fuel pump and carb-to-head cover bracket. Remove the water pump drive belt.

2. Remove the two bolts that retain it and remove the cylinder head cover.

3. Drain the cooling system. Disconnect the upper radiator hose and heater hoses.

4. Turn the crankshaft until No. 1 piston is at the top of its compression stroke (both No. 1 cylinder valves closed and timing marks at Top Center). Remove the distributor cap and matchmark the distributor body with the rotor and the cylinder head. Also matchmark the timing gear and chain.

5. Mark the spark plug wires and disconnect them. Remove the mounting bolt and remove the distributor.

6. Disconnect power brake and any other vacuum hoses that are in the way. Disconnect all wiring that is in the way. Disconnect the carburetor linkage.

7. Remove the camshaft sprocket bolt and sprocket, without disturbing timing chain timing. Remove the distributor drive gear. Disconnect the air feeder hoses from underneath the vehicle.

8. If the car has power steering, unbolt the pump and move aside without disconnecting hoses.

9. Remove the ground wire and dipstick tube. Remove the exhaust manifold heat shield and separate the exhaust manifold from the catalytic converter.

10. Remove the cylinder head bolts in several stages, using the sequence illustrated. Then, pull the cylinder head off the engine.

To install:

11. Install the new gasket without sealer and

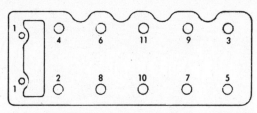

2.6L engine cylinder head bolt loosening sequence

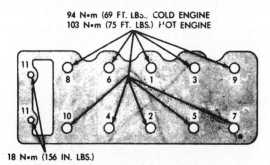

2.6L cylinder head bolt tightening sequence

in a position that causes all bolt holes and the outer border to line up with the bolt holes and outer edge of the block. Lightly oil all the bolts and install them finger tight. Then, torque the bolts to 35 ft. lbs. in the sequence shown. Now, torque the bolts to 69 ft. lbs. in the sequence shown. Torque the cylinder head to timing chain cover bolts to 156 inch lbs.

12. Connect the exhaust manifold to the catalytic converter. Install the ground wire and dipstick tube.

13. Install the power steering pump and belt and adjust the belt tension.

14. Connect the air feeder hoses from underneath the vehicle.

15. Install the camshaft sprocket and bolt and the distributor drive gear. Check the timing chain timing and ensure that it is correct.

16. Reconnect the throttle linkage.

17. Reconnect all wiring.

18. Connect the power brake and any other vacuum hoses that were disconnected.

19. Install the distributor and spark plug wires, according to the markings made at removal.

20. Connect the upper radiator hose and heater hoses. Install the cylinder head cover.

21. Install the fuel pump cover bracket and water pump pulley cover.

22. Reconnect the PCV hose.

23. Install the air cleaner and reconnect all ducting and vacuum hoses securely.

24. Connect the battery. Refill the cooling system. Start the engine and check for leaks. When the engine has reached operating tem-

perature, set the ignition timing. When the engine has cooled back off, refill the cooling system.

1989–92 2.2L And 2.5L Engines
Except DOHC Engine

1. Disconnect the negative battery cable and unbolt it from the head. Relieve the fuel pressure. Drain the cooling system. Remove the dipstick bracket nut from the thermostat housing and remove the ignition coil from the thermostat housing if it is installed there.
2. Remove the air cleaner assembly. Remove the upper radiator hose and disconnect the heater hoses.
3. Disconnect and label the vacuum lines, hoses and wiring connectors from the manifold(s), throttle body and from the cylinder head.
4. Disconnect all linkages and the fuel line from the throttle body. Unbolt the cable bracket. Remove the ground strap attaching screw from the firewall.
5. If equipped with air conditioning, remove the upper compressor mounting bolts. The cylinder head can be remove with the compressor and bracket still mounted. Remove the upper timing belt cover.
6. Raise the vehicle and support safely. Disconnect the exhaust pipe from the exhaust manifold. Disconnect the water hose and oil drain from the turbocharger, if equipped.
7. Rotate the engine by hand until the timing marks align. The No. 1 piston should be at TDC of its compression stroke. Lower the vehicle.
8. With the timing marks aligned, remove the camshaft sprocket. The camshaft sprocket can be suspended to keep the timing intact. Remove the spark plug wires from the spark plugs.
9. Remove the valve cover and curtain. Remove the cylinder head bolts and washers, starting from the outside and working inward.
10. Remove the cylinder head from the engine.
11. Clean the cylinder head gasket mating surfaces.

To install:

NOTE: *Head bolt diameter is 11mm. These bolts are identified with the number "11" on the head of the bolt. The 10mm bolts used on previous vehicles will thread into an 11mm bolt hole, but will permanently damage the cylinder block. Make sure the correct bolts are used when replacing head bolts.*

12. Using new gaskets and seals, install the head to the engine. Using new head bolts assembled with the old washers, torque the cylinder head bolts in sequence, to 45 ft. lbs. (61 Nm). Repeating the sequence, torque the bolts

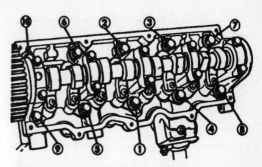

Cylinder head bolt torque sequence—2.2L and 2.5L engines, except 2.2L DOHC engine

to 65 ft. lbs. (88 Nm). With the bolts at 65 ft. lbs., turn each bolt an additional ¼ turn.
13. Install the timing belt.
14. Install or connect all items that were removed or disconnected during the removal procedure.
15. Refill the cooling system. Connect the negative battery cable. Start the engine and check for leaks using the DRB II to activate the fuel pump. Adjust the timing, as required.

2.2L Turbo III Engine

1. Disconnect the negative battery cable and unbolt it from the head. Relieve the fuel pressure. Drain the cooling system.
2. Remove the air cleaner assembly with all ductwork.
3. Remove the timing belt covers. Rotate the engine by hand until the timing marks align (No. 1 piston at TDC). Remove the timing belt.
4. Remove the air conditioning compressor and bracket from the cylinder head.
5. Disconnect the turbocharger coolant lines and separate the intake and exhaust manifolds from the cylinder head.
6. Remove the ignition cable cover and valve covers. Disconnect and label all wiring connectors, hoses and ignition wires from the cylinder head.
7. Remove the cylinder head and gasket from the engine.
8. Clean the cylinder head gasket mating surfaces.

To install:

NOTE: *The head gasket used on the Turbo III engine is unique to the engine. Make sure the replacement head gasket is identical to the original gasket before installing.*

Head bolt diameter is 11mm and the head bolts are unique to this engine. These bolts are identified with the number 11 on the head of the bolt and are not interchangeable with other engines. Make sure the correct bolts are used when replacing head bolts.

9. Using new gaskets and seals, install the

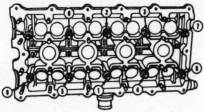

⟵ TIMING BELT END

Cylinder head bolt torque sequence—2.2L DOHC engine

head to the engine. Using new head bolts assembled with the old washers, torque the cylinder head bolts in sequence, to 45 ft. lbs. (61 Nm). Repeating the sequence, torque the bolts to 65 ft. lbs. (88 Nm). With the bolts at 65 ft. lbs., turn each bolt an additional ¼ turn. Final torque must be over 90 ft. lbs. (122 Nm).

10. Install the timing belt and all related items.

11. Install the intake and exhaust manifolds.

12. Install the air conditioning compressor and bracket the cylinder head.

13. Install the valve covers and torque the bolts to 105 inch lbs. (12 Nm).

14. Install the air cleaner assembly and all ductwork.

15. Refill the cooling system. Connect the negative battery cable. Start the engine and check for leaks.

3.0L Engine

1. Disconnect the negative battery cable. Relieve the fuel pressure. Drain the cooling system.

2. Remove the drive belt and the air conditioning compressor from its mount and support it aside. Using a ½ in. drive breaker bar, insert it into the square hole of the serpentine drive belt tensioner, rotate it counterclockwise to reduce the belt tension and remove the belt. Remove the alternator and power steering pump from the brackets and move them aside.

3. Raise the vehicle and support safely. Remove the right front wheel assembly and the right inner splash shield.

4. Remove the crankshaft pulleys and the torsional damper.

5. Lower the vehicle. Using a floor jack and a block of wood positioned under the oil pan, raise the engine slightly. Remove the engine mount bracket from the timing cover end of the engine and the timing belt covers.

6. To remove the timing belt, perform the following procedures:

a. Rotate the crankshaft to position the No. 1 cylinder on the TDC of its compression stroke; the crankshaft sprocket timing mark should align with the oil pan timing indicator

and the camshaft sprockets timing marks (triangles) should align with the rear timing belt covers timing marks.

b. Mark the timing belt in the direction of rotation for reinstallation purposes.

c. Loosen the timing belt tensioner and remove the timing belt.

NOTE: *When removing the timing belt from the camshaft sprocket, make sure the belt does not slip off of the other camshaft sprocket. Support the belt so it can not slip off of the crankshaft sprocket and opposite side camshaft sprocket.*

7. Remove the air cleaner assembly. Label and disconnect the spark plug wires and the vacuum hoses.

8. Remove the valve cover.

9. Install auto lash adjuster retainer tools MD998443 or equivalent, on the rocker arms.

10. If removing the front cylinder head, matchmark the distributor rotor-to-distributor housing and the housing-to-distributor extension locations. Remove the distributor and the distributor extension.

11. Remove the camshaft bearing assembly to cylinder head bolts (do not remove the bolts from the assembly). Remove the rocker arms, rocker shafts and bearing caps as an assembly, as required. Remove the camshafts from the cylinder head and inspect them for damage, if necessary.

12. Remove the intake manifold assembly.

13. Remove the exhaust manifold.

14. Remove the cylinder head bolts, starting from the outside and working inward. Remove the cylinder head from the engine.

15. Clean the gasket mounting surfaces and check the heads for warpage; the maximum warpage allowed is 0.008 in. (0.20mm).

To install:

16. Install the new cylinder head gaskets over the dowels on the engine block.

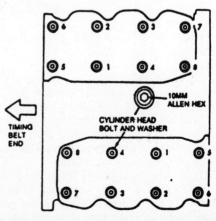

Cylinder head bolt torque sequence—3.0L engine

17. Install the cylinder heads on the engine and torque the cylinder head bolts in sequence using 3 even steps, to 70 ft. lbs. (95 Nm).

18. Install or connect all items that were removed or disconnected during the removal procedure.

19. When installing the timing belt over the camshaft sprocket, use care not to allow the belt to slip off the opposite camshaft sprocket.

20. Make sure the timing belt is installed on the camshaft sprocket in the same position as when removed.

21. Refill the cooling system. Connect the negative battery cable. Start the engine and check for leaks using the DRB II or equivalent to activate the fuel pump. Adjust the timing as required.

3.3L And 3.8L Engines

1. Relieve the fuel pressure. Disconnect the negative battery cable. Drain the cooling system.

2. Remove the intake manifold with the throttle body.

3. Disconnect the coil wires, coolant temperature sending unit wire, heater hoses and by-pass hose.

4. Remove the closed ventilation system hoses, evaporation control system hoses and valve cover.

5. Remove the exhaust manifold.

6. Remove the rocker arm and shaft assemblies. Remove the pushrods and identify them in ensure installation in their original positions.

7. Remove the head bolts and remove the cylinder head from the block.

To install:

8. Clean the gasket mounting surfaces and install a new head gasket to the block.

9. Install the head to the block. Before installing the head bolts, inspect them for

Cylinder head bolt torque sequence—3.3L/3.8L engines

stretching. Hold a straight-edge up to the threads. If the threads are not all on line, the bolt is stretched and should be replaced.

10. Torque the bolts in sequence to 45 ft. lbs. (61 Nm). Repeat the sequence and torque the bolts to 65 ft. lbs. (88 Nm). With the bolts at 65 ft. lbs., turn each bolt an additional ¼ turn.

11. Torque the lone head bolt in the rear of the head to 25 ft. lbs. (33 Nm) after the other 8 bolts have been properly torqued.

12. Install the pushrods, rocker arms and shafts and torque the bolts to 21 ft. lbs. (12 Nm).

13. Place a drop of silicone sealer onto each of the 4 manifold to cylinder head gasket corners.

CAUTION: *The intake manifold gasket is composed of very thin and sharp metal. Handle this gasket with care or damage to the gasket or personal injury could result.*

14. Install the intake manifold gasket and torque the end retainers to 105 inch lbs. (12 Nm).

15. Install the intake manifold and torque the bolts in sequence to 10 inch lbs. Repeat the sequence increasing the torque to 17 ft. lbs. (23 Nm) and recheck each bolt for 17 ft. lbs. After the bolts are torqued, inspect the seals to ensure that they have not become dislodged.

16. Lubricate the injector O-rings with clean oil and position the fuel rail in place. Install the rail mounting bolts.

17. Install the valve cover with a new gasket. Install the exhaust manifold.

18. Install or connect all remaining items that were removed or disconnected during the removal procedure.

19. Refill the cooling system. Connect the negative battery cable. Start the engine and check for leaks using the DRB I or II or equivalent to activate the fuel pump.

1990–92 Dodge Monaco 3.0L Engine

1. Relieve the fuel system pressure.

2. Disconnect the negative battery cable and drain the cooling system.

3. Remove the accessory drive belt and remove the air conditioning compressor from the cylinder head cover.

4. Remove the intake and exhaust manifolds.

5. Remove the spark plug wires. Remove the rocker arm cover.

6. Remove the alternator mounting bracket and remove the top timing case bolts that thread into the cylinder head.

NOTE: *The timing sprocket and chain must be supported in place and not allowed to drop into the timing case. If the chain and sprocket slip into the case the timing case will have to be removed.*

7. Turn the crankshaft until the camshaft

sprocket dowel is straight up. A special tool is available called a timing chain support bracket. This support bracket and dummy bearing attaches to the timing case cover. On the left cylinder head, remove the distributor assembly.

8. Remove the threaded plug on the front of the timing case cover to gain access to the camshaft sprocket bolt.

9. Remove the cylinder head bolts. Remove the rocker shaft assembly.

10. Remove the rear camshaft cover and gasket at the rear of the cylinder head.

11. Loosen the camshaft thrust plate screw, located behind the timing sprocket, and move the thrust plate up. This will allow the camshaft to move back in the head as the sprocket bolt is removed.

12. Loosen the camshaft sprocket bolt and pull the camshaft back until the bolt is free from the camshaft, the bolt will stay in the sprocket. Use an old pushrod or a long thin drift punch as a tool and insert it into the front and rear cylinder head bolt holes on the exhaust manifold side of the head. Tap the dowel down below the head gasket. The reason for this is that the cylinder head is not to be removed by pulling straight upward which would pull the cylinder liners loose from the block. It is to be bumped sideways to break the seal.

NOTE: *Do not pull straight up on the cylinder head to remove it. This will cause the cylinder liners to come out of the block.*

13. Position a block of wood on the intake manifold side of the head and strike it with a hammer, do the same on the exhaust manifold side of the head. Repeat this until the cylinder head is loose. Remove the cylinder head.

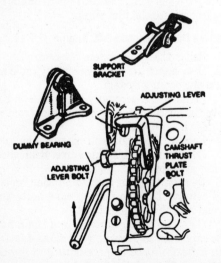

Special tools are recommended to retain cam drive when cylinder head is removed—Dodge Monaco 3.0L engine

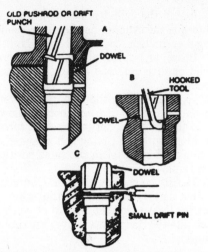

A—Push locating dowel below head gasket so cylinder head can be bumped sideways to be removed; B—Pull dowel out with hook shaped tool; C—Use pin punch to gauge depth of dowel at installation—Dodge Monaco 3.0L engine

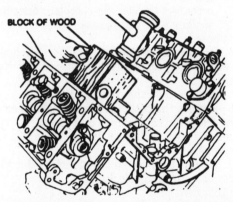

Lifting the cylinder head could dislodge the cylinder liner; instead, bump sideways as shown—Dodge Monaco 3.0L engine

NOTE: *When the cylinder head has been removed, retain the cylinder liners in the block with a liner hold-down clamp. This tool is designed to prevent the cylinder liners from being knocked out of position. If this happens, the sealing rings will dislodge or rip. Do not rotate the engine with the liner clamps in place.*

14. Remove the cylinder head gasket and clean all gasket material from mating surfaces. Remove the cylinder head locating dowels. Check that the cylinder liners protrude between 0.002–0.005 in. (0.0508–0.127mm).

To install:

15. When installing, cut the gasket flush with the cylinder head gasket face at the back of the timing case cover and remove the pieces. Clean

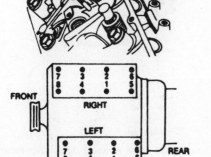

Head bolt torque sequence and angle gauge—Dodge Monaco 3.0L engine

the back of the timing cover. Cut sections of new gasket to replace the pieces removed and attach them with adhesive. Install a small punch into the hole in the block below the locating dowel bolt holes. This will act as a stop for the dowel. Push the dowel into the block until it contacts the punch.

16. Install a new cylinder head gasket over the alignment dowels on the head. Place a small bead of RTV or equivalent, at the point where the head gasket meets the timing case cover.

17. Place the cylinder head on the block and install the top timing case cover-to-cylinder head bolts finger-tight.

18. Remove the timing sprocket support tool. Position the camshaft into the sprocket and align the dowel to the slot in the camshaft. Install the sprocket bolt and lightly tighten it. Slide the thrust plate into position and tighten the thrust plate bolt to 4 ft. lbs. (5.4 Nm).

19. Install the rocker shaft assembly and install new head bolts. Using the proper sequence, tighten the cylinder head bolts in the following order:

a. Starting with bolt No. 1, torque all bolts to 44 ft. lbs. (60 Nm).

b. The following is performed on all bolts, one at a time. Starting with bolt No. 1, loosen the bolt completely, then tighten to 30 ft. lbs. (41 Nm).

c. Place an angle adapter on the torque wrench between the socket and wrench and angle tighten each bolt, in sequence, an additional 180 degrees ± 20 degrees.

d. Repeat Step C to ensure proper torque.

e. Check each bolt for at least 52 ft. lbs. (70 Nm) of torque.

20. Install the rocker covers, intake and exhaust manifolds.

21. Install the timing case plug, spark plug wires and the air conditioning compressor. Reconnect all hoses and fill the cooling system.

22. Install the distributor assembly on the left cylinder head.

23. Install the accessory drive belt and adjust the tension. Connect the negative battery terminal. Start the engine and bleed the cooling system. Check for leaks.

1990–92 Laser And Dodge Stealth

1.8L ENGINE

1. Relieve the fuel system pressure. Disconnect the negative battery cable.

2. Drain the cooling system.

3. Remove the air intake hose and the breather hose.

4. Disconnect the accelerator cable. There will be 2 cables if equipped with cruise-control.

5. Disconnect the high pressure fuel line.

6. Remove the upper radiator hose, the water breather hose, the water bypass hose and the heater hose.

7. Disconnect the PCV hose.

8. Remove the spark plug cables.

9. Disconnect and plug the fuel return line.

10. Disconnect the vacuum line for the brake booster.

11. Disconnect the electrical connections for the oxygen sensor, engine coolant temperature gauge unit and the water temperature sensor.

12. Disconnect the electrical connections for the ISC motor, throttle position sensor, distributor, MPS, fuel injectors, EGR temperature sensor (California vehicles), power transistor, condenser and ground cable.

13. Disconnect the engine control wiring harness.

14. Remove the clamp that holds the power steering pressure hose to the engine mounting bracket.

15. Place a jack and wood block under the oil pan and carefully lift just enough to take the weight off the engine mounting bracket. Then remove the bracket.

16. Remove the valve cover, gasket and half-round seal.

17. Remove the timing belt front upper cover.

18. If possible, rotate the crankshaft clockwise until the timing marks on the cam sprocket and belt align. Remove the sprocket bolt and remove the sprocket with the timing belt attached. Remove the timing belt rear upper cover.

19. Remove the exhaust pipe self-locking nuts and separate the exhaust pipe from the exhaust manifold. Discard the gasket.

20. Loosen the cylinder head mounting bolts

in 3 steps, starting from the outside and working inward. Lift off the cylinder head assembly and remove the head gasket.

To install:

21. Thoroughly clean and dry the mating surfaces of the head and block. Check the cylinder head for cracks, damage or engine coolant leakage. Remove scale, sealing compound and carbon. Clean oil passages throughly. Check the head for flatness. End to end, the head should be within 0.002 in. (0.0508MM) normally with 0.008 in. (0.203mm) the maximum allowed out of true. The total thickness allowed to be removed from the head and block is 0.008 in. (0.203mm) maximum.

22. Place a new head gasket on the cylinder block with the identification marks facing upward. Do not use sealer on the gasket.

23. Carefully install the cylinder head on the block. Using 3 even steps, torque the head bolts in sequence, to 51–54 ft. lbs. (70–75 Nm).

24. Install a new exhaust pipe gasket and connect the exhaust pipe to the manifold. Install the upper rear timing cover.

25. Align the timing marks and install the cam sprocket. Torque the retaining bolt to 58–72 ft. lbs. (80–100 Nm) on 1.8L engine. Check the belt tension and adjust if necessary. Install the outer timing cover.

26. Apply sealer to the perimeter of the half-round seal. Install a new valve cover gasket. Install the valve cover.

27. Install the engine mount bracket. Once secure, remove the jack.

28. Install the clamp that holds the power steering pressure hose to the engine mounting bracket.

29. Connect or install all previously disconnected hoses, cables and electrical connections. Adjust the throttle cable(s).

30. Replace the O-rings and connect the fuel lines.

31. Install the air intake hose. Connect the breather hose.

32. Change the engine oil.

33. Fill the system with coolant.

34. Connect the negative battery cable, run the vehicle until the thermostat opens, fill the radiator completely.

35. Check and adjust the idle speed and ignition timing.

36. Once the vehicle has cooled, recheck the coolant level.

2.0L Engine

1. Relieve fuel system pressure. Disconnect the negative battery cable.

2. Drain the cooling system.

3. Disconnect the accelerator cable. There will be 2 cables if equipped with cruise-control.

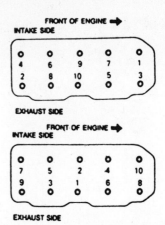

Cylinder head bolt removal and installation sequence—1990–92 Laser 1.8L and 2.0L engines

4. Remove the air cleaner with the air intake hose.

5. Disconnect the oxygen sensor, engine coolant temperature sensor, the engine coolant temperature gauge unit and the engine coolant temperature switch on vehicles with air conditioning.

6. Disconnect the ISC motor, throttle position sensor, crankshaft angle sensor, fuel injectors, ignition coil, power transistor, noise filter, knock sensor on turbocharged engines, EGR temperature sensor (California vehicles), ground cable and engine control wiring harness.

7. Remove the upper radiator hose and the overflow tube.

8. Remove the spark plug cable center cover and remove the spark plug cables.

9. Disconnect and plug the high pressure fuel line.

10. Disconnect the small vacuum hoses.

11. Remove the heater hose and water bypass hose.

12. Remove the PCV hose.

13. If turbocharged, remove the vacuum hoses, water line and eyebolt connection for the oil line for the turbo.

14. Disconnect and plug the fuel return hose.

15. Disconnect the brake booster vacuum hose.

16. Remove the timing belt.

17. Remove the valve cover and the half-round seal.

18. On non-turbocharged engines, remove the exhaust pipe self-locking nuts and separate the exhaust pipe from the exhaust manifold. Discard the gasket.

19. On turbocharged engines, remove the sheet metal heat protector and remove the bolts

that attach the turbocharger to the exhaust manifold.

20. Loosen the cylinder head mounting bolts in 3 steps, starting from the outside and working inward. Lift off the cylinder head assembly and remove the head gasket.

To install:

21. Thoroughly clean and dry the mating surfaces of the head and block. Check the cylinder head for cracks, damage or engine coolant leakage. Remove scale, sealing compound and carbon. Clean oil passages throughly. Check the head for flatness. End to end, the head should be within 0.002 in. (0.0508mm) normally with 0.008 in. (0.203mm) the maximum allowed out of true. The total thickness allowed to be removed from the head and block is 0.008 in. (0.203mm) maximum.

22. Place a new head gasket on the cylinder block with the identification marks facing upward. Do not use sealer on the gasket. Replace the turbo gasket and ring, if equipped.

23. Carefully install the cylinder head on the block. Using 3 even steps, torque the head bolts in sequence, to 65–72 ft. lbs. (90–100 Nm).

24. On turbocharged engine, install the heat shield. On non-turbocharged engine, install a new exhaust pipe gasket and connect the exhaust pipe to the manifold.

25. Apply sealer to the perimeter of the half-round seal and to the lower edges of the half-round portions of the belt-side of the new gasket. Install the valve cover.

26. Install the timing belt and all related items.

27. Connect or install all previously disconnected hoses, cables and electrical connections. Adjust the throttle cable(s).

28. Install the spark plug cable center cover.

29. Replace the O-rings and connect the fuel lines.

30. Install the air cleaner and intake hose. Connect the breather hose.

31. Change the engine oil.

32. Fill the system with coolant.

33. Connect the negative battery cable, run the vehicle until the thermostat opens, fill the radiator completely.

34. Check and adjust the idle speed and ignition timing.

35. Once the vehicle has cooled, recheck the coolant level.

3.0L SOHC Engine

1. Relieve fuel system pressure. Disconnect the negative battery cable.

2. Drain the cooling system.

3. Remove the air intake hose.

4. Remove the exhaust manifold.

5. Remove the air intake plenum and intake manifold.

6. Remove the timing belt.

7. Remove the camshaft sprocket and rear timing belt cover.

8. Remove the power steering pump bracket. If removing the rear (right) side head, remove the alternator brace.

9. Disconnect the water inlet pipe.

10. Remove the purge pipe assembly.

11. Remove the valve cover.

12. Loosen the cylinder head mounting bolts in 3 steps, starting from the outside and working inward. Lift off the cylinder head assembly and remove the head gasket.

To install:

13. Thoroughly clean and dry the mating surfaces of the head and block. Check the cylinder head for cracks, damage or engine coolant leakage. Remove scale, sealing compound and carbon. Clean oil passages throughly. Check the head for flatness. End to end, the head should be within 0.002 in. (0.0508mnm) normally with 0.008 in. (0.0508mm) the maximum allowed out of true. The total thickness allowed to be removed from the head and block is 0.008 in. (0.0508mm) maximum.

14. Place a new head gasket on the cylinder block with the identification marks facing upward. Do not use sealer on the gasket.

15. Carefully install the cylinder head on the block. Make sure the head bolt washers are installed with the chamfered edge upward. Using 3 even steps, torque the head bolts in sequence, to 76–83 ft. lbs. (105–115 Nm).

16. Apply sealer to the lower edges of the half-round portions of the belt-side of the new gasket and install the valve cover.

17. Install the purge pipe assembly.

18. Connect the water inlet pipe.

19. Install the power steering pump bracket and alternator brace.

20. Install the rear timing belt cover and cam sprocket. Torque the retaining bolt to 60–70 ft. lbs. (81–95 Nm).

21. Install the timing belt and all related items.

22. Using all new gaskets, install the intake manifold, air intake plenum and exhaust manifold, following the proper torque sequences.

23. Install the air intake hose.

24. Change the engine oil.

25. Fill the system with coolant.

26. Connect the negative battery cable, run the vehicle until the thermostat opens, fill the radiator completely.

27. Check and adjust the idle speed and ignition timing.

28. Once the vehicle has cooled, recheck the coolant level.

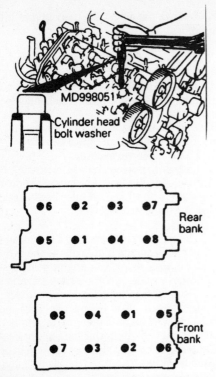

Cylinder head bolt installation sequence—Dodge
Stealth 3.0L engine

3.0L DOHC Engine

1. Reieve fuel system pressure. Disconnect the negative battery cable.

2. Drain the cooling system.

3. Remove the air intake hoses.

4. Remove air intake plenum and intake manifold.

5. Remove the turbocharger if equipped, and exhaust manifold.

6. Remove the timing belt.

7. Remove the triple pipe assembly across the top of the engine.

8. Remove the breather hose.

9. Remove the spark plug cable center cover and remove the spark plug cables.

10. When removing the valve cover, note that bolts for the front head are black and bolts for the rear head are green. Also, all bolts are 10mm long except the 1 closest to the sprockets on the rear head which is 20mm long.

11. To remove the intake camshaft sprocket, hold the camshaft with a wrench on the hexagon near the end of the camshaft and remove the bolt.

12. Remove the center rear timing belt cover.

13. Remove the ignition coil.

14. Disconnect all water hoses from the thermostat housing and remove the housing.

15. Disconnect the water inlet from the front head.

16. Loosen the cylinder head mounting bolts in 3 steps, starting from the outside and working inward. Lift off the cylinder head assembly and remove the head gasket.

To install:

17. Thoroughly clean and dry the mating surfaces of the head and block. Check the cylinder head for cracks, damage or engine coolant leakage. Remove scale, sealing compound and carbon. Clean oil passages throughly. Check the head for flatness. End to end, the head should be within 0.002 in. (0.0508mm) normally with 0.008 in. (0.203mm) the maximum allowed out of true. The total thickness allowed to be removed from the head and block is 0.008 in. (0.203mm) maximum.

18. Place a new head gasket on the cylinder block with the identification marks facing upward. Do not use sealer on the gasket.

19. Carefully install the cylinder head on the block. Make sure the head bolt washers are installed with the chamfered edge upward. Using 3 even steps, torque the head bolts in sequence, to 76–83 ft. lbs. (105–115 Nm) for non-turbocharged engine or 87–94 ft. lbs. (120–130 Nm) for turbocharged engine.

20. Connect the water inlet to the front head.

21. Replace the gaskets and install the thermostat housing and connect the hoses.

22. Install the ignition coil and center rear timing belt cover.

23. Using the same procedure as in removal, install the intake camshaft sprocket. Torque the retaining bolt to 60–70 ft. lbs. (81–95 Nm).

24. Apply sealer to the lower edges of the half-round portions of the belt-side of the new gasket and install the valve cover. Make sure green bolts are installed on the rear head and black bolts are installed on the front head. Also, make sure the longest bolt is installed in its proper location closest to the sprockets on the rear head. Tighten the bolts in the proper sequence to 26

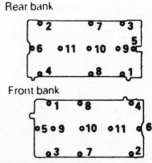

Valve cover bolt installation sequence—Dodge Stealth
3.0L DOHC engine

inch lbs. Then retighten bolts 1–6 to 36 inch lbs.

25. Connect the spark plug cables and install the center cover.

26. Install the breather hose.

27. Install the triple pipe assembly across the top of the engine.

28. Install the timing belt and all related items.

29. Using all new gaskets, install the intake manifold, air intake plenum, turbocharger and exhaust manifold, following the proper torque sequences.

30. Install the air intake hoses.

31. Change the engine oil.

32. Fill the system with coolant.

34. Connect the negative battery cable, run the vehicle until the thermostat opens, fill the radiator completely.

35. Check and adjust the idle speed and ignition timing.

36. Once the vehicle has cooled, recheck the coolant.

CLEANING AND INSPECTION

1. With the valves installed to protect the valve seats, remove deposits from the combustion chambers and valve heads with a scraper and a wire brush. Be careful not to damage the cylinder head gasket surface. After the valves are removed, clean the valve guide bores with a valve guide cleaning tool. Using cleaning solvent to remove dirt, grease and other deposits, clean all bolts holes; be sure the oil passage is clean (V6 engines).

2. Remove all deposits from the valves with a fine wire brush or buffing wheel.

3. Inspect the cylinder heads for cracks or excessively burned areas in the exhaust outlet ports.

4. Check the cylinder head for cracks and inspect the gasket surface for burrs and nicks. Replace the head if it is cracked.

5. On cylinder heads that incorporate valve seat inserts, check the inserts for excessive wear, cracks, or looseness.

RESURFACING

Cylinder Head Flatness

When the cylinder head is removed, check the flatness of the cylinder head gasket surfaces. Refer to a machine shop for cylinder head refinishing specifications and procedure as necessary.

1. Place a straightedge across the gasket surface of the cylinder head. Using feeler gauges, determine the clearance at the center of the straightedge.

2. If warpage exceeds 0.003 in. (0.076mm) in a 6 in. (152mm) span, or 0.006 in. (0.152mm) over the total length, the cylinder head must be resurfaced.

3. If it is necessary to refinish the cylinder head gasket surface, do not plane or grind off more than 0.254mm (0.010 in.) from the original gasket surface.

NOTE: *When milling the cylinder heads of V6 engines, the intake manifold mounting position is altered, and must be corrected by milling the manifold flange a proportionate amount. Consult an experienced machinist about this.*

Valves

REMOVAL AND INSTALLATION

NOTE: *Use the following service procedures as a guide for your engine. Machine shop work requires special training and equipment, it is best to send the cylinder head (valve job) assembly to a reputable machine shop for this kind of repair.*

2.2L and 2.5L Engines

1. Remove the cylinder head described above. Mark all valves and rockers for reinstallation in the same positions.

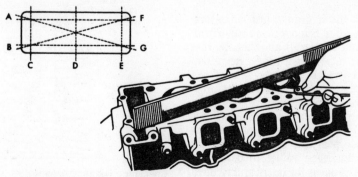

Inspect the cylinder head for flatness in every direction illustrated

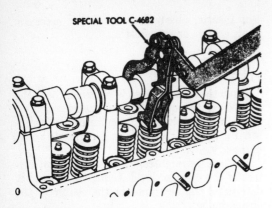

Removing and installing valve springs typical 4-cylinder engine

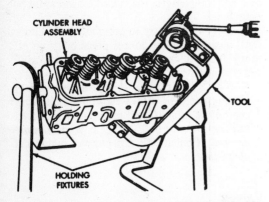

Compress valve springs with special tools typical 6-cylinder engine

2. Situate the head so the valves will be free to move downward. You'll need a valve spring compressor tool such as Chrysler No. 4682. This tool hooks around the thinnest diameter sections of the camshaft and pushes downward on either side of each valve spring retainer. Rotate the camshaft so the first rocker arm is under the base circle of the cam. Then, depress the valve spring with the special tool just until the rocker arm can be slid out.

3. Repeat this procedure for each of the rest of the rockers.

4. Remove all the hydraulic lash adjusters, keeping them in order. Support each valve from underneath as you work on it and then depress each valve spring retainer with the special tool. Remove the keepers from either side of the valve stem and then slowly release spring pressure. Remove the spring.

5. Remove the stem seal by gently prying it side-to-side with a screwdriver blade. Work the seal off the guide post and remove it. Repeat Steps 4 and 5 for each valve. Inspect each valve's stem lock grooves for burrs and remove them prior to removing the valve; otherwise,

valve guides may be damaged. Then, the valves may be removed from the head from underneath.

6. To install, first coat the valve stems with clean engine oil, and then insert each valve into the guide from the lower side of the head.

7. Install new valve seals by pushing each firmly and squarely over the guide so that the center bead of the seal lodges in the valve guide groove. The lower edge of the seal must rest on the valve guide boss. Note that if oversize valves have been installed, oversize seals must also be installed. Install the valve springs.

8. Support the valve you're working on from underneath. Install the valve spring retainer over each spring, depress the spring just enough to expose the grooves for the spring keepers. Make sure to depress the spring squarely so the spring does not touch the valve stem. Install the keepers securely and raise the retainer slowly, making sure the keepers stay in position. Repeat these steps for all valves.

9. Install each of the hydraulic lash adjusters in its proper position.

10. Check the valve spring installed height. If it exceeds specifications, valve spring tension will not be adequate. If necessary, install a spring seat under each spring whose height is too great to make it meet specification.

11. Support the head so that the valves will be free to move downward. Install the rockers, each in its original position, in reverse of the removal procedure. Depress the valve spring retainers only enough to install the rockers, and make sure the keepers stay in place. Check the clearance between the ears of the rocker arm and the spring retainer for each valve with the lash adjuster dry of oil and fully collapsed. If the minimum clearance is not met, the rocker will have to be machined to create it. After clearance specifications are met, remove the rockers and adjusters, immerse adjusters in clean engine oil and pump them to prime them with oil. Finally, reinstall the adjusters and rockers.

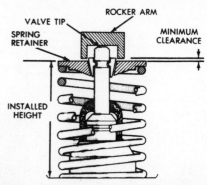

Checking clearance between the valve rocker ears and spring retainers on the 2.2 and 2.5L engines

Make sure, if you're working with the head on the engine, you don't turn the camshaft until lifters have had at least 10 minutes to leak down.

2.6L Engine

1. Remove the cylinder head as described above. Remove the camshaft bearing caps and rocker shafts as an assembly (see the procedure for camshaft removal). Leave the bolts in the front and rear caps.

2. Using a spring compressor designed for use on overhead cam engines with inclined valves, depress each valve spring, remove keepers, and then remove each valve from underneath. Support each valve while doing this so you won't have to depress the spring unnecessarily.

3. Remove each jet valve by unscrewing it with a special socket wrench designed for this purpose. Pull out valve stems seals with a pair of pliers.

4. Valve stems should be coated with oil before each valve is installed. Assemble the springs, retainers, and keepers, making sure you do not depress retainers unnecessarily. Check installed height and compare it with specification. If installed height is excessive, install a thicker spring seat until specifications are met. Disassemble valves, springs, and retainers.

5. Install new valve seals onto the cylinder head by tapping them lightly via a special installer such as Chrysler part No. MD998005. Now, springs, retainers, and keepers may be installed.

6. Install jet valves by screwing them in. Torque to 168 inch lbs. The jet valves themselves have springs, retainers, keepers, and seals. You'll need a special tool No. MD998309 to compress the spring, and another, No. MD998308 to install the seal. Keep all jet valve parts together for each jet valve assembly — do not mix them up. The jet valve stem seal is installed by tapping on the special tool to gently force the seal over the jet body. Also, install a new jet valve O-ring coated with clean engine oil before installing the jet valve back into the head.

7. Make sure in final assembly to set the jet valve clearance after the head bolts are torqued and before setting intake valve clearance. Both must finally be set with the engine hot.

INSPECTION

2.2 and 2.5 Liter Engines

1. Clean the valves thoroughly and discard burned, warped, or cracked valves.

2. If the valve face is only lightly pitted, the

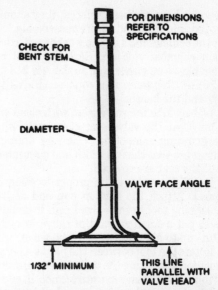

Critical valve dimensions—2.2 and 2.5L engines

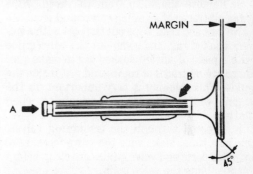

Critical valve dimensions—2.6 liter engine

valve may be refaced to the correct angle by a qualified machine shop.

3. Measure the valve stem for wear at various points and check it against the specifications shown in the "Valve Specifications" chart.

4. Once the valve face has been cleaned up, margin must also be checked. This is the thickness of the valve head below the face. Valves must also meet standards as to head diameter and length.

2.6 Liter Engine

1. Check the tip of the stem for pitting (A).

2. Check stem to guide clearance (B). It must be to specifications.

3. Check margin. It must be to specifications. If reusable, valves should be refaced by a competent automotive machine shop.

REFACING

The valve must be lapped into their seats after resurfacing, to ensure proper sealing. Even if the valve have not been refaced, they should be lapped into the head before reassembly.

Set the cylinder head on the workbench, combustion chamber side up. Rest the head on wooden blocks on either end, so there is 2–3 in. (51–76mm) between the tops of the valve guides and the bench.

1. Lightly lube the valve stem with clean engine oil. Coat the valve seat completely with valve grinding compound. Use just enough compound so that the full width and circumference of the seat are covered.

2. Install the valve in its proper location in the head. Attach the suction cup end of the valve lapping tool to the valve head. It usually helps to put a small amount of saliva into the suction cup to aid it sticking to the valve.

3. Rotate the tool between the palms, changing position and lifting the tool often to prevent grooving. Lap the valve in until a smooth, evenly polished seat and valve face are evident.

4. Remove the valve from the head. Wipe away all traces of grinding compound from the valve face and seat. Wipe out the port with a solvent soaked rag, and swab out the valve guide with a piece of solvent soaked rag to make sure there are no traces of compound grit inside the guide. This cleaning is very important, as the engine will ingest any grit remaining when started.

5. Proceed through the remaining valves, one at a time. Make sure the valve faces, sets, cylinder ports and valve guides are clean before reassembling the valve train.

Valve Springs

REMOVAL AND INSTALLATION

The valve springs are removed and installed as described just above under Valve Removal and Installation.

INSPECTION

Place the valve spring on a flat surface next to a carpenter's square. Measure the height of the spring, and rotate the spring against the edge of the square to measure distortion. If the spring height varies (by comparison) by more than $1/16$ in. (1.6mm) or if the distortion exceeds $1/16$ in. (1.6mm), replace the spring.

Have the valve springs tested for spring pressure at the installed and compressed (installed height minus valve lift) height using a valve spring tester. Springs should be within one pound, plus or minus each other. Replace springs as necessary.

VALVE SPRING INSTALLED HEIGHT

After installing the valve spring, measure the distance between the spring mounting pad and

Testing valve spring with special tool

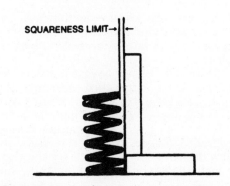

Check spring length and squareness with a steel square tool

Valve stem seals

the lower edge of the spring retainer. Compare the measurement to specifications. If the installed height is incorrect, add shim washers between the spring mounting pad and the spring. Use only washers designed for valve springs, available at most parts houses.

VALVE STEM OIL SEALS

When installing valve stem oil seals, ensure that a small amount of oil is able to pass the seal to lubricate the valve stems and guide walls, otherwise, excessive wear will occur.

Valve Seats

REMOVAL AND INSTALLATION

The seats are integral with the aluminum cylinder head on all engines and so can only be machined to specification, not replaced. If a seat is too worn to be brought to specification, the head must be replaced.

CUTTING THE SEATS

Measuring and, if necessary, cutting the valve seat surfaces of the cylinder head are operations requiring precision instruments and machinery. In some cases, if wear is excessive, the cylinder head may have to be replaced, as seats are integral with the head.

Valve Guides

REMOVAL AND INSTALLATION

2.2 and 2.5 Liter Engines

Valve guides are replaceable, but it is necessary to first make sure the valve seats can be

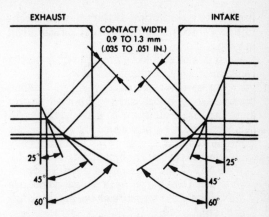

Valve seat dimensions and angles—2.6 liter engine

Measuring valve guide wear

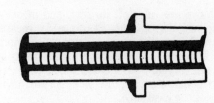

Cross-section of a knurled valve guide

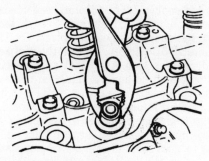

Removing valve stem seals

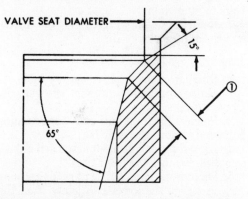

Valve seat dimensions and angles—2.2 liter engine

Lapping a valve in by hand

brought to specification. If the valve seats cannot be refaced, the head must be replaced anyway.

Worn guides should be pressed out from the combustion chamber side and new guides pressed in as far as they will go. In some cases, existing guides can be "knurled" to restore the inside diameter to specifications. All this work must be performed by a competent machine shop, as special skills and extremely sophisticated special equipment are required.

WARNING: *Service valve guides have a shoulder. Once the guide is seated, do not use more than 1 ton pressure or the guide shoulder could break.*

STEM-TO-GUIDE CLEARANCE

Valve stem-to-guide clearance should be checked upon assembling the cylinder head, and is especially necessary if the valve guides have been reamed or knurled, or if oversize valve have been installed. Excessive oil consumption often is a result of too much clearance between the valve guide and valve stem.

1. Clean the valve stem with lacquer thinner or a similar solvent to remove all gum and varnish. Clean the valve guides using solvent and an expanding wire-type valve guide cleaner (a rifle cleaning brush works well here).

2. Mount a dial indicator so that the stem is 90° to the valve stem and as close to the valve guide as possible.

3. Move the valve off its seat, and measure the valve guide-to-stem clearance by rocking the stem back and forth to actuate the dial indicator. Measure the valve stems using a micrometer and compare to specifications, to determine whether stem or guide wear is responsible for excessive clearance.

Oil Pan

REMOVAL AND INSTALLATION

CAUTION: *The EPA warns that prolonged contact with used engine oil may cause a number of skin disorders, including cancer! You should make every effort to minimize your exposure to used engine oil. Protective gloves should be worn when changing the oil. Wash your hands and any other exposed skin areas as soon as possible after exposure to used engine oil. Soap and water, or waterless hand cleaner should be used.*

All Vehicles Except
1990–92 Laser, Dodge Monaco and Stealth

1. Drain the engine oil. On some later model vehicles, remove the engine to transaxle struts if so equipped and torque converter or clutch inspection cover.

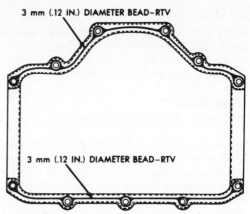

Apply sealer to the oil pan on 2.2 and 2.5L engines as shown

2. Support the pan and remove the attaching bolts.

3. Lower the pan and remove the gasket, if it has one.

4. Clean all gasket surfaces thoroughly. Install the 2.6L pan using gasket sealer and a new gasket.

NOTE: *The 2.2 and 2.5 Liter engine uses a form-in-place type gasket. Chrysler Part Number 4205918 or its equivalent RTV gasket material must be used.*

5. On all 2.2 and 2.5L engines, use new end seals and apply a 1.2 in. (31mm) bead of sealer to the rest of the pan. Make sure to apply sealer where the end seals meet the block. On 1988 and later 2.5L engines, replace the end seals and the side gaskets. Apply RTV to the parting lines between end and side seals on these engines. If necessary, use grease or RTV to hold the side seals in place. On 3.0L, 3.3L and 3.8L engines apply silicone sealer to the chain cover to block mating seam and the rear main seal retainer to block seam-install new oil pan gasket.

6. Torque the pan bolts to 200 inch lbs. (2.2 and 2.5 Liter) and 5 ft. lbs. (2.6 Liter). On 3.0L, 3.3L and 3.8L engines torque oil pan retaining bolts to 50 inch lbs.

7. Refill the engine with oil, start the engine, and check for leaks.

1990–92 Dodge Monco 3.0L Engine

1. Disconnect the negative battery cable.

2. Raise and safely support the vehicle. Drain the oil.

3. Remove the front anti-sway bar retaining bolts and remove the sway bar.

4. Loosen the engine mount stud and nut assemblies. Remove the front tires.

5. Remove the lower ball joint retaining bolts and disengage the lower ball joints from the steering knuckles.

6. Remove the nuts at the center of the transaxle crossmember securing the rear of the transaxle to the crossmember.

7. Lower the vehicle and attach engine support tool MS–1900 to the engine.

8. With the vehicle lowered, loosen the 4 sub-frame attaching nuts. Remove the front 2 first, allowing the sub-frame to pivot to the ground. Support the rear of the sub-frame and remove the 2 rear nuts. Lower the sub-frame away from the vehicle.

9. Raise and support the vehicle. Remove the oil pan retaining bolts and remove the oil pan.

To install:

10. Thoroughly clean and dry the mating surfaces of the pan and block.

11. Install the oil pan to the engine block using a new gasket. Do not use any sealer on the gasket; it must be installed dry. Tighten all of the retaining bolts to 9 ft. lbs. (12 Nm).

12. Install the sub-frame assembly and tighten the mounting nuts to 92 ft. lbs. (125 Nm).

13. Connect the lower ball joints and tighten the attaching nut to 77 ft. lbs. (104 Nm). Tighten the transaxle-to-crossmember bolts to 20 ft. lbs. (27 Nm).

14. Remove the engine support tool. Attach the anti-sway bar and install the front wheels.

15. Lower the vehicle. Fill the crankcase with the appropriate quantity and grade of oil.

16. Connect the negative battery cable and check for leaks.

1990–92 Laser And Dodge Stealth

1. Disconnect the negative battery cable.

2. Raise the vehicle and support safely.

3. Remove the oil pan drain plug and drain the engine oil.

4. On 1.8L engine, disconnect and lower the exhaust pipe.

5. On 2.0L engine, remove the crossmember, disconnect and lower the exhaust pipe and on turbocharged engines, disconnect the return pipe for the turbocharger from the side of the oil pan.

6. Remove the oil pan mounting bolts, separate and remove the engine oil pan.

To install:

7. Thoroughly clean and dry the oil pan, cylinder block bolts and bolt holes.

8. Apply a thin bead of sealer around the surface of the oil pan.

9. Assemble the oil pan to the cylinder block within 15 minutes after applying the sealant.

10. Install the oil pan mounting bolts and torque to 4–6 ft. lbs. (6–8 Nm).

11. Fill the engine with the proper amount of oil.

12. Connect the negative battery cable and check for leaks.

Oil Pump
REMOVAL AND INSTALLATION

CAUTION: *The EPA warns that prolonged contact with used engine oil may cause a number of skin disorders, including cancer! You should make every effort to minimize your exposure to used engine oil. Protective gloves should be worn when changing the oil. Wash your hands and any other exposed skin areas as soon as possible after exposure to used engine oil. Soap and water, or waterless hand cleaner should be used.*

2.2L And 2.5L Engines

NOTE: *Many of the following steps pertain to engines with a distributor. Disregard these steps when working on Turbo III engine. Since that engine does not have a distributor, the oil pump can be installed without timing the distributor gear. The oil pump on all other engines must be properly timed.*

1. Crank the engine so the No. 1 piston is at TDC of its compression stroke. Disconnect the negative battery cable.

2. Matchmark the rotor to the block and remove the distributor to confirm that the slot in the oil pump shaft is parallel to the centerline of the crankshaft. Matchmark the slot to the distributor bore, if desired.

3. Remove the dipstick. Raise the vehicle and support safely. Drain the engine oil and remove the pan.

4. Remove the oil pickup.

5. Remove the 2 mounting bolts and remove the oil pump from the engine.

To install:

6. Prime the pump by pouring fresh oil into the pump intake and turning the driveshaft until oil comes out the pressure port. Repeat a few times until no air bubbles are present.

7. Apply Loctite® 515 or equivalent, to the pump body to block machined surface interface.

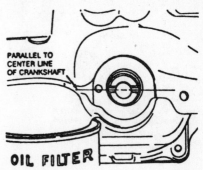

Aligning the slot in the oil pump shaft—2.2L/2.5L engines

Lubricate the oil pump and distributor driveshaft.

8. Align the slot so it will be in the same position as when it was removed. If it is not, the distributor will not be timed correctly. Install the pump fully and rotate back and forth to ensure proper positioning between the pump mounting surface and the machined surface of the block.

9. Install the mounting bolts finger-tight and lower the vehicle to confirm proper slot positioning. If the slot is not properly positioned, raise the vehicle and move the gear as required. If the slot is correct, hold the pump firmly against the block and torque the mounting bolts to 17 ft. lbs. (23 Nm).

10. Clean out the oil pickup or replace, as required. Replace the oil pickup O-ring and install the pickup to the pump.

11. Install the oil pan using new gaskets. Lower the vehicle.

12. Install the distributor.

13. Install the dipstick. Fill the engine with the proper amount of oil.

14. Connect the negative battery cable, check the timing and check the oil pressure.

2.6L Engines

See Timing Chain, Cover, Silent Shaft and Tensioner removal and installation procedure.

3.0L Engine

1. Disconnect the negative battery cable. Remove the dipstick.

2. Raise the vehicle and support safely. Remove the timing belt, drain the engine oil and remove the oil pan from the engine. Remove the oil pickup.

3. Remove the oil pump mounting bolts and remove the pump from the front of the engine.

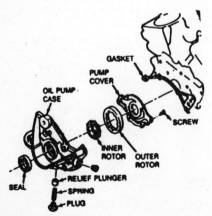

Exploded view of the oil pump assembly—Dodge Monaco 3.0L engine

Note the different length bolts and their position in the pump for installation.

To install:

4. Clean the gasket mounting surfaces of the pump and engine block.

5. Prime the pump by soaking its components with fresh oil and turning the rotors or, using petroleum jelly, pack the inside of the oil pump. Using a new gasket, install the oil pump on the engine and torque all bolts to 11 ft. lbs. (15 Nm).

6. Install the balancer and crankshaft sprocket to the end of the crankshaft.

7. Clean out the oil pickup or replace, as required. Replace the oil pickup gasket ring and install the pickup to the pump.

8. Install the timing belt, oil pan and all related parts.

9. Install the dipstick. Fill the engine with the proper amount of oil.

10. Connect the negative battery cable and check the oil pressure.

3.3L And 3.8L Engines

1. Disconnect the negative battery cable. Remove the dipstick.

2. Raise the vehicle and support safely. Drain the oil and remove the oil pan.

3. Remove the oil pickup.

4. Remove the chain case cover.

5. Disassemble the oil pump and remove its components from the block.

To install:

6. Assemble the pump. Torque the cover screws to 10 ft. lbs. (12 Nm).

7. Prime the oil pump by filling the rotor cavity with fresh oil and turning the rotors until oil comes out the pressure port. Repeat a few times until no air bubbles are present.

8. Install the chain case cover.

9. Clean out the oil pickup or replace, if necessary. Replace the oil pickup O-ring and install the pickup to the pump.

10. Install the oil pan.

11. Install the dipstick. Fill the engine with the proper amount of oil.

12. Connect the negative battery cable and check the oil pressure.

1990–92 Dodge Monaco 3.0L Engine

1. Disconnect the negative battery cable.

2. Remove the timing chain cover assembly.

3. Remove the bolts retaining the oil pump drive sprocket. Remove the sprocket and the oil pump drive chain.

4. Remove the oil pump mounting bolts and remove the oil pump.

To install:

5. Thoroughly clean and dry the mating surfaces of the pump and block. Install the oil

pump to the block using a new gasket. Tighten the bolts to 9 ft. lbs. (12 Nm).

6. Install the oil pump drive sprocket and chain. Coat the threads of the sprocket bolts with a thread locking compound and torque them to 48 inch lbs. (5.4 Nm).

7. Install the timing chain cover.

8. Connect the negative battery cable and check for leaks. Check for sufficient oil pressure.

1990–92 Laser And Dodge Stealth

NOTE: *Whenever the oil pump is disassembled or the cover removed, the gear cavity must be filled with petroleum jelly for priming purposes. Do not use grease.*

1. Disconnect the negative battery cable.

2. Remove the front engine mount bracket and accessory drive belts.

3. Remove timing belt upper and lower covers.

4. Remove the timing belt and crankshaft sprocket.

5. Remove the oil pan.

6. Remove the oil screen and gasket.

7. Remove the front cover mounting bolts.

8. Note and mark the lengths of the mounting bolts as they are removed for proper installation.

9. Remove the front case cover and oil pump assembly. If necessary, the silent shaft can come out with the assembly. Disassemble as required.

To install:

10. Thoroughly clean all gasket material from all mounting surfaces.

11. Apply engine oil to the entire surface of the gears or rotors.

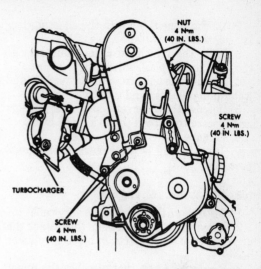

Timing cover attachments—2.2 and 2.5L engines

12. On engines with silent shafts, install the drive/driven gears with the 2 timing marks aligned.

13. Assemble the front case cover and oil pump assembly to the engine block using a new gasket.

14. Install the oil screen with new gasket.

15. Install the oil pan and timing belts.

16. Connect the negative battery cable and check for adequate oil pressure.

Timing Belt Cover
REMOVAL AND INSTALLATION
1981–88 2.2 and 2.5L Engines

1. Loosen the alternator mounting bolts, pivot the alternator and remove the drive belt.

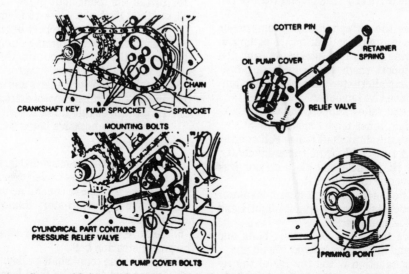

Engine oil pump drive, mount components and priming point—Dodge Monaco 3.0L engine

2. Do the same thing with the air conditioning compressor.

3. Raise the vehicle on a hoist and remove the right inner splash shield.

4. Remove the bolts from the crankshaft and water pump pulleys and remove both.

5. Remove the cover retaining nuts, washers and spacers from both the block and head.

6. Remove the cover.

7. Installation is the reverse of removal procedure.

1989–92 2.2L And 2.5L Engines

1. Disconnect the negative battery cable.

2. Remove the nuts and bolts that attach the upper cover to the valve cover, block or cylinder head.

3. Remove the bolt that attaches the upper cover to the lower cover.

4. Remove the upper cover.

5. Raise the vehicle and support safely. Remove the right wheel and side splash shield.

6. Remove the crankshaft pulley, water pump pulley and the belt(s).

7. Remove the lower cover attaching bolts.

8. Remove the lower cover.

9. The installation is the reverse of the removal procedure.

3.0L Engine

1. Disconnect the negative battery cable.

2. If equipped with air conditioning, loosen the adjustment pulley locknut, turn the screw counterclockwise to reduce the drive belt tension and remove the belt.

3. To remove the serpentine drive belt, insert a ½ in. breaker bar in to the square hole of the tensioner pulley, rotate it counterclockwise to reduce the drive belt tension and remove the belt.

4. Remove the air conditioning compressor and the air compressor bracket, if equipped, power steering pump and alternator from the mounts; support them aside. Remove power steering pump/alternator automatic belt tensioner bolt and the tensioner.

5. Raise and safely support the vehicle. Remove the right inner fender splash shield.

6. Remove the crankshaft pulley bolt and the pulley/damper assembly from the crankshaft.

7. Lower the vehicle and place a floor jack under the engine to support it.

8. Separate the front engine mount insulator from the bracket. Raise the engine slightly and remove the mount bracket.

9. Remove the timing belt cover bolts and the upper and lower covers from the engine.

10. The installation is the reverse of the removal procedure.

1990–92 Laser And Dodge Stealth
EXCEPT 3.0L ENGINE

1. Disconnect the negative battery cable.

2. Remove the engine undercover.

3. Using the proper equipment, slightly raise the engine to take the weight off of the side engine mount. Remove the engine mount bracket.

4. Remove the drive belts, tension pulley brackets, water pump pulley and crankshaft pulley.

5. Remove all attaching screws and remove the upper and lower timing belt covers.

6. The installation is the reverse of the removal procedure. Make sure all pieces of packing are positioned in the inner grooves of the covers when installing.

3.0L SOHC ENGINE

1. Disconnect the negative battery cable.

2. Remove the engine undercover.

3. Remove the cruise control actuator.

4. Remove the accessory drive belts.

5. Remove the air conditioner compressor tension pulley assembly.

6. Remove the tension pulley bracket.

7. Using the proper equipment, slightly raise the engine to take the weight off of the side engine mount. Remove the engine mounting bracket.

8. Remove the power steering pump.

9. Remove the engine support bracket.

10. Remove the crankshaft pulley.

11. Remove the timing belt cover cap.

12. Remove the timing belt upper and lower covers.

To install:

13. Install the timing covers. Make sure all pieces of packing are positioned in the inner grooves of the covers when installing.

14. Install the crankshaft pulley. Torque the bolt to 108–116 ft. lbs. (150–160 Nm).

15. Install the engine support bracket.

16. Install the power steering pump.

17. Install the engine mounting bracket and remove the engine support fixture.

18. Install the tension pulleys and drive belts.

19. Install the cruise control actuator.

20. Install the engine undercover.

21. Connect the negative battery cable.

3.0L DOHC ENGINE

1. Disconnect the negative battery cable.

2. Remove the engine undercover.

3. Remove the cruise control actuator.

4. Remove the alternator. Remove the air hose and pipe.

5. Remove the belt tensioner assembly and the power steering belt.

6. Remove the crankshaft pulley.

7. Disconnect the brake fluid level sensor.

8. Remove the timing belt upper cover.

9. Using the proper equipment, slightly raise the engine to take the weight off of the side engine mount. Remove the engine mount bracket.

10. Remove the alternator/air conditioner idler pulley.

11. Remove the engine support bracket. The mounting bolts are different lengths; mark them for proper installation.

12. Remove the timing belt lower cover.

To install:

13. Make sure all pieces of packing are positioned in the inner grooves of the lower cover and install.

14. Install the engine support bracket. Lubricate the reaming area of the reamer bolt slowly as it is installed.

15. Install the idler pulley.

16. Install the engine mount bracket. Remove the engine support fixture.

17. Make sure all pieces of packing are positioned in the inner grooves of the upper cover and install.

18. Connect the brake fluid level sensor.

19. Install the crankshaft pullet. Torque the bolt to 130–137 ft. lbs. (180–190 Nm).

20. Install the belt tensioner assembly and the power steering belt.

21. Install the air hose and pipe.

22. Install the alternator.

23. Install the cruise control actuator.

24. Install the engine undercover.

25. Connect the negative battery cable.

Timing Belt

REMOVAL AND INSTALLATION

1981–88 2.2L and 2.5L Engines

NOTE: *To perform this procedure, you will need a special tool No. C–4703 or equivalent to apply specified tension to the timing belt. Be careful not to allow the timing belt to come in contact with oil or any solvent, or the teeth will be weakened.*

1. Disconnect the negative battery cable. Remove the timing belt cover as described above.

2. Place a floor jack under the engine. Spread the load is such a way that the oil pan will not be damaged. Then, remove the main through bolt from the right engine mount — the one that is situated right near the timing cover.

3. Raise the engine slightly for access to the crankshaft sprocket.

4. Using the larger bolt on the crankshaft pulley, turn the engine until the #1 cylinder is at TDC of the compression stroke. At this point the valves for the #1 cylinder will be closed and the timing mark will be aligned with the pointer on the flywheel housing. Make sure that the

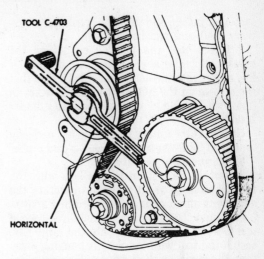

Adjusting timing belt tension—2.2 and 2.5L engines

Camshaft timing

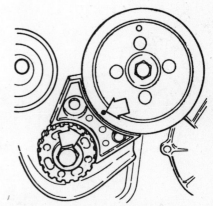

Crankshaft and intermediate shaft timing

dots on the cam sprocket and cylinder head are aligned.

5. Loosen the tensioner pulley center nut. Then, rotate the large hex counterclockwise to reduce belt tension. Now, slide the belt off the

tensioner pulley, and then the crankshaft, auxiliary shaft and camshaft pulleys.

6. Check that the V-notch or dot on the crankshaft pulley aligns with the dot mark or line on the intermediate shaft. Check also that the arrows on the hub of the camshaft are in line with the No. 1 camshaft cap-to-cylinder head line.

NOTE: *If the timing marks are not perfectly aligned, poor engine performance and probable engine damage will result!*

7. Install the belt on the pulleys with the teeth located so as to perfectly maintain the alignment off all pulleys described just above.

8. Adjust the tensioner by installing special tool C–4703 or equivalent onto the large hex. Install the tool with the weight hanging away from the auxiliary shaft drive pulley and allow its weight to tension the belt. Position the tool so that after its tension is applied, the weight will be as close as possible to the height of the center of the pulley (the lever is horizontal). Reset the position of the tool to make sure the tool sits in this position after its tension is applied, if necessary. It must be within 15° of horizontal. Finally, torque the tensioner locknut to 32 ft. lbs.

9. Rotate the engine two full revolutions by the bolt at the center of the crankshaft pulley and recheck the timing. Alter the position of the belt teeth to correct timing and then reset the tension, if necessary.

10. Install the timing belt cover and pulleys, lower the engine and reassemble the engine mount, torquing the through bolt to 70 ft. lbs. Adjust the ignition timing.

1989–92 2.2L And 2.5L Engines Except DOHC

1. If possible, position the engine so the No. 1 piston is at TDC of its compession stroke. Disconnect the negative battery cable.

2. Remove the timing belt covers. Remove

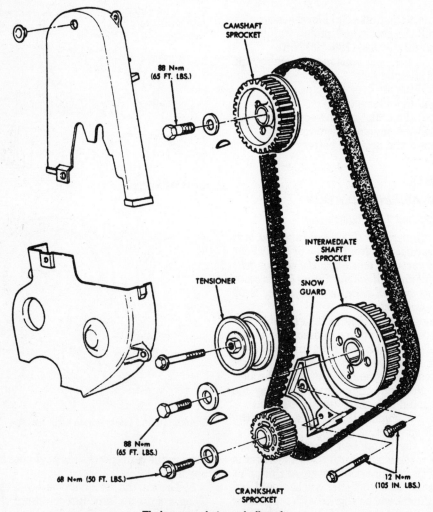

Timing sprockets and oil seals

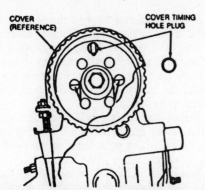

Alignment of arrows on the camshaft sprocket with the camshaft cap to cylinder head mounting line—2.2L/2.5L engines, except 2.2L DOHC

Alignment of the crankshaft sprocket and intermediate shaft sprocket—2.2L/2.5L engines

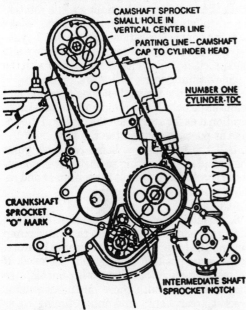

Timing belt installation—2.2L/2.5L engines, except 2.2L DOHC engine

the timing belt tensioner and allow the belt to hang free.

3. Place a floor jack under the engine and separate the right motor mount.

4. Remove the air conditioning compressor belt idler pulley, if equipped, and remove the mounting stud. Unbolt the compressor/alternator bracket and position it aside.

5. Remove the timing belt from the vehicle.

To install:

6. Turn the crankshaft sprocket and intermediate shaft sprocket until the marks are in line. Use a straight-edge from bolt to bolt to confirm alignment.

7. Turn the camshaft until the small hole in the sprocket is at the top and rows on the hub are in line with the camshaft cap to cylinder head mounting lines. Use a mirror to see the alignment so it is viewed straight on and not at an angle from above. Install the belt but let at hang free at this point.

8. Install the air conditioning compressor/alternator bracket, idler pulley and motor mount. Remove the floor jack. Raise the vehicle and support safely. Have the tensioner at an arm's reach because the timing belt will have to be held in position with one hand.

9. To properly install the timing belt, reach up and engage it with the camshaft sprocket. Turn the intermediate shaft counterclockwise slightly, then engage the belt with the intermediate shaft sprocket. Hold the belt against the intermediate shaft sprocket and turn clockwise to take up all tension; if the timing marks are out of alignment, repeat until alignment is correct.

10. Using a wrench, turn the crankshaft sprocket counterclockwise slightly and wrap the belt around it. Turn the sprocket clockwise so there is no slack in the belt between sprockets; if the timing marks are out of alignment, repeat until alignment is correct.

NOTE: *If the timing marks are in line but slack exists in the belt between either the camshaft and intermediate shaft sprockets or the intermediate and crankshaft sprockets, the timing will be incorrect when the belt is tensioned. All slack must be only between the crankshaft and camshaft sprockets.*

11. Install the tensioner and install the mounting bolt loosely. Place the special tensioning tool C–4703 on the hex of the tensioner so the weight is at about the 9 o'clock position (parallel to the ground, hanging toward the rear of the vehicle) plus or minus 15 degrees.

12. Hold the tool in position and tighten the bolt to 45 ft. lbs. (61 Nm). Do not pull the tool past the 9 o'clock position; this will make the belt too tight and will cause it to howl or possibly break.

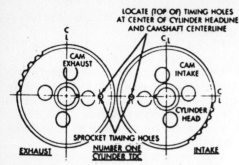

Camshaft sprocket timing—2.2L DOHC engine

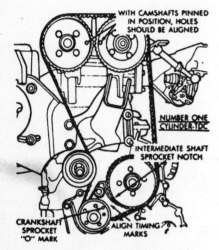

Timing belt installation—2.2L DOHC engine

13. Lower the vehicle and recheck the camshaft sprocket positioning. If it is correct install the timing belt covers and all related parts.

14. Connect the negative battery cable and road test the vehicle.

2.2L Turbo III Engine

1. Disconnect the negative battery cable.

2. Remove the timing belt covers.

3. Place a floor jack under the engine and separate the right motor mount.

4. Raise the vehicle and support safely. Remove the lower accessory drive belt idler pulley bracket assembly.

5. Loosen the timing belt tensioner and remove the timing belt and idler pulley.

To install:

6. Remove the air cleaner fresh air duct, ignition cable cover, spark plugs and valve covers.

7. Loosen the rocker arm retaining bolts about 3 turns in the proper sequence. Check all lash adjusters and replace any that are damaged.

8. Align and pin both camshaft sprockets with $3/16$ in. drills or pin punches.

9. Install a dial indicator so the plunger is in the No. 1 spark plug hole. Rotate the crankshaft until the No. 1 piston is at TDC. Matchmark the crankshaft sprocket to the engine block for reference. Since there is no distributor, the intermediate shaft sprocket does not need to be timed.

10. Install the timing belt and idler pulley starting at the crankshaft and working counterclockwise. Make sure there is no slack between sprockets when installing.

11. Install a suitable belt tension gauge on the timing belt between the camshaft sprockets. Remove the pins from the camshaft sprockets.

12. Rotate the tensioner clockwise to adjust the belt tension to 110 lbs. (445 N). Torque the tensioner bolt 39 ft. lbs. (53 Nm).

13. Rotate the crankshaft clockwise 2 revolutions and recheck the timing and tension. Adjust as required.

14. Torque the rocker arm bolts in sequence to 18 ft. lbs. (24 Nm).

15. Install engine mount and timing belt covers.

16. Install the spark plugs, valve covers, ignition cable cover and air duct.

17. Connect the negative battery cable and road test the vehicle.

3.0L Engine

1. If possible, position the engine so the No. 1 cylinder is at TDC of its compression stroke. Disconnect the negative battery cable. Remove the timing covers from the engine.

2. If the same timing belt will be reused, mark the direction of the timing belt's rotation for installation in the same direction. Make sure the engine is positioned so the No. 1 cylinder is at the TDC of its compression stroke and the sprockets timing marks are aligned with the engine's timing mark indicators.

3. Loosen the timing belt tensioner bolt and remove the belt. If not removing the tensioner, position it as far away from the center of the engine as possible and tighten the bolt.

4. If the tensioner is being removed, paint the outside of the spring to ensure it is not installed backwards. Unbolt the tensioner and remove it along with the spring.

To install:

5. Install the tensioner if removed, and hook the upper end of the spring to the water pump pin and the lower end to the tensioner in exactly the same position as originally installed. If not already done, position both camshafts so the marks align with those on the alternator bracket (rear bank) and inner timing cover (front bank). Rotate the crankshaft so the timing mark aligns with the mark on the oil pump.

6. Install the timing belt on the crankshaft sprocket and while keeping the belt tight on the tension side (right side), install the belt on the front camshaft sprocket.

7. Install the belt on the water pump pulley, then the rear camshaft sprocket and the tensioner.

8. Rotate the front camshaft counterclockwise to tension the belt between the front camshaft and the crankshaft. If the timing marks came out of line, repeat the procedure.

9. Install the crankshaft sprocket flange.

10. Loosen the tensioner bolt and allow the spring to tension the belt.

11. Turn the crankshaft 2 full turns in the clockwise direction only until the timing marks are aligned and torque the tensioner lock bolt to 21 ft. lbs. (29 Nm).

12. Install the timing belt covers and all related parts.

13. Connect the negative battery cable and road test the vehicle.

1990–92 Laser And Dodge Stealth

2.0L ENGINE

1. Disconnect the negative battery cable.

2. Remove the timing belt upper and lower covers.

3. Rotate the crankshaft clockwise and align the timing marks so No. 1 piston will be at TDC of the compression stroke. At this time the timing marks on the camshaft sprocket and the upper surface of the cylinder head should coincide, and the dowel pin of the camshaft sprocket should be at the upper side.

NOTE: *Always rotate the crankshaft in a clockwise direction. Make a mark on the back of the timing belt indicating the direction of rotation so it may be reassembled in the same direction if it is to be reused.*

4. Remove the auto tensioner and remove the timing belt.

5. Remove the timing belt tensioner pulley, tensioner arm, idler pulley, oil pump sprocket, special washer, flange and spacer.

6. Remove the silent shaft (inner) belt tensioner and remove the belt.

To install:

7. Align the timing marks of the silent shaft sprockets and the crankshaft sprocket with the timing marks on the front case. Wrap the timing belt around the sprockets so there is no slack in the upper span of the belt and the timing marks are still aligned.

8. Install the tensioner pulley and move the pulley by hand so the long side of the belt deflects about ¼ in. (6mm).

9. Hold the pulley tightly so the pulley cannot rotate when the bolt is tightened. Tighten the bolt to 15 ft. lbs. (20 Nm) and recheck the deflection amount.

10. Carefully push the auto tensioner rod in until the set hole in the rod aligned up with the hole in the cylinder. Place a wire into the hole to retain the rod.

11. Install the tensioner pulley onto the tensioner arm. Locate the pinhole in the tensioner pulley shaft to the left of the center bolt. Then, tighten the center bolt finger-tight.

12. When installing the timing belt, turn the 2 camshaft sprockets so their dowel pins are located on top. Align the timing marks facing

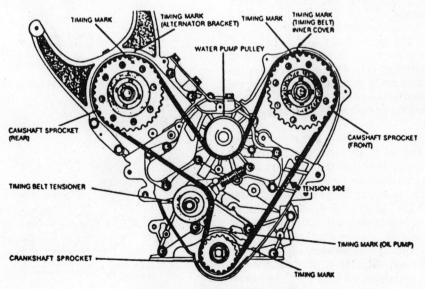

Timing belt installation—3.0L engine

each other with the top surface of the cylinder head. When you let go of the exhaust camshaft sprocket, it will rotate 1 tooth in the counterclockwise direction. This should be taken into account when installing the timing belts on the sprocket.

NOTE: *Both camshaft sprockets are used for the intake and exhaust camshafts and are provided with 2 timing marks. When the sprocket is mounted on the exhaust camshaft, use the timing mark on the right with the dowel pin hole on top. For the intake camshaft sprocket, use the 1 on the left with the dowel pin hole on top.*

13. Align the crankshaft sprocket and oil pump sprocket timing marks. Install the timing belt as follows:

   a. Install the timing belt around the intake camshaft sprocket and retain it with 2 spring clips or binder clips.

   b. Install the timing belt around the exhaust sprocket, aligning the timing marks with the cylinder head top surface using 2 wrenches. Retain the belt with 2 spring clips.

   c. Install the timing belt around the idler pulley, oil pump sprocket, crankshaft sprocket and the tensioner pulley. Remove the 2 spring clips.

   d. Lift upward on the tensioner pulley in a clockwise direction and tighten the center bolt. Make sure all timing marks are aligned.

   e. Rotate the crankshaft a ¼ turn counterclockwise. Then, turn in clockwise until the timing marks are aligned again.

14. To adjust the timing (outer) belt, turn the crankshaft ¼ turn counterclockwise, then turn it clockwise to move No. 1 cylinder to TDC.

15. Loosen the center bolt. Using tool MD998738 or equivalent and a torque wrench, apply a torque of 1.88–2.03 ft. lbs. (2.6–2.8 Nm). Tighten the center bolt.

16. Screw the special tool into the engine left support bracket until its end makes contact with the tensioner arm. At this point, screw the special tool in some more and remove the set wire attached to the auto tensioner, if the wire was not previously removed. Then remove the special tool.

17. Rotate the crankshaft 2 complete turns clockwise and let it sit for approximately 15 minutes. Then, measure the auto tensioner protrusion (the distance between the tensioner arm and auto tensioner body) to ensure that it is within 0.15–0.18 in. (3.8–4.5mm). If out of specification, repeat Step 1–4 until the specified value is obtained.

18. If the timing belt tension adjustment is being performed with the engine mounted in the vehicle, and clearance between the tensioner arm and the auto tensioner body cannot be

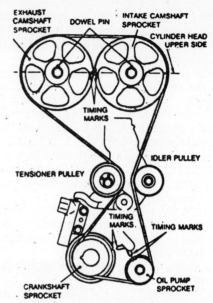

Timing belt installation—1990–92 Laser 2.0L engine

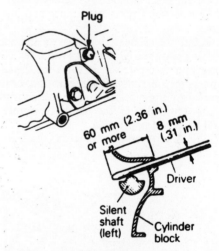

Timing belt installation—1990–92 Laser 1.8L engine

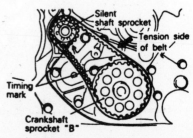

Timing belt installation—1990–92 Laser 1.8L engine

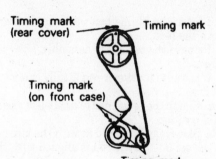

Timing mark (rear cover)

Timing mark

Timing mark (on front case)

Timing mark

Timing belt installation—1990–92 Laser 1.8L engine

measured, the following alternative method can be used:

a. Screw in special tool MD998738 or equivalent, until its end makes contact with the tensioner arm.

b. After the special tool makes contact with the arm, screw it in some more to retract the auto tensioner pushrod while counting the number of turns the tool makes until the tensioner arm is brought into contact with the auto tensioner body. Make sure the number of turns the special tool makes conforms with the standard value of 2½–3 turns.

c. Install the rubber plug to the timing belt rear cover.

19. Install the timing belt covers and all related items.

20. Connect the negative battery cable.

1.8L ENGINE

1. If possible, position the engine so the No. 1 piston is at TDC.

2. Disconnect the negative battery cable.

3. Remove the timing belt covers.

4. Remove the timing (outer) belt tensioner and remove the belt.

5. Remove the outer crankshaft sprocket and flange.

6. Remove the silent shaft (inner) belt tensioner and remove the belt.

To install:

7. Align the timing marks of the silent shaft sprockets and the crankshaft sprocket with the timing marks on the front case. Wrap the timing belt around the sprockets so there is no slack in the upper span of the belt and the timing marks are still aligned.

8. Install the tensioner pulley and move the pulley by hand so the long side of the belt deflects about ¼ in. (6mm).

9. Hold the pulley tightly so the pulley cannot rotate when the bolt is tightened. Tighten the bolt to 15 ft. lbs. (20 Nm) and recheck the deflection amount.

10. Install the timing belt tensioner fully to-

ward the water pump and tighten the bolts. Place the upper end of the spring against the water pump body.

11. Align the timing marks of the camshaft, crankshaft and oil pump sprockets with their corresponding marks on the front case or rear cover.

NOTE: *If the following step is not followed exactly, there is a 50 percent chance that the silent shaft alignment will be 180 degrees off. This will cause a noticeable vibration in the engine and the entire procedure will have to be repeated.*

12. Before installing the timing belt, ensure that the left side (rear) silent shaft is in the correct position.:

a. Remove the plug from the rear of the block and insert a suitable shaft.

b. With the timing marks still aligned, the shaft must be able to go in at least 2⅓ in. (59mm). If it can only go in about 1 in. (25mm), turn the oil pump sprocket 1 complete revolution.

c. Recheck and realign the timing marks.

d. Leave the tool in place to hold the silent shaft while continuing.

13. Install the belt to the crankshaft sprocket, oil pump sprocket, then camshaft sprocket, in that order. While doing so, make sure there is no slack between the sprocket except where the tensioner is installed.

14. Recheck the timing marks' alignment. If all are aligned, loosen the tensioner mounting bolt and allow the tensioner to apply tension to the belt.

15. Remove the tool that is hold the silent shaft and rotate the crankshaft a distance equal to 2 teeth on the camshaft sprocket. This will allow the tensioner to automatically apply the proper tension on the belt. Do not manually overtension the belt or it will howl.

16. Tighten the lower mounting bolt then the upper spacer bolt.

17. To verify the belt tension, check that the deflection of the longest span of the belt is about ½ in. (13mm).

18. Install the timing belt covers and all related items.

19. Connect the negative battery cable.

3.0L SOHC ENGINE

1. If possible, position the engine so the No. 1 cylinder is at TDC of its compression stroke. Disconnect the negative battery cable. Remove the timing covers from the engine.

2. If the same timing belt will be reused, mark the direction of the timing belt's rotation for installation in the same direction. Make sure the engine is positioned so the No. 1 cylinder is at the TDC of its compression stroke and

the sprockets' timing marks are aligned with the engine's timing mark indicators.

3. Loosen the timing belt tensioner bolt and remove the belt. If the tensioner is not being removed, position it as far away from the center of the engine as possible and tighten the bolt.

4. If the tensioner is being removed, paint the outside of the spring to ensure that it is not installed backwards. Unbolt the tensioner and remove it along with the spring.

To install:

5. Install the tensioner, if removed, and hook the upper end of the spring to the water pump pin and the lower end to the tensioner in exactly the same position as originally installed. If not already done, position both camshafts so the marks align with those on the rear. Rotate the crankshaft so the timing mark aligns with the mark on the oil pump.

6. Install the timing belt on the crankshaft sprocket and while keeping the belt tight on the tension side, install the belt on the front camshaft sprocket.

7. Install the belt on the water pump pulley, then the rear camshaft sprocket and the tensioner.

8. Rotate the front camshaft counterclockwise to tension the belt between the front camshaft and the crankshaft. If the timing marks became misaligned, repeat the procedure.

9. Install the crankshaft sprocket flange.

10. Loosen the tensioner bolt and allow the spring to apply tension to the belt.

11. Turn the crankshaft 2 full turns in the clockwise direction until the timing marks align again. Now that the belt is properly tensioned, torque the tensioner lock bolt to 21 ft. lbs. (29 Nm). Measure the belt tension between the rear camshaft sprocket and the crankshaft with belt tension gauge. The specification is 46–68 lbs. (210–310 N).

12. Install the timing belt covers and all related parts.

13. Connect the negative battery cable and road test the vehicle.

3.0L DOHC ENGINE

1. If possible, position the engine so the No. 1 cylinder is at TDC of its compression stroke. Disconnect the negative battery cable. Remove the timing covers from the engine.

2. If the same timing belt will be reused, mark the direction of the timing belt's rotation for installation in the same direction. Make sure the engine is positioned so the No. 1 cylinder is at the TDC of its compression stroke and the sprockets' timing marks are aligned with the engine's timing mark indicators on the valve covers or head.

3. Loosen the timing belt tensioner bolt and remove the belt.

4. Remove the tensioner assembly.

To install:

5. If the auto tensioner rod is fully extended, reset it as follows:

a. Clamp the tensioner in a soft-jaw vice in level position.

b. Slowly push the rod in with the vice until the set hole in the rod is aligned with the hole in the cylinder.

c. Insert a stiff wire into the set holes to retain the position.

d. Remove the assembly from the vice.

6. Leave the retaining wire in the tension and install to the engine. Torque the retaining bolts to 17 ft. lbs. (24 Nm).

7. If the timing marks of the camshaft sprockets and crankshaft sprocket are not aligned at this point, proceed as follows:

NOTE: *Keep fingers out from in between the camshaft sprockets. The sprockets may move unexpectedly because of valve spring pressure and could pinch fingers.*

a. Align the mark on the crankshaft sprocket with the mark on the front case. Then move the sprocket 3 teeth clockwise to lower the piston so the valve can't touch the piston when the camshafts are being moved.

b. Turn each camshaft sprocket 1 at a time to align the timing marks with the mark on the valve cover or head. If the intake and exhaust valves of the same cylinder are opened simultaneously, they could interfere with each other. Therefore, if any resistance is felt, turn the other camshaft to move the valve.

c. Align the timing mark of the crankshaft sprocket, then continue 1 tooth farther in the counterclockwise direction to facilitate belt installation.

8. Using 4 spring loaded paper clips to hold the belt on the cam sprockets, install the belt to the sprockets in the following order:

1st — exhuast camshaft sprocket for the front head

2nd — intake camshaft sprocket for the front head

3rd — water pump pulley

4th — intake camshaft sprocket for the rear head

5th — exhuast camshaft sprocket for the rear head

6th — idler pulley

7th — crankshaft sprocket

8th — tensioner pulley

9. Turn the tensioner pulley so its pin holes are located above the center bolt. Then press the tensioner pulley against the timing belt and simultaneously tighten the center bolt.

10. Make certain that all timing marks are still aligned. If so, remove the 4 clips.

11. Turn the crankshaft ¼ turn counterclockwise, then turn it clockwise until all timing marks are aligned.

12. Loosen the center bolt on the tensioner pulley. Using tool MD998767 or equivalent and a torque wrench, apply a torque of 7.2 ft. lbs. (10 Nm). Tighten the tensioner bolt; make sure the tensioner doesn't rotate with the bolt.

13. Remove the set wire attached to the auto tensioner, if the wire was not previously removed.

14. Rotate the crankshaft 2 complete turns clockwise and let it sit for approximately 5 minutes. Then, make sure the set pin can easily be inserted and removed from the hole in the tensioner.

15. Measure the auto tensioner protrusion (the distance between the tensioner arm and auto tensioner body) to ensure that it is within 0.15–0.18 in. (3.8–4.5mm). If out of specification, repeat Step 1–4 until the specified value is obtained.

16. Install the timing belt covers and all related items.

17. Connect the negative battery cable.

Timing Belt Tensioner

ADJUSTMENT

2.2L And 2.5L Engines Except Turbo III

1. Disconnect the negative battery cable.

2. Raise the vehicle and support safely. Remove the right front inner splash shield.

3. Remove the tensioner cover.

4. Place the special tensioning tool C–4703 on the hex of the tensioner so the weight is at about the 10 o'clock position and loosen the bolt.

5. The tensioner should drop to the 9 o'clock position. Reposition the tool as required in order to have it end up at the 9 o'clock position (parallel to the ground, hanging toward the rear of the vehicle) ± 15 degrees.

6. Hold the tool in position and tighten the bolt. Do not pull the tool past the 9 o'clock position or the belt will be too tight and will cause howling or possible breakage.

7. Install the cover and the splash shield.

2.2L Turbo III Engine

1. Disconnect the negative battery cable.

2. Remove the timing covers.

3. Install a suitable belt tension gauge on the timing belt between the camshaft sprockets.

4. Rotate the tensioner clockwise to adjust the belt tension to 110 lbs. (445 N)

5. Rotate the crankshaft clockwise 2 revolu-

tions and recheck the tension. Adjust as required.

6. Install the timing covers.

3.0L Engine

1. Disconnect the negative battery cable.

2. Remove the timing belt covers.

3. Loosen the bolt that holds the timing belt tensioner in place.

4. Allow the spring only to pull the tensioner in automatically. Do not manually move the tensioner or the belt will be too tight.

5. Tighten the tensioner locking bolt.

6. Install the timing belt covers and all related parts.

1990–92 Laser And Dodge Stealth

1.8L ENGINE

1. Disconnect the negative battery cable.

2. Remove the timing belt covers.

3. On 1.8L engine, adjust the silent shaft (inner) belt tension first. Loosen the idler pulley center bolt so the pulley can be moved.

4. Move the pulley by hand so the long side of the belt deflects about ¼ in. (6mm).

5. Hold the pulley tightly so the pulley cannot rotate when the bolt is tightened. Tighten the bolt to 15 ft. lbs. (20 Nm) and recheck the deflection amount.

6. To adjust the timing (outer) belt, first loosen the pivot side tensioner bolt and then the slot side bolt. Allow the spring to take up the slack.

7. Tighten the slot side tensioner bolt and then the pivot side bolt. If the pivot side bolt is tightened first, the tensioner could turn with bolt, causing over tension.

8. Turn the crankshaft clockwise. Loosen the pivot side tensioner bolt and then the slot side bolt. Tighten the slot bolt and then the pivot side bolt.

9. Check the belt tension on 1.8L engine, the deflection of the longest span of the belt should be about 0.40 in. (10mm). Do not manually overtighten the belt or it will howl.

10. Install the timing belt covers and all related items.

11. Connect the negative battery cable.

2.0L ENGINE

1. Disconnect the negative battery cable.

2. Remove the timing belt covers.

3. Adjust the silent shaft (inner) belt tension first. Loosen the idler pulley center bolt so the pulley can be moved.

4. Move the pulley by hand so the long side of the belt deflects about ¼ in. (6mm).

5. Hold the pulley tightly so the pulley cannot rotate when the bolt is tightened. Tighten

the bolt to 15 ft. lbs. (20 Nm) and recheck the deflection amount.

6. To adjust the timing (outer) belt, turn the crankshaft ¼ turn counterclockwise, then turn it clockwise to move No. 1 cylinder to TDC.

7. Loosen the center bolt. Using tool MD998738 or equivalent and a torque wrench, apply a torque of 1.88–2.03 ft. lbs. (2.6–2.8 Nm). Tighten the center bolt.

8. Screw the special tool into the engine left support bracket until its end makes contact with the tensioner arm. At this point, screw the special tool in some more and remove the set wire attached to the auto tensioner, if the wire was not previously removed. Then remove the special tool.

9. Rotate the crankshaft 2 complete turns clockwise and let it sit for approximately 15 minutes. Then, measure the auto tensioner protrusion (the distance between the tensioner arm and auto tensioner body) to ensure that it is within 0.15–0.18 in. (3.8–4.5mm). If out of specification, repeat Step 1–4 until the specified value is obtained.

10. If the timing belt tension adjustment is being performed with the engine mounted in the vehicle, and clearance between the tensioner arm and the auto tensioner body cannot be measured, the following alternative method can be used:

a. Screw in special tool MD998738 or equivalent, until its end makes contact with the tensioner arm.

b. After the special tool makes contact with the arm, screw it in some more to retract the auto tensioner pushrod while counting the number of turns the tool makes until the tensioner arm is brought into contact with the auto tensioner body. Make sure the number of turns the special tool makes conforms with the standard value of 2½–3 turns.

c. Install the rubber plug to the timing belt rear cover.

11. Install the timing belt covers and all related items.

12. Connect the negative battery cable.

3.0L SOHC ENGINE

1. Disconnect the negative battery cable.

2. Remove the timing belt covers.

3. Loosen the bolt that holds the tensioner in place and allow the spring to automatically apply tension to the belt.

4. Rotate the crankshaft 2 turns clockwise. Tighten the tensioner bolt to 20 ft. lbs. (25 Nm).

5. Measure the belt tension between the rear camshaft sprocket and the crankshaft with belt tension gauge. The specification is 46–68 lbs. (210–310 N).

6. Install the timing belt covers and all related items.

7. Connect the negative battery cable.

3.0L DOHC ENGINE

1. Disconnect the negative battery cable.

2. Remove the timing belt covers.

3. Turn the crankshaft ¼ turn counterclockwise, then turn it clockwise until all timing marks are aligned.

4. Loosen the center bolt on the tensioner pulley. Using tool MD998767 or equivalent and a torque wrench, apply a torque of 7.2 ft. lbs. (10 Nm). Tighten the tensioner bolt; make sure the tensioner doesn't rotate with the bolt.

5. Remove the set wire attached to the auto tensioner, if the wire was not previously removed.

6. Rotate the crankshaft 2 complete turns clockwise and let it sit for approximately 5 minutes. Then, make sure the set pin can easily be inserted and removed from the hole in the tensioner.

7. Measure the auto tensioner protrusion (the distance between the tensioner arm and auto tensioner body) to ensure that it is within 0.15–0.18 in. (3.8–4.5mm). If out of specification, repeat Step 1–4 until the specified value is obtained.

8. Install the timing belt covers and all related items.

9. Connect the negative battery cable.

Timing Cover, Chain, Silent Shafts and Tensioner

REMOVAL AND INSTALLATION

CAUTION: *When draining the coolant, keep in mind that cats and dogs are attracted by the ethylene glycol antifreeze, and are quite likely to drink any that is left in an uncovered container or in puddles on the ground. This will prove fatal in sufficient quantity. Always drain the coolant into a sealable container. Coolant should be reused unless it is contaminated or several years old.*

2.6L Engine

NOTE: *All 2.6 engines are equipped with two Silent Shafts which cancel the vertical vibrating force of the engine and the secondary vibrating forces, which include the sideways rocking of the engine due to the turning direction of the crankshaft and other rolling parts. The shafts are driven by a duplex chain and are turned by the crankshaft. The silent shaft chain assembly is mounted in front of the timing chain assembly and must be removed to service the timing chain.*

1. Disconnect the negative battery terminal.

2. Drain the radiator and remove it from the vehicle.

3. Remove the cylinder head.

4. Remove the cooling fan, spacer, water pump pulley and belt.

5. Remove the alternator and water pump.

6. Raise the front of the vehicle and support it on jackstands.

7. Remove the oil pan and screen. Remove the crankshaft pulley.

8. Remove the timing case cover.

9. Remove the chain guides, side (A), top (B), bottom (C), from the **B** chain (outer).

10. Remove the locking bolts from the **B** chain sprockets.

11. Remove the crankshaft sprocket, silent shaft sprocket and the outer chain.

12. Remove the crankshaft and camshaft sprockets and the timing chain.

13. Remove the camshaft sprocket holder and the chain guides, both left and right.

14. Remove the tensioner.

15. Remove the sleeve from the oil pump. Remove the oil pump by first removing the bolt locking the oil pump driven gear and the right silent shaft, then remove the oil pump mounting bolts. Remove the silent shaft from the engine block.

NOTE: *If the bolt locking the oil pump and the silent shaft is hard to loosen, remove the oil pump and the shaft as a unit.*

16. Remove the left silent shaft thrust washer and take the shaft from the engine block.

Installation is performed in the following manner:

1. Install the right silent shaft into the engine block.

2. Install the oil pump assembly. Do not lose the woodruff key from the end of the silent shaft. Torque the oil pump mounting bolts from 6 to 7 ft. lbs.

3. Tighten the silent shaft and oil pump driven gear mounting bolt.

NOTE: *The silent shaft and the oil pump can be installed as a unit, if necessary.*

4. Install the left silent shaft into the engine block.

5. Install a new O-ring on the thrust plate and install the unit into the engine block, using a pair of bolts without heads, as alignment guides.

CAUTION: *If the thrust plate is turned to align the bolt holes, the O-ring may be damaged.*

6. Remove the guide bolts and install the regular bolts into the thrust plate and tighten securely.

7. Rotate the crankshaft to bring No. 1 piston to TDC.

8. Install the cylinder head.

9. Install the sprocket holder and the right and left chain guides.

10. Install the tensioner spring and sleeve on the oil pump body.

11. Install the camshaft and crankshaft sprockets on the timing chain, aligning the sprocket punch marks to the plated chain links.

12. While holding the sprocket and chain as a unit, install the crankshaft sprocket over the crankshaft and align it with the keyway.

13. Keeping the dowel pin hole on the camshaft in a vertical position, install the camshaft sprocket and chain on the camshaft.

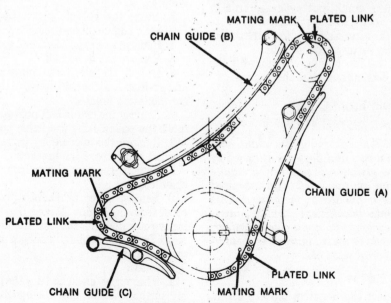

Silent Shaft balancing system on 2.6L engines

NOTE: *The sprocket timing mark and the plated chain link should be at the 2 to 3 o'clock position when correctly installed.*

CAUTION: *The chain must be aligned in the right and left chain guides with the tensioner pushing against the chain. The tension for the inner chain is determined by spring tension.*

14. Install the crankshaft sprocket for the outer or "B" chain.

15. Install the two silent shaft sprockets and align the punched mating marks with the plated links of the chain.

16. Holding the two shaft sprockets and chain, install the outer chain in alignment with the mark on the crankshaft sprocket. Install the shaft sprockets on the silent shaft and the oil pump driver gear. Install the lock bolts and recheck the alignment of the punch marks and the plated links.

17. Temporarily install the chain guides, Side (A), Top (B), and Bottom (C).

18. Tighten Side (A) chain guide securely.

19. Tighten Bottom (C) chain guide securely.

20. Adjust the position of the Top (B) chain guide, after shaking the right and left sprockets to collect any chain slack, so that when the chain is moved toward the center, the clearance between the chain guide and the chain links will be approximately $\frac{9}{64}$ in. (3.5mm). Tighten the Top (B) chain guide bolts.

21. Install the timing chain cover using a new gasket, being careful not to damage the front seal.

22. Install the oil screen and the oil pan, using a new gasket. Torque the bolts to 4.5 to 5.5 ft. lbs.

23. Install the crankshaft pylley, alternator and accessory belts, and the distributor.

24. Install the oil pressure switch, if removed, and install the battery ground cable.

25. Install the fan blades, radiator, fill the system with coolant and start the engine.

Timing Chain Front Cover

REMOVAL AND INSTALLATION

CAUTION: *When draining the coolant, keep in mind that cats and dogs are attracted by the ethylene glycol antifreeze, and are quite likely to drink any that is left in an uncovered container or in puddles on the ground. This will prove fatal in sufficient quantity. Always drain the coolant into a sealable container. Coolant should be reused unless it is contaminated or several years old.*

3.3L And 3.8L Engines

1. Disconnect the negative battery cable. Drain the cooling system.

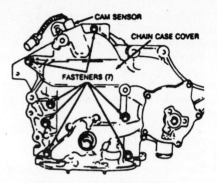

Timing chain cover—3.3L/3.8L engines

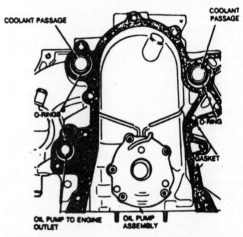

Timing cover removed—3.3L/3.8L engines

2. Support the engine with a suitable engine support device and remove the right side motor mount.

3. Raise the vehicle and support safely. Drain the engine oil and remove the oil pan.

4. Remove the right wheel and splash shield.

5. Remove the drive belt.

6. Unbolt the air conditioning compressor and position it to the side. Remove the compressor mounting bracket.

7. Remove the crankshaft pulley bolt and remove the pulley using a suitable puller.

8. Remove the idler pulley from the engine bracket and remove the bracket.

9. Remove the cam sensor from the timing chain cover.

10. Remove the cover mounting bolts and the cover from the engine. Make sure the oil pump inner rotor does not fall out. Remove the 3 O-rings from the coolant passages and the oil pump outlet.

To install:

11. Thoroughly clean and dry the gasket mating surfaces. Install new O-rings to the block.

12. Remove the crankshaft oil seal from the

cover. The seal must be removed from the cover when installing to ensure proper oil pump engagement.

13. Using a new gasket, install the chain case cover to the engine.

14. Make certain that the oil pump is engaged onto the crankshaft before proceeding or there will be no oil pressure. Install the attaching bolts and torque to 20 ft. lbs. (27 Nm).

15. Use tool C–4992 to install the crankshaft oil seal. Install the crankshaft pulley using a 5.9 in.(150mm) long suitable bolt used with thrust bearing and washer plate L–4524. Make sure the pulley bottoms out on the inner diameter of the crankshaft seal. Install the bolt and torque to 40 ft. lbs. (54 Nm).

16. Install the engine bracket and torque the bolts to 40 ft. lbs. (54 Nm). Install the idler pulley to the engine bracket.

17. To install the cam sensor, perform the following:

    a. Clean off the old spacer from the sensor face completely. A new spacer must be attached to the cam sensor prior to installation; if a new spacer is not used, engine performance will be adversely affected.

    b. Inspect the O-ring for damage and replace, if necessary. Lubricate the O-ring lightly with oil and push the sensor into its bore in the chain case cover until contact is made with the cam timing gear. Hold in this position and tighten the bolt to 9 ft. lbs. (12 Nm).

18. Install the air conditioning compressor and bracket.

19. Install the drive belt.

20. Install the inner splash shield and wheel.

21. Install the oil pan with a new gasket.

22. Install the motor mount.

23. Remove the engine temperature sensor and fill the cooling system until the level reaches the vacant sensor hole. Install the sensor and continue to fill the radiator. Fill the engine with the proper amount of oil.

24. Connect the negative battery cable and check for leaks.

Front Cover Oil Seal

REPLACEMENT

3.3L And 3.8L Engines

1. Disconnect the negative battery cable.

2. Raise the vehicle and support safely. Remove the right front wheel and the inner splash shield.

3. Remove the drive belt.

4. Remove the crankshaft bolt. Using a suitable puller, remove the crankshaft pulley.

5. Use tool C–4991 to remove the seal.

To install:

6. Clean out the bore. Place the seal with the spring toward the engine. Install the new seal using tool C–4992 until it is flush with the cover.

7. Install the crankshaft pulley using a suitable 5.9 in. (150mm) long bolt with thrust bearing and washer plate L–4524. Make sure the pulley bottoms out on the inner diameter of the crankshaft seal. Install the bolt and torque to 40 ft. lbs. (54 Nm).

8. Install the drive belt.

9. Install the splash shield and wheel.

10. Connect the negative battery cable and check for leaks.

Timing Chain and Gears

REMOVAL AND INSTALLATION

CAUTION: *When draining the coolant, keep in mind that cats and dogs are attracted by the ethylene glycol antifreeze, and are quite likely to drink any that is left in an uncovered container or in puddles on the ground. This will prove fatal in sufficient quantity. Always drain the coolant into a sealable container. Coolant should be reused unless it is contaminated or several years old.*

3.3L And 3.8L Engines

1. If possible, position the engine so the No. 1 piston is at TDC of its compression stroke. Disconnect the negative battery cable. Drain the coolant.

2. Remove the timing chain case cover.

3. Remove the camshaft gear attaching cup washer and remove the timing chain with both gears attached. Remove the timing chain snubber.

To install:

4. Assemble the timing chain and gears.

5. Turn the crankshaft and camshaft to line up with the keyway locations of the gears.

6. Slide both gears over their respective

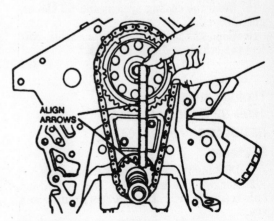

Aligning timing marks—3.3L/3.8L engines

shafts and use a straight-edge to confirm alignment.

7. Install the cup washer and camshaft bolt. Torque the bolt to 35 ft. lbs. (47 Nm).

8. Check camshaft endplay. The specification with a new plate is 0.002–0.006 in. (0.051–0.052mm) and 0.002–0.010 in. (0.51–0.254mm) with a used plate. Replace the thrust plate if not within specifications.

9. Install the timing chain snubber.

10. Thoroughly clean and dry the gasket mating surfaces.

11. Install new O-rings to the block.

12. Remove the crankshaft oil seal from the cover. The seal must be removed from the cover when installing to ensure proper oil pump engagement.

13. Using a new gasket, install the chain case cover to the engine.

14. Make certain that the oil pump is engaged onto the crankshaft before proceeding or severe engine damage will result. Install the attaching bolts and torque to 20 ft. lbs. (27 Nm).

15. Use tool C–4992 to install the crankshaft oil seal. Install the crankshaft pulley using a 5.9 in. (150mm) long suitable bolt and thrust bearing and washer plate L–4524. Make sure the pulley bottoms out on the crankshaft seal diameter. Install the bolt and torque to 40 ft. lbs. (54 Nm).

16. Install all other parts removed during the chain case cover removal procedure.

17. To install the cam sensor, first clean off the old spacer from the sensor face completely. Inspect the O-ring for damage and replace, if necessary. A new spacer must be attached to the cam sensor prior to installation; if a new spacer is not used, engine performance will be adversely affected. Oil the O-ring lightly and push the sensor into its bore in the chain case cover until contact is made with the cam timing gear. Hold in this position and tighten the bolt to 10 ft. lbs. (12 Nm).

18. Refill the cooling system and fill the engine with oil.

19. Connect the negative battery cable, road test the vehicle and check for leaks.

Timing Chain Front Cover
1990–92 Dodge Monaco

REMOVAL AND INSTALLATION

2.5L Engine

1. Disconnect the negative battery cable.

2. Remove the drive belts, engine fan and hub assembly, vibration damper, pulley and key.

3. Remove the alternator bracket. If equipped with air conditioning, remove the compressor.

4. Remove the oil pan-to-cover bolts and the cover-to-engine block bolts.

5. Remove the front cover assembly from the engine.

6. Cut off the oil pan side gasket end tabs flush with the front face of the cylinder block and remove the gasket tabs.

7. Remove the oil seal from the timing cover and clean all gasket material from the sealing surface.

To install:

8. Apply sealant to both sides of the gasket and install on the cover sealing surface.

9. Cut the end tabs from the replacement oil pan side gasket and cement the tabs on the oil pan.

10. Install a new oil seal into the cover assembly.

NOTE: *The oil seal can be installed after the cover has been installed on the engine block, depending upon whether the cover aligning tools are available.*

11. Coat the front cover seal end tab recesses with RTV sealant and position the seal on the cover bottom.

12. Position the cover on the engine block and position an alignment tool into the crankshaft opening.

NOTE: *Two different types of alignment tools are available, without seal in housing or with seal in housing.*

13. Install the cover-to-engine block bolts and the oil pan-to-cover bolts. Tighten the cover-to-engine block bolts to 5 ft. lbs. (7 Nm) and the oil pan-to-cover bolts to 11 ft. lbs. (15 Nm).

14. If not already done, install the seal.

15. Install the vibration damper.

16. Install the compressor and alternator bracket.

17. Install the engine fan and hub assembly. Install the belts and adjust.

18. Connect the negative battery cable and check for leaks.

3.0L Engine

1. Disconnect the negative battery cable.

2. Remove the rocker covers. Hold the camshaft sprocket in place and remove the distributor drive/camshaft sprocket bolt. Remove the distributor assembly.

3. Remove the accessory drive belt. Remove the nuts retaining the front engine vibration damper to the engine and move it toward the radiator.

4. Remove the crankshaft pulley nut and remove the crankshaft pulley.

NOTE: *The crankshaft pulley nut is put on with a threaded lock installed with the nut. It may be necessary to strike the pulley with a brass hammer to loosen it.*

5. Remove the timing cover mounting bolts. Place a suitable prying tool between the cylinder block and a special boss on the front cover and gently pry off the cover. Discard the gaskets.

6. Remove the oil seal from the cover.

To install:

7. To prevent the key from falling into the oil pan, rotate the crankshaft so the keyway points upward.

8. Apply a bead of RTV sealer to the points where the cylinder heads meet the block and the lower case meets the block.

9. Install the cover with new gasket over the alignment dowels. Tighten the bolts to 9 ft. lbs. (12 Nm).

10. Install the distributor assembly and install the rocker covers.

11. Install the crankshaft pulley, apply thread locking compound to the threads of the pulley nut and tighten to 133 ft. lbs. (180 Nm).

12. Install the accessory drive belt and adjust the belt tension.

NOTE: *It is very important the accessory drive belt is routed correctly. If it is incorrectly routed the water pump could be driven in the wrong direction, causing the engine to overheat.*

13. Install the engine vibration damper.

14. Connect the negative battery cable and check for leaks.

Timing Chain and Sprockets 1990–92 Dodge Monaco

REMOVAL AND INSTALLATION

2.5L Engine

1. Disconnect the negative battery cable.

2. Remove the fan shroud assembly, accessory drive belts, water pump pulley, crankshaft vibration damper and timing case cover.

NOTE: *It is a good practice to either remove the radiator or cover the radiator core area when working around the radiator, as damage can result to the radiator core.*

3. Rotate the crankshaft until the 0 timing mark on the crankshaft sprocket aligns with the timing mark on the camshaft sprocket.

4. Remove the oil slinger from the crankshaft.

5. Remove the camshaft retaining bolt, the sprocket and chain assembly.

6. If the timing chain tensioner is to be replaced, the oil pan must also be removed.

To install:

7. Turn the tensioner lever to the **UNLOCK** position and pull the tensioner block toward the

tensioner lever to compress the spring. Hold the block and turn the tensioner lever to the lock **UP** position.

8. Install the crankshaft/camshaft sprockets and timing chain. Make sure the timing marks are aligned as indicated in Step 3.

9. Install the camshaft sprocket retaining bolt and washer. Torque the bolt to 80 ft. lbs. (108 Nm).

NOTE: *To verify correct installation of the timing chain, rotate the crankshaft until the camshaft sprocket timing mark is approximately at the 1 o'clock position. There should be 20 pins (2 per link) between the marks.*

10. Install the oil slinger.

11. Install the timing case cover and all related parts.

12. Connect the negative battery cable and check engine for proper operation.

3.0L Engine

1. Disconnect the negative battery cable. Remove the cylinder head cover.

2. Inspect the chain and sprocket for wear by pulling on the top of the chain. This will produce a gap between the bottom of the timing chain and the bottom of the area between the 2 sprocket teeth. The maximum gap is 0.067 in. (0.17mm). This must not be exceeded. This gap corresponds to a travel of 0.866 in. (2.19mm) by the timing chain tensioner plunger.

3. Use the solid end of a No. 51 drill bit (0.067 in. diameter) to gauge the gap. If the solid end of the drill bit fits into the gap between the timing chain and the 2 sprocket teeth, then the following parts must be replaced: timing chain shoes, tensioners, guides, sprockets, tensioner shoes. Use the following procedure.

4. Disconnect the negative battery cable.

5. Remove the front cover assembly. Turn the crankshaft until piston No. 1 is at TDC of the compression stroke.

NOTE: *Keep all of the components from each side together. This will aid in assembly.*

6. Remove the oil pump sprocket retaining bolts and remove the sprocket/chain assembly.

7. Remove the bolt attaching the right side camshaft sprocket to the camshaft. Remove the right side tensioner and let the tensioner shoe hang down.

8. Remove the right side timing chain and sprocket. Remove the right side chain guide and tensioner shoe.

9. Remove the bolt attaching the left side camshaft sprocket to the camshaft. Remove the left side tensioner and let the tensioner shoe hang down.

10. Remove the left side timing chain and sprocket. Remove the left side chain guide and tensioner shoe.

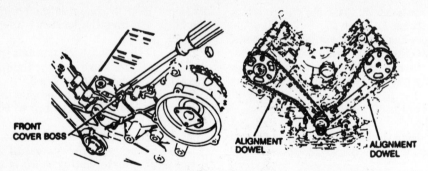

When prying loose front cover assembly, note the two alignment dowels—Dodge Monaco 3.0L engine

To install:

NOTE: *Inspect the timing chain tensioner. An opening shows the tensioner lock inside. This tensioner lock should not be removed. The lock is held in place by a spring that pushes a steel ball against the lock finger. If the lock is removed accidentally, replace the tensioner assembly because there is no way of checking the position of the lock finger in relation to the steel ball. When installing a tensioner use a thin blade tool to turn the ratchet counterclockwise. Then push the tensioner arm in. Position the tensioner over the filter and the tensioner shoe into the arm.*

11. To install, place the left and right chain guides into position and tighten the bolts to 48 inch lbs. (5.4 Nm). Install the tensioner shoes and tighten the mounting bolts to 9 ft. lbs.

12. Turn the left camshaft until the keyway slot is in the 11 o'clock position. Turn the right camshaft so the keyway is in the 8 o'clock position.

13. Turn the crankshaft until the keyway is aligned with the centerline of the left cylinder head.

NOTE: *The crankshaft has 3 sprockets on it. A sprocket each for the left and right timing chains and 1 for the oil pump drive. The timing mark is located on the center sprocket.*

14. Install the left camshaft sprocket. Install the left timing chain on the crankshaft. Position the single painted link of the timing chain on the tooth of the rear sprocket which is directly behind the timing mark of the center sprocket.

15. Install the left timing chain over the camshaft sprocket. The chain must be positioned with the unpainted link which is between 2

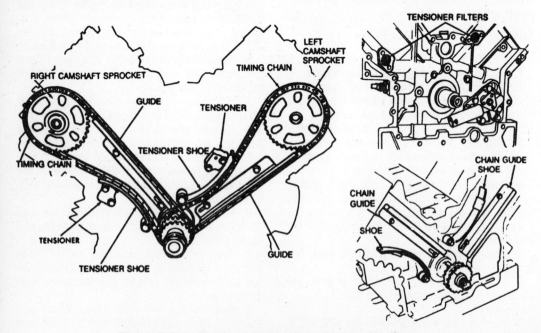

Timing chain and tensioner layout—Dodge Monaco 3.0L engine

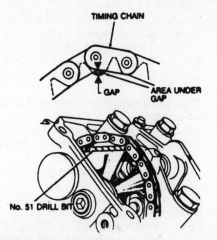

Measuring chain wear using a No. 51 drill as gauge—
Dodge Monaco 3.0L engine

painted links aligned with the stamped timing mark on the camshaft sprocket.

16. Once the left chain is positioned, install the tensioner shoe and turn the tensioner arm inward. Tighten the mounting bolts to 48 inch lbs. (5.4 Nm).

17. Turn the crankshaft until the timing mark on the center sprocket is aligned with the lower oil pump mounting bolt.

18. Install the right side camshaft sprocket. Install the right timing chain over the crankshaft sprocket. Position the single painted link over the timing mark on the crankshaft sprocket.

19. Position the right side timing chain over the camshaft sprocket. The chain must be positioned with the unpainted link which is between 2 painted links aligned with the stamped timing mark on the camshaft sprocket.

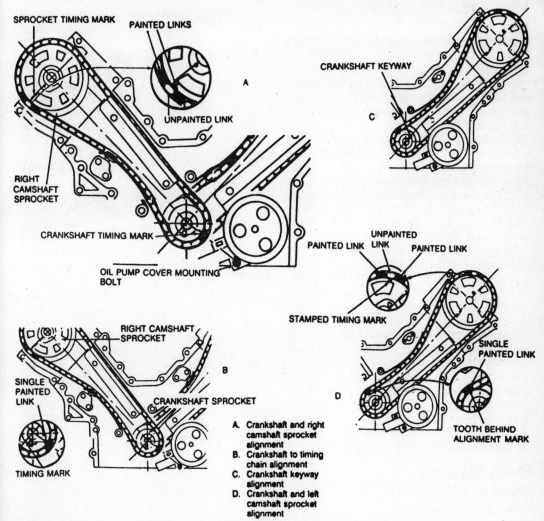

A. Crankshaft and right camshaft sprocket alignment
B. Crankshaft to timing chain alignment
C. Crankshaft keyway alignment
D. Crankshaft and left camshaft sprocket alignment

Engine timing chains and marks are complex; locate and note marks before removal—Dodge Monaco 3.0L engine

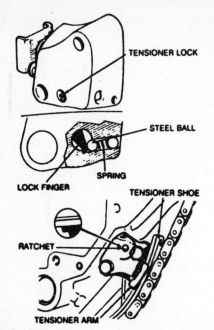

Engine chain tensioner—Dodge Monaco 3.0L engine

20. Once the right side chain is positioned, install the tensioner shoe and turn the tensioner arm inward. Tighten the mounting bolts to 48 inch lbs. (5.4 Nm).

21. Install the right camshaft sprocket bolt and tighten to 59 ft. lbs. (80 Nm). Push both of the chain tensioner shoes in to release them; this will adjust the chain tension.

NOTE: *Once the crankshaft has been rotated, the painted marks on the chain will no longer align with the timing marks. When checking valve timing, it is the relation of the timing marks to each other that is used, not the position of the paint marks on the chains. To check, rotate the crankshaft 180 degrees. Check that the right camshaft sprocket timing mark and the crankshaft sprocket timing mark are aligned. Rotate the crankshaft another 90 degrees. Check that the left camshaft sprocket timing mark and the crankshaft sprocket timing mark are aligned.*

22. Install the oil pump sprocket and chain, apply a suitable thread locking compound to the retaining bolts, and tighten to 48 inch lbs. (5.4 Nm).

23. Install the front cover assembly. Connect the negative battery cable. Check timing.

Timing Sprockets

REMOVAL AND INSTALLATION

2.2 and 2.5L Engines

NOTE: *To hold the camshaft sprocket still while you remove it, it's best to use a special*

tool such as C–4687 or equivalent and, for 2.5 L engines, an adapter such as C–4687–1.

1. Raise and support the car on jackstands.
2. Remove the right inner splash shield.
3. Remove the crankshaft and water pump pulleys.
4. Unbolt and remove both halves of the timing belt cover.
5. Take up the weight of engine with a jack.
6. Remove the right engine mount bolt and raise the engine slightly.
7. Remove the timing belt tensioner and remove the belt.
8. Remove the crankshaft sprocket bolt, and with a puller, remove the sprocket.
9. Using special tool C–4679 or its equivalent (2.2L) or C–4991 or equivalent (2.5L), remove the crankshaft seal.
10. Unbolt and remove the camshaft and intermediate shaft sprockets. Use the special tool or tool and adapter specified in the note above to hold the camshaft sprocket as you loosen the bolt.

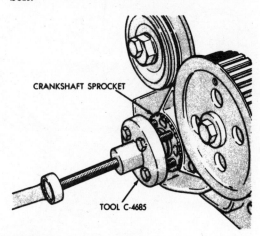

Crankshaft sprocket removal

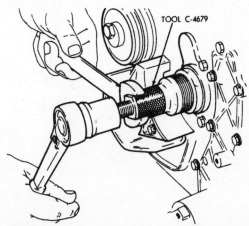

Crankshaft, intermediate shaft, camshaft oil seal removal

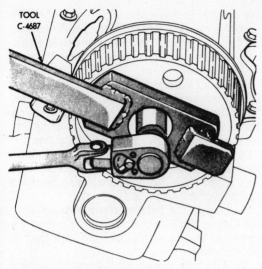

Removing and installing the camshaft and intermediate shaft sprockets

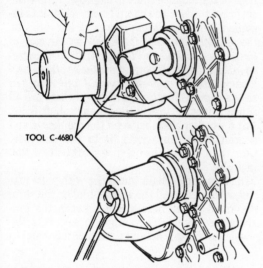

Installing the crankshaft, intermediate shaft and camshaft seal

To install:

11. To install the crankshaft seal, first polish the shaft with 400 grit emery paper. If the seal has a steel case, lightly coat the OD of the seal with Loctite Stud N' Bearing Mount® or its equivalent. If the seal case is rubber coated, generously apply a soap and water solution to facilitate installation. Install the seal with a seal driver. Use C–4680 or equivalent on the 2.2L engine and C–4992 on the 2.5L.

12. Install the sprockets making sure that the timing marks are aligned as illustrated. When installing the camshaft sprocket, make certain the arrows on the sprocket are in line with the #1 camshaft bearing cap-to-cylinder head line.

13. The small hole in the camshaft sprocket must be at the top and in line with the vertical center line of the engine.

14. Rotate the engine two full revolutions and recheck timing mark positioning.

15. Install the belt.

16. Rotate the engine to the #1 piston TDC position.

17. Install the belt tensioner and place tool C-4703 on the large hex nut with the weight hanging away from the auxiliary shaft pulley.

18. Allow the tool to tension the belt. Then, if necessary, reset the tool position so that the axis of the tool is within 15 degrees of horizontal when its tension is positioning the belt.

19. Turn the engine clockwise two full revolutions to #1 TDC.

20. Torque the tensioner locknut to 32 ft. lbs. Other torques are: Timing belt cover bolts, 105 inch lbs.

- Camshaft sprocket bolt, 65 ft. lbs.
- Crankshaft sprocket bolt, 50 ft. lbs.
- Intermediate shaft sprocket bolt, 65 ft. lbs.

2.6L And Other Engines

See the procedures under Timing Chain, Cover and Silent Shafts for the 2.6L engine and the Timing Chain removal and installation for other engines. On all engines that use timing chain instead of timing belt assembly always replace all timing gears (sprockets) when replacing the timing chain.

Balance Shafts

REMOVAL AND INSTALLATION

NOTE: *To complete this procedure, you will need a Tool C–4916 or equivalent or a shim*

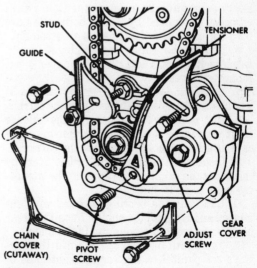

Balance shafts timing chain cover, guide and tensioner (2.5L engines)

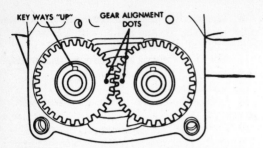

Alignment of timing marks on the balance shaft drive gears

0.039 in. (1mm) thick and 2.75 in. (70mm) long.

1. Drain and remove the oil pan as described above. Remove the attaching bolts and remove the pickup.

CAUTION: *The EPA warns that prolonged contact with used engine oil may cause a number of skin disorders, including cancer! You should make every effort to minimize your exposure to used engine oil. Protective gloves should be worn when changing the oil. Wash your hands and any other exposed skin areas as soon as possible after exposure to used engine oil. Soap and water, or waterless hand cleaner should be used.*

2. Remove the timing belt cover, belt, and crankshaft sprocket as described above. Remove the front crankshaft oil seal retainer as described above.

3. Remove its three mounting bolts and remove the chain cover.

4. Remove the mounting bolt from the chain guide and remove the guide; remove the mounting bolt from the tensioner, and remove it.

5. Remove the bolts which retain the balance shaft gear and chain sprocket (the chain sprocket is retained by Torx® bolts). Remove both sprockets and the chain as an assembly.

6. Remove the gear cover retaining stud with a deep well socket. Then, remove the gear cover. Remove the gears.

7. Unbolt and remove the carrier rear cover. Then, slide the balance shafts out of the carrier.

8. If it is necessary to remove the balance shaft carrier, remove the six carrier-to-crankcase attaching bolts and remove the carrier.

9. Installation is in reverse order. Start by installing the carrier and torquing the mounting bolts to 40 ft. lbs.

10. Lubricate the bearing surfaces with engine oil and reinstall the shafts. Install the rear cover and torque the bolts to 105 inch lbs.

11. Turn both balance shafts until the keyways are parallel to the vertical centerline of the engine and above the shafts. Turn the timing gears so the timing marks align at the center. Install the drive gear with the shorter hub onto the sprocket-driven shaft. Install the gear with the longer hub onto the gear driven shaft.

12. Install the gear cover and torque the stud to 105 inch lbs.

13. Install the crankshaft timing belt sprocket and torque the Torx® bolts to 130 inch lbs. Turn the crankshaft until the timing marks on the chain sprocket line up with the parting line on the left side of No. 1 main bearing cap.

14. Place the chain over the crankshaft sprocket in such a way that the nickel plated link of the chain fits over the timing mark on the crankshaft sprocket.

15. Engage the balance shaft sprocket with the timing chain so that the yellow dot on the sprocket mates with the chain link that is painted yellow.

16. With both balance shaft keyways pointing up, slide the balance shaft sprocket onto the nose of the balance shaft. If necessary, push the nose of the balance shaft in slightly to allow the sprocket to clear the chain cover, when it is installed. Now, *the timing marks on the sprocket, the painted link, and the arrow on the side of the gear cover must all line up with their corresponding marks. If not, retime the shafts as necessary, because improper timing will result in severe engine vibration!* If the sprockets are all timed correctly, install the balance shaft bolts. Put a wooden block between the crankcase and a crankshaft counterweight to prevent rotation; then, torque the balance shaft bolts to 250 inch lbs.

18. Install the chain tensioner with bolts just finger tight. Install the special tool or the shim described in the note above between the tensioner and chain. Then, apply pressure to the tensioner directly behind the adjustment slot to

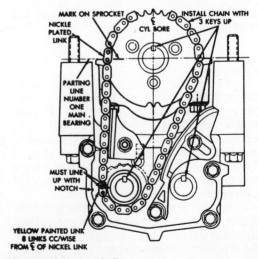

Timing of balance shafts

push the tensioner and shim up against the chain. The shim must contact the shoe of the tensioner from the bottom almost all the way to the top and all slack must be removed. Hold the tension and torque the top tensioner bolt, and then the pivot bolt to 105 inch lbs. Remove the shim or tool. Install the chain guide onto the double-ended stud. Make sure the tab on the guide fits into the slot on the gear cover. Install the nut and washer and torque to 105 inch lbs.

19. Install the carrier covers and torque the bolts to 105 inch lbs.

20. Perform the remaining steps of the installation procedure in reverse of removal.

Intermediate Shaft

REMOVAL AND INSTALLATION

2.2L And 2.5L Engines

1. Disconnect the negative battery cable.

2. Crank the engine so the No. 1 piston is at TDC of its compression stroke. Remove the timing belt covers to confirm that all timing marks are aligned.

3. Remove the distributor, if equipped. Looking down at the oil pump, the slot in the shaft must be parallel with the center line of the crankshaft. Remove the oil pump.

4. Remove the timing belt and the intermediate shaft sprocket.

5. Remove the shaft retainer bolts and remove the retainer from the block.

6. Remove the intermediate shaft from the engine.

7. If necessary, remove the front bushing using tool C–4697–2 and the rear bushing using tool C–4686–2.

To install:

8. Install the front bushing using tool C–4697–1 until the tool is flush with the block. Install the rear bushing using tool C–4686–1 until the tool is flush with the block.

9. Lubricate the distributor drive gear, if equipped, and install the intermediate shaft.

10. Replace the seal in the retainer and apply silicone sealer to the mating surface of the retainer. Install the retainer to the block and torque the bolts to 10 ft. lbs. (12 Nm).

11. Install the intermediate shaft sprocket and the timing belt.

12. With the timing belt properly installed, install the oil pump so the slot is parallel to the center line of the crankshaft. If equipped, install the distributor so the rotor is aligned with the No. 1 spark plug wire tower on the cap.

13. Connect the negative battery cable, check for leaks and adjust the ignition timing, as required.

Camshaft and Bearings

REMOVAL AND INSTALLATION

NOTE: *Use these procedures as a guide for all other engines. Modify service steps as required.*

2.2 and 2.5L Engines

1. Remove the timing belt as described above. Remove the cam cover as described above.

2. Mark the rocker arms for installation identification.

3. Loosen the camshaft bearing capnuts several turns each.

4. Using a wooden or rubber mallet, rap the rear of the camshaft a few times to break it loose.

5. Remove the capnuts and caps being very careful that the camshaft does not cock. Cocking the camshaft could cause irreparable damage to the bearings.

To install:

6. Check all oil holes for blockage.

7. Install the bearing caps with #1 at the timing belt end and #5 at the transmission end. Caps are numbered and have arrows facing forward. Capnut torque is 14 ft. lbs.

8. Apply RTV silicone gasket material to the seal ends.

9. Install the bearing caps BEFORE the seals are installed.

10. The rest of the procedure is the reverse of disassembly.

2.6L Engine

1. Remove the breather hoses and purge hose.

2. Remove the air cleaner and fuel line.

3. Remove the fuel pump. Remove the distributor.

4. Disconnect the spark plug cables.

5. Remove the rocker cover.

6. Remove the breather and semi-circular seal.

7. After slightly loosening the camshaft

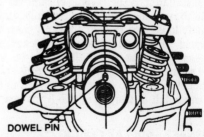

DOWEL PIN

Install the camshaft on 2.6L engines by aligning the dowel pin with the notch in the top of the front bearing cap

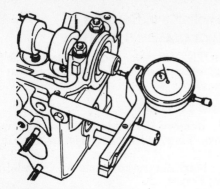

Checking camshaft end play

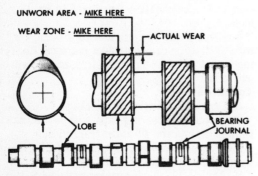

UNWORN AREA - MIKE HERE

WEAR ZONE - MIKE HERE

ACTUAL WEAR

LOBE

BEARING JOURNAL

Measuring cam lobe wear

sprocket bolt, turn the crankshaft until No. 1 piston is at Top Dead Center on compression stroke (both valves closed).

8. Remove the camshaft sprocket bolt and distributor drive gear.

9. Remove the camshaft sprocket with chain and allow it to rest on the camshaft sprocket holder.

10. Remove the camshaft bearing cap tightening bolts. Do not remove the front and rear bearing cap bolts altogether, but keep them inserted in the bearing caps so that the rocker assembly can be removed as a unit.

11. Remove the rocker arms, rocker shafts and bearing caps as an assembly.

12. Remove the camshaft.

13. Installation is the reverse of removal. Lubricate the camshaft lobes and bearings and fit camshaft lobes and bearings and fit camshaft into head. Install the assembled rocker arm shaft assembly. The camshaft should be positioned so that the dowel pin on the front end of the cam is in the 12 o'clock position and in line with the notch in the top of the front bearing cap.

CAMSHAFT ENDPLAY CHECK

1. Move the camshaft as far forward as possible.

2. Install a dial indicator on the end of the camshaft.

3. Zero the indicator, push the camshaft backward, then forward as far as possible and record the play. Maximum play should be 0.006 in. (0.152mm).

INSPECTING THE CAMSHAFT

Measure cam lobe height at the nose or thickest point. Measure at the very edge of the lobe, where there is no wear, and at the center, where wear is at a maximum. On the 2.2 and 2.5 liter engines, 0.010 in. (0.254mm) wear is permitted, while on the 2.6, the figure is 0.020 in. (0.508mm). Replace the camshaft if it is worn excessively.

NOTE: *Use the above procedures as a guide for your engine. Machine shop work requires special training and equipment, it is best to send the camshaft assembly to a reputable machine shop for this kind of repair.*

Pistons and Connecting Rods

IDENTIFICATION

The pistons used in the 2.2 and 2.5 Liter engines have notches in them to indicate the proper installed position. The notch faces the front of the engine, when installed. Connecting rods have markings to indicate proper assembly of the rod to the cap. 2.6 Liter engines have arrows on the pistons. These arrows must face front when installed in the engine. The connecting rods are numbered for easy identification.

REMOVAL AND INSTALLATION

2.2L And 2.5L Engines

1. Follow the instructions under "Cylinder Head" removal and "Timing Belt" or "Timing Chain" removal.

2. Remove the oil pan as described later in this chapter.

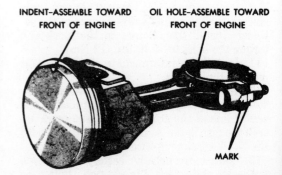

INDENT-ASSEMBLE TOWARD FRONT OF ENGINE

OIL HOLE-ASSEMBLE TOWARD FRONT OF ENGINE

MARK

2.2L pistons for 1981–85 engines

2.6L pistons with connecting rod markings

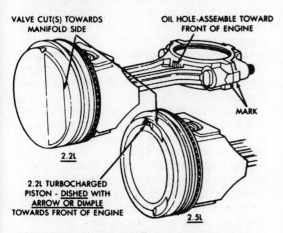

VALVE CUT(S) TOWARDS MANIFOLD SIDE

OIL HOLE-ASSEMBLE TOWARD FRONT OF ENGINE

MARK

2.2L

2.2L TURBOCHARGED PISTON - DISHED WITH ARROW OR DIMPLE TOWARDS FRONT OF ENGINE

2.5L

2.2L pistons for 1986–88 engines, and 2.5L pistons

3. This procedure is much easier performed with the engine of the car.

4. Pistons should be removed in firing order. Turn the crankshaft until the piston to be removed is at the bottom of its stroke.

5. Place a cloth on the head of the piston to be removed and using a ridge reamer, remove the ridge from the upper end of the cylinder bore.

NOTE: *Never remove more than $^1/_{32}$ in. (0.8mm) from the ring travel are when removing the ridges.*

6. Mark all connecting rod bearing caps so that they may be returned to their original locations in the engine. The connecting rod caps are marked with rectangular forge marks which must be mated during assembly and be installed on the intermediate shaft side of the engine. Mark all pistons so they can be returned to their original cylinders.

NOTE: *Don't score the cylinder walls or the crankshaft journal.*

7. Using an internal micrometer, measure the bores across the thrust faces of the cylinder and parallel to the axis of the crankshaft at a minimum of four equally spaced locations. The bore must not be out-of-round by more than 0.005 in. (0.127mm) and it must not taper more than 0.010 in. (0.254mm). Taper is the difference in wear between two bore measurements in any cylinder.

8. If the cylinder bore is in satisfactory condi-

tion, place each ring in the bore in turn and square it in the bore with the head of the piston. Measure the ring gap. If the ring gap is greater than the limit, get a new ring. If the ring gap is less than the limit, file the end of the ring to obtain the correct gap.

9. Check the ring side clearance by installing rings on the piston, and inserting a feeler gauge of the correct dimension between the ring and the lower land. The gauge should slide freely around the ring circumference without binding. Any wear will form a step on the lower land. Remove any pistons having high steps. Before checking the ring side clearance, be sure that the ring grooves are clean and free of carbon, sludge, or grit.

10. Piston rings should be installed so that their ends are at three equal spacings. Avoid installing the rings with their ends in line with the piston pin bosses and the thrust direction.

11. Install the pistons in their original bores, if you are reusing the same pistons. Install short lengths of rubber hose over the connecting rod bolts to prevent damage to the cylinder walls or rod journal.

12. Install a ring compressor over the rings on the piston. Lower the piston and rod assembly into the bore until the ring compressor contacts the block. Using a wooden hammer handle, push the piston into the bore while guiding the rod onto the journal.

NOTE: *On 2.2L and 2.5L engines, the arrow or notch on the piston should face toward the front (drive belt) of the engine.*

CLEANING AND INSPECTION

1. Use a piston ring expander and remove the rings from the piston.

2. Clean the ring grooves using an appropriate cleaning tool, exercise care to avoid cutting too deeply.

3. Clean all varnish and carbon from the piston with a safe solvent. Do not use a wire brush or caustic solution on the pistons.

4. Inspect the pistons for scuffing, scoring, cracks, pitting or excessive ring groove wear. If wear is evident, the piston must be replaced.

5. Have the piston and connecting rod assembly checked by a machine shop for correct alignment, piston pin wear and piston diameter. If the piston has "collapsed" it will have to be replaced or knurled to restore original diameter. Connecting rod bushing replacement, piston pin fitting and piston changing can be handled by the machine shop.

6. On the 2.2L and 2.5L engines, measure the pistons as shown in the illustrations and replace them if they are not to specification. On the 2.6L engine, measure piston diameter with a micrometer in the thrust direction approxi-

mately 0.08 in. (2mm) above the bottom of the skirt. Replace the piston if wear is excessive.

PISTON PIN REPLACEMENT

The pin connecting the piston and connecting rod is press fitted. On the 2.6L engine, the pin bushing in the rod is also press fitted into the top of the rod. You should take the piston/rod assemblies to a machine shop to have pin/bushing wear checked and corrected, if necessary. Installing new rods or pistons requires the use of a press — have the machine shop handle the job for you. The shop should also check the connecting rods for straightness at this time, and replace them, if necessary.

2.6 Liter Engine

Pistons and rods are usually (and most easily) removed as part of a complete engine overhaul. A complete disassembly entails removing the engine from the car and mounting it on a stand, and then removing the cylinder head and oil pan. The front cover, timing chain, and rear main seal are removed. Then, the connecting rod caps are marked and removed and kept in order. The crankshaft is supported or the engine turned upside down and the caps marked, removed, and kept in order. The crankshaft is removed.

Now, the ridge formed at the top of each cylinder by ring wear is removed with a ridge reamer. This is done to prevent damage to the rings or cylinder as the piston is removed. Protect the wear surfaces from grit formed in the reaming process by covering the piston and nearby areas of the cylinder with a clean rag that will catch all the particles. Once the ridges are reamed out, number and remove the pistons and rods.

If, for some reason the engine has suffered ring and cylinder wear but does not require an entire rebuild, you can remove the pistons and rods with the engine in the car. The cylinder head and oil pan must be removed, and connecting rod caps numbered and removed. Turn the crankshaft so each piston is at bottom center position, ream out the ridge as described above, and then mark and remove each piston rod assembly.

In either case, refer to the appropriate procedures above and below for more detailed information.

All four pistons are installed (in original order) with the arrows facing forward — toward the timing chain. Note the relationship between the arrow and marks on the connecting rod and cap. These marks will end up below the number on the top face of the piston.

PISTON RING REPLACEMENT

2.2 and 2.5L Engines

1. Remove the rings from the piston with a ring expander. Clean both the piston ring grooves and the rings thoroughly for more accurate measurement of clearances.

Measuring piston wear—turbocharged 2.2 liter engines. Figures are for 1984–85 engines. Figures for 1985–88 are: 'B' dimension—3.4416–3.4441 in.; Elliptical shape—0.0074–0.0106 in. less at 'A' than at 'B'; Diameter at 'D' should be 0.000–0.0012 in. larger than diameter 'C'

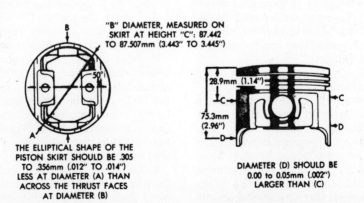

Measuring piston wear for 2.2 and 2.5L engine pistons. Note that the dimension for elliptical wear is as shown for 1981–85 pistons; for 1986–88 pistons, it is 0.30–0.35mm or 0.0118—0.0138 in.

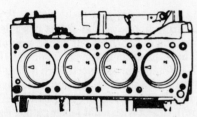

Pistons on the 2.6 liter engine are installed with the arrows facing the timing chain

On the 2.6 liter engine, note the relationship between the arrow on the top of the piston, and numbered marks on both connecting rod and cap

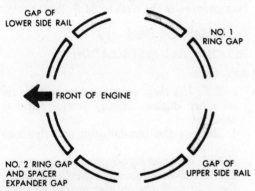

Align the piston ring gaps so they are offset as shown, to prevent ring leakage

2. Inspect the ring grooves on the piston for excessive wear. Install the ring in the groove with a piston ring expander and check side clearance with a feeler gauge. If clearance is excessive, rings will have to be replaced. If new rings cannot restore clearance, replace both the rings and the piston.

3. Take the new piston rings and compress them, one at a time into the cylinder that they will be used in. Press the ring 0.62 in. (16mm) from the bottom of the cylinder they will be used in using an inverted piston.

4. Use a feeler gauge and measure the distance between the ends of the ring, to measure the ring end-gap. Compare the reading to the one called for in the specifications table. File the ends of the ring with a fine file to obtain necessary clearance, if it should be too tight (a rare condition). If ring gap is excessive, the ring must be replaced.

NOTE: *If inadequate ring end-gap is utilized ring breakage will result!*

5. Install new rings on the piston, lower ring first, using a piston ring expander. The "Top" mark on the ring must face upward.

6. When installing oil rings; first, install the ring in the groove. Hold the ends of the ring butted together (they must not overlap) and install the bottom rail (scraper) with the end about 1 in. (25mm) away from the butted end of the control ring. Install the top rail about 1 in. (25mm) away from the butted end of the control but on the opposite side from the lower rail.

7. Install the two compression rings.

8. Consult the illustration for ring positioning, arrange the rings as shown, install a ring compressor and insert the piston and rod assembly into the engine.

2.6L Engine

Piston rings and grooves must be thoroughly cleaned to check side clearance. Remove the rings from each piston with an expander, clean both ring grooves and rings, and reinstall (see below). Measure side clearance with a flat feeler gauge.

The cylinder bores will have to be measured for wear as described below under Cleaning and Inspection. If the bores are satisfactory, and ring side clearance is satisfactory too, each ring must be individually installed in the bottom of its cylinder bore at least 0.63 in. (16mm) from the bottom. Use the piston, inserted part way into the bore, to square the ring's position. Measure end gap with a flat feeler gauge. Excessive dimensions in terms of either side clearance or ring gap require replacement of rings and, if this does not cure excessive side clearance, the rings and piston.

Install the oil ring expander first, and then the upper oil ring rail and, finally the lower oil ring side rail. When installing the side rails, do not use a ring expander, but place one end be-

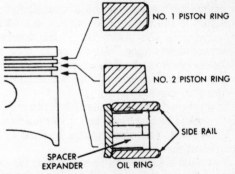

Install the rings on the 2.6L engine as shown. Note the difference between No. 1 and No. 2 rings. Markings on the rings should face upward

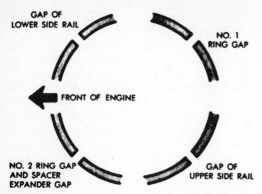

Stagger the rings gaps as shown to prevent ring leakage

tween the piston and ring groove and the ring expander. Hold the end firmly and work your way around the expander from that point to work it down and into position.

With a ring expander, install first the No. 2 ring and, finally, the No. 1 ring. Finally, stagger the ring gaps as shown in the illustration. The oil ring expander gap must be at least 45 degrees from the side rail gaps but not aligned either with the piston pin or the thrust direction.

ROD BEARING REPLACEMENT

The crankshaft must be miked to ensure that it meets wear specifications. See the section below on Crankshaft and Main Bearings. In addition, assuming that connecting rod bearings do not show signs of excess wear or heat (roughness, grooving, blue color from heat, etc.), the bearing clearance must be checked with Plastigage®. This is done by drying all the surfaces and then inserting a Plastigage® insert in between the crankpin and the bearing surface. Assemble the connecting rod cap to the rod. Oil the bolts and then torque them to: 40 ft. lbs. plus ¼ turn on 2.2 and 2.5L engines and 34 ft. lbs. on the 2.6L engine. Do not turn the crankshaft.

Then, remove the cap and read the clearance by comparing the width of the groove left on the crankpin to the width of the marks on a scale provided with the insert kit. If the bearing clearance meets specifications, make sure to clean the insert mark off the crankpin and thoroughly lubricate all parts with clean engine oil before final assembly.

In most cases, if wear is excessive, the crankshaft should be machined and undersize bearings installed. This work should be done by a competent machine shop.

You must also check connecting rods for excessive clearance between the side of the rod and the cheek of the crankshaft. Connecting rod clearance between the rod and crankthrow

casting is checked with a feeler gauge. Pry the rod carefully to one side as far as possible and measure the distance on the other side of the rod. The clearance must be 0.005–0.013 in. (0.127–0.33mm) for new parts with a wear limit of 0.015 in. (0.38mm) on 2.2 and 2.5L engines; on the 2.6L, it must be 0.004–0.010 in. (0.10–0.25mm). Check with a flat feeler gauge. Excess clearance must be corrected by replacing the rod or possibly the rod and crankshaft.

Pistons must be installed into their original bores. All parts must be thoroughly lubricated with engine oil. Use a ring compressor to hold the rings in the compressed position as you slip the piston/rod assembly down into the cylinder. The compressor will rest right against the top of the block. If the crankshaft is still in place, make sure the crankpin is in Bottom Dead Center position. Protect the crankpin from contact with connecting rod studs, if necessary by slipping lengths of rubber hose over the studs. Make sure the rod caps face in the right direction and torque the nuts to 34 ft. lbs.

Rear Main Oil Seal

REMOVAL AND INSTALLATION

2.2L Engine

NOTE: *Use these procedures as a guide for all other engines. Modify service steps as required.*

1. Remove the transmission and flywheel/flex plate.

NOTE: *On some early models, before removing the transmission, align the dimple on the flywheel with the pointer on the flywheel housing. The transmission will not mate with the engine during installation unless this alignment is observed.*

2. Very carefully, pry the oil seal out of the

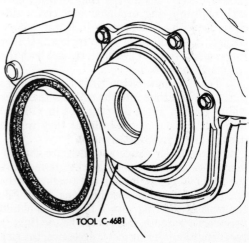

TOOL C-4681

Installing rear oil seal

support ring. Be careful not to nick or damage the crankshaft flange seal surface or retainer bore.

3. Place special tool #C-4681 or its equivalent on the crankshaft.

4. Lightly coat the outside diameter of the seal with Loctite Stud N' Bearing Mount® or its equivalent. Also coat the inside of the seal with engine oil.

5. Place the seal over tool #C-4681 and gently tap it into place with a plastic hammer.

6. Reinstall the remaining parts in the reverse order of removal.

2.6L Engine

The rear main oil seal is located in a housing on the rear of the block. To replace the seal, remove the transmission and flywheel or flex plate and do the work from underneath the vehicle or remove the engine and do the work on the bench.

1. Remove the housing from the block.

2. Remove the separator from the housing.

3. Pry out the old seal.

4. Lightly oil the replacement seal. The oil seal should be installed so that the seal plate fits into the inner contact surface of the seal case. Install the separator with the oil holes facing down.

Crankshaft and Main Bearings
REMOVAL AND INSTALLATION

NOTE: *Use these procedures as a guide for all other engines. Modify service steps as required.*

1. Rod bearings can be installed when the pistons have been removed for servicing (rings etc.) or, in most cases, while the engine is still in the car. Bearing replacement, however, is far easier with the engine out of the car and disassembled.

2. For in-car service, remove the oil pan, spark plugs and front cover if necessary. Turn the engine until the connecting rod to be serviced is at the bottom of its travel. Remove the bearing cap, place two pieces of rubber hose over the rod cap bolts and push the piston and rod assembly up the cylinder bore until enough

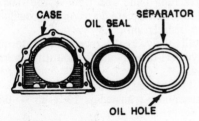

Rear main oil seal on 2.6L engines

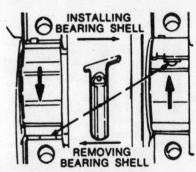

Removing/installing the upper bearing insert with a roll-out pin

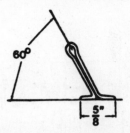

Here's how to make your own roll-out pin

room is gained for bearing insert removal. Take care not to push the rod assembly up too far or the top ring will engage the cylinder ridge or come out of the cylinder and require head removal for reinstallation.

3. Clean the rod journal, the connecting rod end and the bearing cap after removing the old bearing inserts. Install the new inserts in the rod and bearing cap, lubricate them with oil. Position the rod over the crankshaft journal and install the rod caps. Make sure the cap and rod numbers match, torque the rod nuts to specifications.

4. Main bearings may be replaced while the engine is still in the car by "rolling" them out and in.

5. Special roll-out pins are available from automotive parts houses or can be fabricated from a cotter pin. The roll out pin fits in the oil hole of the main bearing journal. When the crankshaft is rotated opposite the direction of the bearing lock tab, the pin engages the end of the bearing and rolls out the insert.

6. Remove main bearing cap and roll out upper bearing insert. Remove insert from main bearing cap. Clean the inside of the bearing cap and crankshaft journal.

7. Lubricate and roll upper insert into position, make sure the lock tab is anchored and the insert is not cocked. Install the lower bearing insert into the cap; lubricate and install on the engine. Make sure the main bearing cap is installed facing in the correct direction. Make

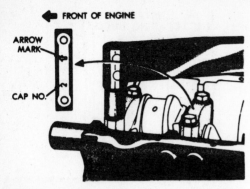

On the 2.6L engine, install the caps in numbered order, arrows facing forward

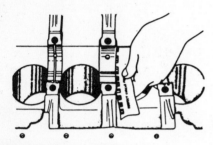

Checking main bearing clearance on 2.6L engine

sure the oil holes line up with those in the block and that the upper shell (grooved) on #3 main bearing is located in the block (rather than in the cap) on the 2.2 and 2.5L engines. Torque to specifications.

8. With the engine out of the car. Remove the intake manifold, cylinder head, front cover, timing gears and/or chain, oil pan, oil pump and flywheel.

9. Remove the piston and rod assemblies. Remove the main bearing caps after marking them for position and direction.

10. Remove the crankshaft bearing inserts and rear main oil seal. Clean the engine block and cap bearing saddles. Clean the crankshaft and inspect for wear. Check the bearing journals with a micrometer for out-of-round condition and to determine what size rod and main bearing inserts to install.

11. Install the main bearing upper inserts and rear main oil seal half (2.2 and 2.5L engines only) into the engine block.

12. Lubricate the bearing inserts and the crankshaft journals. Slowly and carefully lower the crankshaft into position.

13. On the 2.2 and 2.5L engines, install the bearing inserts and rear main seal into the bearing caps, and install the caps from the middle out. Check the cap bolts for "necking down". This is a condition that would prevent the right size nut from being run down until it touches the cap or would cause some threads not to touch a straightedge run along the side of the bolt. Replace if necessary. Torque cap bolts to specifications alternately, in stages.

On the 2.6 liter engine, install the main caps in numbered sequence, No. 1 nearest the timing chain and No. 5 at the transmission end. Make sure the arrows on the caps point toward the timing chain end of the engine. Torque alternately and in three stages to 58 ft. lbs.

14. Remove bearing caps, one at a time, and check the oil clearance with Plastigage® (see the procedure just below). Reinstall if clearance is within specifications. Check the crankshaft end-play as described below, and if it is within specifications install connecting rod and piston assemblies with new rod bearing inserts. Check connecting rod bearing oil clearance and rod side play (see the procedure above); if these are correct, assemble the rest of the engine.

Flywheel and Ring Gear
REMOVAL AND INSTALLATION

The flywheel on manual transmission cars serves as the forward clutch engagement surface. It also serves as the ring gear with which the starter pinion engages to crank the engine. The most common reason to replace the flywheel is broken teeth on the starter ring gear. To remove it, remove the transmission as described in Chapter 7. Then, unbolt and remove the clutch and pressure plate. Finally, *support the flywheel in a secure manner* and then remove the eight attaching bolts and remove the flywheel (matchmark flywheel location if possible for correct installation).

On automatic transmission cars, the torque converter actually forms part of the flywheel. It is bolted to a thin flexplate which, in turn, is bolted to the crankshaft. The flex plate also serves as the ring gear with which the starter pinion engages in engine cranking. The flex plate occasionally cracks; the teeth on the ring gear may also break, especially if the starter is often engaged while the pinion is still spinning. The torque converter and flex plate are separated so the converter and transmission can be removed together. Remove the automatic transaxle as described in Chapter 7. Then, remove the attaching bolts and remove the flexplate (matchmark flexplate location if possible for correct installation).

Install the flywheel in reverse order, torquing the flywheel-to-crankshaft mounting bolts as follows:

- All transaxles, 1986–88 – 70 ft. lbs.
- Automatic transaxles, 1981–85 – 65 ft. lbs.
- Manual transaxles, 1984–86 – 65 ft. lbs.

• Manual transaxles, 1981–83 – 50 ft. lbs.

When the flywheel or flexplate is back in position, reinstall the transmission as described in Chapter 7. Refer to the Torque Specification Chart for torque specifications for flywheel/flexplate installation not listed or for possible changes.

EXHAUST SYSTEM

Exhaust Pipes, Mufflers, and Tailpipes

For a number of different reasons, exhaust system work can be the most dangerous type of work you can do on your car. *Always observe the following precautions:*

1. Support the car extra securely. Not only will you often be working directly under it, but you'll frequently be using a lot of force – say, heavy hammer blows, to dislodge rusted parts. This can cause a car that's improperly supported to shift and possibly fall.

2. Wear goggles. Exhaust system parts are always rusty. Metal chips can be dislodged, even when you're only turning rusted bolts. Attempting to pry pipes apart with a chisel makes chips fly even more frequently.

3. If you're using a cutting torch, keep it at a great distance from either the fuel tank or lines. Stop what you're doing and feel the temperature of fuel bearing pipes or the tank frequently. Even slight heat can expand or vaporize the fuel, resulting in accumulated vapor or even a liquid leak near your torch.

4. Watch where your hammer blows fall. You could easily tap a brake or fuel line when you hit an exhaust system part with a blow. Inspect all lines and hoses in the area where you've been working before driving the car.

REMOVAL AND INSTALLATION

1. Support the vehicle securely. Apply penetrating oil to all clamp bolts and nuts you will be working on. Support the vehicle by the body, if possible, to increase working clearances.

2. If the tailpipe is integral with the muffler, and the muffler must be replaced, cut the tail pipe with a hacksaw right near the front of the muffler. The replacement muffler is then installed using a clamp to attach to the tailpipe.

3. Loosen clamps and supports to permit alignment of all parts, and then retighten. Make sure there is adequate clearance so exhaust parts stay clear of underbody parts.

4. Clean the mating surfaces of pipes or the muffler to ensure a tight seal. Use new insulators, clamps, and supports unless the condition of old parts is very good. Note that the slip joint at the front of the muffler uses a

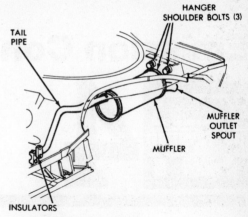

Typical tailpipe and muffler

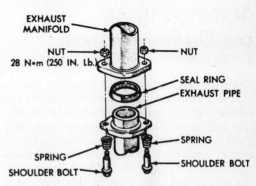

The special exhaust joint coupling is used to allow the engine to move without stressing or cracking exhaust system components

U-clamp. The bolts should be torqued to 270 inch lbs. on cars with normally aspirated engines and to 360 inch lbs. on turbocharged cars.

NOTE: *A number of special exhaust system tools can be rented from auto supply houses or local stores that rent special equipment. A common one is a tail pipe expander, designed to enable you to join pipes of identical diameter. It may also be quite helpful to use solvents designed to loosen rusted bolts or flanges. Soaking rusted parts the night before you do the job can speed the work of freeing rusted parts considerably. Remember that these solvents are often flammable. Apply them only after the parts are cool.*

CAUTION: *Note that a special flexible coupling is used to connect the exhaust pipe to the exhaust manifold. If this important coupling should develop a leak, be sure to replace the seal ring with a quality part, install it in the proper direction, and torque the bolts to specifications. Check also for any cracks in the exhaust pipe, exhaust manifold, or flanges and replace such parts as necessary to prevent carbon monoxide poisoning.*

Emission Controls

4

EMISSION CONTROLS

Crankcase Ventilation System

OPERATION

The PCV system is used to draw the incompletely burned fuel/air mixture that passes the piston rings and valve guides out of the crankcase and valve cover. This mixture contains a great deal of unburnt hydrocarbons. The PCV system conducts it to the engine's air intake system for burning with the fresh mixture in the combustion chambers. In this way, total emissions of unburnt fuel are greatly reduced.

The Chrysler system is unique in that it draws fresh air into the PCV circuit without passing it through the engine crankcase. Fresh air is mixed with the blowby being handled by the system at low rpm, when vacuum is high and blowby minimal. This mixing occurs at the PCV module on carbureted cars. On fuel injected and injected turbo cars, the mixing occurs near the PCV valve or in the top of the valve cover. A filter in the PCV module or air cleaner filters fresh air so that dust will not enter the engine's intake system.

The carburetor or fuel injection system is precisely calibrated to compensate for the extra air the system introduces into the engine's combustion chambers. At the same time, because of the high vacuum the system operates under, the potential exists for it to bleed a great deal of excess air into the system and disturb the mixture. If the engine runs poorly, especially at idle speeds (when vacuum is highest), inspect the PCV system thoroughly for leaks and the PCV valve for clogging or sticking. It may have clogged, failing partly open, so that too much excess air will enter the system causing lean operation.

SERVICE

With the engine idling, remove the PCV valve from the engine. If the valve is operating properly, a hissing noise will be heard and a strong vacuum felt when a finger is placed over the valve inlet. With the engine OFF, the valve should rattle when it is shaken. If the valve is not operating properly it must be REPLACED. Do not attempt to clean the old PCV valve.

Evaporative Emission Controls

This system prevents the release of gasoline vapors from the fuel tank and the carburetor into

The PCV system used on carbureted cars

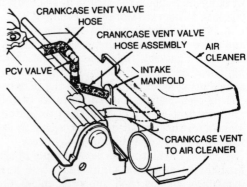

The PCV system used on cars with Throttle Body fuel injection

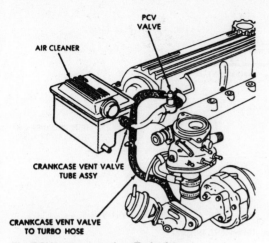

The PCV system used on Turbo I cars

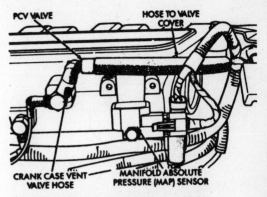

The PCV system used on 3.3/3.8L vehicles

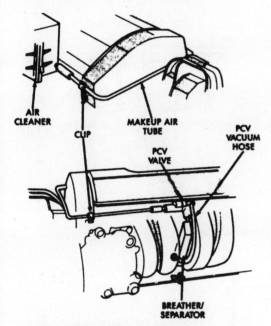

The PCV system used on Turbo II cars

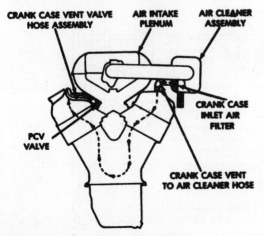

The PCV system used on 3.0L vehicles

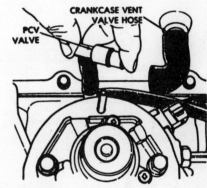

PCV valve test

the atmosphere. It is vacuum operated and draws the fumes into a charcoal canister where they are temporarily held until they are drawn into the intake manifold for burning.

The canister is a sealed, maintenance-free device located in the wheelwell. It is fed from the fuel tank and the carburetor float bowl. When the engine starts, air pump pressure closes off the connection to the carburetor fuel bowl. On most models, an electric solenoid known as a "purge solenoid" opens when the engine temperature exceeds 145°F (63°C). This applies manifold vacuum to the canister to draw the stored fuel vapor out of the charcoal element inside.

SERVICE

For proper operation of the system and to prevent system failure, the lines should be cleaned if they should become plugged, and no gas cap other than the one specified should be used on the fuel tank filler neck. A special fuel-resistant hose is used. If any hoses need replacing, be sure to use hose rated for this type of service.

NOTE: *All vehicles are equipped with a Vehicle Emission Control Information Label which is located in the engine compartment.*

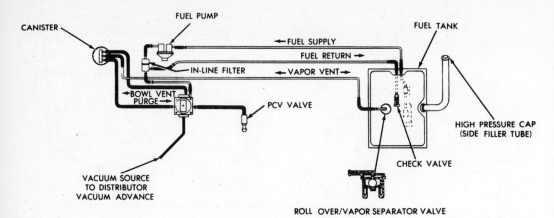

Evaporation control system—2.2L engine

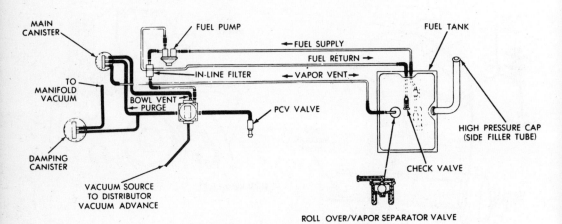

Evaporation control system—2.6L engine

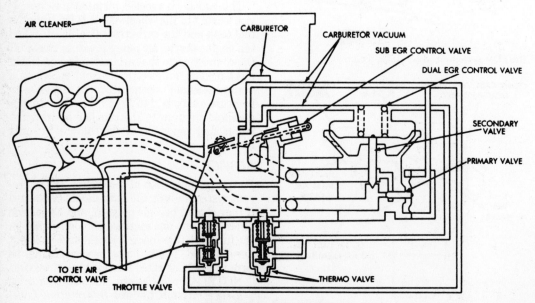

EGR system—2.6L engine

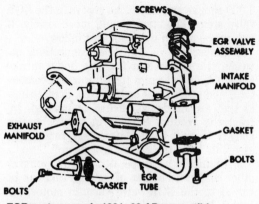

EGR system—early 1991–92 AP convertible

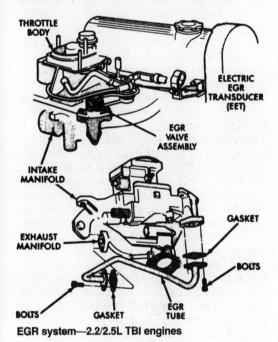

EGR system—2.2/2.5L TBI engines

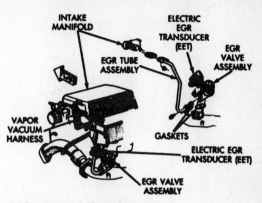

EGR system—3.0L engine

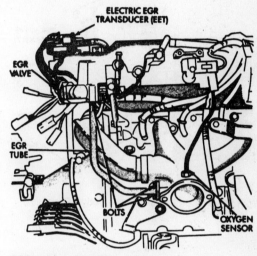

EGR system—3.3/3.8L engines

EGR system—Turbo I engine

The label contains emission specifications and vacuum hose routings. All hoses must be connected and routed as shown on the label.

Exhaust Gas Recirculation System

This system reduces the amount of oxides of nitrogen in the exhaust by allowing a predetermined amount of exhaust gases to recirculate and dilute the incoming fuel/air mixture. The principal components of the system are the EGR valve and the Coolant Control Exhaust Gas Recirculation Valve (CCEGR) used on 1981-86 models or the Coolant Vacuum Switch Cold Closed (CVSCC) used on 1986-88 models. The EGR valve is located in the intake manifold and directly regulates the flow of exhaust gases into the intake. The latter is located in the thermostat housing and overrides the EGR valve when coolant temperature is below 125°F (52°C).

Exhaust system backpressure tends to increase the rate at which the EGR valve flows ex-

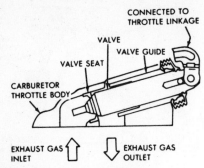

Sub EGR congtrol valve assembly

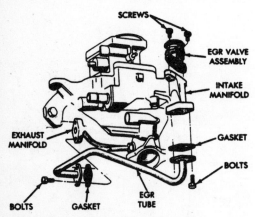

EGR valve mounting for throttle body EFI

haust gas back into the engine. For this reason, on fuel injected and turbocharged engines, an Exhaust Backpressure Transducer is used to regulate the vacuum that opens the EGR valve. When backpressure increases, the transducer will decrease vacuum in such a way that the valve opening will be reduced and gas flow rate will remain correct in spite of that backpressure increase.

2.6 L engines use a Sub EGR Control Valve. This valve is an integral part of the carburetor, and is directly opened and closed by linkage connected to the throttle valve. In conjunction with the standard EGR system the sub EGR more closely modulates EGR flow in response to the throttle valve opening.

SERVICE

The symptoms of possible EGR system failure include: spark knock, engine sag or severe hesitation on acceleration, or rough idle or stalling. Check the following items:

1. Start the engine and allow it to idle in neutral with the throttle closed, for over 70 seconds. Abruptly accelerate the engine to 2,000-3,000 rpm as you watch the groove in the EGR valve stem. The stem should move visibly. If not, proceed with the tests that follow.

2. Inspect all vacuum hose connections between the carburetor/throttle body, intake manifold, and vacuum transducer. All connections and hoses must be leak-free. Replace hoses that are hardened, melted or cracked. Inspect the vacuum passage in the carburetor body or throttle body. If necessary, remove the assembly from the engine and clean it.

3. Connect a hand operated vacuum pump or other confirmed source of vacuum that can be valved to the EGR valve vacuum motor, via rubber hose connections. Tee a vacuum gauge into the line, if you are not using a pump equipped with a vacuum gauge. Have the engine running at normal operating temperature and normal idle speed. Apply vacuum as you read the vacuum gauge. Listen to the engine as you gradually increase vacuum. The engine speed should begin to drop as vacuum reaches 2.0-3.5 in.Hg. The engine may stumble or even stall. This means exhaust gas is flowing through the system the way it is supposed to. If a separate vacuum supply has no effect on engine speed or smoothness, repeat the test, watching the EGR valve stem. If the stem does not move, it will probably be necessary to replace the EGR valve. Unless the stem has been frozen in place by deposits and can be freed up, replace the valve. If the stem moves, but there is no effect on engine operation, clean the EGR system passages — they are clogged.

4. If the EGR system recycles too much exhaust and the system idles roughly, try idling the engine with the EGR valve vacuum line disconnected and plugged. If this has little or no effect, try removing the EGR valve/transducer and inspecting it to make sure the EGR valve poppet is seated. If it will not seat, replace the valve.

5. Check also for an EGR tube-to-manifold leak. On 2.2 and 2.5L engines, torque the EGR tube-to-manifold nut to 300 inch lbs.

REMOVAL AND INSTALLATION

EGR Valve

1. Disconnect the vacuum line going to the EGR valve. Inspect it for cracking, poor seal due to hardness, or other problems and replace if necessary.

2. Remove the two bolts attaching the EGR valve to the intake manifold. Remove the EGR valve.

3. Clean both gasket surfaces and check for cracks. Replace parts as necessary.

4. Install a new gasket and the EGR valve onto the manifold. Install the two attaching

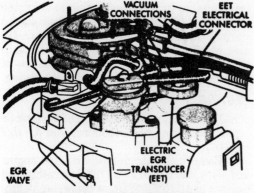

EGR valve mounting 2.2/2.5L TBI engines

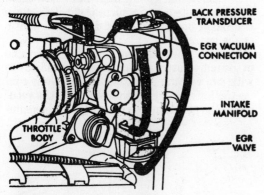

EGR mounting—Turbo I engine

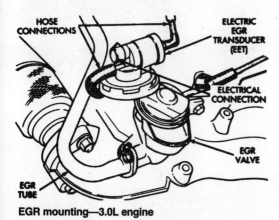

EGR mounting—3.0L engine

bolts and torque to 200 inch lbs. Reconnect the vacuum line.

EGR Tube

1. Remove the four EGR tube attaching bolts from the intake and exhaust manifold connections. Remove the EGR tube.

2. Clean all four gasket surfaces. Inspect gasket surfaces for signs of cracking and replace the EGR tube or manifolds if cracking is found. Discard old gaskets and supply new ones.

3. Assemble the tube and gaskets into place, installing the attaching bolts only loosely.

4. Torque the attaching bolts to 200 inch lbs.

Oxygen Sensor

REMOVAL AND INSTALLATION

NOTE: *To remove the oxygen sensor, a special removal tool is needed. There are two types of sensors — standard and heated. Heated sensors have a multi-prong electrical terminal with three wires, and standard sensors have only a single wire connector. For standard sensors, use tool C-4589 or an equivalent from the aftermarket; for heated sensors, use C-4907 or equivalent. It is necessary to be able to adapt this tool to a torque wrench. Also needed is a tap to clean the sensor mounting threads.*

1. Make sure the engine has been turned off for several hours so all parts will have cooled sufficiently for safe handling. *Pulling on the plug and not the wiring*, disconnect the oxygen sensor electrical lead.

2. Install the special tool and unscrew the sensor from the exhaust manifold.

3. Turn the tap into the sensor threads to chase any corrosion or dirt out.

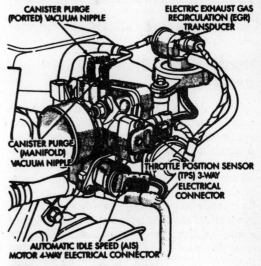

EGR mounting—3.3/3.8L engines

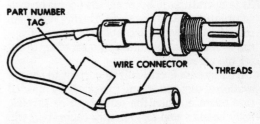

Standard oxygen sensor assembly

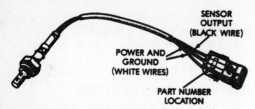

Heated oxygen sensor assembly

Oxygen sensor special socket

4. If installing a new sensor, make sure to get the proper replacement parts. Sensors used with turbo cars have a terminal boot not used on other sensors. As previously mentioned, 1988 and later models use a heated sensor with a multi-prong plug.

5. If the sensor is to be reinstalled, coat the threads with the anti-seize compound. Turn the sensor into the threads and torque it to 20 ft. lbs.

6. Reconnect the electrical connector securely.

Heated Air Inlet System

OPERATION

All 2.2L, 2.5L and 2.6L carbureted and throttle body injected engines are equipped with a vacuum device located in the air cleaner air intake. A small door is operated by a vacuum diaphragm and a thermostatic spring. When the air temperature outside is 65°F (18°C) or lower on carbureted engines, or 115°F (46°C) or lower on throttle body injected engines, the door will block off air entering from outside and allow air channeled from the exhaust manifold area to enter the intake. This air is heated by the hot manifold. At 90°F (32°C) or above on carbureted engines and 140°F (60°C) or above on TBI engines, the door fully blocks off the heated air. At temperatures in between, the door is operated in intermediate positions. During heavy acceleration the door is controlled by engine vacuum to allow the maximum amount of air to enter the carburetor.

This system is critically important to the operation of carbureted and throttle body injected cars because, when the carburetor or throttle body handles cold air, mixture calibration will become incorrect (too lean). The result will be lean running (misfire and hesitation). Engine performance will deteriorate even more during warmup in cold weather. The carburetor will also be more likely to ice up in cool, damp weather. There may also be high emissions of hydrocarbons, as revealed by emissions testing.

TESTING

NOTE: *You'll need a hand vacuum pump or other source of measurable vacuum for this test.*

1. Remove the air cleaner from the engine and allow it to cool to 65°F (18°C) on carbureted engines and 115°F (46°C), or below, on fuel injected engines.

2. Inspect all the vacuum lines associated with the system and replace them if they are cracked or broken or if they do not seal tightly at the connections.

3. Apply 20 in. Hg of vacuum to the inlet side of the temperature sensor, a small round device with two vacuum ports, one of which was connected to the intake manifold. Apply the vacuum to the port that was connected to the mani-

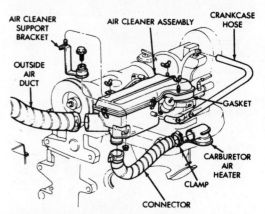

Heated air inlet system—2.2L engine

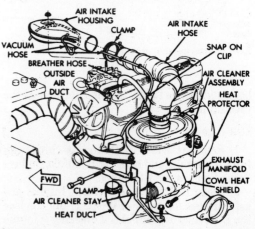

Heated air inlet system—2.6L engine

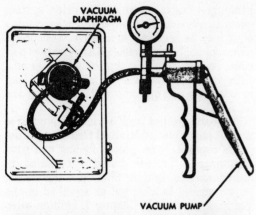

Testing the heated air system vacuum diaphragm

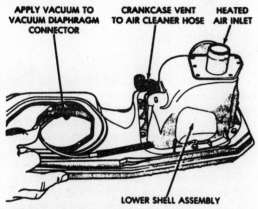

Testing vacuum diaphragm on heated air inlet system—late model

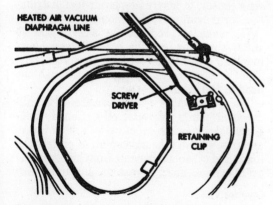

Removing the sensor clips—late model

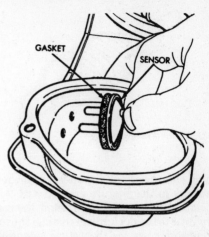

Replacing the air temperature sensor—heated air intake system

fold. Observe the temperature door — it should close.

4. If the door remains open, connect the vacuum source to the vacuum diaphragm on the temperature door. The door should close and then retest the system.

5. If the door now closes, replace the temperature sensor. If the door still does not close, replace the air cleaner, as the temperature door vacuum diaphragm and door are integral parts of it.

REMOVAL AND INSTALLATION

Temperature Sensor

1. Remove the air cleaner. Note routing and then disconnect both vacuum hoses from the sensor.

2. Pry the retaining clips off the sensor connections and discard them. Pull the sensor and gasket out of the wall of the air cleaner.

3. Install the new sensor and gasket and fasten the sensor in place by forcing the new retaining clips all the way onto the vacuum connectors. Make sure to hold the sensor against the air cleaner by its outside diameter as you install the clips so as to compress the gasket.

4. Reconnect the vacuum hoses securely and reinstall the air cleaner.

Catalytic Converter

OPERATION

Two catalysts are used on each car on model years through 1985. On dual catalyst systems, a small one located just after the exhaust manifold ignites early in the engine warm-up cycle, and a larger one located under the car body completes the clean-up process during warmed-up operation of the car. Catalysts promote complete oxidation of exhaust gases through the effect of a platinum and palladium coated mass in the catalyst shell. Three-way catalysts combine oxidation (normal burning) of the fuel with reduction — the removal of oxygen from Nitrogen Oxides. The platinum and palladium are noble metals which accelerate combustion by providing chemical entities necessary for complete

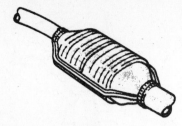

Catalytic converter assembly

burning after nearly all the energy and chemical activity in the mixture are depleted. After the combustion process is completed, the material returns to the noble metal coating; the catalytic converter has the theoretical potential to last indefinitely. If the unit should be damaged, it must be replaced — no service is possible.

1986 and later models employ a 3-way catalyst. Two converters, working under different fuel/air mixture conditions are used. The first catalyst is fed exhaust from the engine that is at the chemically correct mixture ratio of 14.7:1. At this point, the exhaust gases contain oxygen that has combined with the nitrogen in the air to form nitrogen oxides (a pollutant); and unburnt (or oxygen-short) hydrocarbons and carbon monoxide (another pollutant). This converter creates conditions which cause the oxygen in the nitrogen oxides to combine with the unburnt material. This is called "reduction" of the nitrogen oxides. Once the nitrogen oxides have been reduced, the air pump adds extra air (and oxygen). The second converter uses this extra oxygen to complete the job of oxidizing the unburnt material.

Two things act to destroy the catalyst: the use of leaded gas and excessive heat. The use of leaded fuel is the most common cause of catalyst destruction. The lead coats the thin layer of platinum and palladium that actually promotes final combustion of the almost completely burned hydrocarbons that enter the catalytic converter. The coating keeps the mixture from actually contacting the noble metals. The lead may also cause the "substrate" — the material that carries the noble metal coating to clog the passages of the converter, causing the car to run at reduced power or even stop altogether.

The catalyst is fed fuel/air mixture in its least potent form — when combustion is almost 100% complete and nearly all energy has been removed. Excessive heat results in the converter when raw fuel and air with a high oxygen content enter the catalytic converter — a device which greatly accelerates the combustion process. This most often occurs when a spark plug wire is disconnected. Excessive heat during misfiring due to poor vehicle maintenance and prolonged testing with the ignition system wires disconnected are two common ways a catalyst may be rendered ineffective. Test procedures should be accomplished as quickly as possible. The car should be shut off whenever misfiring is noted. Misfiring due to extremely lean or extremely rich mixtures will also damage the catalyst.

While the catalyst itself is a maintenance-free item, it should be understood that long life depends completely on proper fueling and good maintenance. The car should be tuned as required, and fuel and air filters and the oxygen sensor should be changed as specified in the maintenance chart in Chapter 1. Ignition wires and the distributor cap and rotor should be inspected/tested and replaced if necessary to prevent misfire.

Air Injection System
OPERATION

This system is used on all 1981-87 2.2 Liter carburetor-equipped engines. Its job is to reduce carbon monoxide and hydrocarbons to required levels. It adds a controlled amount of air to exhaust gases, causing oxidation of the gases and a reduction in carbon monoxide and hydrocarbons.

The air injection system on the 2.2 Liter engine also includes an air switching system. It has been designed so that air injection will not interfere with the EGR system to control NOx emissions, and on vehicles equipped with an oxygen sensor, to insure proper air-fuel distribution for maximum fuel economy.

The vehicles produced for sale in the 50 states pump air into the base of the exhaust manifold and into the catalytic converter body. The Canadian system pumps air through the head at the exhaust port.

The air injection system consists of a belt-driven air pump, a diverter valve (Canadian engines only) a switch-relief valve, rubber hoses, and check valve tube assemblies to protect the hoses and other components from high temperature exhaust gases in case the air pump fails.

Diverter Valve

The purpose of the diverter valve is to prevent backfire in the exhaust system during sudden deceleration. Sudden throttle closure at the beginning of deceleration temporarily creates an air-fuel mixture too rich to burn. This mixture becomes burnable when it reaches the exhaust area and combines with injector air. The next firing of the cylinder will ignite this air-fuel mixture. The valve senses the sudden increase in manifold vacuum, causing the valve to open, allowing air from the pump to pass through the valve into the atmosphere.

A pressure relief valve incorporated in the same housing as the diverter valve controls pressure within the system by diverting excessive pump output to the atmosphere at high engine speed.

Switch-Relief Valve

The purpose of this valve, an integral part of all U.S. air injection systems, is two-fold. First of all, it directs the air injection flow to either the exhaust port location or to the down-stream injection point. Second, the valve regulates system pressure by controlling the output of the air pump at high speeds. When the pressure reaches a certain level, some of the output is vented to the atmosphere through the silencer.

Check Valve

A check valve is located in the injection tube assemblies that lead to the exhaust manifold and the catalyst injection points on the 50 state engines and to the exhaust port area, through four hollow bolts on the Canadian engines.

This valve has a one-way diaphragm which prevents hot exhaust gases from backing up into the hose and pump. It also protects the system in the event of pump belt failure, excessively high exhaust system pressure, or air hose ruptures.

SERVICE

The most common problem with the air pump system is air pump noise. It first must be understood that a small amount of rattling or chirping noise comes from an air pump in perfect mechanical condition. It should also be understood that, if the air pump requires replacement, the new pump will be extra noisy until it

has broken in. Operate the new pump for 1,000 miles before condemning it as noisy.

If the air pump belt suddenly becomes noisy, first check that tension is correct. If the belt is slipping, noise will often be the result. Retension the belt or, if it is glazed (with smooth, glassy wear surfaces), replace it, making sure to tension the new belt properly and to readjust it a week or two later.

Check also that the pump rotates freely by removing the belt and turning the pump drive pulley by hand. There is normally some slight roughness and rattling when turning the drive pulley. A frozen pump's pulley will be impossible or extremely hard to turn.

If the car is in generally good tune and mechanical condition, and runs well but exhibits high CO and hydrocarbon emissions, the air pump system may not be supplying air to the catalytic converter (or exhaust manifold on Canadian cars). In this case, the best procedure is to disconnect the outlet hose passing from the switch/relief valve to the converter and check for airflow. If there is no flow at idle speed, and noticeable flow above idle speed, which increases when the engine is accelerated, the air pump system is okay and the problem may be in the oxygen sensor or fuel system. If air does not flow at this point in the system, disconnect the hose at the air pump side of the switch/relief valve and repeat the test. If there is air at this point now, and no vacuum actuating the switch/relief valve, replace it.

Check also that all hoses are free of cracks, breaks and clogs and that they are tightly and fully connected.

AIR PUMP REMOVAL AND INSTALLATION

1. Disconnect the negative battery cable. Disconnect the hoses at the air pump. Discon-

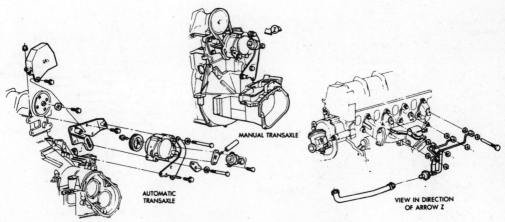

Air injection system—2.2L engine (Canada)

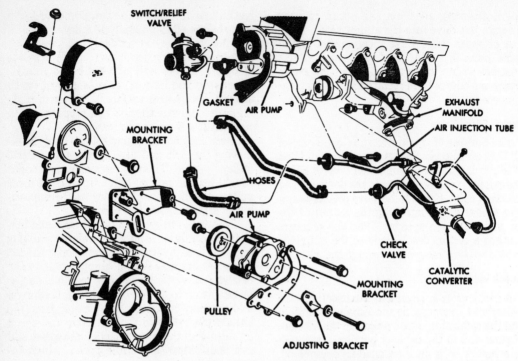

Air pump assembly—1985–87 2.2L carbureted engine

nect the air and vacuum hoses at the switch/relief valve.

2. Remove the air pump drive pulley shield from the engine.

3. Loosen the air pump pivot and and adjusting bolts and remove the air pump drive belt.

4. Remove the air pump attaching bolts and remove the pump and switch/relief valve as an assembly.

5. Remove the switch/relief valve and gasket from the pump. Clean both gasket surfaces. Install a new gasket and the relief valve and torque the mounting bolts to 125 inch lbs.

6. Install the drive pulley on the new air pump and torque the mounting bolt to 12 inch lbs. or less.

7. Position the air pump onto the engine and install the mounting bolts loosely. Loosen the bolts attaching the rear air pump bracket to the transmission housing.

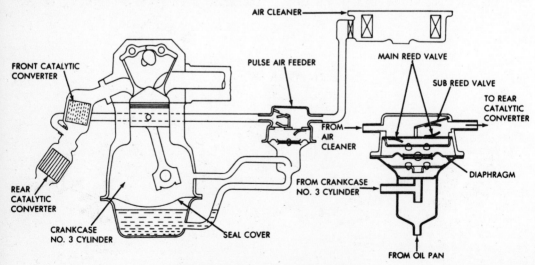

Pulse air feeder system—2.6L engine

8. Install the drive belt onto the air pump drive pulley. Then apply torque with a torque wrench to the adjusting bracket. Use 80-100 ft. lbs. to obtain proper tension. *Do not apply force to the pump body!* Hold this figure and tighten the bracket-to-transmission bolts (maximum – 40 ft. lbs.).

Pulse Air Feeder System

OPERATION

2.6 Liter Engines

Pulse Air Feeder (PAF) is used for supplying secondary air into the exhaust system between the front and rear catalytic converters, for the purpose of promoting oxidation of exhaust emissions in the rear converter.

The PAF consists of a main reed valve and a sub reed valve. The main reed valve is actuated in response to movement of a diaphragm, which is activated by pressure generated when the piston is in the compression stroke. The sub reed valve is opened on the exhaust stroke.

SERVICE

To inspect the system, remove the hose connected to the air cleaner and check for vacuum, with the engine running. If vacuum is not present, check the lines for leaks and evidence of oil leaks. Periodic maintenance of this system is not required.

Air Aspiration System

OPERATION

Some 1983 and later cars with the 2.2 and 2.5L engines use an air aspiration system in place of an air pump. This system operates off the pulses generated in the exhaust system when the exhaust valves open and close. Canadian carbureted engines and U.S. 50 States Throttle Body Injection engines are the most common applications.

SERVICE

The most common part of this system to fail is the aspirator valve. Symptoms of failure are excessive exhaust system noise under the hood at idle speed and hardening of the rubber hose leading from the valve to the air cleaner.

To determine whether or not the system has failed, disconnect the aspirator system intake hose from the at the air cleaner. Start the engine and allow it to idle in neutral.

CAUTION: *Hot exhaust gases may be emitted from the system if the valve has failed.*

Cautiously and gradually place your hand near the open end of the aspirator system intake hose. If the valve is operating, the system will be drawing in fresh air, the area around the

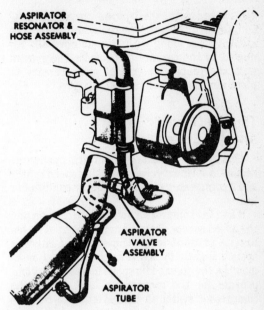

Air aspiration system—TBI system

valve will be cool and you will be able to feel pulses when you touch the open end of the inlet. If the valve has failed, there will be no pulses that can be felt and hot exhaust gas will be emitted.

REMOVAL AND INSTALLATION

The aspirator tube and aspirator valve must be replaced as an assembly. To replace, loosen the hose clamp and disconnect the intake hose at the intake side of the aspirator valve. Then, remove the aspirator tube bracket screw at the converter, unscrew the flared connector collar nut at the converter and remove the assembly.

Install a new tube in reverse order, torquing the flare nut to 40 ft. lbs. Tighten all hose clamps securely.

High Altitude Compensation System

A high altitude compensation system is installed on California vehicles. This modification affects the primary metering system as follows:

A small cylindrical bellows chamber mounted on the body panel in the engine compartment and connected to the carburetor with hoses, is vented to the atmosphere at the top of the carburetor. Atmospheric pressure expands and contracts the bellows.

A small brass tapered-seat valve regulates air flow when it is raised off its seat by expanding the bellows.

If the car travels to a mountainous area, rarefied atmosphere is encountered, producing a rich airfuel mixture. At a predetermined atmospheric pressure, the bellows opens, allowing additional air to enter the main air bleeds. The auxiliary air, along with the air normally inducted by the carburetor provides the system with the proper amount of air necessary to maintain the correct air/fuel mixture.

Throttle Opener (Idle-Up System)

This system consists of a throttle opener assembly, a solenoid valve, an engine speed sensor and a compressor switch for the air conditioner unit.

When the compressor switch is turned on and the speed sensor detects engine speed at or below its present level, the solenoid valve is opened slightly by the throttle opener. Consequently, the engine idle speed increases to compensate for the compressor load. When the compressor switch is turned off, the throttle stops working and returns to normal idle.

Emission Warning Lamps

RESETTING

A Vehicle Maintenance Monitor (VMM) is installed on some (1990–92 Dodge Monaco) vehicles. The dashboard display is activated at 7500 mile intervals to remind the vehicle owner that regular service and maintenance is due. Perform the required service and then press the **RESET** button located on the left side of the instrument panel on the monitor display.

ELECTRONIC ENGINE CONTROLS

Diagnosis and Testing

Diagnosis of a driveability problem requires attention to detail and many times involves com-

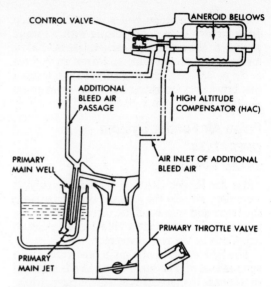

High altitude compensation system

plex procedures and expensive special equipment to carry out. Reading and solving diagnostic codes usually requires this equipment and is best left to a qualified repair facility.

In many cases visual inspection will shorten diagnostic time and often cure a problem without electronic testing. This is possibly the most critical step of diagnosis. Many fault codes or apparent failures are caused by loose, damaged or corroded electrical connectors. A detailed examination of all connectors, wiring and vacuum hoses can often lead to a repair without diagnosis. Performance of this step relies on the the skill of the person performing it; a careful inspector will check the undersides of hoses as well as the integrity of the hard-to-reach hoses blocked by the air cleaner or other components.

Wiring should be checked carefully for any

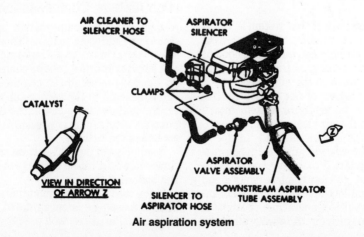

Air aspiration system

sign of strain, burning, crimping or terminal pull-out from a connector. Checking connectors at components or in harnesses is required; usually, pushing them together will reveal a loose fit. Pay particular attention to ground circuits, making sure they are not loose or corroded. Remember to inspect connectors and hose fittings at components not mounted on the engine, such as the evaporative canister or relays mounted on the fender aprons. Any component or wiring in the vicinity of a fluid leak or spillage should be given extra attention during inspection.

Additionally, inspect maintenance items such as belt condition and tension, battery charge and condition and the radiator cap carefully. Any of these very simple items may effect the system enough to set a fault code. The battery itself must be in good condition for the self-diagnostic system to operate properly.

Fuel System

CARBURETED FUEL SYSTEM

Mechanical Fuel Pump

REMOVAL AND INSTALLATION

1. Make sure the battery negative cable is disconnected. Have a metal cup handy to collect any fuel that may spill.
2. Place a drain pan underneath and then remove the oil filter with a strap wrench or equivalent.
3. Disconnect the fuel and vapor lines, catching fuel that spills. Dispose of fuel safely.
4. Plug the lines to prevent fuel leaks.
5. On 1987 models, remove the fuel pump impact blocker strut by removing the three mounting nuts and the bolt.
6. Remove the attaching bolts and remove the fuel pump.

NOTE: *The fuel pump is not repairable. It must be replaced as a complete unit. Always use a new gasket when installing the pump and make certain that the gasket surfaces are clean.*

To install:

7. To install the pump, first position a new gasket against the block. Then, put the pump in position over the gasket with bolt holes lined up squarely. Install the bolts and torque them to 250 inch lbs.
8. Connect the fuel lines to the pump (always start fuel line connections by hand — before using a wrench to tighten) and torque the fittings to 175 inch lbs.
9. On models so-equipped, install the impact blocker strut. Install the three nuts and the bolt finger-tight. Then, refer to the illustration and torque the nuts/bolt in the order listed below to the torque listed there:
   - B: 250 inch lbs.
   - C: 40 ft. lbs.
   - D: 75 ft. lbs.
   - A: 105 inch lbs.

10. Clean the block surface, check the gasket, and then install the oil filter, tightening it by hand only. If the gasket is damaged, replace the filter.
11. Start the engine and check for leaks. Check the crankcase oil level and refill as necessary.

TESTING

The fuel pump may be tested three different ways — for volume, vacuum and pressure. While it is best to test in all three ways, a pressure test will most often reveal a defective pump. Only if pressure meets specifications and there are still fuel supply problems is it necessary to complete all three tests.

NOTE: *To perform these tests, a pressure gauge capable of reading 1–10 psi; a vacuum gauge that will read 0–25 in.Hg; a metal container of just over 1 qt.; several plugs the right diameter for the engine's fuel lines; a watch; and a supply of new fuel hose clamps.*

1. Using a metal cup to collect spilled fuel, disconnect the fuel pump outlet hose at the bottom of the filter and plug it. Connect a pressure gauge into the line.
2. Disconnect the coil-to-distributor high tension wire so the engine won't start. Have a helper crank the engine as you watch the pressure gauge.
3. Read the gauge and compare the pressure to the range shown in the Tune-Up Specifications chart in Chapter 2. If the pressure is either too high or too low, replace the pump. If the pump passes this test and you still have doubts about its performance, proceed with the tests that follow.
4. Remove the pressure gauge from the fuel pump discharge. Disconnect the fuel pump suction line and plug it, collect any spilled fuel, and then connect a vacuum gauge to the suction side of the fuel pump.
5. Again have a helper turn the ignition key

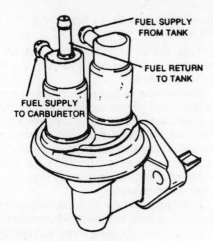

FUEL SUPPLY
FROM TANK

FUEL RETURN
TO TANK

FUEL SUPPLY
TO CARBURETOR

View of mechanical fuel pump

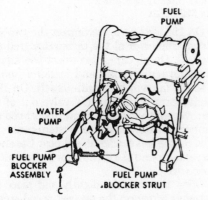

FUEL
PUMP

WATER
PUMP

B

FUEL PUMP
BLOCKER
ASSEMBLY

FUEL PUMP
BLOCKER STRUT

D

C

**Removing and installing the fuel pump used on car-
burated vehicles**

ON while you watch the gauge. The fuel pump should produce a minimum of 11 in.Hg (readings may go as high as 22 in.Hg).

6. If the pump passes these tests, but there is still some question about its ability to produce adequate flow (poor high rpm full throttle performance in spite of a clean filter), proceed with the volume test.

WARNING: *This test must be performed very carefully! It is necessary to run the engine while checking the volume of flow. The potential for spilling and igniting gasoline is very great. Proceed very carefully or, if you are not sure you can perform the test safely, have it performed professionally.*

7. Make sure both fuel filters are clean.

8. Start the engine and allow it to idle a few seconds to stabilize the fuel supply to the carburetor. Make sure the engine is warmed up and off the choke (at normal idle speed). Stop the engine.

9. Disconnect the fuel line at the inlet of the filter-reservoir on the carburetor. Collect any fuel that drains out and dispose of it safely.

10. Plug this line and position it so it will drain into the 1 qt. container. Start the engine and allow it to run a few seconds to stabilize the fuel supply to the carburetor. Make sure the engine is warmed up and at normal idle speed. Have a watch available so you can time the test.

11. Position the 1 qt. container under the fuel line. Pull the plug out and allow the fuel to drain into the container as the engine continues to idle. Run the engine for about 15 seconds, and then stop the engine (before the carburetor begins to run out of fuel). Connect the line to the fuel filter, start the engine, and run it for 15–20 seconds to restore full fuel level to the carburetor.

12. Then, stop the engine, and repeat Steps 10 and 11. There should be a total of four 15–second cycles in which you idle the engine on the fuel in the carburetor and drain the fuel pump output into the container. After four cycles, if the pump has moved 1 qt. or more into the container, it is okay. Otherwise, replace it, even if pressure and vacuum are satisfactory.

Carburetor

ADJUSTMENTS

**Idle Adjustment
Holley 5220/6520**

1. Put the transaxle in neutral and set the parking brake securely. Turn off all accessories. Allow the engine to warm up on the lowest step of the fast idle cam. Install a tachometer.

2. Make the following preparations for adjustment, depending on the year:

    a. Disconnect and plug the vacuum connector at the CVSCC (Coolant Vacuum Switch Cold Closed) on 1984 and earlier engines so-equipped.

    b. Pull the PCV valve out of the vent module and allow it to breathe underhood air.

    c. Disconnect the oxygen feedback system test connector located on the left fender shield if working on a 6520 carburetor.

    d. Disconnect the wiring from the kicker solenoid located on the left fender shield on 1986–87 models. On 1985 and earlier models so-equipped, ground the carburetor switch with a jumper wire.

3. If the tachometer indicates the rpm is not set to specifications, turn the idle speed screw, located on the top of the idle solenoid, until the correct rpm is achieved. See the underhood sticker or the tune-up chart in Chapter 2 for correct idle speed.

4. Restore the PCV system and other vacuum and electrical connections. Roadtest the vehicle for proper operation.

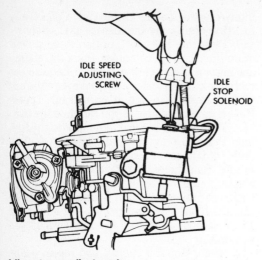

IDLE SPEED
ADJUSTING
SCREW

IDLE
STOP
SOLENOID

Idle set rpm adjustment

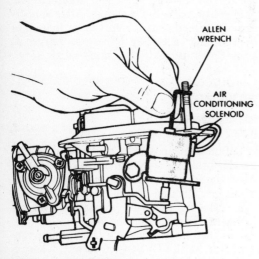

ALLEN
WRENCH

AIR
CONDITIONING
SOLENOID

A/C idle speed adjustment

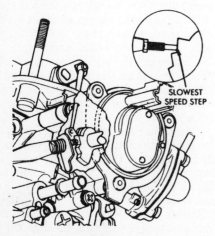

SLOWEST
SPEED STEP

Fast idle speed adjustment

Air Conditioning Idle Speed Adjustment
Holley 5220/6520

1. Turn the air conditioner on and set the blower on low. Disconnect and plug the EGR valve vacuum hose.

2. Remove the adjusting screw and spring from the top of the air conditioning solenoid.

3. Insert a 1/8 in. (3mm) Allen wrench into the solenoid and adjust to obtain the correct idle speed as per the under hood sticker. This adjustment is required on 1981–82 models only. On later models, just verify that the A/C idle speed kicker works.

4. Make sure that the air conditioning clutch is operating during the speed adjustments.

5. Replace the adjusting screw and spring on the solenoid and turn off the air conditioner.

Fast Idle Speed Adjustment
Holley 5220/6520

1. On 1981–82 cars, disconnect the two-way electrical connector at the carburetor (red and tan wires). On all cars, disconnect the jumper wire at the radiator fan and install a jumper wire so the fan will run continuously. On 1983 and later cars: Pull the PCV valve out of the valve cover and allow it to draw underhood air; disconnect the oxygen sensor system connector located on the left fender shield near the shock tower; and ground the carburetor switch with a jumper wire.

2. Open the throttle slightly and place the adjustment screw on the slowest speed step of the fast idle cam. With the choke fully open adjust the fast idle speed to comply with the figure on the under-hood sticker. Return the vehicle to idle, then replace the adjusting screw on the slowest speed step of the fast idle cam to verify fast idle speed. Re-adjust as necessary.

3. Turn the engine off, remove the jumper wire and reconnect the fan. Reinstall the PCV valve and remove the tachometer. On 1983 and later models, reconnect the oxygen sensor system connector, and remove the jumper wire at the carburetor.

Idle Adjustment
Mikuni Carburetor (2.6L Engine)

1. Place the transaxle in neutral, set the parking brake, and turn off all accessories. Disconnect the radiator fan. Run the engine until it reaches operating temperature. On 1983 and earlier models allow the engine to idle for one minute to stabilize RPM.

2. On 1984 models, turn the engine off, and then disconnect the negative battery cable for three seconds and then reconnect it. Disconnect the engine harness lead from the O_2 sensor at the bullet connector. Don't pull on the sensor

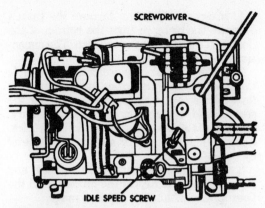

Adjusting idle speed on the Mikuni type carburetor (2.6L engine)

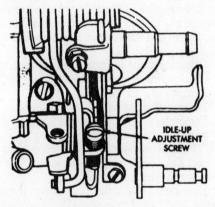

Adjusting the idle-up (air conditioner-on) Mikuni type carburetor (2.6L engine)

wire in doing this. Restart the engine. On 1984 and 1985 vehicles, run the engine at 2,500 rpm for 10 seconds. Then, wait two minutes before checking idle speed.

3. Check the idle speed with a tachometer. If not to specifications, on 1984–84 models, discconnect idle switch connector if the idle speed must be adjusted. Now, adjust the idle speed with the idle screw.

4. On A/C models, turn on the air conditioning with the temperature control lever set to the coldest setting. If the RPM is not 900, turn the idle-up screw to obtain this reading.

5. Turn off the engine and reconnect all connectors. Roadtest the vehicle for proper operation.

Vacuum Kick Adjustment
Holley 5220/6520

If the vacuum kick is adjusted to open the choke too far, the engine may stall or idle very roughly just after cold start. If it is adjusted so the choke does not open enough, there may be black smoke in the exhaust.

NOTE: *To perform this procedure, you will*

need a source of 15 in.Hg or more. The vacuum kick diaphragm may be damaged if you attempt to retract it manually. You will also need a drill or dowel whose diameter is equivalent to the specification for Vacuum Kick in the Carburetor Specifications Chart.

1. Remove the air cleaner. Open the throttle, close the choke and hold it in the closed position, and then release the throttle to trap the fast idle cam in the choke-closed position.

2. Disconnect the vacuum hose at the choke vacuum kick diaphragm. Connect a vacuum pump and apply 15 in.Hg or more of vacuum.

3. Gently move the choke blade toward closed position just until play is eliminated from the vacuum kick linkage (so the vacuum kick is determining choke blade position).

4. Insert the drill or dowel into the gap between the upper edge of the choke blade and the air horn wall, toward the center of the gap. The dowel or drill should just fit into the gap. If necessary, rotate the allen head screw in the center of the diaphragm housing to create the proper gap and then recheck with the measuring device.

5. Restore all vacuum connections and reinstall the air cleaner.

Mixture Adjustment

Chrysler recommends the use of a propane enrichment procedure to adjust the mixture. The equipment needed for this procedure is not readily available to the general public. The complete procedure is given, for reference purposes, Chapter 1.

NOTE: *Mixture screws are sealed under tamperproof plugs. The only time mixture adjustments are necessary is during a major carburetor overhaul. Refer to the instructions supplied with the overhaul kit.*

Float Level Adjustment
HOLLEY 5220/6520

1. Invert the air horn and remove the gasket. Insert a gauge or drill of 12mm diameter be-

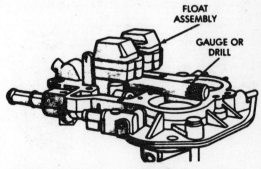

Adjusting float level on the 5220/6520 carburetors

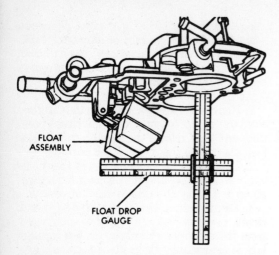

Adjusting the float drop on the 5220/6520 carburetors

tween the air horn and float. The gauge must lay flat along the gasket surface.

2. If the adjustment is incorrect, bend the tang which actuates the needle valve to correct it. Bend the tang up toward the floats to decrease the measurement and downward to increase it.

3. Check float drop with a float drop gauge or using a ruler and straightedge. Float drop must be 47.5mm. Bend the tang on the outer end of the float hinge outward to increase float drop and inward to decrease it.

MIKUNI CARBURETORS
(2.6L ENGINES)

NOTE: *Before attempting to adjust float level, get a shim pack part No. MD606952. These shims are placed under the float needle seat to change its postion and, therefore, the float level.*

1. Invert the air horn. Remove the gasket. Measure the distance from the bottom of the float to the surface of the air horn. The dimension must be 19–21mm.

2. If the dimension is incorrect, disassemble the float, remove the needle and unscrew the float needle seat. Change the shim under the seat or add or subtract shims as necessary. Shims are 0.30mm, 0.40mm and 0.50mm thick. Adding a shim of 0.30mm will lower float level by three times that or 0.90mm.

3. Reassemble the seat, needle and float and recheck the level. Repeat the process until the float level is within the required range.

REMOVAL AND INSTALLATION

NOTE: *When removing the carburetor on the 2.2 Liter engine, it should not be necessary to disturb the isolator (check it for cracks), unless it has been determined that there is a leak in it.*

1. Disconnect the negative battery terminal. Allow the engine to cool thoroughly.

2. Remove the air cleaner.

3. Remove the gas cap.

4. Disconnect the fuel inlet line and all necessary wiring.

NOTE: *It is necessary to drain the coolant on the 2.6 Liter engine before removing the coolant lines at the carburetor.*

5. Disconnect the coolant lines from the carburetor, (2.6 Liter engines only).

6. Disconnect the throttle linkage and all vacuum hoses.

7. Remove the mounting nuts and remove the carburetor. Hold the carburetor level to avoid spilling fuel from the bowl.

8. Installation is the reverse of removal. Start engine, make all necessary adjustments, roadtest for proper operation.

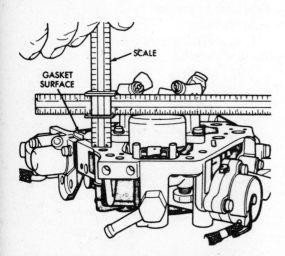

Adjusting float level on Mikuni type carburetor

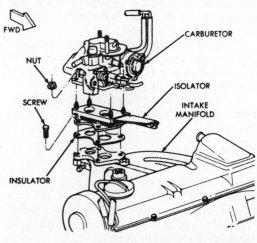

Carburetor removal and installation—2.2L engine

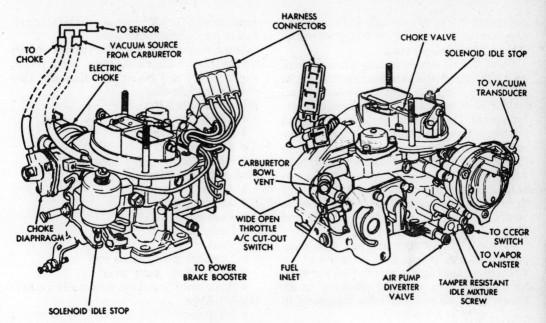

Details of the 2.2L carburetor

Before checking and adjusting any idle speed, check the ignition timing and adjust if necessary. Disconnect the plug the EGR vacuum hose. Unplug the connector at the radiator fan and install a jumper wire so the fan will run continuously. Remove the PCV valve. Allow the PCV valve to draw under hood air and plug the 3/16 in. (5mm) diameter hose at the canister. Connect a tachometer and start the engine. Check the idle speed with the air cleaner in place.

OVERHAUL

Efficient carburetion depends greatly on careful cleaning and inspection during overhaul, since dirt, gum, water, or varnish in or on the carburetor parts are often responsible for poor performance. Overhaul your carburetor in a clean, dust-free area. Carefully disassemble the carburetor, referring often to the exploded views and directions packaged with the rebuilding kit. Keep all similar and look-alike parts

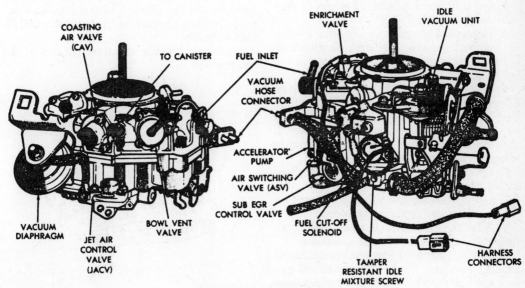

Details of the 2.6L carburetor

segregated during disassembly and cleaning to avoid accidental interchange during assembly. Make a note of all jet sizes.

When the carburetor is disassembled, wash all parts (except diaphragms, electric choke units, pump plunger, and any other plastic, leather, fiber, or rubber parts) in clean carburetor solvent. Do not leave parts in the solvent any longer than is necessary to sufficiently loosen the deposits. Excessive cleaning may remove the special finish from the float bowl and choke valve bodies, leaving these parts unfit for service. Rinse all parts in clean solvent and blow them dry with compressed air or allow them to air dry. Wipe clean all cork, plastic, leather, and fiber part with a clean, lint-free cloth.

Blow out all passages and jets with compressed air and be sure that there are no restrictions or blockages. Never use wire or similar tools to clean jets, fuel passages, or air bleeds. Clean all jets and valve separately to avoid accidental interchange.

Check all parts for wear or damage. If wear or damage is found, replace the defective parts. Especially check the following.

1. Check the float needle and seat for wear. If wear is found, replace the complete assembly.

2. Check the float hinge pin for wear and the float(s) for dents or distortion. Replace the float if fuel has leaked into it.

3. Check the throttle and choke shaft bores for wear or an out-of-round condition. Damage or wear to the throttle arm, shaft, or shaft bore will often require replacement of the throttle body. These parts require a close tolerance of fit; wear may allow air leakage, which could affect starting and idling.

NOTE: *Throttle shafts and bushings are not included in overhaul kits. They can be purchased separately.*

4. Inspect the idle mixture adjusting needles for burrs or grooves. Any such condition requires replacement of the needle, since you will not be able to obtain a satisfactory idle.

5. Test the accelerator pump check valves. They should pass air one way but not the other. Test for proper seating by blowing and sucking on the valve. Replace the valve as necessary. If the valve is satisfactory, wash the valve again to remove breath moisture.

6. Check the bowl cover for warped surfaces with a straightedge.

7. Closely inspect the valves and seats for wear and damage, replacing as necessary.

8. After the carburetor is assembled, check the choke valve for freedom of operation.

Carburetor overhaul kits are recommended for each overhaul. These kits contain all gaskets and new parts to replace those which deteriorate most rapidly. Failure to replace all parts supplied with the kit (especially gaskets) can result in poor performance later.

Some carburetor manufacuturers supply overhaul kits of three basic types: minor repair; major repair; and gasket kits. Basically, they contain the following:

Minor Repair Kits:
- All gaskets
- Float needle valve
- All diaphragms
- Spring for the pump diaphragm

Major Repair Kits:
- All jets and gaskets
- All diaphragms
- Float needle valve
- Pump ball valve
- Float
- Complete intermediate rod
- Intermediate pump lever
- Some cover hold-down screws and washers

Gasket Kits:
- All gaskets

After cleaning and checking all components, reassemble the carburetor, using new parts and referring to the exploded view. When reassembling, make sure that all screws and jets are tight in their seats, but do not overtighten as the tips will be distorted. Tighten all screws gradually, in rotation. Do not tighten needle valves into their seats; uneven jetting will result. Always use new gaskets. Be sure to adjust the float level when reassembling.

Holley Models 5220/6520

DISASSEMBLY

1. Disconnect and remove choke operating rod and choke rod seal.

2. Remove the 2 solenoid retaining screws and remove the solenoid from the carburetor.

3. Remove the vacuum control valve and filter assembly.

4. Remove wiring clip from the top of the carburetor.

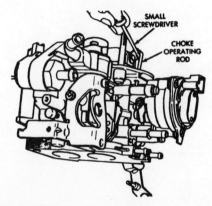

Disconnecting choke operating rod

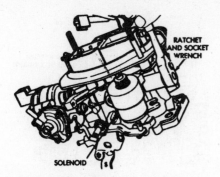

Servicing typical solenoid

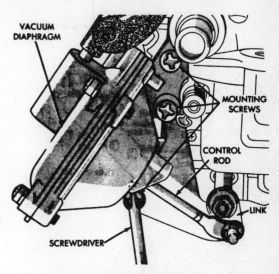

Servicing vacuum control diaphragm

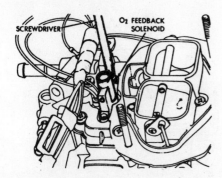

Servicing Oxygen feedback solenoid screws

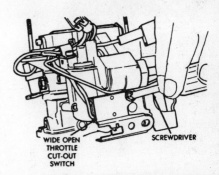

Servicing wide open throttle cut out A/C switch

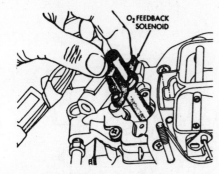

Servicing Oxygen feedback solenoid

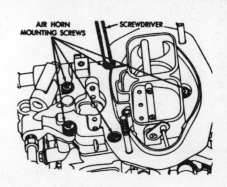

Servicing air horn mounting screws

5. On 6520 models, remove the 2 oxygen feedback solenoid retaining screws and gently lift the solenoid from the air horn.

6. Remove the clip securing vacuum control rod to link, remove vacuum control mounting screws and remove the vacuum control diaphragm.

7. Remove the 2 wide open throttle cutout switch mounting screws. Mark location for proper assembly. Remove the harness mounting screws and open retaining clip.

8. Remove the 5 air horn mounting screws and separate air horn assembly from the carburetor body.

9. Remove the float level pin, float and float inlet needle.

10. Remove fuel inlet seal and gasket.

11. Remove main secondary metering jet. Be sure to note size so that it can be reinstalled in its proper position.

12. Remove main primary metering jet. Be sure to note size so that it can be reinstalled in its proper position.

13. Remove secondary high speed bleed and

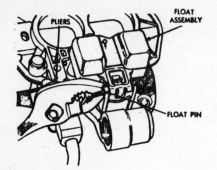

Servicing float level pin

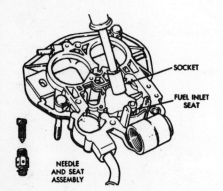

Servicing fuel inlet needle and seat

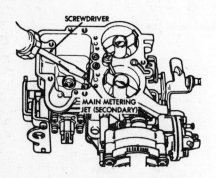

Servicing secondary main metering jet

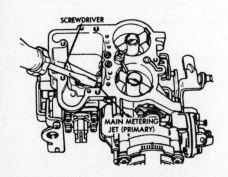

Servicing primary main metering jet

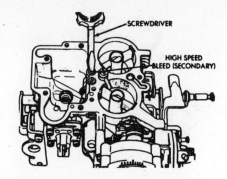

Servicing secondary high speed bleed

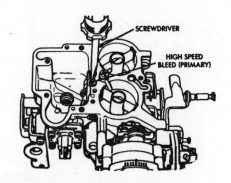

Servicing primary high speed bleed

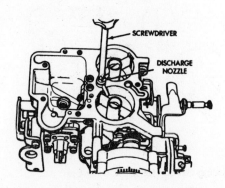

Servicing accelerator pump discharge nozzle

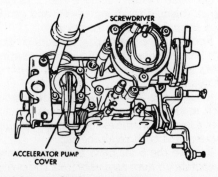

Servicing accelerator pump cover

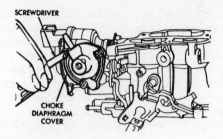

Servicing choke diaphragm cover

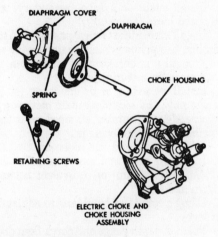

Choke diaphragm assembly

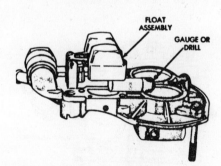

Gauge positioned for dry float setting

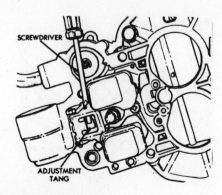

Adjusting dry float level

secondary main well tube. Be sure to note size so that it can be reinstalled in its proper position.

14. Remove primary high speed bleed and primary main well tube. Be sure to note size so that it can be reinstalled in its proper position.

15. Remove the discharge nozzle screw, discharge nozzle and gasket.

16. Invert carburetor body and remove accelerator pump discharge weight ball and checkball (both balls are the same size).

17. Remove the 4 accelerator pump cover screws. Remove the cover, accelerator pump diaphragm and spring.

18. Note the position of the accelerator pump arm pivot pin. If the pin is removed it must be reinstalled in its original position.

19. Remove the 3 choke diaphragm cover screws. Remove the cover and spring.

20. Rotate choke shaft and lever assembly counterclockwise. Rotate choke diaphragm assembly clockwise and reomve from the housing. Remove end of lower screw from housing. If choke diaphragm is to be replaced, diaphragm cover must also be replaced.

21. Remove the concealment plug and remove the idle mixture screw from the carburetor body.

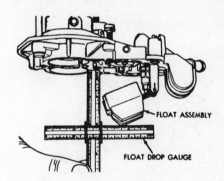

Gauge positioned to check float drop

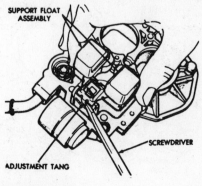

Adjusting float drop

REASSEMBLY

1. If the entire choke assembly was removed, position it on the carburetor and install the 3 retaining screws. If the choke diaphragm was serviced, rotate the choke shaft counterclockwise. Insert the diaphragm with a clockwise motion. Position spring and cover over diaphragm and install retaining screws.

Make certian the fat idle link has been installed properly.

2. Install accelerator pump spring, diaphragm, cover and screws.

3. Install accelerator pump discharge check ball in discharge passage. Check accelerator and seat prior to assembly by filling the fuel bowl with clean fuel.

Hold discharge check ball down with a small brass rod and operate pump plunger by hand. If the check ball and seat are leaking, no resistance will be experienced when operating plunger. If valve is leaking, stake ball using a suitable drift punch. Exercise care when staking ball to avoid damaging bore containing the pump weight. After staking old ball, remove and replace with a new ball for overhaul kit. Install weight ball and recheck for leaks.

4. Install new gaskets, discharge nozzle and screw.

5. Install primary main well tube and primary high speed bleed.

6. Install main well tube (secondary) and high speed bleed (secondary).

7. Install main metering jet (primary) on this assembly, the primary main metering jet will have a small number stamped on it than the secondary main metering jet.

8. Install secondary main metering jet (on this assembly, the secondary main metering jet will have a larger number stamped on it than the primary main metering jet.

9. Install needle and seat assembly.

10. Invert air horn and insert gauge or drill bit 0.480 in. (12.2mm) or equivalent between air horn and float.

11. Using a small tool bend tang to adjust dry float level.

12. Position depth gauge and check float drop.

13. Using a small tool bend tang to adjust float drop to 1⅞ inch (47.6mm).

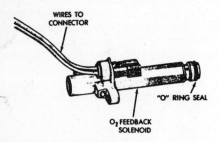

Oxygen feedback solenoid

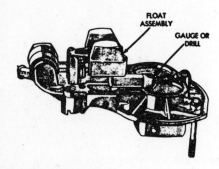

Measuring dry float setting

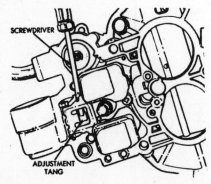

Adjusting dry float level

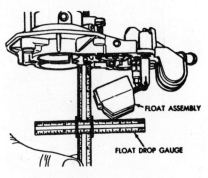

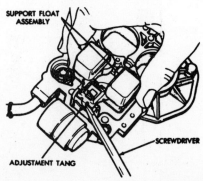

Measuring (above) and adjusting (below) float drop

CARBURETOR SPECIFICATIONS
Holley 5220/6520

Year	Carb. Part No.	Dry Float Setting (in.)	Solenoid Idle Stop (rpm)	Fast Idle Speed (rpm)	Vacuum Kick (in.)
1981	R9060A R9061A	.480	850	1100	.030
	R9125A R9126A	.480	850	1200	.030
	R9052A R9053A	.480	850	1400	.070
	R9054A R9055A	.480	850	1400	.040
	R9602A R9603A	.480	850	1500	.065
	R9604A R9605A	.480	850	1600	.065
1982	R9824A	.480	900	1400	.065
	R9503A R9504A R9750A R9751A	.480	850	1300	.085
	R9822A R9823A	.480	850	1400	.080
	R9505A R9506A R9752A R9753A	.480	900	1600	.100
1983	R-40003A	.480	775	1400	.070
	R-40004A	.480	900	1500	.080
	R-40005A	.480	900	1350	.080
	R-40006A	.480	850	1275	.080
	R-40007A	.480	775	1400	.070
	R-40008A	.480	900	1600	.070
	R-40010A	.480	900	1500	.080
	R-40012A	.480	900	1600	.070
	R-40014A	.480	850	1275	.080
	R-40080A	.480	850	1400	.045
	R-40081A	.480	850	1400	.045
1984	R-40060-1A	.480	see	see	.055
	R-40085-1A	.480	underhood	underhood	.040
	R-40170A R-40171A	.480	sticker	sticker	.060
	R-40067-1A R-40068-1A R-40058-1A	.480	see underhood sticker	see underhood sticker	.070
	R-40107-1A	.480			.055
	R-40064-1A R-40065-1A R-40081-1A R-40082-1A R-40071A R-40122A	.480	see underhood sticker	see underhood sticker	.080

CARBURETOR SPECIFICATIONS
Holley 5220/6520

Year	Carb. Part No.	Dry Float Setting (in.)	Solenoid Idle Stop (rpm)	Fast Idle Speed (rpm)	Vacuum Kick (in.)
1985	R40058A	.480	see	see	.070
	R40060A	.480	underhood	underhood	.055
	R40116A R40117A	.480	sticker	sticker	.095
	R40134A R40135A R40138A R40139A	.480	see underhood sticker	see underhood sticker	.075
1986	U.S.	.480	see	see	.075
	Canada	.480	underhood sticker	underhood sticker	.095
1987	All	.480	see underhood sticker	see underhood sticker	.075

14. Position new gasket on air horn and install choke rod seal and choke operating rod.

15. Carefully locate air horn to carburetor. Install new choke operating rod retainers on choke shaft lever and fast idle cam pickup lever and connect choke operating rod.

16. Install and tighten the 5 airhorn to carburetor body screws evenly in stages to 30 inch lbs.

17. Install and tighten solenoid screws. Reinstall anti-rattle spring.

18. Install wide open throttle cut-out switch, move switch so that A/C clutch circuit is open in throttle position of 10° before to wide open.

19. On 6520 models, position a NEW oxygen feedback solenoid gasket on the air horn. Install new O-ring seal on oxygen feedback solenoid. Lubricate with white grease and carefully install solenoid into carburetor. Install and tighten mounting screws securely.

20. Install vacuum solenoid.

21. Install vacuum control valve.

22. Install and tighten harness mounting screws.

SINGLE POINT FUEL INJECTION SYSTEM

Note also that whenever replacing any fuel lines, it is necessary to use gas hoses marked "EFI/EFM" or an equivalent product from the aftermarket. Whenever replacing hose clamps, use clamps incorporating a rolled edge to prevent hose damage, rather than standard aviation type clamps. This will prevent damage to the hoses that could produce dangerous leaks.

Experience has shown that many complaints that may occur with EFI can be traced to poor wiring or hose connections. A visual check will help spot these most common faults and save unnecessary test and diagnosis time.

Electric Fuel Pump
REMOVAL AND INSTALLATION

An electric fuel pump is used with fuel injection systems in order to provide higher and more uniform fuel pressures. It is located in the tank. To remove it, disconnect the battery, and then remove the fuel tank, as described at the end of this chapter. Then, with a hammer and nonmetallic punch, tap the fuel pump lock ring counterclockwise to release the pump.

To install the pump, first wipe the seal area of the tank clean and install a new O-ring seal. Replace the filter (sock) on the end of the pump if it appears to be damaged. Then position the pump in the tank and install the locking ring. Tighten the ring in the same general way in which you loosened it. Do not overtighten it, as this can cause leakage. Install the tank as described at the end of this chapter.

TESTING

NOTE: *To perform this procedure, you will need a gauge capable of reading 10–20 psi and the extra length of hose, clamps and fittings necessary to Tee the gauge into a $5/16$ in. (8mm) fuel line. Have a metal container handy to collect any fuel that may spill.*

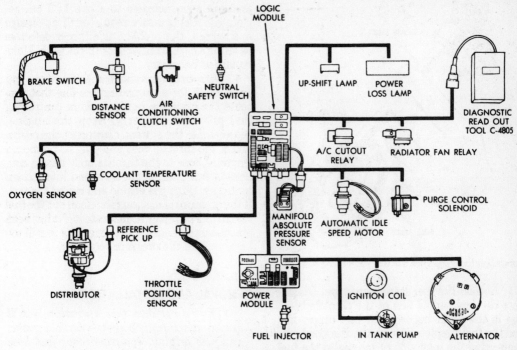

Diagram of the single-point EFI system

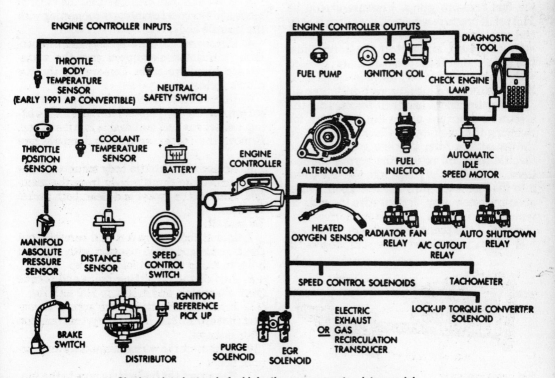

Single point electronic fuel injection components—later models

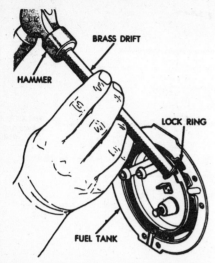

Removing lockring from the fuel tank assembly

1. Release the fuel system pressure. Disconnect the fuel supply line at the throttle body. Tee in the gauge between the fuel supply line and the fuel supply nipple on the throttle body, connecting the inlet side of the tee to the fuel supply line and the throttle body side of the Tee to the throttle body with a rubber hose and clamps.

WARNING: *At the beginning of the next step, watch carefully for fuel leaks. Shut the engine off immediately at any sign of leakage.*

2. Start the engine and run it at idle. Read the fuel pressure gauge. Pressure should be 14.5 psi. If pressure is correct, the pump is okay and you should depressurize the system, remove the gauge, and restore the normal fuel line connections. If the pressure is low, proceed with the next step to test for filter clogging. If the pressure is too high, proceed with Step 4.

3. Stop the engine and then depressurize the system as described under the procedure for changing the fuel filter in Chapter 1. Remove the gauge Tee from the line going into the throttle body and restore the normal connections. Then, Tee the gauge into the line going into the fuel filter. Run the test again. If the pressure is now okay, depressurize the system, replace the fuel filter, and restore normal connections. If the pressure is still low, pinch the fuel return hose closed with your fingers. If

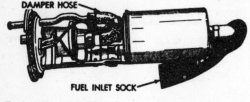

Fuel pump assembly

pressure now increases to above 14.5 psi, replace the fuel pressure regulator. If no change is observed, the problem is either a defective pump or a clogged filter sock in the tank. Make repairs as necessary.

4. With pressure above specification, you must check for a clogged return line that prevents the pressure regulator from controlling fuel pressure properly. Stop the engine, depressurize the system, disconnect the return line at the throttle body and plug it. Connect a length of hose to the throttle body return connection and position the open end into a clean container. Start the engine and repeat the test. If the pressure is now correct, clean out the fuel return line or repair it. Relocate it if it has been pinched or damaged. If the pressure is still too high, replace the pressure regulator.

Throttle Body

REMOVAL AND INSTALLATION

NOTE: *To perform this operation, you'll need a new throttle body-to-manifold gasket and new original equipment-type fuel hose clamps (with rolled edges).*

1. Allow the engine to cool completely. Perform the fuel system pressure release procedure.

2. Disconnect the negative battery cable. Remove the air cleaner and those air hoses which might restrict access to the throttle body.

3. Label and then disconnect all the vacuum hoses and electrical connectors connecting with the throttle body.

4. Disconnect the throttle cable and, on automatic transmission-equipped cars the transmission kickdown cable. Remove the throttle return spring.

5. Disconnect the fuel supply and return hoses by wrapping a rag around the hose and twisting. Collect any fuel that drains in a metal cup. Remove the copper washers and supply new ones.

6. Remove the throttle body mounting bolts and remove the throttle body from the manifold. Remove the gasket and clean both gasket surfaces.

To install:

7. Install the new gasket and carefully put the throttle body into position with the bolt holes in it and the manifold lined up.

8. Install the mounting bolts and torque them alternately and evenly to 200 inch lbs.

9. Install the throttle return spring. Reconnect the throttle and, if necessary, transmission cable linkages.

10. Reconnect the wiring connectors and vacuum hoses.

11. Reconnect the fuel supply hose to the sup-

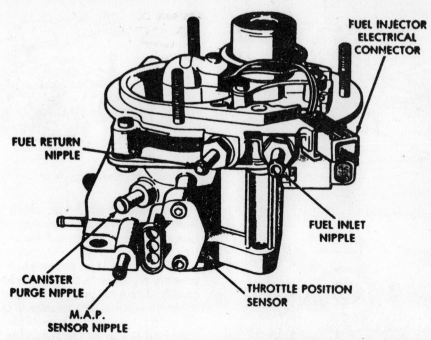

FUEL INJECTOR
ELECTRICAL
CONNECTOR

FUEL RETURN
NIPPLE

FUEL INLET
NIPPLE

CANISTER
PURGE NIPPLE

THROTTLE POSITION
SENSOR

M.A.P.
SENSOR NIPPLE

Throttle body used on TBI system (1988 2.2L engines without turbo and 2.5L engines)

ply connection on the throttle body, using a new copper washer. Reconnect the return hose to the return connection with a new copper washer. Use new clamps and torque to 10 inch lbs.

12. Install the air cleaner and hoses. Reconnect the negative battery cable.

13. Start the engine and check for fuel leaks.

Fuel Injector

REMOVAL AND INSTALLATION

NOTE: *A Torx® screwdriver is required to perform this operation. New O-rings for the injector and cap should also be supplied. A set of three will be required to re-use and old injector, while a new injector will be supplied with a new upper O-ring.*

1. Remove the air cleaner and air hoses. Re-

lease the fuel system pressure as described in Chapter 1. Then, disconnect the negative battery cable.

2. Remove the Torx® head screw with the right tool. With two appropriate, blunt prying instruments located in the screwdriver slot on either side, gently and evenly pry upward to remove the injector cap (refer to illustration).

3. Then, place an appropriate, blunt prying instrument into the screwdriver slot on either side of the electrical connector and gently and evenly pry the injector upward and out of the throttle body unit. Once the injector is removed, check that the lower O-ring has been removed from the throttle body unit.

4. Remove the two O-rings from the injector body and the single O-ring from the cap and re-

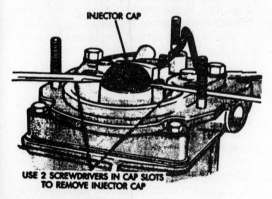

INJECTOR CAP

USE 2 SCREWDRIVERS IN CAP SLOTS
TO REMOVE INJECTOR CAP

Removing fuel injector cap

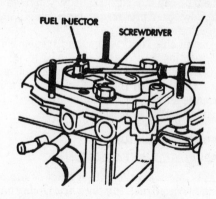

FUEL INJECTOR

SCREWDRIVER

Removing fuel injector

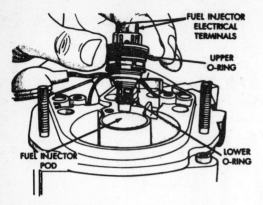

Servicing fuel injector

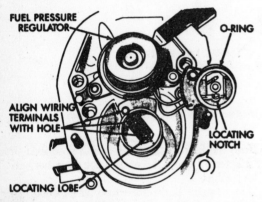

Fuel injector installation

place them. If the injector is being replaced, a new upper O-ring will already be installed.

To install:

5. Carefully assemble the injector and cap together with the keyway and key aligned. Then, align the cap and injector so the cap's hole aligns with the bolt hole in the throttle body. Start the injector/cap assembly into the throttle body without applying downward pressure.

6. With the assembly almost seated, rotate the cap as necessary to ensure perfect alignment of the cap and throttle body. Then apply gentle, downward pressure on both sides to seat the injector and cap.

7. Install the Torx® screw and torque it to 30–35 inch lbs.

8. Connect the battery. Start the engine and check for leaks with the air cleaner off. Then, replace the air cleaner and hoses. Roadtest the vehicle for proper operation.

Pressure Regulator

REMOVAL AND INSTALLATION

NOTE: *Make sure to have a towel or rag on hand to absorb fuel. Supply a new O-ring and gasket for the pressure regulator.*

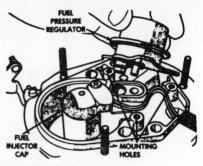

Servicing fuel pressure regulator

1. Remove the air cleaner and air hoses. Release the fuel system pressure as described in Chapter 1. Then, disconnect the negative battery cable.

2. Remove the three screws which attach the pressure regulator to the throttle body. Then, *quickly* place a rag over the fuel inlet chamber to absorb any fuel that remains in the system. When fuel is absorbed, dispose of the rag safely.

3. Pull the pressure regulator from the throttle body. Carefully remove the O-ring and gasket.

To install:

4. Carefully install the new O-ring and gasket onto the regulator.

5. Position the pressure regulator onto the throttle body. Press it into place squarely so as to seal the O-ring and gasket.

6. Install the three attaching screws and torque to 40 inch lbs.

7. Connect the battery. Start the engine and check for leaks with the air cleaner off. Then, replace the air cleaner and hoses.

Idle Speed Adjustment

NOTE: *This procedure applies to vehicles built through 1986. Later models require a "Throttle Body Minimum Airflow Check Procedure". This cannot be performed without utilizing an expensive electronic test system. If airflow is incorrect on these models, the throttle body must be replaced.*

1. Before adjusting the idle on an electronic fuel injected vehicle the following items must be checked.

  a. AIS motor has been checked for operation.

  b. Engine has been checked for vacuum or EGR leaks.

  c. Engine timing has been checked and set to specifications.

  d. Coolant temperature sensor has been checked for operation.

2. Connect a tachometer and timing light to engine.

3. Disconnect throttle body 6-way connector. Remove brown with white trace AIS wire from connector and reconnect the connector.

4. Connect one end of a jumper wire to AIS wire and other end to battery positive post for 5 seconds.

5. Connect a jumper to radiator fan so that it will run continuously.

6. Start and run engine for 3 minutes to allow speed to stabilize.

7. Using tool C–4804 or equivalent, turn idle speed adjusting screw to obtain 800 ± 10 rpm Manual; 725 ± 10 rpm (Automatic) with transaxle in neutral.

NOTE: *If idle will not adjust down, check for binding linkage, speed control servo cable adjustments, or throttle shaft binding.*

8. Check that timing is 18° ± 2° BTDC Manual; 12° ± 2° BTDC Automatic.

9. If timing is not to above specifications turn idle speed adjusting screw until correct idle speed and ignition timing are obtained.

10. Turn off engine, disconnect tachometer and timing light, reinstall AIS wire and remove jumper wire. Roadtest the vehicle for proper operation.

MULTI-POINT FUEL INJECTION

Note also that whenever replacing any fuel lines, it is necessary to use gas hoses marked "EFI/EFM" or an equivalent product from the aftermarket. Whenever replacing hose clamps, use clamps incorporating a rolled edge to prevent hose damage, rather than standard aviation type clamps. This will prevent damage to the hoses that could produce dangerous leaks.

Experience has shown that many complaints that may occur with EFI can be traced to poor wiring or hose connections. A visual check will help spot these most common faults and save unnecessary test and diagnosis time.

Electric Fuel Pump
REMOVAL AND INSTALLATION

An electric fuel pump is used with fuel injection systems in order to provide higher and more uniform fuel pressures. It is located in the tank. To remove it, disconnect the battery, and then remove the fuel tank, as described at the end of this chapter. Then, with a hammer and non-metallic punch, tap the fuel pump lock ring counterclockwise to release the pump.

To install the pump, first wipe the seal area of the tank clean and install a new O-ring seal. Replace the filter on the end of the pump if it appears to be damaged. Then position the pump in the tank and install the locking ring. Tighten the ring in the same general way in which you loosened it. Do not overtighten it, as this can cause leakage. Install the tank as described at the end of this chapter.

TESTING

NOTE: *To perform this test, you will need a pressure gauge capable of reading pressures*

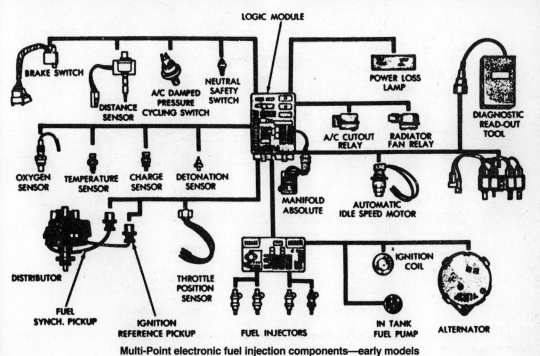

Multi-Point electronic fuel injection components—early models

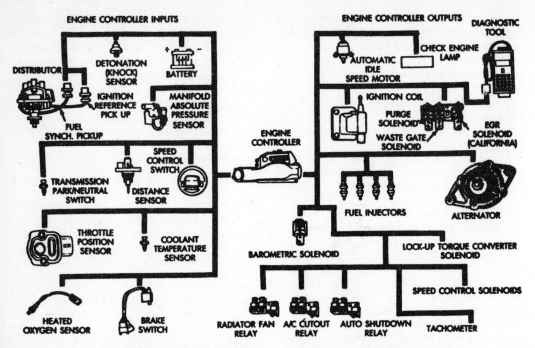

Multi-Point electronic fuel injection components—later models

above 55 psi. The gauge must have a connection that will fit the fuel rail service valve. The gauge will be compatible with Chrysler part No. C–3292 and the connector fitting compatible with C–4805. You may also need a Tee and fittings necessary to Tee the gauge into the fuel supply line at the tank, and a 2 gallon container suitable for collecting fuel.

1. Release the fuel system pressure as described in Chapter 1. Remove the protective cover from the service valve on the fuel rail. On later model vehicles, remove the protective cover from the service valve on the fuel rail (Turbo I, Turbo II, 3.3L and 3.8L engines) or remove fuel hose quick connector from the chassis line (2.2L and 2.5L and 3.0L engines) if so equipped.

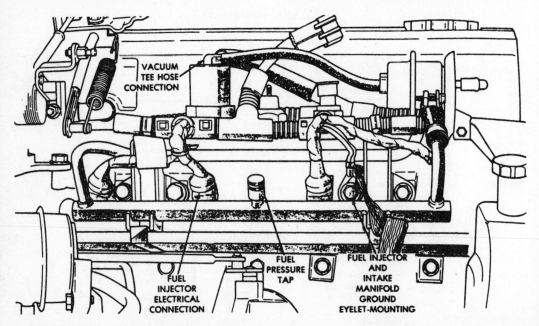

To test the fuel pump pressure on turbocharged cars, connect the fuel pressure gauge to the fuel pressure tap shown at center

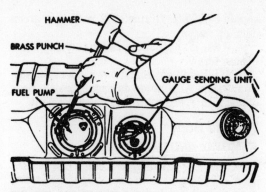

Removing the fuel pump

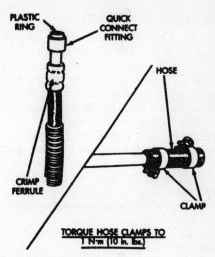

Quick connect fuel fittings

2. Connect the gauge to the pressure tap on the fuel rail. Hold the gauge and have someone start the engine. Run the engine at idle speed in Neutral (manual transmissions) or Park (automatic transmissions).

3. Read the pressure. It should be 53–57 psi. (refer to Tune Up Specification Charts) If it is outside the range, take note of it. Stop the engine, depressurize the system, disconnect the gauge and replace the protective cover. If the pressure is correct, the test is complete. If the pressure is below the range proceed with the steps following; if it is too high, proceed with Step 7.

WARNING: *In the next step, note that fuel may drain from the lines as you disconnect them. Make sure all surrounding exhaust system parts are cool and that all sources of ignition are removed from the area. Collect fuel and dispose of it safely.*

4. Connect the gauge into the fuel supply line running between the tank and the filter which is located at the rear of the vehicle.

WARNING *Make sure all connections are secure.*

5. Have someone start the engine. Read the

pressure gauge. If the pressure has risen more than 5 psi, replace the filter. If the pressure is now within range: allow the engine to cool; remove all sources of ignition; depressurize the system; disconnect the gauge from the lines; replace the fuel filter; and restore connections.

6. If the pressure is still too low, gently and gradually pinch the fuel return line closed as you watch the gauge. If the pressure increases, the fuel pressure regulator is at fault. If there is no change, the problem is either clogging of the filter sock mounted on the pump itself or a defective pump.

7. If the pressure is too high, shut off the engine, allow it to cool, depressurize the system and then disconnect the fuel return hose at the chassis, near the fuel tank. Connect a 3 foot length of hose to the open end of the line running along the chassis. Position the open end of the line into a container suitable for collecting fuel. Have a helper start the engine and check the pressure. If it is now correct, check the in-tank fuel return hose for kinking. If the hose is okay, and the system still exhibits excessive pressure with the tank half full or more, the fuel pump reservoir check valve or aspirator jet may be obstructed and the assembly must be replaced.

8. If the pressure is still too high, shut off the engine, and allow it to cool. Depressurize the system and then reconnect the fuel lines at the rear. Disconnect the fuel return hose at the pressure regulator. Collect all fuel that drains. Then, run the open connection into a large metal container. Connect the fuel gauge back into the fuel rail. Start the engine and repeat the test. If the fuel pressure is now correct, clean a clogged return line or replace pinched or kinked sections of the return line. If no such problems exist, replace the fuel pressure regulator.

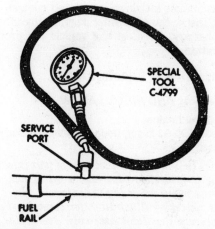

Special tool pressure test gauge

Idle Speed Adjustment

NOTE: *This procedure applies to vehicles built through 1986. Later models require a "Throttle Body Minimum Airflow Check Procedure". This cannot be performed without utilizing an expensive electronic test system. If airflow is incorrect on these models, the throttle body must be replaced.*

Before adjusting the idle on an electronic fuel injected vehicle the following items must be checked:

a. AIS motor has been checked for operation.

b. Engine has been checked for vacuum or EGR leaks.

c. Engine timing has been checked and set to specifications.

d. Coolant temperature sensor has been checked for operation.

Once these checks have been made and you know these components are performing satisfactorily:

1. Install a tachometer.

2. Warm up engine to normal operating temperature (accessories off).

3. Shut engine off and disconnect radiator fan.

4. Disconnect Throttle Body 6-way connector. Remove the brown with white tracer AIS wire from the connector and reconnect connector.

5. Start engine with transaxle selector in park or neutral.

6. Apply 12 volts to AIS brown with white tracer wire. This will drive the AIS fully closed and the idle should drop.

7. Disconnect then reconnect coolant temperature sensor.

8. With transaxle in neutral, idle speed should be 775 ± 25 rpm (700 ± 25 rpm green engine).

9. If idle is not to specifications adjust idle air bypass screw.

10. If idle will not adjust down, check for vacuum leaks, AIS motor damage, throttle body damage, or speed control cable adjustment.

Throttle Body

REMOVAL AND INSTALLATION

NOTE: *The following procedure can be used on all years and models. Slight variations may occur due to extra connections, etc., but the basic procedure should cover all years and models.*

1. Disconnect the negative battery cable. Remove the nuts attaching the air cleaner adaptor to the throttle body, loosen the hose clamps, and remove the air cleaner adaptor.

2. Remove the three control cables — accelerator, accelerator and, if so-equipped, automatic transmission kickdown and speed control cables. Then remove the throttle cable bracket from the throttle body.

3. Note locations and then disconnect the electrical connectors.

4. Note their locations or, if necessary, label them and then disconnect the vacuum hoses from the throttle body.

5. Remove the throttle body-to-adaptor attaching nuts. Then, remove the throttle body and its gasket.

To install:

6. Clean gasket surfaces and install a new gasket. Instal the throttle body-to-adaptor attaching nuts and tighten them alternately and evenly.

7. Reconnect the vacuum hoses, checking the routing and making certain the connections are secure. Reconnect each electrical connector to its connection on the throttle body.

8. Install the throttle and, as necessary, transmission kickdown and speed control cables. Install the air cleaner adaptor. Reconnect the battery. Roadtest the vehicle for proper operation.

Fuel Rail and Injectors

REMOVAL AND INSTALLATION

4 Cylinder Engines
Except 1990–92 Laser, Dodge Stealth and Dodge Monaco

NOTE: *You should have a set of four injector nozzle protective caps and a set of new O-rings before removing the injectors. Refer to the necessary illustration for servicing Fuel Pressure Regulator Assembly.*

1. Release fuel system pressure as described

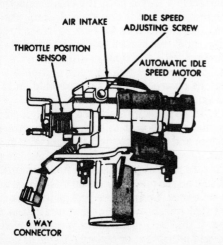

Location of idle speed adjusting screw on the throttle body of the multi-port injection system

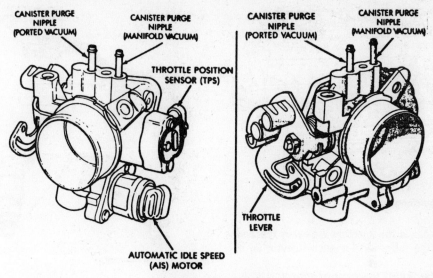

Throttle body assembly

in Chapter 1. Disconnect the negative battery cable.

2. Loosen the hose clamp on the fuel supply hose at the fuel rail inlet and disconnect it. Collect any fuel that may drain out into a metal cup and dispose of it safely.

3. Disconnect the fuel pressure regulator vacuum hose at the intake manifold vacuum tree.

4. Remove the 2 fuel pressure regulator-to-intake manifold bracket screws.

5. Loosen the clamp at the rail end of the fuel rail-to-pressure regulator hose and then remove the regulator and hose. Collect any fuel

that may drain out into a metal cup and dispose of it safely.

6. Remove the bolt from the fuel rail-to-valve cover bracket.

7. Remove the fuel injector head shield clips. Then, remove the four intake manifold-to-rail mounting bolts. Note that one bolt retains a ground strap.

8. Pull the rail away from the manifold in such a way as to pull the injectors straight out of their mounting holes. Pull the injectors out straight so as to avoid damaging their O-rings.

9. To remove individual injectors from the rail, first position the rail on a bench or other

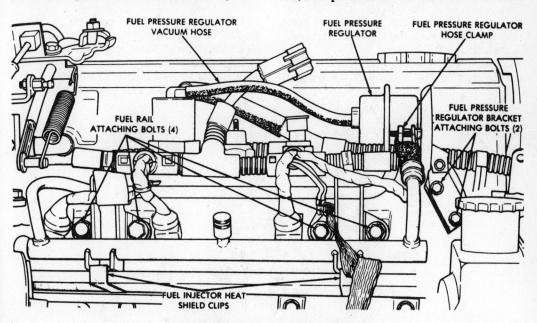

The fuel rail used with Turbo engines

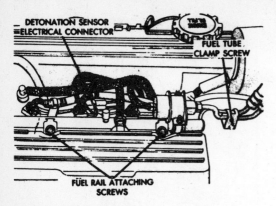

Fuel rail attaching screws

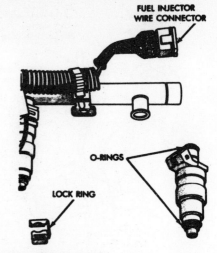

Servicing fuel injectors

surfaces so that the injectors are easily reached. Perform the following for each injector to be removed:

  a. Disconnect the wiring connector.

  b. Remove the lock ring from the rail and injector.

  c. Pull the injector straight out of the injector receiver cup in the fuel rail.

  d. Inspect the injector O-rings for damage. Replace it if necessary. If the injector will be re-used and will be off the rail while other work is performed, install a protective cap over the nozzle.

  e. Lubricate the O-ring that seals the upper end with a drop of clean engine oil. Then, install the inlet end carefully into the fuel rail receiver cup. Proceed slowly and insert the injector straight in to avoid damaging the O-ring.

  f. Slide the open end of the injector lock ring down over the injector, and onto the ridge in the receiver cup. The lock ring must lock into the slot on the top of the injector.

To install:

10. Remove all protective covers installed over the injector tips. Make sure the bores of the injector mounting holes are clean.

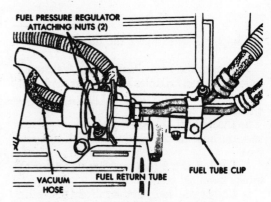

Servicing fuel pressure regulator assembly

11. Put a drop of clean engine oil on the O-ring at the nozzle end of each injector. Then position the rail with the injectors headed squarely into their mounting holes and gently and evenly slide all four injectors into place.

12. Install the four rail mounting bolts and

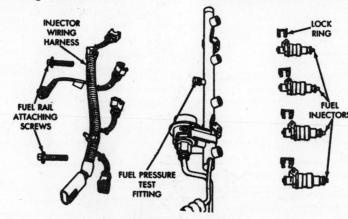

Fuel rail injector assembly

torque them to 250 inch lbs. Make sure to reconnect the ground strap removed earlier.

13. Connect each plug to its corresponding injector. Install each wiring harness into its clips. Connect the injector wiring harness to the main harness.

14. Install the heat shield clips. Install the bolt fastening the rail mounting bracket to the valve cover.

15. Connect the vacuum line for the fuel pressure regulator to the vacuum tree on the manifold. Then, connect the fuel return hose to the fuel pressure regulator (use a wrench to hold the fuel pressure regulator while tightening the fuel tube nut) and position and tighten the clamp. Install the bolts fastening the regulator bracket to the intake manifold.

16. Attach the fuel supply hose to the fuel rail and position and tighten the clamp.

17. Recheck all wiring and hose connections for routing and tightness. Then, connect the battery, start the engine, and check for fuel leaks.

6 Cylinder Engines
Except 1990–92 Laser, Dodge Stealth and Dodge Monaco

3.0L ENGINE

1. Disconnect the negative battery cable.
2. Relieve the fuel pressure.
3. Remove the air cleaner to throttle body hose.
4. Disconnect the throttle cable from the throttle body and disconnect the kickdown linkage. Remove the throttle cable bracket attaching bolts.
5. Disconnect the connectors to the throttle body.
6. Matchmark and carefully remove the vacuum hoses from the throttle body.
7. Remove the PCV and brake booster hoses from the air intake plenum.
8. Remove the ignition coil from the intake plenum, if it is mounted there.
9. Remove the EGR tube flange from the intake plenum, if equipped.
10. Unplug the coolant temperature sensor and charge temperature sensor, if equipped.
11. Remove the vacuum connection from the air intake plenum vacuum connector.
12. Remove the fuel hoses from the fuel rail and plug them.
13. Remove the air intake plenum to intake manifold bolts and remove the plenum and gaskets. Cover the intake manifold openings.
14. Remove the vacuum hoses from the fuel rail.
15. Disconnect the fuel injector wiring harness.

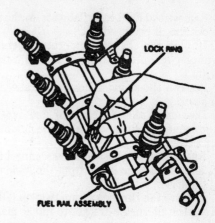

Fuel rail assembly—3.0L engine

16. Remove the fuel rail attaching bolts and remove the fuel rail with the wiring harness from the vehicle. Position the rail on the bench upside down so the injectors are easily accessible.

17. Remove the small connector retainer clip and unplug the injector. Remove the injector clip off the fuel rail and injector. Pull the injector straight out of the rail.

To install:

18. Lubricate the rubber O-ring with clean oil and install to the rail receiver cap. Install the injector clip to the **TOP** slot of the injector, plug in the connector and install the connector clip.

19. Install the fuel rail to the vehicle and plug in the injector harness. Connect the vacuum hoses to the fuel rail.

20. Install new intake plenum gaskets with the beaded sealer side up and install the intake plenum. Torque the attaching bolts and nuts to 115 inch lbs. (13 Nm).

21. Install the fuel hoses to the fuel rail.

22. Install or connect all items that were removed or disconnected from the intake plenum and throttle body.

23. Connect the negative battery cable and check for leaks using the DRB II or equivalent to activate the fuel pump. Roadtest the vehicle for proper operation.

3.3L AND 3.8L ENGINES

1. Disconnect the negative battery cable.
2. Relieve the fuel pressure.
3. Remove the air cleaner and hose assembly.
4. Disconnect the throttle cable. Remove the wiring harness from the throttle cable bracket and intake manifold water tube.
5. Remove the vacuum hose harness from the throttle body.
6. Remove the PCV and brake booster hoses from the air intake plenum.

7. Remove the EGR tube flange from the intake plenum, if equipped.

8. Unplug the charge temperature sensor and unplug all vacuum hoses from the intake plenum.

9. Remove the cylinder head to intake plenum strut.

10. Disconnect the MAP sensor and oxygen sensor connector. Remove the engine mounted ground strap.

11. Release the fuel hose quick disconnect fittings and remove the hoses from the fuel rail. Plug the hoses.

12. Remove the Direct Ignition System (DIS) coils and the alternator bracket-to-intake manifold bolt.

13. Remove the intake manifold bolts and rotate the manifold back over the rear valve cover. Cover the intake manifold.

14. Remove the vacuum harness from the pressure regulator.

15. Remove the fuel tube retainer bracket screw and fuel rail attaching bolts. Spread the retainer bracket to allow for clearance when removing the fuel tube.

16. Remove the fuel rail injector wiring clip from the alternator bracket.

17. Disconnect the cam sensor, coolant temperature sensor and engine temperature sensor.

18. Remove the fuel rail.

19. Position the rail on a work bench so the injectors are easily accessible.

20. Remove the small connector retainer clip and unplug the injector. Remove the injector clip off the fuel rail and injector. Pull the injector straight out of the rail.

To install:

21. Lubricate the rubber O-ring with clean oil and install to the rail receiver cap. Install the injector clip to the slot in the injector, plug in the connector and install the connector clip.

22. Install the fuel rail.

23. Connect the cam sensor, coolant temperature sensor and engine temperature sensor.

24. Install the fuel rail injector wiring clip to the alternator bracket.

25. Install the fuel rail attaching bolts and fuel tube retainer bracket screw.

26. Install the vacuum harness to the pressure regulator.

27. Install the intake manifold with a new gasket. Install the bolts only finger-tight. Install the alternator bracket to intake manifold bolt and the cylinder head to intake manifold strut and bolts. Torque the intake manifold mounting bolts to 21 ft. lbs. (28 Nm) starting from the middle and working outward. Torque the bracket and strut bolts to 40 ft. lbs. (54 Nm).

28. Install or connect all items that were removed or disconnected from the intake manifold and throttle body.

29. Connect the fuel hoses to the rail. Push the fittings in until they click in place.

30. Install the air cleaner assembly.

31. Connect the negative battery cable and check for leaks using the DRB II or equivalent to activate the fuel pump. Roadtest the vehicle for proper operation.

1990–92 Laser And Dodge Stealth

1.8L ENGINE

1. Relieve the fuel system pressure.

2. Disconnect the negative battery cable.

3. Wrap the connection with a shop towel and disconnect the high pressure fuel line at the fuel rail.

4. Disconnect the fuel return hose.

5. Disconnect the connectors from each connector.

6. Remove the injector rail retaining bolts. Make sure the rubber mounting bushings do not get lost.

7. Lift the rail assembly up and away from the engine.

8. Remove the injectors from the rail by pulling gently. Discard the lower insulator. Check the resistance through the injector. The specification is 13–15 ohms at 70°F (20°C).

To install:

9. Install a new grommet and O-ring to the injector. Coat the O-ring with light oil.

10. Install the injector to the fuel rail.

11. Replace the seats in the intake manifold. Install the fuel rail and injectors to the manifold. Make sure the rubber bushings are in place before tightening the mounting bolts.

12. Tighten the retaining bolts to 72 inch lbs. (11 Nm).

13. Connect the connectors to the injectors.

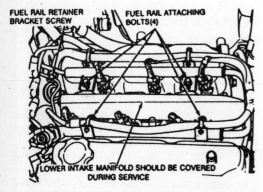

FUEL RAIL RETAINER BRACKET SCREW   FUEL RAIL ATTACHING BOLTS(4)

LOWER INTAKE MANIFOLD SHOULD BE COVERED DURING SERVICE

Fuel rail assembly—3.3/3.8L engines

CHILTON'S
FUEL ECONOMY & TUNE-UP TIPS

Tune-up • Spark Plug Diagnosis • Emission Controls

Fuel System • Cooling System • Tires and Wheels

General Maintenance

CHILTON'S FUEL ECONOMY & TUNE-UP TIPS

Fuel economy is important to everyone, no matter what kind of vehicle you drive. The maintenance-minded motorist can save both money and fuel using these tips and the periodic maintenance and tune-up procedures in this Repair and Tune-Up Guide.

There are more than 130,000,000 cars and trucks registered for private use in the United States. Each travels an average of 10-12,000 miles per year, and, and in total they consume close to 70 billion gallons of fuel each year. This represents nearly ⅔ of the oil imported by the United States each year. The Federal government's goal is to reduce consumption 10% by 1985. A variety of methods are either already in use or under serious consideration, and they all affect you driving and the cars you will drive. In addition to "down-sizing", the auto industry is using or investigating the use of electronic fuel delivery, electronic engine controls and alternative engines for use in smaller and lighter vehicles, among other alternatives to meet the federally mandated Corporate Average Fuel Economy (CAFE) of 27.5 mpg by 1985. The government, for its part, is considering rationing, mandatory driving curtailments and tax increases on motor vehicle fuel in an effort to reduce consumption. The government's goal of a 10% reduction could be realized — and further government regulation avoided — if every private vehicle could use just 1 less gallon of fuel per week.

How Much Can You Save?

Tests have proven that almost anyone can make at least a 10% reduction in fuel consumption through regular maintenance and tune-ups. When a major manufacturer of spark plugs sur-

TUNE-UP

1. Check the cylinder compression to be sure the engine will really benefit from a tune-up and that it is capable of producing good fuel economy. A tune-up will be wasted on an engine in poor mechanical condition.

2. Replace spark plugs regularly. New spark plugs alone can increase fuel economy 3%.

3. Be sure the spark plugs are the correct type (heat range) for your vehicle. See the Tune-Up Specifications.

Heat range refers to the spark plug's ability to conduct heat away from the firing end. It must conduct the heat away in an even pattern to avoid becoming a source of pre-ignition, yet it must also operate hot enough to burn off conductive deposits that could cause misfiring.

The heat range is usually indicated by a number on the spark plug, part of the manufacturer's designation for each individual spark plug. The numbers in bold-face indicate the heat range in each manufacturer's identification system.

Manufacturer	Typical Designation
AC	R **45** TS
Bosch (old)	WA **145** T30
Bosch (new)	HR **8** Y
Champion	RBL **15** Y
Fram/Autolite	4**15**
Mopar	P-**62** PR
Motorcraft	BRF-**42**
NGK	BP **5** ES-15
Nippondenso	W **16** EP
Prestolite	14GR **5** 2A

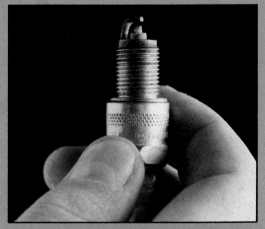

Periodically, check the spark plugs to be sure they are firing efficiently. They are excellent indicators of the internal condition of your engine.

On AC, Bosch (new), Champion, Fram/Autolite, Mopar, Motorcraft and Prestolite, a higher number indicates a hotter plug. On Bosch (old), NGK and Nippondenso, a higher number indicates a colder plug.

4. Make sure the spark plugs are properly gapped. See the Tune-Up Specifications in this book.

5. Be sure the spark plugs are firing efficiently. The illustrations on the next 2 pages show you how to "read" the firing end of the spark plug.

6. Check the ignition timing and set it to specifications. Tests show that almost all cars have incorrect ignition timing by more than 2°.

veyed over 6,000 cars nationwide, they found that a tune-up, on cars that needed one, increased fuel economy over 11%. Replacing worn plugs alone, accounted for a 3% increase. The same test also revealed that 8 out of every 10 vehicles will have some maintenance deficiency that will directly affect fuel economy, emissions or performance. Most of this mileage-robbing neglect could be prevented with regular maintenance.

Modern engines require that all of the functioning systems operate properly for maximum efficiency. A malfunction anywhere wastes fuel. You can keep your vehicle running as efficiently and economically as possible, by being aware of your vehicle's operating and performance characteristics. If your vehicle suddenly develops performance or fuel economy problems it could be due to one or more of the following:

PROBLEM	POSSIBLE CAUSE
Engine Idles Rough	Ignition timing, idle mixture, vacuum leak or something amiss in the emission control system.
Hesitates on Acceleration	Dirty carburetor or fuel filter, improper accelerator pump setting, ignition timing or fouled spark plugs.
Starts Hard or Fails to Start	Worn spark plugs, improperly set automatic choke, ice (or water) in fuel system.
Stalls Frequently	Automatic choke improperly adjusted and possible dirty air filter or fuel filter.
Performs Sluggishly	Worn spark plugs, dirty fuel or air filter, ignition timing or automatic choke out of adjustment.

Check spark plug wires on conventional point type ignition for cracks by bending them in a loop around your finger.

Be sure that spark plug wires leading to adjacent cylinders do not run too close together. (Photo courtesy Champion Spark Plug Co.)

7. If your vehicle does not have electronic ignition, check the points, rotor and cap as specified.

8. Check the spark plug wires (used with conventional point-type ignitions) for cracks and burned or broken insulation by bending them in a loop around your finger. Cracked wires decrease fuel efficiency by failing to deliver full voltage to the spark plugs. One misfiring spark plug can cost you as much as 2 mpg.

9. Check the routing of the plug wires. Misfiring can be the result of spark plug leads to adjacent cylinders running parallel to each other and too close together. One wire tends to pick up voltage from the other causing it to fire "out of time".

10. Check all electrical and ignition circuits for voltage drop and resistance.

11. Check the distributor mechanical and/or vacuum advance mechanisms for proper functioning. The vacuum advance can be checked by twisting the distributor plate in the opposite direction of rotation. It should spring back when released.

12. Check and adjust the valve clearance on engines with mechanical lifters. The clearance should be slightly loose rather than too tight.

SPARK PLUG DIAGNOSIS

Normal

APPEARANCE: This plug is typical of one operating normally. The insulator nose varies from a light tan to grayish color with slight electrode wear. The presence of slight deposits is normal on used plugs and will have no adverse effect on engine performance. The spark plug heat range is correct for the engine and the engine is running normally.

CAUSE: Properly running engine.

RECOMMENDATION: Before reinstalling this plug, the electrodes should be cleaned and filed square. Set the gap to specifications. If the plug has been in service for more than 10-12,000 miles, the entire set should probably be replaced with a fresh set of the same heat range.

Oil Deposits

APPEARANCE: The firing end of the plug is covered with a wet, oily coating.

CAUSE: The problem is poor oil control. On high mileage engines, oil is leaking past the rings or valve guides into the combustion chamber. A common cause is also a plugged PCV valve, and a ruptured fuel pump diaphragm can also cause this condition. Oil fouled plugs such as these are often found in new or recently overhauled engines, before normal oil control is achieved, and can be cleaned and reinstalled.

RECOMMENDATION: A hotter spark plug may temporarily relieve the problem, but the engine is probably in need of work.

Incorrect Heat Range

APPEARANCE: The effects of high temperature on a spark plug are indicated by clean white, often blistered insulator. This can also be accompanied by excessive wear of the electrode, and the absence of deposits.

CAUSE: Check for the correct spark plug heat range. A plug which is too hot for the engine can result in overheating. A car operated mostly at high speeds can require a colder plug. Also check ignition timing, cooling system level, fuel mixture and leaking intake manifold.

RECOMMENDATION: If all ignition and engine adjustments are known to be correct, and no other malfunction exists, install spark plugs one heat range colder.

Carbon Deposits

APPEARANCE: Carbon fouling is easily identified by the presence of dry, soft, black, sooty deposits.

CAUSE: Changing the heat range can often lead to carbon fouling, as can prolonged slow, stop-and-start driving. If the heat range is correct, carbon fouling can be attributed to a rich fuel mixture, sticking choke, clogged air cleaner, worn breaker points, retarded timing or low compression. If only one or two plugs are carbon fouled, check for corroded or cracked wires on the affected plugs. Also look for cracks in the distributor cap between the towers of affected cylinders.

RECOMMENDATION: After the problem is corrected, these plugs can be cleaned and reinstalled if not worn severely.

MMT Fouled

APPEARANCE: Spark plugs fouled by MMT (Methycyclopentadienyl Maganese Tricarbonyl) have reddish, rusty appearance on the insulator and side electrode.

CAUSE: MMT is an anti-knock additive in gasoline used to replace lead. During the combustion process, the MMT leaves a reddish deposit on the insulator and side electrode.

RECOMMENDATION: No engine malfunction is indicated and the deposits will not affect plug performance any more than lead deposits (see Ash Deposits). MMT fouled plugs can be cleaned, regapped and reinstalled.

High Speed Glazing

APPEARANCE: Glazing appears as shiny coating on the plug, either yellow or tan in color.

CAUSE: During hard, fast acceleration, plug temperatures rise suddenly. Deposits from normal combustion have no chance to fluff-off; instead, they melt on the insulator forming an electrically conductive coating which causes misfiring.

RECOMMENDATION: Glazed plugs are not easily cleaned. They should be replaced with a fresh set of plugs of the correct heat range. If the condition recurs, using plugs with a heat range one step colder may cure the problem.

Ash (Lead) Deposits

APPEARANCE: Ash deposits are characterized by light brown or white colored deposits crusted on the side or center electrodes. In some cases it may give the plug a rusty appearance.

CAUSE: Ash deposits are normally derived from oil or fuel additives burned during normal combustion. Normally they are harmless, though excessive amounts can cause misfiring. If deposits are excessive in short mileage, the valve guides may be worn.

RECOMMENDATION: Ash-fouled plugs can be cleaned, gapped and reinstalled.

Detonation

APPEARANCE: Detonation is usually characterized by a broken plug insulator.

CAUSE: A portion of the fuel charge will begin to burn spontaneously, from the increased heat following ignition. The explosion that results applies extreme pressure to engine components, frequently damaging spark plugs and pistons.

Detonation can result by over-advanced ignition timing, inferior gasoline (low octane) lean air/fuel mixture, poor carburetion, engine lugging or an increase in compression ratio due to combustion chamber deposits or engine modification.

RECOMMENDATION: Replace the plugs after correcting the problem.

Photos Courtesy Champion Spark Plug Co.

EMISSION CONTROLS

13. Be aware of the general condition of the emission control system. It contributes to reduced pollution and should be serviced regularly to maintain efficient engine operation.

14. Check all vacuum lines for dried, cracked or brittle conditions. Something as simple as a leaking vacuum hose can cause poor performance and loss of economy.

15. Avoid tampering with the emission control system. Attempting to improve fuel econ-

FUEL SYSTEM

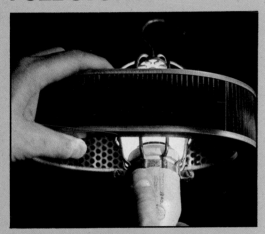

Check the air filter with a light behind it. If you can see light through the filter it can be reused.

Extremely clogged filters should be discarded and replaced with a new one.

18. Replace the air filter regularly. A dirty air filter richens the air/fuel mixture and can increase fuel consumption as much as 10%. Tests show that ⅓ of all vehicles have air filters in need of replacement.

19. Replace the fuel filter at least as often as recommended.

20. Set the idle speed and carburetor mixture to specifications.

21. Check the automatic choke. A sticking or malfunctioning choke wastes gas.

22. During the summer months, adjust the automatic choke for a leaner mixture which will produce faster engine warm-ups.

COOLING SYSTEM

29. Be sure all accessory drive belts are in good condition. Check for cracks or wear.

30. Adjust all accessory drive belts to proper tension.

31. Check all hoses for swollen areas, worn spots, or loose clamps.

32. Check coolant level in the radiator or expansion tank.

33. Be sure the thermostat is operating properly. A stuck thermostat delays engine warm-up and a cold engine uses nearly twice as much fuel as a warm engine.

34. Drain and replace the engine coolant at least as often as recommended. Rust and scale

TIRES & WHEELS

38. Check the tire pressure often with a pencil type gauge. Tests by a major tire manufacturer show that 90% of all vehicles have at least 1 tire improperly inflated. Better mileage can be achieved by over-inflating tires, but never exceed the maximum inflation pressure on the side of the tire.

39. If possible, install radial tires. Radial tires deliver as much as ½ mpg more than bias belted tires.

40. Avoid installing super-wide tires. They only create extra rolling resistance and decrease fuel mileage. Stick to the manufacturer's recommendations.

41. Have the wheels properly balanced.

omy by tampering with emission controls is more likely to worsen fuel economy than improve it. Emission control changes on modern engines are not readily reversible.

16. Clean (or replace) the EGR valve and lines as recommended.

17. Be sure that all vacuum lines and hoses are reconnected properly after working under the hood. An unconnected or misrouted vacuum line can wreak havoc with engine performance.

23. Check for fuel leaks at the carburetor, fuel pump, fuel lines and fuel tank. Be sure all lines and connections are tight.

24. Periodically check the tightness of the carburetor and intake manifold attaching nuts and bolts. These are a common place for vacuum leaks to occur.

25. Clean the carburetor periodically and lubricate the linkage.

26. The condition of the tailpipe can be an excellent indicator of proper engine combustion. After a long drive at highway speeds, the inside of the tailpipe should be a light grey in color. Black or soot on the insides indicates an overly rich mixture.

27. Check the fuel pump pressure. The fuel pump may be supplying more fuel than the engine needs.

28. Use the proper grade of gasoline for your engine. Don't try to compensate for knocking or "pinging" by advancing the ignition timing. This practice will only increase plug temperature and the chances of detonation or pre-ignition with relatively little performance gain.

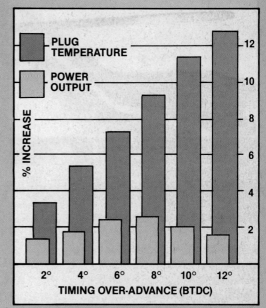

Increasing ignition timing past the specified setting results in a drastic increase in spark plug temperature with increased chance of detonation or preignition. Performance increase is considerably less. (Photo courtesy Champion Spark Plug Co.)

that form in the engine should be flushed out to allow the engine to operate at peak efficiency.

35. Clean the radiator of debris that can decrease cooling efficiency.

36. Install a flex-type or electric cooling fan, if you don't have a clutch type fan. Flex fans use curved plastic blades to push more air at low speeds when more cooling is needed; at high speeds the blades flatten out for less resistance. Electric fans only run when the engine temperature reaches a predetermined level.

37. Check the radiator cap for a worn or cracked gasket. If the cap does not seal properly, the cooling system will not function properly.

42. Be sure the front end is correctly aligned. A misaligned front end actually has wheels going in differed directions. The increased drag can reduce fuel economy by .3 mpg.

43. Correctly adjust the wheel bearings. Wheel bearings that are adjusted too tight increase rolling resistance.

Check tire pressures regularly with a reliable pocket type gauge. Be sure to check the pressure on a cold tire.

GENERAL MAINTENANCE

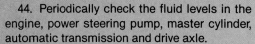

Check the fluid levels (particularly engine oil) on a regular basis. Be sure to check the oil for grit, water or other contamination.

A vacuum gauge is another excellent indicator of internal engine condition and can also be installed in the dash as a mileage indicator.

44. Periodically check the fluid levels in the engine, power steering pump, master cylinder, automatic transmission and drive axle.

45. Change the oil at the recommended interval and change the filter at every oil change. Dirty oil is thick and causes extra friction between moving parts, cutting efficiency and increasing wear. A worn engine requires more frequent tune-ups and gets progressively worse fuel economy. In general, use the lightest viscosity oil for the driving conditions you will encounter.

46. Use the recommended viscosity fluids in the transmission and axle.

47. Be sure the battery is fully charged for fast starts. A slow starting engine wastes fuel.

48. Be sure battery terminals are clean and tight.

49. Check the battery electrolyte level and add distilled water if necessary.

50. Check the exhaust system for crushed pipes, blockages and leaks.

51. Adjust the brakes. Dragging brakes or brakes that are not releasing create increased drag on the engine.

52. Install a vacuum gauge or miles-per-gallon gauge. These gauges visually indicate engine vacuum in the intake manifold. High vacuum = good mileage and low vacuum = poorer mileage. The gauge can also be an excellent indicator of internal engine conditions.

53. Be sure the clutch is properly adjusted. A slipping clutch wastes fuel.

54. Check and periodically lubricate the heat control valve in the exhaust manifold. A sticking or inoperative valve prevents engine warm-up and wastes gas.

55. Keep accurate records to check fuel economy over a period of time. A sudden drop in fuel economy may signal a need for tune-up or other maintenance.

14. Replace the O-ring, lightly lubricate it and connect the fuel pressure regulator.

15. Connect the fuel return hose.

16. Replace the O-ring, lightly lubricate it and connect the high pressure fuel line.

17. Connect the negative battery cable and check the entire system for proper operation and leaks.

2.0L DOHC ENGINE

1. Relieve the fuel system pressure.

2. Disconnect the negative battery cable.

3. Wrap the connection with a shop towel and disconnect the high pressure fuel line at the fuel rail.

4. Disconnect the fuel return hose and remove the O-ring.

5. Disconnect the vacuum hose from the fuel pressure regulator. Remove the fuel pressure regulator and O-ring.

6. Disconnect the PCV hose. Remove the center cover if so equipped.

7. Disconnect the connectors from each injector.

8. Remove the injector rail retaining bolts. Make sure the rubber mounting bushings do not get lost.

9. Lift the rail assembly up and away from the engine.

10. Remove the injectors from the rail by pulling gently. Discard the lower insulator. Check the resistance through the injector. The specification for 2.0L turbocharged engine is 2–3 ohms at 70°F (20°C). The specification for the others is 13–15 ohms at 70°F (20°C).

To install:

11. Install a new grommet and O-ring to the injector. Coat the O-ring with light oil.

12. Install the injector to the fuel rail.

13. Replace the seats in the intake manifold. Install the fuel rail and injectors to the manifold. Make sure the rubber bushings are in place before tightening the mounting bolts.

14. Tighten the retaining bolts to 72 inch lbs. (11 Nm).

15. Connect the connectors to the injectors and install the center cover if so equipped. Connect the PCV hose.

16. Replace the O-ring, lightly lubricate it and connect the fuel pressure regulator.

17. Connect the fuel return hose.

18. Replace the O-ring, lightly lubricate it and connect the high pressure fuel line.

19. Connect the negative battery cable and check the entire system for proper operation and leaks.

3.0L ENGINE

1. Relieve the fuel system pressure.

2. Disconnect the negative battery cable.

3. Drain the coolant.

4. Disconnect all components from the air intake plenum and remove the plenum from the intake manifold. Discard the gaskets.

5. Wrap the connection with a shop towel and disconnect the high pressure fuel line at the fuel rail.

6. Disconnect the fuel return hose and remove the O-ring.

7. Disconnect the vacuum hose from the fuel pressure regulator. Remove the fuel pressure regulator and O-ring.

8. Disconnect the connectors from each injector.

9. Remove the fuel pipe connecting the fuel rails. Remove the injector rail retaining bolts. Make sure the rubber mounting bushings do not get lost.

10. Lift the rail assemblies up and away from the engine.

11. Remove the injectors from the rail by pulling gently. Discard the lower insulator.

To install:

12. Install a new grommet and O-ring to the injector. Coat the O-ring with light oil.

13. Install the injector to the fuel rail.

14. Replace the seats in the intake manifold. Install the fuel rails and injectors to the manifold. Make sure the rubber bushings are in place before tightening the mounting bolts.

15. Tighten the retaining bolts to 72 inch lbs. (11 Nm). Install the fuel pipe with new gasket.

16. Connect the connectors to the injectors.

17. Replace the O-ring, lightly lubricate it and connect the fuel pressure regulator.

18. Connect the fuel return hose.

19. Replace the O-ring, lightly lubricate it and connect the high pressure fuel line.

20. Using new gaskets, install the intake plenum and all related items. Torque the plenum mounting bolts to 13 ft. lbs. (18 Nm).

21. Fill the cooling system.

22. Connect the negative battery cable and check the entire system for proper operation and leaks.

Dodge Monaco

3.0L ENGINE

1. Relieve the fuel system pressure.

2. Disconnect the negative battery cable.

3. Disconnect the fuel lines from the fuel rail assembly.

4. Disconnect and tag the electrical leads from the fuel injectors and lay the harness aside.

5. Disconnect the cruise and accelerator cables from the the throttle body.

6. Remove the 4 screws attaching the engine cover and remove the cover.

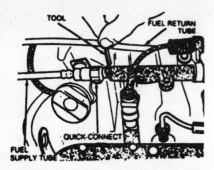

Using special tool to disconnect main fuel supply to injector rail—Dodge Monaco 3.0L engine

Fuel injector and rail—Dodge Monaco 3.0L engine

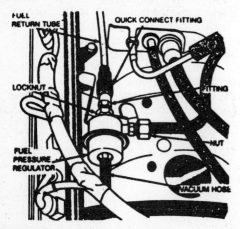

Fuel lines Dodge Monaco 3.0L engine

7. Remove the fuel rail mounting bolts and disconnect the vacuum line from the fuel pressure regulator. Pull the fuel rail and injectors from the engine, using a back and forth twisting motion.

8. Remove the retaining clip and separate the injectors from the fuel rail.

To install:

9. Assemble the fuel rail. Install the fuel rail

and injectors to the engine, be careful not to damage the O-rings on the injectors. Install the fuel rail hold-down bolts and connect the fuel lines.

10. Connect the electrical leads to the injectors. Connect the throttle cable. Install the engine cover plate.

11. Connect the negative battery cable. Turn the ignition to the ON position to pressurize the fuel system and check for leaks.

Fuel Tubes and Quick-Connect Fittings

The fuel system on some late model vehicles utilize plastic fuel tubes with quick-connect fittings that have sealed O-rings; these O-rings do not have to be replaced when the fittings are disconnected. The quick-connect fitting consists of the O-rings, a retainer and the casing. When the fuel tube nipple is inserted into the quick-connect fitting, the shoulder of the nipple is locked in place by the retainer, and the O-rings seal the tube. The fuel tube nipples must first be lubricated with clean 30 weight engine oil prior to reconnecting the quick-connect fitting.

When the fittings are disconnected, the retainer will stay on the nipple of the component that the tube is being disconnected from. A fuel tube should never be inserted into a quick-connect fitting without the retainer being either on the tube or already in the quick-connect fitting. In either case, care must be taken to ensure that the retainer is locked securely into the quick-connect fitting.

If the quick-connect fitting has windows in the side of the casing, the retainer locking ears and the shoulder (stop bead) on the tube must be visible in the windows, or the retainer is not properly installed. After connecting a quick-connect fitting, the connection should be verified by pulling on the lines to ensure that the lock is secure.

There is a factory tool that can be used at the Dodge Monaco 3.0L engine fuel rail and fuel pressure regulator to remove the quick-connect fitting and retainer as an assembly. The retainer will remain in the fitting in the correct position. To install the fuel tube, push it over the nipple until a click is heard. Pull back on the tube to ensure that the connector is locked in place.

FUEL TANK

REMOVAL AND INSTALLATION

NOTE: *ALWAYS EXERCISE CAUTION WHEN SERVICING THE FUEL TANK AS-*

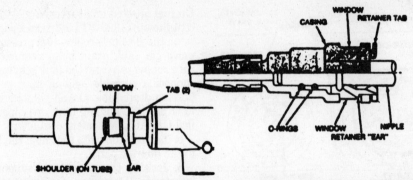

Special quick connect fittings. Use care removing and installing—Dodge Monaco 3.0L engine

SEMBLY AS FUEL VAPORS ARE EX-TREMELY FLAMMABLE. The following procedure can be used on all years and models. Slight variations may occur due to extra connections, etc., some vehicles have a drain plug for fuel tank, but the basic procedure should cover all years and models. To service the Rollover/Vapor Seperator Valve refer to the necessary illustrations.

1. Release the fuel system pressure as described in Chapter 1 on all models with fuel injection.

2. Disconnect the negative battery terminal.

3. Remove the gas cap to relieve any pressure in the tank.

4. On all vehicles without fuel injection, disconnect the fuel supply line at the right front shock absorber tower, and drain the fuel tank.

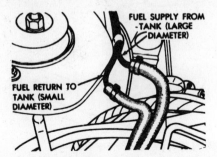

Siphon hose connection location L/M, Z body styles except fuel injection vehicles

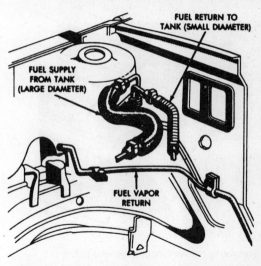

Siphon hose connection location K, E, G body styles except fuel injection vehicles

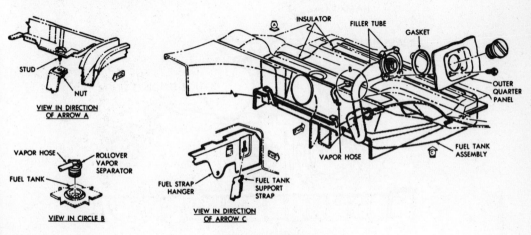

Fuel tank assembly

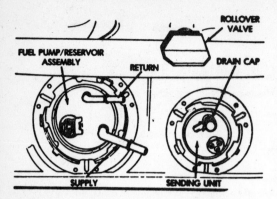

Drain tube connection location—fuel injection vehicles

On fuel injected and turbocharged models (except Stealth, 1990–92 Laser and Dodge Monaco — on these vehicle relieve fuel pressure and remove gas tank drain plug) remove the draft tube rubber cap from the tank sending unit and connect a portable holding tank or a siphon hose to draft tube. On all vehicles drain fuel tank dry into holding tank or properly identified GASAOLINE safety container.

5. Remove the bolts that hold the filler tube to the quarter panel.

6. Jack up the vehicle and support it with jackstands. If necessary for access to the filler tube, remove the right rear wheel.

7. Disconnect the wiring and all hoses from the tank assembly.

8. Remove the screws from the exhaust pipe-to-fuel tank shield, and allow this shield to rest on the exhaust pipe if so equipped.

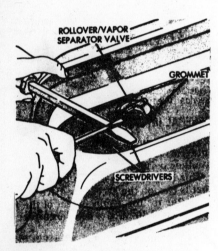

Removing rollover/vapor separator valve

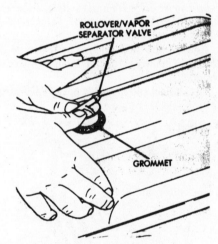

Installing rollover/vapor separator valve

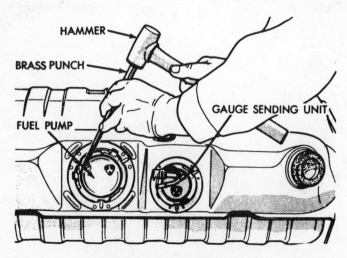

Removing the fuel pump

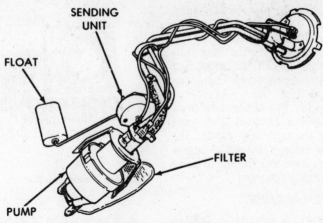

FLOAT

SENDING UNIT

FILTER

PUMP

L-body fuel pump assembly

9. Support the tank with a jack and remove the tank strap bolts.

10. Lower the tank slightly. If there is a roll-over/separator valve hose connecting into the tank, disconnect it at the valve. Carefully remove the filler tube from the tank.

11. Lower the fuel tank assembly and remove it and the insulator pad.

To install:

12. To install the tank, first position the insulator pad on top of the tank and then raise it to within a foot or so of its normal position. Then, connect the filler tube and, if equipped, the roll-over/separator valve hose.

13. Raise the tank into its normal position and install the tank strap bolts (at this point of the service procedure connect all hoses and wiring if necessary to gain access for these connections). Torque strap nuts evenly and check that retaining straps are not twisted or bent.

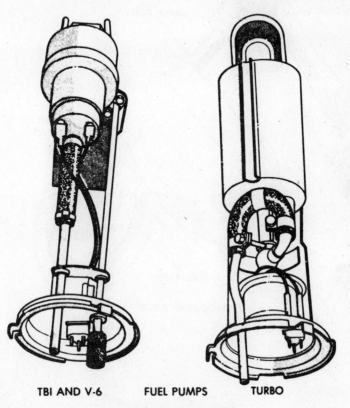

TBI AND V-6   FUEL PUMPS   TURBO

Fuel pump assembly

14. Install the exhaust pipe-to-fuel tank shield. Reconnect the gauge and fuel pump wiring (electric pumps only) and all hoses.

15. Install the bolts attaching the filler tube to the quarter panel. Install the right rear wheel, if it was removed previously. Then, lower the car.

16. Reconnect the fuel line at the right front shock absorber tower if removed. Put some fresh, clean fuel in the tank and reinstall the cap. Reconnect the battery. Start the engine and check for leaks. Road test the car to make sure the tank is securely mounted.

SENDING UNIT REPLACEMENT

1. Remove the fuel tank assembly — refer to the necessary service procedure.

2. Using a tool and brass punch or equivalent (non-metallic) CAREFULLY tap lock ring counterclockwise to release sending unit assembly.

3. Lift the sending unit and O-ring away from the tank assembly. On fuel injected models, remove the internal return line from the sending unit.

To install:

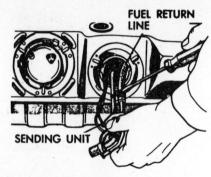

Servicing internal fuel lines

4. Wipe seal area of tank assembly clean and place a new O-ring seal in the proper position.

5. On fuel injected vehicles, inspect internal fuel ine hose and its attachment to the reservoir. Inspect the internal fuel return line does not interfere with the sending unit float travel.

6. Install sending unit in the tank assembly, position lock ring and tap ring in a clockwise direction using proper tools. Install the tank assembly in the vehicle.

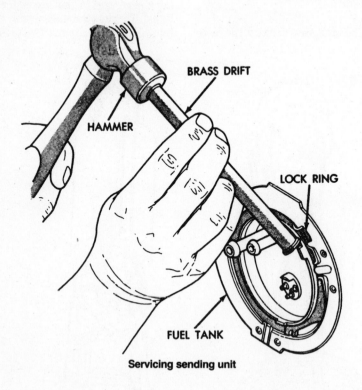

Servicing sending unit

HEATING AND AIR CONDITIONING

Heater Blower Motor

REMOVAL AND INSTALLATION

1981–86 Models

The blower motor is located under the instrument panel on the left side of the heater assembly.

1. Disconnect the negative battery terminal.
2. Disconnect the motor wiring.
3. Remove the two attaching screws and remove the left outlet duct.
4. Remove the motor retaining screws and the motor.
5. Installation is the reverse of removal. Connect the negative battery cable and check the blower motor for proper operation.

Heater and Air Conditioning Blower Motor

REMOVAL AND INSTALLATION

1981–86 Models

1. Disconnect the negative battery terminal.
2. Remove the three screws securing the glovebox to the instrument panel.

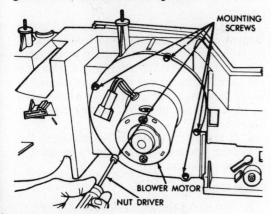

Removing the blower motor assembly

3. Disconnect the wiring from the blower and case.
4. Remove the blower vent tube from the case.
5. Loosen the recirculating door from its bracket and remove the actuator from the housing. Leave the vacuum lines attached.
6. Remove the seven screws attaching the recirculating housing to the air conditioning unit and remove the housing.
7. Remove the three mounting flange nuts and washers.
8. Remove the blower motor from the unit.
9. Installation is the reverse of removal. Replace any damaged sealer. Connect the negative battery cable and check the blower motor for proper operation.

1987 And Later Models
Except 1990–92 Laser, Stealth and Dodge Monaco

1. Disconnect the negative battery cable.
NOTE: *If equipped with an air bag, be sure to disarm it before entering the vehicle. Refer to the end of the service procedure.*
2. Remove the glove box assembly, lower right side instrument panel trim cover and right cowl trim panel, as required. Disconnect the blower lead wire connector.
3. If the vehicle is equipped with air conditioning, disconnect the 2 vacuum lines from the recirculating door actuator and position the actuator aside.
4. Remove the 2 screws at the top of the blower housing that secure it to the unit cover.
5. Remove the 5 screws from around the blower housing and separate the blower housing from the unit.
6. Remove the 3 screws that secure the blower assembly to the heater or air conditioning housing and remove the assembly from the unit. Remove the fan from the blower motor refer to illustration (mark location of fan to blower motor assembly for correct installation).

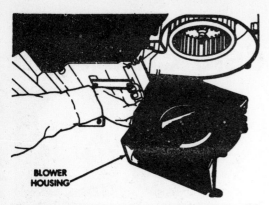

Blower housing

Blower motor and wheel assembly

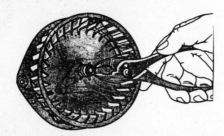

Blower motor wheel retaining ring removal and installation

7. The installation is the reverse of the removal procedure.

8. Connect the negative battery cable and check the blower motor for proper operation.

Chrysler Front Wheel Drive Vehicles

AIR BAG DISARMING

To disarm the air bag, disconnect the negative battery. There is no time lapse built into this sytem, so the system is immediately disabled. No further procedures are needed. Failure to disarm the system may result in deployment of the air bag and possible personal injury.

1990–92 Laser and Dodge Stealth

1. Disconnect the negative battery cable.
NOTE: *If equipped with an air bag, be sure*

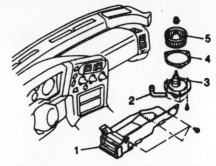

1. Duct, if so equipped
2. Molded hose
3. Blower motor assembly
4. Packing seal
5. Fan

Heater blower assembly 1990–92 Laser

to disarm it before entering the vehicle. Refer to the end of the service procedure.

2. On Laser, remove the right side duct, if equipped. On Stealth, remove the instrument panel undercover.

3. Remove the cooling tube from the blower assembly.

4. Remove the blower motor assembly.

5. Remove the packing seal.

6. Remove the fan retaining nut and fan in order to renew the motor.

To install:

7. Check that the blower motor shaft is not bent and that the packing is in good condition. Clean all parts of dust, etc.

8. Assemble the motor and fan. Install the blower motor and connect the wiring.

9. Install the cooling tube.

10. Install the duct or undercover.

11. Connect the negative battery cable and check the entire climate control system for proper operation.

1990–92 Laser and Dodge Stealth

AIR BAG DISARMING

1. Position the front wheels in the straight ahead position and place the key in the **LOCK** position.

2. Disconnect the negative battery cable and insulate the cable end with high-quality electrical tape or similar non-conductive wrapping.

3. Wait at least 1 minute before working on the vehicle. The air bag system is designed to retain enough voltage to deploy for a short period of time even after the battery has been disconnected.

4. If necessary, enter the vehicle from the passenger side and turn the key to unlock the steering column.

Dodge Monaco

1. Disconnect the negative battery cable.
2. Disconnect the electrical connector from the coolant reservoir.

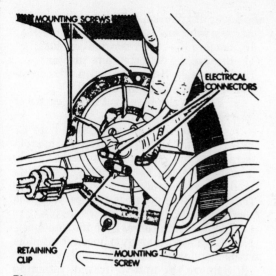

Blower motor removal and installation—Dodge Monaco

3. Remove the coolant reservoir retaining strap and move the reservoir aside.

4. Remove the coolant reservoir mounting bracket. Disconnect the electrical wires from the blower motor.

5. Remove the blower motor mounting bolts and the blower motor.

6. The installation is the reverse of the removal installation.

7. Connect the negative battery cable and check the entire climate control system for proper operation.

Heater Core
REMOVAL AND INSTALLATION
1981–84 Models Without Air Conditioning

1. Remove the heater assembly.

2. Remove the padding from around the heater core outlets and remove the upper core mounting screws.

3. Pry loose the retaining snaps from around the outer edge of the housing cover.

NOTE: *If a retaining snap should break, the housing cover has provisions for mounting screws.*

4. Remove the housing top cover.

5. Remove the bottom heater core mounting screw.

6. Slide the heater core out of the housing.

7. Installation is the reverse of removal.

Heater Assembly
REMOVAL AND INSTALLATION
1981–85 Cars Without Air Conditioning

1. Disconnect the negative battery cable and drain the radiator.

CAUTION: *When draining the coolant, keep in mind that cats and dogs are attracted by the ethylene glycol antifreeze, and are quite likely to drink any that is left in an uncovered container or in puddles on the ground. This will prove fatal in sufficient quantity. Always drain the coolant into a sealable container. Coolant should be reused unless it is contaminated or several years old.*

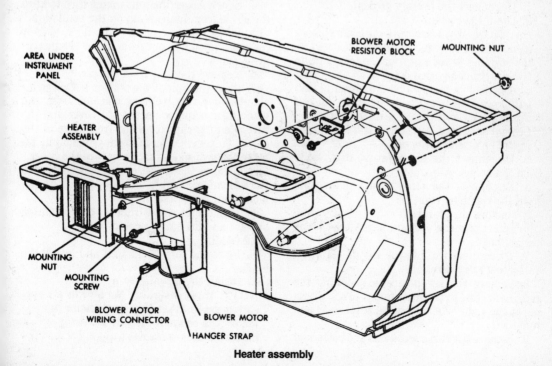

Heater assembly

2. Disconnect the blower motor wiring connector.

3. Reach under the unit, depress the tab on the mode door and temperature control cables, pull the flags from the receivers, and remove the self-adjust clip from the crank arm.

4. Remove the glove box assembly.

5. Disconnect the heater hoses to the unit on the engine side and seal the heater core tube openings and hoses.

6. Through the glove box opening, remove the screw attaching the hanger strap to the heater assembly.

7. Remove the nut attaching the hanger strap to the dash panel and remove the hanger strap.

8. Remove the two nuts attaching the heater assembly to the dash panel. The nuts are on the engine side.

9. Pull out the bottom of the instrument panel and slide out the heater assembly.

10. Installation is the reverse of removal.

1981–84 Air Conditioned Cars

Removal of the Heater-Evaporator Unit is required for heater core removal. Two people will be required to perform the operation. Discharge, evacuation and recharge and leak testing of the refrigerant system must be done at an approved refrigerant recovery facility. See Chapter 1. Just make sure the system is discharged before attempting removal. During installation, a small amount of refrigerant oil will be necessary.

1. Disconnect the battery ground.

2. Drain the coolant.

CAUTION: *When draining the coolant, keep in mind that cats and dogs are attracted by the ethylene glycol antifreeze, and are quite likely to drink any that is left in an uncovered container or in puddles on the ground. This will prove fatal in sufficient quantity. Always drain the coolant into a sealable container. Coolant should be reused unless it is contaminated or several years old.*

3. Disconnect the temperature door cable from the heater-evaporator unit.

4. Disconnect the temperature door cable from the retaining clips.

5. Remove the glovebox.

6. Disconnect the vacuum harness from the control head.

7. Disconnect the blower motor lead and anti-diesel relay wire.

8. Remove the seven screws fastening the right trim bezel to the instrument panel. Starting at the right side, swing the bezel clear and remove it.

9. Remove the three screws on the bottom of the center distribution duct cover and slide the cover rearward and remove it.

10. Remove the center distribution duct.

11. Remove the defroster duct adaptor.

12. Remove the H-type expansion valve, located on the right side of the firewall:

    a. Remove the ⅝ in. bolt in the center of the plumbing sealing plate.

    b. Carefully pull the refrigerant lines toward the front of the car, taking care to avoid scratching the valve sealing surfaces.

    c. Remove the two Allenhead capscrews and remove the valve.

13. Cap the pipe openings at once. Wrap the valve in a plastic bag.

14. Disconnect the hoses from the core tubes.

15. Disconnect the vacuum lines at the intake manifold and water valve.

16. Remove the unit-to-firewall retaining nuts.

17. Remove the panel support bracket.

18. Remove the right cowl lower panel.

19. Remove the instrument panel pivot bracket screw from the right side.

20. Remove the screws securing the lower instrument panel at the steering column.

21. Pull back the carpet from under the unit as far as possible.

22. Remove the nut from the evaporator-heater unit-to-plenum mounting brace and blower motor ground cable. While supporting the unit, remove the brace from its stud.

23. Lift the unit, pulling it rearward to allow clearance. These operations may require two people.

24. Slowly lower the unit taking care to keep the studs from hanging-up on the insulation.

25. When the unit reaches the floor, slide it rearward until it is out from under the instrument panel.

26. Remove the unit from the car.

27. Place the unit on a workbench. On the inside-the-car-side, remove the nut from the mode door actuator on the top cover and the two retaining clips from the front edge of the cover. To remove the mode door actuator, remove the two screws securing it to the cover.

28. Remove the screws attaching the cover to the assembly and lift off the cover. Lift the mode door out of the unit.

29. Remove the screw from the core retaining bracket and lift out the core.

To install:

30. Place the core in the unit and install the bracket.

31. Install the actuator arm.

NOTE: *When installing the unit in the car, care must be taken that the vacuum lines to the engine compartment do not hang-up on the accelerator or become trapped between the unit and the firewall. If this happens, kinked lines will result and the unit will have to be removed to free them. Proper routing of these lines will require two people. The portion of the vacuum harness which is routed through the steering column support MUST be positioned BEFORE the distribution housing is installed. The harness MUST be routed ABOVE the temperature control cable.*

32. Place the unit on the floor as far under the panel as possible.

33. Raise the unit carefully, at the same time pull the lower instrument panel rearward as far as possible.

34. Position the unit in place and attach the brace to the stud.

35. Install the lower ground cable and attach the nut.

36. Install and tighten the unit-to-firewall nuts.

37. Reposition the carpet and install, but do not tighten the right instrument panel pivot bracket screw.

38. Place a piece of sheet metal or thin cardboard against the evaporator-heater assembly to center the assembly duct seal.

39. Position the center distributor duct in place making sure that the upper left tab comes in through thel left center air conditioning outlet opening and that each air take-off is properly inserted in its respective outlet.

NOTE: *Make sure that the radio wiring connector does not interfere with the duct.*

40. Install and tighten the screw securing the upper left tab of the center air distribution duct to the instrument panel.

41. Remove the sheet metal or cardboard from between the unit and the duct.

NOTE: *Make sure that the unit seal is properly aligned with the duct opening.*

42. Install and tighten the two lower screws fastening the center distribution duct to the instrument panel.

43. Install and tighten the screws securing the lower instrument panel at the steering column.

44. Install and tighten the nut securing the instrument panel to the support bracket.

45. Make sure that the seal on the unit is properly aligned and seated against the distribution duct assembly.

46. Tighten the instrument panel pivot bracket screw and install the right cowl lower trim.

47. Slide the distributor duct cover assembly onto the center distribution duct so that the notches lock into the tabs and the tabs slide over the rear and side ledges of the center duct assembly.

48. Install the three screws securing the ducting.

49. Install the right trim bezel.

50. Connect the vacuum harness to the control head.

51. Connect the blower lead and the anti-diesel wire.

52. Install the glovebox.

53. Connect the temperature door cable.

54. Install new O-rings on the evaporator plate and the plumbing plate. Coat the new O-rings with clean refrigerant oil.

55. Place the H-valve against the evaporator sealing plate surface and install the two throughbolts. Torque to 6-10 ft. lb.

56. Carefully hold the refrigerant line connector against the valve and install the bolt. Torque to 14-20 ft. lb.

57. Install the heater hoses at the core tubes.

58. Connect the vacuum lines at the manifold and water valve.

59. Install the condensate drain tube.

60. Have the air conditioning system evacuated, charged and leak tested by an approved facility. See Chapter 1.

All 1985–86 Models

NOTE: *Modify the service steps as necessary — on vehicles not equipped with air conditioning.*

1. Have the air conditioning system dis-

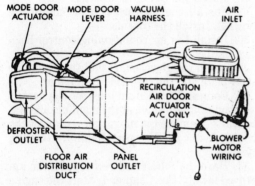

The heater-A/C housing used on 1987 and later models

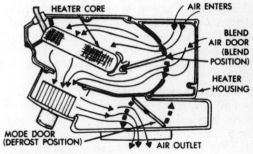

Blend air heater system

charged by an approved refrigerant recovery facility. See Chapter 1.

2. Drain the engine cooling system. Then, disconnnect the heater hoses at the core and plug the core openings with a cork or cap.

CAUTION: *When draining the coolant, keep in mind that cats and dogs are attracted by the ethylene glycol antifreeze, and are quite likely to drink any that is left in an uncovered container or in puddles on the ground. This will prove fatal in sufficient quantity. Always drain the coolant into a sealable container. Coolant should be reused unless it is contaminated or several years old.*

3. Mark and then disconnect the vacuum lines for the heater/air conditioning system at the intake manifold and water valve.

4. Remove the right side scuff plate and the cowl side trim panel.

5. Remove the glovebox.

6. Remove the air conditioning control head as described below.

7. If the car has a console, remove it.

8. Remove the two bolts and two screws which fasten the forward console mounting bracket to the body and remove it.

9. Remove the center distribution duct.

10. Remove the side window demister adapter on those models so-equipped. Pull the defroster adapter from the bottom of the defroster duct.

11. Remove its clamp and remove the L-shaped condensate drain tube. Disconnect the heater/air conditioning unit from the wiring harness at the connector.

12. Disconnect the control cable at the receiver, located near the evaporator assembly. To do this, depress the tab on the red flag and pull the flag out of the receiver.

13. Remove the right side cowl-to-plenum brace. Pull the carpet out from under the unit and fold it back.

14. Remove the screw holding the hanger strap to the unit. Then, remove the 4 mounting nuts for the unit which are located on the engine compartment side of the cowl. Finally, pull the unit toward the rear of the car until the studs clear the dash liner. Allow it to drop down until it rests on the catalytic converter tunnel.

15. Turn the unit so as to clear the lower instrument panel reinforcement without moving it too far to either side. Then, remove the unit from the car and place it on a workbench, standing behind it just as a front seat passenger would.

16. Disconnect the actuator arm at the mounting shaft by squeezing it with a pair of pliers to release it. *Be careful to avoid prying the mounting clips as you do this, as they will probably be broken.* When the arm is free, re-move the retaining clips from the front edge of the cover.

17. Remove the two screws mounting the mode door actuator to the cover and remove it.

18. Remove the 15 screws attaching the cover to the housing and remove it. Then, lift the mode door out.

19. Remove the screw from the heater core tube retaining bracket and lift the core out of the unit.

To install:

20. Slide the new heater core into position and then install the screw into the retaining bracket.

21. Install the mode door. Install the cover to the heater/air conditioning housing and install the 15 attaching screws.

22. Install the mode door actuator and its two attaching screws.

23. Reconnect the actuator arm at the mounting shaft by squeezing it with a pair of pliers to permit it to be installed over the shaft (again be careful not to squeeze the mounting clips). Install the retaining clips on the front edge of the cover.

24. Install the unit back into the car, working it around the instrument panel reinforcement. Raise it until the mounting studs line up with the holes in the cowl and position it so the studs pass through the cowl. Install the four mounting nuts from the engine compartment side.

25. Install the screw attaching the hanger strap to the unit. Work the carpet back into position under the unit. Install the right side cowl-to-plenum brace.

26. Reconnect the control cable at the receiver. Install the L-shaped condensate drain tube. Connect the heater/air conditioning unit wiring harness connector.

27. Install the defroster adapter onto the bottom of the defroster duct. Install the side window demister adapter on those models so-equipped.

28. Install the center distribution duct.

29. Install the forward console mounting bracket. Install the console.

30. Install the air conditioning control head as described below.

31. Install the glovebox. Install the right side scuff plate and the cowl side trim panel.

32. Connect the vacuum lines for the heater/air conditioning system at the manifold and water valve. Remove the plugs and reconnect the heater hoses at the core. Refill the cooling system.

33. Have the refrigerant recharged at an approved facility. See Chapter 1. Start the engine and check for leaks. Refill the cooling system af-

ter the engine has reached operating temperature and then cooled back off.

1987 Models

NOTE: *Modify the service steps as necessary on vehicles not equipped with air conditioning. To complete this procedure, make sure to have suitable caps or plastic sheeting and tape to cover and seal open refrigerant lines. Also needed are caps or plugs for the heater core tubes.*

1. Have the air conditioning system discharged by a facility equipped with a recovery system. Disconnect the battery negative cable.

2. Drain the engine cooling system. Remove the right side cowl cover. Remove the trim panel from the door opening scuff plate.

CAUTION: *When draining the coolant, keep in mind that cats and dogs are attracted by the ethylene glycol antifreeze, and are quite likely to drink any that is left in an uncovered container or in puddles on the ground. This will prove fatal in sufficient quantity. Always drain the coolant into a sealable container. Coolant should be reused unless it is contaminated or several years old.*

3. There is a roll down bolt located behind the instrument panel to the right of the glovebox. Loosen this bolt so that the instrument panel can be shifted later in the procedure.

4. Remove the four instrument cluster center bezel attaching screws, open the glovebox door and remove the bezel.

5. Remove the lower instrument panel module cover, if the car has one.

6. Remove the center console assembly. Position the accessory wiring harness so it will be out of the way when removing the heater/air conditioning unit.

7. Remove the instrument panel center support braces and brackets.

8. Remove the radio as described later in this chapter.

9. Remove the ash tray and then remove its mounting bracket.

10. Remove the cigarette lighter and socket. Remove the glovebox.

11. Remove the heater/air conditioning control as described later in this chapter. Disconnect the temperature cable attaching flag and vacuum harness from the control assembly.

12. Remove the two attaching screws and remove the center air duct.

13. Disconnect the blower motor relay module and wiring lead from the harness and position both so the heater/air conditioning unit can be removed later.

14. The defroster duct adapter is located between the heater/air conditioning unit and the defroster duct. Pull it downward from its installed position and remove it.

15. Remove the attaching nut and 4 screws from the heater/air conditioning unit support bracket and remove it.

16. Remove the 3 attaching screws from the heat outlet duct (located under the unit) and remove the duct.

17. Slide the front passenger's seat as far to the rear as it will go. Then, roll the carpet out from under the unit.

18. Disconnect the lines from the refrigerant expansion "H" valve, and immediately and tightly cover the openings.

19. Disconnect both heater hoses and plug the core tubes.

20. Remove the condensate drain tube.

21. Remove the four heater/air conditioning unit attaching nuts from the engine compartment side of the cowl. Remove the heater/air conditioning unit support brace lower attaching bolt. Then, swing the brace out of the way to the left and behind the dash panel.

22. Pull the unit directly away from the dash panel (do not twist or turn it, so as to avoid damaging the seals). Once the studs clear both the dash panel and liner, allow it to drop down until it rests on the floor tunnel.

23. Remove the demister adapter duct from the top of the unit to provide working clearance.

24. Then, keeping the unit upright, slide it from under the instrument panel and out the right side door opening.

25. Place the unit on a workbench or in some similar spot where you can work on it effectively. Remove the retaining nut from the blend-air door pivot shaft. Then, position a pair of pliers so that the upper jaw rests against the top of the pivot shaft and the lower jaw will tend to pry the crank lever upward. Gently pry the crank lever off the pivot shaft.

26. Disconnect the vacuum lines from the defrost mode and panel mode vacuum actuators and position them out of the way.

27. Remove the two heater/air conditioning unit cover attaching screws located above the cover in the air inlet plenum. Remove the 11 heater/air conditioning unit cover attaching screws located downward from the cover in the housing. Lift the cover off the heater/air conditioning unit.

28. Remove the heater core-to-dash panel seal from the tubes of the core. Then, pull the core out of the unit.

To install:

29. Slide the core into the unit and install the seal. Then install the unit cover and all 13 attaching screws.

30. Reconnect the vacuum lines going to the defrost and panel vacuum actuators. Reinstall the blend air door crank lever onto the pivot shaft.

31. Put the unit back into the car. Install the demister adapter duct. Then, raise the unit until the mounting studs are lined up with the holes in the cowl and work the studs through the holes. Install the support brace and attaching bolt. Install the mounting nuts from the other side of the cowl.

32. Install the condensate drain tube. Reconnect the heater hoses.

33. Reinstall the expansion "H" valve. Uncap the openings and immediately reconnect the refrigerant lines.

34. Install the carpet back under the unit. Then, install the heat outlet duct and the 3 attaching screws.

35. Put the heater/air conditioning unit support bracket into position and then install the attaching nut and 4 screws.

36. Put the defroster duct adapter into position between the heater/air conditioning unit and the defroster duct.

37. Connect the blower motor relay module and wiring lead to the harness.

38. Install the center air duct and install the two attaching screws.

39. Connect the temperature cable attaching flag and vacuum harness to the control assembly. Install the heater/air conditioning control as described later in this chapter.

40. Install the glovebox. Install the cigarette lighter and socket.

41. Install the ash tray and its mounting bracket. Install the radio as described later in this chapter.

42. Install the instrument panel center support braces and brackets.

43. Reposition the accessory wiring harness to its original location. Install the center console assembly.

44. Install the lower instrument panel module cover, if the car has one.

45. Install the instrument cluster bezel and its four attaching screws.

46. Tighten the roll down bolt located behind the instrument panel to the right of the glovebox.

47. Install the trim panel onto the door opening scuff plate. Install the right side cowl cover. Refill the engine cooling system.

48. Reconnect the battery negative cable. Have the air conditioning system charged by an approved facility. See Chapter 1. Operate the engine and check for leaks. After the engine has reached operating temperature and then has cooled back off, bring the coolant level back up to where it belongs.

1988 Models

NOTE: *Modify the service steps as necessary on vehicles not equipped with air conditioning. To complete this procedure, make sure to have suitable caps or plastic sheeting and tape to cover and seal open refrigerant lines. Also needed are caps or plugs for the heater core tubes.*

1. Have the air conditioning system discharged by a facility equipped with a recovery system. Disconnect the battery negative cable.

2. Drain the engine cooling system. Disconnect the heater hoses at the core and plug the openings.

CAUTION: *When draining the coolant, keep in mind that cats and dogs are attracted by the ethylene glycol antifreeze, and are quite likely to drink any that is left in an uncovered container or in puddles on the ground. This will prove fatal in sufficient quantity. Always drain the coolant into a sealable container. Coolant should be reused unless it is contaminated or several years old.*

3. Remove the air conditioner condensate drain. Label and then disconnect the vacuum lines running from the car body to various components on the heater/air conditioning unit.

4. Disconnect/remove the following items, according to the body style of the car:
   a. On LeBaron, remove the right upper and lower underpanel silencers.
   b. On LeBaron with passive restraints, remove the right side underdash lower trim panel.
   c. On Sundance and Shadow, remove the steering column cover.
   d. On Daytona and LeBaron, with passive restraints, remove the inner steering column cover.

5. Put the bench seat or right individual seat all the way to the rear. Then, on the Sundance, remove the right pillar trim. On all cars, remove the right cowl side trim (note that on the LeBaron, this requires pulling the lower end of the right side A-pillar trim outward).

6. Remove the glovebox. Then, perform each of the following procedures on the model indicated:
   a. On Daytona, LeBaron and New Yorker with passive restraints, and on Lancer and LeBaron GTS, remove the right instrument panel reinforcement.
   b. On Sundance and Shadow, Caravelle, 600 and New Yorker Turbo, remove the right instrument panel roll-up screw.

c. On Daytona, LeBaron and New Yorker, remove the forward console bezel, side trim, and lower carpet panels. Then, loosen the floor console and move it to the rear. Remove the forward console. If the car has passive restraints, remove the instrument panel-to-floor reinforcement.

d. On the Sundance and Shadow, remove the center dashboard bezel, lower center module cover, floor console, and instrument support brace (this brace runs from the steering column opening to the right cowl side at the bottom of the instrument panel). Remove also the bracket linking the instrument panel and its support, located under the glovebox. Remove the ashtray. Remove the radio as described later. Remove the instrument panel top cover. Finally, remove the 3 right side panel-to-lower windshield panel attaching screws.

e. On the Caravelle, 600 and New Yorker Turbo, remove the forward console and its mounting bracket.

f. On the Aries, Reliant, LeBaron, New Yorker, and Town & Country, remove the floor console.

g. On the Lancer, remove both front and rear consoles.

h. On the Sundance and Shadow, Aries, Reliant, LeBaron, New Yorker, Town & Country, Caravelle, 600, and New Yorker Turbo pull the right lower side of the instrument panel to the rear.

7. On all models, remove the center distribution and defroster adapter ducts. Then, perform each of the following procedures on the model indicated:

a. On the Sundance and Shadow and Lancer, remove and disconnect the relay module.

b. On the Sundance and Shadow, remove the bracket linking the air conditioning unit and instrument panel. Then, on these models, remove the lower air distribution duct.

c. On the Aries, Reliant, LeBaron, New Yorker, Town & Country, Caravelle, 600 and New Yorker Turbo, remove the audible message center. Then, on these models, remove the right side cowl-to-plenum brace.

8. On all models, disconnect the blower motor wire connector. Then, disconnect the demister hoses at the top of the heater/air conditioning unit.

9. If the car has manual control rather than Automatic Temperature Control:

a. Disconnect the temperature control cable flag from the bottom of the heater/air conditioning unit and unclip the cable from the left side of the heat distribution duct. Then, swing the cable out of the way and to the left.

b. Label and then disconnect the vacuum lines at the unit.

On cars with Automatic Temperature Control: Disconnect the instrument panel wiring from the rear face of the ATC unit.

10. On Lancers, disconnect the right side 25-way connector bracket and fuse block from the panel.

11. Remove the antenna cable from the clip on the top or rear face of the unit, where it is so-routed.

12. Except on Lancers, fold the carpeting back on the right side.

13. Remove the four attaching nuts for the unit from the engine compartment side of the cowl.

14. Remove the lower screw from the unit's hanging strap and then rotate the strap out of the way.

15. Pull the unit to the rear until its studs clear the cowl and liner and then lower it. On the Sundance and Shadow, remove the demister adapter from the top of the unit. Then, on these models, pull the lower right section of the instrument panel rearward and hold it for clearance as you slide the unit out of the car in an upright position. On the other models, rotate the unit as necessary for clearance as you pull it out from under the instrument panel.

To install:

16. Reverse the step above to get the heater assembly into position under the dash. On the Sundance and Shadow, install the demister adapter. Then, raise it, line up the four mounting studs with the holes in the cowl, and work the studs through the cowl.

17. Install the four retaining nuts from the engine compartment side of the cowl.

18. Rotate the hanging strap back into position and install the attaching bolt.

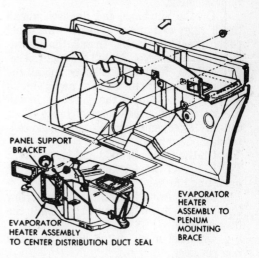

PANEL SUPPORT BRACKET

EVAPORATOR HEATER ASSEMBLY TO PLENUM MOUNTING BRACE

EVAPORATOR HEATER ASSEMBLY TO CENTER DISTRIBUTION DUCT SEAL

Mounting of the heater-A/C unit—1988 models

19. Reposition the carpeting if it was moved.

20. Reclip the antenna cable, if it is clipped to the heater/air conditioning unit.

21. On Lancers, reconnect the right side 25-way connector bracket and fuse block to the panel.

22. If the car has automatic temperature control, reconnect the instrument panel wiring. Otherwise, reconnect the vacuum lines according to the labels and then reconnect and remount the temperature control cable.

23. Reconnect the demister hoses and the blower motor wiring connector.

24. On the Aries, Reliant, LeBaron, New Yorker, Town & Country, Caravelle, 600 and New Yorker Turbo, install the right side cowl-to-plenum brace. Then install the audible message center.

On the Sundance and Shadow and Lancer, connect the relay module.

On the Sundance and Shadow, install the lower air distribution duct. Then, on these models, install the bracket linking the air conditioning unit and instrument panel.

25. On all models, install the center distribution and defroster adapter ducts.

26. Perform each of the following procedures on the model indicated:

a. On Daytona, LeBaron and New Yorker with passive restraints, and on Lancer and LeBaron GTS, install the right instrument panel reinforcement.

b. On Sundance and Shadow, Caravelle, 600 and New Yorker Turbo, install the right instrument panel roll-up screw.

c. On Daytona, LeBaron and New Yorker, install the forward console bezel, side trim, and lower carpet panels. Install the console assemblies. If the car has passive restraints, install the instrument panel-to-floor reinforcement.

d. On the Sundance and Shadow, install the 3 right side panel-to-lower windshield panel attaching screws. Install the instrument panel top cover. Install the radio as described later. Install the ashtray. Install the bracket linking the instrument panel and its support, located under the glovebox. Install the instrument panel support brace, floor console, lower center module cover, and center dashboard bezel.

e. On the Caravelle, 600 and New Yorker Turbo, install the forward console and its mounting bracket.

f. On the Aries, Reliant, LeBaron, New Yorker, and Town & Country, install the floor console.

g. On the Lancer, install both front and rear consoles.

h. On the Sundance and Shadow, Aries, Reliant, LeBaron, New Yorker, Town & Country, Caravelle, 600, and New Yorker Turbo push the right lower side of the instrument panel forward and back into its normal position.

27. Install the glovebox. Install the right pillar trim on the Sundance and right side cowl side trim on all cars.

28. Install/connect the following, according to the model of the car:

a. On LeBaron, install the right upper and lower underpanel silencers.

b. On LeBaron with passive restraints, install the right side underdash lower trim panel.

c. On Sundance and Shadow, install the steering column cover.

d. On Daytona and LeBaron, with passive restraints, install the inner steering column cover.

29. Connect the vacuum lines running from the car body to various components on the heater/air conditioning unit, according to the labeling done during removal. Install the air conditioner condensate drain.

30. Unplug the heater core openings and connect the heater hoses at the core. Refill the cooling system.

31. Have the air conditioning system recharged by an approved facility. See Chapter 1. Operate the engine and check for leaks. After the engine has reached operating temperature and then has cooled back off, bring the coolant level back up to where it belongs.

1989–92 Models
Except Dynasty, New Yorker and Imperial
1990–92 Laser, Stealth and Dodge Monaco

WITHOUT AIR CONDITIONING

NOTE: *The following procedure can be used on all 1989–92 models except where noted above. Slight variations may occur due to extra connections, etc., but the basic procedure should cover all 1989–92 models. Modify the service steps as necessary. Refer to the "Air Bag Disarming" service procedure as necessary.*

1. Disconnect the negative battery cable. Drain the cooling system.

CAUTION: *When draining the coolant, keep in mind that cats and dogs are attracted by the ethylene glycol antifreeze, and are quite likely to drink any that is left in an uncovered container or in puddles on the ground. This will prove fatal in sufficient quantity. Always drain the coolant into a sealable container. Coolant should be reused unless it is contaminated or several years old.*

2. Clamp off the heater hoses near the heater core and remove the hoses from the core tubes.

Plug the hose ends and the core tubes to prevent spillage of coolant.

3. Remove the glove box, right side kick and sill panels and all modules, relay panels and computer components in the vacinity of the heater housing.

4. Remove the lower instrument panel silencers and reinforcements. Remove the radio and other dash-mounted optional equipment, as required.

5. Remove the floor console, if equipped. Remove the floor and defroster distribution ducts.

6. Remove the bolt holding the right side instrument panel to the right cowl.

7. Disconnect the blower motor wiring, antenna, resistor wiring and the temperature control cable.

8. On 1990–92 Daytona and LeBaron, using a suitable cutting device, cut the instrument panel along the indented line along the padded cover to the right of the glove box opening. Cut only plastic, not metal. Remove the reinforcement and the piece of instrument panel that is riveted to it.

9. Disconnect the demister hoses from the top of the housing, if equipped.

10. Disconnect the hanger strap from the package and rotate it aside.

11. Remove the retaining nuts from the package mounting studs at the firewall.

12. Fold the carpeting and insulation back to provide a little more working room and to prevent spillage from staining the carpeting. Pull the right side of the instrument panel out as far as possible.

13. Remove the heater housing from the dash panel and remove it from the passenger compartment. If the passenger seat is preventing removal, remove it.

14. To disassemble the housing assembly, remove the retaining screws from the cover and remove the cover.

15. Remove the retaining screw from the heater core and remove the core from the housing assembly.

To install:

16. Remove the temperature control door from the housing and clean the unit out with solvent. Lubricate the lower pivot rod and its well and install. Wrap the heater core with foam tape and place it in position. Secure it with its screw.

17. Assemble the housing, making sure all cover screws were used.

18. Connect the demister hoses. Install the nuts to the firewall and connect the hanger strap inside the passenger compartment.

19. Fold the carpeting back into position.

20. Install the bolt that attaches the right side of the instrument panel to the cowl.

21. Connect the blower motor wiring, antenna, resistor wiring and the temperature control cable.

22. Install the air distribution ducts.

23. Install the floor console, if equipped.

24. Install the radio and all other dash mounted items that were removed during the disassembly procedure.

25. Install the lower instrument panel reinforcements and silencers.

26. Install all modules, relay panels and computer components that were removed during the disassembly procedure.

27. Install the glove box and right side kick and sill panels. Install the passenger seat.

28. Connect the heater hoses.

29. Fill the cooling system.

30. Connect the negative battery cable and check the entire climate control system for proper operation and leakage.

WITH AIR CONDITIONING

NOTE: *The following procedure can be used on all 1989–92 models except where noted above. Slight variations may occur due to extra connections, etc., but the basic procedure should cover all 1989–92 models. Modify the service steps as necessary. Refer to the "Air Bag Disarming" service procedure as necessary.*

1. Disconnect the negative battery cable. Have the air conditioning system discharged by an approved refrigerant recovery facility. See Chapter 1. Drain the cooling system.

CAUTION: *When draining the coolant, keep in mind that cats and dogs are attracted by the ethylene glycol antifreeze, and are quite likely to drink any that is left in an uncovered container or in puddles on the ground. This will prove fatal in sufficient quantity. Always drain the coolant into a sealable container. Coolant should be reused unless it is contaminated or several years old.*

2. Clamp off the heater hoses near the heater core and remove the hoses from the core tubes. Plug the hose ends and the core tubes to prevent spillage of coolant.

3. Disconnect the H-valve connection at the valve and remove the H-valve. Remove the condensation tube.

4. Disconnect the vacuum lines at the brake booster and water valve.

5. Remove the glove box, right side kick and sill panels and all modules, relay panels and computer components in the vacinity of the housing.

6. Remove the lower instrument panel silencers and reinforcements. Remove the radio and other dash-mounted optional equipment, as required.

7. Remove the floor console, if equipped. Remove the floor and center distribution ducts.

8. Remove the bolt holding the right side instrument panel to the right cowl.

9. Disconnect the blower motor wiring, antenna, resistor wiring and the temperature control cable. Disconnect the vacuum harness at the connection at the top of the housing.

10. On 1990–92 Daytona and LeBaron, using a suitable cutting device, cut the instrument panel along the indented line along the padded cover to the right of the glove box opening. Cut only plastic, not metal. Remove the reinforcement and the piece of instrument panel that is riveted to it.

11. Disconnect the demister hoses from the top of the housing, if equipped.

12. Disconnect the hanger strap from the package and rotate it aside.

13. Remove the retaining nuts from the package mounting studs at the firewall.

14. Fold the carpeting and insulation back to provide a little more working room and to prevent spillage from staining the carpeting. Pull the right side of the instrument panel out as far as possible.

15. Remove the entire housing assembly from the dash panel and remove it from the passenger compartment. Remove the passenger seat, if it is preventing removal.

16. To disassemble the housing assembly, remove the vacuum diaphragm and retaining screws from the cover and remove the cover.

17. Remove the retaining screw from the heater core and remove the core from the housing assembly.

To install:

18. Remove the temperature control door from the housing and clean the unit out with solvent. Lubricate the lower pivot rod and its well and install. Wrap the heater core with foam tape and place it in position. Secure it with its screw.

19. Assemble the housing, making sure all vacuum tubing is properly routed.

20. Feed the vacuum lines through the hole in the firewall and install the assembly to the vehicle. Connect the vacuum harness and demister hoses. Install the nuts to the firewall and connect the hanger strap inside the passenger compartment.

21. Fold the carpeting back into position.

22. Install the bolt that attaches the right side of the instrument panel to the cowl.

23. Connect the blower motor wiring, antenna, resistor wiring and the temperature control cable.

24. Install the center and floor distribution ducts.

25. Install the floor console, if equipped.

26. Install the radio and all other dash mounted items that were removed during the disassembly procedure.

27. Install the lower instrument panel reinforcements and silencers.

28. Install all modules, relay panels and computer components that were removed during the disassembly procedure.

29. Install the glove box and right side kick and sill panels. Install the passenger seat, if removed.

30. Connect the vacuum lines at the brake booster and water valve.

31. Using new gaskets, install the H-valve and condensation tube.

32. Connect the heater hoses.

33. Have the air conditioning system evacuated and recharged by an approved facility.

34. Fill the cooling system.

35. Connect the negative battery cable and check the entire climate control system for proper operation and leakage.

1989–92 Models
Dynasty, New Yorker and Imperial

1. Disconnect the negative battery cable. Refer to the "Air Bag Disarming" service procedure as necessary. Have the air conditioning system discharged by an approved refrigerant recovery facility. Drain the cooling system.

CAUTION: *When draining the coolant, keep in mind that cats and dogs are attracted by the ethylene glycol antifreeze, and are quite likely to drink any that is left in an uncovered container or in puddles on the ground. This will prove fatal in sufficient quantity. Always drain the coolant into a sealable container. Coolant should be reused unless it is contaminated or several years old.*

2. Clamp off the heater hoses near the heater core and remove the hoses from the core tubes. Plug the hose ends and the core tubes to prevent spillage of coolant.

3. Disconnect the H-valve connection at the valve and remove the H-valve. Remove the condensation tube.

4. Disconnect the vacuum lines at the brake booster and water valve, if equipped.

5. Remove the right upper and lower under-panel silencers.

6. Remove the steering column cover and the ash tray.

7. Remove the left side under-panel silencer.

8. Remove the right side cowl trim piece.

9. Remove the glove box assembly and the right side instrument panel reinforcement.

10. Remove the center distribution and defroster adaptor ducts.

11. Disconnect the relay module, blower mo-

tor wiring and 25-way connector bracket and
fuse block from the panel.

12. Disconnect the demister hoses from the
top of the package.

13. Disconnect the temperature control cable
and vacuum harness, if equipped. If equipped
with Automatic Temperature Control (ATC),
disconnect the instrument panel wiring from
the rear of the ATC unit.

14. Disconnect the hanger strap from the
package and rotate it out of the way.

15. Remove the retaining nuts from the package mounting studs at the firewall.

16. Fold the carpeting and insulation back to
provide a little more working room and to prevent spillage from staining the carpeting.

17. Move the package rearward to clear the
mounting studs and lower.

18. Pull the right side of the instrument panel
out as far as possible. Rotate the package while
removing it from under the instrument panel.

19. To disassemble the housing assembly, remove the vacuum diaphragm, if equipped. Then
remove the retaining screws from the cover and
remove the cover.

20. Remove the retaining screw from the
heater core and remove the core from the housing assembly.

To install:

21. Remove the temperature control door
from the housing and clean the unit out with
solvent. Lubricate the lower pivot rod and its
well and install. Wrap the heater core with
foam tape and place it in position. Secure it
with its screw.

22. Assemble the package, making sure all
vacuum tubing is properly routed.

23. If equipped, feed the vacuum lines
through the hole in the firewall and install the
assembly to the vehicle. Connect the vacuum
harness and demister hoses. Install the nuts to
the firewall and connect the hanger strap inside
the passenger compartment.

24. Fold the carpeting back into position.

25. Connect the wiring to the ATC unit, if
equipped.

26. Install the fuse block. Connect the 25-way
connector, relay module and blower motor
wiring.

27. Install the center distribution and defroster adaptor ducts.

28. Install the right side instrument panel reinforcement and the glove box assembly.

29. Install the right side cowl trim piece, left
side under-panel silencer, steering column cover, ash tray and right side under-panel
silencers.

30. Connect the vacuum lines at the brake
booster and water valve.

31. Using new gaskets, install the H-valve
and condensation tube.

32. Connect the heater hoses.

33. Have the air conditioning recharged by an
approved facility.

34. Fill the cooling system.

35. Connect the negative battery cable and
check the entire climate control system for
proper operation and leakage.

1990–92 Laser

1. Disconnect the negative battery cable. Refer to the "Air Bag Disarming" service procedure as necessary.

2. Drain the cooling system and have the air
conditioning system discharged by an approved
refrigerant recovery facility. Disconnect the refrigerant lines from the evaporator. Cover the
exposed ends of the lines to minimize
contamination.

CAUTION: *When draining the coolant, keep
in mind that cats and dogs are attracted by
the ethylene glycol antifreeze, and are quite
likely to drink any that is left in an uncovered
container or in puddles on the ground. This
will prove fatal in sufficient quantity. Always
drain the coolant into a sealable container.
Coolant should be reused unless it is contaminated or several years old.*

3. Remove the floor console by first removing the plugs, then the screws retaining the side
covers and the small cover piece in front of the
shifter. Remove the shifter knob, manual
transmission, and the cup holder. Remove both
small pieces of upholstery to gain access to retainer screws. Disconnect both electrical connectors at the front of the console. Remove the
shoulder harness guide plates and the console
assembly.

4. Locate the rectangular plugs in the knee
protector on either side of the steering column.
Pry these plugs out and remove the screws. Remove the screws from the hood lock release lever and the knee protector.

5. Remove the upper and lower column
covers.

6. Remove the narrow panel covering the instrument cluster cover screws, and remove the
cover.

7. Remove the radio panel and remove the
radio.

8. Remove the center air outlet assembly by
reaching through the grille and pushing the
side clips out with a small flat-tipped tool while
carefully prying the outlet free.

9. Pull the heater control knobs off and remove the heater control panel assembly.

10. Open the glove box, remove the plugs
from the sides and the glove box assembly.

11. Remove the instrument gauge cluster and

the speedometer adapter by disconnecting the speedometer cable at the transaxle, pulling the cable sightly towards the vehicle interior, then giving a slight twist on the adapter to release it.

12. Remove the left and right speaker covers from the top of the instrument panel.

13. Remove the center plate below the heater controls.

14. Remove the heater control assembly installation screws.

15. Remove the lower air ducts.

16. Drop the steering column by removing the bolts.

17. Remove the instrument panel mounting screws, bolts and the instrument panel assembly.

18. Remove both stamped steel reinforcement pieces.

19. Remove the lower duct work from the heater box.

20. Remove the upper center duct.

21. Vehicles without air conditioning will have a square duct in place of the evaporator; remove this duct if present. If equipped with air conditioning, remove the evaporator assembly:

    a. Remove the wiring harness connectors and the electronic control unit.

    b. Remove the drain hose and lift out the evaporator unit.

    c. If servicing the assembly, disassemble the housing and remove the expansion valve and evaporator.

22. With the evaporator removed, remove the heater unit. To prevent bolts from falling inside the blower assembly, set the inside/outside air-selection damper to the position that permits outside air introduction.

23. Remove the cover plate around the heater tubes and remove the core fastener clips. Pull the heater core from the heater box, being careful not to damage the fins or tank ends.

To install:

24. Thoroughly clean and dry the inside of the case. Install the heater core to the heater box. Install the clips and cover.

25. Install the heater box and connect the duct work.

26. Assemble the housing, evaporator and expansion valve, making sure the gaskets are in good condition. Install the evaporator housing.

27. Using new lubricated O-rings, connect the refrigerant lines to the evaporator.

28. Install the electronic transaxle ELC box. Connect all wires and control cables.

29. Install the instrument panel assembly and the console by reversing their removal procedures.

30. Have the air conditioning system evacuated and recharged by an approved facility. If the evaporator was replaced, add 2 oz. of refrigerant oil during the recharge.

31. Connect the negative battery cable and check the entire climate control system for proper operation. Check the system for leaks.

Dodge Stealth

1. Disconnect the negative battery cable. Refer to the "Air Bag Disarming" service procedure as necessary.

2. Drain the coolant and disconnect the heater hoses from the core tubes.

CAUTION: *When draining the coolant, keep in mind that cats and dogs are attracted by the ethylene glycol antifreeze, and are quite likely to drink any that is left in an uncovered container or in puddles on the ground. This will prove fatal in sufficient quantity. Always drain the coolant into a sealable container. Coolant should be reused unless it is contaminated or several years old.*

3. To remove the console, perform the following:

    a. Remove the cup holder and console plug.

    b. Remove the rear console.

    c. Remove the radio bezels and radio.

    d. Remove the switch bezel.

    e. Remove the side covers and front console garnish.

    f. If equipped with a manual transaxle, remove the shifter knob.

    g. Remove the mounting screws and remove the console assembly.

4. Remove the hood lock release handle from the instrument panel.

5. Remove the interior and dash lights rheostat and switch bezel to its right.

6. Remove the driver's knee protector. Remove the steering column covers.

7. Remove the glove box and cover.

8. Remove the center air outlet assembly.

9. Remove the climate control switch assembly.

10. Remove the instrument cluster bezel and cluster.

11. If equipped with front speakers, remove them. If not, remove the plug in their place.

12. Disconnect the wiring harnesses on the right side of the instrument panel.

13. Remove the steering shaft support bolts and lower the steering column.

14. Remove the instrument panel mounting hardware and remove the instrument panel from the vehicle.

15. Remove the center reinforcement.

16. Remove the foot warmer ducts and lap duct.

17. If equipped with air conditioning, remove the evaporator case mounting bolt and nut to allow clearance for heater unit removal.

18. Remove the center duct above the heater unit.

19. Remove the heater unit and disassemble on a workbench. Remove the heater core from the heater case.

To install:

20. Thoroughly clean and dry the inside of the case and install the heater core and all related parts.

21. Install the heater unit to the vehicle and install the mounting screws.

22. Install the center duct above the unit.

23. Secure the evaporator case with the bolt and nut.

24. Install the lap duct and foot warmer ducts.

25. Install the center reinforcement.

26. Install the instrument panel by reversing its removal procedure.

27. Install the hood lock release cable handle.

28. Install the console.

29. Fill the cooling system.

30. Connect the negative battery cable and check the entire climate control system for proper operation and leaks.

Dodge Monaco

1. Disconnect the negative battery cable.

2. Drain the coolant. Have the air conditioning system discharged by an approved refrigerant recovery facility.

CAUTION: *When draining the coolant, keep in mind that cats and dogs are attracted by the ethylene glycol antifreeze, and are quite likely to drink any that is left in an uncovered container or in puddles on the ground. This will prove fatal in sufficient quantity. Always drain the coolant into a sealable container. Coolant should be reused unless it is contaminated or several years old.*

3. Remove the instrument panel lower trim cover, which is retained by 3 screws.

4. Remove the instrument panel support rod. Remove the screw attaching the steering column wiring harness bulkhead connector.

5. Disconnect the automatic transaxle shift cable from the lever.

   a. Compress the cable retainer tangs with pliers and slide the cable from the column mounting bracket.

   b. Loosen the screw that holds the anchoring bracket in place, move the bracket to the keyhole position and remove it from its mounting bracket.

6. Lift the indicator wire off of the pulley.

7. Pull the plastic sleeve down to expose the steering column universal joint.

8. Make a reference mark on the steering column shaft and intermediate shaft.

9. Remove the bolt from the intermediate shaft.

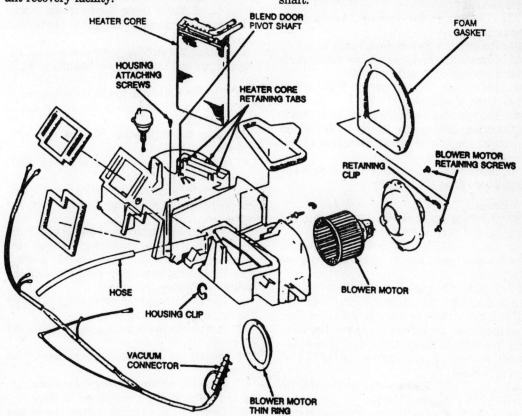

Heater core and related parts—Dodge Monaco

10. Remove the 4 bolts and nuts that hold the steering column to the instrument panel and carefully lower to the vehicle floor.

11. Separate the steering column shaft from the intermediate shaft and remove the steering column assembly from the vehicle.

12. Remove the defroster grille from the top of the instrument panel.

13. Loosen but do not remove the nut located near the parking brake release handle and the nut which is located on the passenger side kick panel.

14. Remove the screws and lower the parking brake release handle.

15. Remove the ashtray.

16. Disconnect the cigarette lighter connectors.

17. Remove the screw from the ashtray cavity.

18. Disconnect all electrical connections.

19. Remove the bolts that hold the instrument panel to the center floor bracket.

20. Disconnect the interior temperature sensor.

21. Remove the floor duct extension.

NOTE: *The heater core inlet and outlet tubes are made of plastic and may break if too much pressure is applied.*

22. Remove the heater hoses from the heater core spouts.

23. Disconnect the coolant level switch connector.

24. Remove the coolant reservoir.

25. Disconnect the blower motor connector.

26. Disconnect the vacuum hoses.

27. Disconnect the refrigerant lines at the dash panel, if equipped.

28. Remove the retaining nuts from inside and outside of the vehicle and carefully pull the heater/air conditioning housing rearward to remove it.

29. Release the plastic tabs and remove the heater core from the housing.

To install:

30. Carefully insert the heater core into the housing and push until it snaps in place.

31. Before installing the housing, make sure the housing seals are in place and in good condition.

32. Position the heater/air conditioning housing to the dash panel. Make sure the drain tube extends through its opening in the upper floor and the blower motor connector and the vacuum line extends through the dash panel. Ensure that the ECU connectors are to the right of the drain tube.

33. Install new housing retaining nuts. Install the floor duct extension.

34. Install new O-rings on the refrigerant

lines and lubricate with clean refrigerant oil. Press each line into its connector until it snaps into place.

35. Connect the vacuum hose and the blower electrical connector.

36. Install the coolant reservoir bracket and reservoir.

37. Reconnect the coolant level switch connector.

38. Carefully reconnect the heater hoses to the core.

39. Place the instrument panel into position so the mounting brackets engage the studs on the kick panels. Make sure the wiring harness is behind the center mounting bracket and connect all electrical connections.

40. Install the bolt to the brake support.

41. Install the screw into the ashtray cavity.

42. Install the 2 bolts to the center support bracket.

43. Connect the cigarette lighter connectors and the ashtray.

44. Tighten the nut located near the parking brake release handle and the nut located on the passenger side kick panel.

45. Install the parking brake release handle.

46. Install the bolts under the defroster grille, then install the grille.

47. Position and install the steering column shaft in the intermediate steering shaft U-joint. Align the 2 shafts using the reference marks made during removal. Install but do not tighten the U-joint bolt.

48. Attach the steering column to the instrument panel and tighten the bolts/nuts to 35 ft. lbs.

49. Tighten the bolt in the intermediate steering shaft U-joint and move the plastic sleeve into position.

50. Snap the shift cable into the mounting bracket.

51. Snap the shift cable head onto the mounting ball in the shift arm.

52. Loop the shift indicator wire over the pulley. Position the anchoring bracket over the screw.

53. Move the gearshift lever into N and check the position of the shift indicator. If the pointer is not aligned with the N mark on the display, slide the bracket forward/rearward to align the indicator. Tighten the screw.

54. Install the bulkhead connector and install the connector attaching screw.

55. Install the instrument panel support rod securely.

56. Install the instrument panel lower trim cover.

57. Have the air conditioning system evacuated and recharged by an approved facility.

58. Connect the negative battery cable and

check the entire climate control system for proper operation. Check the system for leaks.

Air Conditioning Control Head

REMOVAL AND INSTALLATION

Manual Control

1. Disconnect the negative battery cable.
2. Remove the necessary bezel(s) in order to gain access to the control head.
3. Remove the screws that fasten the control head to the instrument panel.
4. Pull the unit out and unplug the electrical and vacuum connectors. Disconnect the temperature control cable by pushing the flag in and pulling the end from its seat.
5. Remove the control head from the instrument panel.
6. The installation is the reverse of the removal procedure.
7. Connect the negative battery cable and check the entire climate control system for proper operation.

NOTE: *Manual control cables are self-adjusting. If the cable is not fuctioning properly, check for kinks and lubricate dry moving parts. The cable cannot be disassembled; replace if faulty.*

Electronic Control

1. Disconnect the negative battery cable.
2. Remove the necessary bezel(s) in order to gain access to the control head.
3. Remove the screws that fasten the control head to the instrument panel.
4. Pull the unit out and unplug the wire harness.
5. Remove the control head from the instrument panel.
6. The installation is the reverse of the removal procedure.
7. Connect the negative battery cable and check the entire climate control system for proper operation.

Evaporator Core

REMOVAL AND INSTALLATION

The evaporator core can be removed only after the entire heater/air conditioning unit (this unit is equipped with a drain tube located on right side of dash panel — if tube becomes obstructed water will enter passenger compartment floor) is removed from the vehicle. Refer to the "Heater Assembly" equipped with air conditioning service procedures.

Remove the heater A/C unit top cover. Remove the expansion valve sealing plate seal and seal retaining screw from under the sealing plate. Lift the evaporator coil from the heater

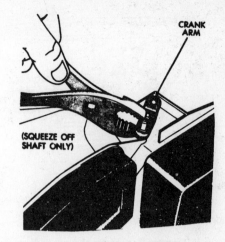

Blend air door crank linkage removal

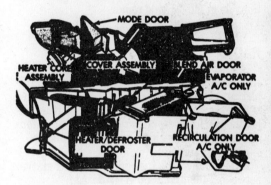

Heater A/C unit cover removal and installation

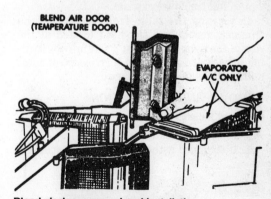

Blend air door removal and installation

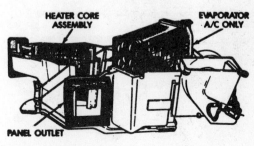

Evaporator assembly removal and installation

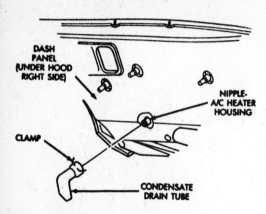

Condensate water drain tube

A/C unit. To install, reverse the preceding service operation. Refer to the necessary illustrations as guide for this repair.

RADIO

AM, AM/FM monaural, or AM/FM stero multiplex units are available. All radios are trimmed at the factory and should require no further adjustment. However, after repair or if the antenna trim is to be verified, proceed as follows:

1. Turn radio on.
2. Manually tune the radio to a weak station between 1400 and 1600 KHz on AM.
3. Increase the volume and set the tone control to full treble (clockwise).
4. Viewing the radio from the front, the trimmer control is a slot-head located at the rear of the right side. Adust it carefully by turning it back and forth with a screwdriver until maximum loudness is achieved.

REMOVAL AND INSTALLATION

Aries and Reliant

1. Remove the bezel.
2. If equipped with a mono (single) speaker,

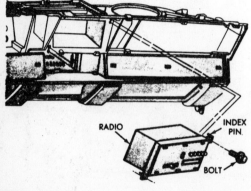

Radio assembly

remove the instrument panel top cover, speaker, and disconnect the wires from the radio.
3. Remove the two screws attaching the radio to the base panel.
4. Pull the radio thru the front of the base, then disconnect the wiring harness, antenna lead and ground strap.
5. Installation is the reverse of removal.

Daytona and LeBaron

1. Remove the two screws from the bottom of the console trim bezel. Then, lift the bezel out of the console.
2. Remove the two attaching screws fastening the radio to the console.
3. Pull the radio through the front face of the console far enough for access to the wiring. Then, disconnect the wiring harness, antenna lead, and ground strap. Remove the radio.
4. Installation is the reverse of removal.

Lancer

1. Remove the instrument cluster bezel. Then, remove the two radio attaching screws.
2. Disconnect the wiring connectors and antenna cable.
3. Remove the ground strap attaching screw. Remove the radio.
4. Installation is the reverse of removal.

Sundance and Shadow

1. Remove the center module bezel.
2. If the car has a short console, remove the lower center module cover. If the car has a full-length console, remove the right console sidewall.
3. Remove the two radio mounting screws and pull it out of the dash far enough to reach the wiring. Disconnect the power wiring and the antenna cable. Disconnect the ground strap and remove the radio.
4. Installation is the reverse of removal.

All Other Late Model Vehicles
Except 1990–92 Laser and Dodge Stealth

NOTE: *On vehicles equipped with a compact disc player, removal and installation procedures are the same as for the radio.*
1. Disconnect the negative battery cable.
2. Remove the console or cluster bezel, as required.
3. Remove the screws that attach the radio to the instrument panel.
4. Pull the radio out, disconnect the connectors, ground cable and antenna, and remove the radio.
5. The installation is the reverse of the removal procedure.
6. Connect the negative battery cable and

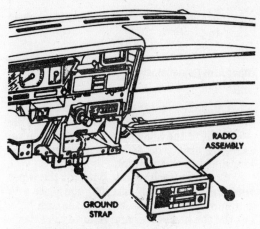

Radio assembly—AA body

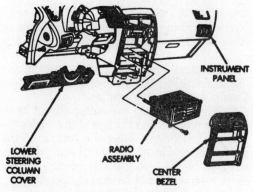

Radio assembly—AG and AJ bodies

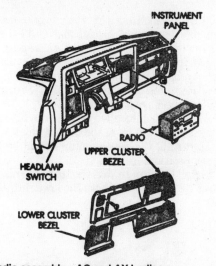

Radio assembly—AC and AY bodies

check all functions of the radio for proper operation.

1990–92 Laser and Dodge Stealth

1. Disconnect battery negative cable.
NOTE: *If equipped with an air bag, be sure*

to disarm it before entering the vehicle. Refer to the "Air Bag Disarming" service procedure as necessary.

2. Remove the panel from around the radio. Use a plastic trim tool to pry the lower part of the radio panel loose. Remove it from the center console.

3. Remove the radio or radio/tape player. Depending on the speaker installation, it may save time at installation to identify and tag all wires before they are disconnected.

4. Separate amplifiers and/or CD player can be removed by first removing the side cover of the console box.

5. Remove the mounting brackets from the radio.

To install:

6. The installation is the reverse of the removal procedure. Make all electrical and antenna connections before fastening the radio assembly in place.

7. Install the center panel.

8. Connect the negative battery cable and check the entire audio system for proper operation.

WINDSHIELD WIPERS

The windshield wipers can be operated with the wiper switch only when the ignition switch is in the Accessory or Ignition position. A circuit breaker, integral with the wiper switch or fuse in the fuse box, protects the circuitry of the wiper system and the vehicle.

Wiper blades, exposed to the weather for a long period of time, tend to lose their wiping effectiveness. Periodic cleaning of the the wiper blade element is suggested. The wiper blade element, arms and windshield should be cleaned with a sponge or cloth and a mild detergent or non-abrasive cleaner. If the the wiper element continues to streak or smear, replace the wiper blade element on or arm.

Blade and Arm
REMOVAL AND INSTALLATION

Wiper Blade Replacement

1. Lift the wiper arm away from the glass.
2. Depress the release lever on the bridge and remove the blade assembly from the arm. On later model vehicles, remove the blade assembly from the arm by inserting a small tool into the release slot of the wiper blade and push downward, or by pushing the release button. Refer to the necessary illustration.
3. To remove the wiping element from the blade assembly: Lift the tab and pinch the end bridge to release it from the center bridge.

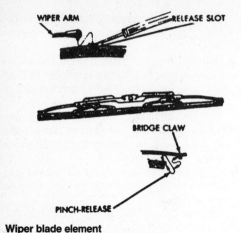

Wiper blade element

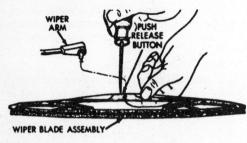

Blade assembly from the wiper arm

Wiper element from the blade assembly

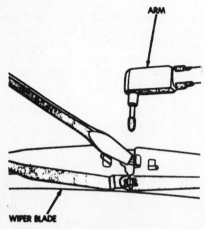

Wiper blade removal—Dodge Monaco

4. Slide the end bridge from the blade element and the element from the opposite end bridge.

5. Assembly is the reverse of removal. Make sure that the element locking tabs are securely locked in position.

Wiper Arm Replacement

FRONT

1. On latch release type: lift the arm (note installation position) so that the latch can be pulled out to the holding position and then release the arm. The arm will remain off the windshield in this position.

2. On arm attaching nut type: lift the wiper arm (note installation position) and place a ⅛ in. (3mm) pin or equivalent into the arm hole. Lift the the head cover and remove the attaching nut.

3. On all types, remove the arm assembly off the pivot using a rocking motion.

NOTE: *On 1990–92 Laser and Stealth vehicles, the driver's side wiper arm should be marked* **D** *and the passenger's side wiper arm should be marked* **A**. *The identification marks should be located at the base of the arm, near the pivot. Always install the wiper arms in the correct location.*

4. When installing, the motor should be in the park position and the tips of the blades ¾–1½ in. (19–38mm) above the bottom of the windshield moulding. Torque for arm attaching nut type is 120 inch lbs. Operate the wipers, check all components for proper operation.

REAR

NOTE: *To remove the rear wiper arm assembly the use of special tool C–3982 or equivalent is necessary. The use of a screwdriver is not recommended as it will distort and damage the arm. Refer to "Wiper Arm Removal and Installation Front" service procedure as a guide.*

1. With the tool installed on the arm, lift the arm then remove it from the output shaft.

2. To install, the wiper motor should be in the park position.

3. Install the arm so that the tip of the blade is about 1.3 in. (33mm) above the lower liftgate gasket.

Removing wiper arm—AG and AJ bodies

Front Windshield Wiper Motor

REMOVAL AND INSTALLATION

1981–85 Vehicles

1. Disconnect the negative battery terminal.
2. Disconnect the linkage from the motor crank arm.
3. Remove the wiper motor plastic cover.
4. Disconnect the wiring harness from the motor.
5. Remove the three mounting bolts from the motor mounting bracket and remove the motor.
6. Installation is the reverse of removal.

1986–88 Aries, Reliant, Caravelle, New Yorker and New Yorker Turbo, Daytona and LeBaron with Passive Restraint System

1. With the ignition switch ON, turn the wiper switch on until the wipers have run halfway across the windshield and then turn the switch OFF. Leave the ignition switch ON until the wipers are fully parked and then turn it OFF.
2. Remove the wiper arms and blades as described above. On the Daytona, disconnect the washer fluid reservoir hose at the tee connector.
3. Remove the plastic screen from the top of the cowl.

4. Remove the mounting bolts from the two pivots for the wiper arms.
5. Remove the plastic cover for the wiper motor from the cowl. Disconnect the motor electrical connector. Remove the three motor mounting nuts.
6. Push the pivots down into the plenum chamber behind the cowl. Then, pull the motor outward, past the point where it clears the mounting studs, and then as far toward the driver's side of the car as it will go. At this point, pull the right pivot and link out through the opening, and then shift the motor to the opposite side of the opening to remove it, the passenger's side link, and that side's pivot.
7. Carefully clamp the motor bracket in a vise and remove the nut from the end of the motor shaft. Separate the linkage from the shaft. If the motor is to be reinstalled, be careful not to turn it out of the "park" position.
8. If the motor's position is disturbed or if installing a new motor that is obviously not in the "park" position: Connect the wiring connector, turn ON the ignition switch, turn the wiper switch on briefly and then turn it back off. When the motor has reached the "park" position, turn OFF the ignition switch.

To install:

9. Connect the linkage to the motor with the

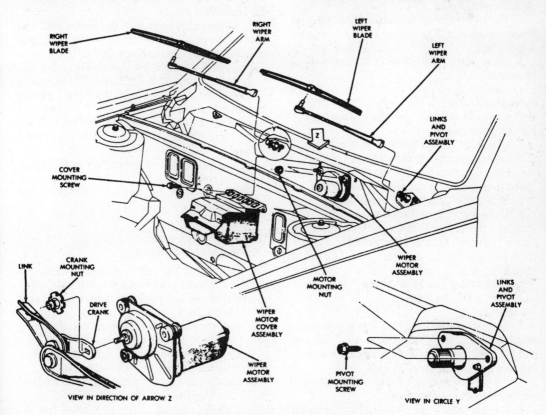

Removing wiper arm—AA, AC, AP and AY bodies

crank by installing the crank so its D-shaped slot fits over the motor shaft. Install the attaching nut and torque it to 95 inch lbs.

10. Maneuver the left pivot and its link into the chamber behind the cowl. Slide the assembly all the way to the left (toward the driver's side of the car) until the motor clears the mounting studs and the crank is positioned behind the sheet metal. Push the right pivot and link through the opening in the cowl; then, maneuver the assembly to the right until the motor is lined up with the mounting studs and install it over those studs.

11. Install the 3 motor mounting nuts and torque to 55 inch lbs.

12. Position the pivots and install the pivot mounting bolts, torquing them to 55 inch lbs. Connect the motor wiring connector.

13. Install the plastic motor cover onto the cowl. On Daytona with passive restraints, connect the washer fluid reservoir hose to the Tee connector. Note that the hoses passes through a special hole in the cowl screen. Then, mount the screen to the cowl, on these cars.

14. Install the wiper arms and connect their washer hoses to the Tee connectors.

1986–88 Lancer, LeBaron GTS

1. Remove the wiper arms as described above. Open the hood.

2. Remove the cover from the top of the cowl. Then, remove the 3 attaching screws from each wiper pivot.

3. Disconnect the wiper motor wiring connector.

4. Remove the 3 bolts that attach the motor mounting bracket to the body. Then, remove the motor, its bracket, and the linkage assembly from the cowl plenum.

5. Carefully clamp the motor bracket in a vise and remove the nut from the end of the motor shaft. Separate the linkage from the shaft. If the motor is to be reinstalled, be careful not to turn it out of the "park" position.

6. If the motor's position is disturbed or if installing a new motor that is obviously not in the "park" position: Connect the wiring connector, turn ON the ignition switch, turn the wiper switch on briefly and then turn it back off. When the motor has reached the "park" position, turn OFF the ignition switch.

To install:

7. Connect the linkage to the motor with the crank by installing the crank so its D-shaped slot fits over the motor shaft. Install the attaching nut and torque it to 95 inch lbs.

8. Install the motor, bracket and linkage assembly into the cowl plenum.

9. Loosely install the 3 attaching screws for each pivot. Then, install the 3 motor mounting

bracket attaching bolts. Finally, tighten the pivot attaching screws.

10. Connect the motor electrical connector. Install the cowl cover. Install and adjust the wiper arms as described above.

1986–88 Sundance and Shadow

1. Remove the wiper arms as described above. Open the hood.

2. Remove the cowl cover. Remove the 2 retaining nuts from each wiper pivot.

3. Disconnect the wiper motor wiring connector.

4. Remove the 3 bolts that attach the motor mounting bracket to the body and remove the motor, bracket, and linkage from the cowl plenum.

5. Carefully clamp the motor bracket in a vise and remove the nut from the end of the motor shaft. Separate the linkage from the shaft. If the motor is to be reinstalled, be careful not to turn it out of the "park" position.

6. If the motor's position is disturbed or if installing a new motor that is obviously not in the "park" position: Connect the wiring connector, turn ON the ignition switch, turn the wiper switch on briefly and then turn it back off. When the motor has reached the "park" position, turn OFF the ignition switch.

To install:

7. Connect the linkage to the motor with the crank by installing the crank so its D-shaped slot fits over the motor shaft. Install the attaching nut and torque it to 95 inch lbs.

8. Install the motor, bracket and linkage into the cowl plenum. Position the pivots so the mounting studs pass through the cowl and loosely install the pivot mounting nuts. Then, install and tighten the three motor mounting bolts.

9. Tighten the pivot mounting nuts. Install the cowl cover.

10. Install the wiper arm assemblies as described above.

1989–92 Models Except
1990–92 Laser and Stealth

1. Disconnect the negative battery cable.

2. If the cowl top plastic cover must be removed, remove the wiper arms and blades and remove the cover.

3. Remove the wiper motor cover and disconnect the motor wiring harness.

4. Disconnect the linkage drive crank from the motor crank arm.

5. Remove the motor mounting nuts and remove the wiper motor from the vehicle.

6. The installation is the reverse of the removal procedure.

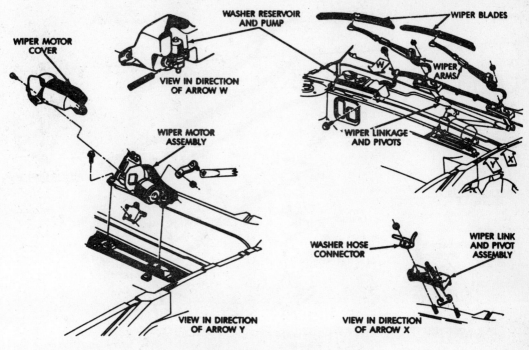

Windshield wiper motor and linkage—AP body

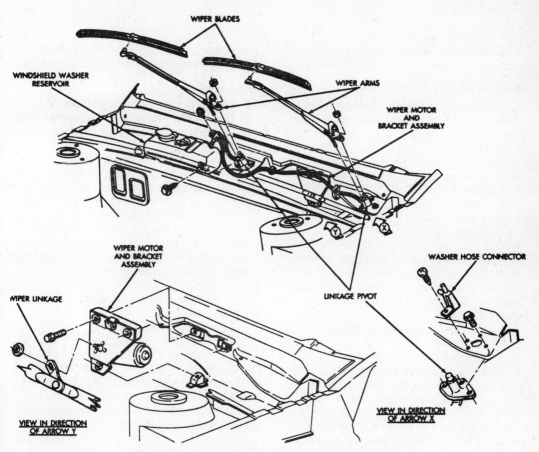

Windshield wiper motor and linkage—AC and AY bodies

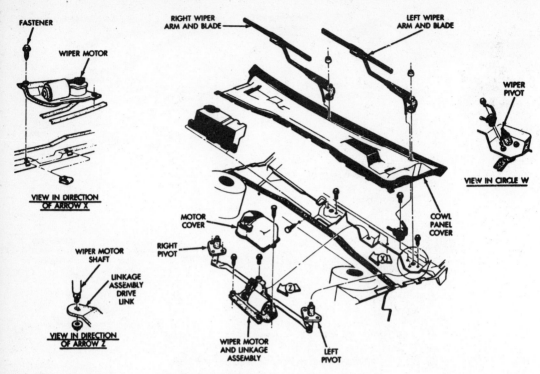

FASTENER

WIPER MOTOR

RIGHT WIPER ARM AND BLADE

LEFT WIPER ARM AND BLADE

WIPER PIVOT

VIEW IN DIRECTION OF ARROW X

VIEW IN CIRCLE W

WIPER MOTOR SHAFT

LINKAGE ASSEMBLY DRIVE LINK

MOTOR COVER

RIGHT PIVOT

COWL PANEL COVER

VIEW IN DIRECTION OF ARROW Z

WIPER MOTOR AND LINKAGE ASSEMBLY

LEFT PIVOT

Windshield wiper motor and linkage—AA body

7. Connect the negative battery cable and check the wiper motor for proper operation.

1990–92 Laser

1. Disconnect the negative battery cable.
2. Remove the windshield wiper arms by unscrewing the cap nuts and lifting the arms from the linkage posts.
3. Remove the front garnish panel.
4. Remove the air inlet trim pieces.
5. Remove the hole cover.
6. Remove the wiper motor by loosening the mounting bolts, removing the motor assembly, then disconnecting the linkage.
NOTE: *The installation angle of the crank arm and motor has been factory set; do not remove them unless it is necessary to do so. If they must be removed, remove them only after marking their mounting positions.*

To install:

7. Install the windshield wiper motor and connect the linkage.
8. Reinstall all the trim pieces.
9. Reinstall the wiper blades. Note that the driver's side wiper arm should be marked **D** and the passenger's side wiper arm should be marked **A**. The identification marks should be located at the base of the arm, near the pivot. Install the arms so the blades are 1 in. (25mm) from the garnish molding when parked.

10. Connect the negative battery cable and check the wiper system for proper operation.

Dodge Stealth

1. Disconnect the negative battery cable.
2. Remove the windshield wiper arms by unscrewing the cap nuts and lifting the arms from the linkage posts.
3. Remove the access hole cover.
4. Remove the wiper motor mounting bolts.
5. Detach the motor crank arm from the wiper linkage and remove the motor.
NOTE: *The installation angle of the crank arm and motor has been factory set; do not remove them unless it is necessary to do so. If they must be removed, remove them only after marking their mounting positions.*

To install:

6. Install the windshield wiper motor and connect the linkage.
7. Install the access hole cover.
8. Reinstall the wiper blades. Note that the driver's side wiper arm should be marked **D** and the passenger's side wiper arm should be marked **A**. The identification marks should be located at the base of the arm, near the pivot. Install the arms so the blades are parallel to the garnish molding when parked.
9. Connect the negative battery cable and check the wiper system for proper operation.

Rear Wiper Motor

REMOVAL AND INSTALLATION

1981–85 Vehicles

1. Disconnect the negative battery terminal.
2. Remove the blade and arm assembly.
3. Open the liftgate.
4. Remove the motor cover and disconnect the wiring connector.
5. Remove the four bracket retaining screws and remove the motor.
6. Installation is the reverse of removal.

1986–88 Aries, Sundance and Shadow

1. Open the liftgate.
2. Remove the arm and blade as described above. Remove the trim panel from the inside of the liftgate.
3. Disconnect the four screws that mount the motor mounting bracket to the liftgate. Then, remove the motor.
4. Installation is the reverse of removal.

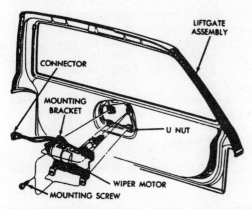

Rear wiper motor installation 1986–88 Aries, Sundance and Shadow

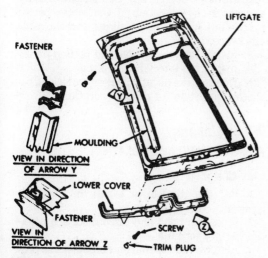

Liftgate cover assembly

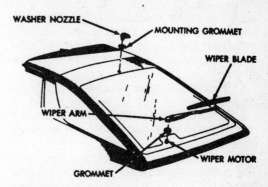

Liftgate wiper grommet

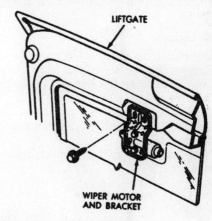

Liftgate wiper motor—AG body

1986–88 Daytona

1. Remove the wiper arm/blade assembly as described above. Remove the grommet from the motor driveshaft.
2. Open the liftgate. Remove the trim panel from inside the liftgate.
3. Disconnect the motor electrical connector.
4. Remove the two screws that mount the motor bracket onto the liftgate and remove the motor and bracket.
5. Installation is the reverse of removal.

1986–88 Lancer, LeBaron GTS

1. Remove the wiper arm/blade assembly as described above. Remove the grommet and escutcheon from the motor driveshaft.
2. Open the liftgate. Remove the trim panel from inside the liftgate.
3. Disconnect the motor wiring connector. Then, remove the four screws attaching the motor bracket and the motor to the liftgate. Remove the motor.
4. Installation is the reverse of removal.

1989–92 Daytona

1. Disconnect the negative battery cable.
2. To remove the wiper arm, lift the arm

against its spring tension and release the latch. Lift the arm off of the motor shaft.

3. Open the liftgate and remove the trim panel. Disconnect the connector from the motor.

4. Remove the grommet from the liftgate glass.

5. Remove the screws that fasten the bracket to the liftgate and remove the motor assembly from the vehicle.

6. Use a new grommet when assembling. The installation is the reverse of the removal procedure.

7. Connect the negative battery cable and check the liftgate wiper system for proper operation.

1990–92 Laser

1. Disconnect the negative battery cable.

2. Remove the rear wiper arm by removing the cover, unscrewing the nut and lifting the arm from the linkage post.

3. Remove the large interior trim panel. Use a plastic trim stick to unhook the trim clips of the liftgate trim.

4. If equipped with rear air spoiler, remove the grommet.

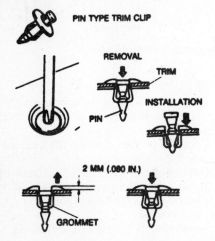

Remove the pin clips with care so they can be reused

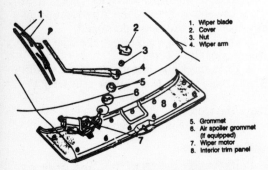

Rear glass wiper removal 1990–92 Laser

5. Remove the rear wiper assembly. Do not loosen the grommet for the wiper post.

To install:

6. Install the motor and grommet. Mount the grommet so the arrow on the grommet is pointing upward.

7. Install the wiper arm.

8. Connect the negative battery cable and check the rear wiper for proper operation.

9. If operation is satisfactory, fit the tabs on the upper part of the liftgate trim into the liftgate clips and secure the liftgate trim.

Dodge Stealth

1. Disconnect the negative battery cable.

2. Remove the liftgate lower trim. Remove the clips that hold the trim by using the following procedure:

  a. Remove the clip by pressing down on the center pin with a suitable blunt pointed tool. Press down a little more than $1/16$ in. (1.6mm). This releases the clip. Pull the clip outward to remove it.

  b. Do not push the pin inward more than necessary because it may damage the grommet, or if pushed too far, the pin may fall in. Once the clips are removed, use a plastic trim stick to pry the trim cover loose.

3. Remove the rear spoiler, center brace and center brake light.

4. Lift the small cover, remove the retaining nut and remove the wiper arm and spacer.

5. Remove the mounting bolts and remove the wiper motor.

To install:

6. Install the motor and install the retaining bolts.

7. Install the spacer, wiper arm and retaining nut. The arm should be positioned so the upper tip points to the upper left corner of the rear window when parked. Connect the battery and check the operation of the motor before proceeding. If satisfactory, disconnect the cable and proceed.

8. Install the rear spoiler and related parts.

9. Install the interior trim piece.

10. Connect the negative battery cable and recheck the system for proper operation.

Wiper Linkage
REMOVAL AND INSTALLATION

1981–85 Models

1. Put the windshield wipers in the park position.

2. Raise the hood and disconnect the negative battery terminal.

3. Remove the wiper arms and blades as previously described.

4. Disconnect the hoses from the tee connector.

5. Remove the pivot screws.

6. Remove the wiper motor plastic cover, and disconnect the wiring harness.

7. Remove the plastic screen from the cowl.

8. Remove the three motor mounting bolts.

9. Push the pivots down into the plenum chamber. Pull the motor out until it clears the mounting studs and then move it to the driver's side as far as it will go. Pull the right pivot and link out through the openin, then shift the motor to the right and remove the motor, the left link and pivot.

NOTE: *Do not rotate the motor output shaft from the park position.*

10. Installation is the reverse of removal.

1986 and Later Vehicle

On all these cars, the linkage is removed along with the front windshield wiper motor, using an identical procedure. Refer to the appropriate procedure above.

INSTRUMENTS AND SWITCHES

Instrument Cluster

REMOVAL AND INSTALLATION

1981–85 Conventional Cluster

1. Disconnect the negative battery terminal.

2. Apply the parking brake and block the wheels. Place the gearshift lever in position 1.

3. Remove the instrument panel trim strip.

4. Remove the left upper and lower cluster bezel screws.

5. Remove the right lower cluster bezel screw and retaining clip.

6. Remove the instrument cluster bezel by snapping the bezel off of the five retaining clips.

7. Remove the seven retaining screws and remove the upper right bezel.

8. Remove the four rear instrument panel top cover mounting screws.

9. Lift the rear edge of the panel top cover and remove the two screws attaching the upper trim strip retainer and cluster housing to the base panel.

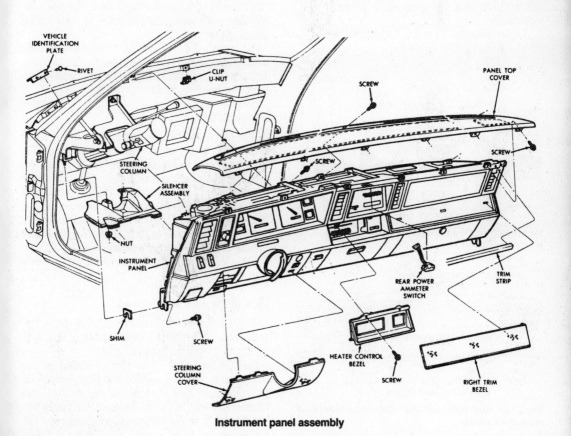

Instrument panel assembly

10. Remove the trim strip retainer.

11. Remove the two screws attaching the cluster housing to the base panel of the lower cluster.

12. Lift the rearward edge of the panel top cover and slide the cluster housing rearward.

13. Disconnect the right printed circuit board connector from behind the cluster housing.

14. Disconnect the speedometer cable connector.

15. Disconnect the left printed circuit connector.

16. Remove the cluster assembly.

17. Installation is the reverse of removal.

1981–85 Electronic Cluster

The electronic cluster is removed in the same manner as the conventional cluster, except for that there is no speedometer cable. When replacing the electronic cluster, the odometer memory chip can be removed from the old cluster and placed in the new one. To remove the chip, special tool C–4817 must be used.

1986–88 Conventional Cluster except Daytona and LeBaron

1. Disconnect the negative battery cable. Apply the parking brake and block the wheels. If the car has an automatic transmission with column shift, put the gearshift lever in "1" position.

2. Remove the 6 screws from the cluster be-

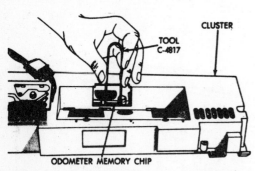

Removing/installing the odometer memory chip in the electronic cluster

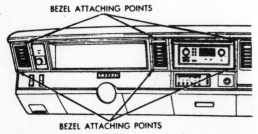

Bezel attaching points on the 1986–88 conventional instrument cluster

zel. Then, remove the bezel by snapping it off all 5 retaining clips.

3. Remove the rear-facing screws from the instrument panel upper pad. Then, lift the rearward edge of the pad and, holding it up, remove the 2 screws from the top of the cluster.

4. Remove the 2 screws from the bottom of the cluster (these attach it to the dash panel). Lift the rear edge of the pad on top of the dash and hold it upward as you pull the cluster out far enough to reach the wiring.

5. Unscrew the speedometer outer cable retaining collar and then pull the inner cable out of the rear of the speedometer. If necessary, mark the wiring connectors. Then, disconnect all of them.

6. Remove the cluster.

To install:

7. To install the cluster, first position it in front of the dash. Then, reconnect the wiring connectors to their original locations. Insert the square end of the speedometer cable into the rear of the speedometer, turning it slightly to line it up, if necessary. Install and tighten the speedometer cable collar nut.

8. Lift the rear edge of the dash pad and hold it upward as you slide the cluster back into position.

9. Install the 4 cluster attaching screws (2 at the bottom and 2 at the top, under the pad). Install the rear-facing screws into the instrument panel upper pad.

10. Install the bezel so all the retaining clips lock. Then, install the 6 bezel attaching screws. Return the gearshift lever to "Park" and reconnect the battery cable.

Electronic Cluster

The electronic cluster is removed in the same manner as the conventional cluster, except for that there is no speedometer cable. When replacing the electronic cluster, the odometer memory chip can be removed from the old cluster and placed in the new one. To remove the chip, special tool C–4817 must be used.

NOTE: *On some later models the odometer memory is no longer retained in the cluster. This information is stored in the body computer.*

1986–88 Daytona and LeBaron

1. Disconnect the battery negative cable. Remove the 5 screws attaching the top of the cluster bezel to the instrument panel.

2. Pull the bezel to the rear to disengage the 3 clips on its bottom surface and then remove it.

3. Remove the four screws attaching the cluster housing to the dash panel. Pull the cluster assembly to the rear to gain clearance to the

wiring. Then, reach underneath it to disconnect the wiring harness. Remove the cluster.

4. To install, connect the wiring harness. Then, put the cluster in position and install the four mounting screws.

5. Install the cluster bezel, first engaging the 3 clips on its bottom surface. Install the 5 screws at the top of the bezel. Reconnect the battery.

1989–92 Conventional Cluster

EXCEPT 1990–92 DAYTONA AND LEBARON
1990–92 LASER, STEALTH AND DODGE MONACO

1. Disconnect the negative battery cable.

2. Remove the instrument cluster bezel. Cluster removal is not necessary if just removing gauges.

3. When only removing gauge(s) or the speedometer, remove the trip odometer reset knob, if necessary, remove the mask and lens

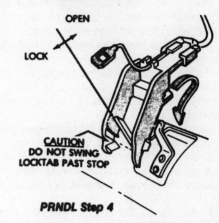

PRNDL Step 4

Removing PRNDL cable column shift type

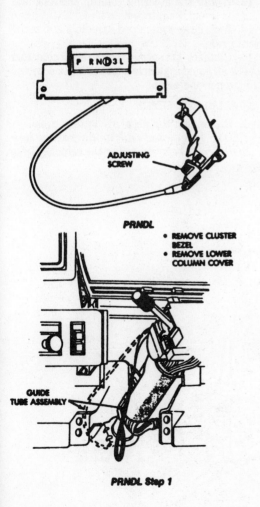

PRNDL

PRNDL Step 1

PRNDL Step 2

PRNDL Step 3

Removing PRNDL cable column shift type

assembly, and remove the desired gauge from the cluster. Disconnect the speedometer cable, if equipped, when removing the speedometer.

4. If equipped with automatic transaxle and column shift, remove the lower column cover and disconnect the gear indicator cable.

5. Remove the screws attaching the cluster to the instrument panel.

6. Pull the cluster out and disconnect all wiring harnesses and the speedometer cable, if equipped. Remove the cluster from the vehicle.

To install:

7. Position the cluster and feed the gear indicator cable through its slot.

8. Connect all wiring and install the speedometer cable to the speedometer, if removed; make sure the cable end is securely clicked in place.

9. Install the cluster retaining screws. Connect the gearshift indicator cable.

10. Install the cluster bezel.

11. Connect the negative battery cable, check all gauges and the speedometer for proper operation. Make sure the gearshift indicator is properly aligned.

1990-92 DAYTONA AND LEBARON

1. Disconnect the negative battery cable.

2. Remove the panel vent grille above the switch pod assembly and remove the 2 revealed pod mounting screws.

3. Remove the 2 remaining screws under the pod and pull the pod out to disconnect the wiring harnesses. Remove the pod from the instrument panel.

4. Unscrew the tilt column lever, if equipped, remove the screws from under the upper steering column shrouds and remove the shrouds.

5. Pull rearward to disengage the cluster trim bezel retaining clips and remove the bezel.

6. When only removing gauges or the speedometer, remove the mask and lens assembly and remove the desired assembly from the cluster.

7. Remove the screws attaching the cluster to the instrument panel.

8. Pull the cluster out and disconnect all wiring harnesses and the turbo gauge hose, if equipped. Remove the cluster from the vehicle.

To install:

9. Position the cluster and connect all wiring and the turbo hose, if it was disconnected.

10. Install the cluster mounting screws.

11. Install the cluster trim bezel.

12. Install the steering column shrouds and the tilt lever, if equipped.

13. Install the switch pod assembly and panel vent grille.

14. Connect the negative battery cable and check all gauges, switches and the speedometer for proper operation.

1990-92 LASER AND STEALTH

1. Disconnect the negative battery cable.

NOTE: *If equipped with an air bag, be sure to disarm it before entering the vehicle. Refer*

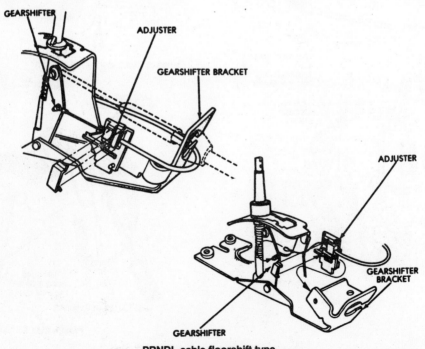

PRNDL cable floorshift type

to the necessary service procedure in this chapter.

2. On Stealth, remove the hood lock release handle and switches from the knee protector below the steering column. Then remove the exposed retaining screws and remove the knee protector.

3. Remove the screw cover at the side of the bezel.

4. Remove the instrument cluster bezel.

5. Remove the instrument cluster. Disassemble and remove gauges or the speedometer as required.

NOTE: *If the speedometer cable adapter must be serviced, disconnect the cable at the transaxle end. Pull the cable slightly toward the vehicle interior, release the lock by turning the adapter to the right or left and remove the adapter.*

6. The installation is the reverse of the removal procedure. Use care not to damage the printed circuit board or any gauge components.

7. Connect the negative battery cable and check all cluster-related items for proper operation.

DODGE MONACO

1. Disconnect the negative battery cable.

2. Remove the screws retaining the instrument cluster bezel and remove the bezel.

3. Remove the cluster retaining screws and tilt the cluster forward. Disconnect the electrical connectors.

4. If necessary, disconnect the speedometer cable.

5. Remove the lower instrument panel cover and remove the cluster.

6. Install the cluster and lower trim cover. Connect the electrical leads to the cluster.

7. Install the instrument panel bezel. Connect the negative battery cable.

Windshield Wiper Switch
REMOVAL AND INSTALLATION

The front wiper switch on most vehicles (exceptions below) is part of the combination turn signal/cruise control/wiper switch or column mounted assembly. Refer to the appropriate procedure in Chapter 8 or the service procedures below.

1990–92 Daytona And LeBaron

1. Disconnect the negative battery cable.

2. Remove the panel vent grille above the switch pod assembly and remove the 2 revealed pod mounting screws.

3. Remove the 2 remaining screws under the pod and pull the pod out to disconnect the wiring harnesses. Remove the pod from the instrument panel.

4. Remove the inner panel from the pod. Disconnect the switch linkage from the buttons.

5. Remove the windshield wiper switch mounting screws and remove the entire switch assembly.

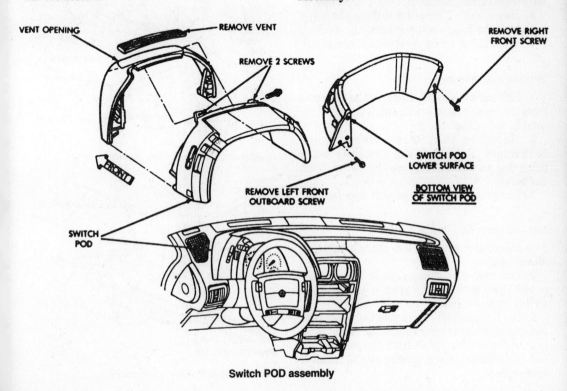

Switch POD assembly

6. The installation is the reverse of the removal procedure.

7. Connect the negative battery cable and check the entire wiper system for proper operation.

Dodge Monaco

Refer to the Headlight (Combination Switch) service procedures in this chapter.

Rear Window Washer/Wiper Switch

REMOVAL AND INSTALLATION

NOTE: *Use these service procedures as guide. Slight variations may occur due to extra connections, etc., but the basic procedure should work on applicable models.*

Conventional Cluster except Daytona and LeBaron

1. On 1985 and later models, remove the instrument cluster bezel (you can refer to "Instrument Cluster Removal and Installation" above, for attaching screw locations). On 1981–84 models, remove the pull the bottom of the steering column cover to the rear and snap it off the column.

2. Remove the left lower trim bezel by pulling it off the two attaching clips. Pull it out of the dash just far enough to reach the wiring connectors. Then, noting which is which for easy installation, disconnect the connectors.

3. Remove the 2 screws attaching the wiper switch to the bezel assembly and pull it off.

4. Installation is the reverse of removal.

Daytona and LeBaron

1. Lift the console lid. Remove the 2 screws from the console bezel and then lift the bezel assembly out of the console.

2. Disconnect the rear wiper/wash switch connectors. Remove the 2 switch-to-bezel mounting screws and remove the switch from the bezel.

3. Installation is the reverse of removal.

1990–92 Laser And Dodge Stealth

1. Disconnect the negative battery cable on all vehicles.

2. On 1990–92 Laser, remove the cluster panel then remove the rear wiper/washer switch from the holder.

3. On Dodge Stealth, remove the knee protector and column upper cover then remove the rear wiper/washer switch from the holder.

4. Installation is the reverse of the removal procedure.

Headlight Switch

REMOVAL AND INSTALLATION

1981–88 Models
Except Sundance and Shadow

1. Remove the cluster bezel as necessary. Remove the three screws securing the headlamp switch mounting plate to the base panel.

2. Pull the switch and plate rearward and disconnect the wiring connector.

3. Depress the button on the switch and remove the knob and stem.

4. Snap out the escutcheon, then remove the nut that attaches the switch to the mounting plate.

5. Installation is the reverse of removal.

Sundance and Shadow

1. Remove the headlamp switch bezel from the instrument panel by unsnapping the attaching tangs.

2. Remove the 3 screws securing the switch mounting plate to the instrument panel. Then, pull the switch and mounting plate rearward and out of the instrument panel opening.

3. Disconnect the electrical connector at the switch. Press the release button on the bottom of the switch and then pull the knob and shaft out of the switch.

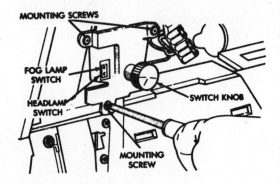

Headlamp switch mounting screws

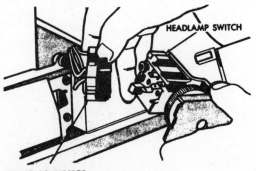

Headlamp switch wiring connectors

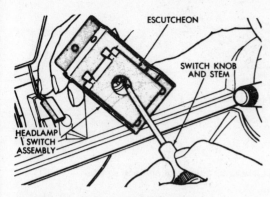

Headlight switch knob and stem

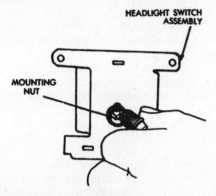

Headlamp switch mounting nut

4. Detach the headlamp switch escutcheon from the mounting plate by unsnapping the attaching tangs and removing it. Then, unscrew the switch-to-mounting plate retaining nut and pull the switch off the mounting plate.

To install:

5. Position the switch onto the mounting plate and install the retaining nut. Then, snap the headlamp switch escutcheon back into position.

6. Slide the knob shaft into the switch until it locks. Reconnect the switch electrical connector.

7. Install the mounting plate onto the instrument panel. Install the 3 attaching screws.

8. Snap the headlamp switch bezel back into position.

1989–92 All Models Except:
1990–92 Daytona And LeBaron
1990–92 Laser And Stealth
Dodge Monaco

1. Disconnect the negative battery cable.

2. Remove the headlight switch bezel or cluster bezel, as required.

3. Remove the screws securing the headlight switch mounting plate to the instrument panel. Pull the assembly out and disconnect the connectors from the switch.

4. Depress the spring button and remove the headlight switch knob and stem.

5. Remove the escutcheon, if equipped, and remove the nut that attaches the switch to the mounting plate.

6. The installation is the reverse of the removal procedure.

7. Connect the negative battery cable and check the switch for proper operation.

1990–92 Daytona And LeBaron

1. Disconnect the negative battery cable.

2. Remove the panel vent grille above the switch pod assembly and remove the 2 revealed pod mounting screws.

3. Remove the 2 remaining screws under the pod and pull the pod out to disconnect the wiring harnesses. Remove the pod from the instrument panel.

4. Remove the turn signal switch lever by pulling it straight out of the pod.

5. Remove the inner panel from the pod. Remove the turn signal switch in order to gain access to the headlight switch.

6. Disconnect the switch linkage from the buttons.

7. Remove the switch mounting screws and remove the entire switch assembly.

8. The installation is the reverse of the removal procedure.

9. Connect the negative battery cable and check the system for proper operation.

1990–92 Laser And Stealth

The headlights, turn signals, dimmer switch, windshield/washer and, on some models, the cruise control function are all built into 1 multifunction combination switch that is mounted on the steering column. Refer to the appropriate procedure in Chapter 8.

Dodge Monaco

The windshield wiper, turn signal, headlight and dimmer switches are all combined in the "Combination Switch" on the left side of the steering column.

1. Disconnect the negative battery cable.

2. If not equipped with passive restraint, remove the lower instrument panel cover. If equipped with passive restraint, perform the following:

    a. Pull the ashtray from the receptacle, remove the receptacle and unplug the lighter.

    b. Remove the 2 screws fastening the console to the front bracket.

    c. Remove the armrest and the 2 screws fastening the console to the rear bracket.

    d. Reach inside the console and push out the seatbelt guides. Remove the console.

    e. Remove the bolts fastening the pivot

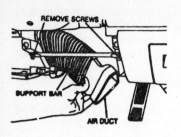 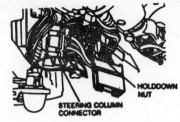 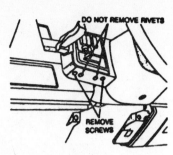

To remove combination switch, remove duct, electrical connector and pod screws

bracket to the knee bolster. Loosen, but do not remove, the 2 bolts fastening the pivot bracket to the front console bracket.

f. Remove the screw and the 2 Torx® screws that attach the bracket to the floor and slide the bracket back.

g. Remove the screw located at the top of the knee bolster to the left of the steering column.

h. Remove the screw attaching the air duct to the knee bolster.

i. Remove the screw located at the bottom of the instrument panel holding the garnish penal.

j. Remove both bolster end caps and the revealed nuts.

k. Move the knee bolster toward the rear of the vehicle enough to gain access to the 2 screws holding the parking brake handle, then lower the handle.

l. Remove the knee bolster.

3. Remove the screws, remove the support rod and pull the air duct aside.

4. Cut the plastic tie-wrap straps.

5. Loosen the hold-down nut in the center of the steering column electrical connector and separate the connector.

6. Separate the left side pod switch connector from the steering column connector by placing a flat blade tool between the connectors to disengage the locking tab. Push on the wire side of the left side pod switch connector and slide the connector out of the channels of the steering column connector.

7. Disconnect the electrical connector, then remove the bottom 2 screws (not the rivets) from the pod assembly.

8. To gain access to the inside of the pod, remove the screws from the back of the left side switch pod assembly and remove the switch pod housing back cover.

NOTE: *There are small retaining clips on the left side pod that may fall off when the switch is removed.*

9. Carefully pull the switch pod far enough from the housing to expose the 2 screws, remove them and gently pull the switch forward

and pull the harness out through the housing to remove the switch.

To install:

10. Route the switch assembly connector through the housing and along the underside of the steering column.

11. Connect the switch connector.

12. Connect the steering column connector and install the hold-down nut. Secure with a new tie.

13. Position the switch and secure with the screws.

14. Connect the air duct.

15. Install the lower support bar.

16. Install the knee bolster and console by reversing their removal procedure, if equipped, or install the lower instrument cover.

17. Connect the negative battery cable and check all functions of the combination switch for proper operation.

Clock
REMOVAL AND INSTALLATION
1981–84 Models

1. Remove the 2 attaching screws and remove the heater control bezel. Then, remove the 2 screws attaching the clock to the base panel.

2. Pull the clock to the rear to gain clearance to reach the electrical connector. Then, disconnect the electrical connector and remove the clock.

3. Installation is the reverse of removal.

1985 And Later Models

All 1985 and later models use digital clocks only. Digital clocks are part of the radio unit. For removal, refer to the "Radio Removal and Installation" procedure above.

Back-up Light Switch
REMOVAL AND INSTALLATION

On both manual and automatic cars, this switch is mounted on the transaxle. Refer to the appropriate service procedure in Chapter 7.

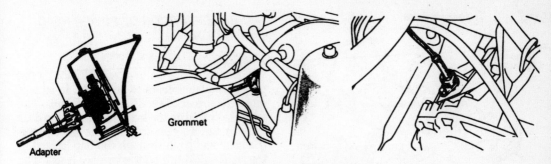

Typical speedometer cable installation

Speedometer Cable

REMOVAL AND INSTALLATION

1. Reach under the instrument panel and depress the spring clip retaining the cable to the speedometer head. Pull the cable back and away from the head.

2. If the core is broken, raise and support the vehicle and remove the cable retaining screw from the cable bracket. Carefully slide the cable out of the transaxle.

To install:

3. Coat the new core sparingly with speedometer cable lubricant and insert it in the cable. Install the cable at the transaxle, lower the car and install the cable at the speedometer head. Do not bend cable or cable housing, a bend will cause incorrect indication or abnormal noise in the speedometer assembly.

LIGHTING

Headlights

REMOVAL AND INSTALLATION

Seal Beam Headlamp Type

NOTE: *If vehicle is equipped with headlamp doors turn the headlight switch ON. Open the hood and locate the power distribution center. This center is located in the front of the left front strut tower. Remove the cover from the center and remove the Headlamp Close Relay. This will prevent the headlamp doors from closing to provide easier servicing. Turn the headlight switch to OFF then perform this repair.*

1. Remove the headlight bezel.

2. Unhook the spring from the headlight retaining ring if so equipped.

3. Unscrew the retaining ring and remove it.

NOTE: *Do not disturb the two long aiming screws. Conventional and Halogen headlamp sealed beams units are interchangeable, but it is recommended that they not be interchanged.*

4. Unplug the old sealed beam.

5. Connect the replacement bulb and install into the receptacle (check operation of headlight before completing repair).

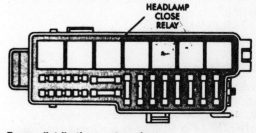

Power distribution center relays

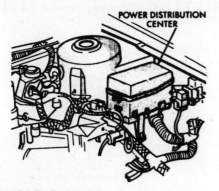

Power distribution center

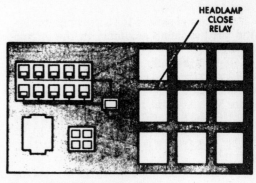

Power distribution center relays

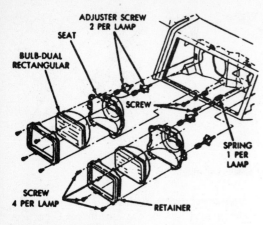

Sealed beam replacement

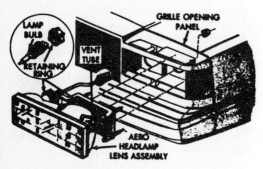

Aero headlamp assembly

6. Install the retaining ring and connect the spring.

7. Install the headlight bezel.

Aero Headlamp Type

Aero headlamp system use a replaceable halogen bulb that is mounted in an aerodynamic, molded plastic lens reflector assembly.

NOTE: *Lens fogging is a normal condition and does not require service, as moisture will vent from tubes behind lens on Aero headlamp type system.*

1. Locate and remove the wire connector behind the headlamp assembly in the engine compartment.

2. Rotate the bulb retaining ring counterclockwise ¼ turn and remove the ring, bulb and bulb holder from the lens assembly. The bulb holder has alignment notches.

3. DO NOT TOUCH THE BULB WITH FINGERS OR ANY POSSIBLY OILY SURFACE, REDUCED BULB LIFE WILL RESULT!

4. To install the bulb reverse the the preceding service operation.

MANUAL OPERATION OF POWER HEADLAMP DOORS

Except 1990–92 Laser and Dodge Stealth

A manual over-ride hand wheel permits the power headlamp doors to be opened in case of motor failure or to service the headlamps. The wheel is located on the top of the headlamp door drive motor. To gain access to the wheel, open the hood and go in through the flap located in the sight shield behind the bumper fascia. The wheel must be turned a number of turns to remove play and then open the doors.

1. Disconnect the negative battery cable.

2. Locate the manual override knob. On Daytona, they are located under access shields behind the bumper facia and under the center of the front bumper on LeBaron and other models.

3. Remove the protective cover boot.

4. Rotate the manual override knob to raise the headlight cover(s).

5. Connect the negative battery cable.

1990–92 Laser And Dodge Stealth

If the headlight covers will not raise electrically, remove the fusible link from the relay box, then remove the boot on the rear area of the pop-up motor and turn the manual knob clockwise until the cover is open. Perform this procedure on both the left and right sides.

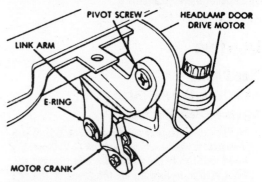

The power headlamp drive mechanism—Note the location of the manual actuating wheel on the top of the drive motor

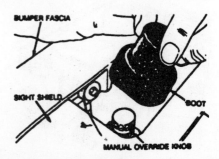

Manual override knob—Daytona

Signal and Marker Lights
REMOVAL AND INSTALLATION
Front Turn Signal and Parking Lights

The marker lights are replaced by removing the lamp assembly from the bumper or quarter panel, twisting and pulling the socket out of the assemby, and then twisting the lamp to release it from the socket.

Where the lamp is located in an assembly separate from the headlamp, remove the screws from the lens and pull the assembly out of the bumper fascia.

Where the lamp is located in the side of the headlamp bezel, remove the two nuts from the rear of the turn signal/parking light assembly. These are located in the wall of the bezel, directly in front of the headlight and will also release the lens (catch it and remove it to a safe place to keep it from being damaged).

Remove the lamp by turning it to release it from the socket. Install the new lamp by inserting it into the socket so the prongs line up with the internal grooves, permitting it to be turned and locked easily. If the lamp cannot be fully inserted and turned readily, turn it 180° and try again. Insert the socket into the assembly and turn it tight to lock it. Then, install the lamp assembly. On separate designs, install the mounting screws. On intergral designs, install the lens

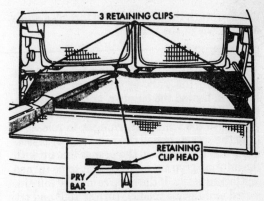

Front turn signal lamp shield—AY body

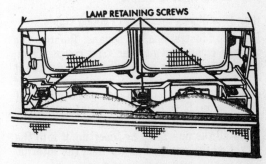

Front turn signal lamp mounting screws—AY body

Front lamp assembly—AY body

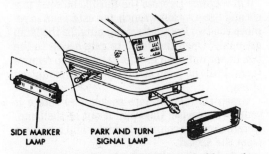

Removing the turn signal/parking and side marker lights on the 1988 Sundance/Shadow

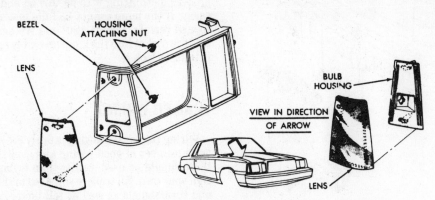

Removing the side marker/turn signal lamp on the 1982 Aries and Reliant

and then turn the nuts over the threaded studs on the back of the lens.

Side Marker Lights

The side marker lights are located in a socket locked into the back of the lamp assembly. Reach in behind the bumper, grasp the socket, turn it to release, and pull it from the lamp.

Remove the lamp by turning it to release it from the socket. Install the new lamp by inserting it into the socket so the prongs line up with the internal grooves, permitting it to be turned and locked easily. If the lamp cannot be fully inserted and turned readily, turn it 180° and try again. Insert the socket into the lamp assembly and turn it tight to lock it.

Rear Turn Signal, Brake, and Parking Lights

Refer to illustrations, on sedans: Remove the luggage compartment rear trim cover. Then, loosen the quarter panel silencer and shift it out of the way. Grasp the appropriate socket and rotate it counterclockwise; then pull it out of the lamp. Rotate the bulb counterclockwise and remove it from the socket.

Install the new lamp by inserting it into the socket so the prongs line up with the internal

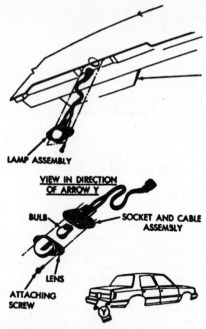

License plate lamp—AA body

grooves, permitting it to be turned and locked easily. If the lamp cannot be fully inserted and turned readily, turn it 180° and try again. Insert the socket into the lamp assembly and turn it tight to lock it.

On wagons: Depress the flexible bumper fascia and use a socket wrench and extension to remove the two lower attaching nuts for the lamp assembly. Open the hatch to gain access to the two upper nuts and use the same tool to remove them. Pull the lamp assembly off the mounting studs.

Grasp the appropriate socket and rotate it counterclockwise; then pull it out of the lamp. Rotate the bulb counterclockwise and remove it from the socket.

Install the new lamp by inserting it into the socket so the prongs line up with the internal grooves, permitting it to be turned and locked easily. If the lamp cannot be fully inserted and turned readily, turn it 180° and try again. Insert the socket into the lamp assembly and turn it tight to lock it.

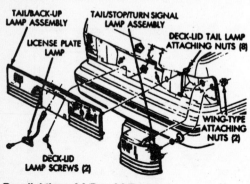

Rear lighting—AA/P or AA/D body

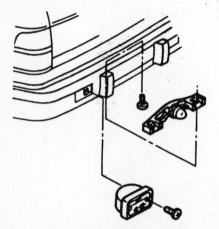

Back-up and license plate lamps—AA/C body

TRAILER WIRING

Wiring the car for towing is fairly easy. There are a number of good wiring kits available and these should be used, rather than trying to design your own. All trailers will need brake lights and turn signals as well as tail lights and side marker lights. Most states require extra marker lights for overly wide trailers. Also, most states have recently required back-up lights for trailers, and most trailer manufacturers have been building trailers with back-up lights for several years.

Additionally, some Class I, most Class II and just about all Class III trailers will have electric brakes.

Add to this number an accessories wire, to operate trailer internal equipment or to charge the trailer's battery, and you can have as many as seven wires in the harness.

Determine the equipment on your trailer and buy the wiring kit necessary. The kit will contain all the wires needed, plus a plug adapter set which included the female plug, mounted on the bumper or hitch, and the male plug, wired into, or plugged into the trailer harness.

When installing the kit, follow the manufacturer's instructions. The color coding of the wires is standard throughout the industry.

One point to note, some domestic vehicles, and most imported vehicles, have separate turn signals. On most domestic vehicles, the brake lights and rear turn signals operate with the same bulb. For those vehicles with separate turn signals, you can purchase an isolation unit so that the brake lights won't blink whenever the turn signals are operated, or, you can go to your local electronics supply house and buy four diodes to wire in series with the brake and turn signal bulbs. Diodes will isolate the brake and turn signals. The choice is yours. The isolation units are simple and quick to install, but far more expensive than the diodes. The diodes, however, require more work to install properly, since they require the cutting of each bulb's wire and soldering in place of the diode.

One final point, the best kits are those with a spring loaded cover on the vehicle mounted socket. This cover prevents dirt and moisture from corroding the terminals. Never let the vehicle socket hang loosely. Always mount it securely to the bumper or hitch.

CIRCUIT PROTECTION 1981–88 MODEL YEARS

Fuses

The fuse box is located behind an access panel in the glovebox on 1981–85 models and under the steering column in 1986–88 models. Remove the panel by unsnapping the clips at the bottom (pulling out hard). Then, slide the retaining tabs out at the top. On earlier models, a special fuse removal tool is located on the back of the access panel. On the later models, slide the fuse block to the left and off the retaining bracket to remove it for easy access to the fuses.

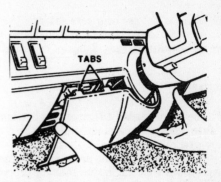

Removing the fuse access panel on 1986 and later models

The later models use blade type fuses. Standard fuses have the amperage rating stamped on the silver connector at either end. Blade fuses have the amperage printed on the outer edge and are also color coded according to amperage rating. *Make sure to note the amperage rating before discarding a blown fuse! Always replace the fuse with one of exactly the same rating, as use of a rating even slightly higher than standard could result in a dangerous vehicle fire.*

If a circuit continues to blow a fuse of the proper rating, leave the fuse out and check the circuit or the accessories it runs for an electrical short or mechanical overload.

Remember, in replacing the access panel, to insert the tabs at the top first and then to snap the locking tabs at the bottom into place.

Fusible Links

CAUTION: *Do not replace blown fusible links with standard wire. Only fusible type wire with hypalon insulation can be used, or damage to the electrical system will occur!*

When a fusible link blows it is very important to find out why. They are placed in the electrical system for protection against dead shorts to ground, which can be caused by electrical component failure or various wiring failures.

CAUTION: *Do not just replace the fusible link to correct a problem!*

When replacing all fusible links, they are to be replaced with the same type of prefabricated link available from your Chyrsler dealer.

REPLACEMENT

1. Cut the fusible link including the connection insulator from the main harness wire.

2. Remove 1 in. (25mm) of insulation from both new fusible link, and the main harness, and wrap together.

3. Heat the splice with a soldering gun, and apply rosin type solder.

NOTE: *Do not use acid core solder.*

4. Allow the connection to cool, and wrap the new splice with at least 3 layers of electrical tape.

Flashers

Flashers are located either on the bottom of the fuse block or on a module under the dash. They are replaced by simply pulling them straight out. Note that the prongs are arranged in such a way that the flasher must be properly oriented before attempting to install it. Turn the flasher until the orientation of the prongs is correct and simply push it firmly in until the prongs are fully engaged.

CIRCUIT PROTECTION 1989–92 MODEL YEARS

Fuses, Circuit Breakers and Relays
LOCATION
ARIES, RELIANT, 600, CARAVELLE, LEBARON (K BODY) AND NEW YORKER

The fuse block is located behind a removeable access panel, below the steering column. The hazard and turn signal flashers along with the time delay and horn relays are also located behind the panel. Additional relays are mounted on the inner fender panel near the battery.

SPIRIT, ACCLAIM, SHADOW AND SUNDANCE

The fuse block is located behind the steering column cover, accessible by removing the fuse access panel above the hood latch release lever. The relay and flasher module is located behind an access panel in the glovebox. Included in the module are the hazard and turn signal flashers along with the time delay and horn relays. Additional relays are mounted on the inner fender panel near the battery.

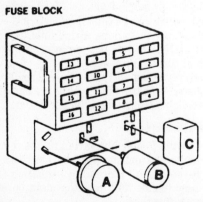

FUSE BLOCK

The fuse and flasher block used on 1985 Reliant. "A" is the turn signal flasher, "B" the ignition time delay relay and "C" the horn relay

LANCER AND LEBARON GTS

The fuse block is located behind the glove box door, accessible by removing the fuse access panel. The relay and flasher module is located behind the cupholder in the center of the instrument panel. The entire module can be removed by pushing it up and off of of its mounting bracket. Included in the module are the hazard and turn signal flashers along with the time delay and horn relays. Additional relays are mounted on the inner fender panel near the battery.

DAYTONA AND LEBARON (J BODY)

The fuse block is located behind a removeable access panel to the left of the lower portion of the steering column. On 1988–89 Daytona and LeBaron, the hazard and turn signal flashers along with the time delay and horn relays are also located behind the panel.

On 1990–92 Daytona and LeBaron, a relay bank is located on the left side kick panel. The Power Distribution Center, which contains additional relays and fuses, is located in the engine compartment behind the battery. Each item is identified on the cover.

DYNASTY AND IMPERIAL

On vehicles without a Power Distribution Center, fusible links are part of the the large wiring harness behind the battery. On vehicles with a Power Distribution Center, fusible links in the form of cartridge fuses, which resemble small relays but serve as fusible links, are located in the Center. Each item is identified on the cover of the Power Distribution Center.

The fuse panel, which contains fuses and circuit breakers, is located behind the glove box door. To remove the panel, pull it out from the bottom and slide the tabs out from the top. Additional fuses are in the Power Distribution Center located near the left side strut tower in the engine compartment. Each item is identified on the cover of the Power Distribution Center.

1990–92 LASER

The 1990–92 Laser has several fuse panels. There are 3 main fusible links the MPI circuit — 20 amp, the radiator fan motor circuit — 30 amp and the ignition switch circuit — 30 amp. They are found under the hood in a centralized junction with the battery positive cable clamp. Another fuse panel is located on the passenger side, under the hood, just forward of the strut tower. It shares the panel with a bank of relays. This panel contains fuses and several fusible links. Another fuse panel is on the driver's side, under the hood, back against the firewall. A fourth fuse panel is the multi-purpose fuse block located inside the vehicle, on the left side behind the driver's knee protector.

The 1990–92 Laser uses a number of relays. A centralized fuse/relay panel on the passenger side, under the hood, just forward of the strut tower contains the taillight relay, headlight relay, radiator fan motor relay, pop-up (retractable light) motor relay, power window relay, alternator relay and fog light relay. Also in the engine compartment on the driver's side a panel are 2 air conditioning condenser fan relays and the air conditioning compressor clutch relay. Inside the vehicle, the interior relay box contains the door lock relay, starter relay, defogger timer and room of other relays as required (use in Canada, etc).

The turn signal and hazard flasher unit is located in the multi-purpose fuse panel located under the driver's left side knee protector.

DODGE STEALTH

The Stealth has several fuse panels. One fuse panel is located on the passenger side, under the hood, just forward of the air flow box. It shares the panel with a bank of relays. This panel also contains several fusible links. Another fuse panel is the multi-purpose fuse block located under the instrument panel, on the left side behind the driver's knee protector.

The Stealth uses a number of relays. A centralized fuse/relay panel on the driver side, under the hood, just forward of the strut tower contains the radiator fan relay, air conditioning system relays and others. Also in the engine compartment in front of the air flow box is a relay bank containing the the taillight relay, headlight relay, pop-up (retractable light) motor relay, horn relay, alternator relay and fog light relay. Inside the vehicle, relays above the

fuse box are for the blower motor and theft alarm horn.

The turn signal and hazard flasher unit is mounted to the lower portion of the sheet metal behind the left side kick panel.

DODGE MONACO

The fuse panel is located above the parking brake release lever, under the instrument panel. On Monaco built on or after October 9, 1991, various cartridge fuses are in the Power Distribution Center, located on the left side of the engine compartment,

Circuit breakers are an integral part of the headlight switch, the wiper switch and the air conditioning circuit. They are used to protect each circuit from an overload. Other circuit breakers are on the fuse panel.

Relays are used throughout the system in various locations. When replacing a protective electrical relay, be very sure to install the same type of relay. Verify that the schematic imprinted on the original and replacement relays are identical. Relay part numbers may change. Do not rely on them for identification. Instead, use the schematic imprinted on the relay for positive identification.

On vehicles built before October 9, 1991, a relay bank is located on the left side of the engine compartment. On vehicles built on or after October 9, 1991, the Power Distribution Center is used in the same location and is equipped with additional fuses. Additional relay locations are as follows:

The turn signal flasher is located behind the left side of the instrument panel. The hazard flasher is located behind the left side of the instrument panel.

Drive Train

7

MANUAL TRANSAXLE

Identification

The Transaxle Identification Number is stamped on a boss located on the upper part of the transaxle housing. Every transaxle also carries an assembly part number, which is also required for parts ordering purposes. On the A-412 manual transaxle, it is located on the top of the housing, between the timing window and the differential.

On the manual transaxles except the A-520 and A-555, this number is located on a metal tag attached to the front of the transaxle. On the A-520 and A-555, the tag is attached to the top of the unit.

NOTE: *The transaxle model, assembly number, build date and final drive ratio are stamped on a tag that is attached to the top of the transaxle. Certain transaxle assemblies utilize high-strength steel in various gears to provide adequate life in heavy duty applications. The correct transaxle assembly number must be used when ordering service parts.*

Adjustments

NOTE: *Identify the correct manual transaxle model for your vehicle before starting this procedure.*

SHIFTER

Model A-412

1. Place the transmission in neutral at the 3-4 position.
2. Loosen the shift tube clamp.
3. Place a 16mm spacer between the slider and blocker bracket.
4. Tighten the shift tube clamp and remove the spacer.

Model A-460, 465, 525 with Shift Rod

1. From the left side of the car, remove the lockpin from the transaxle selector shaft housing.
2. Reverse the lockpin and insert it in the same threaded hole while pushing the selector shaft into the selector housing. A hole in the selector shaft will align with the lockpin, allowing the lockpin to be screwed into the housing. This will lock the selector shaft in the 1-2 neutral position.
3. Raise and support the vehicle on jackstands.
4. Loosen the clamp bolt that secures the gearshift tube to the gearshift connector.
5. Make sure that the gearshift connector slides and turns freely in the gearshift tube.
6. Position the shifter mechanism connector assembly so that the isolator is contacting the standing flange and the rib on the isolator is aligned front and back with the hole in the block-out bracket. Hold the connector in this position while tightening the clamp bolt on the gearshift tube to 14 ft. lb.
7. Lower the car.
8. Remove the lockpin from the selector shaft housing and install it the original way in the housing.
9. Tighten the lockpin to 105 inch lbs.
10. Check the shifter action.

Model A-525, A-555 with Shift Cable

NOTE: *To adjust the shift cable, two 140mm lengths of rod (except Daytona and K-body LeBarons) and an inch-pound torque wrench are required. The rod stock should be 5mm diameter for Aries, Reliant, LeBaron, Town & Country, Sundance and Shadow; for Lancer and LeBaron GTS, it should be 4mm.*

1. Work over the left front fender and remove the lockpin from the transaxle selector shaft housing.

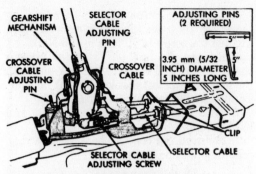

Make 2 cable adjusting pins (H-body)

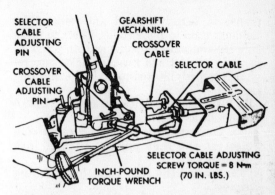

Adjusting the selector cable with the 2 adjusting pins installed

2. Turn the lockpin so the long end faces downward. Gently attempt to insert it into the same threaded hole while you gradually push the selector shaft into the selector housing. When the pin fits into the selector shaft, stop sliding the shaft into the housing and screw the pin into the housing. If done correctly, this will lock the selector shaft into the Neutral fore and aft position and into the 1-2 shift plane. Make sure that these conditions are met.

3. Unscrew and remove the gearshift knob. Then coat the shift shaft with a soap and water solution and pull the shift boot up and over the pull-up ring.

4. Remove the console as follows:

  a. Remove its two attaching screws and remove the forward console bezel.

  b. Remove the two attaching screws from the inside of the console storage area. Remove the two attaching screws from underneath the forward section of the console.

  c. Disconnect all the console electrical connectors.

  d. Remove the console.

5. The selector (fore and aft) and crossover (side-to-side) shift cables, located on either side of the shifter, each have slotted slides. A bolt locks the position of the slide to the gear lever mechanism. Loosen *both* bolts enough so that the slides can move freely.

6. On all but Daytonas and K-body LeBarons, bend the end of each of the two lengths of rod so the longer portion is just 127mm long. On Daytonas and K-Body LeBarons, pull the adjusting screw tool off the shifter support bracket (it's taped there).

7. On all but Daytonas and K-body LeBarons, move the gearshift in the fore and aft plane while attempting to insert the rod into the side of the shifter support bracket until it locks the gearshift in place. Repeat the operation in the side-to-side plane, attempting to insert the other rod into the rear of the shifter support bracket. On Daytonas and K-Body LeBarons, pass the bolt portion of the adjusting screw tool through the spacer block and then insert the tool through the shifter support bracket. Move the gearshift until you can turn the bolt and thread it into the shifter, locking in place. Torque the bolt to 20 inch lbs.

8. Once the shifter is properly locked in place, torque both the lockbolts for the shift cable slides to 70 inch lbs. Then, remove the fabricated rod pins or the adjusting screw tool. Unscrew the adjusting screw tool and tape it back where it was.

9. Unscrew and remove the lock pin from the

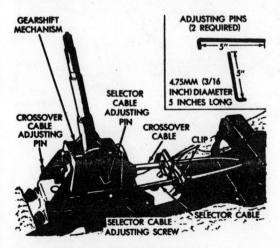

Make 2 cable adjusting pins (K, P-body)

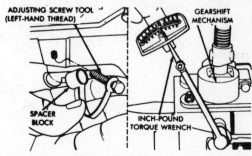

Adjusting the selector cable with the adjusting screw tool installed

transaxle, turn it around, and reinstall it, torquing again to 105 inch lbs. Check to make sure the transmission shifts smoothly and effectively into 1st and reverse. Make sure reverse is properly blocked out until the shift ring is raised.

10. Install the gearshift knob and boot. Install the console as follows:

a. Connect all the matching electrical connectors and then put the console into position.

b. Install the four console attaching screws.

c. Install the forward console bezel and its attaching screws.

Model A-523, A-543 and A-568 with Shift Cable

1. Working over the left front fender, remove the lock pin from the transaxle selector shaft housing.

2. Reverse the lock pin so the long end is down and insert it into the same threaded hole while pushing the selector shaft into the selector housing. A hole in the selector shaft will align with the lock pin, allowing the lock pin to be screwed into the housing. This operation locks the selector shaft in the neutral position between 3rd and 4th gears.

3. Remove the gearshift knob, the retaining nut and the pull-up ring from the gearshift lever.

4. If necessary, remove the shift lever boot and console to expose the gearshift linkage. The selector cable is not adjustable.

5. Loosen the crossover cable adjusting screw and allow the cable to move in the slot. Tighten the screw to 70 inch lbs. (8 Nm).

6. Remove the lock pin from the selector shaft housing and reinstall the lock pin, with the long end up, in the selector shaft housing. Torque the lock pin to 10 ft. lbs. (12 Nm).

7. Check the first/reverse shifting and blockout into reverse.

8. Reinstall the console, boot, pull-up ring, retaining nut and knob.

Dodge Stealth And 1990–92 Laser

SELECT CABLE

NOTE: *Refer to "Select Cable Adjustment Procedure" illustration as necessary.*

1. Move the transaxle shift lever to the **N** position. The select lever will be set to the neutral position when the transaxle shift lever is moved to the neutral position.

2. Move lever B to the neutral position.

3. Adjust, by using the adjuster, so that the end of the select cable is positioned in the correct postion relative to lever B.

4. The flange side of the resin bushing at the select cable end should be at the lever B end surface.

SHIFT CABLE

NOTE: *Refer to "Shift Cable Adjustment Procedure" illustration as necessary.*

1. On the transaxle, put select lever in **N** and move the transaxle shift lever to put it in **4th** gear. Depress the clutch, if necessary, to shift.

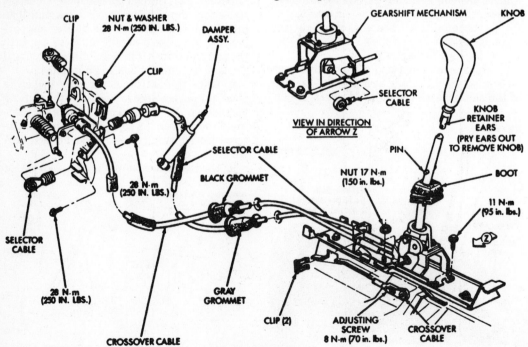

Gearshift mechanism

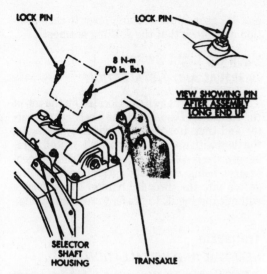

Manual transaxle pinned in the (N) neutral position to adjust gearshift

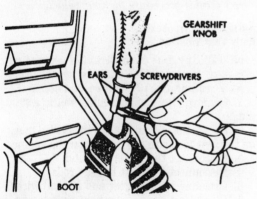

Remove gearshift knob

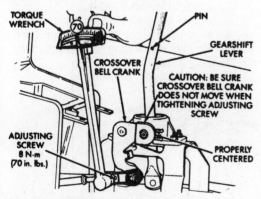

Adjusting crossover cable

the flange side of the plastic bushing at the shift cable end is on the cotter pin side.

4. The cables should be adjusted so the clearance between the shift lever and the 2 stoppers are equal when the shift lever is moved to 3rd

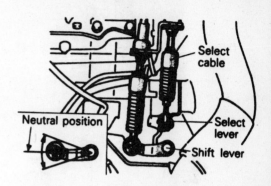

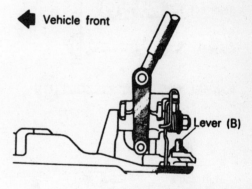

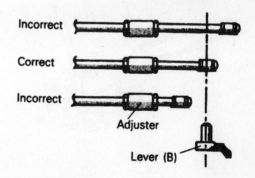

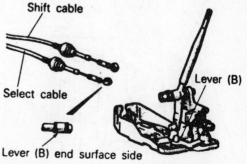

Lever (B) end surface side

Select cable adjustment procedure—1990–92 Laser and Stealth

2. Move the shift lever in the vehicle to the 4th gear position until it contacts the stop.

3. Turn the adjuster turn buckle so the shift cable eye aligns with the eye in the gear shift lever. When installing the cable eye, make sure

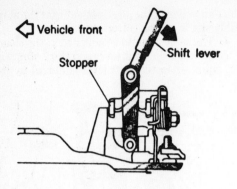

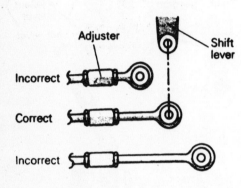

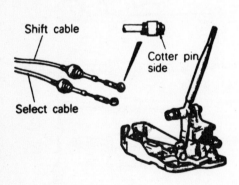

and 4th gear. Move the shift lever to each position and check that the shifting is smooth.

Back-Up Light Switch
REMOVAL AND INSTALLATION

The back-up light switch is located on the top of the transaxle. Disconnect the electrical connector and then unscrew the switch by engaging the flats with an open-end wrench. Install in reverse order (replace the gasket or O-ring as necessary) being especially careful to start the switch into the threaded bore of the transaxle without forcing it, to prevent cross-threading.

Transaxle
REMOVAL AND INSTALLATION

NOTE: *Identify the correct manual transaxle model, year coverage or vehicle model before starting this procedure. Refer to the correct service procedure for your vehicle.*

A-412 Model Transaxle
Early Year Vehicles

NOTE: *Any time the differential cover is removed, a new gasket must be formed from RTV sealant. See illustration in Chapter 1.*

1. Remove the engine timing mark access plug.
2. Rotate the engine to align the drilled mark on the flywheel with the pointer on the engine.
3. Disconnect the battery ground.
4. Disconnect the shift linkage rods.
5. Disconnect the starter and ground wires.
6. Disconnect the backup light switch wire.
7. Remove the starter.
8. Disconnect the clutch cable.
9. Disconnect the speedometer cable.
10. Support the weight of the engine from above, preferably with a shop hoist or the fabricated holding fixture.
11. Raise and support the vehicle.

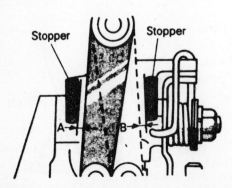

Shift cable adjustment procedure—1990–92 Laser and Stealth

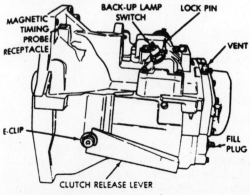

Location of the back-up lamp switch

12. Disconnect the driveshafts and support them out of the way.

13. Remove the left splash shield.

14. Drain the transaxle.

15. Unbolt the left engine mount.

16. Remove the transaxle-to-engine bolts.

17. Slide the transaxle to the left until the mainshaft clears, then, carefully lower it from the car.

To install:

18. To install the transaxle, position it so the mainshaft will slide straight into the center of the clutch. Turn the transaxle slightly, if necessary, and change the angle until the mainshaft engages, and then slide the transaxle to the right until the bell housing boltholes line up with the corresponding bores in the block.

19. Install the transaxle-to-engine bolts. Reinstall the through bolt for the left engine mount.

20. Install the left side splash shield.

21. Install the driveshafts back into the transaxle (see "Halfshafts Removal and Installation" below).

22. Lower the vehicle to the ground. Remove the engine support system.

23. Reconnect the speedometer and clutch cables.

24. Install the starter. Connect the backup light switch wire.

25. Reconnect the shift rods. Reconnect the battery. Install the engine timing mark access plug.

26. Adjust the clutch cable and the shift linkage.

27. Fill the transaxle with the recommended fluid (See Chapter 1).

1981–88 Model Years

1. Disconnect the battery.

2. Install a shop crane or equivalent and lifting eye under the #4 cylinder exhaust manifold bolt to securely support the engine. Position a suitable transmission jack under the transaxle assembly to securely support the transaxle.

3. Disconnect the shift linkage.

4. Remove both front wheel and tire assemblies.

5. Remove the left front splash shield, and left engine mount from the transaxle.

6. Follow the procedures under "'Halfshaft Removal and Installation" in this chapter. Remove both halfshafts.

7. On 1987 and later models, disconnect the anti-rotation link or damper *at the crossmember*, leaving it connected at the transaxle.

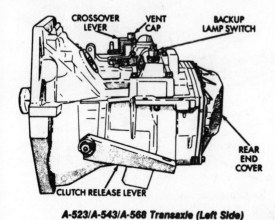

A-523/A-543/A-568 Transaxle (Left Side)

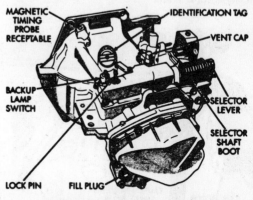

A-523/A-543/A-568 Transaxle Identification

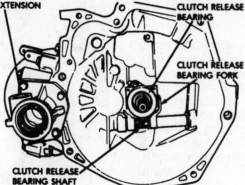

Transaxle assembly—late model Chrysler FWD

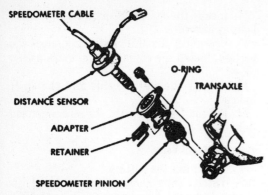

Speedometer drive

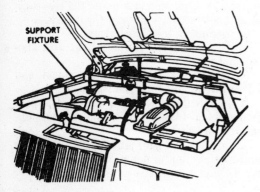

Engine support fixture

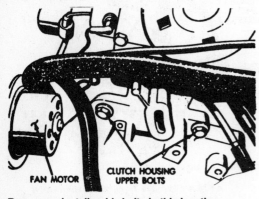

Remove or install guide bolts in this location

8. Remove all necessary components, wiring and or cables to gain removal and installation access clearance to the transaxle assembly.

9. Remove all transaxle retaining bolts. Slowly, slide the transaxle directly away from the engine so the input shaft will slide smoothly out of the clutch release bearing and clutch/ pressure plate assembly. Lower the transaxle (transaxle assembly must be properly supported with transmission jack) from the engine compartment.

NOTE: *It will be easier upon installation to*

locate the transaxle, so as to align the bell housing boltholes with those in the block, if two locating pins are fabricated and are used in place of the top two locating bolts. To fabricate the pins: Buy two extra bolts. Hacksaw the heads off the bolts. Then, cut slots in the ends of the bolts for a flat-bladed screwdriver. Finally, remove all burrs with a grinding wheel. Before installing the transaxle onto the engine block, install the two locating pins into the top two engine block holes.

To install:

10. Support the transaxle unit securely and raise it into precise alignment with the engine block. Then, move it toward the engine block, inserting the transmission input shaft (grease input shaft lightly) into the release bearing and clutch/pressure plate assembly onto the transaxle mounting guide pins.

11. Complete the remaining part of installation by reversal of the removal procedures.

12. Make all necessary adjustments and fill the transaxle if necessary with the specific fluid to the correct level. Roadtest the vehicle for proper operation.

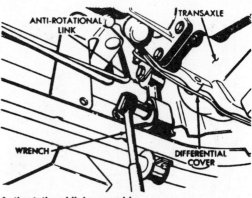

Anti-rotational link assembly

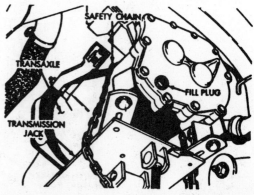

Positioning transmission jack in the correct manner

**1989–92 Model Years
Except 1990–92 Laser And Stealth**

NOTE: *If the vehicle is going to be rolled while the transaxle is out of the vehicle, obtain 2 outer CV-joints to install to the hubs. If the vehicle is rolled without the proper torque applied to the front wheel bearings, the bearings will no longer be usable.*

Different transaxles are used according to application. It is important to use the round identification tag screwed to the top of the case when obtaining parts for exact parts matching. The tag should be reinstalled for future reference.

1. Disconnect the negative battery cable.
2. Remove the air cleaner assembly with all ducts. Remove the upper bellhousing bolts. Disconnect the reverse light switch and the ground wire.
3. Remove the starter attaching nut and bolt at the top of the bellhousing.
4. Raise the vehicle and support safely. Remove the tire and wheel assemblies. Remove the axle end cotter pins, nut locks, spring washers and axle nuts.
5. Remove the ball joint retaining bolts and pry the control arm from the steering knuckle. Position a drainpan under the transaxle where the axles enter the differential or extension housing. Remove the axles from the transaxle or center bearing. Unbolt the center bearing and remove the intermediate axle from the transaxle, if equipped.
6. Remove the anti-rotation link from the crossmember. Disconnect the shifter cables from the transaxle and unbolt the cable bracket.
7. Remove the speedometer gear adaptor bolt and remove the adaptor from the transaxle.
8. Remove the rear mount from the starter, unbolt the starter and position it aside.
9. Using the proper equipment, support the weight of the engine.
10. Remove the front motor mount and bracket.
11. Position a suitable transaxle jack under the transaxle.
12. Remove the lower bellhousing bolts.
13. Remove the left side splash shield. Remove the transaxle mount bolts.
14. Carefully pry the transaxle from the engine.
15. Slide the transaxle rearward until the input shaft clears the clutch disc.
16. Pull the transaxle completely away from the clutch housing and remove it from the vehicle.
17. To prepare the vehicle for rolling, support

the engine with a suitable support or reinstall the front motor mount to the engine. Then reinstall the ball joints to the steering knuckle and install the retaining bolt. Install the obtained outer CV-joints to the hubs, install the washers and torque the axle nuts to 180 ft. lbs. (244 Nm). The vehicle may now be safely rolled.

To install:

18. Lubricate the pilot bushing and input shaft splines very lightly with high temperature lubricant.
19. Mount the transaxle securely on a suitable jack. Lift it in place until the input shaft is centered in the clutch housing opening. Roll the transaxle forward until the input shaft splines fully engage with the clutch disc and install the transaxle to clutch housing bolts.
20. Raise the transaxle and install the left side mount bolts.
21. Install the front motor mount and bracket.
22. Remove the engine and transaxle support fixtures.
23. Install the starter to the transaxle and install the lower bolt finger-tight.
24. Install a new O-ring to the speedometer cable adaptor and install to the extension housing; make sure it snaps in place. Install the retaining bolt.
25. Install the shift cable bracket and snap the cable ends in place. Install the anti-rotation link.
26. Install the axles and center bearing, if equipped. Install the ball joints to the steering knuckles. Torque the axle nuts to 180 ft. lbs. (244 Nm) and install new cotter pins. Fill the transaxle with SAE 5W-30 engine oil until the level is even with the bottom of the filler hole. Install the splash shield and install the wheels. Lower the vehicle.
27. Install the upper bellhousing bolts.
28. Install the starter attaching nut and bolt at the top of the bellhousing. Raise the vehicle and tighten the starter bolt from under the vehicle. Lower the vehicle.
29. Connect the reverse light switch and the ground wire.
30. Install the air cleaner assembly.
31. Connect the negative battery cable and check the transaxle for proper operation. Make sure the reverse lights are on when in Reverse.

1990–92 Laser

NOTE: *If the vehicle is going to be rolled while the halfshafts are out of the vehicle, obtain 2 outer CV-joints or proper equivalent tools and install to the hubs. If the vehicle is rolled without the proper torque applied to the front wheel bearings, the bearings will no longer be usable.*

1. Remove the battery.

2. Remove the auto-cruise actuator and bracket underhood, on the passenger side inner fender wall.

3. Drain the transaxle and transfer case.

4. Remove the air intake hose.

5. Remove the cotter pin securing the select and shift cables and remove the cable ends from the transaxle.

6. Remove the connection for the clutch release cylinder and without disconnecting the hydraulic line, secure aside.

7. Disconnect the backup light switch and the speedometer cable.

8. Disconnect the starter electrical connections and remove the starter motor.

9. Remove the transaxle mount bracket.

10. Raise the vehicle and support safely. Remove the undercover.

11. Remove the cotter pin and disconnect the tie rod end from the steering knuckle.

12. Remove the self-locking nut and remove the lower arm ball joint.

13. Remove the halfshafts by inserting a prybar between the transaxle case and the driveshaft and prying the shaft from the transaxle. Do not pull on the driveshaft. Doing so damages the inboard joint. Use the prybar. Do not insert the prybar so far that the oil seal in the case is damaged. On AWD, remove the right side shaft as just described. The left side shaft can be removed by tapping with a plastic hammer. Remove the shaft with the hub and knuckle as an assembly. Don't tap on the center bearing or it will be damaged. Tie the shafts aside. Note the circle clip on the end of the inboard shafts. These should not be reused.

14. On AWD vehicle, disconnect the front exhaust pipe.

15. On AWD vehicle, remove the transfer case by removing the attaching bolts, moving the transfer case to the left and lowering the front side. Remove it from the rear driveshaft. Be careful of the oil seal. Do not allow the prop shaft to hang; tie it up. Cover the transfer case openings to keep out dirt.

16. Remove the underpan from the transaxle bellhousing. On AWD, also remove the crossmember and the triangular gusset.

17. Remove the transaxle lower coupling bolt. It is just above the halfshaft opening on 2WD or transfer case opening on AWD.

18. Remove the transaxle assembly. On turbocharged vehicle, take care to prevent damaging the lower radiator hose with the transaxle housing. Wind tape around the lower hose and put tape on the transaxle housing. Support the transaxle assembly using the proper jack, move the transaxle to the right and lower it.

To install:

19. Install the transaxle to the engine and install the mounting bolts.

20. Install the transaxle lower coupling bolt.

21. Install the underpan, crossmember and the triangular gusset.

22. Install the transfer case on AWD vehicles and connect the exhaust pipe.

23. When installing the halfshafts, use new circlips on the axle ends. Take care to get the inboard joint parts straight, not bent relative to the axle. Care must be taken to ensure that the oil seal lip of the transaxle is not damaged by the serrated part of the driveshaft.

24. Connect the tie rod and ball joint to the steering knuckle.

25. Install the transaxle mount bracket.

26. Install the starter motor.

27. Connect the backup light switch and the speedometer cable.

28. Install the clutch release cylinder.

29. Connect the select and shift cables and install new cotter pins.

30. Install the air intake hose.

31. Install the auto-cruise actuator and bracket underhood, on the passenger side inner fender wall.

32. Install the battery.

33. Make sure the vehicle is level when refilling the transaxle. Use Hypoid gear oil or equivalent, GL-4 or higher.

34. Connect the negative battery cable and check the transaxle and transfer case for proper operation. Make sure the reverse lights come on when in reverse.

Dodge Stealth

NOTE: *If the vehicle is going to be rolled while the halfshafts are out of the vehicle, obtain 2 outer CV-joints or proper equivalent tools and install to the hubs. If the vehicle is rolled without the proper torque applied to the front wheel bearings, the bearings will no longer be usable.*

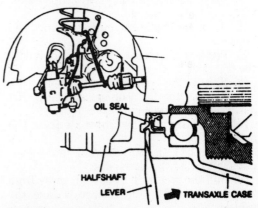

Pry halfshaft from the transaxle case as shown and tie back out of the way

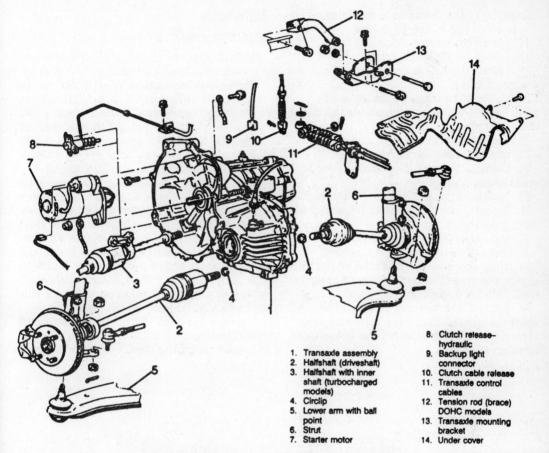

1. Transaxle assembly
2. Halfshaft (driveshaft)
3. Halfshaft with inner shaft (turbocharged models)
4. Circlip
5. Lower arm with ball point
6. Strut
7. Starter motor
8. Clutch release– hydraulic
9. Backup light connector
10. Clutch cable release
11. Transaxle control cables
12. Tension rod (brace) DOHC models
13. Transaxle mounting bracket
14. Under cover

Manual transaxle layout—1990–92 Laser and Stealth

1. Remove the battery and battery tray. Raise the vehicle and support safely. Drain the transaxle oil and remove the transfer case if equipped.

2. Remove the left side splash shield.

3. Remove the air cleaner assembly and all adjoining duct work.

4. Disconnect the shifter control cables and speedometer connector.

5. Remove the clutch release cylinder.

6. Disconnect the reverse light switch.

7. Support the weight of the transaxle and remove the transaxle mount through bolt. Remove the access plug, remove the bolts for the bracket and remove the brackets.

8. Disconnect the transaxle ground cable.

9. Disconnect the tie rod end and ball joint from the steering knuckle.

10. Remove the right frame member.

11. Remove the starter motor.

12. Remove the halfshafts by inserting a prybar between the transaxle case and the driveshaft and prying the shaft from the transaxle. Do not pull on the driveshaft. Doing so damages the inboard joint. Use the prybar. Do

not insert the prybar so far that the oil seal in the case is damaged. On AWD, remove the right side shaft as just described. The left side shaft can be removed by tapping with a plastic hammer. Remove the shaft with the hub and knuckle as an assembly. Don't tap on the center bearing or it will be damaged. Tie the shafts aside. Note the circle clip on the end of the inboard shafts. These should not be reused.

13. Remove the transaxle brackets.

14. Remove the transaxle assembly. On turbocharged vehicles, take care to prevent damaging the lower radiator hose with the transaxle housing. Wind tape around the lower hose and put tape on the transaxle housing. Support the transaxle assembly using the proper jack, move the transaxle away from the engine and lower it.

To install:

15. Install the transaxle to the engine and install the mounting bolts.

16. When installing the halfshafts, use new circlips on the axle ends. Take care to get the inboard joint parts straight, not bent relative to the axle. Care must be taken to ensure that the

oil seal lip of the transaxle is not damaged by the serrated part of the driveshaft.

17. Install the starter motor and cover.

18. Install the right side frame member.

19. Install the ball joint and tie rod to the steering knuckle.

20. Connect the transaxle ground cable.

21. Install the side mount brackets and install the access plug.

22. Connect the reverse light switch.

23. Install the clutch release cylinder.

24. Connect the shifter control cables and speedometer connector.

25. Install the transfer case on AWD vehicles.

26. Install the air cleaner assembly and all adjoining duct work.

27. Install the left side splash shield.

28. Install the battery tray and battery.

29. Make sure the vehicle is level when refilling the transaxle. Use Hypoid gear oil or equivalent, GL-4 or higher.

30. Connect the negative battery cable and check the transaxle and transfer case for proper operation. Make sure the reverse lamps come on when in reverse.

Halfshafts

IDENTIFICATION

NOTE: *Refer to the necessary illustrations on later model vehicles to identify each driveshaft (halfshaft) assembly. Vehicles can be equipped with any of these driveshafts (halfshaft) assemblies. Chrysler front wheel drive vehicles use two different driveshaft systems. Some vehicles use an equal length system while other vehicles use an unequal length system (refer to the illustration).*

The driveshaft assemblies are three-piece units. Each driveshaft has an inner sliding constant velocity (Tripod) joint and an outer constant velocity (Rzeppa) joint with a stub shaft splined into the hub. On 2.2 L engines with turbocharging, the shafts are of equal length and both are short and of solid construction. With this setup, there is a short, intermediate shaft with a bearing and bracket on the outer side and a Cardan (U-joint) on the inner side.

On vehicles with the normally aspirated (non-turbocharged) 2.2 and 2.5 L engines, the connecting shafts for the CV-joints are unequal

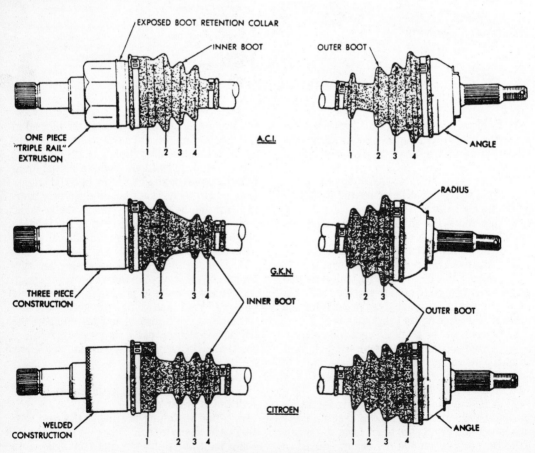

Halfshaft identification for 1981–85 models

in length and construction. The left side is a short solid shaft and the right is longer and tubular.

It is impossible to classify driveshaft type according to model and year designations. However, each type of shaft is clearly identifiable according to the design features pointed out on the enclosed illustrations. Use these to classify the joint according to brand and type so that if parts are to be replaced, you can order by manufacturer name as well as the year and model of the car.

REMOVAL AND INSTALLATION

1981–85 A-412 Manual Transaxle

1. With the vehicle on the floor and the brakes applied, loosen the hub nut.

NOTE: *The hub and driveshaft are splined together and retained by the hub nut which is torqued to at least 180 ft.lbs.*

2. Raise and support the vehicle and remove the hub nut and washer.

NOTE: *Always support both ends of the driveshaft during removal.*

3. Disconnect the lower control arm ball joint stud nut from the steering knuckle.

4. Remove the six 1.6mm Allen head screws which secure the CV-joint to the transmission flange.

5. Holding the CV-joint housing, push the outer joint and knuckle assembly outward while disengaging the inner housing from the flange face. Quickly turn the open end of the joint upward to retain as much lubricant as pos-

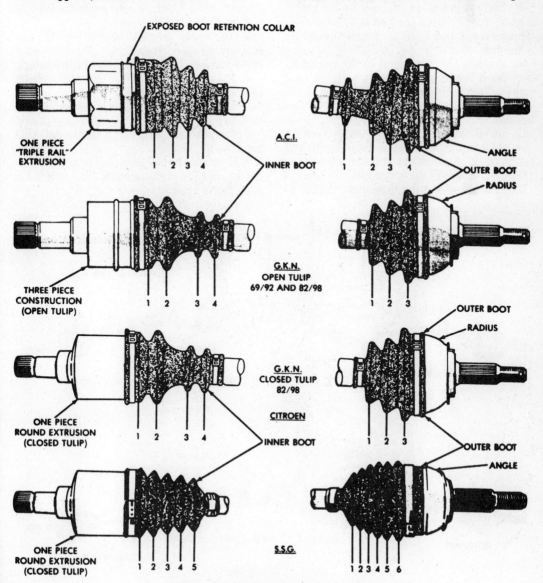

Halfshaft identification for 1986–90 models

sible, then carefully pull the outer joint spline out of the hub. Cover the joint with a clean towel to prevent dirt contamination.

NOTE: *The outer joint and shaft must be supported during disengagement of the inner joint.*

6. Before installation, make sure that any lost lubricant is replaced. The only lubricant specified is Chrysler part number 4131389. No other lubricant of any type is to be used, as premature failure of the joint will result.

To install:

7. Clean the joint body and mating flange face.

8. Install the outer joint splined shaft into the hub. Do not secure with the nut and washer.

9. Early production vehicles were built with a cover plate between the hub and flange face. This cover is not necessary and should be discarded.

10. Position the inner joint in the transmission drive flange and secure it with six new screws. Torque the screws to 37-40 ft.lb.

11. Connect the lower control arm to the knuckle.

12. Install the outer joint and secure it with a new nut and washer. Torque the nut with the car on the ground and the brake set. Torque is 180 ft.lbs. Reinstall the cotter pin.

13. After attaching the driveshaft, if the in-

board boot appears to be collapsed or deformed, vent the inner boot by inserting a round-tipped, small diameter rod between the boot and the shaft. As venting occurs, boot will return to its original shape.

1981–83 A460, 465, 525 Manual Transaxle and Automatic Transaxle

The inboard CV-joints are retained by circlips in the differential side gears. The circlip tangs are located on a machined surface on the inner end of the stub shaft.

1. With the car on the ground, loosen the hub nut.

2. Drain the transaxle differential and remove the cover.

NOTE: *Any time the transaxle differential cover is removed, a new gasket should be formed from RTV sealant.*

3. To remove the right hand driveshaft, disconnect the speedometer cable and remove the cable and gear before removing the driveshaft.

4. Rotate the driveshaft to expose the circlip tangs.

5. Compress the circlip with needle nose pliers and push the shaft into the side gear cavity.

6. Remove the clamp bolt from the ball stud and steering knuckle.

7. Separate the ball joint stud from the steering knuckle, by prying against the knuckle leg and control arm.

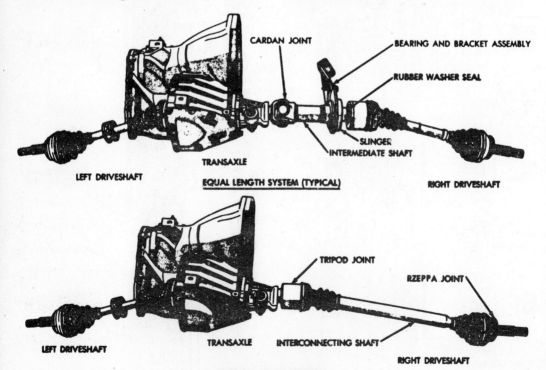

Front wheel drive halfshaft systems

8. Separate the outer CV-joint splined shaft from the hub by holding the CV-joint housing and moving the hub away. Do not pry on the slinger or outer CV-joint.

9. Support the shaft at the CV-joints and remove the shaft. Do not pull on the shaft.

NOTE: *Removal of the left shaft may be made easier by inserting the blade of a thin prybar between the differential pinion shaft* *and prying against the end face of the shaft.*

To install:

10. Support the shaft at the CV-joints and position the shaft for reinstallation. Hold the inner joint assembly at the housing. Align the splined joint with the splines in the differential side gear, and guide it into the housing. Be sure the circlip tangs are positioned against the flattened end of the shaft before installing the

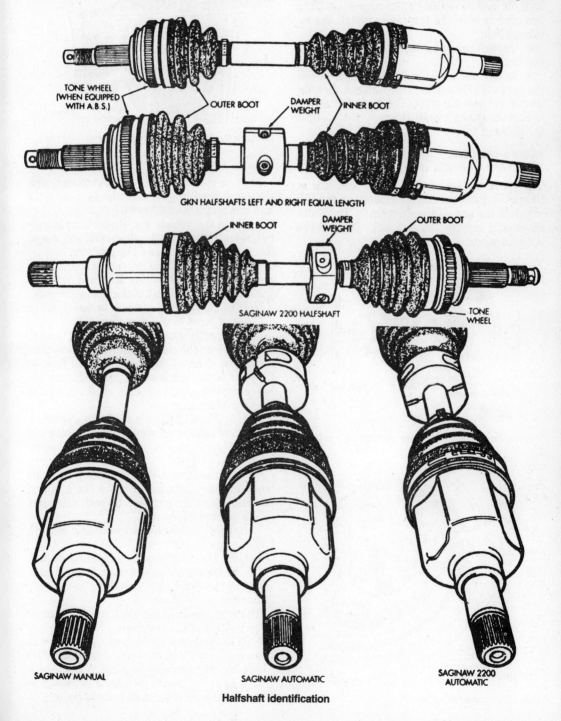

Halfshaft identification

shaft. A quick thrust will lock the circlip in the groove.

11. Push the hub and knuckle assembly outward and insert the outer splined CV-joint shaft into the hub. Then, insert the ball joint stud into the knuckle assembly. Install the clamp bolt and nut and torque to 70 ft. lbs.

12. If it has been removed, insert the speedometer pinion back into the transaxle with the bolthole in the retaining collar aligned with the threaded hole in the transaxle. Install the retaining bolt.

13. Install the specified lubricant into the transaxle.

14. Install the wheel and wheel nuts. Lower the car to the floor. Clean the hub nut threads, located at the outer end of the shaft. Install the washer and then install the nub nut. Torque the hub nut to 180 ft. lbs.

All 1984–88 Models
Manual And Automatic Transaxles

1. Drain the transaxle fluid as described in Chapter 1. Bend the cotter pin straight and pull it out of the end of the driveshaft. Then, unscrew and remove the nut lock. Remove the spring washer.

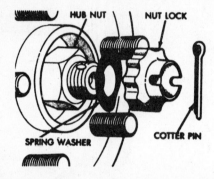

Remove the cotter pin, nut lock and spring washer

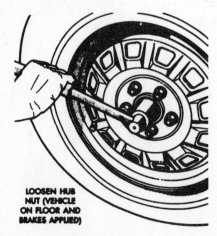

Loosen hub nut in this manner

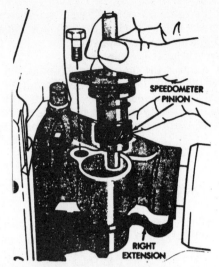

Remove the speedometer pinion clamp

2. Have someone apply the brakes and, with the car still resting on the wheels, loosen the hub nut and the wheel nuts.

3. Raise the vehicle and support it securely by the body. Remove the wheel nuts and wheel. Remove the hub nut and the washer.

4. If removing the right side driveshaft, remove the single attaching bolt and pull the speedometer pinion out of the transaxle case.

NOTE: *Do not pry against the ball joint or CV-joint boots in the next step.*

5. Remove the nut and bolt clamping the ball joint stud into the steering knuckle. Then, carefully *so as to avoid damaging the ball joint or CV-joint boots*, use a small prybar to pry the lower control arm ball joint stud out of the steering knuckle.

NOTE: *Be careful not to pry against or otherwise use excessive force on the wear sleeve of the CV-joint as you perform the following step.*

6. Hold the outer CV-joint housing with one hand and use the other to move the hub and knuckle assembly outward to pull the outer joint shaft out of the hub.

7. Support the driveshaft assembly at both CV-joint housings.

NOTE: *The axle must be supported at both CV-joints during this operation to avoid pulling on the shaft. Any stretching forces may damage the U-joints!*

Then, pull on the inner joint housing in order to pull it out of the transaxle.

NOTE: *Note that the driveshaft, when in its normal, installed position, acts to keep the hub/bearing assembly in place. If the vehicle is to be supported by its wheels or moved on them while the driveshaft is out of the car, in-*

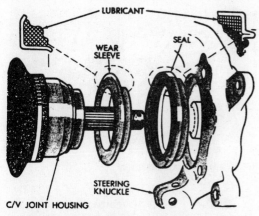

Lubricating the seal and wear sleeve on the outboard end of the halfshaft

stall a bolt through the hub to ensure the hub bearing assembly cannot loosen.

To install:

8. Thoroughly clean the seal located between the outer end of the driveshaft and the steering knuckle with a safe solvent. Make sure solvent does not get onto the driveshaft boot. Apply a bead of a lubricant such as Mopar Multipurpose Lubricant Part No. 4318063 or the equivalent. Apply it to the full circumference and make the bead ¼ in. (6mm) wide. Fill the lip-to-housing cavity on the seal around its complete circumference; wet the seal lip with the lubricant, as well.

9. To install the driveshaft assembly, first inspect units on turbocharged cars to make sure the rubber washer seal is in place on the right inner joint. Relocate the seal, if necessary.

10. Support the driveshaft by both CV-joints. Hold the inner joint assembly at the housing. Align the splined joint with the splines in the differential side gear, guide it into the housing, and insert it until it locks.

NOTE: *If installing an A.C.I. brand shaft, make sure the tripod joint engages in the housing and is not twisted.*

11. If necessary, remove the bolt installed through the hub earlier. Push the hub and knuckle assembly outward and insert the outer splined CV-joint shaft into the hub. Then, insert the ball joint stud into the knuckle assembly. Install the clamp bolt and nut and torque to 70 ft. lbs. *Note that, if replacing the the clamp bolt, it is a prevailing torque type and must be replaced with an equivalent part.*

12. If it has been removed, insert the speedometer pinion back into the transaxle with the bolthole in the retaining collar aligned with the threaded hole in the transaxle. Install the retaining bolt.

13. Install the specified lubricant into the transaxle.

14. Install the wheel and wheel nuts. Lower the car to the floor. Clean the hub nut threads, located at the outer end of the shaft. Install the washer and then install the nub nut. Torque the hub nut to 180 ft. lbs.

15. Install the lock finger tight. Then, back it off until the cotter pin slot aligns with the hole in the end of the driveshaft. Install the cotter pin until it is pulled all the way through. Bend the prongs tightly around the outer end of the nut lock. Make sure the prongs wrap tightly. Torque the wheel nuts to 95 ft. lbs.

16. If the boot on the transaxle end of the shaft is deformed (collapsed), it must be vented and restored to its normal shape. To do so, first remove and discard the clamp on the shaft side (if the shaft has one); then, insert a round, small diameter rod between the boot and the shaft to vent it; then, work the boot back into its normal shape, being careful to keep dirt from getting in or grease from getting out. When the boot has reached its normal shape, remove the rod and install a new service clamp.

All 1989–92 Models
Manual And Automatic Transaxles
Except 1990–92 Laser, Stealth And Dodge Monaco

1. Disconnect the negative battery cable.

2. Raise the vehicle and support safely. DO NOT ROLL VEHICLE WITH HALFSHAFTS REMOVED FROM THE VEHICLE.

3. Remove the tire and wheel assembly.

4. Remove the cotter pin from the end of the halfshaft. Remove the nut lock, spring washer, axle nut and washer.

5. Remove the ball joint retaining bolt and pry the control arm down to release the ball stud from the steering knuckle.

6. Position a drainpan under the transaxle where the halfshaft enters the differential or extension housing. Remove the halfshaft from

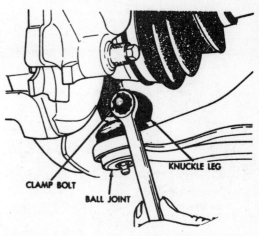

Remove the ball joint to steering knuckle clamp bolt

the transaxle or center bearing. Unbolt the center bearing from the block and remove the intermediate shaft from the transaxle, if equipped.

To install:

7. Install the halfshaft or intermediate shaft to the transaxle, being careful not to damage the side seals. Make sure the inner joint clicks into place inside the differential. Install the center bearing retaining bolts if equipped, then install the outer shaft to the center bearing.

Removing halfshaft assembly

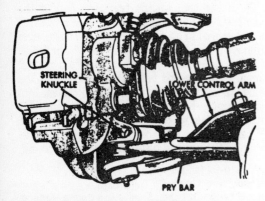

Separate ball joint from the steering knuckle

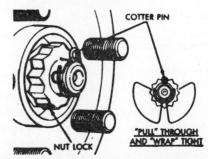

Install spring washer, nut lock and new cotter pin

8. Pull the front strut out and insert the outer joint into the front hub.

9. If necessary, turn the ball joint stud to position the bolt retaining indent to the inside of the vehicle. Install the ball joint stud into the steering knuckle. Install the retaining bolt and nut and torque to 70 ft. lbs. (95 Nm). THIS NUT AND BOLT COMBINATION IS UNIQUE TO THIS APPLICATION AND SHOULD NOT BE REPLACED WITH CONVENTIONAL HARDWARE! USE ORIGINAL EQUIPMENT PARTS IF REPLACING!

10. Install the axle nut washer and nut and torque the nut to 180 ft. lbs. (244 Nm). Install the spring washer, nut lock and a new cotter pin.

11. Install the tire and wheel assembly.

1990–92 Laser And Stealth

NOTE: *If the vehicle is going to be rolled while the halfshafts are out of the vehicle, obtain 2 outer CV-joints or proper equivalent tools and install to the hubs. If the vehicle is rolled without the proper torque applied to the front wheel bearings, the bearings will no longer be usable.*

1. Disconnect the negative battery cable.

2. Remove the cotter pin, halfshaft nut and washer. It is recommended that the halfshaft nut is removed while the vehicle is on the floor with the brakes applied.

3. Raise the vehicle and support safely. Re-

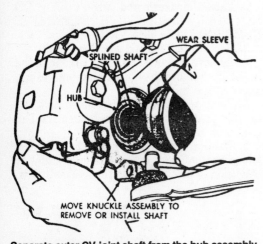

Separate outer CV-joint shaft from the hub assembly

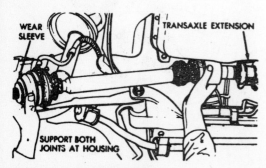

Removing halfshaft assembly

move the lower ball joint and the tie rod end from the steering knuckle.

4. On vehicles with an inner shaft, remove the center support bearing bracket bolts and washers.

5. On vehicles with an inner shaft, remove the halfshaft by setting up a puller on the outside wheel hub and pushing the halfshaft from the front hub. Then tap the joint case with a plastic hammer to remove the halfshaft shaft and inner shaft from the transaxle.

6. On vehicles without an inner shaft, remove the halfshaft by setting up a puller on the outside wheel hub and pushing the halfshaft from the front hub. After pressing the outer shaft, insert a prybar between the transaxle case and the halfshaft and pry the shaft from the transaxle. Do not pull on the shaft; doing so damages the inboard joint. Do not insert the prybar too far or the oil seal in the case may be damaged.

To install:

7. Inspect the halfshaft boot for damage or deterioration. Check the ball joints and splines for wear.

8. Replace the circlips on the ends of the halfshafts.

9. Insert the halfshaft into the transaxle. Make sure it is fully seated.

10. Pull the strut assembly out and install the other end to the hub.

11. Install the center bearing bracket bolts and tighten to 33 ft. lbs. (45 Nm).

12. Install the washer so the chamfered edge faces outward. Install the nut and tighten temporarily.

13. Install the tie rod end and ball joint.

14. Install the wheel and lower the vehicle to the floor. Tighten the axle nut with the brakes applied. Tighten the nut to a maximum torque of 188 ft. lbs. (260 Nm) maximum. Install the cotter pin and bend it securely.

Dodge Monaco

The halfshafts are comprised of an inner CV-joint, an interconnecting shaft and an outer Rzeppa CV-joint with a stub shaft. The inner tripod CV-joint can be disassembled but must be replaced as a unit. The outer Rzeppa joint CV-joint cannot be disassembled and must be replaced as a unit. The protective rubber boots and clamps that cover each CV-joint are replaceable components.

1. Disconnect the negative battery cable. Raise the vehicle and support safely.

2. Remove the wheels.

3. Remove the brake caliper but do not disconnect the brake hose from the caliper. Wire it aside. Do not allow the brake hose to support the weight of the caliper.

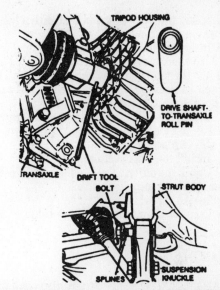

Remove the halfshaft by driving out the roll pin and remove joint from the knuckle

4. Remove the halfshaft hub nut. A holding fixture may be required to hold the wheel hub/rotor when removing the nut.

5. Spiral wound roll pin(s) are used to retain each halfshaft at the transaxle. Using a drift type tool, remove the halfshaft-to-transaxle roll pin(s).

NOTE: *Before proceeding to the next step, be certain the front suspension is hanging free. The strut body to suspension knuckle bolts are splined. Remove the bolts only as instructed in the following steps.*

6. Remove the 2 splined bolts that attach the strut body to the suspension knuckle. Do this by first loosening and turning the nuts (do not turn the bolt heads) until they are almost at the end of the bolt threads. Tap the nuts with a brass hammer to loosen the bolts and disengage the splines. Remove the nuts and slide the bolts out of the strut body and suspension knuckle.

7. Place a drain pan under the transaxle end of the halfshaft.

8. Wrap a shop towel around the halfshaft outer rubber boot to prevent damaging the boot.

9. Tilt the suspension knuckle out and away from the strut body and remove the halfshaft. If the halfshaft cannot be pushed through the hub by hand, use a puller.

To install:

10. Install the halfshaft to the transaxle shaft and align the roll pin holes in each shaft.

NOTE: *One side of the roll pin hole in the transaxle shaft is beveled. Align the beveled side of that hole with the side of the hole in the CV-joint housing that is located in the housing "valley."*

11. Insert the roll pin(s) and seat with a hammer and a drift type tool.

12. Insert the halfshaft end through the hub.

13. Tilt the knuckle back into position and install the bolts. Hold the bolt heads with a wrench to prevent them from turning and tighten the nuts to 123 ft. lbs. (167 Nm).

14. Install the halfshaft end nut and tighten to 181 ft. lbs. (245 Nm), while holding the rotor and hub in place.

15. Install the brake caliper.

16. Check the differential fluid level. Fill with recommended synthetic gear oil.

17. Install the wheels.

18. Connect the negative battery cable.

CLUTCH

CAUTION: *The clutch driven disc contains asbestos, which has been determined to be a cancer-causing agent. Never clean clutch surfaces with compressed air! Avoid inhaling any dust emitted from any clutch surface! When cleaning clutch surfaces, use a commercially available brake cleaning fluid.*

Adjustments

FREE PLAY

All Chrysler Front Wheel Drive Except 1990–92 Laser And Dodge Stealth

The clutch cable requires no adjustment (on all transaxle models except A-412) for clutch disc wear on the following: A-460, A-465, A-520, A-523, A-525, A-555, A-543 and A-568

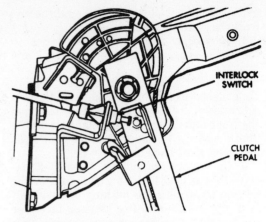

Starter interlock switch location

transaxles. Unless improperly installed, the spring in the clutch pedal holds the cable in the proper position.

A-412 Transaxle

1. Pull up on the clutch cable.

2. While holding the cable up, rotate the adjusting sleeve downward until a snug contact is made against the grommet.

3. Rotate the sleeve slightly to allow the end of the sleeve to seat in the rectangular hole in the grommet.

PEDAL HEIGHT/FREE-PLAY ADJUSTMENT

1990–92 Laser And Dodge Stealth

1. Measure the clutch pedal height (clutch pedal height adjustment-refer to illustration) from the face of the pedal pad to the firewall. If

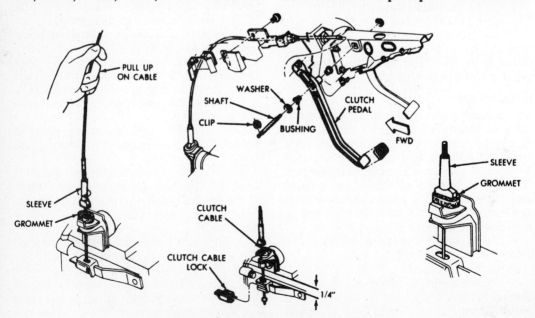

Adjusting clutch freeplay A-412 manual transaxle

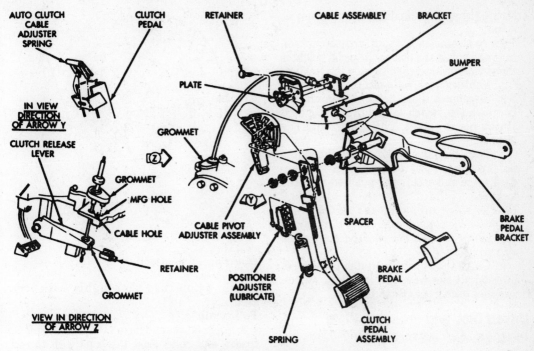

AUTO CLUTCH CABLE ADJUSTER SPRING

CLUTCH PEDAL

RETAINER

CABLE ASSEMBLEY

BRACKET

BUMPER

IN VIEW DIRECTION OF ARROW Y

PLATE

CLUTCH RELEASE LEVER

GROMMET

GROMMET

MFG HOLE

CABLE HOLE

CABLE PIVOT ADJUSTER ASSEMBLY

RETAINER

POSITIONER ADJUSTER (LUBRICATE)

SPACER

BRAKE PEDAL BRACKET

BRAKE PEDAL

GROMMET

VIEW IN DIRECTION OF ARROW Z

SPRING

CLUTCH PEDAL ASSEMBLY

Self-adjusting clutch release mechanism

the pedal height is not within 6.93–7.17 in (176–182mm) for Laser and Stealth, adjustment is necessary.

2. Measure the clutch pedal clevis pin play (clutch pedal free play adjustment-refer to illustration) at the face of the pedal pad. If the clutch pedal clevis pin play is not within 0.04–0.12 in. (1–3mm) for Laser or 0.24–0.51 in. (6–13mm) for Stealth, adjustment is necessary.

3. If the clutch pedal height or clevis pin play

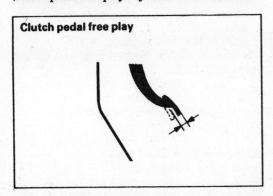

Clutch pedal free play

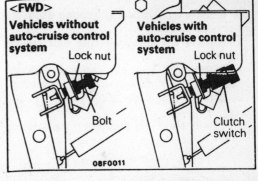

<FWD>

Vehicles without auto-cruise control system

Lock nut

Bolt

Vehicles with auto-cruise control system

Lock nut

Clutch switch

08F0011

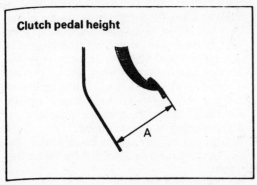

Clutch pedal height

A

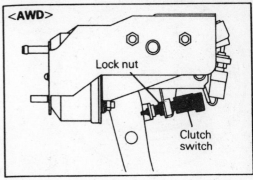

<AWD>

Lock nut

Clutch switch

Clutch pedal adjustments 1990–92 Laser and Stealth

are not within the standard value, adjust as follows:

a. For vehicles without cruise control, turn and adjust the bolt so the pedal height is the standard value, then tighten the locknut.

b. Vehicles with auto-cruise control system, disconnect the clutch switch connector and turn the switch to obtain the standard clutch pedal height. Then, lock with the locknut.

c. Turn the pushrod to adjust the clutch pedal clevis pin play to agree with the standard value and secure the pushrod with the locknut.

NOTE: *When adjusting the clutch pedal height or the clutch pedal clevis pin play, be careful not to push the pushrod toward the master cylinder.*

d. Check that when the clutch pedal is depressed all the way, the interlock switch switches over from **ON** to **OFF**.

Driven Disc and Pressure Plate

REMOVAL AND INSTALLATION

A-412 Transaxle

NOTE: *Chrysler recommends the use of special tool L-4533 for disc alignment.*

1. Remove the transaxle as described earlier in this chapter.
2. Loosen the flywheel-to-pressure plate bolts diagonally, one or two turns at a time to avoid warpage.
3. Remove the flywheel and clutch disc from the pressure plate.
4. Remove the retaining ring and release plate.
5. Diagonally loosen the pressure plate-to-crankshaft bolts. Mark all parts for reassembly.
6. Remove the bolts, spacer and pressure plate.
7. The flywheel and pressure plate surfaces

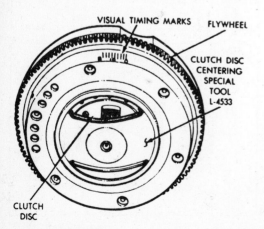

Centering clutch disc

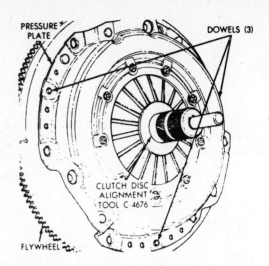

Clutch disc aligning tool

should be cleaned thoroughly with fine sandpaper.

To install:

8. Align marks and install the pressure plate, spacer, and bolts. Coat the bolts with thread compound and torque them to 55 ft. lbs.
9. Install the release plate and retaining ring.
10. Using special tool L-4533 or its equivalent, install the clutch disc and flywheel on the pressure plate.

NOTE: *Make certain that the drilled mark on the flywheel is at the top, so that the two dowels on the flywheel align with the proper holes in the pressure plate.*

11. Install the six flywheel bolts and tighten them to 15 ft. lbs.
12. Remove the aligning tool.
13. Install the transmission.
14. Adjust the freeplay as described above.

**All Chrysler Front Wheel Drive
A-460, A-465, A-520, A-523,
A-525, A-555, A-543 and A-568 Transaxles
Except 1990–92 Laser And Dodge Stealth**

NOTE: *Chrysler recommends the use of special tool #C-4676 for disc alignment. Clean the flywheel face with crocus cloth or fine sandpaper (400-600 grade), then wipe the surface with mineral spirits. If the flywheel surface is severely scored, heat cracked or warped replace the flywheel. Always replace the clutch assembly, pressure plate and release bearing as a matched set.*

1. Disconnect the negative battery cable. Remove the transaxle as described earlier in this chapter.
2. Matchmark the clutch cover and flywheel for installation in the same positions.

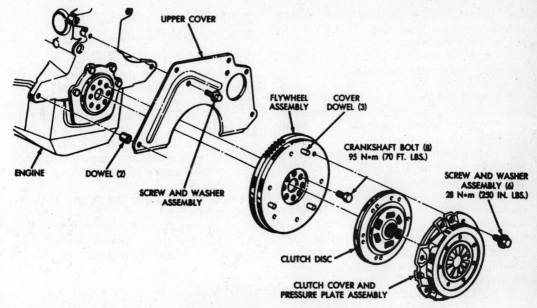

UPPER COVER

FLYWHEEL ASSEMBLY

COVER DOWEL (3)

CRANKSHAFT BOLT (8) 95 N•m (70 FT. LBS.)

ENGINE

DOWEL (2)

SCREW AND WASHER ASSEMBLY

SCREW AND WASHER ASSEMBLY (6) 28 N•m (250 IN. LBS.)

CLUTCH DISC

CLUTCH COVER AND PRESSURE PLATE ASSEMBLY

Manual transaxle clutch assembly

3. Insert special tool C-4676 or its equivalent to hold the clutch disc in place.

4. Loosen the cover attaching bolts. Do this procedure in a diagonal manner, a few turns at a time to prevent warping the cover.

5. Remove the cover assembly and disc from the flywheel. Be careful to keep any dirt or other contamination off the friction surfaces.

6. Remove the clutch release shaft and slide the release bearing off the input shaft seal retainer.

7. Remove the fork from the release bearing thrust plate.

To install:

8. Inspect the rear main seal for leakage. Repair the seal at this point, if there is leakage.

9. Make sure the friction surfaces of both the flywheel and the pressure plate are uniform in appearance. If there is evidence of heavy contact at one point and very light contact 180° away, the flywheel or pressure plate may be improperly mounted (torqued) or sprung due to mechanical damage. If there is evidence that the flywheel may not be true, it should be checked with a dial indicator or replaced (always replace the flywheel retaining bolts-with new bolts coated with Loctite sealant-torque to specifications). The indicator must be mounted so that its plunger is in contact with the flywheel wear circle. In a full turn, the indicator should read no more than 0.076mm. Make sure to push forward on the flywheel before you begin taking the reading and zeroing the indicator and press forward on it continuously as you turn to keep any crankshaft endplay out of the reading (refer to local machine shop if neces-

sary-the flywheel assembly can be machined if still in specifications).

10. With a straightedge, check the pressure plate for flatness. The inner surface of the pressure plate should be straight within 0.5mm. It should also be free of discoloration, cracks, grooves, or ridges. Otherwise, replace it.

11. Spin the clutch bearing to make sure it turns freely and smoothly.

12. Install the fork, release bearing, and clutch release shaft in the reverse order of the removal procedure.

13. Install the clutch assembly onto the flywheel, carefully aligning the dowels on the flywheel with the holes in the assembly. Make sure the alignment marks made earlier also align. Then, apply pressure to the clutch alignment tool to precisely center it as you snug the clutch attaching bolts sufficiently to hold the clutch disc in the proper position.

14. Tighten the clutch cover bolts alternately and evenly until they all are seated. Then, torque to 21 ft. lbs. Remove the disc alignment tool.

1990–92 Laser And Dodge Stealth

NOTE: *Always replace the clutch assembly, pressure plate and release bearing as a matched set.*

1. Disconnect the negative battery cable.

2. Remove the transaxle assembly from the vehicle.

3. Remove the pressure plate attaching bolts. If the pressure plate is to be reused, loosen the bolts in succession, 1 or 2 turns at a time to prevent warping the the cover flange.

4. Remove the pressure plate release bearing assembly and the clutch disc. Do not use solvent to clean the bearing.

5. Inspect the condition of the clutch components and replace any worn parts.

To install:

6. Inspect the flywheel for heat damage or cracks. Use new bolts and replace if necessary.

7. Using the proper alignment tool, install the clutch disc to the flywheel. Install the pressure plate assembly and tighten the pressure plate bolts evenly to 11–16 ft. lbs. (15–22 Nm). Remove the alignment tool.

8. Apply a very light coat of high temperature grease to the clutch fork at the ball pivot and where the fork contacts the bearing. Also a little bit of grease can be applied to end of the release cylinder's pushrod and to the pushrod hole on the fork. Apply a light coat of grease on the transaxle input shaft splines.

9. Install a new clutch release bearing. Pack its inner surface with grease.

10. Install the transaxle assembly and check for proper clutch operation.

Clutch Master Cylinder

REMOVAL AND INSTALLATION

1990–92 Laser And Dodge Stealth

1. Disconnect the negative battery cable.

2. Remove necessary underhood components in order to gain access to the clutch master cylinder.

3. Loosen the line at the cylinder and allow the fluid to drain. Use care; brake fluid damages paint.

4. On Laser and FWD Stealth, remove the cotter pin at the clutch pedal and remove the washer and clevis pin. AWD Stealth has a clutch pedal booster which directly activates the master cylinder.

5. Remove the 2 nuts and pull the cylinder from the firewall. A seal should be between the mounting flange and firewall. This seal should be replaced.

6. The installation is the reverse of the removal procedure.

6. Lubricate all pivot points with grease.

7. Bleed the system (refer to service procedure below) at the slave cylinder using DOT 3 brake fluid.

OVERHAUL

Refer to the exploded view illustration as guide for this repair. If overhaul is in doubt replace the complete assembly.

Clutch Slave/Release Cylinder

REMOVAL AND INSTALLATION

1990–92 Laser And Dodge Stealth

1. Disconnect the negative battery cable. Remove necessary underhood components in order to gain access to the clutch slave cylinder.

2. Remove the hydraulic line and allow the system to drain.

3. Remove the bolts and pull the cylinder from the transaxle housing (the clutch slave/release cylinder uses a pushrod bearing against the clutch arm).

4. The installation is the reverse of the removal procedure.

5. Lubricate all pivot points with grease.

6. Bleed the system (refer to service procedure below) using DOT 3 brake fluid.

OVERHAUL

Refer to the exploded view illustration as guide for this repair. If overhaul is in doubt replace the complete assembly.

HYDRAULIC CLUTCH SYSTEM BLEEDING

1. Fill the reservoir with brake fluid.

2. Loosen the bleed screw, have the clutch pedal pressed to the floor.

3. Tighten the bleed screw and release the clutch pedal.

4. Repeat the bleeding operation until the fluid is free of air bubbles.

NOTE: *It is suggested to attach a hose to the bleeder and place the other end into a container at least ½ full of brake fluid during the bleeding operation. Do not allow the reservoir to run out of fluid during the bleeding operation.*

AUTOMATIC TRANSAXLE

Identification

Transaxle operation requirements are different for each vehicle and engine combination. Some internal parts will be different to provide for this. When you order replacement parts, refer to the seven digit part number stamped (on most applications) on the rear of the transaxle oil pan flange.

On the Dodge Monaco vehicles with the ZF-4 type transaxle, the transaxle ID plate is on the left side of the transaxle case above the oil pan.

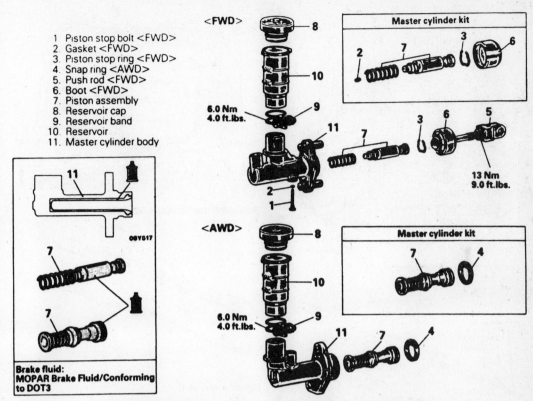

1. Piston stop bolt <FWD>
2. Gasket <FWD>
3. Piston stop ring <FWD>
4. Snap ring <AWD>
5. Push rod <FWD>
6. Boot <FWD>
7. Piston assembly
8. Reservoir cap
9. Reservoir band
10. Reservoir
11. Master cylinder body

<FWD>

8
10
6.0 Nm
4.0 ft.lbs.
9
11
2
1

Master cylinder kit

2 7 3 6
6
3
5
13 Nm
9.0 ft.lbs.

<AWD>

8
10
6.0 Nm
4.0 ft.lbs.
9
11 7 4

Master cylinder kit

7 4

06Y517

7
7

Brake fluid:
MOPAR Brake Fluid/Conforming
to DOT3

Exploded view clutch master cylinder 1990–92 Laser and Stealth

Fluid Pan

REMOVAL, INSTALLATION AND FILTER SERVICE

NOTE: *To prevent dirt and water from entering the automatic transaxle after checking or replenishing fluid, make certain the the dipstick cap is seated properly.*

On all vehicles refer to Vehicle Owner's Manual or Maintenance Interval Chart for mileage interval to perform the necessary service.

1. Jack up the vehicle and support safely it with jackstands.

2. Place a drain pan under the transaxle. On some vehicles a drain plug is located on the bottom of transaxle assembly. Remove the drain plug and allow fluid to drain. On Dodge Monaco loosen nut attaching fill tube to drain fluid. Retaining torque is 50 ft. lbs. after fluid is drained.

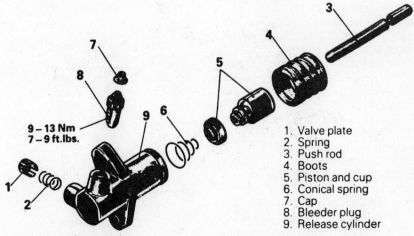

9 – 13 Nm
7 – 9 ft.lbs.

1
2

7
8
9
5
6
4
3

1. Valve plate
2. Spring
3. Push rod
4. Boots
5. Piston and cup
6. Conical spring
7. Cap
8. Bleeder plug
9. Release cylinder

Exploded view clutch slave/release cylinder 1990–92 Laser and Stealth

SERIAL NUMBER LOCATION

Automatic transaxle assembly

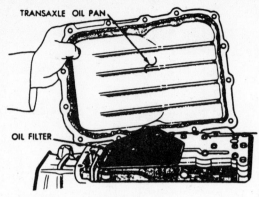

TRANSAXLE OIL PAN

OIL FILTER

Removing the transaxle fluid pan

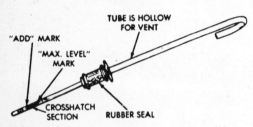

TUBE IS HOLLOW FOR VENT

"ADD" MARK

"MAX. LEVEL" MARK

CROSSHATCH SECTION   RUBBER SEAL

Dipstick and transaxle vent

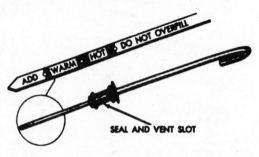

ADD WARM HOT DO NOT OVERFILL

SEAL AND VENT SLOT

Dipstick and vent

3. If vehicle is not equipped with drain plug, loosen the pan bolts (do not remove all oil pan retaining bolts/clamps — as oil pan will fall down). Gently tap the pan at one corner to loosen it, thereby, allowing the fluid to drain.

4. Remove the pan and the transaxle oil filter. On Dodge Monaco ZF-4 automatic transaxle 2 piece type oil filter is used.

To install:

5. Install a new filter (with new gasket or O-ring as equipped) and tighten the filter bolts evenly to 40 in. lbs except on Dodge Monaco, torque transaxle oil filter retaining bolts according to illustration.

6. Clean both gasket surfaces (transaxle case and oil pan) of all gasketing material if a gasket is used. If RTV sealer is used, clean all sealer from both surfaces.

7. Reinstall the transaxle oil pan with a new gasket or a new bead of RTV sealant and tighten the bolts evenly in 2 or 3 stages to 14 ft. lbs. on Chrysler front wheel drive and 9 ft. lbs. on Dodge Stealth/1990–92 Laser and 5 ft. lbs. (retaining clamps) on Dodge Monaco.

8. Refill the automatic transaxle with the specified fluid to the correct level (about 4 quarts on most Chrysler FWD vehicles and 1990–92 Laser — 4.8 quarts on Dodge Stealth

— add small amounts until the correct level is reached on the the Dodge Monaco).

9. Start the engine and allow it to run for at least 2 minutes. While the engine is running, FIRMLY hold your foot on the service brake, apply the emergency brake and shift the transaxle through all gear ranges, then shift back to the Park position.

10. Check the fluid in the N (neutral) or P

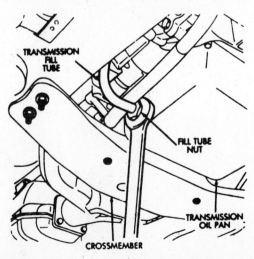

TRANSMISSION FILL TUBE

FILL TUBE NUT

TRANSMISSION OIL PAN

CROSSMEMBER

Draining transmission fluid—Dodge Monaco

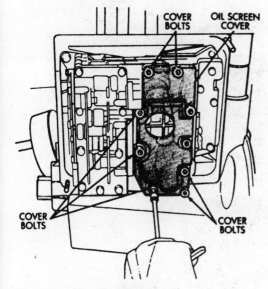

Oil pan—Dodge Monaco

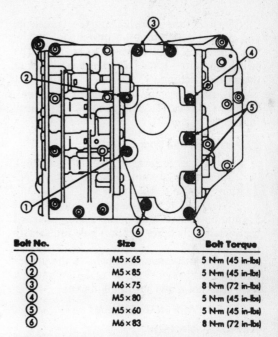

Bolt No.	Size	Bolt Torque
①	M5×65	5 N-m (45 in-lbs)
②	M5×85	5 N-m (45 in-lbs)
③	M6×75	8 N-m (72 in-lbs)
④	M5×80	5 N-m (45 in-lbs)
⑤	M5×60	5 N-m (45 in-lbs)
⑥	M6×83	8 N-m (72 in-lbs)

Oil screen bolt torque chart—Dodge Monaco

Oil screen cover—Dodge Monaco

(park) position, and add more if necessary. Recheck the fluid after it has reached normal operating temperature. The fluid level should be between the "Max" and "Add" lines on the dipstick. On some later model vehicles, recheck the fluid level, at curb idle speed, in the P (park) position after the automatic transaxle is at normal operating temperature. The level should be in the "Hot" region.

Adjustments

NEUTRAL SAFETY/BACK-UP LIGHT SWITCH ADJUSTMENT

Except 1990–92 Laser And Dodge Stealth

The neutral safety switch is the center terminal of the three terminal switch, located on the transaxle. The back-up light switch uses the two outside terminals. The center terminal provides a ground for the starter solenoid circuit through the selector lever in the Park and Neutral positions only.

1. Disconnect the negative battery terminal.

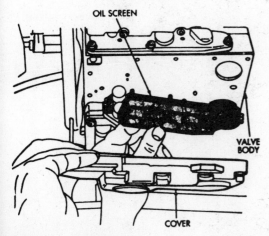

Oil screen—Dodge Monaco

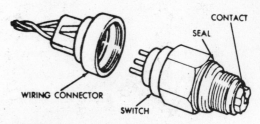

Neutral switch and back-up light switch

2. Unscrew the switch from the transaxle, and allow the fluid to drain into a pan.

3. Move the selector lever to see that the switch operating lever fingers are centered in the switch opening.

4. Install the new switch and new seal. Tighten the switch assembly to 24 ft. lbs. Check for proper operation.

1990–92 Laser And Dodge Stealth

1. Place selector lever in the "N" position.

2. Place manual control lever in the "N" position.

3. To adjust, rotate the switch body so that the manual control lever 5mm (0.2 in.) hole and the switch body 5mm (0.2 in.) hole are exactly aligned.

4. Tighten the mounting bolts of the inhibitor switch body to 7–9 ft. lbs. make sure switch body does not move out of alignment.

SHIFT LINKAGE ADJUSTMENT

1981-83 Chrysler FWD

NOTE: *When it is necessary to disassembly the linkage cable from the lever, which uses plastic grommets as retainers, the grommets should be replaced with new ones.*

1. Make sure that the adjustable swivel block is free to slide on the shift cable.

2. Place the shift lever in Park.

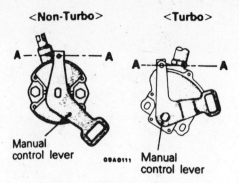

<Non-Turbo>   <Turbo>

Manual control lever   Manual control lever

09A0111

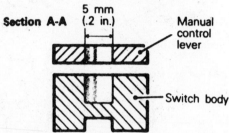

Section A-A   5 mm (.2 in.)   Manual control lever

Switch body

Nuetral safety switch adjustment 1990–92 Laser and Dodge Monaco

3. With the linkage assembled, and the swivel lock bolt loose, move the shift arm on the transaxle all the way to the front detent.

4. Hold the shift arm in this position with a

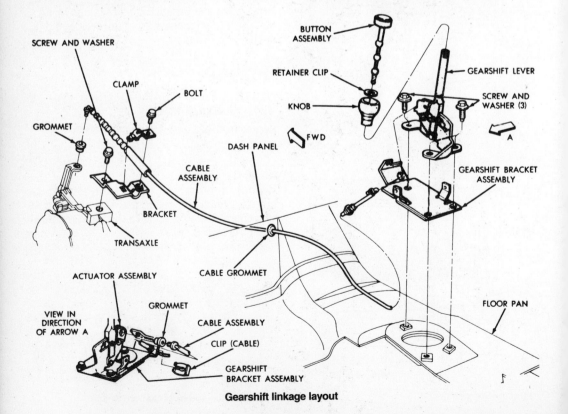

Gearshift linkage layout

force of about 10 lbs. and tighten the adjust swivel lock bolt to 8 ft. lb.

5. Check the linkage action.

NOTE: *The automatic transaxle gear selector release buttom may pop up in the knob when shifting from PARK to DRIVE. This is caused by inadequate retension of the selector release knob retaining tab. The release button will always work but the loose button can be annoying. A sleeve (Chrysler Part No. 5211984) and washers (Chrysler Part No. 6500380) are available to cure this condition.*

1984 And Later Chrysler FWD

1. Put the gearshift in "PARK". Loosen the clamp bolt located on the gearshift cable bracket.

2. On column shifts, make sure that the pre-load adjustment spring engages the fork on the transaxle bracket.

3. Pull the shift lever (on the transaxle) all the way to the front detent position (which puts the transaxle in "PARK"). Then, tighten the lockbolt to 90 inch lbs. on 1984–87 models and 100 ft. lbs. on 1988 and later model cars.

4. Check the adjustment as follows:

a. The detent positions of the transaxle shift lever for "NEUTRAL" and "DRIVE" should be within the limits of the corresponding gate stops on the hand shift lever.

b. The starter must operate with the key only if the shift lever is in "PARK" or "NEUTRAL" position.

SHIFTER CONTROL CABLE ADJUSTMENT

1990–92 Laser And Dodge Stealth

1. The shifter cable adjustment is done at the neutral safety switch (inhibitor switch). Locate the switch on the transaxle and note the alignment holes in the arm and the body of the switch. Place the selector lever in **N**. Place the manual lever of the transaxle in the neutral position.

2. Align the holes on the switch.

3. If the cable needs to be adjusted, loosen the nut on the cable end and pull the cable end by hand until the alignment holes match. Tighten the nut. Check that the transaxle shifts and conforms to the positions of the selector lever.

SHIFT LINKAGE ADJUSTMENT

Dodge Monaco

1. Disconnect the negative battery cable.

2. Shift into the **P** detent.

3. Remove the shifter cover and locate the shift cable cross-lock where the cable meets the shifter bracket. Release the shift cable cross-lock by pulling it upward.

4. Move the transaxle shift lever all the way rearward into the **P** detent. Be sure the lever is centered in the detent. Verify positive engagement of the park lock by attempting to rotate the halfshafts. The shafts cannot be turned if the park lock is properly engaged.

5. On 3.0L engine, adjust by performing the following:

a. Verify that the cable is properly routed and secured and the cable grommet is fully seated in the floor pan. Press the cable cross-lock downward until it snaps in place.

b. Position the cable self-adjusting unit in the fork of the lower cable mounting bracket at the transaxle. Use the index key to properly index and seat the cable within the bracket.

c. Seat the cable core end fitting onto the transaxle operating lever pin.

d. At the transaxle end fitting, push the core-adjust slider mechanism until it snaps into a locked position. This will properly adjust and lock the gearshift cable.

6. Check the shift cable adjustment. The engine should start in **P** and **N** only.

THROTTLE PRESSURE CABLE ADJUSTMENT

1981-85 Chrysler FWD

NOTE: *This adjustment should be performed while the engine is at normal operating temperature. Make sure that the carburetor is not on fast idle by disconnecting the choke.*

1. Loosen the adjustment bracket lock screw.

2. To insure proper adjustment, the bracket must be free to slide on its slot.

3. Hold the throttle lever firmly to the left (toward the engine) against its internal stop and tighten the adjusting bracket lock to 105 inch lbs. (8¾ ft. lbs.).

4. Reconnect the choke. Test the cable operation by moving the throttle lever forward and slowly releasing it to confirm it will return fully rearward.

1986 And Later Chrysler FWD 4 Cyl. Engines

1. Make sure the engine is at operating temperature. On carbureted cars, disconnect the choke to make sure the throttle is completely off the fast idle cam.

2. Loosen the bracket lock screw that is mounted on the cable.

3. The bracket should be positioned with both its alignment tabs touching the surface of the transaxle. If not, position it that way. Then tighten the lock bolt to 105 inch lbs.

4. Release the cross lock on the cable assembly by pulling it upward. Make sure that the cable is then free to slide all the way toward the engine (until it is against its stop).

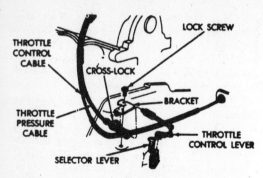

THROTTLE
CONTROL
CABLE

LOCK SCREW

CROSS-LOCK

BRACKET

THROTTLE
PRESSURE
CABLE

THROTTLE
CONTROL LEVER

SELECTOR LEVER

Adjusting the throttle cable on 1986–88 vehicles

5. Now turn the transaxle throttle control lever fully clockwise — until it hits its internal stop. Press the cross lock downward and into its locked position. This will automatically remove all cable backlash.

6. Reconnect the choke, if it has been disconnected. Turn the transaxle throttle lever forward (or counterclockwise) and then slowly release it. It should return to the full clockwise position, indicating that the cable operates freely.

THROTTLE PRESSURE ROD ADJUSTMENT

1988 And Later Chrysler FWD 6 Cyl. Engines

1. Run the engine until it reaches normal operating temperature.

2. Loosen the adjustment swivel lock screw.

3. To ensure proper adjustment, the swivel must be free to slide along the flat end of the throttle rod. Disassembly, clean and lubricate as required.

4. Hold the transaxle throttle control lever firmly toward the engine and tighten the swivel screw.

5. Road test the vehicle and check the shift points.

THROTTLE CONTROL CABLE ADJUSTMENT

1990–92 Laser And Dodge Stealth

Some vehicles do not use a throttle linkage. Instead, the throttle position sensor provides an electric signal to the transaxle, so no linkage adjustment is required.

1. Check that the throttle lever is in the curb idle position, with the engine **OFF** but at normal operating temperature.

2. At the lower cable bracket, raise the cone shaped cover to uncover a small fitting on the cable. By loosening the locknut and adjuster nut, make the distance between the fitting on the cable and the lower collar is 0.020–0.060 in. (0.5–1.5mm).

3. With the throttle in the wide open position, check that the cable does not bind.

THROTTLE VALVE CABLE ADJUSTMENT

Dodge Monaco

1. Disconnect negative battery cable.

2. Loosen the cable locknuts and lift the threaded shank of the cable out of the engine bracket.

3. Place the throttle lever in the curb idle position.

4. An accurate measurement must now be made. Vernier calipers are suggested. If accurate calipers are not available, fabricate a cable adjustment gauge from a small piece of sheet stock or other material that can be slipped over the throttle cable wire. The gauge must be 1.55 in. (39.5mm) long.

5. Pull the cable wire forward and position the vernier calipers or fabricated gauge on the wire between the cable connector and cable end.

6. Pull the cable shank rearward to the detent position but not to the wide open throttle position; the detent position feels similar to a stop when reached.

7. Hold the cable shank at the detent position, then insert the cable shank into the cable bracket and tighten the cable locknuts.

8. Remove the vernier calipers or gauge and verify the adjustment. The cable detent position should be reached when the cable wire travels 1.55 in. ± 0.039 in. (39.5mm ± 1mm).

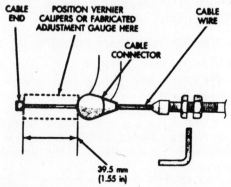

CABLE
END

POSITION VERNIER
CALIPERS OR FABRICATED
ADJUSTMENT GAUGE HERE

CABLE
WIRE

CABLE
CONNECTOR

39.5 mm
(1.55 in)

Setting throttle valve cable adjustment—Dodge Monaco

Upshift and Kickdown Learning Procedure

A-604 ULTRADRIVE TRANSAXLE

In 1989, the A–604 4 speed, electronic transaxle was introduced; it is the first to use fully adaptive controls. The controls perform their functions based on real time feedback sensor information. Although, the transaxle is conventional in design, functions are controlled by its computer.

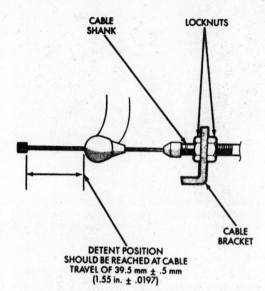

CABLE SHANK   LOCKNUTS

CABLE BRACKET

DETENT POSITION
SHOULD BE REACHED AT CABLE
TRAVEL OF 39.5 mm ± .5 mm
(1.55 in. ± .0197)

Verifying throttle valve cable adjustment—Dodge Monaco

Since the A–604 is equipped with a learning function, each time the battery cable is disconnected, the ECM memory is lost. In operation, the transaxle must be shifted many times for the learned memory to be re-inputed to the ECM; during this period, the vehicle will experience rough operation. The transaxle must be at normal operating temperature when learning occurs.

1. Maintain constant throttle opening during shifts. Do not move the accelerator pedal during upshifts.
2. Accelerate the vehicle with the throttle ⅛–½ open.
3. Make fifteen to twenty 1/2, 2/3 and 3/4 upshifts. Accelerating from a full stop to 50 mph each time at the aforementioned throttle opening is sufficient.
4. With the vehicle speed below 25 mph, make 5–8 wide open throttle kickdowns to 1st gear from either 2nd or 3rd gear. Allow at least 5 seconds of operation in 2nd or 3rd gear prior to each kickdown.
5. With the vehicle speed greater than 25 mph, make 5 part throttle to wide open throttle kickdowns to either 3rd or 2nd gear from 4th gear. Allow at least 5 seconds of operation in 4th gear, preferably at road load throttle prior to performing the kickdown.

Neutral Safety and Backup Lamp Switch

REMOVAL AND INSTALLATION

Chrysler FWD

1. Remove the wiring connector from the switch.

2. Place a drain pan underneath the switch to catch drain fluid and unscrew the switch from the case.
3. Install the new switch with a new seal, torque it to 24 ft. lbs. and replace lost fluid.

1990–92 Laser And Dodge Stealth

1. Disconnect the negative battery cable.
2. Disconnect the selector cable from the lever.
3. Remove the 2 retaining screws and lift off the switch.
4. The installation is the reverse of the removal procedure. Do not tighten the bolts until the switch is adjusted.
5. Make sure the engine only starts in **P** and **N**. Also make sure the reverse lights come on in **R**.

Dodge Monaco

1. Disconnect battery negative cable.
2. Disconnect the neutral switch harness connector located in the engine compartment.
3. Raise and support the vehicle safely. Remove the splash shield.
4. Remove the bolt attaching the switch bracket to transaxle case and remove switch from case. Replace the O-ring.
5. The installation is the reverse of the removal procedure. Connect the negative battery cable and check the switch for proper operation.

ADJUSTMENT

Refer to the necessary service adjustment procedures listed above in this chapter.

Transaxle

REMOVAL AND INSTALLATION

1981–88 Chrysler FWD

The automatic transaxle can be removed with the engine installed in the car, but the transaxle and torque converter must be removed as an assembly. Otherwise, the drive plate, pump bushing or oil seal could be damaged. The drive plate will not support a load — no weight should be allowed to bear on the drive plate as the unit is removed; it must be fully disconnected from the converter before the transmission is shifted out of its normal position.

1. Disconnect the positive battery cable.
2. Disconnect the throttle and shift linkage from the transaxle.
3. Put a drain pan underneath and then disconnect both the upper and lower oil cooler hoses. If the car has a lockup converter, unplug the electrical connector, which is located near the dipstick.
4. Install a positive means of supporting the

engine, such as a support fixture that runs across between the two front fenders.

5. Remove the upper bolts — those that are accessible from above from the bell housing.

6. For 1986 and later vehicles, refer to the appropriate procedure earlier in this chapter to remove or install the driveshafts. This will include removing both front wheels and raising the car and supporting it securely so it can be worked on from underneath. On 1985 and earlier vehicles, remove the driveshafts as follows:

  a. Remove the left splash shield. Drain the differential and remove the cover.

  b. Remove the speedometer adapter, cable and gear.

  c. Remove the sway bar.

  d. Remove both lower ball joint-to-steering knuckle bolts.

  e. Pry the lower ball joint from the steering knuckle.

  f. Remove the driveshaft from the hub.

  g. Rotate both driveshafts to expose the circlip ends. Note the flat surface on the inner ends of both axle tripod shafts. Pry the circlip out.

  h. Remove both driveshafts.

7. On 1986 and later vehicles, remove the left side splash shield.

8. Remove the dust cover from under the torque converter. Remove the access plug in the right splash shield to rotate the engine. Matchmark the torque converter and drive plate. Then, remove the torque converter mounting bolts, rotating the engine after each bolt is removed for access to the next one.

9. Disconnect the plug for the neutral safety/backup light switch.

10. Remove the engine mount bracket from the front crossmember.

11. Support the transmission from underneath. It must be supported in a positive manner and without the weight resting on the pan; it should be supported by its corners.

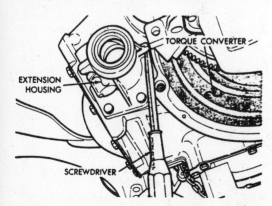

Prying the transaxle away from the engine for clearance

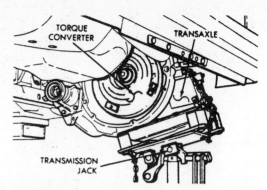

Lowering the transaxle out of the car. Note that the transmission support jig must support the unit by the corners of the oil pan—and not by the oil pan itself

12. Remove the front mount insulator through-bolts.

13. Remove the long through-bolt from the left hand engine mount.

14. Remove the starter. Then, remove any bell housing bolts that are still in position.

15. Pry the transaxle away from the engine to ensure that the torque converter will clear the drive plate. If removing a manual transaxle, slide the transaxle directly away from the engine so the transmission input shaft will slide smoothly out of the bearing in the flywheel and the clutch disc. Lower the transaxle and remove it from the engine compartment.

To install:

16. To install the transaxle, first support the unit securely and raise it into precise alignment with the engine block. Then, move it toward the block, inserting the transmission input shaft into the clutch disc, if it is a manual transaxle (turn the input shaft slightly, if necessary, to get the splines to engage). With automatic units, make sure to align the lower boltholes in the transaxle bell housing with those in the block.

17. Install the lower bell housing bolts and the starter. Bell housing bolts are torqued to 105 inch lbs.

18. Turn the engine via the crankshaft pulley bolt as necessary to align the torque converter boltholes with those in the flex drive plate. Make sure the matchmarks made prior to disassembly are aligned. Install each bolt and torque it to 40 ft. lbs. on 1981-85 models, and 55 ft. lbs. on 1986-88 models. Then, turn the crank for access to the next set of boltholes and install the bolt in that position.

19. Install the long through-bolt into the left hand engine mount.

20. Install the front mount insulator through-bolts.

21. Remove the jack supporting the transmis-

sion. Then, install the engine mount bracket onto the front crossmember.

22. Reconnect the electrical connector for the backup light/neutral safety switch.

23. Install the dust cover under the torque converter. Install the access plug in the right splash shield.

24. Install the driveshafts by reversing the removal procedure. Install the left side splash shield.

25. With the wheels remounted and the car back on the floor, install the remaining bell housing bolts and torque them to 105 inch lbs.

26. Remove the engine support fixture.

27. Connect both the upper and lower oil cooler hoses. If the car has a lockup converter, replug the electrical connector.

28. Reconnect the throttle and shift cables and adjust them.

29. Install the differential cover on those transmissions from which it was removed. Form a new gasket from RTV sealant when installing the cover. See Chapter 1. Fill the differential or combined transmission and differential with the approved automatic transmission fluid. Reconnect the battery.

1989–92 Chrysler FWD

NOTE: *If the vehicle is going to be rolled while the transaxle is out of the vehicle, obtain 2 outer CV-joints to install to the hubs. If the vehicle is rolled without the proper torque applied to the front wheel bearings, the bearings will no longer be usable.*

1. Disconnect the negative battery cable. If equipped with 3.0L, 3.3L or 3.8L engine, drain the coolant. Remove the dipstick.

2. Remove the air cleaner assembly if it is preventing access to the upper bellhousing bolts. Remove the upper bellhousing bolts and water tube, where applicable. Unplug all electrical connectors from the transaxle.

3. If equipped with a 2.2L or 2.5L engine, remove the starter attaching nut and bolt at the top of the bellhousing.

4. Raise the vehicle and support safely. Remove the tire and wheel assemblies. Remove the axle end cotter pins, nut locks, spring washers and axle nuts.

5. Remove the ball joint retaining bolts and pry the control arm from the steering knuckle. Position a drainpan under the transaxle where the axles enter the differential or extension housing. Remove the axles from the transaxle or center bearing. Unbolt the center bearing and remove the intermediate axle from the transaxle, if equipped.

6. Drain the transaxle. Disconnect and plug the fluid cooler hoses. Disconnect the shifter and kickdown linkage from the transaxle, if equipped.

7. Remove the speedometer cable adaptor bolt and remove the adaptor from the transaxle.

8. Remove the starter. Remove the torque converter inspection cover, matchmark the torque converter to the flexplate and remove the torque converter bolts.

9. Using the proper equipment, support the weight of the engine.

10. Remove the front motor mount and bracket.

11. Position a suitable transaxle jack under the transaxle.

12. Remove the lower bellhousing bolts.

13. Remove the left side splash shield. Remove the transaxle mount bolts.

14. Carefully pry the transaxle from the engine.

15. Slide the transaxle rearward until dowels disengage from the mating holes in the transaxle case.

16. Pull the transaxle completely away from the engine and remove it from the vehicle.

17. To prepare the vehicle for rolling, support the engine with a suitable support or reinstall the front motor mount to the engine. Then reinstall the ball joints to the steering knuckle and install the retaining bolt. Install the obtained outer CV-joints to the hubs, install the washers and torque the axle nuts to 180 ft. lbs. (244 Nm). The vehicle may now be safely rolled.

To install:

18. Install the transmission securely on the transmission jack. Rotate the converter so it will align with the positioning of the flexplate.

19. Apply a coating of high temperature grease to the torque converter pilot hub.

20. Raise the transaxle into place and push it forward until the dowels engage and the bellhousing is flush with the block. Install the transaxle to bellhousing bolts.

21. Raise the transaxle and install the left side mount bolts. Install the torque converter bolts and torque to 55 ft. lbs. (74 Nm).

22. Install the front motor mount and bracket. Remove the engine and transaxle support fixtures.

23. Install the starter to the transaxle. Install the bolt finger-tight if equipped with a 2.2L or 2.5L engine.

24. Install a new O-ring to the speedometer cable adaptor and install to the extension housing; make sure it snaps in place. Install the retaining bolt.

25. Connect the shifter and kickdown linkage to the transaxle, if equipped.

26. Install the axles and center bearing, if equipped. Install the ball joints to the steering

knuckles. Torque the axle nuts to 180 ft. lbs. (244 Nm) and install new cotter pins. Install the splash shield and install the wheels. Lower the vehicle. Install the dipstick.

27. Install the upper bellhousing bolts and water pipe, if removed.

28. If equipped with 2.2L or 2.5L engine, install the starter attaching nut and bolt at the top of the bellhousing. Raise the vehicle again and tighten the starter bolt from under the vehicle. Lower the vehicle.

29. Connect all electrical wiring to the transaxle.

30. Install the air cleaner assembly, if removed. Refill all fluid levels. Fill the transaxle with the proper amount of the specified fluid to the correct level.

31. Connect the negative battery cable and check the transaxle for proper operation. Refer to "Upshift and Kickdown Learning Procedure" in the Adjustment section if necessary in this chapter.

1990–92 Laser

NOTE: *If the vehicle is going to be rolled while the halfshafts are out of the vehicle, obtain 2 outer CV-joints or proper equivalent tools and install to the hubs. If the vehicle is rolled without the proper torque applied to the front wheel bearings, the bearings will no longer be usable.*

1. Remove the battery and battery tray.

2. If equipped with auto-cruise, remove the control actuator and bracket.

3. Drain the transaxle fluid.

4. Remove the air cleaner assembly, intercooler and air hose.

5. Remove the adjusting nut and disconnect the shift cable.

6. Disconnect and tag the electrical connectors for the solenoid, neutral safety switch (inhibitor switch), the pulse generator kickdown servo switch and oil temperature sensor.

7. Disconnect the speedometer cable and oil cooler lines.

8. Disconnect the wires to the starter motor and remove the starter.

9. Remove the upper transaxle to engine bolts.

10. Support the transaxle and remove the transaxle mounting bracket.

11. Raise the vehicle and support safely. Remove the sheet metal under guard.

12. Remove the tie rod ends and the ball joints from the steering knuckle.

13. Remove the halfshafts by inserting a prybar between the transaxle case and the driveshaft and prying the shaft from the transaxle. Do not pull on the driveshaft. Doing so damages the inboard joint. Use the prybar. Do

not insert the prybar so far the oil seal in the case is damaged. Tie the halfshafts aside.

14. On AWD, disconnect the exhaust pipe, remove the frame pieces, and remove the transfer case.

15. Remove the lower bellhousing cover and remove the special bolts holding the flexplate to the torque converter. To remove, turn the engine crankshaft with a box wrench and bring the bolts into position 1 at a time. After removing the bolts, push the torque converter toward the transaxle so it doesn't stay on the engine side and allow oil to pour out the converter hub.

16. Remove the lower transaxle to engine bolts and remove the transaxle assembly.

To install:

17. After the torque converter has been mounted on the transaxle, install the transaxle assembly on the engine. Tighten the drive plate bolts to 34–38 ft. lbs. (46–53 Nm). Install the bell housing cover.

18. On AWD, install the transfer case and frame pieces. Connect the exhaust pipe using a new gasket.

19. Replace the circlips and install the halfshafts to the transaxle.

20. Install the tie rods and ball joint to the steering arm.

21. Install the transaxle mounting bracket.

22. Install the under guard.

23. Install the starter.

24. Connect the speedometer cable and oil cooler lines.

25. Connect the solenoid, neutral safety switch (inhibitor switch), the pulse generator kickdown servo switch and oil temperature sensor.

26. Install the shift control cable.

27. Install the air hose, intercooler and air cleaner assembly.

28. If equipped with auto-cruise, install the control actuator and bracket.

29. Refill with Dexron®II, Mopar ATF Plus type 7176, or equivalent automatic transaxle fluid.

30. Start the engine and allow to idle for 2 minutes. Apply parking brake and move selector through each gear position, ending in **N**. Recheck fluid level and add if necessary. Fluid level should be between the marks in the **HOT** range.

Dodge Stealth

NOTE: *If the vehicle is going to be rolled while the halfshafts are out of the vehicle, obtain 2 outer CV-joints or proper equivalent tools and install to the hubs. If the vehicle is rolled without the proper torque applied to the front wheel bearings, the bearings will no longer be usable.*

1. Remove the battery, battery tray and washer tank.

2. Remove the air cleaner assembly and adjoining duct work.

3. Disconnect the shifter control cable.

4. Disconnect and plug the oil cooler hoses.

5. Disconnect the inhibitor switch, kickdown servo switch, pulse generator, oil temperature sensor, shift control solenoid valve, and ground cable.

6. Disconnect the speedometer cable.

7. Raise the vehicle and support safely. Remove the undercovers.

8. Support the weight of the transaxle and remove the mount bracket. Remove the upper bellhousing bolts.

9. Disconnect the tie rod end and ball joint from the steering knuckle.

10. Remove the right frame member.

11. Remove the starter.

12. Remove the halfshafts by inserting a prybar between the transaxle case and the driveshaft and prying the shaft from the transaxle. Do not pull on the driveshaft. Doing so damages the inboard joint. Use the prybar. Do not insert the prybar so far the oil seal in the case is damaged. Tie the halfshafts aside.

13. Remove the remaining mounting brackets.

14. Remove the bellhousing cover plate.

15. Remove the special bolts holding the flexplate to the torque converter.

16. After removing the bolts, push the torque converter toward the transaxle so it doesn't stay on the engine side and allow oil to pour out the converter hub.

17. Remove the lower transaxle to engine bolts and remove the transaxle assembly.

To install:

18. After the torque converter has been mounted on the transaxle, install the transaxle assembly on the engine. Tighten the driveplate bolts to 34–38 ft. lbs. (46–53 Nm). Install the bell housing cover.

19. Install the mounting brackets.

20. Replace the circlips and install the halfshafts to the transaxle.

21. Install the starter and frame member.

22. Install the tie rods and ball joint to the steering arm.

23. Install the upper bellhousing bolts.

24. Install the transaxle mounting bracket.

25. Install the undercovers.

26. Connect the speedometer cable.

27. Connect the inhibitor switch, kickdown servo switch, pulse generator, oil temperature sensor, shift control solenoid valve, and ground cable.

28. Connect the oil cooler hoses.

29. Connect the shifter control cable.

30. Install the air cleaner assembly and adjoining duct work.

31. Install the washer tank, battery tray and battery.

32. Refill with Dexron®II, Mopar ATF Plus type 7176, or equivalent automatic transaxle fluid.

33. Start the engine and allow to idle for 2 minutes. Apply parking brake and move selector through each gear position, ending in **N**. Recheck fluid level and add if necessary. Fluid level should be between the marks in the **HOT** range.

Dodge Monaco

ZF-4 TYPE TRANSAXLE

1. Disconnect the negative battery cable.

2. Loosen the throttle valve cable adjusting nut and remove the cable from the engine bracket.

3. Remove the upper steering knuckle mounting nut, remove the bolt, and loosen the lower bolt.

4. Remove the halfshaft retaining pin. Swing each rotor and steering knuckle outward and slide the halfshafts from the transaxle.

5. Remove the underbody splash shield. Loosen the nut attaching the fill tube to the pan and drain the transaxle. When fluid has drained, tighten the nut.

6. Remove the converter housing covers. Remove the converter-to-flexplate bolts. Support the transaxle.

7. Remove the nuts attaching the crossmember to the side sills. Remove the large bolt and nut that attach the rear cushion to the support bracket.

8. Remove the support bracket and rear cushion.

9. Disconnect the header pipes from the exhaust manifold and the catalytic converter.

10. Loosen the engine cradle bolts only until there is ½–⅞ in. (13–19mm) clearance between the cradle and the side sill.

11. Remove the front exhaust pipe. Remove the starter, plate and dowel.

12. Disconnect the shift cable from the transaxle lever. Remove the cable bracket bolts and separate the bracket from the case. Remove the brace rod.

13. Disconnect and remove the TDC sensor, speedometer sensor, and engine speed sensor. Disconnect and plug the transaxle cooling lines.

14. Using a suitable transaxle jack, support the weight of the transaxle. Remove the transaxle-to-engine bolts, then pull the transaxle back and away from the engine.

To install:

15. Position the transaxle to the engine. In-

stall the transaxle-to-engine bolts and tighten to 31 ft. lbs. 42 Nm).

16. Install removed sensors and connect all electrical leads. Connect the transaxle cooler lines. Install the brace rod.

17. Attach the shift bracket to the case and tighten the bolts to 125 inch lbs. (14 Nm). Install the shift cable to the bracket.

18. Install the starter. Connect the exhaust head pipes to the manifolds and he converter.

19. Install the rear support and cushion, install the mounting bolts and tighten to 49 ft. lbs. (66 Nm).

20. Tighten the engine cradle bolts to 92 ft. lbs. (125 Nm). Install the halfshafts.

21. Coat the threads with Loctite® and install the converter-to-flexplate bolts. Tighten to 24 ft. lbs. (33 Nm). Install the converter housing covers.

22. Install the halfshafts. Tilt the steering knuckles in and install the top bolts. Tighten the nuts to 148 ft. lbs. (200 Nm).

23. Install the front wheels. Install the under body splash shield. Attach the throttle valve cable.

24. Fill the transaxle with Mopar Mercon™ transaxle fluid. Check the differential fluid level. If it is low, fill with synthetic type 75W–140 gear oil.

25. Connect the negative battery cable and check the transaxle for proper operation.

Halfshafts

Removal and installation procedures for all halfshafts, whether used with automatic or manual transaxles, are covered under the appropriate portions of the "Manual Transaxle Section". Refer to the necessary service procedures in this chapter.

TRANSFER CASE

Case Assembly

REMOVAL AND INSTALLATION

1990–92 Laser And Dodge Stealth

1. Disconnect the battery negative cable.
2. Raise the vehicle and support safely. Drain the transfer oil.
3. On Stealth, remove necessary front bumper components. Disconnect the front exhaust pipe.
4. Unbolt the transfer case assembly and remove by sliding it off the rear driveshaft. Be careful not to damage the oil seal in the transfer case output housing. Do not let the rear driveshaft hang; suspend it from a frame piece. Cover the opening in the transaxle and transfer

case to keep oil from dripping and to keep dirt out.

To install:

5. Lubricate the driveshaft sleeve yoke and oil seal lip on the transfer extension housing. Install the transfer case assembly to the transaxle. Use care when installing the rear driveshaft to the transfer case output shaft.

6. Tighten the transfer case to transaxle bolts to 40–43 ft. lbs. (55–60 Nm) on Laser with manual transaxle; 43–58 ft. lbs. (60–80 Nm) on Laser with automatic transaxle; 64 ft. lbs. (88 Nm) on Stealth.

7. Install the exhaust pipe using a new gasket. Install removed bumper components.

8. Refill the transfer case and check oil levels in transaxle and transfer case.

DRIVELINE

Driveshaft and U-Joints

REMOVAL AND INSTALLATION

1990–92 Laser And Stealth AWD

1. Disconnect the negative battery cable. Raise the vehicle and support safely.

2. The rear driveshaft is a 3-piece unit, with a front, center and rear propeller shaft. Remove the nuts and insulators from the center support bearing. Work carefully. There will be a number of spacers which will differ from vehicle to vehicle. Check the number of spacers and write down their locations for reference during reassembly.

3. Matchmark the rear differential companion flange and the rear driveshaft flange yoke. Remove the companion shaft bolts and remove the driveshaft, keeping it as straight as possible so as to ensure that the boot is not damaged or pinched. Use care to keep from damaging the oil seal in the output housing of the transfer case.

NOTE: *Damage to the boot can be avoided and work will be easier if a piece of cloth or similar material is inserted in the boot.*

4. Do not lower the rear of the vehicle or oil will flow from the transfer case. Cover the opening to keep dirt out.

To install:

5. Install the driveshaft to the vehicle and align the matchmarks at the rear yoke. Install the bolts and torque to 22–25 ft. lbs. (30–35 Nm) on Laser or 36–43 ft. lbs. (50–60 Nm) on Stealth.

6. Install the center support bearing with all spacers in place. Torque the retaining nuts to 22–25 ft. lbs. (30–35 Nm).

7. Check the fluid levels in the transfer case and rear differential case.

REAR AXLE

Rear Axle Shaft, Bearing and Seal

REMOVAL AND INSTALLATION

1990–92 Laser And Stealth AWD

1. Disconnect the negative battery cable. Raise the vehicle and support safely.
2. Remove the bolts that attach the rear halfshaft to the companion flange.
3. Use a prybar to pry the inner shaft out of the differential case. Don't insert the prybar too far or the seal could be damage.
4. Remove the rear halfshaft from the vehicle.
5. If equipped with ABS, remove the rear wheel speed sensor.
6. Remove the caliper, pads and brake rotor.
7. Hold the axle shaft stationary and remove the axle shaft self-locking nut and washer.
8. Using a slide hammer, separate the axle shaft from the companion flange and remove.
9. Use a vice and gear puller tool to disassemble the axle shaft and companion flange assemblies.

To install:

10. Assemble the axle shaft and companion shaft assemblies using new parts as required.
11. Install the axle shaft to the housing and slide the axle shaft over it. Install the washer and new self-locking nut. Hold the axle shaft stationary and torque the nut to 116–159 ft. lbs. (160–220 Nm) for Laser and non-turbocharged Stealth. Torque to 188–217 ft. lbs. (260–300 Nm) for turbocharged Stealth.
12. Install the brake rotor, pads and caliper.
13. Install the ABS rear wheel speed sensor.
14. Replace the circlip and install the rear halfshaft to the differential case. Make sure it snaps in place. Torque the companion flange bolts to 40–47 ft. lbs. (55–65 Nm).
15. Check the fluid level in the rear differential.

Pinion Seal

REMOVAL AND INSTALLATION

Front Differential

1. Disconnect the negative battery cable.
2. Remove the front halfshaft.
3. Using a suitable prying tool, pry the seal from the case.

To install:

4. Apply a thin coat of multi-purpose grease to the seal lip and the seal contact surface.
5. Install the new seal with a suitable driver.
6. Install the front halfshaft.

Rear Differential

1. Raise the vehicle and support safely.
2. Matchmark the rear driveshaft and companion flange and remove the shaft. Don't let it hang from the transaxle. Tie it up to the underbody.
3. Hold the companion flange stationary and remove the large self-locking nut in the center of the companion flange.
4. With a suitable puller, remove the flange. Pry the old seal out.

To install:

5. Apply a thin coat of multi-purpose grease to the seal lip and the companion flange seal contacting surface. Install the new seal with a suitable driver.
6. Install the companion flange. Install a new locknut and torque to 116–160 ft. lbs. (157–220 Nm). The rotation torque of the drive pinion should be about 2 inch lbs.
7. Install the rear driveshaft.

Differential Carrier

REMOVAL AND INSTALLATION

1990–92 Laser And Stealth AWD

1. Raise the vehicle and support safely.
2. Drain the differential gear oil and remove the center exhaust pipe.
3. Matchmark and remove the rear driveshaft.
4. Remove the rear halfshafts.
5. On Stealth, remove or disconnect the 4 wheel steering oil pump.
6. The large mounting bolts that hold the differential carrier support plate to the underbody may use self-locking nuts. Before removing them, support the rear axle assembly in the middle with a suitable transaxle jack. Remove the nuts, then remove the support plate(s) and the square dynamic damper from the rear of the carrier.
7. Lower the differential carrier and remove from the vehicle.

To install:

8. Install the unit and all mounting brackets. Replace all locknuts.
9. Use new circlips on the inboard joints and install.
10. Install the rear driveshaft, matching up the marks made at disassembly.
11. With the vehicle level, fill the rear differential.

Suspension and Steering

FRONT SUSPENSION

On all Chrysler front wheel drive cars use a MacPherson Type front suspension, with vertical shock absorbers attached to the upper fender reinforcement and the steering knuckle. Lower control arms, attached inboard to a crossmember and outboard to the steering knuckle through a ball joint, provide lower steering knuckle position. During steering manuevers, the upper strut (through a pivot bearing in the upper retainer assembly) and steering knuckle turn as an assembly.

On 1990–92 Laser, Dodge Stealth and Monaco these vehicles use a MacPherson Type front suspension.

MacPherson Struts

REMOVAL AND INSTALLATION

Chrysler Front Wheel Drive Vehicles Except 1990–92 Laser, Dodge Stealth And Monaco

REGULAR SUSPENSION STRUT ASSEMBLY

NOTE: *A large C-clamp — 4 in. (102mm) or larger — is needed to perform this operation.*

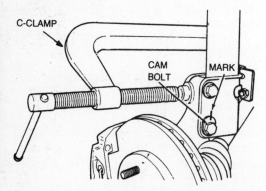

Using a C-clamp to position the lower end of the strut assembly on the steering knuckle

1. Loosen the wheel nuts. Jack up the vehicle and support it with jackstands.
2. Remove the wheel.
3. If the same strut and knuckle will be re-used together, mark the cam adjusting bolt (do this service step on these models later year — AA, AG, AJ bodies) except on Sundance, Shadow, Lancer, and LeBaron GTS. On those models, mark the outline of the strut on the knuckle (do this service step on later year — AC, AY, AP bodies).
4. Remove the cam adjusting bolt, through bolt, washer plates, and brake hose bracket screw.
5. Have someone support the strut from underneath. Remove the strut mounting nuts and washers from the fender well. Lower and remove the strut assembly.

NOTE: *INSPECT STRUT ASSEMBLY FOR FLUID LEAKAGE, ACTUAL LEAKAGE WILL BE A STREAM OF FLUID RUNNING DOWN THE SIDE AND DRIPPING OFF THE LOWER END OF THE UNIT. A SLIGHT AMOUNT OF SEEPAGE IS NOT UNUSUAL AND DOES NOT AFFECT PERFORMANCE.*

To install:

6. Install the strut assembly by raising it into position and then supporting it from underneath. Have someone support the strut at the bottom as you do this and hold it until it can be bolted to the knuckle. Install the washers and nuts and torque the nuts to 20 ft. lbs.
7. Position the neck of the knuckle in between the strut brackets, and install the cam and knuckle bolts and, if there are any washers, those also. Attach the brake hose retainer to the damper and torque the mounting bolt to 10 ft. lbs.
8. Index the strut to align the mark made on the knuckle neck at disassembly with the edge of the strut bracket.

9. Install a C-clamp onto the strut so as to pull the strut onto the knuckle neck. The rotating part of the clamp should rest against the neck. While tightenening the clamp, constantly check the fit of the knuckle neck into the strut, feeling for looseness. At the point where looseness is just eliminated, stop tightening the clamp. Make sure the index marks made earlier are aligned. If necessary, loosen the clamp and change the position of the strut to align them, and then retighten the clamp.

10. Torque the bolts to 75 ft. lbs. on 1984 and later models, 45 ft. lbs. on 1983 and earlier models. Then, turn them another ¼ turn. Remove the C-clamp.

11. Install the wheel and tire and torque the bolts to 95 ft. lbs. on 1985 and later models and 80 ft. lbs. on 1981–84 models. Check front wheel alignment if necessary.

AIR SUSPENSION STRUT

1. Disconnect the negative battery cable.

2. Raise the vehicle and support safely. Remove the wheel and tire assembly.

3. To disconnect the air line, pull back on the plastic ring and pull the air line from the fitting.

4. Disconnect the electrical leads from the solenoid and the height sensor.

5. The solenoid has a molded square tang that fits into stepped notches in the air spring housing to provide for exhaust and a retaining positions. To vent the air spring:

a. Release the retaining clip.

b. Rotate the solenoid to the first step in the housing and allow the air presure to vent.

c. Rotate the solenoid farther to the release slot and remove it from the housing.

6. Matchmark the assembly to the knuckle.

1. FRONT SUSPENSION CROSSMEMBEP
2. FRONT PIVOT BOLT
3. LOWER CONTROL ARM
4. SWAY ELIMINATOR SHAFT ASSEMBLY
5. LOWER ARM BALL JOINT ASSEMBLY
6. STEERING GEAR
7. TIE ROD ASSEMBLY
8. DRIVE SHAFT
9. STEERING KNUCKLE
10. STRUT DAMPER ASSEMBLY
11. COIL SPRING
12. UPPER SPRING SEAT
13. REBOUND STOP
14. UPPER MOUNT ASSEMBLY
15. JOUNCE BUMPER
16. DUST SHIELD

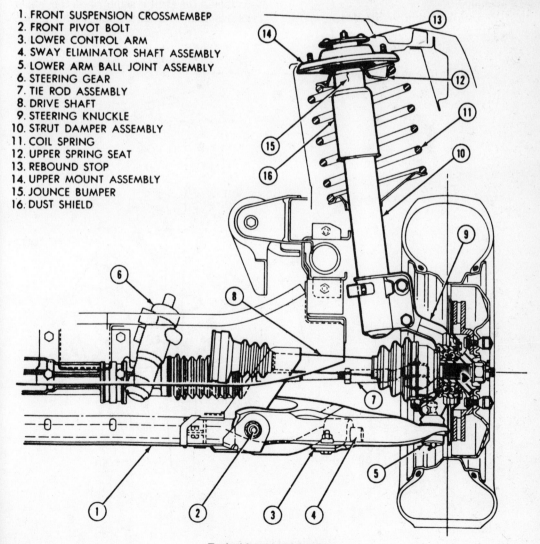

Typical front suspension

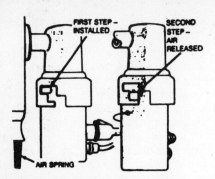

Air suspension spring solenoid positions

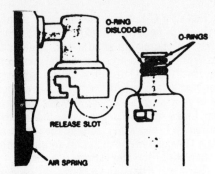

Air suspension solenoid removed

7. Remove cam bolt, knuckle bolt, and washers. Disconnect the brake hose bracket retaining bolt.

8. Hold or support the strut. Remove the upper nuts from the shock tower. Remove the strut assembly.

NOTE: *Disassembly is restricted to the upper* *mount and bearing housing. The strut, air* *spring, height sensor, solenoid and wiring* *harness cannot be disassembled or serviced.* *They are replaced as a unit.*

To install:

9. Install the strut assembly into the fender reinforcement, then install the retaining nuts

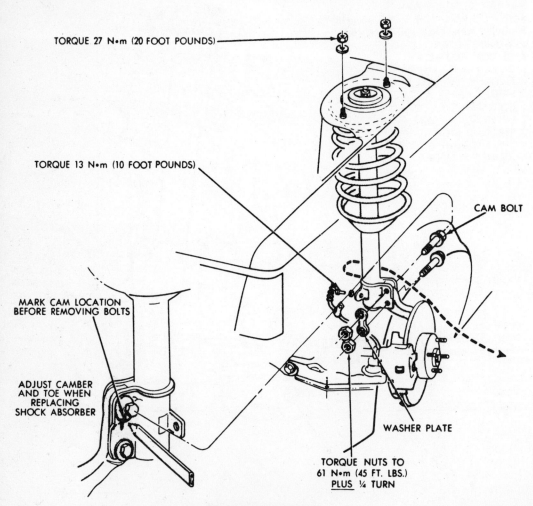

Strut assembly removal

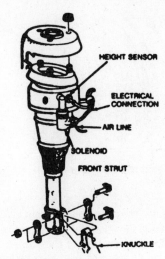

Air suspension strut assembly

and washers. Tighten to 20 ft. lbs. (27 Nm).

10. Position the knuckle into strut. Install washers with cam and knuckle bolts.

11. Attach brake hose retainer and tighten to 10 ft. lbs. (13 Nm).

12. Index the strut to the marks made during removal.

13. Use C-clamp to hold strut and knuckle. Tighten the clamp just enough to eliminate any looseness between the knuckle and the strut.

14. Check alignment of matchmarks. Tighten the nuts on the cam and knuckle bolts to 75 ft. lbs. (100 Nm) plus ¼ turn.

15. Remove the C-clamp.

16. Install the solenoid to the top step in the housing.

17. Connect the electrical leads to the solenoid and height sensor.

18. Connect the air line by pushing it into place; it will lock in place.

19. Connect the negative battery cable.

20. To recharge the air spring:

a. To activate the left front spring solenoid, ground Pin 7 (dark green with orange tracer) to Pin 19 (gray with black tracer) of the controller connector.

b. To activate the right front spring solenoid, ground Pin 6 (dark blue with orange tracer) to Pin 19 (gray with black tracer) of the controller connector.

c. Run the compressor for 60 seconds by jumping from pin No. 9 (black wire with red tracer) to pin No. 19 (gray wire with black tracer) of the controller connector.

d. The air suspension controller is located behind the right side trunk trim panel.

21. Install the wheel and tire.

22. Check the system for proper operation.

1990–92 Laser And Stealth

1. Disconnect the negative battery cable. Raise and safely support vehicle.

2. Remove the brake hose and tube bracket. Do not pry the brake hose and tube clamp away when removing it.

3. Support the lower arm and remove the strut to knuckle bolts. Use a piece of wire to suspend the knuckle to keep the weight off the brake hose.

4. If equipped with ECS, disconnect the ECS connector at the top of the strut.

5. Before removing the top bolts, make matchmarks on the body and the strut insulator for proper reassembly. If this plate is installed improperly, the wheel alignment will be wrong. Remove the strut upper bolts and remove the strut assembly from the vehicle.

To install:

6. Install the strut to the vehicle and install the top bolts.

7. Connect the ECS connector.

8. Install to the knuckle and install the bolts.

9. Install the brake hose bracket.

10. Perform a front end alignment.

Dodge Monaco

1. Raise and safely support vehicle. Do not support vehicle by placing supports under the suspension arms.

2. Remove the wheel and tire assemblies.

3. Remove the outer tie rod ends with a screw type puller.

CAUTION: *Do not remove the strut strut-to-tower cushion locknut (the center nut). The coil spring is compressed and has very strong tension. Bodily injury could result.*

4. Remove the 3 strut tower cushion-to-tower attaching bolts.

NOTE: *Before proceeding to the next step, make sure the suspension is hanging free. There must not be any pressure or tension on any front suspension components. Note too that the strut body-to-knuckle bolts are splined. Do not try to turn the bolt head. Turn the nuts only. Follow the procedure below.*

Also, make sure brake hoses and/or ABS wiring will not be damaged.

5. Remove the splined bolts by loosening the nuts until they are almost at the end of the bolt threads. Tap the nuts with a brass hammer to loosen the bolts and disengage the splines. Remove the nuts, then the bolts.

6. For protection, wrap the halfshaft boot with heavy shop towels. Then press down on the suspension arm and pull the strut out of the wheel well.

To install:

7. Carefully route the strut into place and in-

stall the 3 upper strut tower cushion-to-body bolts finger-tight. Make sure the splines are aligned on the bolts and tap into place. Tighten the nuts only. Do not allow the bolt heads to turn or the splines will strip. Hold the bolt heads with a wrench while the nuts are tightened. Torque the nuts to 123 ft. lbs. (167 Nm).

8. Torque the 3 upper bolts to 17 ft. lbs. (23 Nm).

9. Install the tie rod end and install the wheel.

10. Perform a front end alignment.

OVERHAUL

Chrysler Front Wheel Drive Vehicles

STANDARD STRUT MOUNT TYPE

NOTE: *To perform this procedure, a special spring compressor such as Tool C-4838 (C-4514 on 1981–82 models) or equivalent is required. Also needed is a special large socket and adapter L-4558 and L-4558-1 which must be used to produce correct torque on the strut rod retaining nut.*

This service repair requires above average mechanical ability or skill and special tools. Extreme care should be exercised when performing this operation.

Use this service procedure as a guide for all other models.

1. Remove the strut as previously outlined.

2. Compress the spring, using a reliable coil spring compressor.

CAUTION: *Make sure the spring is locked securely into the compressor and that all tension has been removed before beginning the next step.*

3. Install a large box or open-end wrench onto the rod nut and a smaller wrench onto the end of the strut rod. Hold the strut rod stationary with the small box wrench and use the larger wrench to remove the rod nut.

4. Remove the isolator, dust shield, jounce bumper, spacer (if used), and spring seat.

5. Remove the spring. Mark the spring as to "RIGHT" or "LEFT" side of the vehicle as

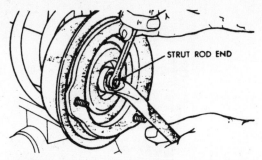

Hold the strut rod stationary as you remove the retaining nut

they are *not* interchangeable from side to side.

6. Inspect the strut damper mount assembly for severe deterioration of the rubber isolator, cracked retainers, and distorted retainers and isolators or those with a failure of the bond holding rubber and metal parts together. Inspect the bearings for noise, roughness, or looseness. Pull the shock through its full stroke to make sure its resistance is even. Replace all defective parts.

7. If the spring is being replaced, carefully unscrew and then remove the compressor. Then, compress the new spring in the same manner as the original was compressed – until it will fit onto the strut and permit assembly of all parts without interference. Install the spring with the single small coil at the top. The end of the lower coil must line up with the recess in the seat.

8. Install the spring seat, spacer (if used), jounce bumper, dust shield, and isolator.

9. Torque rod nut to 55 ft. lbs. (plus ¼ turn 1990–92 vehicles) before removing the spring compressor. Be sure the lower coil end of the spring is seated in the recess. Use a crow's foot adaptor L-4558-1 to tighten the nut while holding the rod with an open end wrench.

NOTE: *The use of the adapter is necessary to ensure the proper torque is actually applied to the nut.*

10. Release the tension on the spring compressor. Install the strut back into the car as described above.

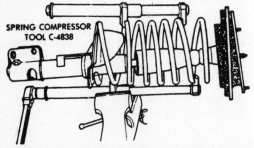

Using a spring compressor to remove all tension from the strut assembly

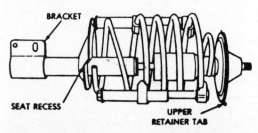

Installing/locating the spring—note that the lower end of the spring must align with the seat recess

VARIABLE DAMPING STRUT MOUNT TYPE

Refer to the service procedure above as this service procedure should be followed with these exceptions.

Position the spring seat alignment notch or tab correctly with respect to bottom bracket (refer to illustration). Also vehicles equipped with "Variable Damping" require strut rod alignment for electrical connection. Align flat on strut rod and one retaining stud on mount assembly within 15° in OPPOSITE direction from the spring seat alignment notch.

With this type strut assembly use special tool 6430 to hold retaining plate and strut rod position. Tighten retaining nut to 75 ft. lbs. This step MUST BE DONE before the spring compressor is released.

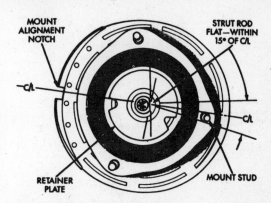

Align Variable damping strut rod and mount assembly

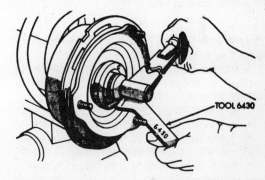

Hold Variable damping retaining plate with special tool

AIR SUSPENSION STRUT MOUNT TYPE

On this system disassembly is restricted to the upper mount and bearing housing. The strut, air spring, height sensor, solenoid and wiring harness cannot be disassembled or serviced. They are replaced as a unit.

Lower Ball Joints

INSPECTION

Chrysler Front Wheel Drive

The lower front suspension ball joints operate with no free play. The ball joint housing is pressed into the lower control arm with the joint stud retained in the steering knuckle with a (clamp) bolt.

With the weight of the vehicle resting on the ground, grasp the ball joint grease fitting with the fingers, and attempt to move it. If the ball joint is worn the grease fitting will move easily. If movement is noted, replacement of the ball joint is recommended.

1990–92 Laser and Stealth

The lower ball joints on these vehicles are not serviceable. If defective, the entire lower arm must be replaced. The ball joints can be checked using the following procedure:

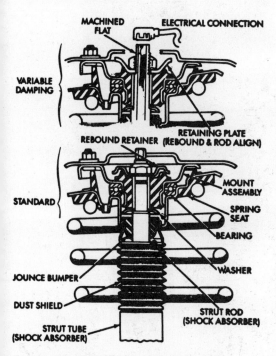

Standard and Variable damping strut mounts

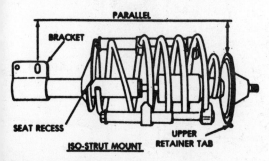

Spring seat alignment position to bracket

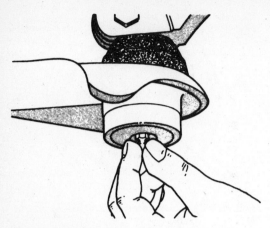

Checking ball joint wear

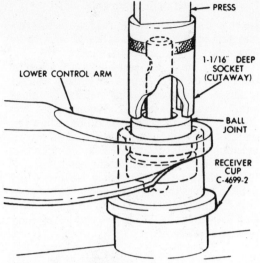

Removoving the ball joint

1. Wiggle the ball joint a few times to make sure it is free.

2. Double-nut the stud and use a torque wrench to measure how much torque is required to turn it. Starting torque should be:

   a. Laser: 26–87 inch lbs. (3–10 Nm).

   b. Stealth: 86–191 inch lbs. (10–22 Nm).

3. If the stud has more resistance than specified, replace the lower arm assembly. If the resistance is less, it may still be reused unless it has excessive play.

4. A new grease boot can be installed using a large socket for a driver.

Dodge Monaco

On this vehicle inspect the ball joint assembly. Replace it if the protective rubber boot is damaged, or the ball stud is loose or defective.

REMOVAL AND INSTALLATION

Except 1990–92 Laser, Stealth
Dodge Monaco

REMOVABLE TYPE

NOTE: *Due to the change in design some lower ball joints are not removable, in this case the entire lower control arm must be replaced. Before starting this repair check at your local parts store or Chrysler dealership for the availability of the suspension part.*

1. Pry off the seal.

2. Position a receiving cup, special tool #C-4699-2 or its equivalent to support the lower control arm.

3. Install a $1\frac{1}{16}$ in. (27mm) deep-well socket over the stud and against the joint upper housing.

4. Press the joint assembly from the arm.

To install:

5. Position the ball joint housing into the control arm cavity.

6. Position the assembly in a press with spe-

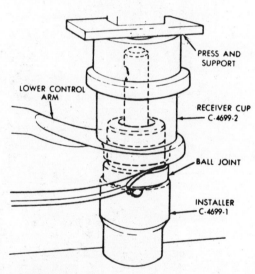

Installing ball joint

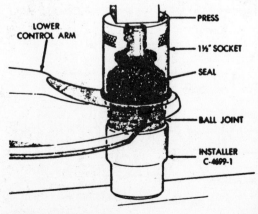

Installing ball joint seal

cial tool #C-4699-1 or its equivalent, supporting the control arm.

7. Align the ball joint assembly, then press it until the housing ledge stops against the control arm cavity down flange.

8. To install a new seal, support the ball joint housing with tool #C-4699-2 and place a new seal over the stud, against the housing.

9. With a 1½ in. (38mm) socket, press the seal onto the joint housing with the seat against the control arm.

NON-REMOVABLE (WELDED TO CONTROL ARM) TYPE

On this type, the ball joints are welded to the lower control arms. This necessitates replacement of the control arm assembly. Do not attempt to replace ball joints that are welded to the control arm; replacement control arms are equipped with a new ball joint.

1990–92 Laser And Stealth

On these vehicles, the lower ball joints on these vehicles are not serviceable. If defective, the entire lower arm must be replaced.

Dodge Monaco

1. Disconnect the negative battery cable. Raise and safely support vehicle.

2. Remove the wheel and tire assemblies.

3. Wrap a heavy shop cloth or towel around the halfshaft outer boot to protect it.

4. Loosen but do not remove the stabilizer bar inner bracket retaining bolts at the engine cradle. Remove the stabilizer bar outer bracket nuts at the suspension arm and remove the bracket. Note that the outer bracket nuts and bolts also fasten the ball joint to the suspension arm.

5. Remove the ball joint pinch bolt from the suspension knuckle. Loosen but do not remove the nuts and bolts at the bushings that attach the suspension arm to the engine cradle.

6. Disengage the ball joint stud from the suspension knuckle and remove the plastic washer from the stud. Remove the ball joint from the suspension arm by removing the bolts and tapping upward on it with a brass hammer.

To install:

7. Install the replacement ball joint assembly to the suspension arm. Crimp the sleeves, but do not tighten the nuts yet. Install a new plastic washer on the stud.

8. Install to the knuckle. When installing the pinch bolt that holds the ball joint stud to the knuckle, make sure the bolt aligns with the groove in the stud. Torque to 77 ft. lbs. (105 Nm).

9. Do not tighten the stabilizer bar nuts or bolts until the vehicle is lowered and the tires are supporting the weight of the vehicle. At that time, torque the suspension arm-to-engine cradle nuts and bolts to 103 ft. lbs. (140 Nm), the stabilizer outer bracket nuts to 60 ft. lbs. (81 Nm), and the stabilizer bar inner bracket nuts to 21 ft. lbs. (29 Nm).

10. Perform a front end alignment.

Sway Bar

REMOVAL AND INSTALLATION

Except 1990–92 Laser, Stealth And Dodge Monaco

NOTE: *Lubricate the sway bar rubber bushings liberally with suitable grease before assembling.*

1. Raise the vehicle and support it in a secure manner.

2. Remove the nuts, bolts, and retainers at the ends of the sway bar — where it meets the control arms.

3. Remove the bolts from the mounting clamps attached to the crossmember and remove the swaybar.

To install:

4. Put the busings that attach the swaybar to the crossmember into position on the swaybar with the curved surface facing upward and the slit facing forward.

5. Raise the swaybar into position and install the mounting clamps and their bolts.

6. Position the outboard retainers at the control arms, and install the bolts and nuts.

7. Lower the vehicle to the ground and make sure it is at design height by loading it normally. Then, torque all retaining bolts evenly.

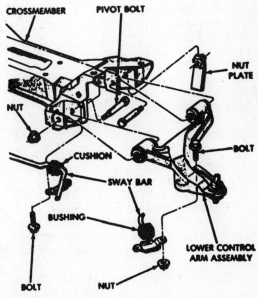

Exploded view lower control arm assembly—Chrysler cars

1990–92 Laser

1. Disconnect the negative battery cable.
2. Raise and safely support vehicle. Remove the front exhaust pipe if necessary.
3. Remove the tie rod end from the steering knuckle.
4. Remove the center crossmember rear bolts.
5. Remove the stabilizer link bolts. On the ball stud type, hold ball stud with a hex wrench and remove the self-locking nut with a box wrench.
6. Remove the stabilizer bar mounts and remove the bar from the vehicle.
7. The installation is the reverse of the removal procedure. Lubricate all rubber parts when installing. Note that the bar brackets are marked left and right.
8. Tighten link bolts with rubber bushings just until the bushings are squashed to the width of the washer.

Stealth

1. Disconnect the negative battery cable.
2. Raise the vehicle and support safely.
3. Remove the front exhaust pipe and engine undercover.
4. Remove the left and right frame members.
5. On AWD vehicles with automatic transaxle, remove the transfer case bracket and transfer case.
6. Remove the sway bar link.
7. Remove the sway bar brackets and remove the sway bar from the vehicle.

To install:

8. Note that the bar brackets are marked left and right. Lubricate all rubber parts and install the bushings, the sway bar and brackets.
9. Install the sway bar link.
10. Install the transfer case and bracket.
11. Install the frame members.
12. Install the engine undercover and exhaust pipe.
13. Connect the negative battery cable.

Dodge Monaco

1. For ease of stabilizer bar (sway bar) removal and installation, do not raise the vehicle. Leave the vehicle's weight on the tires.
2. Remove the bolts that hold the stabilizer bar inner brackets to the engine cradle.
3. Remove the retaining nuts from the stabilizer bar outer bracket bolts at the suspension arms. Note that the outer bracket nuts and bolts also fasten the ball joint to the suspension arm. Remove the stabilizer bar and brackets from the vehicle. Reinstall a nut to keep the ball joint from separating from the arm.

To install:

4. Inspect the stabilizer bushings and replace, if necessary.
5. Tighten stabilizer bar nuts or bolts only finger-tight until all the fasteners are in place. Then tighten the stabilizer outer bracket nuts to 60 ft. lbs. (81 Nm) and the stabilizer bar inner bracket nuts to 21 ft. lbs. (29 Nm).

Lower Control Arm

REMOVAL AND INSTALLATION

Except 1990–92 Laser, Stealth and Dodge Monaco

NOTE: *Ball joints and pivot bushings that are welded to the control arms must be serviced by replacement of the complete control arm assembly.*

1. Jack up your vehicle and support it with jackstands.
2. Remove the front inner pivot through bolt, and rear stub strut nut, retainer and bushing. On the 1991 vehicle, remove the front and rear control arm pivot bolts. Remove the ball joint-to-steering knuckle clamp bolt.
3. Separate the ball joint stud from the steering knuckle by prying between the ball stud retainer on the knuckle and the lower control arm.

NOTE: *Pulling the steering knuckle out from the vehicle after releasing it from the ball joint can separate the inner CV-joint.*

4. Remove the sway bar-to-control arm nut and reinforcement and rotate the control arm over the sway bar. Remove the rear stub strut bushing, sleeve and retainer. Inspect lower control arm for distortion. Check bushings for severe deterioration.

NOTE: *The substitution of fasteners other than those of the grade originally used is not recommended.*

To install:

5. Install the retainer, bushing and sleeve on the stub strut.
6. Position the control arm over the sway bar and install the rear stub strut and front pivot into the crossmember.
7. Install the front pivot bolt and loosely install the nut.
8. Install the stub strut bushing and retainer and loosely assemble the nut. On the 1991 vehicles, install the front and rear control arm pivot bolts.
9. Install the ball joint stud into the steering knuckle and install the clamp bolt. Torque the clamp bolt to 70 ft. lb.
10. Position the sway bar bracket and stud through the control arm and install the retainer nut. Tighten the nut to 25 ft. lb.
11. Lower the car so that it is resting on the wheels. Tighten the front pivot bolt to 105 ft.

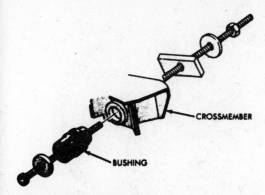

Installing stub strut bushings

lb. (95 ft. lbs. on 1986 and later cars) and the stub strut nut to 70 ft. lb. On the 1991 vehicles, tighten pivots to 125 ft. lbs. with suspension supporting vehicle (control arm at design height).

1990–92 Laser And Stealth

1. Disconnect the negative battery cable.
2. Raise the vehicle and support safely.
3. Remove the sway bar and links.
4. Disconnect the ball joint stud from the steering knuckle.

5. Remove the inner mounting frame through bolt and nut.
6. Remove the rear mount bolts. Remove the clamp if equipped.
7. Remove the rear rod bushing if servicing.

To install:

8. Assemble the control arm and bushing.
9. Install the control arm to the vehicle and install the through bolt. Replace the nut and snug temporarily.
10. Install the rear mount clamp, bolts and replacement nuts. Torque the bolts to 70 ft. lbs. (95 Nm) on Laser and Stealth. The nut is torqued to 30 ft. lbs. (41 Nm).
11. Connect the ball joint stud to the knuckle. Install a new nut and torque to 43–52 ft. lbs. (60–72 Nm).
12. Install the sway bar and links.
13. Lower the vehicle to the floor for the final torquing of the frame mount through bolt.
14. Once the full weight of the vehicle is on the floor, torque the nuts to 75–90 ft. lbs. (102–122 Nm).
15. Connect the negative battery cable.

Dodge Monaco

1. Raise and safely support vehicle.
2. Remove the wheel and tire assemblies.

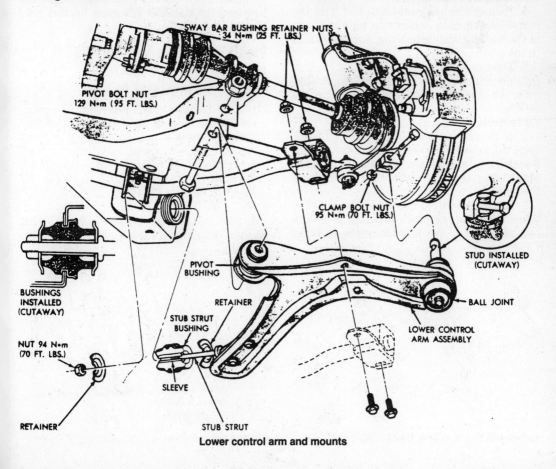

Lower control arm and mounts

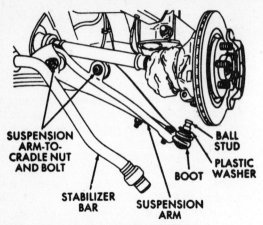

Suspension arm removal—Dodge Monaco

3. Wrap a heavy shop cloth or towel around the halfshaft outer boot to protect it.

4. Loosen but do not remove the stabilizer bar inner bracket retaining bolts at the engine cradle. Remove the stabilizer bar outer bracket nuts at the suspension arm and remove the bracket. Note that the outer bracket nuts and bolts also fasten the ball joint to the suspension arm. Reinstall a nut to keep the ball joint from separating from the arm.

5. Remove the ball joint pinch bolt from the suspension knuckle. Remove the nuts and bolts at the bushings that attach the suspension arm to the engine cradle.

6. Disengage the ball joint stud from the suspension knuckle, remove the plastic washer from the stud and remove the arm from the vehicle.

To install:

7. If reuseable, transfer the ball joint. Inspect the suspension arm bushings and replace if necessary. Install the cradle bolts, but do not tighten until the full weight of the vehicle is on the ground.

8. Install the ball joint stud to the knuckle. When installing the pinch bolt that holds the ball joint stud to the knuckle, make sure the

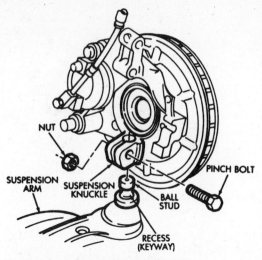

Ball joint stud installation—Dodge Monaco

bolt aligns with the groove in the stud. Torque to 77 ft. lbs. (105 Nm).

9. Do not tighten the stabilizer bar nuts or bolts until the vehicle is lowered and the tires are supporting the weight of the vehicle. At that time, torque the suspension arm-to-engine cradle nuts and bolts to 103 ft. lbs. (140 Nm), the stabilizer outer bracket nuts to 60 ft. lbs. (81 Nm) and the stabilizer bar inner bracket nuts to 21 ft. lbs. (29 Nm).

Steering Knuckle and Spindle
REMOVAL AND INSTALLATION
Chrysler Front Wheel Drive Vehicles

NOTE: *Use this service procedure as a guide for all other models. Refer to "Front Hub And Bearing" service procedures for "Steering Knuckle" removal and installation for all other models not listed below. DEPRESS THE BRAKE PEDAL SEVERAL TIMES TO SEAT THE BRAKE PADS BEFORE MOVING THE VEHICLE.*

1. Remove the cotter pin, nut lock and spring washer from the threaded outer end of the driveshaft.

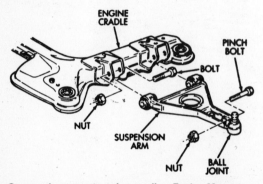

Suspension arm at engine cradle—Dodge Monaco

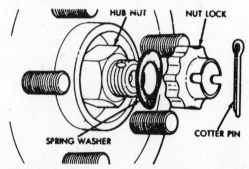

Remove the cotter pin, nut lock and spring washer

2. The car should be resting on the floor with brakes applied. Loosen the hub nut. Then, raise the vehicle and remove the wheel.

3. Remove the hub nut. Then, raise the vehicle and support it securely by the crossmembers.

NOTE: *In all the following steps, be aware that stretching stresses on the driveshaft must be avoided. Avoid moving the knuckle so as to avoid stretching stress. Prior to removing it, make sure the driveshaft will slide freely out of the splines on the knuckle.*

4. Press the tie rod end off the steering arm with an appropriate tool (C-3894 or equivalent).

5. Disconnect the brake hose retainer from the strut damper. Then, remove the clamp bolt that holds the ball joint stud in the steering knuckle and remove the stud from the knuckle.

6. Remove the bolts and washers attaching the brake caliper to the steering knuckle. Slide the caliper off the knuckle and support it in a position that will not put excess pressure on the brake hose.

7. Slide the rotor off the wheel studs. Mark the cam adjusting bolt except on Sundance, Shadow, Lancer, and LeBaron GTS. On those models, mark the outline of the strut on the knuckle. Remove the cam adjusting bolt, through bolt, and washer plates attaching the knuckle to the bottom of the strut.

8. Slide the driveshaft out of the center of the knuckle *without putting any stretching*

stresses on it. If necessary, lightly tap the center of the driveshaft to ease it out of the knuckle. Remove the knuckle.

To install:

9. Clean the knuckle wear sleeve and the related seal. Lubricate the entire circumference of the seal and wear sleeve with Multi-Purpose grease. To install the steering knuckle, slide the splined outer end of the driveshaft through the splined center of the hub and then position the knuckle neck into the lower end of the strut. Install a C-clamp onto the strut so as to pull the strut onto the knuckle neck. The rotating part of the clamp should rest against the neck. While tightenening the clamp, constantly check the fit of the knuckle neck into the strut, feeling for looseness. At the point where looseness is just eliminated, stop tightening the clamp. Make sure the index marks made earlier are aligned. If necessary, loosen the clamp and change the position of the strut to align them, and then retighten the clamp. Install the bolts, washer and nuts. Torque the bolts to 75 ft. lbs. on 1984 and later models, 45 ft. lbs. on 1983 and earlier models. Then, turn them another ¼ turn.

10. Install the lower ball joint stud through the opening in the steering knuckle and then install the knuckle clamp bolt and nut, torquing to 70 ft. lbs.

11. Install the stud of the tie rod end into the steering arm. Install the nut and torque it to 35 ft. lbs. Then, install a NEW cotter pin.

12. Install the brake disc over the wheel

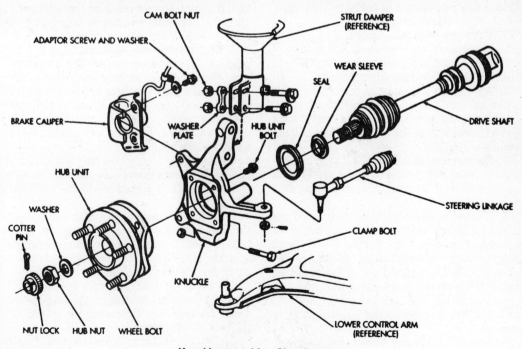

Knuckle assembly—Chrysler cars

studs. Then, install the brake caliper over the disc. Position the caliper adapter over the steering knuckle. Install the bolts and torque them to 160 ft. lbs.

13. Attach the brake hose retainer to the strut damper and tighten its mounting screw to 10 ft. lbs. Install the washer and axle hub nut. Then, have someone appply the brakes and torque the hub nut to 180 ft. lbs. Install the spring washer, nut lock, and a NEW cotter pin (the nut lock has a slot in the outer edge which must line up with the hole through the end of the driveshaft). Finally, wrap the two ends of the cotter pin tightly around the end of the nut lock.

14. Install the wheel and tire and torque the wheel nuts to 95 ft. lbs.

Dodge Monaco

The front wheel hub and bearing must be removed as a unit before the suspension knuckle can be removed. This is the only service situation where the wheel hub and bearing are removed together.

1. Disconnect the negative battery cable. Raise and safely support the vehicle.

2. Remove the tire and wheel assembly. Wrap a heavy shop cloth or towel around the outer CV-joint boot to protect it.

3. Remove the brake caliper. Do not disconnect the brake hose from the caliper. Wire it aside. Do not allow the brake hose to support the caliper weight.

4. Remove the halfshaft hub nut. A holding fixture may be required to hold the wheel hub/rotor when removing the nut.

5. Push the halfshaft inward, to disengage the shaft splines from the wheel hub splines. If it does not push out easily, use a screw type puller to press the shaft from the hub.

6. Install a puller plate that can be used with a slide hammer and pull the rotor/hub assembly from the suspension knuckle. Use care to keep dirt and debris from the bearing as the hub assembly is removed.

7. Remove the rotor from the hub by removing the rotor safety nuts. If these safety nuts are damaged by removal, always replace with new ones.

8. Rotate the wheel hub as necessary and use the access hole in the hub to remove each wheel bearing-to-suspension knuckle Torx® head bolt. Reinstall the brake rotor, attach a puller plate to it that can be used with a slide hammer and pull the rotor/hub assembly from the suspension knuckle. Use care to keep dirt and debris from the bearing as the hub assembly is removed.

9. Loosen but do not remove the stabilizer bar inner bracket retaining bolts at the engine cradle. Remove the stabilizer bar outer bracket retaining nuts at the suspension arm and remove the bracket from the retaining bolts. Note that the stabilizer bar outer bracket retaining nuts also retain the ball joint to the suspension arm. Move the stabilizer bar away from the suspension arm and reinstall one of the nuts on either of the ball joint retaining bolts.

10. Loosen but do remove the nuts and bolts at the bushings that attach the suspension arm to the engine cradle.

11. Remove the ball joint stud pinch bolt and disengage the ball joint stud from the suspension knuckle.

12. Note that the 2 bolts that hold the bottom of the MacPherson strut to the suspension knuckle have splines under the bolt head. This keeps the bolt from rotating. Turn the nuts (not the bolt heads) until they are almost at the end of the bolt threads. Tap the nuts with a brass hammer to loosen the bolts and disengage the splines. Remove the nuts and pull out the bolts. Remove the knuckle from the halfshaft.

To install:

13. Position the steering knuckle over the halfshaft and insert the ball joint stud into the knuckle. Install the pinch bolt. Note that there is a recess, groove or keyway machined into the ball joint stud. The pinch bolt must be seated in this groove. Torque to 77 ft. lbs. (104 Nm).

14. Position the knuckle to the strut and install the through bolts. Note that the splines under the bolt heads must be properly aligned in the strut hole. Tap the bolts in place and install the nuts. Use a wrench on the bolt head to keep the bolt from turning and stripping the splines when the nut is tightened.

15. Remove the ball joint retaining nut and position the stabilizer bar at the suspension arm. Position the outer bracket on the stabilizer bar and install the nuts but do not tighten yet. The ball joint nuts must not be tightened until the vehicle is lowered and the tire and wheel assembly is installed and supporting the weight of the vehicle.

16. Position the wheel bearing and hub over the halfshaft and insert into the knuckle with the hub splines mated with the halfshaft splines.

17. Remove the brake rotor from the hub. Rotate the hub, as necessary, and use the access hole in the hub to install each wheel bearing-to-knuckle Torx® head bolt. Tighten each bolt to 11 ft. lbs. (15 Nm). Install the brake rotor.

18. Install the halfshaft-to-wheel hub nut. Use an appropriate holding tool to keep the hub from rotating while tightening the nut to 181 ft. lbs. (245 Nm) torque.

NOTE: *Do not use an impact wrench to tighten the halfshaft-to-wheel hub nut. Use a*

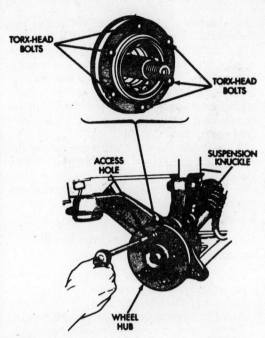

Bearing to knuckle bolt removal—Dodge Monaco

torque wrench only to tighten the nut. It is also essential that the halfshaft-to-wheel hub nut be tighten to the specified torque. In addition to retaining the wheel hub on the halfshaft, the specified torque also establishes the wheel bearing preload.

19. Install the brake caliper, tire and wheel assembly and lower the vehicle.

20. With the vehicle weight being supported by the tire and wheels, torque the suspension arms-to-engine cradle nuts and bolts at the bushings to 103 ft. lbs. (140 Nm), torque the stabilizer bar outer bracket retaining nuts to 60

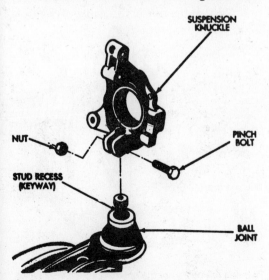

Suspension knuckle installation—Dodge Monaco

ft. lbs. (81 Nm) and tighten the stabilizer bar inner bracket retaining bolts to 21 ft. lbs. (29 Nm).

21. Connect the negative battery cable. DEPRESS THE BRAKE PEDAL SEVERAL TIMES TO SEAT THE BRAKE PADS BEFORE MOVING THE VEHICLE!

Front Hub and Bearing
REMOVAL AND INSTALLATION
1981–88 Chrysler Front Wheel Drive Vehicles

NOTE: *It is not necessary to disassemble and repack wheel bearings. In fact, the bearings must be broken to disassemble them. This procedure is for replacement of damaged or worn bearings only. This procedure requires a set of special tools C-4811 or equivalent.*

1. Remove the knuckle assembly from the car as described above.

2. Back one of the bearing retainer screws out of the hub and install bracket C-4811-17 or equivalent between the head of the screw and the retainer. Then, insert the thrust button C-4811-6 or equivalent into the bore of the hub.

3. Position C-4811-14 so its two bolts will screw into the caliper mounting threads on the knuckle, passing through the tapped brake adapter extensions. Install the tool's nut and washer onto the bracket bolt of the tool. Then, tighten the bolt to pull the hub off the bearing.

4. If the outboard race stays on the hub, use a C-clamp and universal puller to remove it. Use the thrust button and the fabricated washer from C-4811-6 or equivalent used above; use the C-clamp to keep the puller jaws over the edges of the outboard inner race.

5. Remove the tool and attach the bolts from the steering knuckle.

6. Remove its three retaining screws and remove the bearing retainer from the steering knuckle.

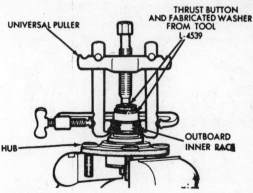

Removing the inner race with a universal puller and C-clamp

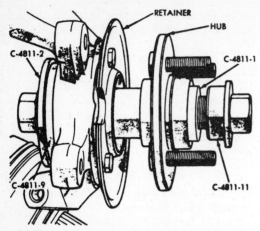

Pressing a new bearing into the knuckle with a tool set such as C-4811 set

7. Pry the bearing seal out of the machined recess in the knuckle, being careful not to scratch the surfaces of the recess.

8. Install a tool set such as C–4811 through the knuckle hub. Hold the nut with one wrench as you turn the bolt with another to pull the bearing out of the knuckle and into the ring. Then, be sure to discard both the bearing and seal, as they **are not** reuseable.

9. Inspect the inner surfaces of the hub (where the bearing interfaces with the outside of the bearing). **If these surfaces are rough or damaged in any way, the knuckle must be replaced.**

10. Turn the bearing so that the **Red** seal will face outward and be located near the brake disc.

WARNING: *Failure to do this would cause heat from the brakes to damage the type of seal used on the opposite side.*

Then, with C–4811 or an equivalent toolset, press the new bearing into the knuckle until it seats. Install a new seal and the bearing retainer and then torque the retainer bolts to 20 ft. lbs.

11. Press the hub into the bearing with C–4811–1, –2, –9 and –11 or equivalent.

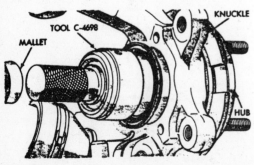

Installing a new seal in the bearing recess—assemble the tool as shown

12. Position a new seal into the recess and then install Tool C–4698. Note that this tool has a handle and dual-purpose drive head provided for installing the seal into the knuckle and for installing the wear sleeve into the CV-Joint housing. Assemble the tool as shown, make sure it and the seal are positioned squarely, and then lightly tap the seal into place with a lightweight mallet.

13. Lubricate the entire circumference of the seal and wear sleeve with Multi-Purpose grease.

14. Install the driveshaft into the knuckle and install the knuckle back into the car as described above.

1989–92 Chrysler Front Wheel Drive Vehicles

PRESSED IN (TWO-PIECE HUB AND BEARING)

NOTE: *Some hub and bearing replacement packages include the one-piece unit described below. If this is the case, follow the installation steps for one-piece unit instead of for the two-piece unit described here.*

1. Raise the vehicle and support safely.

2. Remove the tire and wheel assembly. Remove the brake caliper from the adaptor and remove the adaptor. Remove the brake disc.

3. Remove the halfshaft.

NOTE: *Knuckle removal is not necessary for bearing and hub replacement.*

4. Disconnect the tie rod from the knuckle.

5. Matchmark the lower strut mount to the knuckle. Remove the 2 strut clamp bolts and remove the knuckle from the vehicle.

6. Attach the hub removal tool C–4811 or equivalent, and the triangular adapter, to the 3 rear threaded holes of the steering knuckle housing with the thrust button inside the hub bore.

7. Tighten the bolt in the center of the tool,

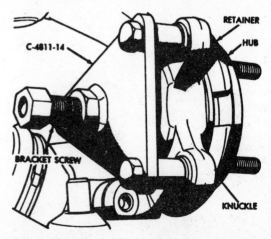

Remove the hub from the steering knuckle—2 piece hub assembly

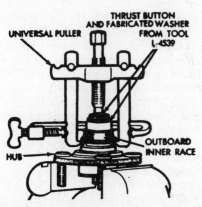

Remove the outboard inner race—2 piece hub assembly

to press the hub from the steering knuckle. Remove the removal tools.

8. Remove the bolts and bearing retainer from the outside of the steering knuckle.

9. Carefully pry the bearing seal from the machined recess of the steering knuckle and clean the recess.

10. Insert tool C–4811, or equivalent through the hub bearing and install bearing removal adapter to the outside of the steering knuckle. Tighten the tool to press the hub bearing from the steering knuckle. Discard the bearing and the seal.

To install:

11. Use tool C–4811 or equivalent, and the bearing installation adapter to press in the hub bearing into the steering knuckle.

12. Install a new seal, the bearing retainer and the bolts to the steering knuckle. Torque the bearing retainer bolts to 20 ft. lbs.

13. Use the tool C–4811 or equivalent, and the hub installation adapter, to press the hub into the hub bearing.

14. Using the bearing installation tool C–4698 or equivalent, drive the new dust seal into

the rear of the steering the hub and bearing from the knuckle as required.

15. The installation of the knuckle and halfshaft is the reverse of the removal procedure. Torque the tie rod nut to 35 ft. lbs. (47 Nm).

16. Align the front end.

BOLT IN (ONE-PIECE HUB AND BEARING)

NOTE: *Knuckle removal is not necessary for bearing and hub replacement.*

1. Raise the vehicle and support safely.

2. Remove the tire and wheel assembly. Remove the brake caliper from the adaptor and remove the adaptor. Remove the brake disc.

3. Remove the halfshaft.

4. Disconnect the tie rod from the knuckle.

5. Matchmark the lower strut mount to the knuckle. Remove the 2 strut clamp bolts and remove the knuckle from the vehicle.

6. Remove the 4 hub and bearing assembly mounting bolts from the rear of the knuckle and remove the assembly from the knuckle.

7. Carefully pry the bearing seal from the machined recess of the steering knuckle and clean the recess.

8. Thoroughly clean and dry the knuckle and bearing mating surfaces and the seal installation area.

To install:

9. Install the hub and bearing assembly to the knuckle and torque the bolts in a criss-cross pattern to 45 ft. lbs. (65 Nm).

10. Install a new seal and wear sleeve. Lubricate the circumferences of the seal and sleeve liberally with grease.

11. The installation of the knuckle and halfshaft is the reverse of the removal proce-

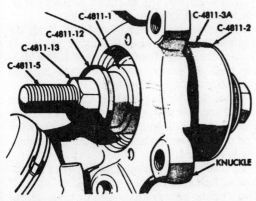

Remove the bearing from the knuckle—2 piece hub assembly

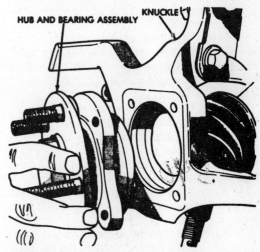

Remove the hub and bearing assembly—1 piece hub assembly

dure. Torque the tie rod nut to 35 ft. lbs. (47 Nm).

12. Align the front end.

1990–92 Laser And Dodge Stealth

1. Disconnect the negative battery cable.

2. Remove the cotter pin, halfshaft nut and washer. It is recommended that the halfshaft nut is removed while the vehicle is on the floor with the brakes applied.

3. Raise the vehicle and support safely. If equipped with ABS, remove the front wheel speed sensor. Remove the ball joint and tie rod end from the steering knuckle.

4. Remove the caliper and pads and suspend with a wire.

5. On vehicles with an inner shaft, remove the center support bearing bracket bolts and washers. Remove the halfshaft by setting up a puller on the outside wheel hub and pushing the halfshaft from the front hub. Then tap the joint case with a plastic hammer to remove the halfshaft shaft and inner shaft from the transaxle.

6. On vehicles without an inner shaft, remove the halfshaft by setting up a puller on the outside wheel hub and pushing the halfshaft from the front hub. After pressing the outer shaft, insert a prybar between the transaxle case and the halfshaft and pry the shaft from the transaxle.

7. On Stealth with AWD, the front hub/bearing assembly can be serviced at this point as a unit. If the knuckle is being removed, proceed. All others require knuckle removal.

8. Unbolt the lower end of the strut and remove the hub and steering knuckle assembly.

9. Set up a puller with the knuckle/hub in a vise and pull the hub from the knuckle. Do not use a hammer to accomplish this or the bearing will be damaged.

10. Once the hub and outer bearing inner race are removed with a puller, the bearing outer races can be removed by tapping out with a brass drift pin and a hammer.

To install:

11. Assemble the hub/knuckle assembly with pressing tools, using new parts as required.

12. Install the knuckle assembly to the vehicle and install the strut bolts.

13. On AWD Stealth, torque the front hub/bearing assembly nuts to 76 ft. lbs. (105 Nm).

14. Apply a thin coat of grease to the outside of the outer races and install into the hub with a bearing driver.

15. Apply multi-purpose grease to the bearings, inside surface of the hub and the lip of the grease seal. Place the outside bearing into the knuckle and install the seal with a driver.

16. The hub is assembled to the knuckle with a puller. Draw the parts together firmly to seat the bearings. Use a small torque wrench to check the bearing turning torque. It should be 16 inch lbs. or less. for Laser and Stealth. Check that the bearings feel smooth when rotated.

17. Apply a thin coat of grease to the lip of the halfshaft side axle seal and drive into place until it contacts the inner bearing outer race.

18. Replace the circlips on the ends of the halfshafts.

19. Insert the halfshaft into the transaxle. Make sure it is fully seated.

20. Pull the strut assembly out and install the other end to the hub.

21. Install the center bearing bracket bolts and tighten to 33 ft. lbs. (45 Nm).

22. Install the washer so the chamfered edge faces outward. Install the nut and tighten temporarily.

23. Install the tie rod end and ball joint.

24. Install the wheel and lower the vehicle to the floor. Tighten the axle nut with the brakes applied. Tighten the nut to a maximum torque of 188 ft. lbs. (260 Nm) maximum. Install the cotter pin and bend it securely.

Dodge Monaco

The front wheel hub can be removed without removing the bearing from the steering knuckle. However, the wheel hub must be removed before the bearing can be removed from the knuckle. The wheel hub and bearing are independently replaceable.

When servicing the steering knuckle, the wheel hub and bearing can and should be removed as a unit. Although the wheel bearing components can be disassembled for inspection, the bearing must be replaced as a unit only. If any of the bearing components are worn, damaged or defective, the complete bearing must be replaced.

1. Disconnect the negative battery cable. Raise and safely support the vehicle.

2. Remove the halfshaft end nut. Push the halfshaft inward and disengage the shaft splines from the wheel hub splines. If it does not push out easily, use a screw type puller to press the shaft from the hub.

3. Install a puller plate that can be used with a slide hammer and pull the rotor/hub assembly from the steering knuckle. Use care to keep dirt and debris from the bearing as the hub assembly is removed.

4. If necessary, the rotor and hub can be separated by removing the rotor safety nuts. If these safety nuts are damaged by removal, replace with new ones.

5. Remove the Torx® bolts that attach the

wheel bearing to the knuckle. Remove the bearing.

6. If the wheel hub and/or bearing are being replaced without the other, remove the outer race from the hub with a shop press and the appropriate adapters.

To install:

7. If a new wheel hub is being installed, force the original bearing outer race on the replacement hub with a shop press and a suitable length of steel pipe that has the correct inside diameter to fit around the hub. If a new bearing is being installed, do the same with the new race.

8. If the original wheel bearing is being installed, pack the bearing and lubricate both races (inner and outer) with an extreme pressure type wheel bearing lubricant.

9. If a replacement wheel bearing is being installed, prepare the bearing as follows:

    a. Remove and discard the plastic protective covers.

    b. Locate, remove and discard the plastic protective sleeve from the replacement bearing bore.

    c. Remove the inner and outer bearing races from the bearing.

    d. Pack the bearing with lubricant which may be supplied with the replacement bearing.

    e. Insert the bearing inner race in the bearing and force the bearing outer race on the wheel hub with a press and suitable length of steel pipe.

10. Install the bearing to the knuckle and install the bolts. Torque the bolts to 11 ft. lbs. (15 Nm).

11. Lubricate the bearing mating surface on the wheel hub bearing outer race with an extreme pressure type wheel bearing lubricant.

12. Position the wheel hub on the halfshaft and insert the hub into the wheel bearing. Tap the wheel hub with a brass hammer until 3 or 4 of the halfshaft threads extend beyond the hub.

13. If removed, install the brake rotor on the wheel hub, using new safety nuts if required.

14. Install the halfshaft-to-wheel hub nut. Use an appropriate holding tool to keep the hub from rotating while tightening the nut to 181 ft. lbs. (245 Nm) torque.

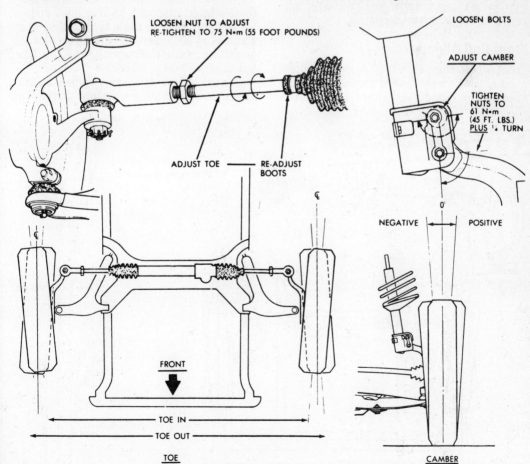

Front end alignment adjustments—early Chrysler models

Wheel Alignment Specifications

(Caster is not adjustable)

| Year | Front Camber | | Rear Camber | | Toe-Out (in.) | |
	Range (deg.)	Preferred	Range (deg.)	Preferred	Front	Rear
'81–'85	¼N to ¾P	⁵⁄₁₆P	1N-0	½N	⁷⁄₃₂ out to ⅛ in	³⁄₁₆ out to ³⁄₁₆ in
'86–'88	¼N to ¾P	⁵⁄₁₆P	1¼N–¼P	½N	⁷⁄₃₂ in to ⅛ out	¹⁄₁₆ in

NOTE: *Do not use an impact wrench to tighten the driveshaft-to-wheel hub nut. Use a torque wrench only to tighten the nut. It is also essential that the halfhaft-to-wheel hub nut be tighten to the specified torque. In addition to retaining the wheel hub on the halfshaft, the specified torque also establishes the wheel bearing preload.*

15. Install the brake caliper, tire and wheel assembly and lower the vehicle.

16. Connect the negative battery cable. DEPRESS THE BRAKE PEDAL SEVERAL TIMES TO SEAT THE BRAKE PADS BEFORE MOVING THE VEHICLE.

Front End Alignment

Front wheel alignment is the proper adjustment of all the inter-related suspension angles affecting the running and steering of the front wheels. There are six basic factors which are the foundation of front wheel alignment. These are: height, caster, camber, toe-in, steering axis inclination, and toe-out/toe-in on turns. Of these basic factors, only camber and toe-out/toe-in are mechanically adjustable.

REAR SUSPENSION

All Chrysler front wheel drive vehicles use a flexible beam axle with trailing links and coil (or air) springs. The blade type trailing arms, attached to body mounted pivots, provide fore and aft location of the suspension while a Track Bar provides lateral location.

Located in line with the spindles, an open channel section beam axle assures that the rear

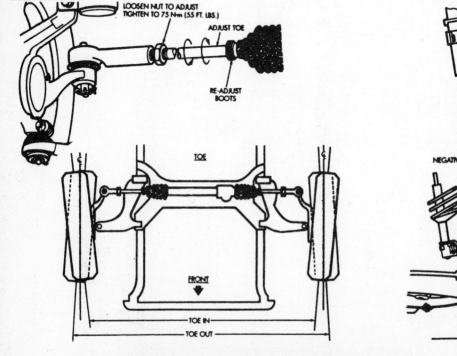

Front end alignment adjustments—later Chrysler models

SPECIFICATIONS 1989–91

FRONT WHEEL ALIGNMENT	ACCEPTABLE ALIGNMENT RANGE AT CURB HEIGHT	PREFERRED SETTING
Camber – All (Except AY with Air Suspension) .... AY with Air Suspension	-0.2° to + 0.8° (1/4" to 3/4") -0.3 to + 0.5	+0.3° (+5/16")
TOE – All models .... Specified in inches .... Specified in degrees	7/32" in to 1/8" out 0.4° in to 0.2° out	1/16" in ± 1/16" 0.1° in ± 0.1°
CASTER*	**REFERENCE ANGLE**	
AY (with Air Suspension) All (Except AY with Air Suspension)	2.9° 2.8°	
*Side-to-Side Caster should not exceed 1.5 degrees.		
REAR WHEEL ALIGNMENT	**ACCEPTABLE ALIGNMENT RANGE AT CURB HEIGHT**	**PREFERRED SETTING**
CAMBER – All models	-1.3° to -0.2° (-1¼" to +1/4")	-0.5 ± 0.5 (1/2")
TOE* – All models Specified in inches .... Specified in degrees	5/16" out to 5/16" in 0.60° out to 0.60° in	0" ± 1/8" 0 ± 0.25
Thrust Angle	-0.40° to +0.40°	-0.40° to +0.40°
*TOE OUT when backed on alignment rack is TOE IN when driving.		

Alignment specifications at curb height

TORQUE		
Ⓐ	54 N•m	40 FT. LBS.
Ⓑ	108 N•m	80 FT. LBS.
Ⓒ	61 N•m	45 FT. LBS.
Ⓓ	8 N•m	70 IN. LBS.

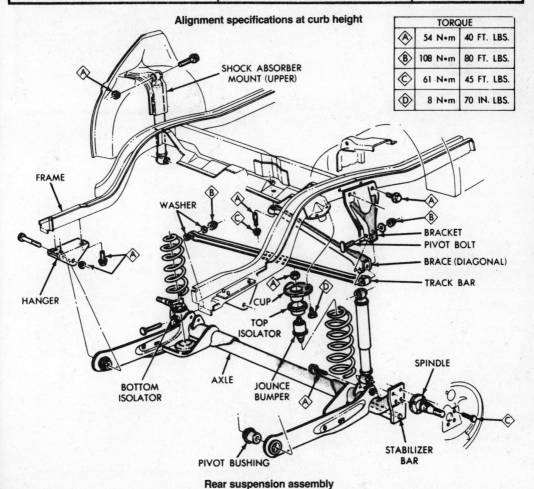

SHOCK ABSORBER MOUNT (UPPER)

FRAME

WASHER

BRACKET
PIVOT BOLT
BRACE (DIAGONAL)
TRACK BAR

HANGER

CUP

TOP ISOLATOR

SPINDLE

BOTTOM ISOLATOR

AXLE

JOUNCE BUMPER

PIVOT BUSHING

STABILIZER BAR

Rear suspension assembly

tires remain parallel to each other and essentially perpendicular to the road surface. While being able to twist as one wheel moves vertically with respect to the other.

Roll resistance is provided partly by the axle's resistance to twist. But primarily by a torque tube or rod depending (on the rear suspension) running through the channel and attached rigidly to its end plates by welding. Because the torque tube or rod is an integral part of the axle assembly, it cannot be individually replaced.

One shock absorber on each side is mounted outside the coil spring and attached to the body and the beam axle. Wheel spindles are bolted to the outer ends of the axle and can be individually replaced if necessary.

Rear wheel alignment changes require the use of shims between the spindle and the axle end plates.

Coil Springs

REMOVAL AND INSTALLATION

1. Jack up the vehicle and support it with jackstands.
2. Support the rear axle with a floor jack.
3. Remove the bottom bolt from both rear shock absorbers.
4. Lower the axle assembly until the spring and support isolator can be removed.

NOTE: *Do not stretch the brake hoses.*

5. Remove the spring and isolator. Note position of spring and isolator for correct installation.
6. Installation is the reverse of removal. With suspension supporting vehicle, torque the lower shock bolts to 40–45 ft. lb.

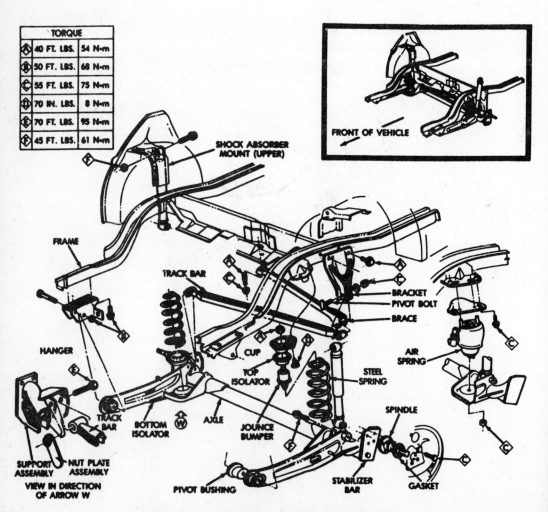

TORQUE	
Ⓐ 40 FT. LBS.	54 N-m
Ⓑ 50 FT. LBS.	68 N-m
Ⓒ 55 FT. LBS.	75 N-m
Ⓓ 70 IN. LBS.	8 N-m
Ⓔ 70 FT. LBS.	95 N-m
Ⓕ 45 FT. LBS.	61 N-m

Trailing arm rear suspension—late model Chrysler cars

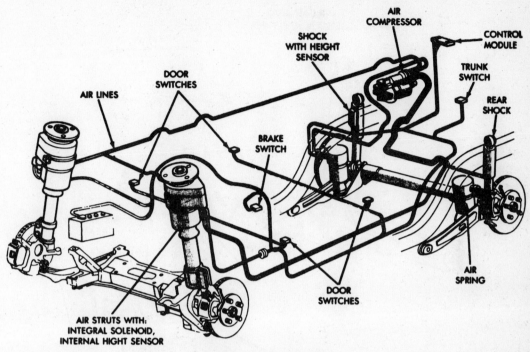

Automatic air suspension

Air Springs

REMOVAL AND INSTALLATION

Chrysler Front Wheel Drive Vehicles

1. Disconnect the negative battery cable.
2. Raise the vehicle and support safely. Remove the wheel.

3. To disconnect the air line, pull back on the plastic ring and pull the air line from the fitting.
4. Disconnect the electrical leads from the solenoid and the height sensor.
5. The solenoid has a molded square tang that fits into stepped notches in the air spring housing to provide for exhaust and a retaining positions. To vent the air spring:

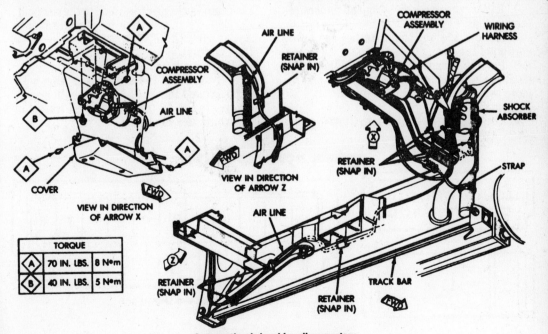

TORQUE		
A	70 IN. LBS.	8 N•m
B	40 IN. LBS.	5 N•m

Automatic air load leveling system

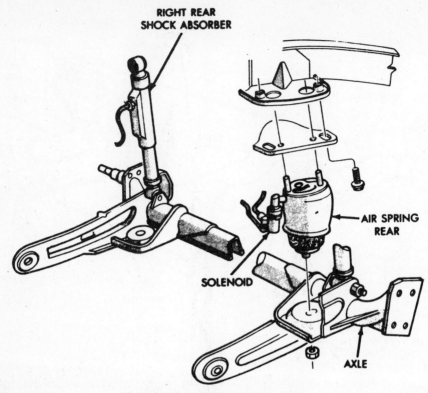

RIGHT REAR
SHOCK ABSORBER

AIR SPRING
REAR

SOLENOID

AXLE

Automatic air suspension component

a. Release the retaining clip.

b. Rotate the solenoid to the first step in the housing and allow the air presure to vent.

c. Rotate the solenoid farther to the release slot and remove it from the housing.

6. Release the upper air spring alignment/retaining clips.

7. Remove the nut that attaches the lower portion of the spring to the axle.

8. Pry the assembly down, pull the alignment studs through the retaining clips and remove the assembly from the vehicle.

To install:

9. Position the lower stud into its seat in the axle and the upper alignment pins through the frame rail adaptor. Install the retaining clips.

10. Loosely install the lower mounting nut.

11. Install the solenoid to the top step in the housing.

12. Connect the electrical lead to the solenoid.

13. Connect the air line by pushing it into place; it will lock in place.

14. Connect the negative battery cable.

15. To partially recharge the air spring:

a. To activate the right rear spring solenoid, ground Pin 10 (light green with orange tracer) to Pin 19 (gray with black tracer) of the controller connector.

CONTROL MODULE CONNECTOR

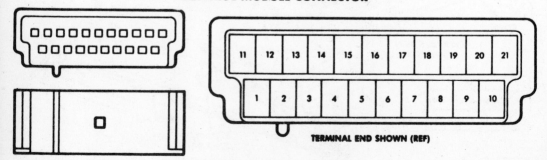

| 11 | 12 | 13 | 14 | 15 | 16 | 17 | 18 | 19 | 20 | 21 |

| 1 | 2 | 3 | 4 | 5 | 6 | 7 | 8 | 9 | 10 |

TERMINAL END SHOWN (REF)

Automatic air suspension connector

b. Run the compressor for 60 seconds by jumping from pin No. 9 (black wire with red tracer) to pin No. 19 (gray wire with black tracer) of the controller connector.

c. The air suspension controller is located behind the right side trunk trim panel.

16. When the air spring is properly inflated, torque the lower mounting nut to 50 ft. lbs. (68 Nm).

17. Install the wheel and tire.

18. Check the system for proper operation.

Torsion Bars

Since torque is developed at different angles, the rear torsion bars at each side of the vehicle twist in different directions. The bars are machined differently and must be installed at the correct location in the rear suspension. The left side bar is identified by the letter **G** stamped twice on its outer end. The right side bar is identified by the letter **D** stamped twice on its outer end. In addition, the outer end of each torsion bar has 31 splines and the inner end has 30 splines. The torsion bars have a dot stamped onto their outer ends to assist in end identification and installation reference. This end with the dot must always be installed facing outward.

The front and rear torsion bars serve different purposes on Monaco vehicles. The front torsion bar is the actual suspension component, while the rear is used mostly as an anti-sway bar. The front bar is 26.25 in. (667mm) in length. The rear bar is 23.26 in. (591mm) in length. Also, the rear torsion bar in a vehicle is dependent upon the suspension package originally installed on the vehicle. The bars are color-coded to identify its diameter. The color codes are as follows:

- White/blue − 0.96 in. (24mm)
- Red/white − 1 in. (25mm)
- Brown/green − 1.04 in. (26mm)

Never raise a Dodge Monaco vehicle with a lift positioned under the V-shaped rear crossmember. Never let the hoist arms come into contact with the lower edge of the rocker panel. If necessary, place a small block of wood between the hoist pad and the body lifting points so the vehicle does not rest on the rocker panels. The manufacturer does not recommend use of a twin post under-the-vehicle hoist.

REMOVAL AND INSTALLATION

Dodge Monaco

NOTE: *This service repair requires above average mechanical ability or skill and special tools. Extreme care should be exercised when performing this operation.*

1. Disconnect the negative battery cable.

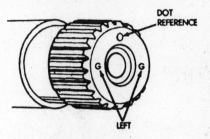

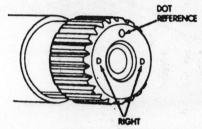

Torsion bar identification—Dodge Monaco

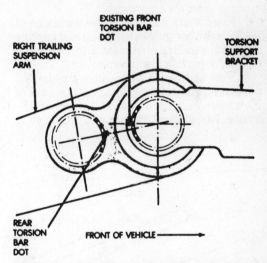

Torsion bar installation reference marks—Dodge Monaco

2. Raise the vehicle and support safely.

3. Remove the both rear wheels and shocks.

4. Pry the protective end caps and remove them from the front torsion bars.

5. Unthread the protective end caps and remove them from the rear torsion bars.

6. Pry the retaining clips away from the ends of the torsion bars and remove.

NOTE: *Each torsion bar bracket has an existing dot stamped into it that provides a reference for the initial installation position of the front torsion bar. An additional installation position mark must be punched into the*

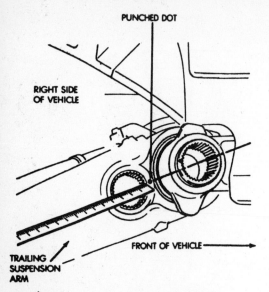

Installation reference marks—Dodge Monaco

trailing suspension arm before the bar is removed from the crossmember.

7. Place a straightedge on the centerline of the 2 torsion bar installation holes and punch a dot into the trailing suspension arm adjacent to the rear torsion bar spline groove.

8. Note and record the relative positions of the installation reference dots on the ends of the torsion bars in respect to the dots on the torsion bar support bracket and the trailing suspension arm. In other words, count the number of splines between the dot on the bar and the dot made on the bracket or trailing arm. These dots will ensure that the proper "initial twist" is applied to the torsion bar upon installation, according to the suspension package originally installed in the vehicle.

9. Loosen and extract the front torsion bars using a slide hammer. Pull the bars out far enough to disengage the splines from the connecting link and the torsion support brackets.

10. Loosen and extract the rear torsion bars using a slide hammer. Pull the bars out far enough to disengage the splines from the connecting link and the trailing suspension arms.

11. The crossmember must be lowered before the torsion bars can be removed from it. Using the proper equipment, support the weight of the rear crossmember. Do not apply lifting force to the crossmember.

12. Loosen both torsion support bracket front bolts about 4 turns. Do not remove these bolts.

13. Loosen both torsion support bracket rear bolts about 10 turns. Do not remove these bolts.

14. Slowly allow the torsion support bracket and crossmember to lower about 1 in. (25mm).

15. Remove the torsion bars and connecting link from the crossmember.

To install:

16. Make sure the correct torsion bar will be installed to the correct side — **G** is stamped on left side bars; **D** is stamped on right side bars.

17. Insert the torsion bars into the rear cross-

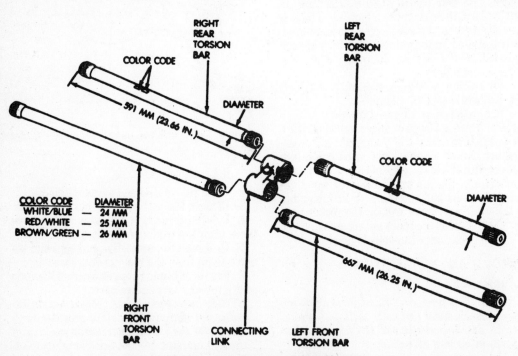

Front and rear torsion bars—Dodge Monaco

member. At this time, do not insert it so far as to engage the torsion bar splines with the splines in the support brackets or suspension arms.

18. Raise the crossmember and torsion support bracket and tighten the attaching bolts to 68 ft. lbs. (92 Nm).

NOTE: *Before the torsion bar splines are meshed with the connecting link splines, the torsion support bracket splines and the trailing suspension arm splines must be positioned at the correct location in relation to the vehicle chassis.*

19. Position the trailing suspension arms in the correct location on each side of the vehicle using 2 sets of special tool 6049 (threaded rod). Two spacers from tool set 7466 must also be used. Adjust each positioning tool so the distance between the center of the rod eyelet and the center of the hub is on the adjusting bracket is $17^{15}/_{16}$ in. (456mm).

20. After the distance has been properly set, install the positioning tools where the rear shocks are installed.

21. Insert the upper attaching bolt through the eyelet and loosely tighten it. Insert the spacer into the lower shock attaching bolt hole and insert the adjustable bracket hub into the spacer.

22. Liberally apply all-purpose lubricant to all torsion bar splines.

NOTE: *If the bars are not being replaced, they must be installed in their exact original*

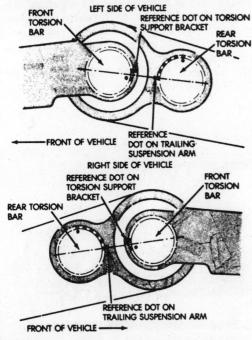

Torsion bar installation positions—Dodge Monaco

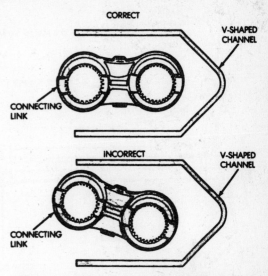

Center link centered correctly—Dodge Monaco

locations. The dot reference positions must be the same on both sides of the vehicle to prevent added stress from being applied to the bars.

23. Refer to the previously made torsion bar dot reference positions and correctly mesh the splines of the torsion bars with the trailing suspension arm splines.

24. Mesh the connecting link splines with the splines of the previously positioned rear torsion bar so the connecting link is correctly centered within the V-shaped channel in the rear crossmember. Use large pliers to assist in this operation if necessary.

25. Mesh the splines of the opposite rear torsion bar with the trailing suspension arm splines and the connecting link splines.

26. Mesh the splines of one of the front torsion bars with the torsion support bracket splines and the connecting link splines.

27. Mesh the splines of the opposite front torsion bar with the torsion support bracket splines and the connecting link splines. Recheck all bars for correct re-installation.

NOTE: *Do not directly contact the splined ends of the bars with a hammer because this could damage the splines.*

28. After all 4 bars have been installed, the ends must be centered in the torsion support brackets and the trailing suspension arms. Tap on the ends of the front torsion bars using a hammer and brass drift to position. Adjust so the outer end of each bar is recessed $^{13}/_{16}$ in. ± $^{1}/_{16}$ in. (20.6mm ± 1.6mm) from the outer edge of the torsion support bracket boss.

29. Tap on the ends of the rear torsion bars using a hammer and brass drift to position. Adjust so the outer end of each bar is recessed $^{1}/_{4}$

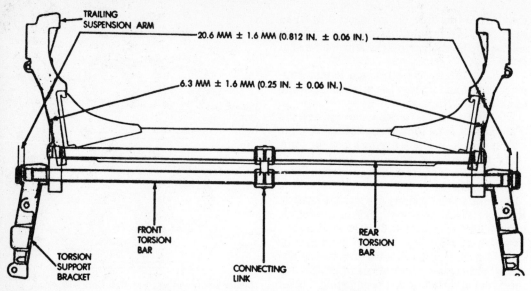

Torsion bar centering adjustment—Dodge Monaco

in. ± $\frac{1}{16}$ in. (6.3mm ± 1.6mm) from the outer edge of the trailing suspension arm.

30. Position and press the retaining clips inward against the ends of the torsion bars.

31. Install the protective caps.

32. Remove the position tools from the vehicle and install the shock absorbers.

33. Install the wheels and lower the vehicle.

34. Measure the vehicle height using the following procedure:

a. The vehicle should be unloaded, on a flat level surface, with a full tank of fuel, and with the tires all adjusted to the same proper pressure.

b. Measure from the centerline of the front wheel hubs to the ground (H1) and from the rear wheel hubs to the ground (H4).

c. Measure from the engine cradle at the wheel hub vertical centerline to the ground on each side (H2).

d. Measure from the front torsion bar horizontal center line to the ground on each side (H3).

e. Subtract H2 from H1. This value should be 3.36–3.98 in. (85–101mm). If this height is not within specification, replace worn front end parts.

f. Subtract H3 from H4. This value should be 1.25–1.87 in. (31.5–47.5mm).

35. If the rear vehicle height is not within specification, reposition the front torsion bar(s). This is accomplished by adjusting the length of special tool 6049 (threaded rod) when re-installing the bar (Step 19 in the procedure). Do not attempt to adjust vehicle height with the rear torsion bars.

36. Connect the negative battery cable and road test the vehicle.

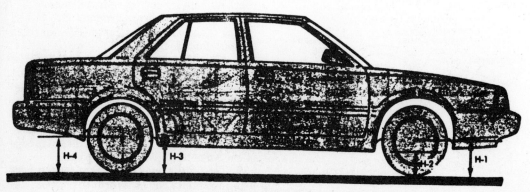

Vehicle height measurement locations—Dodge Monaco

Shock Absorbers

TESTING

Shock absorbers require replacement if the car fails to recover quickly after hitting a large bump or if it sways excessively following a directional change.

Always check shock absorbers for signs of oil fluid leaks, if shock absorber is leaking replace it.

A good way to test the shock absorbers is to intermittently apply downward pressure to the side of the car until it is moving up and down for almost its full suspension travel. Release it and observe its recovery. If the car bounces once or twice after having been released and then comes to a rest, the shocks are alright. If the car continued to bounce, the shocks will probably require replacement.

REMOVAL AND INSTALLATION

Chrysler Front Wheel Drive Vehicles

1. Jack up the vehicle and support it with jackstands.
2. Support the rear axle with a floor jack. Disconnect the height sensor and air line, if equipped. The air line is released by pulling back on the plastic retaining ring.
3. Remove the top and bottom shock absorber bolts.
4. Remove the shock absorbers.
5. Installation is the reverse of removal. Torque the upper and lower bolts to 40 ft. lb. Torque lower retaining bolt with suspension supporting vehicle.

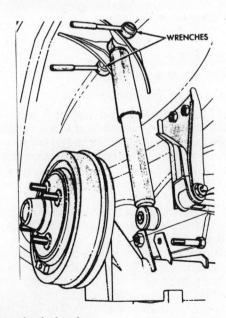

Rear shock absorber

Dodge Monaco

Never raise a Dodge Monaco vehicle with a lift positioned under the V-shaped rear crossmember. Never let the hoist arms come into contact with the lower edge of the rocker panel. If necessary, place a small block of wood between the hoist pad and the body lifting points so the vehicle does not rest on the rocker panels. The manufacturer does not recommend use of a twin post under-the-vehicle hoist.

1. Raise and safely support the rear of the vehicle.
2. Lift upward on the trailing arm to relieve the weight from the shock absorber.
3. Remove the top and bottom bolts and remove the shock absorber.
4. Installation is the reverse of removal. Torque the top bolt to 60 ft. lbs. (81 Nm) and the bottom bolt to 85 ft. lbs. (115 Nm).

MacPherson Struts

REMOVAL AND INSTALLATION

1990–92 Laser And Stealth

1. Disconnect the negative battery cable. Remove the trim panel inside the trunk or hatch area for access to the top mounting nuts.
2. Remove the top cap and mounting nuts. Disconnect the ECS connector if equipped.
3. Raise and safely support vehicle.
4. Remove the brake tube bracket bolt if necessary, then remove the strut lower mounting bolt.
5. Remove the rear strut assembly from the vehicle.
6. Installation is the reverse of the removal procedure. Do not tighten the lower mounting nut until the full weight of the vehicle is on the ground.

OVERHAUL

Refer to "Front Suspension" section as a guide for overhaul service procedures.

Rear Control Arms

REMOVAL AND INSTALLATION

1990–92 Laser With AWD And Stealth

1. Disconnect the negative battery cable. On FWD Stealth, remove the rear strut assembly. Raise and safely support vehicle. Remove the brake line clamp bolt.
2. Remove the ball joint(s) from the rear trailing arm/steering knuckle.
3. If removing the lower arm, disconnect the sway bar link from the arm.
4. Matchmark and remove the inboard lower arm pivot bolt, if necessary, and remove the arm from the vehicle.

5. Installation is the reverse of the removal procedure. Replace all self-locking nuts. Do not torque the inboard pivot nuts until the full weight of the vehicle is on the ground.

6. On Laser, torque the lower inboard pivot nut to 65–80 ft. lbs. (90–110 Nm). All other nuts are torqued to 101–116 ft. lbs. (140–160 Nm).

7. Perform a rear wheel alignment. Roadtest the vehicle.

Rear Trailing Arm

REMOVAL AND INSTALLATION

1990–92 Laser With AWD And Stealth

1. Disconnect the negative battery cable. Raise and safely support vehicle.

2. Remove the rear caliper from the brake disc and suspend with a wire. Remove the brake disc. Disconnect the parking brake cable and remove the mounting bolts along the trailing arm.

3. Remove the bolt(s) holding the speed sensor bracket to the knuckle and remove the assembly from the vehicle.

NOTE: *The speed sensor has a pole piece projecting from it. This exposed tip must be protected from impact or scratches. Do not allow the pole piece to contact the toothed wheel during removal or installation.*

4. On AWD, remove the rear axle to companion flange bolts and nuts and separate the axle from the companion flange. Remove the self-locking nut and remove the axle hub and companion flange. Remove the dust shield.

5. On FWD Stealth, remove the axle hub unit, parking brake shoes and backing plate. Remove the sway bar link bolt.

6. Remove the lower strut mounting bolt.

7. Remove the control arms from the trailing arm.

8. Remove the trailing arm front mounting nuts and bolts and remove the trailing arm from the vehicle. On AWD, remove the connecting rod at the front of the arm using tool MB991254 or equivalent.

To install:

9. Assemble the trailing arm and connecting rod. Install the trailing arm to the vehicle and install the install the front mounting nuts and bolts. Complete the final tightening of these when the full weight of the vehicle is on the ground.

10. Install the control arms to the trailing arm, using new self-locking nuts.

11. Install the lower strut bolt.

12. On FWD Stealth, install the sway bar

link. Install the parking brake parts and axle hub unit.

13. On AWD, install the dust shield, axle hub and companion flange with a new self-locking nut. Connect the rear axle to the companion flange.

14. Temporarily install the speed sensor to the knuckle; tighten the bolts only finger-tight.

15. Route the cable correctly and loosely install the clips and retainers. All clips must be in their original position and the sensor cable must not be twisted. Improper installation may cause cable damage and system failure.

NOTE: *The wiring in the harness is easily damaged by twisting and flexing. Use the white stripe on the outer insulation to keep the sensor harness properly placed.*

16. Use a brass or other non-magnetic feeler gauge to check the air gap between the tip of the pole piece and the toothed wheel. Correct gap is 0.012–0.035 in. (0.3–0.9mm). Tighten the 2 sensor bracket bolts to 10 ft. lbs. (14 Nm) with the sensor located so the gap is the same at several points on the toothed wheel. If the gap is incorrect, it is likely that the toothed wheel is worn or improperly installed.

17. Install the brake disc, caliper and connect the parking brake cable, if not already done. Install the mounting clamps bolts.

18. Double check everything for correct routing and installation. Lower the vehicle so its full weight is on the floor.

19. On Laser and FWD Stealth, torque the front mount nuts to 101–116 ft. lbs. (140–160 Nm). On AWD Stealth, tighten to 145–174 ft. lbs. (200–240 Nm).

20. Perform a rear wheel alignment. Roadtest the vehicle.

Track Bar

REMOVAL AND INSTALLATION

Chrysler Front Wheel Drive vehicles

1. Raise the vehicle and support it securely by the body. Then, raise the rear axle to approximately its normal curb height and support it *securely* with an axle stand under either side.

2. If the car has a load-leveling system, disconnect the link from the sensor to the track bar.

3. Remove the track bar-to-axle pivot bolt and the track bar-to-frame pivot bolt. Then, remove the track bar.

4. Installation is the reverse of the service removal procedures. Torque the support bracket retaining bolts 40 ft. lbs., diagonal brace and track bar to frame retaining bolt to 55 ft.lbs. and track bar to axle retaining bolt to 70 ft. lbs.

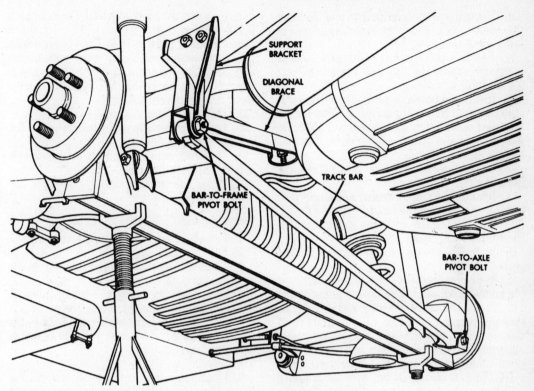

Track bar brace bracket—Chrysler cars

REAR AXLE ASSEMBLY (SUSPENSION TYPE)

REMOVAL AND INSTALLATION

Chrysler Front Wheel Drive Vehicles

1. Raise the vehicle and support safely.

2. Disconnect the parking brake cable at the connection.

3. Disconnect the brake tubes from the hoses and unclip the brake tubes from the axle housing. Disconnect the rear wheel speed sensors, if equipped with anti-lock brakes.

4. Disconnect the link from the sensor to the track bar used for automatic load leveling system, if equipped. Remove the rear air spring, if equipped.

5. Using the proper equipment, support the weight of the axle.

6. Unbolt the shock absorbers and remove the track bar to axle pivot bolt. Suspend the track bar with a wire.

7. Lower the axle and remove the coil springs.

8. Remove the axle from the vehicle.

9. The installation is the reverse of the removal procedure. Refer to the illustrations in this chapter.

1990–92 Laser

1. Raise the vehicle and support safely.

2. Remove the tire and wheel assembly.

3. If equipped with ABS, remove the bolts holding the speed sensor bracket to the trailing arm and remove the sensor assembly from the vehicle.

NOTE: *The speed sensor has a pole piece projecting from it. This exposed tip must be protected from impact or scratches. Do not allow the pole piece to contact the toothed wheel during removal or installation.*

4. If equipped with rear disc brakes, remove the caliper from the disc and remove the brake disc.

5. Remove the dust cap and bearing nut. Do not use an air gun to remove the nut.

6. Remove the outer wheel bearing.

7. Remove the drum and/or axle hub with the inner wheel bearing and the grease seal.

8. Remove the parking brake cable, brake hose, tube bracket and brake shoes with backing plate from the axle.

9. Remove the lateral rod mounting bolt and nut and secure the lateral rod to the axle beam with a piece of wire.

10. Using the proper equipment, slightly raise the torsion axle and arm assembly. Remove lower strut mounting bolt.

11. Remove the front trailing arm mount bolts and remove the rear axle assembly.

To install:

12. Install the rear axle assembly to the vehicle and install the strut mounting bolts. Install the front mount bolts and lateral rod bolts. Do not tighten these until the full weight of the vehicle is on the ground.

13. Install the backing plate, brake shoes, cable and hose.

14. Install the tounged washer and a new self-locking nut. Torque the nut to 144–188 ft. lbs. (200–260 Nm), align with the indentation in the spindle, and crimp.

15. Install the grease cap and all related brake parts.

16. Temporarily install the speed sensor to the knuckle; tighten the bolts only finger-tight.

17. Route the cable correctly and loosely install the clips and retainers. All clips must be in their original position and the sensor cable must not be twisted. Improper installation may cause cable damage and system failure.

NOTE: *The wiring in the harness is easily damaged by twisting and flexing. Use the white stripe on the outer insulation to keep the sensor harness properly placed.*

18. Use a brass or other non-magnetic feeler gauge to check the air gap between the tip of the pole piece and the toothed wheel. Correct gap is 0.012–0.035 in. (0.3–0.9mm). Tighten the 2 sensor bracket bolts to 10 ft. lbs. (14 Nm) with the sensor located so the gap is the same at several points on the toothed wheel. If the gap is incorrect, it is likely that the toothed wheel is worn or improperly installed.

19. Install the wheel.

20. Lower the vehicle so the full weight of vehicle is on the floor.

21. On Laser vehicles, torque the trailing arm bolt to 72–87 ft. lbs. ((100–120 Nm).

22. Torque the lateral rod nut to 58–72 ft. lbs. (80–100 Nm).

Dodge Monaco

1. Raise and safely support the vehicle.

2. Remove the rear wheels.

3. Remove the parking brake cables from the body support.

4. Disconnect and plug the brake hoses at the axle. Remove the shock absorbers.

5. Support the axle assembly and remove the support bracket bolts. Lower the axle assembly and remove.

To install:

6. Installation is the reverse of removal. Position the axle under the vehicle and raise it into place. Install and tighten the support bracket bolts, tighten to 68 ft. lbs. (92 Nm).

7. Connect the brake hoses at the axle. Connect the parking brake cables. Install the shock

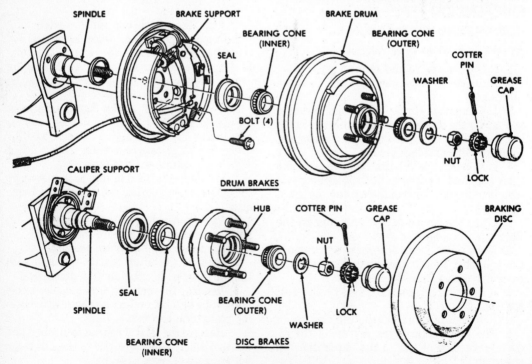

Exploded view of drum (above) and disc (below) brake assemblies

absorbers, tighten the upper shock bolt to 60 ft. lbs. (81 Nm) and the lower bolt to 85 ft. lbs. (115 Nm).

8. Install the rear wheels, bleed the brake system and adjust the parking brake cable.

Rear Wheel Bearings

REPLACEMENT

Chrysler Front Wheel Drive Vehicles — Drum Brakes

CAUTION: *Brake linings contain asbestos. Avoid using compressed air or any other means to remove dust from the drum or brake shoes or areas nearby. Failure to heed this warning could cause inhalation of asbestos fibers, a known carcinogen!*

1. Raise the car and support it securely. Remove the wheel and tire.

2. Remove the grease cap, cotter pin, nut lock and retaining nut.

3. Slide the washer off the spindle. Refer to Chapter 9 and adjust the rear brakes away from the drum if necessary. Then, pull the brake drum and outer bearing off the spindle. Remove the bearing from the drum.

4. Slide the inner bearing cone off the spindle. Slide the seal off the spindle.

5. Inspect the bearing rollers. If they turn roughly or the surfaces are cracked, rough or brinneled, replace them.

6. Inspect the inner diameter of the brake drum where the bearing rolls. If the surface is cracked, rough or brinneled, replace the drum.

7. Inspect the cone-shaped bearing surface of the spindle. If it is cracked, rough or brinneled, replace the spindle.

8. If the spindle must be replaced:

a. Disconnect the brake hydraulic tube from the back of the wheel cylinder. Disconnect the parking brake cable at the adjustment. Remove the four mounting bolts and remove the brake backing plate, spindle, and seal.

b. Route the parking brake cable through the trailing arm opening and route the brake tube over the trailing arm. Put the spindle, seal, and backing plate into position on the axle (with boltholes aligned). Install the four bolts and tighten them finger tight to position all parts. Then, torque them to 55 ft. lbs. Bleed the brake system as described in the next chapter.

9. Make sure all spindle surfaces and the inner diameter bearing surface in the brake drum are clean.

10. Very thoroughly pack the wheel bearings with *wheel bearing grease* (ordinary Multi-Purpose grease is *not* satisfactory). Work the grease

thoroughly into the spaces between the rollers by forcing grease through them repeatedly.

11. Install the seal, inner bearing cone, brake drum, and outer bearing cone onto the spindle. Note that the inner cone's larger diameter goes on first, while the outer cone's outer diameter goes on last.

12. Align the tab in the washer with the groove in the threaded portion of the spindle and slide it on. Screw the nut onto the spindle threads.

13. Rotating the drum, torque the nut to 240–300 inch lbs. Then back off the nut until preload is completely eliminated (the nut turns freely). Then, finger tighten the nut.

14. Install the nut lock until it touches the wheel bearing nut. Then, turn it backward *just* until the next slot aligns with the cotter pin hole.

15. Reconnect the parking brake cable and adjust it as described in Chapter 9.

16. Clean and install the grease cap. Install the wheel and tire and lower the vehicle to the floor.

Chrysler Front Wheel Drive Vehicles — Rear Disc Brakes

CAUTION: *Brake linings contain asbestos. Avoid using compressed air or any other means to remove dust from the rotor or brake calipers or linings or areas nearby. Failure to heed this warning could cause inhalation of asbestos fibers, a known carcinogen!*

1. Raise the car and support it securely. Remove the wheel and tire.

2. Disconnect the brake hose mounting bracket from the caliper support. Remove the parking brake cable and brake hose from the caliper assembly. Then, remove the caliper assembly as described in Chapter 9.

3. Unbolt and remove the caliper adapter. Slide the disc off the wheel studs.

4. Remove the grease cap, cotter pin, nut lock and retaining nut.

5. Remove the outer bearing cone. Then, slide the hub off the spindle. Remove the inner bearing cone. Remove the inner seal.

6. Inspect the bearing rollers. If they turn roughly or the surfaces are cracked, rough or brinneled, replace them.

7. Inspect the inner diameter of the brake hub where the bearing rolls. If the surface is cracked, rough or brinneled, replace the hub.

8. Inspect the cone-shaped bearing surface of the spindle. If it is cracked, rough or brinneled, replace the spindle.

9. If the spindle must be replaced:

a. Remove the bolts and remove the caliper support and the spindle.

b. Position the caliper support and new

spindle onto the axle with the boltholes aligned. Install the four retaining bolts finger tight. Then, torque to 55 ft. lbs.

10. Make sure all spindle surfaces and the inner diameter bearing surface in the brake hub are clean.

11. Very thoroughly pack the wheel bearings with *wheel bearing grease* (ordinary Multi-Purpose grease is *not* satisfactory). Work the grease thoroughly into the spaces between the rollers by forcing grease through them repeatedly.

12. Install the caliper adapter. Install the seal, inner bearing cone, brake hub and outer bearing cone onto the spindle. Note that the inner cone's larger diameter goes on first, while the outer cone's outer diameter goes on last.

12. Align the tab in the washer with the groove in the threaded portion of the spindle and slide it on. Screw the nut onto the spindle threads.

13. Install the rotor onto the wheel studs. Rotating the rotor, torque the nut to 240–300 inch lbs. Then back off the nut until preload is completely eliminated (the nut turns freely). Then, finger tighten the nut.

14. Install the nut lock until it touches the wheel bearing nut. Then, turn it backward *just* until the next slot aligns with the cotter pin hole.

15. Install the caliper as described in Chapter 9.

16. Clean and install the grease cap. Install the wheel and tire and lower the vehicle to the floor.

Do not add grease to wheel bearing that already has grease packed in it. Relubricate complete. Mixing of different types of grease in wheel bearings should be avoided since it may result in excessive thinning and leakage of the grease.

To clean bearings, soak them in appropriate cleaning solvent. Strike the flat surface of the bearing inner race against a hardwood block several times, immersing the bearings in solvent between the blows to jar loose and wash old particles of hardened grease form the bearings. Repeat this operation until bearings are clean.

Do not drag seal or inner bearing over the

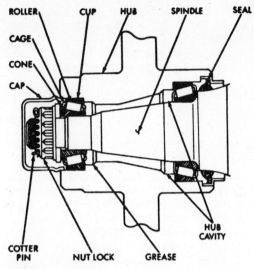

Rear wheel bearings

threaded area of the stub axle. Always replace grease seals when servicing rear wheel bearings.

1990–92 Laser And Stealth

1. Raise the vehicle and support safely.
2. Remove the tire and wheel assembly.
3. Remove the bolt(s) holding the speed sensor bracket to the knuckle and remove the assembly from the vehicle.

NOTE: *The speed sensor has a pole piece projecting from it. This exposed tip must be protected from impact or scratches. Do not allow the pole piece to contact the toothed wheel during removal or installation.*

4. Remove the caliper from the brake disc and suspend with a wire.
5. Remove the brake disc.
6. Remove the grease cap, self-locking nut and tounged washer.
7. Remove the rear hub assembly. This assembly is not serviceable and must be replaced as a unit.

To install:

8. Install the hub assembly.
9. Install the tounged washer and a new self-locking nut. Torque the nut to 144–188 ft. lbs. (200–260 Nm), align with the indentation in the spindle, and crimp.
10. Set up a dial indicator and measure the endplay while moving the hub in and out. If the endplay exceeds 0.004 in. (0.01mm) for Laser or 0.002 in. (0.005mm) for Stealth, retorque the nut. If still beyond the limit, replace the hub unit.
11. Install the grease cap and brake parts.
12. Temporarily install the speed sensor to the knuckle; tighten the bolts only finger-tight.
13. Route the cable correctly and loosely in-

Packing wheel bearings

stall the clips and retainers. All clips must be in their original position and the sensor cable must not be twisted. Improper installation may cause cable damage and system failure.

NOTE: *The wiring in the harness is easily damaged by twisting and flexing. Use the white stripe on the outer insulation to keep the sensor harness properly placed.*

14. Use a brass or other non-magnetic feeler gauge to check the air gap between the tip of the pole piece and the toothed wheel. Correct gap is 0.012–0.035 in. (0.3–0.9mm). Tighten the 2 sensor bracket bolts to 10 ft. lbs. (14 Nm) with the sensor located so the gap is the same at several points on the toothed wheel. If the gap is incorrect, it is likely that the toothed wheel is worn or improperly installed.

15. Install the wheel.

Dodge Monaco

The rear wheel bearings and hubs are replaced as assemblies only. They are non-adjustable. The maximum allowable bearing endplay is 0.001 in. (0.025mm). If the endplay exceeds this, the bearing/hub assembly should be replaced.

1. Raise and safely support the rear of the vehicle. Remove the wheel.
2. Remove the brake drum from the axle shaft hub.
3. Remove the axle shaft hub nut and remove the hub/bearing assembly.

To install:

4. Lightly oil the axle shaft before installing the hub/bearing assembly. Install the hub to the axle shaft using a new nut. Tighten the nut to 123 ft. lbs. (167 Nm).
5. Install the brake drum and wheel.

Rear Axle Alignment

Chrysler front wheel drive vehicles are equipped with a rear suspension, using wheel spindles, thereby making it possible to align the camber and toe of the rear wheels.

Alignment adjustment, if required, is made by adding shims (Part #5205114 or equivalent) between the spindle mounting surface and axle mounting plate.

Because of the specialized equipment needed to perform this procedure it is best left to your Chrysler dealer or a reliable repair facility.

On the Dodge Monaco and 1990–92 Laser vehicles the rear camber and toe are not adjustable.

On the Stealth vehicle the rear camber and toe by an eccentric bolt in the rear suspension.

STEERING

Steering Wheel

REMOVAL AND INSTALLATION

CAUTION: *On vehicles equipped with an air bag, the negative battery cable must be disconnected and isolated before working on the system. Failure to do so may result in deployment of the air bag and possible personal injury.*

Without Airbag System

1. Disconnect the negative battery cable.
2. Straighten the steering wheel so the front tires are pointing straight forward.
2. Remove the horn pad.
3. Remove the steering wheel hold-down nut and remove the damper, if equipped. Matchmark the steering wheel to the shaft.
4. Using a suitable steering wheel puller, pull the steering wheel off of the shaft.
5. The installation is the reverse of the removal procedure. Torque the hold-down nut to 45 ft. lbs. on 1982 and later vehicle (60 ft. lbs. on 1981 models) Do not torque the nut against the steering column lock or damage will occur.

With Airbag System

NOTE: *This service repair requires above average mechanical ability, skill and special*

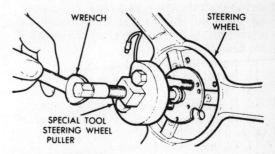

Steering wheel removal

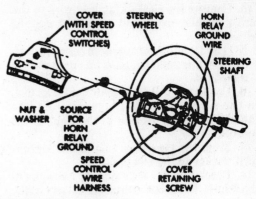

Horn pad removal (typical)

tools. Extreme care should be exercised when performing this operation.

1. Disconnect the negative battery cable.

2. Straighten the steering wheel so the front tires are pointing straight forward.

3. Remove the 4 nuts located on the back side of the steering wheel that attach the airbag module to the steering wheel.

4. Lift the module and disconnect the connectors. Remove the speed control switch, if equipped.

NOTE: *All columns except Acustar are equipped with a clockspring set screw held by a plastic tether on the steering wheel. Acustar-mounted clocksprings are auto-locking. If the steering column is not an Acustar and is lacking the set screw, obtain one before proceeding.*

5. If equipped with the set screw, place it in the clockspring to ensure proper positioning when the steering wheel is removed.

6. Remove the steering wheel hold-down nut and remove the damper, if equipped. Matchmark the steering wheel to the shaft.

7. Using a suitable steering wheel puller, pull the steering wheel off of the shaft.

To install:

8. Position the steering wheel on the steering column. Make sure the flats on the hub of the steering wheel are aligned with the formations on the clockspring.

9. Pull the airbag and speed control connectors through the lower, larger hole in the steering wheel and pull the horn wire through the smaller hole at the top. Make sure the wires are not pinched anywhere.

10. Install the damper, if equipped.

11. Install the hold-down nut and torque to 45 ft. lbs. (60 nm).

12. If equipped with a clockspring set screw, remove the screw and place it in its storage location on the steering wheel.

13. Connect the horn wire.

14. Connect the speed control wire and install the speed control switch.

15. Connect the clockspring lead wire to the airbag module and install module to steering wheel.

NOTE: *Do not allow anyone to enter the vehicle from this point on, until this procedure is completed.*

16. Connect a DRB II, or equivalent scan tool, to the Airbag System Diagnostic Module (ASDM) connector located to the right of the console.

17. From the passenger side of the vehicle, turn the key to the **ON** position.

18. Check to make sure nobody has entered the vehicle. Connect the negative battery cable.

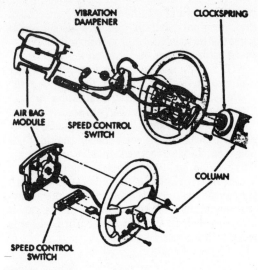

Airbag module

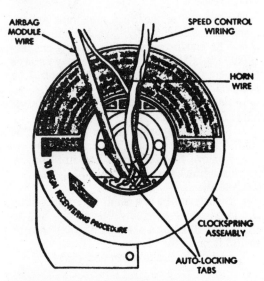

Clockspring auto-locking-airbag system

19. Using the DRB II, read and record any active fault data or stored codes.

20. If any active fault codes are present, perform the proper diagnostic procedures before continuing.

21. If there are no active fault codes, erase the stored fault codes; if there are active codes, the stored codes will not erase.

22. From the passenger side of the vehicle, turn the key **OFF**, then **ON** and observe the instrument cluster airbag warning light. It should come on for 6–8 seconds, then go out, indicating the system is functioning normally. If the warning light either fails to come on, or stays lit, there is a system malfunction and further diagnostics are needed.

1990–92 Laser

1. Disconnect the negative battery cable.
2. Remove the horn pad and disconnect horn button connector.
3. Remove steering wheel retaining nut.
4. Matchmark the steering wheel to the shaft.
5. Use a steering wheel puller to remove the steering wheel. Do not hammer on steering wheel to remove it. The collapsible column mechanism may be damaged.

To install:

6. Line up the matchmarks and install the steering wheel. Torque the retaining nut to 29 ft. lbs. (40 Nm).
7. Install the steering wheel attaching nut and torque to 33 ft. lbs. (45 Nm).
8. Reconnect the horn connector and install the horn pad.

Stealth

NOTE: *If equipped with an air bag, be sure to disarm it before entering the vehicle. Refer to the service procedure below.*

1. Disconnect the negative battery cable.
2. Remove the air bag module mounting nut from behind the steering wheel.
3. Carefully disconnect the module connector.
4. Store the air bag module in a clean, dry place with the pad cover facing up.
5. Remove the steering wheel retaining nut. Matchmark the steering wheel to the shaft. Use a steering wheel puller to remove the wheel. Do not use a hammer or the collapsible mechanism in the column could be damaged. from the steering column.

To install:

6. Center the clock spring by aligning the **NEUTRAL** mark on the clock spring with the mating mark on the casing.
7. Line up the matchmarks and install the steering wheel. Torque the retaining nut to 29 ft. lbs. (40 Nm).

AIR BAG DISARMING

1. Position the front wheels in the straight ahead position and place the key in the **LOCK** position.
2. Disconnect the negative battery cable and insulate the cable end with high-quality electrical tape or similar non-conductive wrapping.
3. Wait at least 1 minute before working on the vehicle. The air bag system is designed to retain enough voltage to deploy for a short period of time even after the battery has been disconnected.
4. If necessary, enter the vehicle from the passenger side and turn the key to unlock the steering column.

Turn Signal Switch

REMOVAL AND INSTALLATION

1981–87 Chrysler FWD – Without Tilt Wheel

1. Disconnect the negative battery terminal.
2. Remove the steering wheel as described earlier.
3. On vehicles equipped with intermittend wipe or intermittend wipe with speed control, remove the two screws that attach the turn signal lever cover to the lock housing and remove the turn signal lever cover.
4. Remove the wash/wipe switch assembly.
5. Pull the hider up the control stalk and remove the two screws that attach the control stalk sleeve to the wash/wipe shaft.
6. Rotate the control stalk shaft to the full clockwise position and remove the shaft from the switch by pulling straight out of the switch.
7. Remove the turn signal switch and upper bearing retainer screws. Remove the retainer and lift the switch up and out.

1981–87 Chrysler FWD – With Tilt Wheel

1. Disconnect the negative battery terminal.
2. Remove the steering wheel as previously described.
3. Remove the tilt lever and push the hazard warning knob in and unscrew it to remove it.
4. Remove the ignition key lamp assembly.
5. Pull the knob off the wash/wipe switch assembly.
6. Pull the hider up the stalk and remove the two screws that attach the sleeve to the wash/wipe switch and remove the sleeve.
7. Rotate the shaft in the wiper switch to the full clockwise position and remove the shaft by pulling straight out of the wash/wipe switch.
8. Remove the plastic cover from the lock plate. Depress the lock plate with tool C–4156 and pry the retaining ring out of the groove. Remove the lock plate, canceling cam and upper bearing spring.

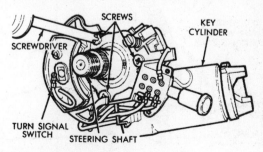

Turn signal switch assembly removal

9. Remove the switch actuator screw and arm.

10. Remove the three turn signal switch attaching screws and place the shift bowl in low position. Wrap a piece of tape around the connector and wires to prevent snagging then remove the switch and wires.

11. Installation is the reverse of removal.

1988–89 Chrysler FWD — With Standard Column

1. Disconnect the negative battery cable.
2. Remove the lower steering column cover, if equipped.
3. Straighten the steering wheel so the tires are pointing straight-ahead.

NOTE: *If equipped with an airbag, it is imperative that the "Steering Wheel" removal and installation procedure under Steering is followed.*

4. Remove the steering wheel.
5. Remove the plastic wiring channel from the under the steering column and disconnect the turn signal switch connector.
6. Remove the hazard switch knob. Remove the slotted hex-head screw that attaches the wiper switch to the turn signal switch.
7. Remove the 3 screws and pull the turn signal switch out of the column.

To install:

8. Run the wiring through the opening and down the steering column, position the switch

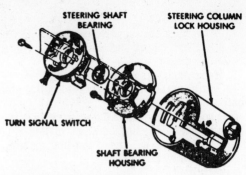

Turn signal switch assembly

and install the hex-head screw. Make sure the dimmer switch rod is properly engaged.

9. Install the 3 screws and the hazard switch knob.
10. Connect the wires and install the wiring channel.
11. Install the steering wheel and torque the nut to 45 ft. lbs. (61 Nm).
12. Install the horn pad.
13. Connect the negative battery cable and check the turn signal switch and dimmer switch for proper operation.
14. Install the lower column cover, if equipped.

1988–89 Chrysler FWD — With Tilt Wheel

1. Disconnect the negative battery cable.
2. Remove the lower steering column cover,

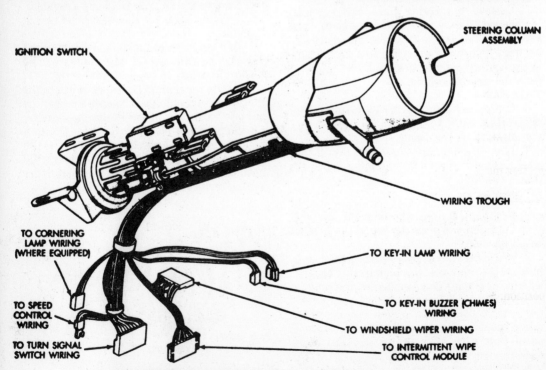

Steering column wiring connectors—K, E, G, H, J, P, C body styles

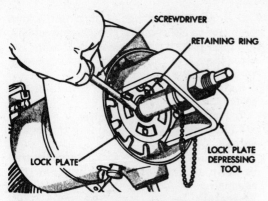

Removing lock plate retaining ring using special tools

if equipped and remove the plastic wiring channel from the under the steering column.

3. Straighten the steering wheel so the tires are pointing straight-ahead.

NOTE: *If equipped with an airbag, it is imperative that the "Steering Wheel" removal and installation procedure under Steering is followed.*

4. Remove the steering wheel.

5. Depress the lockplate with the proper depressing tool, remove the retaining ring from its groove and remove the tool, ring, lockplate, cancelling cam and spring.

6. Remove the stalk actuator screw and arm.

7. Remove the hazard switch knob.

8. Disconnect the turn signal switch connector.

9. Remove the 3 screws and remove the turn signal switch. Tape the connector to the wires to aid in removal.

To install:

10. Run the wiring through the opening and down the steering column, install the turn signal switch, switch stalk actuator arm and hazard switch knob.

11. Install the spring, cancelling cam, lockplate and ring on the steering shaft. Depress the plate with the depressing tool and install the ring securely in the groove. Remove the tool slowly.

12. Connect the turn signal switch connector and install the channel.

13. Install the steering wheel and torque the nut to 45 ft. lbs. (61 Nm).

14. Install the horn pad.

15. Connect the negative battery cable and check the turn signal switch and dimmer switch for proper operation.

16. Install the lower column cover, if equipped.

1990–92 Daytona And LeBaron

1. Disconnect the negative battery cable.

2. Remove the panel vent grille above the

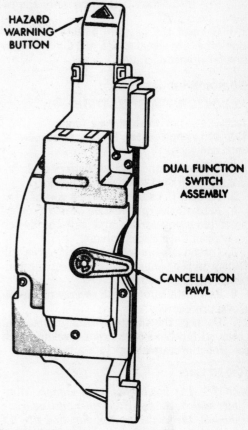

Dual function switch—AG and AJ body styles

switch pod assembly and remove the 2 revealed pod mounting screws.

3. Remove the 2 remaining screws under the pod and pull the pod out to disconnect the wiring harnesses. Remove the pod from the instrument panel.

4. Remove the turn signal switch lever by pulling it straight out of the pod.

5. Remove the inner panel from the pod. Unplug the switch from the printed circuit board.

6. Remove the turn signal switch mounting screws and slide the switch out of the slot.

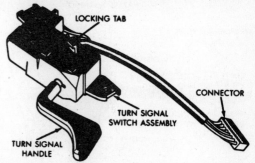

Remote turn signal switch assembly—AG and AJ body styles

7. The installation is the reverse of the removal procedure.

8. Connect the negative battery cable and check the turn signal switch and dimmer function for proper operation.

Combination Switch

REMOVAL AND INSTALLATION

1990–92 Dynasty, Imperial, New Yorker
1990–92 LeBaron Landau, Shadow, Sundance, Spirit and Acclaim

1. Disconnect the negative battery cable.
2. Remove the tilt lever, if equipped.
3. Remove the steering column covers.
4. Remove the combination switch tamper-proof mounting screws and pull the switch away from the steering column.
5. Loosen the connector screw; the screw will remain in the connector. Disconnect the connector from the switch.
6. The installation is the reverse of the removal procedure.
7. Connect the negative battery cable and check all functions of the combination switch for proper operation.

1990–92 Laser

NOTE: *The headlights, turn signals, dimmer switch, windshield/washer and, on some models, the cruise control function are all built into 1 multi-function combination switch that is mounted on the steering column.*

1. Disconnect the negative battery cable.
2. Remove the knee protector panel under the steering column, then the upper and lower column covers.
3. Remove the horn pad by pulling the lower end.
4. Matchmark and remove the steering wheel with a steering wheel puller. Do not hammer on the steering wheel to remove it or the collapsible mechanism may be damaged.

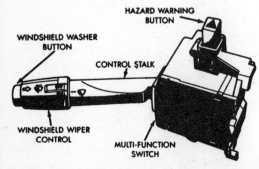

HAZARD WARNING BUTTON

WINDSHIELD WASHER BUTTON

CONTROL STALK

WINDSHIELD WIPER CONTROL

MULTI-FUNCTION SWITCH

Multi-function switch—AA, AC, AP, AY body styles

5. Locate the rectangular plugs in the knee protector on either side of the steering column. Pry these plugs out and remove the screws. Remove the screws from the hood lock release lever and remove the knee protector.
6. Remove the upper and lower column covers.
7. Remove the lap cooler ducts.
8. Remove the band retaining the switch wiring.
9. Disconnect all connectors, remove the wiring clip and remove the column switch assembly.

To install:

10. Install the switch assembly and secure the clip. Make sure no wires are pinched or out of place.
11. Install the lap cooler ducts.
12. Install the column covers and knee protector.
13. Install the steering wheel. Torque the steering wheel-to-column nut to 29 ft. lbs. (40 Nm).
14. Connect the negative battery cable and check all functions of the combination switch for proper operation.

Stealth

NOTE: *The headlights, turn signals and dimmer switch are all built into 1 multi-function combination switch that is mounted on the left side of the steering column.*

1. Disconnect the negative battery cable.

NOTE: *If equipped with an air bag, be sure to disarm it before entering the vehicle. Refer to the service procedure below.*

2. Remove the steering wheel:
   a. Remove the air bag module mounting nut from behind the steering wheel.
   b. Carefully disconnect the module connector.
   c. Store the air bag module in a clean, dry place with the pad cover facing up.
   d. Remove the steering wheel retaining nut and use a steering wheel puller to remove the wheel. Do not use a hammer or the collapsible mechanism in the column could be damaged.
3. Remove the hood lock release handle.
4. Remove the switches from the knee protector below the steering column, and remove the exposed retaining screws. Then remove the knee protector.
5. Remove the column covers.
6. Remove necessary duct work and disconnect the combination switch connectors.
7. Remove the retaining screws and remove the combination switch assembly from the steering column.

To install:

8. Install the switch to the steering column and connect the connectors.

9. Install any removed duct work.

10. Install the column covers.

11. Install the knee protector and switches.

12. Install the hood release handle.

13. Center the clock spring by aligning the **NEUTRAL** mark on the clock spring with the mating mark on the casing. Then install the steering wheel and torque the retaining nut to 29 ft. lbs. (40 Nm).

14. Connect the negative battery cable and check all functions of the combination switch for proper operation.

AIRBAG DISARMING

1. Position the front wheels in the straight ahead position and place the key in the **LOCK** position.

2. Disconnect the negative battery cable and insulate the cable end with high-quality electrical tape or similar non-conductive wrapping.

3. Wait at least 1 minute before working on the vehicle. The air bag system is designed to retain enough voltage to deploy for a short period of time even after the battery has been disconnected.

4. If necessary, enter the vehicle from the passenger side and turn the key to unlock the steering column.

Dodge Monaco

NOTE: *The windshield wiper, turn signal, headlight and dimmer switches are all combined in the combination switch on the left side of the steering column.*

1. Disconnect the negative battery cable.

2. If not equipped with passive restraint, remove the lower instrument panel cover. If equipped with passive restraint, perform the following:

a. Pull the ashtray from the receptacle, remove the receptacle and unplug the lighter.

b. Remove the 2 screws fastening the console to the front bracket.

c. Remove the armrest and the 2 screws fastening the console to the rear bracket.

d. Reach inside the console and push out the seatbelt guides. Remove the console.

e. Remove the bolts fastening the pivot bracket to the knee bolster. Loosen, but do not remove, the 2 bolts fastening the pivot bracket to the front console bracket.

f. Remove the screw and the 2 Torx® screws that attach the bracket to the floor and slide the bracket back.

g. Remove the screw located at the top of the knee bolster to the left of the steering column.

h. Remove the screw attaching the air duct to the knee bolster.

i. Remove the screw located at the bottom of the instrument panel holding the garnish penal.

j. Remove both bolster end caps and the revealed nuts.

k. Move the knee bolster toward the rear of the vehicle enough to gain access to the 2 screws holding the parking brake handle, then lower the handle.

l. Remove the knee bolster.

3. Remove the screws, remove the support rod and pull the air duct aside.

4. Cut the plastic tie-wrap straps.

5. Loosen the hold-down nut in the center of the steering column electrical connector and separate the connector.

6. Separate the left side pod switch connector from the steering column connector by placing a flat blade tool between the connectors to disengage the locking tab. Push on the wire side of the left side pod switch connector and slide the connector out of the channels of the steering column connector.

7. Disconnect the electrical connector, then remove the bottom 2 screws (not the rivets) from the pod assembly.

8. To gain access to the inside of the pod, remove the screws from the back of the left side switch pod assembly and remove the switch pod housing back cover.

NOTE: *There are small retaining clips on the left side pod that may fall off when the switch is removed.*

9. Carefully pull the switch pod far enough from the housing to expose the 2 screws, remove them and gently pull the switch forward and pull the harness out through the housing to remove the switch.

To install:

10. Route the switch assembly connector through the housing and along the underside of the steering column.

11. Connect the switch connector.

12. Connect the steering column connector and install the hold-down nut. Secure with a new tie.

13. Position the switch and secure with the screws.

14. Connect the air duct.

15. Install the lower support bar.

16. Install the knee bolster and console by reversing their removal procedure, if equipped, or install the lower instrument cover.

17. Connect the negative battery cable and check all functions of the combination switch for proper operation.

Ignition Switch and Keylock
REMOVAL AND INSTALLATION
Chrysler Front Wheel Drive
Vehicles Without Tilt Wheel

NOTE: *Use this service procedure as guide for all other models. Refer to "Turn Signal Switch" removal and installation procedures in this chapter.*

1. Follow the turn signal switch removal procedure previously described.

2. Unclip the horn and key light ground wires.

3. Remove the retaining screw and move the ignition key lamp assembly out of the way.

4. Remove the four screws that hold the bearing housing to the lock housing.

5. Remove the snapring from the upper end of the steering shaft.

6. Remove the bearing housing from the shaft.

7. Remove the lock plate spring and lock plate from the steering shaft.

8. Remove the igniton key, then remove the screw and lift out the buzzer/chime switch.

9. Remove the two screws attaching the igniton switch to the column jacket.

10. Remove the ignition switch by rotating the switch 90 degrees on the rod then sliding off the rod.

11. Remove the two mounting screws from the dimmer switch and disengage the switch from the actuator rod.

12. Remove the two screws that mount the bellcrank and slide the bellcrank up in the lock housing until it can be disconnected from the ignition switch actuator rod.

13. To remove the lock cylinder and lock lever places the cylinder in the lock position and remove the key.

14. Insert a small diameter screwdriver or similar tool into the lock cylinder release holes and push into the release spring loaded lock retainers. At the same time pull the lock cylinder out of the housing bore.

15. Grasp the lock lever and spring assembly and pull straight out of the housing.

16. If necessary the lock housing may be removed from the column jacket by removing the hex head retaining screws.

17. Installation is the reverse of removal. If the lock housing was removed tighten the lock housing screws to 90 inch lbs.

18. To install the dimmer switch, firmly seat the push rod into the switch. Compress the switch until two $\frac{3}{32}$ in. drill shanks can be inserted into the alignment holes. Reposition the upper end of the push rod in the pocket of the wash/wipe switch. With a light rearward pressure on the switch, install the two screws.

19. Grease and assemble the two lock levers, lock lever spring and pin.

20. Install the lock lever assembly in the lock housing. Seat the pin firmly into the bottom of the slots and make sure the lock lever spring leg is firmly in place in the lock casting notch.

21. Install the ignition switch actuator rod from the bottom through the oblong hole in the lock housing and attach it to the bellcrank. Position the bellcrank assembly into the lock housing while pulling the ignition switch rod down the column, install the bellcrank onto its mounting surface. The gearshift lever should be in the park position.

22. Place the ignition switch on the ignition switch actuator rod and rotate it 90 degrees to lock the rod into position.

23. To install the ignition lock, turn the key to the lock position and remove the key. Insert the cylinder far enough into the housing to contact the switch actuator. Insert the key and press inward and rotate the cylinder. When the parts align the cylinder will move inward and lock into the housing.

24. With the key cylinder in the lock position and the ignition switch in the lock position (second detent from top) tighten the igniton switch mounting screws.

25. Feed the buzzer/chime switch wires behind the wiring post and down through the space between the housing and the jacket. Remove the igniton key and position the switch in the housing and tighten the mounting screws. The igniton key should be removed.

26. Install the lock plate on the steering shaft.

27. Install the upper bearing spring, then the upper bearing housing.

28. Install the upper bearing snapring on the steering shaft, locking the assembly in place.

29. Install the four screws attaching the bearing housing to the lock housing.

30. Install the key lamp and turn signal switch, following the procedure given previously.

Lock Cylinder
REMOVAL AND INSTALLATION
Chrysler Front Wheel Drive
Vehicles With Tilt Wheel

NOTE: *Use this service procedure as a guide for all other models. This service repair requires above average mechanical ability or skill. Refer to "Turn Signal Switch" removal and installation procedures in this chapter.*

1. Remove the turn signal switch as previously described.

2. Place the lock cylinder in the lock position.

3. Insert a thin tool into the slot next to the switch mounting screwing boss (right hand slot) and depress the spring latch at the bottom of the slot and remove the lock.

4. Installation is the reverse of removal. Turn the ignition lock to the **Lock** position and remove the key. Insert the cylinder until the spring loaded retainer snaps into place.

Ignition Switch

REMOVAL AND INSTALLATION

Chrysler Front Wheel Drive Vehicles With Tilt Wheel

NOTE: *Use this service procedure as a guide for all other models. This service repair requires above average mechanical ability or skill. Refer to "Turn Signal Switch" removal and installation procedures in this chapter.*

1. Remove the turn signal switch as described above. Remove the ignition lock cylinder as described above.

NOTE: *If the wedge spring described in the next step is dropped, it could drop into the column, requiring complete disassembly. Follow the directions and work carefully to avoid dropping it.*

2. Bend a paper clip or similar type of wire into a hook. Insert the curved end of the hook into the exposed loop of the buzzer/chime switch wedge spring. Pull the wire hook straight up to remove both the buzzer/chime switch and the spring.

3. Remove the three housing cover screws and remove the housing cover. Then, remove the wash/wipe switch.

4. Adjust the column into the full up position. Then, to remove the tilt spring retainer, insert a large Phillips screwdriver into the tilt

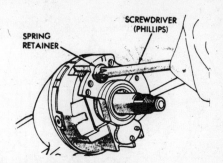

Removing the tilt spring retainer

spring opening, press the lockscrew in about $3/16$ in. (5mm) and then turn it approximately $1/8$ turn clounterclockwise to align the ears with the grooves in the housing. Remove the spring and guide.

5. Pull the actuating rod out of the dimmer switch. Remove the dimmer switch mounting screws and remove the switch.

6. Push the upper steering shaft inward far enough to remove the inner race and inner race seat, and remove both.

7. Turn the ignition switch to the **ACCESSORY** position, remove its mounting screws, and remove it.

8. To install the new switch, first turn it to the **ACCESSORY** position and slide it into place. Install the mounting screws.

9. Hold the steering shaft inward and replace the inner race seat and inner race.

10. Put the dimmer switch into position and then install its retaining screws. Install the actuating rod.

11. Install the tilt spring and guide. Put the tilt spring retainer into position. Then, use a Phillips screwdriver to re-engage the spring retainer lockscrew.

12. Install the wash/wipe switch. Install the housing cover and install the three housing cover screws.

13. Insert the curved end of the hook used in

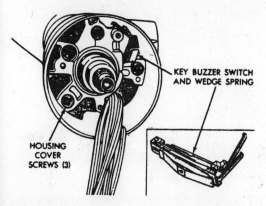

Location of the steering housing cover screws

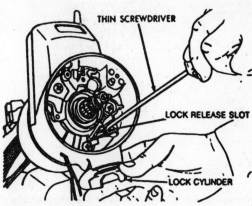

Removing the key lock cylinder—tilt wheel column

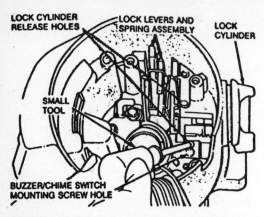

Removing the key lock cylinder—standard column

removal into the loop of the buzzer/chime switch wedge spring. Use it to install both the buzzer/chime switch and the spring without allowing the spring to drop into the column.

14. Install the ignition lock cylinder as described above. Install the turn signal switch as described above.

Ignition Lock/Switch

REMOVAL AND INSTALLATION

Late Model Chrysler Front Wheel Drive Vehicles

ACUSTAR STEERING COLUMN

NOTE: *The Acustar column can be identified by the "halo" light around the ignition key cylinder. This service repair requires above average mechanical ability or skill.*

1. Disconnect the negative battery cable.
2. Remove the tilt lever, if equipped.
3. Remove the upper and lower column covers.
4. Remove the 3 ignition switch Torx®

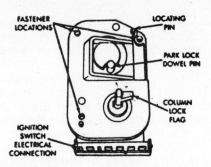

Preparing the ignition switch for installation—Acustar steering column

screws; APEX 440–TX20H or equivalent required.

5. Pull the switch away from the column. Release the connector locks on the 2 wiring connectors and disconnect them from the switch.

6. Remove the key lock cylinder from the ignition switch:

a. Insert the key and turn the switch to the **LOCK** position. Using a suitable small tool, depress the key cylinder retaining pin flush with the key cylinder surface.

b. Rotate the key clockwise to the **OFF** position to unseat the key cylinder from the ignition switch assembly. The cylinder bezel should be about ⅛ in. (3mm) above the ignition switch halo light ring. Do not attempt to remove the key cylinder yet.

c. With the key cylinder in the unseated position, rotate the key counterclockwise to the **LOCK** position and remove the key.

d. Remove the key cylinder from the ignition switch.

To install:

7. Connect the wiring connectors.

8. Mount the ignition switch to the column:

a. Position the shifter in **PARK** position. The park lock dowel pin on the ignition switch assembly must engage with the column park lock slider linkage.

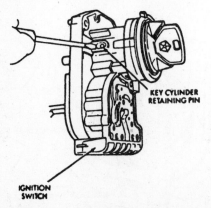

Depressing the key cylinder retaining pin—Acustar steering column

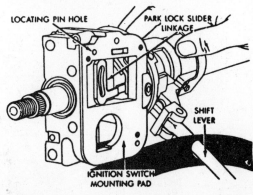

Ignition switch mounting pad—Acustar steering column

b. Verify that the ignition switch is in the **LOCK** position; the flag should be parallel to the ignition switch terminals. Apply a small amount of grease to the flag and pin.

c. Position the park lock link to mid-travel.

d. Align the locating pin hole and its pin, position the ignition switch against the lock housing face and make sure the pin is inserted into the park lock link contour slot. Torque the retaining screws to 17 inch lbs.

9. With the key cylinder and ignition switch in the **LOCK** position, key not in cylinder, gently insert the key cylinder into the ignition switch until it bottoms.

10. Insert the key. Simultaneously, push in on the cylinder and rotate the key to the **RUN** position. This action should fully seat the cylinder in the ignition switch.

11. Install the column covers and the tilt lever, if equipped.

12. Connect the negative battery cable and check the push-to-lock and park lock functions, halo lighting and all ignition switch positions for proper operation.

Steering Column

REMOVAL AND INSTALLATION
Chrysler Front Wheel Drive Vehicles

NOTE: *Use this service procedure as a guide for all other models. Refer to the exploded view illustrations in this chapter.*

CAUTION: *On vehicles equipped with an air bag, the negative battery cable must be disconnected and isolated before working on the system. Failure to do so may result in deployment of the air bag and possible personal injury.*

1. Disconnect the negative battery cable.

2. If the car has a column shift, disconnect the cable rod by prying the rod out of the grommet in the shift lever. On these cars, also remove the cable clip and remove the cable from the lower bracket.

3. Disconnect the wiring connectors at the steering column jacket. Remove the steering wheel center pad assembly. Disconnect the horn wires.

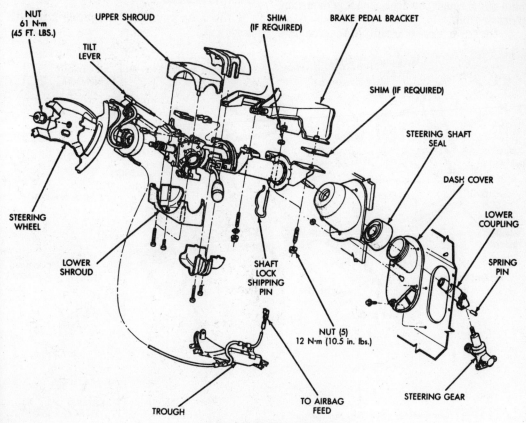

Acustar tilt steering column

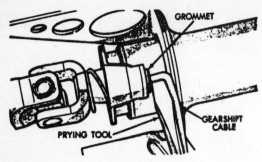

Removing rod out of grommet

4. Remove the steering wheel as described above.

5. Remove the instrument panel steering column cover and lower reinforcement. Disconnect the bezel.

6. Remove the indicator set screw and gearshift indicator pointer from the shift housing.

7. Remove the nuts which attach the column bracket to the instrument panel support and lower the bracket. Make sure to retain the washers used on the breakaway capsules. *Do not remove the roll pin!*

8. Grasp the column assembly and pull it to the rear so as to disconnect the stub shaft from the steering gear coupling. Then, pull the column out through the door, avoiding damaging paint or trim.

9. Grease a *new* gearshift lever grommet.

The grommet must be forced into place with a pair of pliers, working so as to install it from the side of the lever. Close the pair of pliers around the portion of the lever where the grommet goes and the grommet, with a washer located between the one jaw of the pair of pliers and the grommet to protect it from the teeth.

To install:

10. Position it in the car, align the stub shaft with the coupling in the steering gear, and gently thrust it forward to engage the two.

11. Raise the column and engage it with the 5 studs. Put the bracket in place below the column. Loosely install the 5 nuts, making sure to install washers on the breakaway capsules. Exert a force which will pull the column to the rear and then torque the nuts to 105 inch lbs.

12. Connect the gearshift cable rod to the shift lever on column shift-equipped cars. Grease the cable rod and then use a pair of pliers to force the rod to snap into the grommet. Check the linkage adjustment.

13. Install the steering wheel as described above.

Steering Linkage
REMOVAL AND INSTALLATION
Outer Tie Rod End

1. Jack up your car and support it with jackstands.

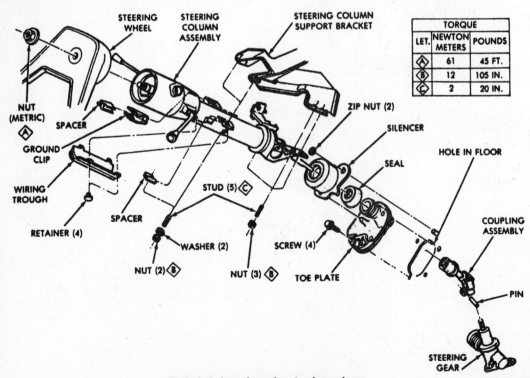

TORQUE		
LET.	NEWTON METERS	POUNDS
△	61	45 FT.
◇	12	105 IN.
◇	2	20 IN.

Exploded view of regular steering column

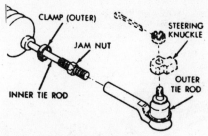

CLAMP (OUTER)

JAM NUT

STEERING KNUCKLE

INNER TIE ROD

OUTER TIE ROD

Outer tie rod assembly (typical)

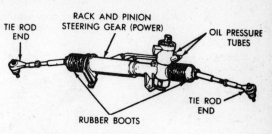

RACK AND PINION STEERING GEAR (POWER)

TIE ROD END

OIL PRESSURE TUBES

TIE ROD END

RUBBER BOOTS

Power steering gear assembly

2. Loosen the jam nut which connects the tie rod end to the rack.

3. Mark the tie rod position on the threads.

4. Remove the tie rod cotter pin and nut.

5. Using a puller, remove the tie rod from the steering knuckle.

6. Unscrew the tie rod end from the rack. Count the number of complete turns it takes to remove the tie rod end from the rack assembly.

To install:

7. Install a new tie rod end assembly (install new grease fitting if equipped) the same of amount turns it took to remove, and retighten the jam nut to 55 ft. lbs.

8. Toe adjustment is made by turning the tie rod end. Install nut with NEW cotter pin. Recheck the wheel alignment.

Manual and Power Steering Gear

REMOVAL AND INSTALLATION

Chrysler Front Wheel Drive Vehicles

NOTE: *An assistant will be needed to perform this procedure. Use this service procedure as a guide for all other models.*

1. Loosen the wheel nuts. Raise the vehicle and support it securely by the body.

2. Detach the tie rod ends at the steering knuckles as described above.

3. Support the lower front suspension crossmember securely with a jack. Then, remove all four suspension crossmember attaching bolts. Lower the crossmember with the jack until it is possible to gain access to the steering gear and the lower steering column. Slide the gear off the steering column coupling.

4. Remove the splash shields and boot seal shields.

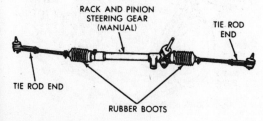

RACK AND PINION STEERING GEAR (MANUAL)

TIE ROD END

TIE ROD END

RUBBER BOOTS

Manual steering gear assembly

5. If the car has power steering, remove the fasteners from the hose locating bracket attachment points. Get a drain pan and disconnect both hoses at the opening nearest the steering gear and drain them into the pan. Discard the O-rings.

6. Remove the bolts attaching the power steering unit to the crossmember.

7. Remove the steering gear from the crossmember by pulling it off the steering column coupling and then removing it.

To install:

8. To install, first bolt the steering gear to the crossmember, torquing them to 250 inch lbs. on vehicles to 1988, 50 ft. lbs. on 1989–90 vehicles and 90 ft. lbs. on 1991 vehicles.

9. Raise the crossmember into position with the jack, lining up the steering column coupling and the corresponding fitting on the end of the steering rack pinion shaft. Have an assistant inside the car help to position the column. If the car has manual steering, make sure the master serrations are lined up. Then, maneuver the crossmember/rack assembly so as to engage the column coupling and pinion shaft.

10. Position the crossmember so the boltholes will line up. Install the bolts, but do not tighten them — merely start the threads. Tighten the right rear bolt, which serves as a pilot bolt to properly located the crossmember. Then, torque all four bolts to 90 ft. lbs. PROPER TORQUE TO THESE CROSSMEMBER BOLTS IS VERY IMPORTANT.

11. Reconnect the tie rod ends, as described above.

12. Wipe the ends of the power steering pump hoses and the ports in the steering gear. Install new O-rings on the hose tube ends and coat them with power steering fluid. Then, route the hose carefully in all clips and in such a way as to avoid kinks or close proximity to any exhaust system parts.

13. Make the hose connections and torque them to 25 ft. lbs. Refill the power steering pump with approved fluid.

14. Adjust toe in. Bleed the power steering system. Run the engine and check for leaks.

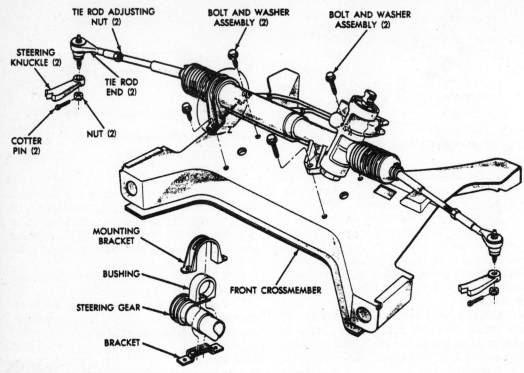

Steering gear mounting

Power Steering Pump
REMOVAL AND INSTALLATION
Chrysler Front Wheel Drive vehicles

NOTE: *Use this service procedure as a guide for all other models.*

1. Disconnect the vapor separator hose from the carburetor/throttle body. If the car has air conditioning, disconnect the two wires from the air conditioning clutch cycling switch.

2. Remove the drive belt adjustment lockbolt (refer to illustrations on later model vehicles) from the front of the power steering pump. Remove drive belt. Remove the pump end hose bracket nut, if the pump has one.

3. Raise the vehicle and support it securely.

4. Place a drain pan under the pump. Disconnect the return hose from the tube on the steering gear and and lower the end of the hose into the pan to drain the fluid from the pump (fluid will continue to drain during the next step).

5. Remove the right side splash shield (this protects the drive belts).

6. Disconnect both power steering hoses from the pump.

7. Cap the open hose ends as well as the ports in the pump to keep dirt out of the system.

8. Remove the lower stud nut and the pivot bolt from the pump.

9. Lower the vehicle. Remove the belt from the pump pulley.

10. Remove the pump rearward and to clear the mounting bracket and remove the adjusting bracket.

11. Rotate the pump clockwise so the pulley faces the rear of the vehicle and pull it upwards to remove it.

To install:

12. To replace the pump, position it as it was when it came out (pulley to the rear) and lower it into position. Then, turn it to its normal ori-

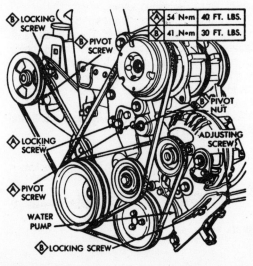

△	54 N·m	40 FT. LBS.
⑧	41 N·m	30 FT. LBS.

P/S pump mounting—2.2L and 2.5L engines

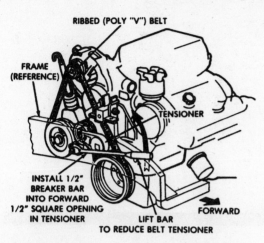

RIBBED (POLY "V") BELT

FRAME (REFERENCE)

TENSIONER

INSTALL 1/2" BREAKER BAR INTO FORWARD 1/2" SQUARE OPENING IN TENSIONER

LIFT BAR TO REDUCE BELT TENSIONER

FORWARD

P/S pump mounting—late model Chrysler vehicles

entation. Install the adjustment bracket onto the pump with the tab in the lower left mounting hole in the front of the housing.

13. Raise the vehicle and support it securely. Then, install the lower pump stud nut and pivot bolt *only finger tight*.

14. Install new O-rings on the pressure hose and connect both hoses. Torque the tube nuts to 25 ft. lbs. Install the belt into both pulley grooves.

15. Lower the vehicle to the floor. Install the belt adjusting screw into the bracket and then and adjust the belt tension.

NOTE: *Do not pry on the pump reservoir. Be careful not to create excessive belt tension* Torque the bolt to 30 ft. lbs.

16. Again raise and support the vehicle securely. Torque the lower stud nut and pivot bolt to 40 ft. lbs. Install the splash shield that protects the belt.

17. Lower the vehicle to the ground and connect the vapor separator and vent hoses to the carburetor/throttle body. Connect the two wires to the air conditioning cycling switch, if the car has air conditioning.

18. Fill the pump reservoir to the correct (cold) level with approved fluid. Bleed the system as described immediately below.

BLEEDING THE SYSTEM

1. Check the fluid level in the reservoir and fill to the correct level with the approved power steering fluid.

2. Start the engine and allow it to idle with the transmission in Neutral (manual) or Park (automatic).

3. Slowly turn the steering wheel all the way to the left and then all the way to the right. Turn it from lock to lock like this through several cycles. Then, refill the fluid reservoir.

Brakes

BRAKE SYSTEM

Adjustments

DRUM BRAKES

Chrysler Front Wheel Drive Vehicles

The brakes are self-adjusting and require no periodic adjustment. If the pedal is low and there are no apparent hydraulic problems, the rear drum brake linings are excessively worn or the automatic adjusters may be defective. The brakes are adjusted (the automatic adjusters are actuated) after drum removal or lining replacement.

In removing or installing the drums, the adjusters will have been adjusted down so the linings will be located well inside the drum. First, pump the pedal through its full stroke and with firm pressure repeatedly until the adjusters bring the linings out to fit the drum (the pedal comes up to a normal level). Then, adjust the parking brake cable as described later in this chapter. Finally, drive the car and stop normally several times to allow the adjusters to reach their final position.

Dodge Monaco

1. Raise the rear of vehicle and remove the rear wheels.
2. Remove access plate from the backing plate.
3. Working through access plug hole, tighten adjuster screw with brake tool or equivalent until drum is at moderate drag condition.

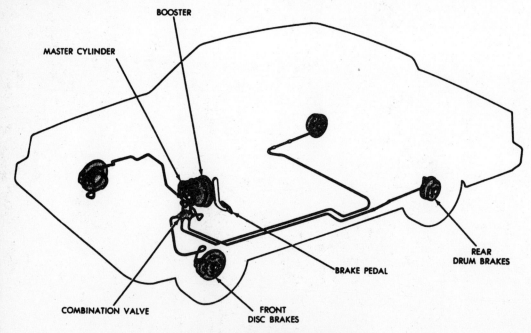

Split braking system (Non ABS system)

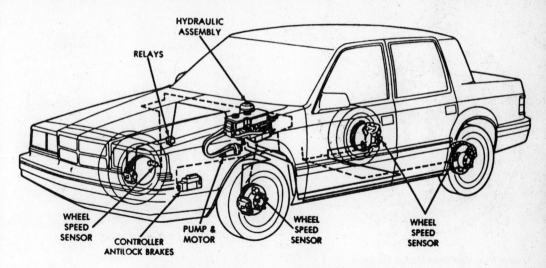

Anti-Lock brake system components—AC and AY body

4. Hold adluster lever away from the adjuster screw with a thin blade tool. Back off adjuster screw until rear wheels spin freely without noticeable brake shoe to rear brake drum drag.

5. Install access plug into bqacking plate, install wheel and lower the vehicle. Roadtest the the vehicle for proper operation.

Brake Light Switch

REMOVAL AND INSTALLATION

Chrysler Front Wheel Drive

1. The stop lamp switch is incorporated with its mounting bracket. To replace the switch,

first disconnect the negative battery cable. Then, unplug the two connector plugs.

2. Remove the wiring harness for the switch from the clip. Remove the nut and washer from the mounting bracket stud and remove the mounting bracket.

3. Install the switch/retaining bracket and install the nut and lockwasher. Tighten the retaining nut for the bracket. Connect the electrical connector plugs and route the wire through the retainer clip.

4. Push the switch forward as far as it will go (this will cause the brake pedal to move forward slightly).

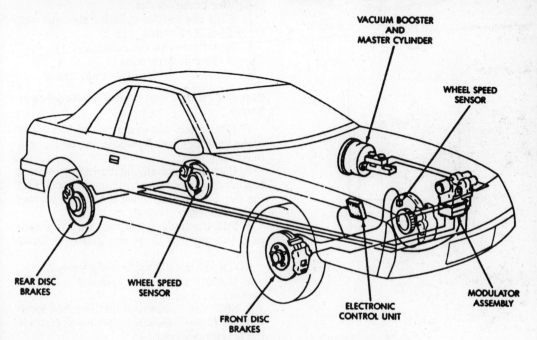

Anti-Lock brake system components—AA, AG/AJ body

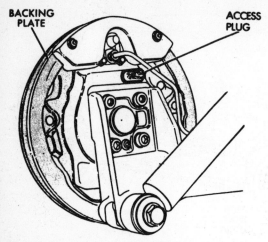

Access plug location—Dodge Monaco

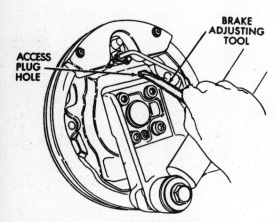

Tightening adjuster star screw—Dodge Monaco

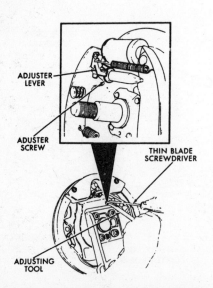

Backing off adjuster star screw—Dodge Monaco

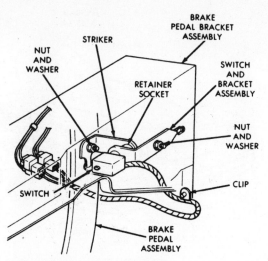

Mounting of the stop light switch

5. Gently pull backward on the brake pedal until the pedal lever rests against the stop. This will ratchet the switch back to its properly adjusted position.

Master Cylinder

REMOVAL AND INSTALLATION

Chrysler Front Wheel Drive With Power Brakes

1. Disconnect the primary and secondary brake lines from the master cylinder. Plug the openings.

2. Remove the nuts attaching the cylinder to the power brake booster.

3. Slide the master cylinder straight out, away from the booster.

4. Installation is the reverse of removal. Torque the mounting bolts to 15–25 ft. lbs.

5. Remember to bleed the brake system.

Chrysler Front Wheel Drive With Non-Power Brakes

1. Disconnect the primary and secondary brake lines and install plugs in the master cylinder openings.

2. Disconnect the stoplight switch mounting bracket from under the instrument panel. Pull the stop light switch out of the way to prevent switch damage.

3. Pull the brake pedal backward to disengage the pushrod from the master cylinder piston.

NOTE: *This will destroy the grommet.*

4. Remove the master cylinder-to-firewall nuts.

5. Slide the master cylinder out and away from the firewall. Be sure to remove all pieces of the broken grommet.

To install:

6. Install the boot on the pushrod.

7. Install a new grommet on the pushrod.

8. Apply a soap and water solution to the grommet and slide it firmly into position in the primary piston socket. Move the pushrod from side to side to make sure it's seated.

9. From the engine side, press the pushrod through the master cylinder mounting plate and align the mounting studs with the holes in the cylinder.

10. Install the nuts and torque them to 250 inch lbs.

11. From under the instrument panel, place the pushrod on the pin on the pedal and install a new retaining clip. Be sure to lubricate the pin.

12. Install the brake lines on the master cylinder.

13. Bleed the system.

1990–92 Laser And Stealth

1. Disconnect the negative battery cable.

2. Disconnect the fluid level sensor connector.

3. Disconnect the brake lines from the master cylinder. On Laser vehicles, a separate reservoir is used. Plug the lines to prevent drainage.

4. On Stealth, disconnect the low pressure hose.

5. Remove the 2 nuts securing the master cylinder and lift off.

To install:

6. Bench bleed the master cylinder.

7. Install to the studs and install the nuts.

8. Install the brake lines to the master cylinder.

9. Connect the negative battery cable and check the brakes for proper operation.

Dodge Monaco

1. Disconnect the negative battery cable.

2. Disconnect the fluid sensor electrical connector, if equipped.

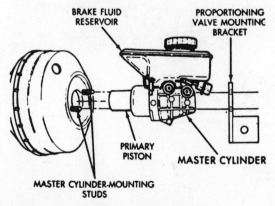

Installing master cylinder—Dodge Monaco

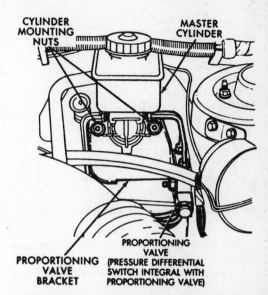

Master cylinder mounting—Dodge Monaco

3. Disconnect and plug the brake lines. Cover the master cylinder outlet ports and brake lines to prevent the entry of dirt.

4. If equipped with manual brake, disconnect the master cylinder pushrod at the brake pedal.

5. Remove the master cylinder retaining bolts or nuts.

6. Remove the proportioning valve bracket, if required.

7. Remove the master cylinder from the vehicle.

8. Before installing the replacement master cylinder on the vehicle, bench bleed the master cylinder.

9. Installation is the reverse of the removal procedure.

10. The entire brake system must be bled after installing the master cylinder.

OVERHAUL

NOTE: *Use this service procedure and exploded view diagrams as a guide for overhaul of the master cylinder assembly for all years/models. If in doubt about overhaul condition or service procedure REPLACE the complete assembly with a new master cylinder.*

1. Remove the master cylinder as previously outlined.

2. Clean the housing and reservoir.

3. Remove the caps and empty the brake fluid.

4. Remove the reservoir by rocking it from side to side.

5. Remove the housing-to-reservoir grommets.

6. Use needle-nose pliers to remove the sec-

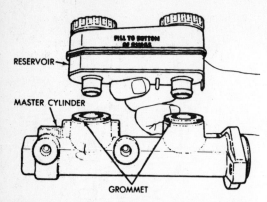

Removing the reservoir—master cylinder assembly

ondary piston stop pin from inside the master cylinder housing.

7. Remove the snapring from the outer end of the cylinder bore.

8. Slide the piston out of the cylinder bore.

9. Gently tap the end of the master cylinder on the bench to remove the secondary piston.

NOTE: *If the piston sticks in the bore use air pressure to force the piston out. New cups must be installed, if air pressure is used to force the piston out as the old cups will be damaged.*

10. Remove the rubber cups from the pistons (except the primary cup of the primary piston), after noting the position of the cup lips.

NOTE: *Do not remove the primary cup of the primary piston. If the cup is damaged, the entire piston assembly must be replaced.*

Install new piston cups in every case but the primary cup of the primary piston, unless it is certain that cups are in perfect condition. They must be flexible and free of cracks or wear, especially at the outer edges.

11. If the brass tube seats are not reuseable, remove them with an Easy-out®, and insert new ones.

12. Wash the cylinder bore with clean brake fluid. Check for scoring, pitting or scratches. If any of these conditions exist replace the master cylinder. Replace the pistons if they are corroded. Replace the cups and seals. Discard all used rubber parts.

13. During installation, coat all components with clean brake fluid. This will protect them from corrosion and moisture and permit assembly without damaging rubber cups and seals.

14. With the rubber cups and master cylinder bore thoroughly lubricated, slide the secondary piston back into the bore. Follow it with the primary piston.

15. Install the snapring into the outer end of the cylinder bore. Then, use needle-nose pliers to install the secondary piston stop pin from inside the master cylinder housing.

MASTER CYLINDER BLEEDING

1. Place the master cylinder in a vise.

2. Connect two lines to the fluid outlet orifices, and into the reservoir.

3. Fill the reservoir with brake fluid.

4. Using a wooden dowel, depress the pushrod slowly, allowing the pistons to return. Do this several times until the air bubbles are all expelled.

5. Remove the bleeding tubes from the master cylinder, plug the outlets and install the caps.

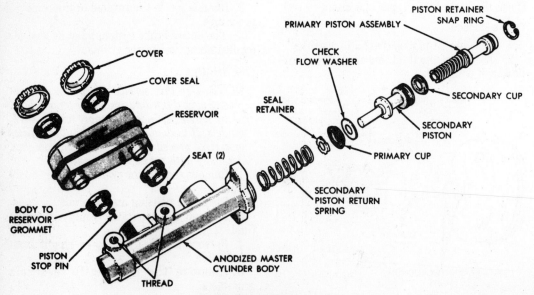

Master cylinder assembly

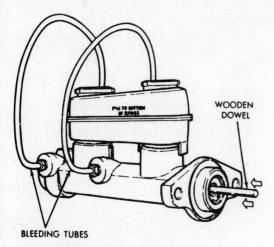

Bench bleeding the master cylinder

NOTE: *It may not be necessary to bleed the entire system after replacing the master cylinder, provided the master cylinder has been bled and filled upon installation.*

Power Brake Booster

REMOVAL AND INSTALLATION

Chrysler Front Wheel Drive Vehicles

1. Remove the brake lines from the master cylinder.

2. Remove the nuts attaching the master cylinder to the brake booster, and remove the master cylinder.

3. Release its tension with a pair of pliers and slide the vacuum hose retaining clamp back from the check valve. Then, disconnect the vacuum line supplying the brake booster at the check valve. *Do not remove the check valve.* On 1985 and later models with a manual transmission: Remove the clutch cable mounting bracket and then pull the wiring harness away from and up the strut tower.

4. Working underneath the instrument panel, remove the retainer clip from the brake pedal pin. To do this, position a small, bladed instrument between the center tang of the retainer clip and the pin on the brake pedal and twist it. Use this method to cause the tang on the clip

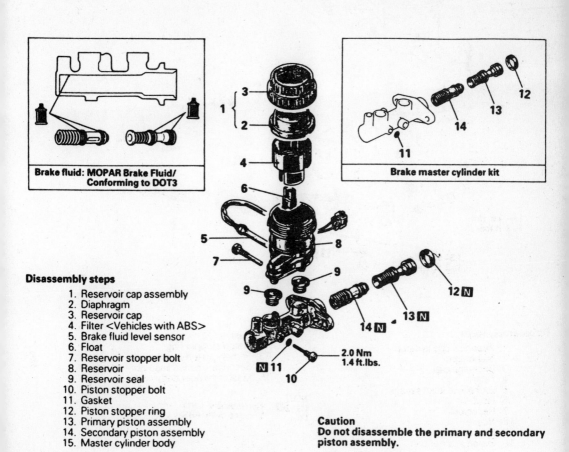

Disassembly steps

1. Reservoir cap assembly
2. Diaphragm
3. Reservoir cap
4. Filter <Vehicles with ABS>
5. Brake fluid level sensor
6. Float
7. Reservoir stopper bolt
8. Reservoir
9. Reservoir seal
10. Piston stopper bolt
11. Gasket
12. Piston stopper ring
13. Primary piston assembly
14. Secondary piston assembly
15. Master cylinder body

Caution
Do not disassemble the primary and secondary piston assembly.

Exploded view brake master cylinder—Dodge Stealth

to pass over the end of the brake pedal pin. Discard the retainer clip because it will no longer lock safely.

5. Remove the brake light switch and striker plate.

6. Remove the four power booster attaching nuts.

7. Remove the booster from the car. The power brake booster is not repairable. Do not attempt to disassemble it.

To install:

8. Postion the booster on its mounting bracket and install its four mounting nuts. Torque them to 250 inch lbs.

9. Coat the load bearing surface of the brake pedal pin with Lubriplate® or equivalent to reduce wear. Then, connect the pushrod to the pedal pin and install a new retaining clip through the end. Lock the retaining clip securely.

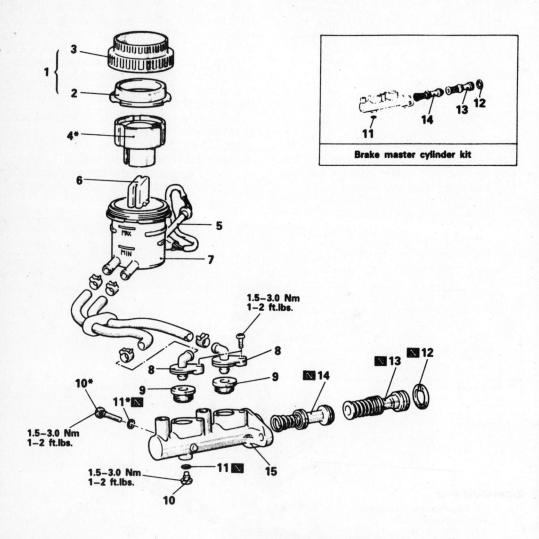

Brake master cylinder kit

Disassembly steps

1. Reservoir cap assembly
2. Diaphragm
3. Reservoir cap
4. Filter
5. Brake fluid level sensor
6. Float
7. Reservoir
8. Nipple
9. Reservoir seal
10. Piston stopper bolt
11. Gasket
12. Piston stopper ring
13. Primary piston assembly
14. Secondary piston assembly
15. Master cylinder body

NOTE
(1) ⌐N⌐ : Non-reusable parts
(2) * : Vehicles with ABS

Exploded view brake master cylinder—1990–92 Laser

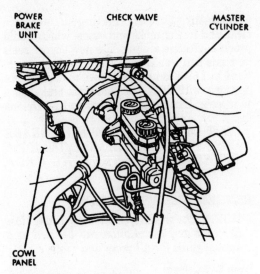

POWER BRAKE UNIT

CHECK VALVE

MASTER CYLINDER

COWL PANEL

Power brake unit mounting

10. Position the master cylinder onto the brake booster, install the mounting nuts and torque them to 250 inch lbs.

11. Route the vacuum hose carefully to the booster, ensuring that it is not kinked or pinched. Then, position its retaining clamp carefully.

12. Install each brake hydraulic tube into its correct master cylinder opening and torque the retaining flare nut to 145 inch lbs.

13. Slide the wiring harness down over the strut tower and reinstall the retaining clips. On 1985 and later models with a manual transmission, install the clutch cable mounting bracket.

14. Bleed the brake system, making sure to keep the master cylinder full of the approved brake fluid throughout the procedure. Make sure the unit is filled to the correct level when bleeding is completed. Road test the vehicle for proper operation.

1990–92 Laser And Stealth

1. Disconnect the negative battery cable.

2. Disconnect the vacuum hose from the booster. Pull it straight off. Prying off the vacuum hose could damage the check valve installed in the brake booster.

3. Remove the nuts attaching the master cylinder to the booster and remove the master cylinder.

4. From inside the passenger compartment, remove the cotter pin and clevis pin that secures the booster pushrod to the brake pedal.

5. Remove the nuts that attach the booster to the dash panel and remove it from the vehicle.

6. The installation is the reverse of the removal procedure.

7. Connect the negative battery cable, bleed the brakes and check for proper operation.

Dodge Monaco

1. Disconnect the negative battery cable.

2. Disconnect the vacuum line from the booster.

3. Remove the clip retaining the throttle cables to the bracket on the booster. Remove the master cylinder.

4. Inside the vehicle, disconnect the connector from the brake light switch. Remove the pushrod from the brake pedal.

5. Remove the booster retaining nuts and remove the booster. Inspect the seal for damage.

To install:

6. Transfer parts to the replacement booster. Install the booster to the firewall and connect the pushrod to the brake pedal. Connect the brake light switch.

7. Install the master cylinder and clip the throttle cables in place.

8. Connect the negative battery cable and bleed the brake system.

Proportioning Valve

REMOVAL AND INSTALLATION

1. Disconnect the negative battery cable.

2. Disconnect and plug the brake lines from the proportioning valve.

3. Remove the bolt and nut attaching the valve to the bracket.

4. Remove the valve from the vehicle.

5. Installation is the reverse of removal.

6. Bleed the brakes after installation.

Combination Control Valve

REMOVAL AND INSTALLATION

1. Unplug the electrical connector from the valve.

2. Place a drain pan underneath the valve. Disconnect all six hydraulic line flare nuts.

3. Remove the mounting bolt and remove the valve from the fender well.

4. To install: bolt the new valve onto the fender well.

5. Reconnect all six flare nut fittings. Torque to 145 inch lbs.

6. Reconnect the electrical connector.

7. Thoroughly bleed the brake system as described below. Then, repeatedly stop the vehicle with firm application on the pedal to center the warning switch spool valve and extinguish the brake light.

Brake Hoses

It is important to use quality brake hose intended specifically for the application. Hose of

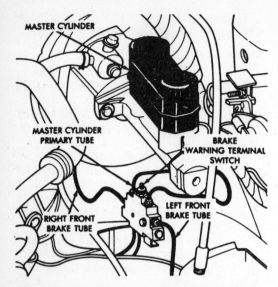

Mounting and hydraulic line identification for the brake combination valve

less than the best quality, or hose not made to the specified length will tend to fatigue and may therefore create premature leakage and, consequently, a potential for brake failure. Note also that brake hose differs from one side of the car to the other and should therefore be ordered specifying the side on which it will be installed.

Make sure hose end mating surfaces are clean and free of nicks and burrs, which would prevent effective sealing. Use new copper seals on banjo fittings. Torque brake tubing connections to 115–170 inch lbs.; hose-to-caliper connections to 19–29 ft. lbs.; and front brake hose-to-intermediate bracket fittings to 75–115 inch lbs.

CAUTION: *WHEN ROUTING A BRAKE HOSE TO A VEHICLE, MINIMIZE HOSE TWISTING AND BENDING UPON INSTALLATION!*

REMOVAL AND INSTALLATION

NOTE: *The procedures below for Brake Hose Removal and Installation can be used as a service guide for all years and models.*

Front Brake Hose

1. Place a drain pan under the hose connections. First, disconnect the hose where it connects to the body bracket and steel tube.

2. Unbolt the hose bracket from the strut assembly.

3. Remove the bolt to disconnect the banjo connection at the caliper.

4. Position the new hose, noting that the body bracket and the body end of the hose are keyed to prevent installation of the hose in the

LETTER	TIGHTENING TORQUE	
Ⓐ	105 IN. LB.	12 N·m
Ⓑ	95 IN. LB.	11 N·m
Ⓒ	70 IN. LB.	8 N·m
Ⓓ	145 IN. LB.	16 N·m
Ⓔ	40 IN. LB.	5 N·m
Ⓕ	35 FT. LB.	25 N·m

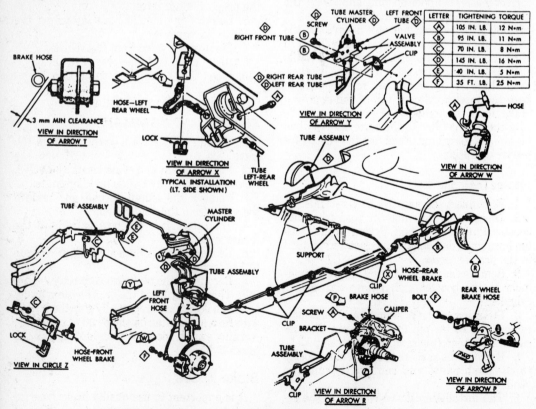

Brake line routing

wrong direction. First attach the hose to the banjo connector on the caliper.

5. Bolt the hose bracket located in the center of the hose to the strut, allowing the bracket to position the hose so it will not be twisted.

6. Attach the hose to the body bracket and steel brake tube.

7. Torque the banjo fitting on the caliper to 19–29 ft. lbs.; the front hose to intermediate bracket to 75–115 inch lbs.; and the hose to brake tube to 115–170 inch lbs. Bleed the system thoroughly, referring to the procedure below.

Rear Brake Hose (Trailing Arm-to-Floor Pan)

1. Place a drain pan under the hose connections. Disconnect the double nut (using a primary wrench and a backup wrench) at the tube mounted on the floor pan. Then, disconnect the hose at the retaining clip.

2. Disconnect the hose at the trailing arm tube. Install the new tube to the trailing arm connection first. Torque the connection to 115–170 inch lbs. Then, making sure it is not twisted, connect it to the tube on the floor pan. Again, torque the connection to 115–170 inch lbs. Bleed the system thoroughly, referring to the procedure below.

Caliper Hose – Rear Disc Brakes

1. Place a drain pan under the hose connections. Disconnect the double nut (using a primary wrench and a backup wrench) at the tube mounted on the clip, located on the caliper-mounted bracket. Then, disconnect the banjo connector by removing the through bolt.

2. Install the new hose by connecting the banjo connector first, using new copper seals and torquing the through-bolt to 19–29 ft. lbs.

3. Making sure the hose is not twisted, make the connection to the tube, torquing to 115–170 in lbs.

4. Secure the hose to the bracket with the retaining clip. Bleed the system thoroughly, referring to the procedure below.

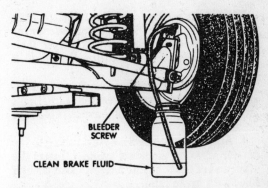

Proper method for bleeding brake system

Bleeding The System

NOTE: *For bleeding of the Anti-Lock Brake system refer to the service procedure in the "Anti-Lock Brake Section" in this chapter.*

The purpose of bleeding the brakes is to expel air trapped in the hydraulic system. The system must be bled whenever the pedal feels spongy, indicating that compressible air has entered the system. It must also be bled whenever the system has been opened or repaired. You will need a helper for this job.

NOTE: *Never reuse brake fluid which has been bled from the brake system. It contains moisture and corrosion products and should therefore always be replaced with fresh fluid.*

1. The sequence for bleeding is right rear, left front, left rear and right front for Chrysler front wheel drive vehicles without ABS system. If the car has power brakes, remove the vacuum by applying the brakes several times. Do not run the engine while bleeding the brakes.

2. Clean all the bleeder screws. You may want to give each one a shot of penetrating solvent to loosen it up; seizure is a common problem with bleeder screws, which then break off, sometimes requiring replacement of the part to which they are attached.

3. Fill the master cylinder with DOT 3 brake fluid.

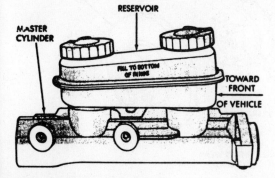

Master cylinder level information

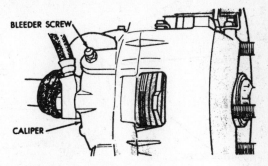

Bleeder screw location

NOTE: *Brake fluid absorbs moisture from the air. Don't leave the master cylinder or the fluid container uncovered any longer than necessary. Be careful handling the fluid—it eats paint.*

Check the level of the fluid often when bleeding, and refill the reservoirs as necessary. Don't let them run dry, or you will have to repeat the process.

4. Attach a length of clear vinyl tubing to the bleeder screw on the wheel cylinder. Insert the other end of the tube into a clear, clean jar half filled with brake fluid.

5. Have your assistant slowly depress the brake pedal. As this is done, open the bleeder screw ⅓–½ turn, and allow the fluid to run through the tube. Then close the bleeder screw before the pedal reaches the end of its travel. Have your assistant slowly release the pedal. Repeat this process until no air bubbles appear in the expelled fluid.

6. Repeat the procedure on the other three brakes, checking the lever of fluid in the master cylinder reservoir often.

After finishing, there should be no feeling of sponginess in the brake pedal. If there is, either there is still air in the line, in which case the process must be repeated, or there is a leak somewhere, which, of course, must be corrected before the car is moved. After all repairs and service work is finished roadtest the vehicle for proper operation.

FRONT DISC BRAKES

CAUTION: *Brake shoes contain asbestos, which has been determined to be a cancer-*

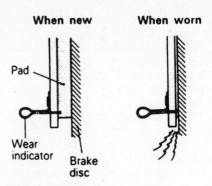

Brake pad wear indicators

causing agent. Never clean the brake surfaces with compressed air! Avoid inhaling any dust from any brake surface! When cleaning brake surfaces, use a commercially available brake cleaning fluid.

Brake Pads
INSPECTION

Measure lining wear by measuring the combined thickness of the shoe and lining at the thinnest point. It must be $5/16$ in. (8mm) on front disc brakes on Chrysler front wheel drive and Dodge Monaco vehicles.

Measure lining wear by measuring the brake pad at the thinnest point. It must be at least ⅛ inch (3mm) on front disc brakes on 1990–92 Laser and Stealth.

Some vehicles are equipped with a wear sensor on the outboard pad of the front disc brake assemblies. This sensor when emitting a sound signals that brake linings may need inspection and or replacement.

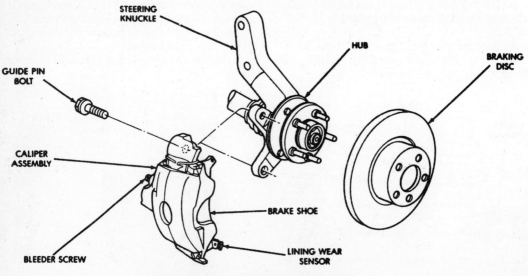

Front disc brake assembly (Chrysler caliper)

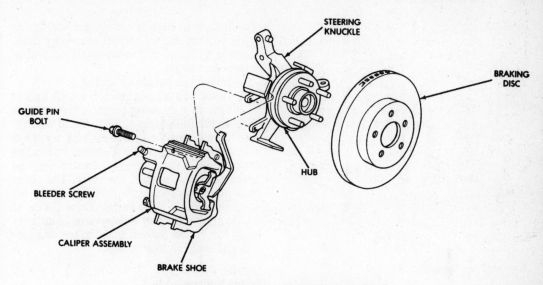

Front disc brake assembly (Non-Chrysler caliper)

Always replace both front brake pad assemblies (inboard and outboard pad) on both front wheels whenever necessary. The specifications given above on front disc brake lining wear should be used as guide for replacement.

Disc Brake Pads and Calipers

REMOVAL AND INSTALLATION

NOTE: *When replacing the front disc brake pads remove some of the brake fluid from the master cylinder first, then after removing the caliper use a large C-clamp or equivalent and slowly compress the piston back into the cailper bore to aid installation. On vehicles equipped with ABS system refer to the necessary service procedures.*

Chrysler FWD
ATE Type Brake Caliper

1. Raise and support the front end on jackstands.
2. Remove the front wheels.
3. Remove the caliper holddown spring by pushing in on the center of the spring and pushing outward.
4. Loosen but do not remove the guide pins, until the caliper is free. Remove the guide pins only if the bushings are being replaced.
5. Lift the caliper away from the rotor. The inboard pad will remain with the caliper. Remove the pad by pulling it away from the caliper piston to unsnap the retaining clip.
6. Remove the outboard pad by simply pulling it away from the caliper adapter.

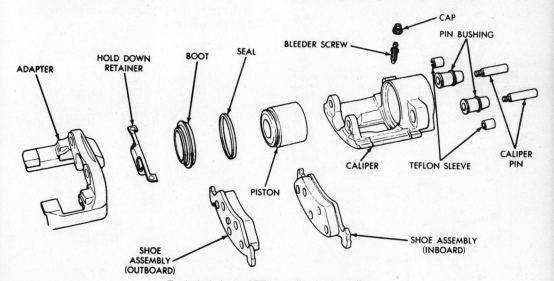

Exploded view—ATE type disc brake caliper

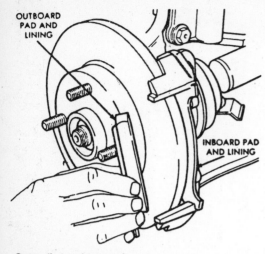

Outer disc pad removal

7. If the caliper is being removed, disconnect and cap the brake line. If only the pads are being removed, support the caliper with wire in such a way that the brake line will not be stressed.

8. Lubricate both bushing channels with silicone lubricant.

9. Remove the protective backing from the noise suppression gasket on the inner pad assembly.

10. Install the new inboard pad in the caliper, centering the retainer in the piston bore.

11. Remove the protective backing from the noise suppression gasket on the outboard pad and position the pad on the adapter.

12. Carefully lower the caliper over the rotor and inboard pad.

13. Install the guide pins and torque to 18–22 ft. lbs.

NOTE: *It is easy to crossthread the guide pins. Start them carefully, turning them gently by hand and allowing them to find their own angle.*

14. Install the holddown spring.

15. Install the wheels and torque the lugs to ½ torque in a crossing pattern, then torque them to the full torque of 95 ft. lbs. If the caliper was removed, bleed the system throroughly, as described above. Pump the brake pedal several times to ensure that the brake pads seat against the rotor. *The pedal must give resistance at the normal position before attempting to drive the car.* Drive the car at moderate speeds in an isolated area in order to apply the brakes several times to test the system and seat the new linings.

Chrysler FWD
Dodge Monaco
Kelsey-Hayes Type Brake Caliper

1. Raise and support the front end on jackstands. Refer to the illustrations in this chapter.

2. Remove the front wheels.

3. Remove the caliper guide pin. To do this, unscrew it until it is free from the threads and then pull it out of the caliper adapter.

4. Using a small prybar, gently wedge the caliper away from the rotor, breaking the adhesive seals.

5. Slowly slide the caliper away from the rotor and off the caliper adapter. Support the caliper securely by hanging it from the body with wire (this is necessary to keep its weight from damaging the brake hose).

6. Slide the outboard pad off the caliper adapter. Then remove the disc by simply sliding it off the wheel studs.

7. Remove the inboard pad by sliding it off the caliper adapter.

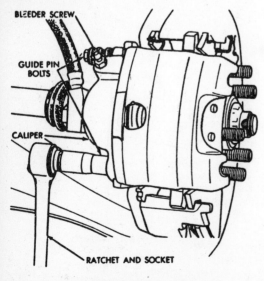

Removing or installing guide pin bolts

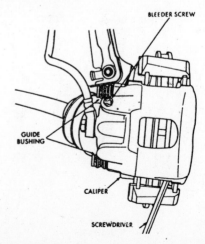

Loosening family caliper assembly from the adapter

8. If the caliper is to be removed, disconnect and cap the brake line. Then, remove it from the hanger and remove it.

9. Lubricate both bushing channels with silicone grease.

10. Remove the protective paper backing from the anti-squeal surfaces on both pads. Install the inboard pad on the adapter. Be careful to keep grease from the bushing channels from getting onto the pad as you do this.

11. Install the rotor onto the wheel studs of the steering knuckle. Install the outboard pad in the caliper and carefully slide it into place over the rotor.

12. If necessary, reconnect the brake line or remove the caliper from the hanger. Lower the caliper into position over the rotor and pads. Install the guide pin and torque it to 35 ft. lbs.

NOTE: *It is easy to crossthread the guide pin. Start it carefully, turning it by hand gently and allowing it to find its own angle.*

13. Install the wheels and torque the lugs to half the specified torque in a criss-cross pattern. Then, torque the lugs to full torque (95 ft. lbs.). If the brake line was disconnected, bleed the system thoroughly as described above.

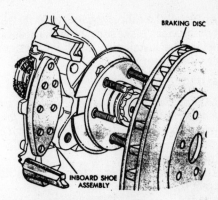

Removing or installing brake disc

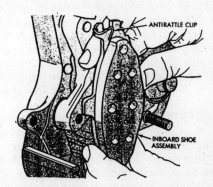

Removing or installing inboard shoe assembly

Pump the brake pedal several times to ensure that the brake pads seat against the rotor. *The pedal must give resistance at the normal position before attempting to drive the car.* Drive the car at moderate speeds in an isolated area in order to apply the brakes several times to test the system and seat the new linings.

1990–92 Laser And Stealth

1. Disconnect battery negative cable.
2. Raise the vehicle and support safely.
3. Remove appropriate wheel assembly.
4. On the front of AWD Stealth, remove the pad retaining pins and pull the pads out of the caliper body.
5. On others, remove the caliper from its adaptor but do not allow the caliper to hang by the brake line. On some vehicles, the caliper can be flipped up by leaving the upper pin in place and using it as a pivot point. Take note of the clips, pins, anti-squeal shims and other parts for reference at assembly. On some applications, the lock pins or guide pins are matched marked to the caliper body for proper installation.

To install:

6. Use a large C-clamp to compress the piston(s) back into the caliper bore. Install the pads and all other small parts.

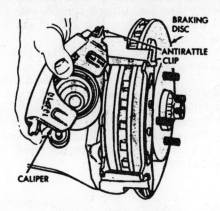

Removing or installing caliper assembly

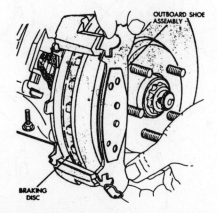

Removing or installing outboard shoe assembly

8. Install the caliper (torque is 50 ft. lbs. on retaining pins). Make sure the brake hose is not twisted after installation. Refill the master cylinder if necessary.

CALIPER OVERHAUL

NOTE: *Use this service procedure as a guide for overhaul of the caliper assembly for all years/models. If in doubt about overhaul condition or service procedure REPLACE the complete assembly.*

1. Remove the caliper as previously outlined, leaving the brake line connected.

2. Carefully have a helper depress the brake pedal to hydraulically push the piston out of the bore. When the piston has passed out of the bore, fluid and pedal pressure will drop. As soon as pedal pressure drops, hold the pedal in position with the foot and then devise a means to keep it there during work—this will minimize fluid loss and difficulty bleeding the system later.

CAUTION: *Under no condition should air pressure be used to remove the piston. Personal injury could result from this practice.*

3. Disconnect the flexible brake line at the frame bracket and immediately plug the open end of the line. If the piston from the caliper on the opposite side of the car must now be removed, it can be removed in the same way. When the piston has been removed, disconnect and plug the other flexible line.

4. Place the caliper in a vise which has soft jaws, clamping it as lightly as possible.

NOTE: *Excessive vise pressure will cause bore distortion and piston binding.*

5. Remove the dust boot and discard it.

6. Use a plastic rod to work the piston seal

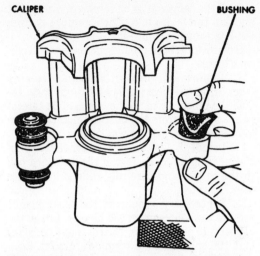

Removing bushings from the caliper assembly

out of its groove in the piston bore. Discard the old seal.

NOTE: *Do not use a metal tool for this procedure, because of the possiblity of scratching the piston bore or damaging the edges of the seal.*

7. Remove the bushings from the caliper by pressing them out, using a suitable tool. Discard the old bushings. If a Teflon® sleeve is used, discard this also.

8. Clean all parts using alcohol and blow dry with compressed air.

NOTE: *Whenever a caliper has been disassembled, a new boot and seal must be installed.*

9. Inspect the piston bore for scoring or pitting. Bores with light scratches can be cleaned up. If the bore is scratched beyond repair, the caliper should be replaced.

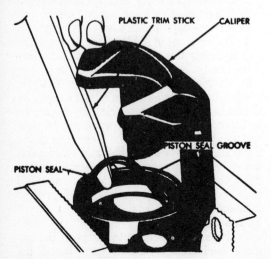

Removing piston seal

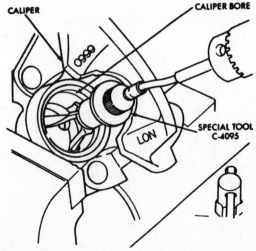

Honing piston bore

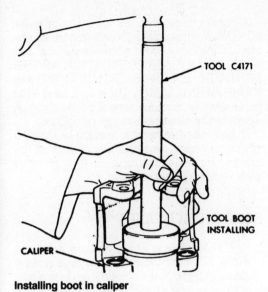

Installing boot in caliper

17. Be sure the flanges extend over the caliper casting evenly on both sides.

18. When reinstalling the calipers use new seal washers and torque the brake hose connections to the specified torque. Follow the installation procedure above.

19. Bleed the brake system. Pump the brake pedal several times to ensure that the brake pads seat against the rotor. *The pedal must give resistance at the normal position before attempting to drive the car.* Drive the car at moderate speeds in an isolated area in order to apply the brakes several times to test the system.

Brake Disc

REMOVAL AND INSTALLATION

1. Raise and support the front end on jackstands.

2. Remove the caliper from the rotor, but do not disconnect the brake line.

3. Suspend the caliper out of the way with wire. Do not put stress on the brake hose.

4. On ATE type brake caliper systems, remove the adapter from the knuckle.

5. Remove the rotor (some applications have 2 hold down in the brake disc or rotor screws that must be removed) from the drive flange studs.

To install:

6. Coat both sides of the rotor with alcohol or equivalent (to clean assembly) and slide it onto the studs.

7. Install the adapter ATE type brake caliper.

8. Install the caliper as described above.

INSPECTION

Light scoring is acceptable. Heavy scoring or warping will necessitate refinishing or replace-

10. Dip the new piston seal in clean brake fluid and install it in the bore groove.

NOTE: *Never use an old piston seal.*

11. Coat the new piston with clean brake fluid, leaving a generous amount inside the boot.

12. Position the dust boot over the piston.

13. Install the piston into the bore, pushing it past the piston seal until it bottoms in the bore.

NOTE: *Force must be applied uniformly to avoid cocking the piston.*

14. Position the dust boot in the counterbore.

15. Using tools #C–4689 and C–4171 or their equivalents install the dust boot.

16. Remove the Teflon® sleeves from the guide pin bushings before installing the bushings into the caliper. After the new bushings are installed in the caliper, reinstall the Teflon® sleeves into the bushings.

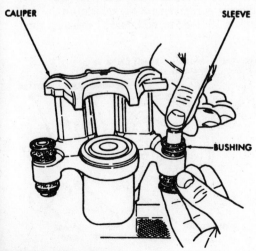

Installing caliper sleeves

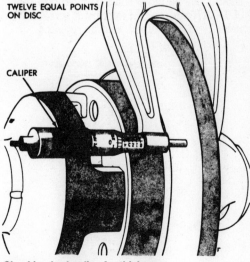

Checking brake disc for thickness

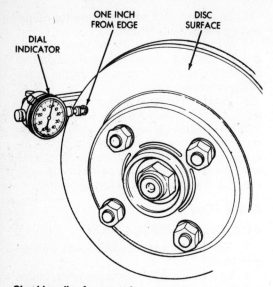

Checking disc for run-out

ment of the disc. The brake disc must be replaced if cracks or burned marks are evident.

Check the thickness of the disc. Measure the thickness at 12 equally spaced points 1 in. (25.4mm) from the edge of the disc. If thickness varies more than 0.0005 in. (0.013mm) the disc should be refinished, provided equal amounts are out from each side and the thickness does not fall below 0.882 inch (22.4mm) on Chrysler front wheel drive vehicles.

Check the run-out of the disc. Total runout of the disc installed on the car should not exceed 0.005 in. (0.013mm). The disc can be resurfaced to correct minor variations as long as equal amounts are cut from each side and the thickness is at least 0.882 inch (22.4mm) on Chrysler front wheel drive vehicles after resurfacing.

Check the run-out of the hub (disc removed). It should not be more than 0.002–0.003 inch (0.050–0.076mm) on Chrysler front wheel drive vehicles If so, the hub should be replaced.

All brake discs or rotors have markings for MINIMUM allowable thickness cast on an unmachined surface or an alternate surface. ALWAYS USE THIS SPECIFICATION AS THE MINIMUM ALLOWABLE THICKNESS OR REFINISHING LIMIT. Refer to a local auto parts store or machine shop if necessary shop where brake disc or rotors are resurfaced.

If the brake disc or rotor needs to be replaced with a new part, the protective coating on the braking surface of the rotor must be removed with an appropriate solvent.

REAR DRUM BRAKES

CAUTION: *Brake shoes contain asbestos, which has been determined to be a cancer-causing agent. Never clean the brake surfaces with compressed air! Avoid inhaling any dust from any brake surface! When cleaning brake surfaces, use a commercially available brake cleaning fluid.*

Brake Drums

REMOVAL AND INSTALLATION

Chrysler Front Wheel Drive Vehicles

1. Jack up the car and support it with jack stands.

2. Remove the rear wheels.

3. On 1984 and later models, loosen the parking brake cable adjustment by backing off the adjusting nut if necessary. On all models, remove the plug from the support plate and insert a brake spoon or similar tool and release the brake shoe drag (to gain further clearance for brake drum removal if necesary). Do this by moving up (up rotating motion on automatic adjuster – left side of vehicle) on the left side and down (down rotating motion on automatic adjuster – right side of the vehicle) on the right side on 1981–83 models, and by using an rotat-

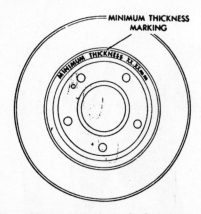

Minimum thickness markings—brake rotor

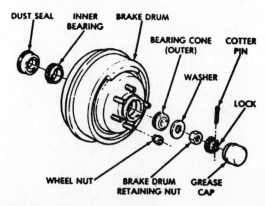

Brake drum and hub assembly

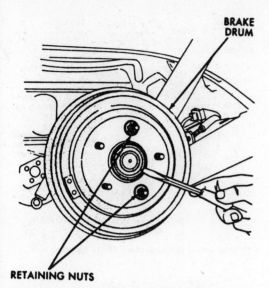

RETAINING NUTS

Removing or installing drum retaining clips

ing upward motion on both sides of the vehicle on later models. Refer to illustration in this chapter.

4. Remove the grease cap.

5. Remove the cotter pin, locknut, retaining nut and washer.

6. Remove the brake drum and bearings.

7. Installation is the reverse of removal. Adjust the wheel bearings and brake system. Refer to chapter 8 if necessary for additional information. Tighten wheel bearing adjusting nut to 240–300 inch lbs. while rotating hub this seats the bearing — Back off adjusting nut ¼ turn or 90° — Then tighten adjusting nut finger tight — Position locknut with a pair of slots in line with cotter pin — Install cotter pin, always use a NEW cotter pin upon installation.

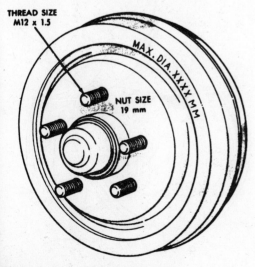

Maximum drum diameter identification

Dodge Monaco

1. Raise and safely support vehicle.

2. Remove wheel and tire assemblies.

3. Remove drum retaining nuts and pull the drum from the hub.

4. If the drum is difficult to remove, the brake shoes are probably holding the drum in place and must be backed off. Remove the access plug from the backing plate. Unseat the adjuster lever with a small pointed tool and back off the adjuster screw with a brake tool.

5. Installation is the reverse of removal. Adjust the brake shoes as necessary.

INSPECTION

Measure drum run-out and diameter. If the drum is not to specifications, have the drum resurfaced. The run-out should not exceed 0.006 in. (0.15mm). The diameter variation (ovalness) of the drum must not exceed 0.0025 in. (0.06mm) in 30° or 0.0035 in. (0.089mm) in 360°. All brake drums will show markings of the maximum allowable diameter.

All brake drums have markings for MINIMUM allowable thickness. ALWAYS USE THIS SPECIFICATION AS THE MINIMUM ALLOWABLE THICKNESS OR REFINISHING LIMIT. Refer to a local auto parts store or machine shop if necessary shop where brake drums are resurfaced.

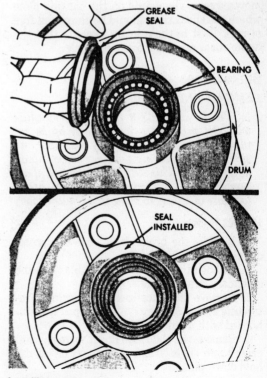

Installing grease seal

Once the drum is off, clean the shoes and springs with a damp rag to remove the accumulated brake dust.

CAUTION: *Do not use compressed air to blow brake dust off the linings or other brake system parts. Brake dust contains asbestos, a known cancer causing agent.*

Grease on the shoes can be removed with alcohol or fine sandpaper.

After cleaning, examine the brake shoes for glazed, oily, loose, cracked or improperly (unevenly) worn linings. Light glazing is common and can be removed with fine sandpaper. Linings that are worn improperly or below $\frac{1}{16}$ in. (1.5mm) above rivet heads or brake shoe should be replaced. The NHSTA advises states with inspection programs to fail vehicles with brake linings less than $\frac{1}{32}$ in. (0.8mm). A good "eyeball" test is to replace the linings when the thickness is the same as or less than the thickness of the metal backing plate (shoe).

Wheel cylinders are a vital part of the brake system and should be inspected carefully. Gently pull back the rubber boots; if any fluid is visible, it's time to replace or rebuild the wheel cylinders. Boots that are distorted, cracked or otherwise damaged, also point to the need for service. Check the flexible brake lines for cracks, chafing or wear.

Check the brake shoe retracting and holddown springs; they should not be worn or distorted. Be sure that the adjuster mechanism moves freely. The points on the backing plate where the shoes slide should be shiny and free of rust. Rust in these areas suggests that the brake shoes are not moving properly.

Brake Shoes

REMOVAL AND INSTALLATION

NOTE: *If you are not thoroughly familiar with the procedures involved in brake replacement, disassemble and assemble one side at a time, leaving the other wheel intact, as a reference. This will reduce the risk of assembling brakes incorrectly. Special brake tools are available to make this repair easier.*

1981–83 Models

1. Remove the brake drum. See the procedure earlier in this chapter.

2. Unhook the parking brake cable from the secondary (trailing) shoe.

3. Remove the shoe-to-anchor springs (retracting springs). They can be gripped and unhooked with a pair of pliers.

4. Remove the shoe hold down springs: compress them slightly and slide them off of the hold down pins.

5. Remove the adjuster screw assembly by

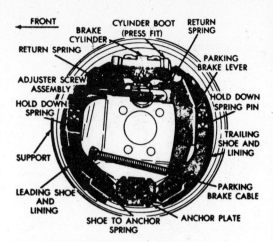

Left rear wheel brake system 1981–83 cars

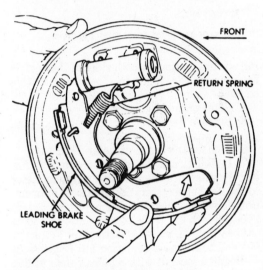

Installing front brake shoe 1981–83 cars

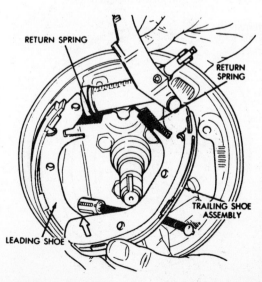

Installing trailing brake shoe and lever 1981–83 cars

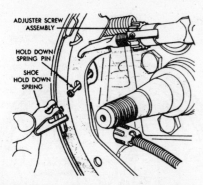

Installing shoe holddown spring 1981–83 cars

spreading the shoes apart. The adjuster nut must be fully backed off.

6. Raise the parking brake lever. Pull the secondary (trailing) shoe away from the backing plate so pull-back spring tension is released.

7. Remove the secondary (trailing) shoe and disengage the spring end from the backing plate.

8. Raise the primary (leading) shoe to release spring tension. Remove the shoe and disengage the spring end from the backing plate.

9. Inspect the brakes (see procedures under Brake Drum Inspection).

To install:

10. Lubricate the six shoe contact areas on the brake backing plate and the web end of the brake shoe which contacts the anchor plate. Use a multi-purpose lubricant or a high temperature brake grease made for this purpose.

11. Chrysler recommends that the rear wheel bearings be cleaned and repacked whenever the brakes are renewed. Be sure to install a new bearing seal. Refer to the illustration in this chapter.

12. With the leading shoe return spring in position on the shoe, install the shoe at the same time as you engage the return spring in the end support.

13. Position the end of the shoe under the anchor.

14. With the trailing shoe return spring in position, install the shoe at the same time as you engage the spring in the support (backing plate).

15. Position the end of the shoe under the anchor.

16. Spread the shoes and install the adjuster screw assembly making sure that the forked end that enters the shoe is curved down.

17. Insert the shoe hold down spring pins and install the hold down springs.

18. Install the shoe-to-anchor springs.

19. Install the parking brake cable onto the parking brake lever.

20. Replace the brake drum and tighten the nut to 240–300 inch lbs. while rotating the wheel.

21. Back off the nut enough to release the bearing preload and position the locknut with one pair of slots aligned with the cotter pin hole. Refer to service procedures in this chapter.

22. Install the cotter pin. The end play should be 0.001–0.003 inch (0.025–0.076mm).

23. Install the grease cap.

1984 And Later Models

NOTE: *Refer to the brake component illustrations in this chapter as a service guide for this repair.*

1. Remove the brake drum as described above. Remove the automatic adjuster spring by disconnecting the upper hook with a pair of pliers and then disconnecting it at the bottom. Then, remove the automatic adjuster lever.

2. Rotate the adjuster screw assembly to

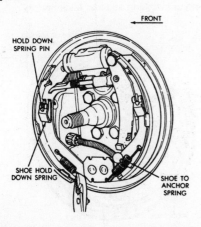

Installing shoe-to-anchor springs 1981–83 cars

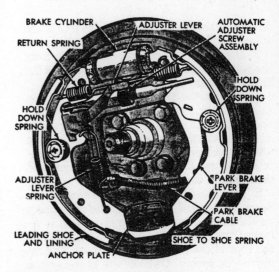

Drum brake system for 1984 and later models

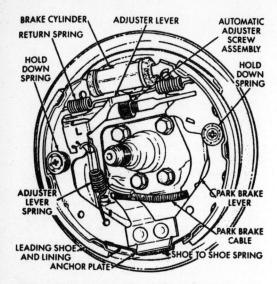

Kelsey-Hayes left rear wheel brake component

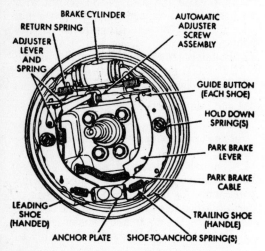

Varga left rear wheel components 1984 and later

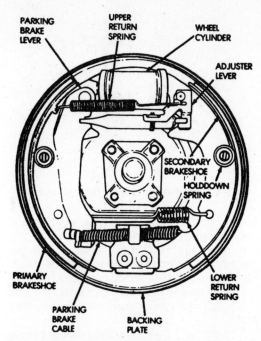

Brake components right rear wheel—Dodge Monaco

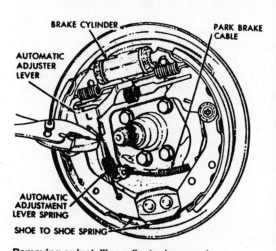

Removing or installing adjuster lever spring

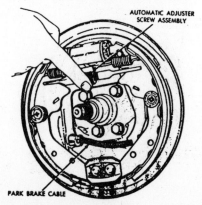

Expand or retract adjuster screw

move each shoe out far enough to be free of the wheel cylinder boots.

3. Disconnect the parking brake cable from the parking brake actuating lever located at the brake mounting plate.

4. Remove the two shoe holddown springs (use special brake tool if possible) by depressing and then turning each mounting washer so the narrow cut in the center of the clip is lined up with the locking bar. When the washer is properly lined up, slowly remove the tension and then remove the washer and spring.

5. Rock the shoes away from the wheel cylinder at the top and then loosen the adjustment on the automatic adjuster until tension is removed from the brake return spring (linking the tops of the shoes). Then, unhook and remove this spring. Unhook the shoe-to-shoe spring from the bottoms of the shoes, too.

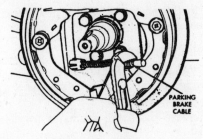

Disconnect parking brake cable

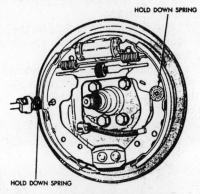

Removing or installing holddown springs

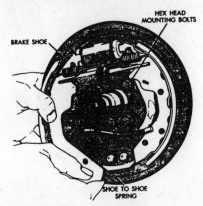

Removing or installing brake shoes

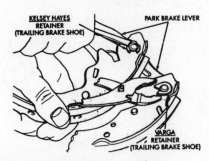

Installing parking brake lever retainer

6. Pull the shoes down and away from the support plate and remove them. In the case of the trailing shoe, use a suitable small lever to pull the C-clip off the retaining post. Remove

the C-clip and the wave washer underneath, and then disconnect the parking brake lever at the shoe.

7. Clean the metal parts of the brake shoes and inspect them to ensure that they are not bent or severely worn. Inspect the lining to make sure it contacts the drum evenly. Also inspect it to make sure that the minimum lining thickness requirement shown in the Brake Specifications chart and any applicable state inspection standards for lining thickness are met. Always use these specifications as a guide. Replace the brake shoes before damage to the brake drum starts.

To install:

8. Clean and inspect the brake support plate and the self-adjuster threads. Apply Multipurpose grease to the threads. Replace the self-adjuster if the threads are corroded. Inspect the springs for overheating (signs are burned paint or distorted end coils) and replace as necessary.

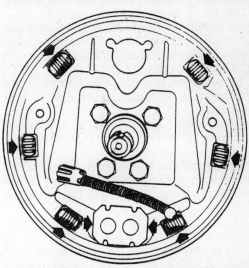

Apply multipurpose grease to the eight areas shown on 1984 and later models to ensure smooth brake operation

The self adjuster and lever used on 1984 and later models—note that the adjuster must be installed only in the proper direction and with each end turned so the stepped side is outboard

9. Lubricate all 8 contact areas of the support plate with Multipurpose grease. Insert the post of the parking brake lever through the trailing shoe. Install the wave washer and a new C-clip.

10. Attach the return (upper) spring between the two shoe assemblies; then install the brake automatic adjuster with the two stepped sides of the forks facing to the front or outboard sides of the shoes. The longer fork must face toward the rear.

11. Connect the shoe-to-shoe spring to the bottoms of the shoes. Then, expand the automatic adjuster assembly by turning the screw until the shoes are far enough apart that they will not disturb the wheel cylinder boots when installing them. Move the shoes upward and into position on the support plate, sliding the bottoms under the retaining clip at the bottom of the plate.

12. Install the holddown springs by forcing the locks over the retainers and then turning them 90° to ensure they lock positively.

13. Install the automatic adjuster lever and its retaining spring. Connect the parking brake cable to the parking brake actuating lever on the mounting plate.

14. Adjust the automatic adjuster well inward so the brake drum can be installed without resistance.

NOTE: *Make sure the adjuster nut stays in contact with the tubular strut of the adjuster when you do this.*

15. Install the brake drum. Readjust the wheel bearings as described in chapter 8 and install a new cotter pin. Install the wheel and torque the bolts.

16. After lowering the car, pump the brake pedal several times to adjust the brakes. When there is adequate pedal, road test the car in an isolated area at lower speeds applying the brakes repeatedly to ensure that they are performing well and to complete the adjustment.

Refer to the necessary service procedures in this book.

Wheel Cylinders

REMOVAL AND INSTALLATION

1. Jack up your vehicle and support it with jack stands.

2. Remove the brake drums as previously outlined.

3. Visually inspect the wheel cylinder boots for signs of excessive leakage. Replace any boots that are torn or broken.

NOTE: A slight amount of fluid on the boots may not be a leak but may be preservative fluid used at the factory.

4. If a leak has been discovered, remove the brake shoes and check for contamination. Replace the linings if they are soaked with grease or brake fluid.

5. Disconnect the brake line from the wheel cylinder.

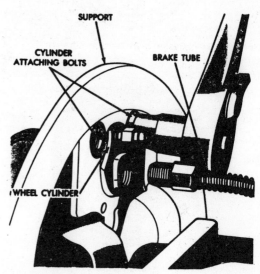

Wheel cylinder brake line

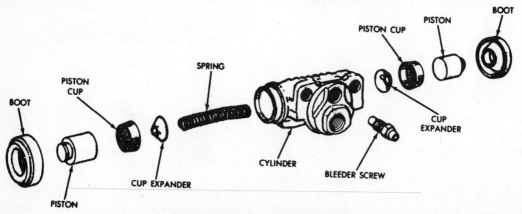

Exploded view of rear wheel cylinder

6. Remove the wheel cylinder attaching bolts, then pull the wheel cylinder out of its support.

7. Installation is the reverse of removal. Torque the wheel cylinder mounting bolts to 75 inch lbs. and the brake line connection to 115–170 inch lbs.

8. Bleed the brake system.

REAR DISC BRAKES

CAUTION: *Brake shoes contain asbestos, which has been determined to be a cancer-causing agent. Never clean the brake surfaces with compressed air! Avoid inhaling any dust from any brake surface! When cleaning brake surfaces, use a commercially available brake cleaning fluid.*

Brake Pads

INSPECTION

Measure lining wear by measuring the combined thickness of the shoe and lining at the thinnest point. It must be $9/32$ on rear disc brakes for Chrysler front drive vehicles and Dodge Monaco.

Measure lining wear by measuring the brake pad at the thinnest point. It must be at least $1/8$ inch (3mm) or more on rear disc brakes on 1990–92 Laser and Stealth.

Use these specifications as a guide for rear disc brake pad replacement.

WHENEVER THE DISC BRAKE PAD IS TO BE REPLACED, REPLACE THE PADS ON THE RIGHT AND LEFT WHEELS AS A SET!

Brake Caliper and Pads

REMOVAL AND INSTALLATION

NOTE: *On all vehicles covered in this manual, the rear disc brake caliper piston (for brake pad and caliper R&R) is retracted in several different service procedures. Refer to the necessary service procedure for your vehicle. On ABS equipped vehicles read the necessary procedures in this chapter.*

1988 Chrysler Front Wheel Drive Vehicles

NOTE: *You'll need a metric size Allen wrench (4mm) to perform this operation.*

1. Raise the vehicle and support it securely by the body structure or rear axle. Remove the rear wheels.

2. There is an access plug on the inboard side of the caliper that looks like an ordinary bolt. It is located just under the parking brake cable lever. Clean the plug and the area around it to

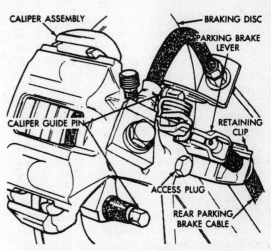

Rear disc brake caliper assembly—Chrysler cars

keep dirt out of the caliper and then remove it.

3. Install the 4mm Allen wrench into the access hole and turn it counterclockwise to retract the pads from the disc. Turn the retractor a few turns—until there is daylight between the disc and the pads.

4. Remove the anti-rattle spring by prying it off the outside of the caliper with a small, blunt instrument. Be careful to pry outward on the spring just far enough to release it, in order to avoid damaging it.

5. Clean the guide pins and the areas around them of dirt and then unscrew them. Pull them out just far enough to free the caliper from the adapter if it is not necessary to replace the caliper bushings. If the bushings are to be replaced, remove the guide pins.

6. Lift the caliper (and the inboard pad, which will remain with it) upward and away from the braking disc and then suspend it securely on a piece of wire, so as to prevent putting stress on the brake hose.

7. Pull the inboard pad away from the caliper piston and remove it. Pull the outboard pads off the caliper adapter.

NOTE: *In the following step, be careful to retract the piston very slowly and carefully and by using only a minimum of effort. The use of excessive force will damage the retraction and actuation shafts.*

8. Insert the Allen wrench into the access hole and retract the piston all the way by rotating the wrench *very gently just until the rotating effort increases very slightly.*

9. Install a new inboard brake pad to the bore of the caliper piston. Then, install a new outboard pad marked **L** or **R**, according to the side of the vehicle you are working on. This pad is installed by sliding it onto the caliper adaptor

10. Lower the caliper over the disc and out-

board pad. Gently and cautiously turn the guide pins *in order to start them in their threads without cross-threading them.* Use a minimum amount of force and allow the pins to find their own angle so the threads will not be damaged. Torque the guide pins to 18–26 ft. lbs.

11. Install the anti-rattle spring. Then, insert the Allen wrench back through the access hole and turn the retraction shaft clockwise just until there is a slight amount of tension on it and the clearance between the pads and disc has been removed. Then, retract the shaft ⅓ of a turn.

12. If the brake line has been disconnected, bleed the brake system. Pump the brake pedal several times to ensure that the brake pads seat against the rotor. *The pedal must give resistance at the normal position before attempting to drive the car.* Drive the car at moderate speeds in an isolated area in order to apply the brakes several times to test the system.

1989–92 Chrysler Front Wheel Drive Vehicles
1990–92 Laser And Stealth

NOTE: *All brake pins, shims and other parts must be installed in the the proper location. Record location before removing any brake hardware. On vehicles equipped with ABS system refer to the necessary service procedures in this chapter.*

1. Remove some of the fluid from the master cylinder.

2. Raise the vehicle and support safely. Remove the tire and wheel assemblies.

3. Remove the hold-down spring if necessary. Remove the caliper mounting pin(s). Lift the caliper off the rotor assembly and remove the caliper and outer pad.

4. Remove the inner pad from the adaptor.

To install:

5. Use a large C-clamp to (SLOWLY) compress the piston back into the caliper bore.

6. Install the inner pad to the adaptor.

7. Position the caliper over the rotor so the caliper engages the adaptor correctly (tighten guide pins to 25–35 ft. lbs.) and install the retainer pin(s).

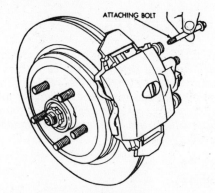

Removing caliper attaching bolts

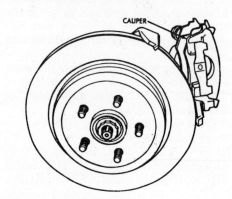

Removing caliper assembly

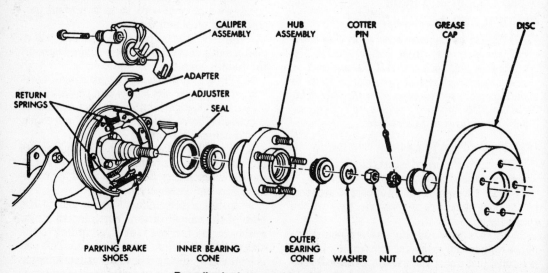

Rear disc brake assembly—Chrysler cars

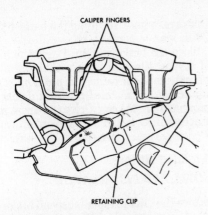

Removing outboard shoe assembly

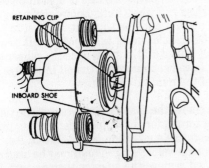

Removing inboard shoe assembly

8. Install the hold-down spring, if removed.
9. Refill the master cylinder as necessary.

Dodge Monaco

1. Raise and safely support vehicle.
NOTE: *Do not attempt to press the caliper piston back into the bore at this time. A special spanner type tool #6366 is required for this operation to rotate the piston into the bore. Refer to the illustration in this chapter.*
2. Remove wheel and tire assemblies.
3. Unseat the operating lever return spring at the caliper.
4. Remove the operating lever attaching bolt

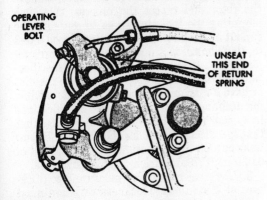

Operating lever and return spring attachment—Dodge Monaco

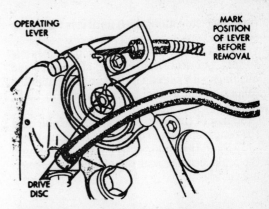

Mark operating lever position—Dodge Monaco

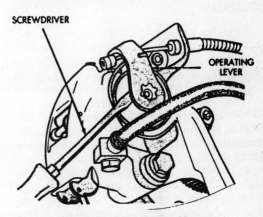

Removing operating lever—Dodge Monaco

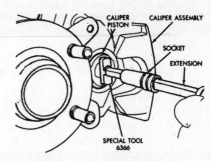

Rear disc brake service—Dodge Monaco

and pry the lever (matchmark before removal) off the drive disc.
5. Remove the lever return spring.
6. Remove the operating lever from the parking brake cable. Pull the parking brake cable out of the mounting flange.
7. Remove caliper slide pins and remove the caliper. Remove the brake shoe retaining pin and remove the brake pads and anti-rattle spring.

To install:
8. A spanner tool may be required, along with an appropriate socket and extension, to

turn the piston **clockwise** until it is fully seated in the bore.

9. Install the brake pads and anti-rattle spring. Lubricate the caliper slide pins and bushings with silicone lubricant and install the caliper assembly. (tighten guide pins to 22 ft. lbs.)

10. Install the operating lever assemble and the return spring to the brake operating lever.

11. Bleed the brakes after installation. Pump the brake pedal to seat the brakes before moving vehicle.

Brake Caliper

OVERHAUL

Rear disc brake calipers are not overhauled, but are replaced on most vehicles. Check with local Auto Supply store or Dealership for the availability of service related parts. Only the dust boots and guide pin bushings are serviced, as described here. If a new caliper assembly complete with dust boots and guide pin bushings is to be installed, make sure to transfer useable pads and related parts and replace those which are worn.

1. Disconnect and plug the brake line. Disconnect the parking brake cable retaining clips from the hanger bracket and caliper. Disconnect the cable at the parking brake lever. Then, remove the caliper.

2. Check the caliper dust boot and inboard pad area for piston seal leaks. If there is a visible leak, the caliper must be replaced (they are not serviceable).

3. Inspect the dust boot and the caliper pin bushings. Replace them if they are damaged, dry, or embrittled.

4. Clean the area around the dust boot with alcohol or a suitable solvent and wipe it dry. Remove the dust boot retainer with a finger or a blunt instrument and remove the dust boot from the caliper and piston grooves and discard it.

5. Clean the grooves in the piston and caliper and then coat a new boot with clean brake fluid, leaving a heavy coating inside. Position the boot over the piston and into the grooves of both piston and caliper. Install a boot retainer over the groove in the caliper.

6. Pry the bushings from the caliper with a small, dull tool. Discard the bushings and Teflon® sleeves.

7. Remove the Teflon® sleeves from new bushings. Install the bushings by putting pressure on their flanges with the fingers to press them in until seated. Reinstall the Teflon® sleeves.

8. Install the caliper as described above. Con-

nect the brake hose, torquing the banjo bolt to 19–29 ft. lbs.

9. Bleed the brake system. Pump the brake pedal several times to ensure that the brake pads seat against the rotor. *The pedal must give resistance at the normal position before attempting to drive the car.* Drive the car at moderate speeds in an isolated area in order to apply the brakes several times to test the system.

Brake Disc Rotor

REMOVAL AND INSTALLATION

Remove the brake caliper (suspend brake caliper — do not disconnect the caliper) and pads as described above. The disc is held in place by the wheel and wheel nuts. Before removing the disc, mark it and one adjacent wheel stud so it may be installed in the same position. It may be simply pulled off the studs once the caliper and pads have been removed. Install in reverse order of the removal procedure.

On the 1988 ATE front and rear brake system remove the adapter if necessary. The tightening torque for the caliper adapter mounting bolts on this application is 130–190 ft. lbs.

On some vehicles an adapter may be used unbolt and remove the adapter then remove the rear disc brake rotor.

INSPECTION

Inspect the disc for scoring, rust, impregnated lining material and ridges, and replace or machine it if serious problems in these areas are visible. Take the following specific measurements:

1. With the wheel removed, install the lugnuts to hold the disc snugly in place against the hub. Then, mount a dial indicator so it will read runout about 1 in. (25.4mm) from the outer edge of the rotor. Zero the indicator, rotate the disc, and read the maximum reading. It must be 0.005 in. (0.13mm) or less.

2. If the specification is excessive, remove the rotor and repeat the process, this time mounting the indicator so as to measure the runout of the hub. This must not exceed 0.003 in. (0.076mm). If it does, the hub requires replacement. If hub runout meets the specification and disc runout does not, replace the disc or have it machined, if it can be trued up while maintaining minimum thickness specifications (stamped on an unmachined surface). Note that this specification includes 0.030 in. (0.76mm) wear beyond the maximum machining limit of 0.030 in. (0.76mm) from original thickness.

3. Use a micrometer to measure disc thickness at 4 locations. Thickness variation must not exceed 0.0005 in. (0.013mm). If thickness variation can be corrected by machining the

disc while maintaining maximum thickness limits, this may be done.

All brake discs or rotors have markings for MINIMUM allowable thickness cast on an unmachined surface or an alternate surface. ALWAYS USE THIS SPECIFICATION AS THE MINIMUM ALLOWABLE THICKNESS OR REFINISHING LIMIT. Refer to a local auto parts store or machine shop if necessary shop where brake disc or rotors are resurfaced.

If the brake disc or rotor needs to be replaced with a new part, the protective coating on the braking surface of the rotor must be removed with an appropriate solvent.

PARKING BRAKE

Cable

ADJUSTMENT

Chrysler FWD Vehicles
Except 1990–92 Daytona, Daytona Shelby (AG) And LeBaron (AJ)

NOTE: *The service brakes must be properly adjusted before adjusting the parking brake.*

1. Release the parking brake lever, then back off the parking brake cable adjuster so there is slack in the cable.
2. Before loosening cable adjusting nut, clean and lubricate the threads.
3. Tighten the parking brake adjuster (after service brake adjustment if necessary) until a slight drag is felt while rotating the wheels.
4. Loosen the cable adjusting nut until the rear wheels can be rotated freely, then back the cable adjuster nut off 2 full turns.
5. Apply and release the parking brake several times.
6. Test the parking brake. The rear wheels should rotate freely without dragging when parking brake is released. To check operation, make sure the parking brake holds on an incline.

1990–92 Daytona, Daytona Shelby And LeBaron

The parking brake hand lever contains a self-adjusting loaded clockspring feature. Routine parking brake adjustment is not required. Refer to the "Parking Brake Cable Removal and Installation" below for additional information.

1990–92 Laser And Stealth

1. Make sure the parking brake cable is free and is not frozen or sticking. With the engine running, forcefully depress the brake pedal 5–6 times. Check the parking brake stroke. It should be 5–7 notches on Laser and 3–5 notches on Stealth. If not, adjust using the following procedure.

2. On rear drum brakes, adjust the rear brakes. On rear disc brakes, make sure the parking brake mechanism is not frozen or sticking.
3. On Laser, remove the console carpeting. On Stealth, remove the coin holder and plug. This will expose the adjusting nut within the console.
4. Rotate the adjusting nut to adjust the parking brake stroke to the 5–7 notch setting. After making the adjustment, check there is no looseness between the adjusting nut and the parking brake lever, then tighten the locknut.

NOTE: *Do not adjust the parking brake too tight. If the number of notches is less than specification, the cable has been pulled too much and the automatic adjuster will fail or the brakes will drag.*

5. After adjusting the lever stroke, raise the rear of the vehicle. With the parking brake lever in the released position, turn the rear wheels to confirm that the rear brakes are not dragging.
6. Check that the parking brake holds the vehicle on an incline.

Dodge Monaco

1. Adjust the rear brakes if necessary.
2. Apply and release the parking brake 5 times to center the shoes in the drums. Set the pedal on the first notch from the released position.
3. Raise and support the vehicle safely.
4. Tighten the cable at the equalizer so the wheels can just barely be turned forward, then loosen 1 turn. Be sure to hold the end of the cable screw to prevent the cable from turning.
5. Release the parking brake and check for rear brake drag. The wheels should rotate freely with the parking brake no applied.

REMOVAL AND INSTALLATION

NOTE: *Use these service procedures as a guide for all models/years. Refer to the "Parking Brake Cable Routing" illustrations in this chapter. On the 1990–92 Daytona, Daytona Shelby (AG) And LeBaron (AJ) a one piece cable is used refer to the correct service procedure below.*

Chrysler FWD — Front Cable

1. Jack up your car and support it with jack stands.
2. Loosen the cable adjusting nut and disengage the cable from the connectors.
3. Lift the floor mat for access to the floor pan.
4. Remove the floor pan seal panel.
5. Pull the cable end forward and disconnect it from the clevis.
6. Pull the cable assembly through the hole.

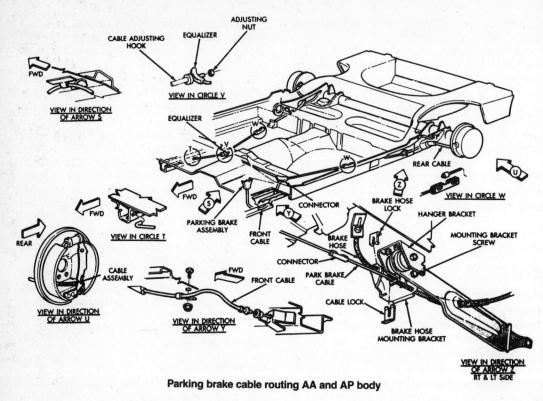

Parking brake cable routing AA and AP body

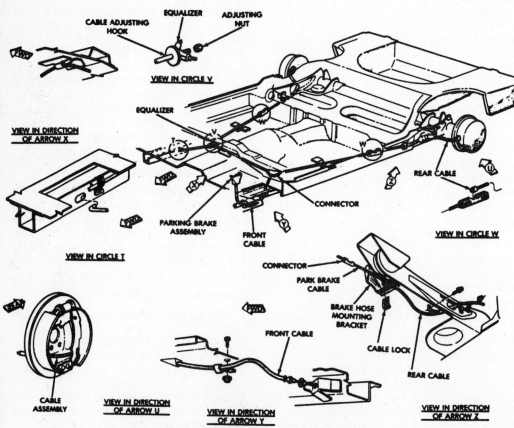

Parking brake cable routing AC and AY body

7. Installation is the reverse of removal.

8. Adjust the service and parking brakes.

Chrysler FWD — One Piece Cable
1990–92 Daytona And LeBaron

CAUTION: *The parking brake hand lever contains a self-adjusting loaded clockspring loaded to about 30 lbs. Care must be taken when handling components in the vicinity of the hand lever or serious personal injury may result.*

1. Disconnect the negative battery cable.

2. Disengage the cable from the equalizer bracket in the console.

4. Lift the carpet and floor matting and remove the floor pan seal.

5. Separate the cable from the rear parking brake shoes lever.

6. Pull the cable through the hole and remove.

To install:

7. Install the cable and connect to the rear shoes and equalizer bracket. Install the floor pan seal and position the carpet.

8. To reload, lockout and adjust the system:

    a. Pull on the equalizer output cable with at least 30 lbs. pressure to wind up the spring. Continue until the self-adjuster lockout pawl is positioned about midway between the self-adjuster sector.

    b. Rotate the lockout pawl into the self-adjuster sector by turning the Allen screw clockwise. This action requires very little effort; do not force the screw.

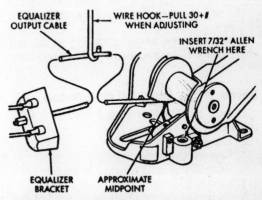

Self adjuster parking brake lever assembly 1990–92 Daytona and LeBaron

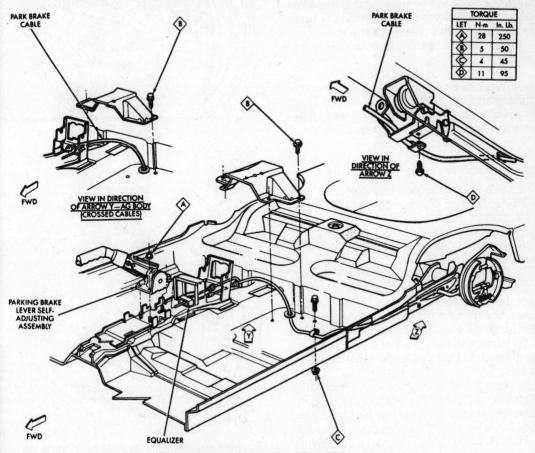

Parking brake cable routing AG and AJ body

c. Adjust the rear drum-in-hat parking brake shoes.

d. Turn the Allen screw counterclockwise about 15 degrees. When turning the lockout device, self-adjuster release is a snapping noise followed by a detent that should be felt. Very light effort is required to seat the lockout device into the detent. Make sure to follow through into the detent.

e. Cycle the lever a few times to complete the adjustment. The wheels should rotate freely.

9. Connect the negative battery cable and check the parking brakes for proper operation.

Chrysler FWD — Rear Cable (Drum Brakes)

1. Jack up your vehicle and support it with jack stands.

2. Remove the rear wheels.

3. Remove the brake drums.

4. Back off the cable adjuster to provide slack in the cable.

5. Compress the retainers on the end of the cable and remove the cable from the brake backing plate or support plate. A worm gear type hose clamp can be used for this procedure (remove the clamp before removing the brake cable assembly from the support plate).

6. Disconnect the cable from the brake shoe lever.

7. Remove the clip from brake cable at support bracket. Pull the brake cable from the trailing arm.

8. Installation is the reverse of removal. Adjust the service and parking brakes.

Chrysler FWD — Rear Cable (Disc Brakes)

1. Jack up your vehicle and support it with jack stands. Back off the cable adjuster to provide slack in the cable.

2. Remove the rear wheels.

3. Remove the brake cailper and disc assembly.

4. Compress the retainers on the end of the cable and remove the cable from the adapter. A worm gear type hose clamp can be used for this procedure (remove the clamp before removing the brake cable assembly from the adapter).

5. Remove the clip from brake cable at support bracket. Pull the brake cable from the trailing arm.

6. Installation is the reverse of removal. Be sure that the retainers on the brake cable are expanded around the mounting hole in adapter. Adjust the parking brake shoe diameter to 6.75 inch (171.5mm). Install the brake disc, caliper and wheel/tire assembly.

Parking Brake Shoes

REMOVAL, INSTALLATION AND ADJUSTMENT

Chrysler Front Wheel Drive Vehicles

1. Remove the caliper from the disc assembly. Refer to the necessary service procedures in this chapter.

2. Remove the brake disc from the hub assembly. Refer to the necessary service procedures in this chapter.

3. Remove the grease cap, cotter pin, lock nut, retaining nut and washer.

4. Remove the hub and bearing assembly.

5. Remove the forward hold down clip on brake shoes.

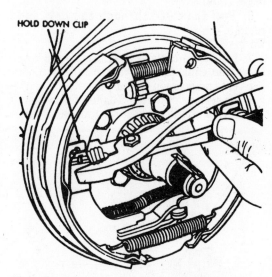

Removing hold down clip—parking brake assembly

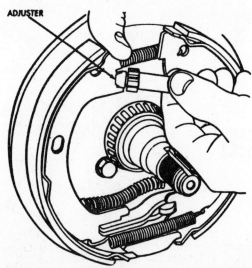

Removing adjuster assembly—parking brake assembly

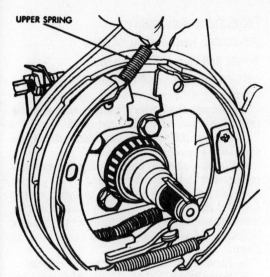

Removing upper spring—parking brake assembly

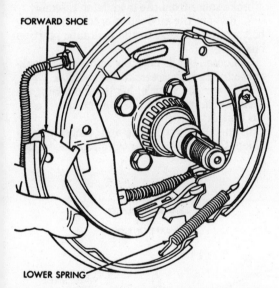

Removing shoe and lower spring—parking brake assembly

6. Turn adjuster wheel until adjuster is at shortest length. Remove the adjuster assembly.

7. Remove the upper shoe to shoe spring. Pull front shoe away from anchor and remove the front shoe and lower spring.

8. Remove the rear hold-down clip and shoe.

To install:

9. Install rear shoe and holddown clip.

10. Install the lower shoe to shoe spring. Pull forward shoe over anchor block until properly located on adapter.

11. Install upper shoe to shoe spring. Install adjuster assembly (grease threads with suitable grease before installation) with star wheel forward.

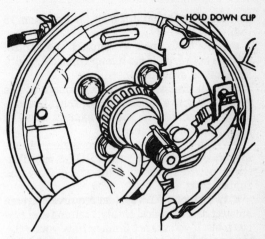

Removing rear holddown clip and shoe—parking brake asembly

12. Install front holddown clip.

13. Adjust parking brake shoe diameter to 6.75 inch (171mm). Install hub assembly on the spindle.

14. Install outer bearing, thrust washer and nut. Tighten wheel bearing adjusting nut to 240–300 inch lbs. while rotating hub this seats the bearing.

15. Back off adjusting nut ¼ turn or 90° then tighten adjusting nut finger tight.

16. Position locknut with a pair of slots in line with cotter pin. Install cotter pin, always use a NEW cotter pin upon installation.

17. Install grease cap, brake disc, cailper and wheel/tire assemblies.

18. Test the parking brake. The rear wheels should rotate freely without dragging when parking brake is released. To check operation, make sure the parking brake holds on an incline.

BENDIX ANTI-LOCK 6 BRAKE SYSTEM SERVICE

Chrysler FWD Daytona, LeBaron, LeBaron Landau, Spirit And Acclaim

PRECAUTIONS

Failure to observe the following precautions may result in system damage.

● Before performing electric arc welding on the vehicle, disconnect the control module and the hydraulic unit connectors.

● When performing painting work on the vehicle, do not expose the control module to temperatures in excess of 185°F (85°C) for longer than 2 hrs. The system may be exposed to temperatures up to 200°F (95°C) for less than 15 min.

• Never disconnect or connect the control module or hydraulic modulator connectors with the ignition switch ON.

• Never disassemble any component of the Anti-Lock Brake System (ABS) which is designated non-servicable; the component must be replaced as an assembly.

• When filling the master cylinder, always use brake fluid which meets DOT-3 specifications; petroleum-based fluid will destroy the rubber parts.

• Working on ABS system requires extreme amount of mechanical ability, training and special tools. If you are not familiar have your vehicle repaired by a certified mechanic or refer to a more advanced publication on this subject.

Pump/Motor Assembly

REMOVAL AND INSTALLATION

Bendix Anti-Lock 6 Brake System

DAYTONA, LEBARON, LEBARON LANDAU, SPIRIT AND ACCLAIM

The pump and motor assembly used on the Bendix Anti-lock 6 brake system is not removable. If the pump or motor fails, the modulator assembly must be replaced.

Modulator Assembly

REMOVAL AND INSTALLATION

Bendix Anti-Lock 6 Brake System

DAYTONA, LEBARON, LEBARON LANDAU, SPIRIT AND ACCLAIM

1. Remove the battery, battery tray and the protective cover from the modulator.
2. Disconnect the electrical connector from the Delta P switch.
3. Remove the top bolt holding the modulator bracket to the fender shield.
4. Disconnect the 2 master cylinder supply tubes at the modulator. Loosen (but do not remove) the other end of the tubes at the master cylinder; swing the tubes aside without kinking them.
5. Elevate and safely support the vehicle.
6. From below, disconnect the modulator 10-pin electrical connector. Remove the remaining 4 brake tubes from the modulator assembly.
7. Remove the modulator bracket mounting bolt which is closest to the hydraulic junction block.
8. Loosen but do not fully remove the bracket mounting bolt closest to the radiator.
9. Lower the vehicle; lift the modulator assembly and bracket out of the vehicle.

To install:

10. Install the modulator and bracket into position. Use the protruding tab on the modulator

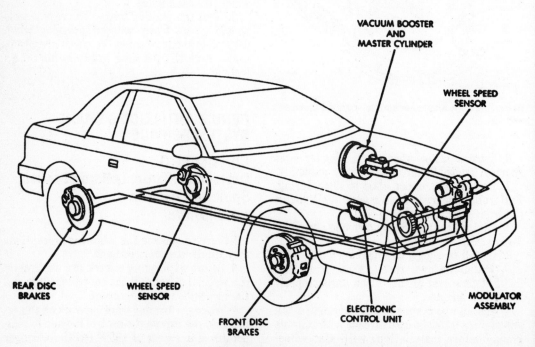

Anti-Lock brake system components AG/AJ body—Bendix Anti-Lock 6 brake system

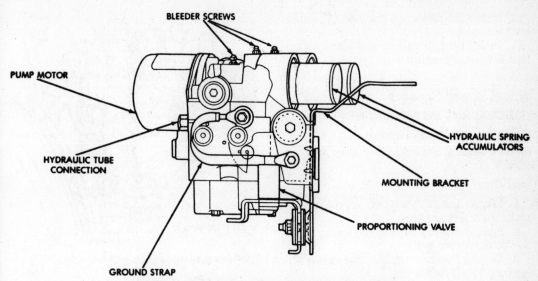

BLEEDER SCREWS

PUMP MOTOR

HYDRAULIC TUBE CONNECTION

HYDRAULIC SPRING ACCUMULATORS

MOUNTING BRACKET

PROPORTIONING VALVE

GROUND STRAP

Modulator assembly—Bendix Anti-Lock 6 brake system

to locate and hold the assembly. Make certain the bracket is held by the front mounting bolt.

11. Install but do not tighten the bolt holding the bracket to the fender shield.

12. Elevate and safely support the vehicle.

13. Install the bracket mounting bolt closest to the junction block. Tighten both lower mounting bracket bolts to 21 ft. lbs. (28 Nm).

14. Install the 4 hydraulic lines at the modulator; tighten the fittings to 12 ft. lbs. (16 Nm).

15. Reconnect the 10-pin electrical connector to the modulator.

16. Lower the vehicle. Connect the 2 supply tubes from the master cylinder to the modulator. Tighten the fittings at both ends of the tubes to 12 ft. lbs. (16 Nm).

17. Tighten the bolt holding the bracket to the fender shield (Step 11) to 21 ft. lbs. (28 Nm).

18. Bleed the base brake system in the usual fashion.

19. Bleed the modulator assembly following the correct sequences and procedure.

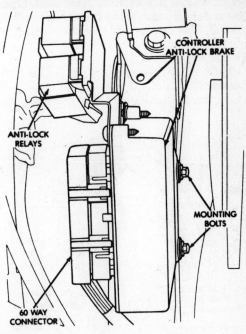

ACID SHIELD

BRAKE LINES

FRAME RAIL

MODULATOR ASSEMBLY

CONTROLLER ANTI-LOCK BRAKE

ANTI-LOCK RELAYS

MOUNTING BOLTS

60 WAY CONNECTOR

Modulator assembly removal—Bendix Anti-Lock 6 brake system

ABS controller location—Bendix Anti-Lock 6 brake system

20. Install the protective cover on the modulator assembly.

21. Install the battery tray and battery. Connect the battery cables.

Wheel Speed Sensors
REMOVAL AND INSTALLATION

Bendix Anti-Lock 6 Brake System

DAYTONA, LEBARON, LEBARON LANDAU, SPIRIT AND ACCLAIM

Front Wheel

1. Elevate and safely support the vehicle. Remove the wheel and tire.

2. Remove the clip holding the wiring grommet to the fender well.

3. Remove the screws holding the sensor wiring tube to the fender well.

4. Carefully remove the grommet from the fender shield.

5. Make certain the ignition switch is **OFF**. Disconnect the sensor wiring from the ABS harness.

6. Remove the triangular retaining clip from the bracket on the strut. Not all vehicles have this clip.

7. Remove the sensor wiring grommets from the bracket.

8. Remove the fastener holding the sensor head.

9. Carefully remove the sensor head from the steering knuckle. Do not use pliers on the sensor head; if it is seized in place, use a hammer and small punch to tap the edge of the sensor ear. The tapping and side-to-side motion will free the unit.

To install:

10. Connect the speed sensor to the ABS harness.

11. Push the sensor assembly grommet into

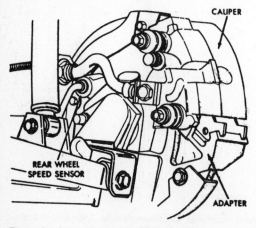

Rear wheel speed sensor—Chrysler cars

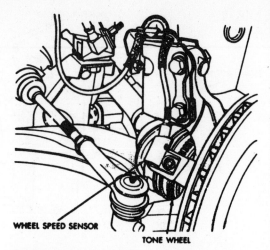

Front wheel speed sensors—Chrysler cars

the the the hole in the fender shield. Install the retainer clip and screw.

12. Install the sensor wiring tube and tighten the retaining bolts to 35 inch lbs. (4 Nm).

13. Install the sensor grommets into the brackets on the fender shield and strut. Install the retainer clip at the strut.

14. Install the sensor to the knuckle. Install the retaining screw and tighten it to 60 inch lbs. (7 Nm).

NOTE: *Proper installation of the sensor and its wiring is critical to system function. Make certain that wiring is installed in all retainers and clips. Wiring must be protected from moving parts and not be stretched during suspension movements.*

15. Install the tire and wheel. Lower the vehicle to the ground.

Rear Wheel

1. Elevate and safely support the vehicle. Remove the wheel and tire.

2. Remove the sensor assembly grommet from the underbody and pull the harness through the hole in the body.

3. Make certain the ignition switch is **OFF**. Disconnect the sensor wiring from the ABS harness.

4. Remove the clip retaining screw from the bracket just forward of the trailing arm bushing.

5. Remove the sensor and brake tube assembly clip from the inboard side of the trailing arm.

6. Remove the sensor wire retainer from the rear brake hose bracket.

7. Remove the outboard sensor assembly nut. This nut is also used to hold the brake tube clip.

8. Remove the fastener holding the sensor head.

9. Carefully remove the sensor head from the adapter assembly. Do not use pliers on the sensor head; if it is seized in place, use a hammer and small punch to tap the edge of the sensor ear. The tapping and side-to-side motion will free the unit.

To install:

10. Before installation, coat the sensor with high temperature multi-purpose grease.

11. Install the sensor; install the retaining screw and tighten it to 60 inch lbs. (7 Nm).

12. Install the outboard retaining nut.

13. Install the clips and nuts at and around the trailing arm.

14. Connect the sensor wiring to the ABS harness; make sure the connector lock is engaged.

15. Push the sensor assembly grommet into the the hole in the underbody.

NOTE: *Proper installation of the sensor and its wiring is critical to system function. Make certain that wiring is installed in all retainers and clips. Wiring must be protected from moving parts and not be stretched during suspension movements.*

16. Install the tire and wheel.

17. Lower the vehicle to the ground.

BRAKE SYSTEM BLEEDING

Bendix Anti-Lock 6 Brake System

DAYTONA, LEBARON, LEBARON LANDAU, SPIRIT AND ACCLAIM

The brake system must be bled any time air is permitted to enter the system through loosened or disconnected lines or hoses, or anytime the modulator is removed. Excessive air within the system will cause a soft or spongy feel in the brake pedal.

When bleeding any part of the system, the reservoir must remain close to **FULL** at all

times. Check the level frequently and top off fluid as needed.

The Bendix Anti-lock 6 brake system must be bled as 2 separate brake systems. Proper procedures must be followed if the system is to work correctly. The normal portion of the brake system is bled in the usual fashion with either pressure or manual bleeding equipment and must be fully and properly bled before bleeding the modulator.

Bleeding the Modulator Assembly

To bleed the ABS unit, the battery must be relocated outside the vehicle and connected to the vehicle with jumper cables. This allows access to the 4 bleeder screws on top of the modulator assembly. Additionally, the DRB II must be connected to the diagnostic plug before bleeding begins; the DRB II is used to activate the system(s) during the procedure. The 4 components to be bled within the modulator are (in order) the secondary sump, the primary sump, the primary accumulator and the secondary accumulator. Use the following procedure to bleed the modulator assembly.

CAUTION: *Wear eye protection when bleeding the modulator assembly and always use a hose on the bleed screw to direct the flow of fluid away from painted surfaces. Bleeding the modulator may result in the release of very high pressure fluid.*

1. Connect a clear hose to the secondary sump bleeder screw and route the hose to a clear container.

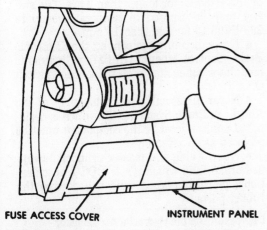

FUSE ACCESS COVER   **INSTRUMENT PANEL**

ABS diagnostic connector location—Bendix Anti-Lock 6 brake system

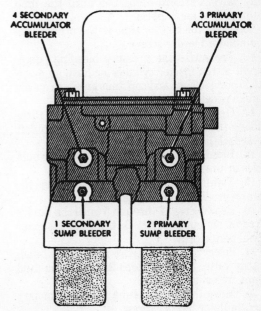

Bleeding ABS modulator assembly—Bendix Anti-Lock 6 brake system

2. Either install and pressurize the pressure bleeding equipment at the master cylinder or have an assistant provide light and constant pressure on the brake pedal.

3. Open the bleeder screw about ½–¾ turn. Use the DRB II to select the ACTUATE VALVES test; actuate the left front build/decay valve.

4. Bleed until the fluid flows free of air bubbles or until the brake pedal bottoms.

5. Tighten the bleeder screw and release the brake pedal if it was being held.

6. Repeat Steps 2 through 5 until the fluid is free of air bubbles. Remember to check the fluid reservoir level periodically.

7. Select and actuate the right rear build/decay valve and perform Steps 2–5 until the fluid flows without air bubbles.

8. Move the bleeder tube to the primary sump bleeder screw.

9. Pressurize the pressure bleeding equipment at the master cylinder or have an assistant provide light and constant pressure on the brake pedal.

10. Open the bleeder screw about ½–¾ turn. Using the DRB II, actuate the right front build/decay valve.

11. Bleed until the fluid flows free of air bubbles or until the brake pedal bottoms.

12. Tighten the bleeder screw and release the brake pedal if it was being held.

13. Repeat Steps 2 through 5 until the fluid is free of air bubbles. Remember to check the fluid reservoir level periodically.

14. Select and actuate the left rear build/decay valve. Perform Steps 2–5 until the fluid runs free of air bubbles.

15. Move the bleeder tube to the primary accumulator bleeder screw.

16. Pressurize the pressure bleeding equipment at the master cylinder or have an assistant provide light and constant pressure on the brake pedal.

17. Open the bleeder screw about ½–¾ turn. Using the DRB II, actuate the right front/left rear isolation valve.

18. Bleed until the fluid flows free of air bubbles or until the brake pedal bottoms.

19. Tighten the bleeder screw and release the brake pedal if it was being held.

20. Repeat Steps 2 through 5 until the fluid is free of air bubbles. Check the fluid reservoir level periodically.

21. Select and actuate the right front build/decay valve. Perform Steps 2–5 until the fluid runs free of air bubbles.

22. Move the bleeder tube to the secondary accumulator bleeder screw.

23. Pressurize the pressure bleeding equipment at the master cylinder or have an assis-

tant provide light and constant pressure on the brake pedal.

24. Open the bleeder screw about ½–¾ turn. Using the DRB II, actuate the left front/right rear isolation valve.

25. Bleed until the fluid flows free of air bubbles or until the brake pedal bottoms.

26. Tighten the bleeder screw and release the brake pedal if it was being held.

27. Repeat Steps 2 through 5 until the fluid is free of air bubbles. Check the fluid reservoir level periodically.

28. Select and actuate the left front build/decay valve. Perform Steps 2–5 until the fluid runs free of air bubbles.

29. Remove the bleeding apparatus; fill the brake fluid reservoir to the correct level and install the cap.

BOSCH ABS III BRAKE SYSTEM SERVICE (1989–90) BENDIX ANTI-LOCK 10 BRAKE SYSTEM (1991–92)

Chrysler FWD
Dynasty, Imperial And New Yorker
PRECAUTIONS

Failure to observe the following precautions may result in system damage.

• Before performing electric arc welding on the vehicle, disconnect the Electronic Brake Control Module (EBCM) and the hydraulic modulator connectors.

• When performing painting work on the vehicle, do not expose the Electronic Brake Control Module (EBCM) to temperatures in excess of 185°F (85°C) for longer than 2 hrs. The system may be exposed to temperatures up to 200°F (95°C) for less than 15 min.

• Never disconnect or connect the Electronic Brake Control Module (EBCM) or hydraulic modulator connectors with the ignition switch ON.

• Never disassemble any component of the Anti-Lock Brake System (ABS) which is designated non-serviceable; the component must be replaced as an assembly.

• When filling the master cylinder, always use brake fluid which meets DOT-3 specifications; petroleum-based fluid will destroy the rubber parts.

Depressurizing the Hydraulic Accumulator

1. With the ignition OFF, pump the brake pedal a minimum of 40 times, using approxi-

mately 50 lbs. (222 N) pedal force. A noticeable change in pedal feel will occur when the accumulator is discharged.

2. When a definite increase in pedal effort is felt, stroke the pedal a few additional times. This should remove all hydraulic pressure from the system.

Pump/Motor Assembly

REMOVAL AND INSTALLATION

1989–90 Vehicles

BOSCH ABS III SYSTEM

1. Disconnect the negative battery cable. Depressurize the hydraulic accumulator.

CAUTION: *Failure to depressurize the hydraulic accumulator, prior to performing this operation may result in personal injury and/ or damage to the painted surfaces.*

2. Remove the fresh air intake ducts.

3. Disconnect all electrical connectors to the pump motor.

4. Disconnect the high and low pressure hoses from the hydraulic assembly. Cap the spigot on the reservoir.

5. Disconnect the shift selection cable bracket from the transaxle and move it aside.

6. Loosen the nuts on the 2 studs that position the pump/motor to the transaxle differential cover.

7. Remove the retainer bolts that are used to mount hose bracket and pump/motor. The engine inlet water extension pipe is also held in position by these bolts.

NOTE: *Do not disturb the inlet water extension pipe, or engine coolant will leak out.*

8. Disconnect the wiring harness retaining clip from the hose bracket.

9. Lift the pump/motor assembly off of the studs and out of the vehicle.

10. Remove the heat shield from the pump/ motor, if equipped and discard.

To install:

11. Place a new heat shield to the pump/motor bracket, using fasteners provided.

12. Install the pump/motor assembly in the reverse order of the removal.

13. Readjust the gearshift linkage, if it was disturbed.

14. Connect the negative battery cable and check the assembly for proper operation.

1991–92 Vehicles

BENDIX SYSTEM 10

1. Disconnect the negative battery cable.

CAUTION: *Failure to depressurize the hydraulic accumulator, prior to performing this operation may result in personal injury and/ or damage to the painted surfaces.*

2. Depressurize the brake system.

3. Remove the fresh air intake ducts from the engine.

4. Remove the clip holding the high pressure line to the battery tray.

5. Disconnect the electrical connectors running across the engine compartment in the vicinity of the pump/motor high and low pressure hoses. One of these connectors is the one for the pump/motor assembly.

6. Disconnect the high and low pressure hoses from the hydraulic assembly. Cap or plug the reservoir fitting.

7. Disconnect the pump/motor electrical connector from the engine mount.

8. Remove the heat shield bolt from the front of the pump bracket. Remove the heat shield.

9. Lift the pump/motor assembly from the bracket and out of the vehicle.

To install:

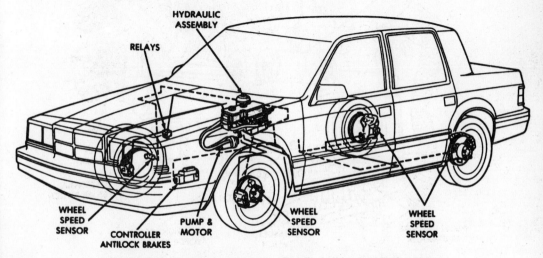

Anti-Lock brake system components—Bendix Anti-Lock 10 brake system

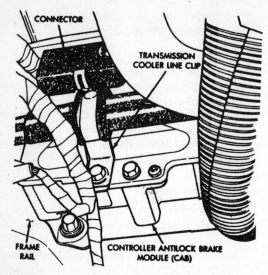

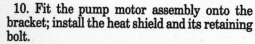

ABS controller location—Bendix Anti-Lock 10 brake system

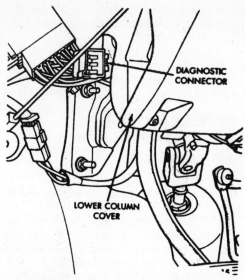

ABS diagnostic connector location—Bendix Anti-Lock 10 brake system

10. Fit the pump motor assembly onto the bracket; install the heat shield and its retaining bolt.

11. Install the pump/motor electrical connector to the engine mount.

12. Connect the high and low pressure hose to the hydraulic assembly. Tighten the high pressure line to 145 inch lbs. (16 Nm). Tighten the hose clamp on the low pressure hose to 10 inch lbs (1 Nm).

13. Connect the electrical connectors which were removed for access.

14. Install the high pressure line retaining clip to the battery tray if it was removed.

15. Install the fresh air intake ducts.

16. Bleed the brake system.

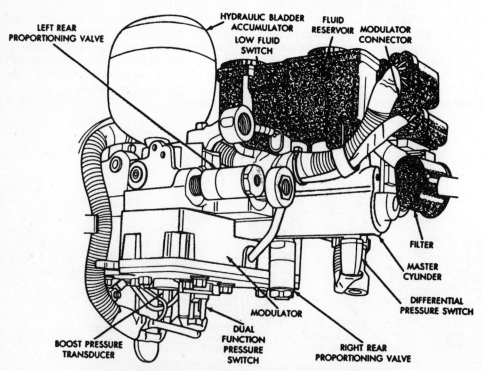

Hydraulic assembly—Bendix Anti-Lock 10 brake system

Hydraulic Assembly

REMOVAL AND INSTALLATION

1. Disconnect the negative battery cable. Depressurize the hydraulic accumulator.

CAUTION: *Failure to depressurize the hydraulic accumulator, prior to performing this operation may result in personal injury and/or damage to the painted surfaces.*

2. Remove the fresh air intake ducts.

3. Disconnect all electrical connectors from the hydraulic unit and pump/motor.

4. Remove as much of the fluid as possible from the reservoir on the hydraulic assembly.

5. Remove the pressure hose fitting (banjo bolt) from the hydraulic assembly. Use care not to drop the 2 washers used to seal the pressure hose fitting to the hydraulic assembly inlet.

6. Disconnect the return hose from the reservoir nipple. Cap the spigot on the reservoir.

7. Disconnect all brake tubes from the hydraulic assembly.

8. Remove the driver's side sound insulation panel.

9. Disconnect the pushrod from the brake pedal by using a small, flat tool to release the retainer clip on the brake pedal pin. The center tang on the clip must be moved back enough to allow the lock tab to clear the pin. Disconnect the pushrod from the pedal pin.

10. Remove the 4 underdash hydraulic assembly mounting nuts.

11. Remove the hydraulic assembly.

To install:

12. Position the hydraulic assembly on the vehicle.

13. Install and torque the mounting nuts to 21 ft. lbs. (28 Nm).

14. Using Lubriplate® or equivalent, coat the bearing surface of the pedal pin.

15. Connect the pushrod to the pedal and install a new retainer clip.

16. Install the brake tubes. If the proportioning valves were removed from the hydraulic assembly, reinstall valves and tighten to 20 ft. lbs. (27 Nm).

17. Install the return hose to the nipple on the reservoir.

18. Install the pressure hose to the hydraulic assembly; be sure the 2 washers are in there proper position. Tighten the banjo bolt to 13 ft. lbs. (18 Nm).

19. Fill the reservoir to the top of the screen.

20. Connect all electrical connectors to the hydraulic assembly.

21. Bleed the entire brake system.

22. Install the cross-car brace, if disturbed. Install the fresh air intake duct.

23. Connect the negative battery cable and check the assembly for proper operation.

Sensor Block

REMOVAL AND INSTALLATION

1989–90 Vehicles

BOSCH ABS III SYSTEM

1. Disconnect the negative battery cable. Depressurize the hydraulic accumulator.

CAUTION: *Failure to depressurize the hydraulic accumulator, prior to performing this operation may result in personal injury and/or damage to the painted surfaces.*

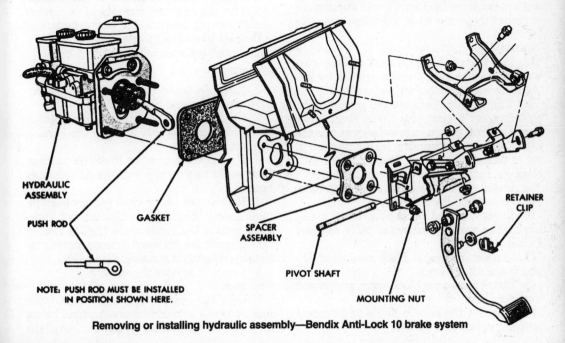

HYDRAULIC ASSEMBLY

PUSH ROD

GASKET

SPACER ASSEMBLY

PIVOT SHAFT

RETAINER CLIP

MOUNTING NUT

NOTE: PUSH ROD MUST BE INSTALLED IN POSITION SHOWN HERE.

Removing or installing hydraulic assembly—Bendix Anti-Lock 10 brake system

2. Disconnect all electrical connectors from the reservoir on the hydraulic assembly.

3. Working from under the dash, disconnect the pushrod from the brake pedal.

4. Remove the driver's side sound insulator panel.

5. Remove the 4 hydraulic assembly mounting nuts.

6. Working from under the hood, pull the hydraulic assembly away from the dash panel and rotate the assembly enough to gain access to the sensor block cover.

NOTE: *The brake lines should not be removed or deformed during this procedure.*

7. Remove the sensor block cover retaining bolt and remove the sensor block cover. Care should be used not to damage the cover gasket during removal.

8. Disengage the locking tabs and disconnect the valve block connector (12 pin) from the sensor block.

9. Disengage the reed block connector, marked PUSH, by carefully pulling outward on the orange connector body. The connector is partially retained by a plastic clip and will only move outward approximately ½ in. (13mm).

10. Remove the 3 block retaining bolts.

11. Carefully disengage the sensor block pressure port from the hydraulic assembly and remove the sensor block from the vehicle. The sensor block pressure port is sealed with an O-ring and extra care should be taken to prevent damage to the seal.

12. Inspect the sensor block pressure port O-ring for damage. Replace the O-ring if cut or damaged. Check the sensor block wiring for any mis-positioning or damage. Correct any damage or replace the sensor block, if damage cannot be corrected.

To install:

13. Pull the reed block connector (2 pin) outward to the disengage position prior to installing the sensor block on the hydraulic unit.

14. Thoroughly lubricate the sensor block pressure port O-ring with fresh, clean brake fluid. Carefully insert the pressure port into the hydraulic assembly's orifice, taking care not to cut or damage the O-ring. Position the sensor block for installation of the mounting bolts.

15. Install the sensor block mounting bolts. Tighten to 11 ft. lbs. (15 Nm).

16. Engage the reed block connector by pressing on the orange connector body marked **PUSH.**

17. Connect the valve block connector (12 pin) to the sensor block.

18. Install the sensor block cover, gasket and mounting bolt.

19. Connect the sensor block and control pressure switch connectors.

20. Install the hydraulic assembly by reversing the removal procedure.

21. Connect the negative battery cable and check the sensor block for proper operation.

Wheel Speed Sensors

REMOVAL AND INSTALLATION

Chrysler FWD
Dynasty, Imperial And New Yorker

FRONT SENSOR

1. Raise the vehicle and support safely. Remove the wheel and tire assembly.

2. Remove the screw from the clip that holds the sensor to the fender shield.

3. Carefully pull the sensor assembly grommet from the fender shield.

4. Unplug the connector from the harness. Remove the retainer clip from the strut damper bracket.

5. Remove the sensor mounting screw.

6. Carefully remove the sensor.

To install:

7. Coat the sensor with high temperature multi-purpose anti-corrosion compound before installing into the steering knuckle. Install the screw and tighten to 60 inch lbs. (7 Nm).

8. Connect the sensor connector to the harness and install the sensor connector lock.

9. Install the sensor assembly grommet and attach the clip to the fender shield.

NOTE: *Proper installation of the wheel speed sensor cables is critical to continued system operation. Be sure the cables are installed in retainers. Failure to install the cables in the retainers may result in contact with moving parts and/or over-extension of the cables, resulting in an open circuit.*

10. Install the wheel.

REAR SENSOR

1. Raise the vehicle and support safely. Remove the wheel and tire assembly.

2. Carefully pull the sensor assembly grommet from the underbody and pull the harness through the hole.

3. Unplug the connector from the harness. Remove the retainer clip from the strut damper bracket.

4. Remove the sensor spool grommet clip retaining screw from the body hose bracket, located in front of the inside of the trailing arm.

5. Remove the outboard sensor assembly retaining nut and sensor mounting screw.

6. Carefully remove the sensor.

To install:

7. Coat the sensor with high temperature multi-purpose anti-corrosion compound before installing into the steering knuckle. Install the

screw and tighten to 60 inch lbs. (7 Nm). Install the retaining nut.

8. Install the sensor spool grommet clip retaining screw.

9. Feed the sensor connector wire through the grommet and connect to the harness.

10. Install the sensor assembly grommet.

11. Install the wheel.

BRAKE SYSTEM BLEEDING

Chrysler FWD
Dynasty, Imperial And New Yorker

BOOSTER BLEEDING
BOSCH ABS III (1989-90)

1. The hydraulic accumulator must be depressurized.

2. Connect all pump/motor and hydraulic assembly electrical connections, if previously disconnected. Be sure all brake lines and hose connections are tight.

3. Fill the reservoir to the full level.

4. Connect a transparent hose to the bleeder screw location on the right side of the hydraulic assembly. Place the other end of the hose into a clear container to receive brake fluid.

5. Open the bleeder screw ½-¾ of a turn.

6. Turn the ignition switch to the **ON** position. The pump/motor should run, discharging fluid into the container. After a good volume of fluid has been forced through the hose, an air-free flow in the plastic hose and container will indicate a good bleed.

7. Turn the ignition switch **OFF**.

NOTE: *If the brake fluid does not flow, it may be due to a lack of prime to the pump/motor. Try shaking the return hose to break up air bubbles that may be present within the hose.*

Should the brake fluid still not flow, turn the ignition switch to the OFF position. Remove the return hose from the reservoir and cap nipple on the reservoir. Manually fill the return hose with brake fluid and connect to the reservoir. Repeat the bleeding process.

8. Remove the hose from the bleeder screw. Tighten the bleeder screw to 7.5 ft. lbs. (10 Nm). Do not overtighten.

9. Top off the reservoir to the correct fluid level.

10. Turn the ignition switch to the **ON** position. Allow the pump to charge the accumulator, which should stop after approximately 30 seconds.

Pressure Bleeding

The brake lines may be pressure bled, using a standard diaphragm type pressure bleeder. Only diaphragm type pressure bleeding equipment should be used to bleed the system.

1. The ignition should be turned **OFF** and remain **OFF** throughout this procedure.

2. Depressurize the hydraulic accumulator.
CAUTION: *Failure to depressurize the hydraulic accumulator, prior to performing this operation may result in personal injury and/or damage to the painted surfaces.*

3. Remove the electrical connector from fluid level sensor on the reservoir cap(s) and remove the reservoir cap(s).

4. Install the pressure bleeder adapter.

5. Attach the bleeding equipment to the bleeder adapter. Charge the pressure bleeder to approximately 20 psi (138 kPa).

6. Connect a transparent hose to the caliper bleed screw. Submerge the free end of the hose in a clear glass container, which is partially filled with clean, fresh brake fluid.

7. With the pressure turned **ON**, open the caliper bleed screw ½-¾ turn and allow fluid to flow into the container. Leave the bleed screw open until clear, bubble-free fluid slows from the hose. If the reservoir has been drained or the hydraulic assembly removed from the vehicle prior to the bleeding operation, slowly pump the brake pedal 1-2 times while the bleed screw is open and fluid is flowing. This will help purge air from the hydraulic assembly. Tighten the bleeder screw to 7.5 ft. lbs. (10 Nm).

8. Repeat Step 7 at all calipers. Calipers should be bled in the following order:
   a. Left rear
   b. Right rear
   c. Left front
   d. Right front

9. After bleeding all 4 calipers, remove the pressure bleeding equipment and bleeder adapter by closing the pressure bleeder valve and slowly unscrewing the bleeder adapter from the hydraulic assembly reservoir. Failure to release pressure in the reservoir will cause spillage of brake fluid and could result in injury or damage to painted surfaces.

10. Using a syringe or equivalent method, remove excess fluid from the reservoir to bring the fluid level to full level.

11. Install the reservoir cap and connect the fluid level sensor connector. Turn the ignition **ON** and allow the pump to charge the accumulator.

MANUAL BLEEDING

1. Depressurize the hydraulic accumulator.
CAUTION: *Failure to depressurize the hydraulic accumulator, prior to performing this operation may result in personal injury and/or damage to the painted surfaces.*

2. Connect a transparent hose to the caliper bleed screw. Submerge the free end of the hose

in a clear glass container, which is partially filled with clean, fresh brake fluid.

3. Slowly pump the brake pedal several times, using full strokes of the pedal and allowing approximately 5 seconds between pedal strokes. After 2 or 3 strokes, continue to hold pressure on the pedal, keeping it at the bottom of its travel.

4. With pressure on the pedal, open the bleed screw ½–¾ turn. Leave the bleed screw open until fluid no longer flows from the hose. Tighten the bleed screw and release the pedal.

5. Repeat this procedure until clear, bubble-free fluid flows from the hose.

6. Repeat all steps at each of the calipers. Calipers should be bled in the following order:
   a. Left rear
   b. Right rear
   c. Left front
   d. Right front

BRAKE SPECIFICATIONS
1990–92 Laser

All measurements given are (in.) unless noted.

Year	Lug Nut Torque (ft. lbs.)	Master Cylinder Bore	Brake Disc		Brake Drum			Minimum Lining Thickness	
			Minimum Thickness	Maximum Runout	Diameter	Max. Machine O/S	Max. Wear Limit	Front	Rear
1990	(Front) 87–101	①	0.882	0.003	—	—	—	0.080	0.080
	(Rear) 87–101	—	0.331	0.003	—	—	—	0.080	0.080
1991–92	(Front) 87–101	②	0.882	0.003	—	—	—	0.080	0.080
	(Rear) 87–101	—	0.331	0.003	—	—	—	0.080	0.080

NOTE: Minimum lining thickness is as recommended by the manufacturer. Because of variations in state inspection regulations, the minimum allowable thickness may be different than recommended by the manufacturer.

① Non-turbocharged engine: ⅞ inch
  Turbocharged engine: ¹⁵/₁₆ inch
② Non-turbocharged without ABS: ⅞ inch
  Non-turbocharged with ABS: ¹⁵/₁₆ inch
  Turbocharged with FWD: ¹⁵/₁₆ inch
  Turbocharged with AWD: 1 inch

BRAKE SPECIFICATIONS
1991–92 Dodge Stealth

All measurements given are (in.) unless noted.

Year	Model	Lug Nut Torque (ft. lbs.)	Master Cylinder Bore	Brake Disc		Brake Drum			Minimum Lining Thickness	
				Minimum Thickness	Maximum Runout	Diameter	Max. Machine O/S	Max. Wear Limit	Front	Rear
1991–92	FWD	(Front) 87–101	①	0.880	0.003	—	—	—	0.080	0.080
		(Rear) 87–101	—	0.650	0.003	—	—	—	0.080	0.080
	AWD	(Front) 87–101	1¹/₁₆	1.12	0.003	—	—	—	0.080	0.080
		(Rear) 87–101	—	0.720	0.003	—	—	—	0.080	0.080

NOTE: Minimum lining thickness is as recommended by the manufacturer. Because of variations in state inspection regulations, the minimum allowable thickness may be different than recommended by the manufacturer.
FWD: Front Wheel Drive
AWD: All Wheel Drive
① Without ABS: 1 inch
  With ABS: 1¹/₁₆ inch

BRAKE SPECIFICATIONS
1990–92 Dodge Monaco
All measurements given are (in.) unless noted.

Year	Lug Nut Torque (ft. lbs.)	Master Cylinder Bore	Brake Disc		Brake Drum			Minimum Lining Thickness	
			Minimum Thickness	Maximum Runout	Diameter	Max. Machine O/S	Max. Wear Limit	Front	Rear
1990–92	(Front) 63	0.945	0.890	0.003	—	—	—	0.06	0.06
	(Rear) 63	—	0.380	0.003	8.92	①	①	0.06	0.06

NOTE: Minimum lining thickness is as recommended by the manufacturer. Because of variations in state inspection regulations, the minimum allowable thickness may be different than recommended by the manufacturer.
① See figure stamped on the drum

BRAKE SPECIFICATIONS
Acclaim, Aries, Caravelle, Daytona, Dynasty, E-Class, Executive, Sedan, Imperial, Lancer, Laser (1984–86), LeBaron, New Yorker, Reliant, Shadow, Spirit, Sundance, Town & Country, 400 and 600 Models
All measurements given are (in.) unless noted.

Year	Lug Nut Torque (ft. lbs.)	Master Cylinder Bore	Brake Disc		Brake Drum			Minimum Lining Thickness	
			Minimum Thickness	Maximum Runout	Diameter	Max. Machine O/S	Max. Wear Limit	Front	Rear
1981–85	95	.827	.882⑤	.004	7.87②	①	①	.300	5/16④
1986–92	95	.827	.882⑤	.005	7.87③	①	①	5/16	5/16④

NOTE: Minimum lining thickness is as recommended by the manufacturer. Because of variations in state inspection regulations, the minimum allowable thickness may be different than recommended by the manufacturer.
① See figure stamped on the drum
② Caravelle, 600 and New Yorker: 8.66
③ Caravelle, 600 and New Yorker, and Daytona, Aries, Reliant, LeBaron and Town and Country with Heavy Duty Brakes and towing option: 8.66
④ Applied to drum brakes. Rear disc: 9/32
⑤ Front Disc Brakes—On Rear Disc Brake Applications, see figure stamped on Disc Assembly

Body

10

EXTERIOR

Doors

REMOVAL AND INSTALLATION

All Chrysler Front Wheel Drive cars are equipped with doors the hinges of which are welded to both the door panel and the door pillar. Doors are removed and installed basically by disconnecting them at the hinges.

NOTE: *To perform this procedure, you'll need a hinge alignment tool C–4741 and a removal tool C–4614 or C–4716 (depending on the size of the hinge). It will also be helpful to have a grinding wheel.*

1. Disconnect the negative battery cable. If there is any kind of wiring harness to the door, remove the door panel as described later in this chapter. Then, label all electrical connectors. Unplug each connector. Route the harness through the grommet in the edge of the door, coil it and tape it in a spot where it will be kept away from the area of the door hinges.

2. Open the door and, using a padded device of some kind, support it securely from underneath near the outer end.

3. Use the hinge removal tool to remove the *lower* hinge pin. Then, immediately install the hinge alignment tool in place of the hinge pin.

4. Make sure the door is steadied against falling over. Use the appropriate sized hinge removal tool to remove the upper hinge pin. Then, remove the alignment tool and remove the door.

5. Grind a chamfer on the lower end of both hinge pins to ease installation.

6. Position the door so as to fit its hinge-halves into the hinge-halves welded to the body. Align the door precisely and install two hinge alignment tools.

7. Position the upper hinge pin under the upper hinge and use a small hammer to tap it upward and through the hinge. Install the lower hinge pin from the upper side of the lower hinge in a similar manner. Remove the two alignment tools.

8. Route the wiring harness through the door, connecting all connectors to their original locations. Install the door panel as described later in this chapter.

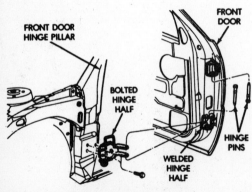

Front door assembly—Chrysler cars

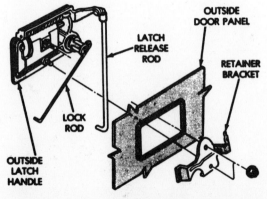

Outside front door latch release handle—Chrysler cars

ADJUSTMENT

Except Laser and Stealth

The door hinges are welded to both the door panels and door pillars. Because of this fact, adjustments can be performed only through the use of a special door hinge adjusting tool (C-4736), which bends the hinges in a controlled way.

Before adjusting either hinge, check these items:

• The alignment of the striker plate. Is it correct?

• The fit and condition of the hinge roll pins. If there is looseness, they must be replaced.

• The installation of the door seal. Sealing problems which may seem to be door misalignment may actually be due to irregular/incorrect positioning of the seal on the body.

1. If it is necessary to adjust the striker plate:

a. Scribe around the striker plate to mark its location against the door jamb. Then, loosen the mounting screws just slightly.

b. Open and close the door slowly to watch engagement of the door with the striker. The door should not rise or fall as it is closed. Reposition the striker vertically to ensure that this requirement is met.

c. Close the door and inspect its outer surface to see if it is flush with adjacent sheet metal. If not, adjust the striker inward or outward until the door rests in a flush position.

d. Tighten the striker adjustments securely.

2. If these other checks fail to resolve door alignment problems, it is necessary to bend the hinges. Keep in mind that this process must be done gradually to fine tune the door position. First, determine the exact angle/area of misalignment.

3. Slip the hinge bending tool *completely* over the hinge to be bent. Then, slowly and gradually apply pressure so the change in door position can be monitored accurately. Stop the process and check the point of misalignment frequently.

LATCH ADJUSTMENT

The latch adjustment affects both the smoothness of door latch operation and the door handle-to-skin position.

1. Insert a $^5/_{32}$ in. (4mm) Allen wrench through the access hole in the end of the door and engage it with the Allen screw in the latch mechanism. Slide the screw up or down in the slot to adjust the latch position and then tighten the Allen screw to about 30 inch lbs. Remove the wrench.

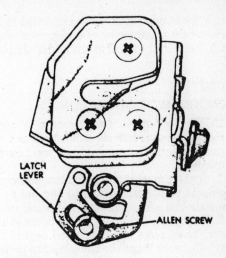

Adjusting the door latch

2. Close the door and check the operation of the latch as well as the door handle position.

3. Readjust as described in Steps 1 and 2 until the door closes smoothly and the door handle is flush.

1990–92 Laser And Dodge Stealth

1. Use a special tool MB99034 or equivalent to loosen the hinge mounting bolts on the body side and then adjust the clearance around the door so that it is uniform on all sides.

2. When the hinge is replaced, loosen hinge mounting bolts on door side and adjust alignment of the fender panel with door assembly.

3. Loosen door striker mounting screws to adjust alignment of door panel. Increase or de-

Door adjustment procedures 1990–92 Laser and Dodge Stealth

crease the number of shims and move the striker to adjust engagement of striker with door latch. Refer to the illustrations in this chapter.

Hood

REMOVAL AND INSTALLATION

NOTE: *To perform this operation a cover that will protect both the windshield and the two fenders is required, as well as an assistant.*

1. Scribe a mark around each hinge where it connects to the underside of the hood for reinstallation with a minimum of adjustment.

2. Protect the windshield and fenders with a cover. Then, place blocks of wood behind the hood – between it and the windshield to protect the windshield in case the hood should slide to the rear.

3. As an assistant supports the hood, remove the hood bolts. With one person on either side, remove the hood from the car. If the hood is being replaced with a new one, transfer the latch striker and safety catch by removing the attaching bolts and reinstalling these components onto the new hood with them.

To install:

4. To install the hood, first position it as precisely as possible – with the bolt holes of the upper hinge and the hood lined up. Then, with the assistant both supporting the front of the hood and keeping the assembly from sliding back toward the windshield, install the bolts until their heads are just a turn or two below the lower hood surface.

5. Shift the hood on both sides to align the matchmarks and hinges precisely. Tighten one bolt on either side gradually, checking that the

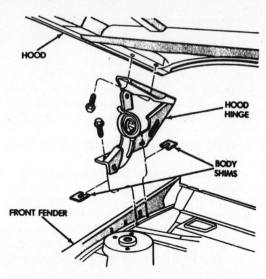

Hood hinge—Chrysler cars

hood remains in position and shifting it to maintain alignment (refer to service procedure below) as necessary. Tighten one bolt on either side to hold the hood in position.

6. Have the assistant hold the hood up as you tighten all the remaining bolts slightly. Then, torque all bolts evenly and tight.

7. Remove the cover and blocks.

ALIGNMENT

Except Laser and Stealth

1. Inspect the clearances (about 0.160 in. or 4mm) between the hood edges in relation to the cowl, fenders and grille panel.

2. If the hood requires adjustment, loosen the mounting bolts located on the underside of the hood.

3. Shift the hood forward or rearward to change the dimension between its rear and the cowl first, if this adjustment is necessary. Once this is correct, shift the hood right or left as necessary.

4. Torque all bolts evenly and tight.

1990–92 Laser And Dodge Stealth

1. Loosen the hood mounting bolts, and then adjust the hood by moving it so that the clearance is equal on all sides.

2. Turn the hood bumpers, adjust the height of the hood.

3. Loosen the hood latch mounting bolts, and move the hood latch to adjust the attachment between the hood latch and hood striker.

Trunk Lid

REMOVAL AND INSTALLATION

NOTE: *This operation requires the help of an assistant to prevent possible physical inju-*

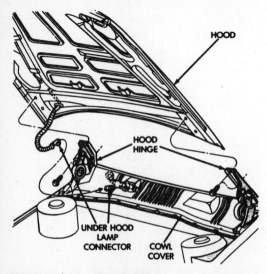

Hood assembly—Chrysler cars

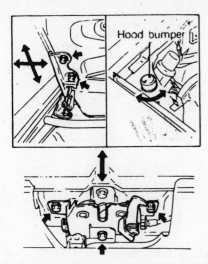

Hood adjustment 1990–92 Laser and Dodge Stealth

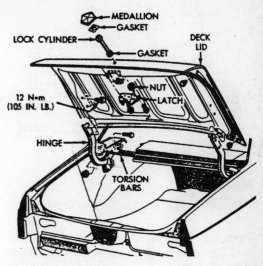

Replacing the trunk lid

ry or damage to the rear window and fenders.

1. Scribe a mark around each hinge where it connects to the underside of the trunk lid for reinstallation with a minimum of adjustment.

2. As an assistant supports the trunk lid remove the bolts (2 on on either side) which fasten it to the outer arm of the hinge. Then, with one person on either side, remove the lid from the car. If a new trunk lid is to be installed, unbolt and transfer the lock cylinder, Chrysler medallion and gasket, lock cylinder and gasket, and latch.

To install:

4. To install the trunk lid, first position it as precisely as possible—with the bolt holes of the upper hinge and the lid lined up. Then, with the assistant both supporting the rear of the lid and keeping the assembly from sliding forward toward the rear window, install the bolts until their heads are just a turn or two below the lower hood surface.

5. Shift the lid on both sides to align the matchmarks and hinges precisely. Tighten one bolt on either side gradually, checking that it remains in position and shifting it to maintain

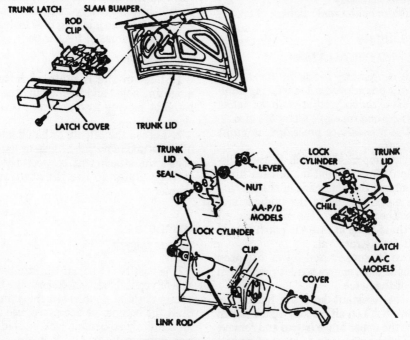

Trunk lid lock assembly

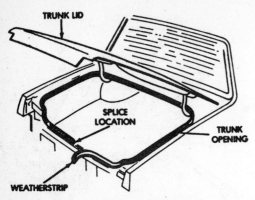

Trunk opening weatherstrip—Chrysler cars

alignment (about 0.160 in. or 4mm) as necessary. Tighten one bolt on either side to hold the trunk lid in position.

6. Have the assistant hold it up as you tighten all the remaining bolts slightly. Then, torque all bolts evenly tight.

ADJUSTMENT

1. Inspect the clearances (about 0.160 in. or 4mm) between the edges of the trunk lid in relation to the rear of the body under the rear window, the fenders, and the rear panel.

2. If the lid requires adjustment, loosen the mounting bolts located on its underside.

3. Shift the lid forward or rearward to change the dimension between its front end and the fore and after seals first, if this adjustment is necessary. Once this is correct, shift the hood right or left as necessary.

4. Torque the bolts evenly tight.

Hatch or Liftgate

REMOVAL AND INSTALLATION

NOTE: *It is necessary to use an assistant to perform this procedure without risking damage to areas of the body adjacent to the hatch. Masking tape and rope type sealer are also required. Use this service procedure as guide for this repair.*

1. Securely support the hatch in the wide-open position. Mark the outline of each hinge where it contacts the underside of the hatch.

2. Apply masking tape to the underside of the door and the rear edge of the roof to prevent damage to these areas in case the hatch should slip or shift during removal.

3. Remove the upper and lower lift prop mounting bolts and remove the lift props from both sides of the hatch.

4. Have the assistant hold the hatch. Remove the two bolts on either side which fasten the hatch to the upper hinge halves and remove the hatch. If the hatch is to be re-used, unbolt

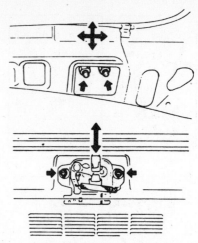

Liftgate or hatch adjustment 1990–92 Laser and Dodge Stealth

and transfer the bumper, latch, and lock cylinder.

To install:

5. To install the hatch, position it against the hinges with the holes in the hinges and those in the hatch precisely aligned. Have the assistant hold the hatch in position. Apply rope type sealer to the outer edges of the hinges where they will fit against the hatch.

6. Install the hinge mounting bolts and tighten them alternately and evenly.

7. Locate one of the lift props, having the assistant adjust the height of the hatch so hinge holes will align. Install the attaching bolts. Have the assistant hold the opposite side as you install the prop and bolts on the other side.

8. Remove the masking tape installed to protect various areas of the car body.

ADJUSTMENT

1. Loosen the liftgate or hatch hinges mounting bolts, and then adjust the liftgate or hatch by moving it so clearance is equal on all sides.

2. Loosen the liftgate or hatch latch mounting bolts and move the liftgate or hatch latch to adjust the attachment between the latch and striker. Refer to the illustrations in this chapter.

Bumpers

ADJUSTMENT

It is possible to adjust the bumper's side-to-side or vertical location. Loosen the bumper-to-energy absorber (outer) attaching nuts or bolts. Shift the bumper as necessary, use a helper or an infinitely adjustable jack to hold it in position and torque to 105 inch lbs. on 1981–85 models and 250 inch lbs. on later models. Refer to illustrations.

REMOVAL AND INSTALLATION

CAUTION: *Energy absorbing units may become stuck in the retracted position because of an impact. DO NOT DRILL THE ABSORBER TO REMOVE PRESSURE! This could result in the release of this pressure! If loosening the bolts or nuts at either end to relieve torque on the energy absorber does not cause it to expand, it MUST BE DISCARDED.*

1. Refer to the illustrations in this chapter as a guide for this repair. Place supports under the bumper. If the bumper has a fascia, remove the retaining nuts and remove it.

2. Remove the bumper-to-energy absorber (outer end) retaining nuts or bolts. Then, lower the bumper assembly to the floor.

To install:

3. To install the bumper, raise it into its normal position and install the retaining nuts/bolts loosely. Now, shift the bumper as necessary, use a helper or an infinitely adjustable jack to hold it in position and then torque that attaching nuts or bolts to 105 inch lbs. on 1981–85 models and 250 inch lbs. on later models.

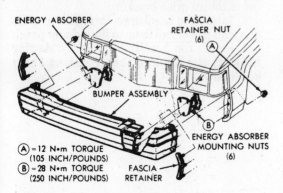

A = 12 N•m TORQUE (105 INCH/POUNDS)
B = 28 N•m TORQUE (250 INCH/POUNDS)

Replacing the bumper on 1981 K car

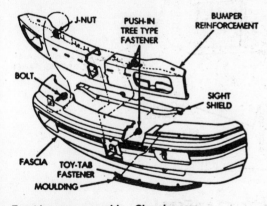

Front bumper assembly—Chrysler cars

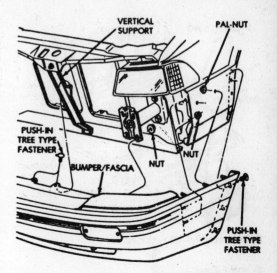

Wrap around front bumper assembly—Chrysler cars

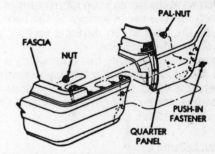

Wrap around rear bumper assembly—Chrysler cars

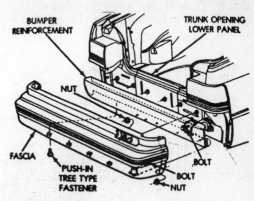

Standard rear bumper assembly—Chrysler cars

4. Install the bumper fascia and retaining nuts as necessary.

Grille

REMOVAL AND INSTALLATION

NOTE: *Use these service procedures as guide for all years/models. Carefully install the grille assembly to create even spacing on either side upon installation. Refer to the illustrations in this chapter.*

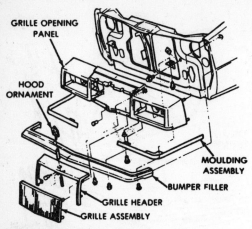

GRILLE OPENING PANEL

HOOD ORNAMENT

MOULDING ASSEMBLY

BUMPER FILLER

GRILLE HEADER

GRILLE ASSEMBLY

Grille assembly—Chrysler cars

K- and E-Cars

The grille on these cars is retained by 2 mounting screws at the top and two return springs at the bottom. The use of springs at the bottom permits the grille to flex during a parking lot type of low-speed collision.

To replace the grille, all that is necessary is to open the hood, remove the two top mounting screws, disconnect the two return springs at the bottom, and pull the grille out. Reverse this procedure to install it.

Lancer, LeBaron GTS

The grille on these models is retained very simply. There is once screw on either side, accessible from in front of the car. Simply remove both these screws to remove the grille. Install it in reverse order.

Daytona AND Laser

The grille on the Daytona AND Laser is retained by two screws at the top (reached from in front of the car) and two at the bottom, accessible from above and by going behind the grille. These screws are accessible once the hood is open. Remove the four screws and remove the grille. Replace the grille in reverse order.

Sundance and Shadow

1. Open the hood. Then remove the headlamp bezel by removing the screws and rotating it upward at the bottom and then out of the grille.

2. Remove the headlamps.

3. Loosen the bolts attaching the grille to the outboard mounting brackets. Remove the bolts attaching the grille to the radiator panel.

4. Remove the grille. To install the grille, position the slotted ends over the bolts in the outboard mounting brackets and then carefully shift the grille from left to right to create even spacing on either side.

5. Install the bolts attaching the grille to the brackets in the radiator panel.

6. Tighten the bolts attaching the grille to the outboard grille brackets.

7. Insert the headlamps through the grille openings and install them to the radiator panel.

8. Install the headlamp bezels by starting them at the top and then rotating them downward.

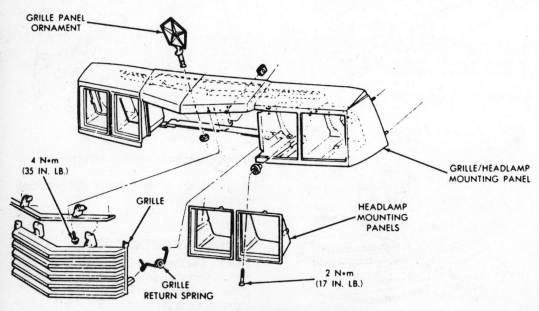

GRILLE PANEL ORNAMENT

4 N•m (35 IN. LB.)

GRILLE

GRILLE RETURN SPRING

2 N•m (17 IN. LB.)

HEADLAMP MOUNTING PANELS

GRILLE/HEADLAMP MOUNTING PANEL

Replacing the grille assembly on K and E cars

Mirrors

REMOVAL AND INSTALLATION

1. Remove the mirror bezel mounting screw to release the bezel from the channel bracket. If the mirror is the remote control type, loosen the bezel set screw (this will release the cable control).

2. If the mirror is the power type, remove the door trim panel, and then disconnect the mirror wiring harness at the connector.

3. Remove the 3 screws from the inboard side of the channel bracket.

4. Remove the 2 screws from the door frame. Release the mirror and seal from the channel bracket.

5. To install the mirror, assemble the mirror and seal to the channel bracket. Install the 2 screws to the door frame and then install the 3 screws to the inboard side of the channel bracket.

6. If working with a power mirror, reconnect the wiring harness connector and install the trim panel.

7. On remote control mirrors, tighten the bezel set screw. Then, on all mirrors, install the mirror bezel-to-channel bracket mounting screw.

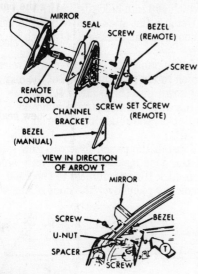

VIEW IN DIRECTION OF ARROW T

Side mirror mounting

Antenna

REPLACEMENT

NOTE: *To perform this operation, a special antenna cap nut (much like a socket wrench), Tool C–4816, is required. On some vehicles the radio must be remove to gain access to the antenna connection. Some vehicles use a two piece cable do not remove the radio but dis-*

connect the cable at harness connection. Refer to the illustrations in this chapter.

1. The radio may have to be removed from the car to gain access to the antenna connection. Remove the radio if necessary. Then, unplug the antenna lead at the radio or harness connection.

2. Use an open-end wrench of appropriate size across the flats at the bottom of the antenna mast to unscrew the mast from the antenna adapter. Then, remove the mast.

3. Use the special tool to unscrew the antenna cap nut from the fender. Then, remove the cap nut and the adapter and gasket underneath it.

4. If access to the antenna body from underneath the fender is blocked by an inner fender shield, remove the 3 screws from the rear of the shield and bend it away to gain access.

5. Then, remove the antenna lead and body assembly.

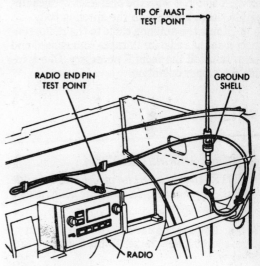

Antenna assembly

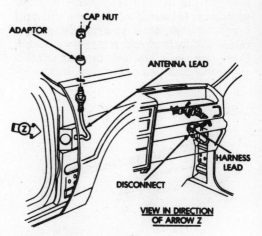

VIEW IN DIRECTION OF ARROW Z

Two piece antenna assembly

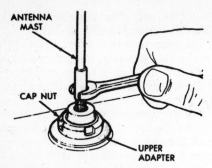

Antenna mast removal and installation

To install:

6. To install the antenna, first insert the antenna body and cable through the hole in the fender from underneath. Then, install the gasket, adapter and cap nut torquing the cap nut to 100–150 inch lbs. with the special tool.

7. Screw the antenna mast into the antenna body. Tighten it with the open-end wrench until its sleeve bottoms on the antenna body.

8. Route the antenna cable to the radio, connect it to the radio (or harness connection) and then reinstall the radio if necessary. Check radio for proper operation.

INTERIOR

Door Panels

REMOVAL AND INSTALLATION

NOTE: *Use these service procedures as guide to all years/models. Refer to the illustrations in this chapter.*

Aries, Reliant, LeBaron, Town & Country, Caravelle, 600, New Yorker Turbo, Sundance and Shadow

NOTE: *If the watershield must be removed to work on the window mechanism or other items mounted inside the door, you will need a soft, water-resistant material designed to retain the watershield to the door metal. Since rain water that gets into the window slit drains down inside the door, it is neces-*

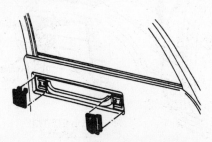

Removing the pull straps appliques K-body cars

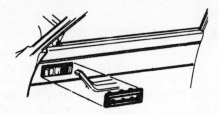

Removing the remote bezel from the right side door K-body cars

sary to seal the watershield carefully so there will not be leakage inside the car.

1. Unsnap the plastic appliques from the door pull strap and the remote bezel. Then, pull the front edge of the bezel outward and push the bezel backward to release it.

2. Remove the mounting screws at either end of the pull strap and remove it from the door panel.

3. Note the installation angle of the window crank handle and then remove it. To do this, use an Allen wrench to remove the Allen screw from the center of the window mechanism shaft.

4. Remove the retaining screws from the lower side of the door handle and remove it.

5. There are spring clips mounted to the door panel which slip into holes drilled into the door metal. Using a flat stick, gently pry the panel off the door at front, back and bottom to release the clips.

6. Lift the panel straight upward to release clips which retain it to the inside of the door by running down into the window slot.

7. If the watershield must be removed, carefully pull it off the retaining material.

To install:

8. To install the panel, first run new sealer around the door metal under the watershield and then stick the watershield to the door.

9. Hook the panel over the door at the win-

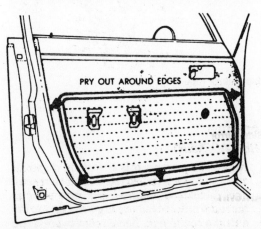

Door panel retaining clip locations

dow slit and hang it down over the door. Make sure the retaining clips line up with their corresponding holes and then press the panel inward directly over each clip to engage it with the door.

10. Install the door handle with the retaining screws if the car has one.

11. Install the window crank handle at the same angle by engaging its internal splines with those on the window mechanism shaft. Then, install the retaining screw and tighten it with the Allen wrench.

12. Install the pull strap, its retaining screws and the bezels.

13. Install the remote bezel.

Daytona AND Laser

1. Lower the window all the way. Disconnect the battery negative cable.

2. If the car has manual windows, remove the Allen screw from the end of the window mechanism shaft and remove the crank handle.

3. With a piece of thin, relatively soft material (such as a strip of wood), gently pry the electric mirror/door lock bezel out of the armrest. Then, disconnect the wiring connectors for the electric mirror and the door lock switch.

4. Remove the bezel surrounding the remote lock/latch release switches.

5. Disconnect the four armrest electrical plugs at the armrest. Remove the screw located behind each plug and the single screw in the opening of the switch bezel.

6. Rotate the armrest to release it and remove it.

7. Remove the one remaining trim panel retaining screw from the area of the door near the body pillar.

8. There are spring clips mounted to the door panel which slip into holes drilled into the door metal. Using a flat stick, gently pry the panel off the door at front, back and bottom to release the clips.

9. Disconnect the wire connector at the courtesy lamp.

10. Lift the panel straight upward to release clips which retain it to the inside of the door by running down into the window slot.

11. If the watershield must be removed, carefully pull it off the retaining material.

To install:

12. To install the panel, first run new sealer around the door metal under the watershield and then stick the watershield to the door.

13. Hook the panel over the door at the window slit and hang it down over the door. Make sure the retaining clips line up with their corresponding holes and then press the panel inward directly over each clip to engage it with the

door. Connect the wire connector at the courtesy lamp.

14. Install the trim panel retaining screw located in the area of the door near the body pillar.

15. Rotate the armrest into position.

16. Install the screw located behind the location of each plug in the armrest and the single screw in the opening of the switch bezel. Connect the four armrest electrical plugs.

17. Install the bezel surrounding the remote lock/latch release switches.

18. Connect the wiring connectors for the electric mirror and the door lock switch. Then, install the electric mirror/door lock bezel into the armrest.

19. If the car has manual windows, install the crank handle and then install the Allen screw into the end of the window mechanism shaft.

20. Reconnect the negative battery cable.

Lancer, LeBaron GTS

FRONT DOOR WITH MANUAL WINDOW REGULATOR

1. Roll the window all the way down. With an Allen wrench, remove the window crank handle retaining screw. Note the installation angle of the handle and remove it.

2. Snap off the mirror remote control bezel. Then, remove the two screws at the mirror remote control. Slide the inside handle bezel rearward and remove it.

3. Remove the door panel retaining screw from the forward/upper corner of the panel. There are spring clips mounted to the door panel which slip into holes drilled into the door metal. Using a flat stick, gently pry the panel off the door at the bottom, at the rear and half way up the front. Then, flex the panel at the forward, upper corner to to disengage the two additional clips located there.

4. Disconnect the courtesy light electrical connector.

5. Lift the panel straight upward to release clips which retain it to the inside of the door by running down into the window slot.

6. If the watershield must be removed, carefully pull it off the retaining material.

To install:

7. To install the panel, first run new sealer around the door metal under the watershield and then stick the watershield to the door.

8. Hook the panel over the door at the window slit and hang it down over the door. Make sure the retaining clips line up with their corresponding holes and then press the panel inward directly over each clip to engage it with the door. Connect the wire connector at the courtesy lamp.

9. Install the door panel retaining screw to the forward/upper corner of the panel.

10. Slide the inside handle bezel rearward and install it. Install the two screws at the mirror remote control. Snap the mirror remote control bezel back on.

11. Reinstall the crank handle at its original angle.

FRONT DOOR WITH ELECTRIC WINDOW REGULATOR

1. Lower the glass all the way. Then, disconnect the negative battery cable.

2. Remove the single retaining screw located at the electric window switch plate's forward edge. Lift the switch plate off the door panel, note how the connectors are hooked up, and then disconnect the connectors.

3. Follow Steps 2 through 6 of the procedure above to complete removal. Then, follow 7 through 10.

4. Remake the electrical connections to the window switch. Then, slip the switchplate into the door panel. Install the switchplate retaining screw. Reconnect the battery.

REAR DOOR WITH MANUAL REGULATOR

1. Roll the glass all the way down. Disconnect the negative battery cable.

2. Using an Allen wrench, remove the retaining screw for the window crank handle from the regulator shaft. Note the angle of the crank handle and remove it.

3. Remove the retaining screw from the pull cup behind the armrest. Then, slide the remote control bezel rearward to remove it.

4. There are spring clips mounted to the door panel which slip into holes drilled into the door metal. Using a flat stick, gently pry the panel off the door at the bottom, at the rear and half way up the front (there are 6 clips).

5. Disconnect the courtesy lamp electrical connector.

6. Lift the panel straight upward to release clips which retain it to the inside of the door by running down into the window slot.

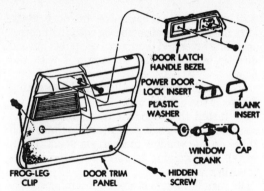

Front door trim panel with manual windows—Chrysler cars

7. If the watershield must be removed, carefully pull it off the retaining material.

To install:

8. To install the panel, first run new sealer around the door metal under the watershield and then stick the watershield to the door.

9. Hook the panel over the door at the window slit and hang it down over the door. Make sure the retaining clips line up with their corresponding holes and then press the panel inward directly over each clip to engage it with the door. Connect the wire connector at the courtesy lamp.

10. Position the remote control bezel into the panel and slide it forward to install it. Install the retaining screw into the pull cup behind the armrest.

11. Install the crank handle at its original installation angle. Reconnect the battery.

REAR DOOR WITH ELECTRIC REGULATOR

1. Roll the glass all the way down. Disconnect the negative battery cable.

2. Unsnap the window lift bezel and pull the switch out of the door panel just far enough to reach wiring. Note the wiring connector locations and disconnect them.

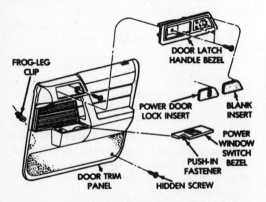

Front door trim panel with power windows—Chrysler cars

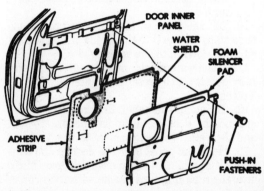

Front door silencer and water shield—Chrysler cars

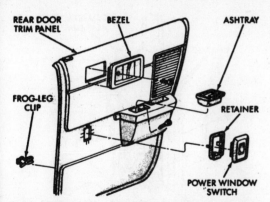

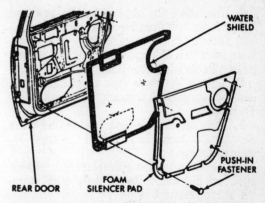

Rear door trim panel with power windows—Chrysler cars

Rear door silencer and watershield—Chrysler cars

3. Follow Steps 2 through 10 of the procedure above.

4. Reconnect the electric window motor wiring connectors to the correct terminals. Locate the switch into the door panel and snap the bezel back in.

5. Reconnect the battery.

LeBaron

1. Lower the window all the way.

2. Remove the switch bezel and the radio speaker from the door.

3. Remove the screw from the opening in which the switch bezel was located.

4. Remove the 2 screws attaching the door panel from the through-slits in the carpeted area of the map pocket.

5. If the car has manually operated windows, remove the retaining Allen screw for the regulator handle from the center of the window regulator shaft. Note the installation angle of the regulator handle and then remove it. Remove the spacer behind the handle.

6. Pull the bottom of the trim panel outward carefully to disengage the the lower clips. Pull it

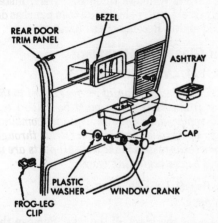

Rear door trim panel with manual windows—Chrysler cars

out just far enough to gain access to the courtesy lamp connection. Then, reach behind the panel and disconnect the courtesy lamp wire.

7. Pull the panel in order to remove the remaining clips from the door. Lift the panel straight upward to release clips which retain it to the inside of the door by running down into the window slot.

8. If the watershield must be removed, carefully pull it off the retaining material.

To install:

9. To install the panel, first run new sealer around the door metal under the watershield and then stick the watershield to the door.

10. Hook the panel over the door at the window slit and hang it down over the door. Connect the wire connector at the courtesy lamp. Make sure the retaining clips line up with their corresponding holes and then press the panel inward directly over each clip to engage it with the door.

11. Reinstall the regulator handle at its original installation angle.

12. Install the 2 screws attaching the door panel working through the slits in the carpeted area of the map pocket.

13. Install the panel retaining screw into the opening in which the switch bezel was located.

14. Install the switch bezel and the radio speaker into the door.

Door Locks

REMOVAL AND INSTALLATION

Except Daytona and Laser

NOTE: *On Sundance, Shadow, Lancer and LeBaron GTS a Torx® screwdriver is required to remove the lock mechanism mounting screws.*

1. Raise the glass until it is up all the way. Remove the trim panel and plastic air shield as described above.

2. Disconnect the outside handle link and key cylinder link from the lock mechanism.

3. Disconnect the remote control link, remote latch lock link and, if the car has electric locks, the electric motor link.

4. Remove the three lock attaching screws and remove the lock through the access hole.

To install:

5. Reposition the lock inside the door through the access hole. Install the three attaching screws.

6. Reconnect the remote control link, remote latch lock link and, if the car has electric locks, the electric motor link.

7. Reconnect the outside handle link and key cylinder link from the lock mechanism.

8. Install the water shield and trim panel as described above. Adjust the latch as described above.

Daytona and Laser

NOTE: *If the car has electric door locks, you will need two short ¼–20 bolts and corresponding nuts.*

1. Roll the window down all the way. Disconnect the battery.

2. Remove the door panel as described above. Peel the water shield away at the top/rear to gain access to the hole located on the inside of the door and near the lock mechanism.

3. Raise the window all the way (if the car has electric windows, reconnect the battery to do this and then disconnect it again).

4. Disconnect the lock cylinder-to-lock link. Disconnect the outside handle-to-lock mechanism link.

5. Disconnect the inside handle-to-lock link and the inside remote lock actuator-to-lock link.

6. If the car is equipped with electric door locks, drill out the two rivets that retain the locking motor.

7. Remove the three bolts attaching the lock mechanism to the door. Remove the lock and, if the car has electric locks, the locking motor.

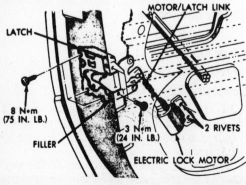

Door lock components on Daytona with power locks

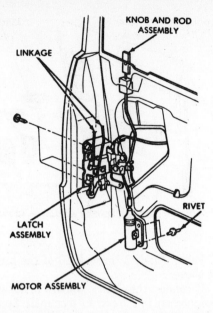

Front door latch assembly—AC body style Chrysler cars

To install:

8. To install the mechanism, first transfer the locking motor to the new mechanism (on cars with electric locks).

9. Position the latch assembly on the door and install the three attaching bolts. Torque these bolts to 75 inch lbs.

10. If the car has electric locks, attach the locking motor to the door with two short ¼–20 bolts and corresponding nuts. Torque these to 90 inch lbs.

11. Connect the lock cylinder to the latch link.

12. Connect the outside handle to the latch link. Do the same with the inside handle.

13. Connect the inside lock remote switch to the latch link.

14. Lower the window all the way (temporarily connecting the battery on cars equipped with electric windows to do so). Then, install the air shield, water shield and trim panel as described above. Reconnect the battery.

Door Glass and Regulator

REMOVAL AND INSTALLATION

NOTE: *Window regulators are riveted to the door frame. The rivets must be drilled out and replaced by bolts or bolt/nut combinations of certain specification. Read through the procedure and make sure all parts are in hand before beginning work.*

Aries, Reliant, LeBaron, Town & Country

FRONT DOOR

1. Lower the glass all the way. Remove the trim panel as described above.

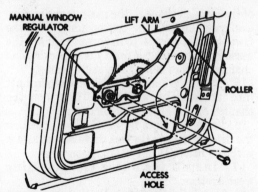

Manual front door window regulator—AA body style Chrysler cars

2. Gently pull the air and water shields off the door.

3. Remove the three nuts that attach the glass to the regulator channel. Then, lower the glass all the way.

4. Remove the outer glass-sealing weatherstrip by disengaging the spring clip tabs from the slots in the outer door panel. To do this, grasp the weatherstrip between the thumb and forefinger on either side of each spring clip. Pull out slightly and then up at each clip until the weatherstrip is free.

5. Work the glass off the mounting studs and remove it through the slot in the top of the lower door.

6. To remove the regulator, drive the center pin of each regulator mounting rivet out with a hammer and drift punch. Then, drill the rivets out with a 1/4 in. (6mm) drill.

7. Disengage the regulator arm from the lift plate and then remove the regulator through the access hole in the inside of the door.

To install:

8. To install the new regulator, load it through the access hole and engage the access arm with the lift plate. Then, bolt the regulator

to the door with 1/4–20 nuts and short screws, *making sure these screws will not interfere with regulator operation.* Torque the screws and nuts to 90–115 inch lbs.

9. Install the new glass by lowering it into the door. Position the glass on the mounting studs.

10. Install the outer weatherstrip by sliding the clips into the door panel slots and sliding them downward until they lock.

11. Raise the glass to the top of its travel and then install the three retaining nuts, but without tightening them. Seat the glass fully in the upper glass run to adjust it, and then tighten the mounting nuts gently.

12. Install the air and water shields and the trim panel as described above.

Aries, Reliant, LeBaron, Town & Country, Caravelle, 600, New Yorker Turbo

REAR DOOR

1. Remove the trim panel as described above.

2. Remove the watershield and air shield. Remove the end seals from the front and rear of the door at the beltline.

3. Remove its two mounting bolts and remove the support bracket from underneath the fixed glass at the rear of the door.

4. Remove, from inside the door, the two brackets that attach the "division" channel (dividing the moveable and stationary glass sections).

5. Remove the glass run weatherstrip from the forward and top edges of the door where the moveable glass contacts it.

6. Remove the mounting screw from the top of the division channel.

7. Remove the fixed glass.

8. Remove the outer glass-sealing weatherstrip by disengaging the spring clip tabs from

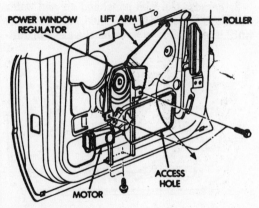

Power front door window regulator—AA body style Chrysler cars

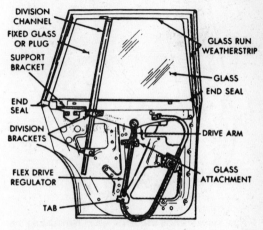

Rear door glass component locations on K and E models

the slots in the outer door panel. To do this, grasp the weatherstrip between the thumb and forefinger on either side of each spring clip. Pull out slightly and then up at each clip until the weatherstrip is free.

9. Remove the bolt (it has a shoulder on it) which attaches the glass to the drive arm of the flex drive mechanism.

10. Then, remove the division channel, moveable glass and drive arm together by raising the assembly. Rotate it 90 degrees, so the lower division channel bracket is parallel to the opening. Then, lift the assembly out through the belt opening.

11. Drive the center pins from the 6 mounting rivets (7 with electric windows) for the regulator using a hammer and drift pin. Then drill the rivets out with a ¼ in. (6mm) drill. Then, rotate the regulator as necessary for clearance and remove it through the access hole in the door.

12. If re-using the same regulator, clean and lubricate the flex drive teeth. Then, orient the regulator so it can be installed through the access hole and locate it inside the door with its locating tab engaging the appropriate hole.

NOTE: *The torque sequence specified for the following step must be followed to prevent binding of the flex drive unit for the window.*

13. Use ¼–20 bolts and nuts to remount the regulator, *tightening the nuts as specified in the illustration.* Torque to 90 inch lbs.

14. To install the new glass, start the bottom of the division channel, the glass, and the drive arm assembly into the belt opening. With the lower bracket parallel to the opening, lower the assembly into the door until the upper division channel bracket is near the belt opening.

15. Rotate the assembly 90 degrees to bring it into its normal orientation. Then, rest the channel on the bottom of the door.

16. Raise the glass by hand. Then, position the drive arm onto the flex drive and secure it with the bolt with the shoulder on it.

17. Install the outer glass-sealing weatherstrip.

18. Install the fixed-glass bracket, but do not tighten the bolts. Then, position the fixed-glass into the opening and rock it into position. Allow it to rest lightly on the support bracket.

19. Fit the rear edge of the division channel over the front edge of the fixed-glass. Then, install the mounting screw into the top of the division channel.

20. Install the glass run weatherstrip into the forward and top door channels.

21. Install the upper bracket retaining the division channel. Then, install the lower bracket retaining the division channel.

22. Push the fixed glass bracket upward and secure it in place.

23. Install the end seals at the belt opening. Install the air and water shields.

24. Install the door trim panel as described above.

Daytona and Laser

CAUTION: *If the glass has shattered, wear gloves and work cautiously. Use a protective, heavy cloth to cover all painted surfaces, plastic parts, and interior trim near the glass. Remove the glass from the window frame before removing the gloves.*

1. Roll the window all the way down. Disconnect the battery.

2. Remove the trim panel and air and water shields as described above. Then, raise the glass until it is possible to work on the glass mount-

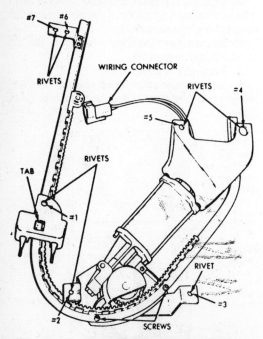

Follow the numerical sequence when remounting the rear door window regulator assembly on K and E body cars

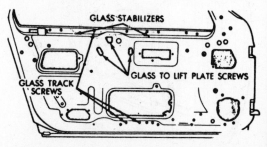

Location of components involved in removal/installation of door glass on Daytona and Laser

ing nuts through the lower access hole (reconnecting the battery temporarily to operate the window motor, if the car has electric windows).

CAUTION: *If the glass is still in position, make sure to support it during the next step.*

3. Remove the three lift plate-to-glass attaching nuts.

4. Remove the two glass stabilizers. If the glass is intact, remove it through the window frame.

CAUTION: *If the glass has been shattered, wear gloves and goggles and then use a heavy duty vacuum to carefully remove all glass particles from the door and glass run at this point.*

5. Remove the lift plate-to-regulator screw and remove the lift plate from the door.

6. Using a hammer and drift punch, drive out the center pin in each of the 8 rivets (7 on cars with electric windows) that mount the regulator to the door. Then, drill out each rivet with a ¼ in. (6mm) drill.

7. Turn the regulator as necessary and then remove it through the access hole in the door.

8. Remove the flex window drive and install it onto the new regulator. Clean and lubricate the teeth.

9. Work the assembly back into the door through the access hole, and position it so its mounting holes line up with the holes where rivets where installed. Install ¼–20 bolts and corresponding nuts to mount the regulator. Torque to 90 inch lbs.

10. Attach the lift plate to the regulator with an M6 × 25 bolt.

11. Attach the three glass-to-lift plate mounting studs to the new glass. Then, install the glass through the window opening. It must initially be cocked to the rear to work it into position and then leveled. Install the retaining nuts without tightening them.

12. Attach the two inner stabilizers without tightening them. Then, loosen the three glass track mounting screws.

13. Connect the battery if the car has electric windows and install the crank handle if it has manually operated windows. Then, guiding the glass, move the window up carefully until it has reached its uppermost position.

14. Tighten the three lift plate-to-glass attaching nuts, starting with the one in the middle, to 85 inch lbs.

15. Tighten the three glass track mounting screws to 115 inch lbs.

16. Adjust the inner glass stabilizers so they just touch the glass and then tighten them to 115 inch lbs.

17. Lower the glass and disconnect the battery or remove the window regulator handle. Install the door trim panel as described above.

Sundance and Shadow, Lancer, LeBaron, and LeBaron GTS

FRONT DOOR W/MANUAL REGULATOR

NOTE: *A special tool must be used to remove the glass, or the glass-run channel may be damaged. Use Miller Tool No. C–4867 or equivalent.*

1. Remove the door trim panel as described above. Carefully remove the watershield as described there also.

2. Lower the glass to gain the best possible access to the rear glass sliders. Then, use the special tool to disengage the sliders from the rear glass guide, holding the glass to keep it from rotating and falling.

3. Rotating the glass on the regulator roller, slide it rearward and lower the rear until it reaches a 45 degree angle. Then, remove it.

4. Temporarily install the regulator handle and set the position of the unit for easy access to the regulator mounting rivets (just below the position where the window would normally be all the way up).

5. Drill out the three rivets on the regulator with a ¼ in. (6mm) drill. Then, slide the regulator off the glass lift channel. Cock the regulator to an appropriate angle and remove it through the access hole.

To install:

6. Angle and position the regulator appropriately and work it through the access hole in the door.

7. Line up the regulator mounting and rivet holes and then install short ¼–20 bolts and nuts (it may be easier to install the bolts if you reset the position of the regulator by temporarily installing the handle). Torque the bolts to 90–115 inch lbs. and make sure they are short enough that they will not interfere with the moving parts as the window is raised and lowered.

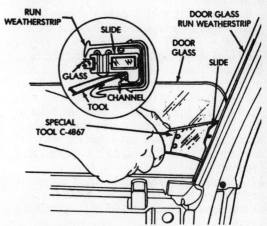

Front or rear door glass removal—AP body style Chrysler cars

8. Transfer the lift channel and sliders to the new glass. Then, slide the glass back into the door at the angle at which it was removed.

9. Rotate the glass to its normal position and slide it forward on the regulator roller in reverse of the removal procedure.

10. Position the glass for best possible access to the rear sliders, holding it to keep it from rotating and falling. Then, use the special tool to engage the sliders with the rear glass guide.

11. Install the watershield and trim panel as described above.

FRONT DOOR W/ELECTRIC REGULATOR

NOTE: *A special tool must be used to remove the glass, or the glass-run channel may be damaged. Use Miller Tool No. C–4867 or equivalent.*

1. Remove the door trim panel as described above. Carefully remove the watershield as described there also.

2. Follow Steps 2–3 of the procedure above to remove the glass from the door.

3. Adjust the position of the regulator until there is access to all the regulator mounting rivets (this is just below the position where the glass is all the way up).

4. Disconnect the negative battery cable. Then, disconnect the window motor electrical connector.

5. Drill out the 6 regulator mounting rivets with a ¼ in. (6mm) drill. Then, slide the regulator off the glass channel.

6. Remove the motor from the regulator. Then, remove the regulator from the door, turning it as necessary so it will fit easily through the access hole.

7. If the regulator is being re-used, clean and lubricate the teeth on the flex drive rack. Then, load the regulator assembly through the door access panel.

8. Install the motor onto the regulator. Then, engage the regulator roller with the lift channel.

9. Line up the regulator mounting and rivet holes and then install short ¼-20 bolts and nuts (it may be easier to install the bolts if you reset the position of the regulator by temporarily installing the handle). Torque the bolts to 90–115 inch lbs. and make sure they are short enough that they will not interfere with the moving parts as the window is raised and lowered.

10. Connect the regulator wiring connector and the negative battery cable. Install the window as described in Steps 8–10 of the procedure above.

11. Install the watershield and trim panel as described above.

REAR DOOR W/MANUAL REGULATOR

Follow the procedure above for the front door, noting that there are only 3 or 4 mounting rivets for the regulator assembly.

REAR DOOR W/ELECTRICAL REGULATOR

Follow the procedure above for the front door through Step 4. Remove the regulator-to-regulator arm bolt; then proceed with the remaining steps of the procedure. Note that the rear door electric window regulator is retained by only 5 mounting rivets.

Electric Window Motor
REMOVAL AND INSTALLATION
Cars w/Conventional (Gear Type) Regulators

CAUTION: *The electric window regulator incorporates a very powerful spring which forces the window toward the top of the window frame at all times. Failure to ensure that the window is in this position before beginning this operation could result in a dangerous situation. The same is true of failing to support the window upward, in case a malfunction of this spring should occur. RAISE WINDOW TO FULL UP POSITION AND KEEP IT THERE AT ALL TIMES WHILE REPLACING MOTOR!*

1. Remove the trim panel as described in the appropriate procedure above. Raise the window until it is in the full up position. Then, *securely* prop the window in this position.

2. Disconnect the negative battery cable. Then, disconnect the electric window motor electrical connector located about 11 in. (28cm) away from the motor in the wiring harness.

3. Remove the 3 mounting screws which attach the motor gearbox to the window regulator. On most models, there are three holes in the inner panel to provide access to these screws. On AJ body cars, go in through the opening in the inner panel and reach around to the rear of the regulator to gain access to these screws.

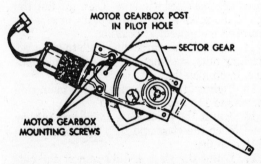

Electric motor mounting—conventional window regulator

CHILTON'S
AUTO BODY
REPAIR TIPS

Tools and Materials • Step-by-Step Illustrated Procedures
How To Repair Dents, Scratches and Rust Holes
Spray Painting and Refinishing Tips

With a little practice, basic body repair procedures can be mastered by any do-it-yourself mechanic. The step-by-step repairs shown here can be applied to almost any type of auto body repair.

TOOLS & MATERIALS

You may already have basic tools, such as hammers and electric drills. Other tools unique to body repair — body hammers, grinding attachments, sanding blocks, dent puller, half-round plastic file and plastic spreaders — are relatively inexpensive and can be obtained wherever auto parts or auto body repair parts are sold. Portable air compressors and paint spray guns can be purchased or rented.

Auto Body Repair Kits

The best and most often used products are available to the do-it-yourselfer in kit form, from major manufacturers of auto body repair products. The same manufacturers also merchandise the individual products for use by pros.

Kits are available to make a wide variety of repairs, including holes, dents and scratches and fiberglass, and offer the advantage of buying the materials you'll need for the job. There is little waste or chance of materials going bad from not being used. Many kits may also contain basic body-working tools such as body files, sanding blocks and spreaders. Check the contents of the kit before buying your tools.

BODY REPAIR TIPS

Safety

Many of the products associated with auto body repair and refinishing contain toxic chemicals. Read all labels before opening containers and store them in a safe place and manner.

• Wear eye protection (safety goggles) when using power tools or when performing any operation that involves the removal of any type of material.

• Wear lung protection (disposable mask or respirator) when grinding, sanding or painting.

Sanding

1 Sand off paint before using a dent puller. When using a non-adhesive sanding disc, cover the back of the disc with an overlapping layer or two of masking tape and trim the edges. The disc will last considerably longer.

2 Use the circular motion of the sanding disc to grind *into* the edge of the repair. Grinding or sanding away from the jagged edge will only tear the sandpaper.

3 Use the palm of your hand flat on the panel to detect high and low spots. Do not use your fingertips. Slide your hand slowly back and forth.

WORKING WITH BODY FILLER

Mixing The Filler

Cleanliness and proper mixing and application are extremely important. Use a clean piece of plastic or glass or a disposable artist's palette to mix body filler.

1 Allow plenty of time and follow directions. No useful purpose will be served by adding more hardener to make it cure (set-up) faster. Less hardener means more curing time, but the mixture dries harder; more hardener means less curing time but a softer mixture.

2 Both the hardener and the filler should be thoroughly kneaded or stirred before mixing. Hardener should be a solid paste and dispense like thin toothpaste. Body filler should be smooth, and free of lumps or thick spots.

Getting the proper amount of hardener in the filler is the trickiest part of preparing the filler. Use the same amount of hardener in cold or warm weather. For contour filler (thick coats), a bead of hardener twice the diameter of the filler is about right. There's about a 15% margin on either side, but, if in doubt use less hardener.

3 Mix the body filler and hardener by wiping across the mixing surface, picking the mixture up and wiping it again. Colder weather requires longer mixing times. Do not mix in a circular motion; this will trap air bubbles which will become holes in the cured filler.

Applying The Filler

1 For best results, filler should not be applied over ¼" thick.

Apply the filler in several coats. Build it up to above the level of the repair surface so that it can be sanded or grated down.

The first coat of filler must be pressed on with a firm wiping motion.

Apply the filler in one direction only. Working the filler back and forth will either pull it off the metal or trap air bubbles.

REPAIRING DENTS

Before you start, take a few minutes to study the damaged area. Try to visualize the shape of the panel before it was damaged. If the damage is on the left fender, look at the right fender and use it as a guide. If there is access to the panel from behind, you can reshape it with a body hammer. If not, you'll have to use a dent puller. Go slowly and work the metal a little at a time. Get the panel as straight as possible before applying filler.

1 This dent is typical of one that can be pulled out or hammered out from behind. Remove the headlight cover, headlight assembly and turn signal housing.

2 Drill a series of holes ½ the size of the end of the dent puller along the stress line. Make some trial pulls and assess the results. If necessary, drill more holes and try again. Do not hurry.

3 If possible, use a body hammer and block to shape the metal back to its original contours. Get the metal back as close to its original shape as possible. Don't depend on body filler to fill dents.

4 Using an 80-grit grinding disc on an electric drill, grind the paint from the surrounding area down to bare metal. Use a new grinding pad to prevent heat buildup that will warp metal.

5 The area should look like this when you're finished grinding. Knock the drill holes in and tape over small openings to keep plastic filler out.

6 Mix the body filler (see Body Repair Tips). Spread the body filler evenly over the entire area (see Body Repair Tips). Be sure to cover the area completely.

7 Let the body filler dry until the surface can just be scratched with your fingernail. Knock the high spots from the body filler with a body file ("Cheesegrater"). Check frequently with the palm of your hand for high and low spots.

8 Check to be sure that trim pieces that will be installed later will fit exactly. Sand the area with 40-grit paper.

9 If you wind up with low spots, you may have to apply another layer of filler.

10 Knock the high spots off with 40-grit paper. When you are satisfied with the contours of the repair, apply a thin coat of filler to cover pin holes and scratches.

11 Block sand the area with 40-grit paper to a smooth finish. Pay particular attention to body lines and ridges that must be well-defined.

12 Sand the area with 400 paper and then finish with a scuff pad. The finished repair is ready for priming and painting (see Painting Tips).

Materials and photos courtesy of Ritt Jones Auto Body, Prospect Park, PA.

REPAIRING RUST HOLES

There are many ways to repair rust holes. The fiberglass cloth kit shown here is one of the most cost efficient for the owner because it provides a strong repair that resists cracking and moisture and is relatively easy to use. It can be used on large and small holes (with or without backing) and can be applied over contoured areas. Remember, however, that short of replacing an entire panel, no repair is a guarantee that the rust will not return.

1 Remove any trim that will be in the way. Clean away all loose debris. Cut away all the rusted metal. But be sure to leave enough metal to retain the contour or body shape.

2 Grind away all traces of rust with a 24-grit grinding disc. Be sure to grind back 3-4 inches from the edge of the hole down to bare metal and be sure all traces of paint, primer and rust are removed.

3 Block sand the area with 80 or 100 grit sandpaper to get a clear, shiny surface and feathered paint edge. Tap the edges of the hole inward with a ball peen hammer.

4 If you are going to use release film, cut a piece about 2-3″ larger than the area you have sanded. Place the film over the repair and mark the sanded area on the film. Avoid any unnecessary wrinkling of the film.

5 Cut 2 pieces of fiberglass matte to match the shape of the repair. One piece should be about 1″ smaller than the sanded area and the second piece should be 1″ smaller than the first. Mix enough filler and hardener to saturate the fiberglass material (see Body Repair Tips).

6 Lay the release sheet on a flat surface and spread an even layer of filler, large enough to cover the repair. Lay the smaller piece of fiberglass cloth in the center of the sheet and spread another layer of filler over the fiberglass cloth. Repeat the operation for the larger piece of cloth.

7 Place the repair material over the repair area, with the release film facing outward. Use a spreader and work from the center outward to smooth the material, following the body contours. Be sure to remove all air bubbles.

8 Wait until the repair has dried tack-free and peel off the release sheet. The ideal working temperature is 60°-90° F. Cooler or warmer temperatures or high humidity may require additional curing time. Wait longer, if in doubt.

9 Sand and feather-edge the entire area. The initial sanding can be done with a sanding disc on an electric drill if care is used. Finish the sanding with a block sander. Low spots can be filled with body filler; this may require several applications.

10 When the filler can just be scratched with a fingernail, knock the high spots down with a body file and smooth the entire area with 80-grit. Feather the filled areas into the surrounding areas.

11 When the area is sanded smooth, mix some topcoat and hardener and apply it directly with a spreader. This will give a smooth finish and prevent the glass matte from showing through the paint.

12 Block sand the topcoat smooth with finishing sandpaper (200 grit), and 400 grit. The repair is ready for masking, priming and painting (see Painting Tips).

Materials and photos courtesy Marson Corporation, Chelsea, Massachusetts

PAINTING TIPS

Preparation

1 SANDING — Use a 400 or 600 grit wet or dry sandpaper. Wet-sand the area with a $1/4$ sheet of sandpaper soaked in clean water. Keep the paper wet while sanding. Sand the area until the repaired area tapers into the original finish.

2 CLEANING — Wash the area to be painted thoroughly with water and a clean rag. Rinse it thoroughly and wipe the surface dry until you're sure it's completely free of dirt, dust, fingerprints, wax, detergent or other foreign matter.

3 MASKING — Protect any areas you don't want to overspray by covering them with masking tape and newspaper. Be careful not get fingerprints on the area to be painted.

4 PRIMING — All exposed metal should be primed before painting. Primer protects the metal and provides an excellent surface for paint adhesion. When the primer is dry, wet-sand the area again with 600 grit wet-sandpaper. Clean the area again after sanding.

Painting Techniques

P aint applied from either a spray gun or a spray can (for small areas) will provide good results. Experiment on an old piece of metal to get the right combination before you begin painting.

SPRAYING VISCOSITY (SPRAY GUN ONLY) — Paint should be thinned to spraying viscosity according to the directions on the can. Use only the recommended thinner or reducer and the same amount of reduction regardless of temperature.

AIR PRESSURE (SPRAY GUN ONLY) — This is extremely important. Be sure you are using the proper recommended pressure.

TEMPERATURE — The surface to be painted should be approximately the same temperature as the surrounding air. Applying warm paint to a cold surface, or vice versa, will completely upset the paint characteristics.

THICKNESS — Spray with smooth strokes. In general, the thicker the coat of paint, the longer the drying time. Apply several thin coats about 30 seconds apart. The paint should remain wet long enough to flow out and no longer; heavier coats will only produce sags or wrinkles. Spray a light (fog) coat, followed by heavier color coats.

DISTANCE — The ideal spraying distance is 8″-12″ from the gun or can to the surface. Shorter distances will produce ripples, while greater distances will result in orange peel, dry film and poor color match and loss of material due to overspray.

OVERLAPPING — The gun or can should be kept at right angles to the surface at all times. Work to a wet edge at an even speed, using a 50% overlap and direct the center of the spray at the lower or nearest edge of the previous stroke.

RUBBING OUT (BLENDING) FRESH PAINT — Let the paint dry thoroughly. Runs or imperfections can be sanded out, primed and repainted.

Don't be in too big a hurry to remove the masking. This only produces paint ridges. When the finish has dried for at least a week, apply a small amount of fine grade rubbing compound with a clean, wet cloth. Use lots of water and blend the new paint with the surrounding area.

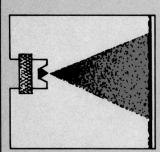

WRONG

Thin coat. Stroke too fast, not enough overlap, gun too far away.

CORRECT

Medium coat. Proper distance, good stroke, proper overlap.

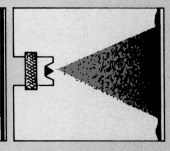

WRONG

Heavy coat. Stroke too slow, too much overlap, gun too close.

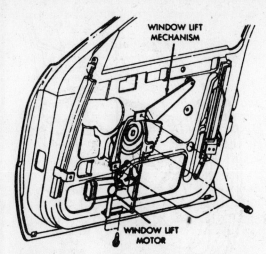

Front door power window assembly—AA body style Chrysler cars

4. Remove the motor from the regulator by grabbing the motor housing and pulling it toward either the inner or outer panel.

CAUTION: *Keep fingers well away from the gears while disengaging the motor. Gears may turn a small amount, and could pinch!*
Rock or twist the motor as necessary to get it to disengage from the regulator.

5. To install the motor, position it onto the regulator, gaining access as during removal. Work the motor into a position that will ensure the motor gear engages the regulator sector teeth *and* the center post on the motor gearbox enters the pilot hole in the mounting plate. As the motor approaches its final position, rock it to ensure easy engagement of the gear teeth.

6. Align the motor screw holes with those in the mounting plate. Install the 3 motor gearbox screws and the single tie-down bracket screw. Torque them to 50–60 inch lbs.

7. Remove the blocking device. Connect the multi-prong connector and then the battery.

Cars w/Flex-Drive Type Regulators

NOTE: *To perform this procedure, a center punch, a ¼ in. (6mm) drill, and 7 #8–32 × ½ in. screws are required.*

1. Remove the trim panel as described in the appropriate procedure above. Then, the screw that attaches the flexible rack to the drive arm must be removed. Adjust the position of the window up and down until the position is right for access to this screw and then remove it. Now, *securely* prop the window in this position. If the motor will not operate on its own, try assisting it cautiously. If this fails, see the note below.

2. Disconnect the battery. Disconnect the motor electrical connector.

3. Remove the regulator/ motor attaching rivets by knocking out the rivet center mandrels with a hammer and the center punch. Then, drill the rivets out with the ¼ in. (6mm) drill.

4. Start the motor end of the flex drive regulator out through the largest access hole in the door panel, maneuvering and rotating the unit out. Remove the screws attaching the motor to the flexible track.

NOTE: *If the motor will not move, it will be necessary follow steps 2 and 3 to drill out the attaching rivets. Then, move the motor/flexible drive assembly as necessary to gain access to the screws mounting the motor to the flex drive. Manually lift the window upward until it is possible to access the screw that attaches the flexible rack to the drive arm and then remove it.*

5. Remove the 2 screws attaching the motor to the flex drive.

6. To install the motor, feed the top of the flexible drive track into the access hole and then

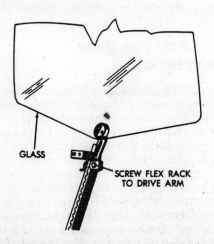

Rear door power window assembly—AA body style Chrysler cars

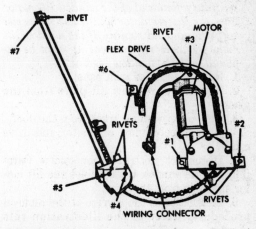

Front door flex drive window regulator

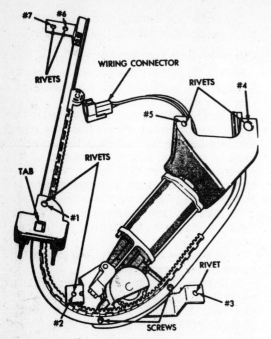

Rear door flex drive window regulator

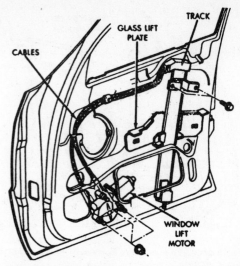

Front door power window assembly—AC and AY body style Chrysler cars

rotate it toward the door pillar until the motor is horizontal. Then, rotate the assembly (about ¼ turn) in the opposite direction to align the bracket tab with the slot in the inner door panel.

7. Install the mounting screws and torque them to 40 inch lbs. in the sequence shown. Refer to the illustrations in this chapter.

8. Connect the motor electrical connector. Reconnect the battery. Position the window drive so the flex rack fitting lines up with the window drive arm. Install the screw and torque to 40 inch lbs. Remove the window prop.

Cars w/Cable And Drum Type Regulators

NOTE: *The window lift motor is not serviced separately. Removal of the window lift motor from the the regulator will cause the assist spring to unwind rapidly. If the window lift motor requires replacement, it must be replaced with the window regulator.*

1. Remove the door trim panel.

2. Disconnect window lift plate from the glass.

3. Disconnect window track from the door.

4. Disconnect window lift motor and drive cables.

5. Disconnect electrical connections. Carefully remove window track, cables and lift motor assembly from the door.

6. Installation is the reverse of the removal procedure. Refer to the illustration this chapter.

Quarter Glass Module
REMOVAL AND INSTALLATION
Daytona Series

1. Remove the quarter trim panel as necesary to gain access to quarter glass module.

2. Remove nuts holding quarter glass module to quarter glass opening.

3. Cut urethane sealer around perimeter of quarter glass opening fence.

4. Push quarter glass module from quarter glass opening. separate module from vehicle.

To install:

5. Clean all surfaces of opening fence and glass module.

6. Prepare fence and glass module using method described in the "Windshield removal and installation" service procedures in this chapter. Reverse the necessary removal steps for installation.

Inside Rear View Mirror
REPLACEMENT

The mirror is mechanically attached to the mirror button, and if it should become cracked or develop a a mechanical problem which prevents easy adjustment, it can be replaced very simply by disconnecting it from the button. The button, in turn, serves to mount the mirror to the windshield. If it should be damaged or the adhesive bond should become partly broken, it can be removed and replaced after the mirror is detached. Note that removal of the button and/or remaining adhesive requires the use of a controllable electric heat gun. Also needed, if the button must be replaced, are a rag soaked in al-

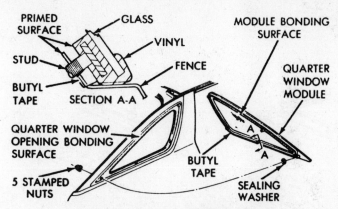

Quarter glass module—Dodge Daytona

cohol, ordinary kitchen cleanser, and fine-grit sandpaper. The new button is installed using a special adhesive kit 4054099 or an equivalent available in the aftermarket.

1. Loosen the setscrew with a standard screwdriver until all tension is removed. Slide the base of the mirror upward and off the mounting button.

2. If the mirror mounting button must be removed, first mark the location of the button on the outside of the windshield with a wax pencil. Then, apply low heat with the electric heat gun to soften the vinyl. When it is soft, peel the button off the glass.

3. Clean the surface of the windshield where the button was mounted with a rag soaked in alcohol and the cleanser. Then, wipe the surface with an alcohol soaked rag. Do not touch this area of the windshield glass!

4. Crush the vial in the plastic housing of the accelerator in the new button kit to saturate the applicator.

5. Remove the paper sleeve and then apply a

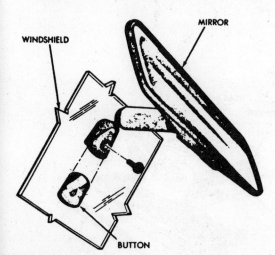

Mounting of the rearview mirror to the button and windshield

generous amount of the accelerator to the onto the mounting surface of the mirror button.

6. Allow the accelerator to dry for 5 minutes; during this time, be careful not to touch the mounting surface of the button.

7. Apply a thin film of the accelerator to the inner surface of the windshield where the button will be mounted. Allow this to dry for 1 minute.

8. Apply one drop of the adhesive to the center of the mounting surface of the button. Then, use the bottom of the adhesive tube, distribute the adhesive evenly over the entire button bonding surface.

NOTE: *Precise alignment of the button is essential in the following step from the beginning, as the adhesive sets up very fast!*

9. Position the bottom edge of the button against the lower edge of the mark made earlier with the button lined up side-to-side. Then, rock the button upward until it touches the windshield over its entire surface. Press it firmly to the glass and hold it there firmly for 1 full minute.

10. Remove the pressure, but allow 5 minutes more time for the button mounting adhesive to dry.

11. With an alcohol-dampened cloth, remove any adhesive which may have spread beyond the mounting surface of the button.

NOTE: *Be careful not to over-tighten the mirror mounting screw in the following procedure, as the mirror mounting button could be distorted, destroying its bond with the windshield.*

12. Slide the mirror downward and over the mount. Tighten the screw gently!

Seats

REMOVAL AND INSTALLATION

NOTE: *Use these service procedures as a guide for all models/years. Refer to the "Seat Assembly" illustrations as necessary.*

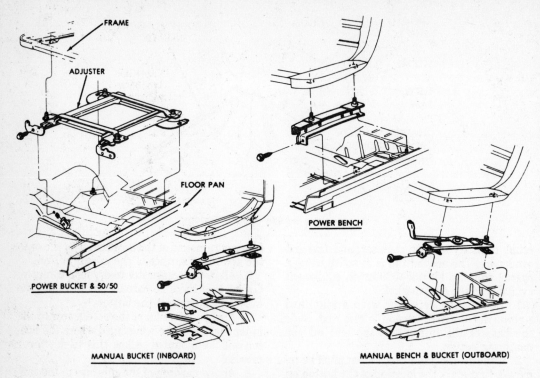

FRAME

ADJUSTER

FLOOR PAN

POWER BENCH

POWER BUCKET & 50/50

MANUAL BUCKET (INBOARD)

MANUAL BENCH & BUCKET (OUTBOARD)

E-body seat mountings for 1986 and later models

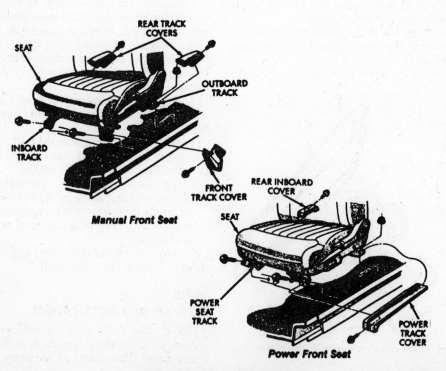

REAR TRACK COVERS

SEAT

OUTBOARD TRACK

INBOARD TRACK

FRONT TRACK COVER

REAR INBOARD COVER

Manual Front Seat

SEAT

POWER SEAT TRACK

POWER TRACK COVER

Power Front Seat

Seat mounting—Chrysler cars

Caravelle, 600, New Yorker Turbo

FRONT

1. Move the seat forward all the way. Then, remove the mounting nuts from the vertical studs welded into the floor (one on each side).

2. Move the seat all the way to the rear. On all but power bench seats, there are 2 bolts, oriented horizontally, on either side (on power bench there is only 1). Remove the bolts.

3. If the car has power seats, disconnect the battery and then disconnect the motor electrical connector. Remove the seat from the car by lifting upward on the rear until the stud clears the mounting hole in the frame and then lifting and angling the seat as necessary to maneuver it out. If the seat must be detached from the mounting frame, remove the four nuts from the studs and separate the two.

4. To install the seat, first, attach it to the frame and install the attaching nuts, torquing them to 250 inch lbs. Then, install the assembled seat into the car, positioning the forward mount over the beam on the floor, shifting the seat side-to-side to line up the bolt holes in the frame and beam. Then, tilt the seat rearward to cause the rear of the frame to sit down over the stud. Install the bolts and nuts and torque to 250 inch lbs.

Arles, Reliant, LeBaron, Town & Country

FRONT

1. Move the seat forward all the way. Then, remove the mounting bolts from the crossmember. Note that bucket seats use a nut and washer, accessible from underneath, to retain the bolt at the rear.

2. Move the seat all the way to the rear. Remove the bolts (one on either side) that retain the seat adjuster frame at the front. These sit in a horizontal position.

3. If the car has power seats, disconnect the battery and then disconnect the motor electrical connector. Remove the seat from the car by lifting it upward and out. If the seat must be detached from the mounting frame, remove the four nuts from the studs and separate the two.

4. To install the seat, first, attach it to the frame and install the attaching nuts, torquing them to 250 inch lbs. Then, install the assembled seat into the car, positioning the forward mount over the beam on the floor, shifting the seat side-to-side to line up the bolt holes in the frame and beam. Install the bolts and nuts and torque to 250 inch lbs.

1986 and Later Caravelle, 600, New Yorker Turbo Arles, Reliant, LeBaron, Town & Country

REAR BENCH SEAT

1. To remove the rear cushion, remove the 2 screws from the underside of the front of the

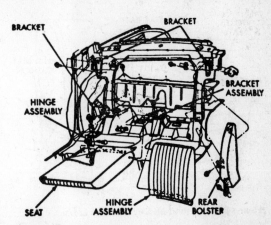

Rear seat cushion and back assembly—Chrysler cars

rear seat cushion. Remove the cushion from the vehicle.

2. To remove the seat back, remove the 2 screws from the bottom/rear of the seat back. Then, unsnap the 2 seatbelt retainers. Lift the seat back upward to disengage the seatback wires from the support pockets.

3. Install the seatback and rear cushion by reversing the removal procedure.

Daytona, Laser, Lancer, LeBaron GTS, LeBaron, Sundance AND Shadow

FRONT SEAT

1. Move the seat forward all the way. Remove the mounting nuts attaching the seat to the floor at the rear.

2. Move the seat all the way to the rear and remove the two seat frame-to-crossmember bolts, located horizontally, from the front on either side. Remove the seat.

3. Install in reverse order, torquing the nuts/bolts to 250 inch lbs.

Daytona and Laser

REAR SEAT

The seat backs are hinged. The hinge mounting bolts are accessible directly under the seat back. Remove the bolt on either side to remove the seat back. To install, reverse the procedure, torquing the bolt to 350 inch lbs.

The seat cushions are bolted to the floor pan. Remove the mounting bolt at the rear on either side and remove the seat cushion. Reverse the procedure to install, torquing the bolts to 40 ft. lbs.

1986 and Later Lancer, LeBaron GTS, Sundance, Shadow, LeBaron

REAR SEAT CUSHION

The rear seat cushion is bolted to the floorpan. Simply remove the bolts and remove the cushion. Install in reverse order.

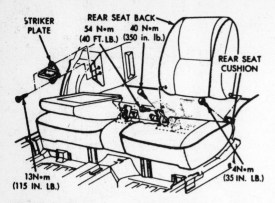

Rear seat mounting on Daytona and Laser

REAR BENCH SEAT BACK

1. Peel back the corner of the carpet from the back of the rear seat by pulling it free from the Velcro® retainers.

2. Remove the seat back-to-hinge arm screws from both sides. Remove the seat back.

3. Reverse this procedure to install the seat back.

REAR 60/40 SEAT BACK

To remove the seat back, simply remove the seat back-to-hinge arm screws from the seat back. Then, remove the seat back. Reverse the procedure to install the seat back.

1981–85 Cars

REAR SEAT CUSHION AND BACK

1. To remove the rear seat cushion, remove the 2 screws from the underside of the rear seat cushion and remove it from the vehicle. Install it in reverse order.

2. To remove the seat back, first remove the 2 screws from the bottom of the seat back. Then, unsnap the 2 seat belt retainers.

3. Remove the seat back by lifting it upward so as to disengage the seatback retaining wires from the support pockets.

4. To install the seat back, lower it into position so as to engage the retaining wires.

Seat Belt Systems

REMOVAL AND INSTALLATION

Front

1. Remove the necessary trim panel(s).

2. Remove the bolt holding seat belt retractor to B-pillar.

3. Separate retractor from the vehicle.

4. Installation is the reverse of the removal procedure. Refer to the illustrations. Torque for seat belt retaining bolts is 350 inch lbs.

Rear

1. Remove the necessary trim panel(s).

2. Remove the bolt holding lap belt to floor at wheelhouse kickup.

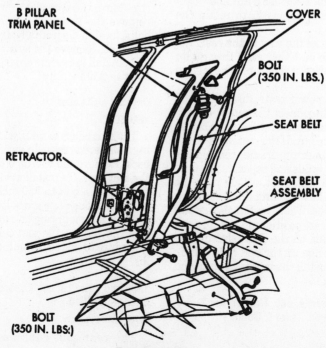

Front seat belts

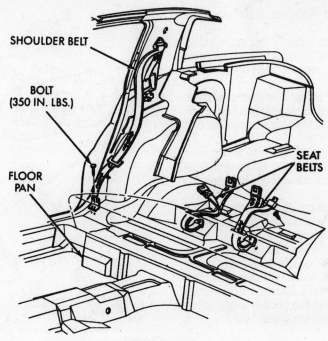

SHOULDER BELT

BOLT
(350 IN. LBS.)

FLOOR
PAN

SEAT
BELTS

Rear seat belts

3. Remove the bolt holding seat belt retractor to quarter panel.

4. Installation is the reverse of the removal procedure. Refer to the illustrations. Torque for seat belt retaining bolts is 350 inch lbs.

Power Seat Motor

REMOVAL AND INSTALLATION

1. Move the seat adjuster as required for easy access to the mounting bolts, if possible.

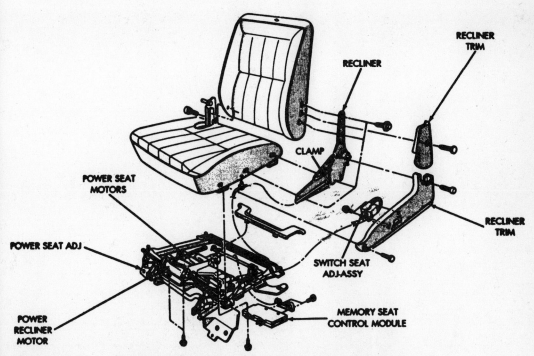

RECLINER
TRIM

RECLINER

CLAMP

RECLINER
TRIM

POWER SEAT
MOTORS

POWER SEAT ADJ

SWITCH SEAT
ADJ-ASSY

POWER
RECLINER
MOTOR

MEMORY SEAT
CONTROL MODULE

Exploded view of power memory seat assembly—Chrysler cars

Remove the adjuster mounting bolts/nuts from the floor pan.

2. Disconnect the battery negative cable. Disconnect the wiring harness motor connector at the carpet. Then, remove the seat from the car.

3. Lay the seat on its back on a clean surface. Then, remove the motor mounting screws from the motor bracket and the single mounting bolt from the adjuster.

4. Note the routing of cable to the motor. Then, carefully disconnect the housing and cables from the motor assembly. Remove the motor.

5. To install the motor, first position it in its mounted position. Then, connect the cables and the housing to the motor.

6. Install the transmission-to-motor mounting screws. Install the bolt fastening the motor to the adjuster. Then, install the seat in reverse of the removal procedure. Reconnect the wiring harness connector and the battery negative cable. Check seat for proper operation.

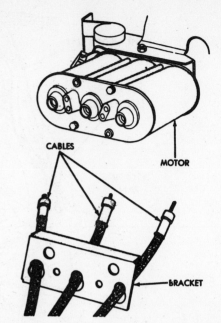

Cable and housing assembly power bench seat—Chrysler cars

Mechanic's Data

11

General Conversion Table

Multiply By	To Convert	To	
LENGTH			
2.54	Inches	Centimeters	.3937
25.4	Inches	Millimeters	.03937
30.48	Feet	Centimeters	.0328
.304	Feet	Meters	3.28
.914	Yards	Meters	1.094
1.609	Miles	Kilometers	.621
VOLUME			
.473	Pints	Liters	2.11
.946	Quarts	Liters	1.06
3.785	Gallons	Liters	.264
.016	Cubic inches	Liters	61.02
16.39	Cubic inches	Cubic cms.	.061
28.3	Cubic feet	Liters	.0353
MASS (Weight)			
28.35	Ounces	Grams	.035
4536	Pounds	Kilograms	2.20
—	To obtain	From	Multiply by

Multiply By	To Convert	To	
AREA			
.645	Square inches	Square cms.	.155
.836	Square yds.	Square meters	1.196
FORCE			
4.448	Pounds	Newtons	.225
.138	Ft./lbs.	Kilogram/meters	7.23
1.36	Ft./lbs.	Newton-meters	.737
.112	In./lbs.	Newton-meters	8.844
PRESSURE			
.068	Psi	Atmospheres	14.7
6.89	Psi	Kilopascals	.145
OTHER			
1.104	Horsepower (DIN)	Horsepower (SAE)	.9861
.746	Horsepower (SAE)	Kilowatts (KW)	1.34
1.60	Mph	Km/h	.625
.425	Mpg	Km/1	2.35
—	To obtain	From	Multiply by

Tap Drill Sizes

National Coarse or U.S.S.

Screw & Tap Size	Threads Per Inch	Use Drill Number
No. 5	40	.39
No. 6	32	.36
No. 8	32	.29
No. 10	24	.25
No. 12	24	.17
1/4	20	8
5/16	18	F
3/8	16	5/16
7/16	14	U
1/2	13	27/64
9/16	12	31/64
5/8	11	17/32
3/4	10	21/32
7/8	9	49/64

National Coarse or U.S.S.

Screw & Tap Size	Threads Per Inch	Use Drill Number
1	8	7/8
1 1/8	7	63/64
1 1/4	7	17/64
1 1/2	6	1 11/32

National Fine or S.A.E.

Screw & Tap Size	Threads Per Inch	Use Drill Number
No. 5	44	.37
No. 6	40	.33
No. 8	36	.29
No. 10	32	.21

National Fine or S.A.E.

Screw & Tap Size	Threads Per Inch	Use Drill Number
No. 12	28	15
1/4	28	3
6/16	24	1
3/8	24	Q
7/16	20	W
1/2	20	29/64
9/16	18	33/64
5/8	18	37/64
3/4	16	11/16
7/8	14	13/16
1 1/8	12	13/64
1 1/4	12	1 11/64
1 1/2	12	1 27/64

Drill Sizes In Decimal Equivalents

Inch	Decimal	Wire	mm
1/64	.0156		.39
	.0157		.4
	.0160	78	
	.0165		.42
	.0173		.44
	.0177		.45
	.0180	77	
	.0181		.46
	.0189		.48
	.0197		.5
	.0200	76	
	.0210	75	
	.0217		.55
	.0225	74	
	.0236		.6
	.0240	73	
	.0250	72	
	.0256		.65
	.0260	71	
	.0276		.7
	.0280	70	
	.0292	69	
	.0295		.75
	.0310	68	
1/32	.0312		.79
	.0315		.8
	.0320	67	
	.0330	66	
	.0335		.85
	.0350	65	
	.0354		.9
	.0360	64	
	.0370	63	
	.0374		.95
	.0380	62	
	.0390	61	
	.0394		1.0
	.0400	60	
	.0410	59	
	.0413		1.05
	.0420	58	
	.0430	57	
	.0433		1.1
	.0453		1.15
	.0465	56	
3/64	.0469		1.19
	.0472		1.2
	.0492		1.25
	.0512		1.3
	.0520	55	
	.0531		1.35
	.0550	54	
	.0551		1.4
	.0571		1.45
	.0591		1.5
	.0595	53	
	.0610		1.55
1/16	.0625		1.59
	.0630		1.6
	.0635	52	
	.0650		1.65
	.0669		1.7
	.0670	51	
	.0689		1.75
	.0700	50	
	.0709		1.8
	.0728		1.85

Inch	Decimal	Wire	mm
	.0730	49	
	.0748		1.9
	.0760	48	
	.0768		1.95
5/64	.0781		1.98
	.0785	47	
	.0787		2.0
	.0807		2.05
	.0810	46	
	.0820	45	
	.0827		2.1
	.0846		2.15
	.0860	44	
	.0866		2.2
	.0886		2.25
	.0890	43	
	.0906		2.3
	.0925		2.35
	.0935	42	
3/32	.0938		2.38
	.0945		2.4
	.0960	41	
	.0965		2.45
	.0980	40	
	.0981		2.5
	.0995	39	
	.1015	38	
	.1024		2.6
	.1040	37	
	.1063		2.7
	.1065	36	
	.1083		2.75
7/64	.1094		2.77
	.1100	35	
	.1102		2.8
	.1110	34	
	.1130	33	
	.1142		2.9
	.1160	32	
	.1181		3.0
	.1200	31	
	.1220		3.1
1/8	.1250		3.17
	.1260		3.2
	.1280		3.25
	.1285	30	
	.1299		3.3
	.1339		3.4
	.1360	29	
	.1378		3.5
	.1405	28	
9/64	.1406		3.57
	.1417		3.6
	.1440	27	
	.1457		3.7
	.1470	26	
	.1476		3.75
	.1495	25	
	.1496		3.8
	.1520	24	
	.1535		3.9
	.1540	23	
5/32	.1562		3.96
	.1570	22	
	.1575		4.0
	.1590	21	
	.1610	20	

Inch	Decimal	Wire & Letter	mm
	.1614		4.1
	.1654		4.2
	.1660	19	
	.1673		4.25
	.1693		4.3
	.1695	18	
11/64	.1719		4.36
	.1730	17	
	.1732		4.4
	.1770	16	
	.1772		4.5
	.1800	15	
	.1811		4.6
	.1820	14	
	.1850	13	
	.1850		4.7
	.1870		4.75
3/16	.1875		4.76
	.1890		4.8
	.1890	12	
	.1910	11	
	.1929		4.9
	.1935	10	
	.1960	9	
	.1969		5.0
	.1990	8	
	.2008		5.1
	.2010	7	
13/64	.2031		5.16
	.2040	6	
	.2047		5.2
	.2055	5	
	.2067		5.25
	.2087		5.3
	.2090	4	
	.2126		5.4
	.2130	3	
	.2165		5.5
7/32	.2188		5.55
	.2205		5.6
	.2210	2	
	.2244		5.7
	.2264		5.75
	.2280	1	
	.2283		5.8
	.2323		5.9
	.2340	A	
15/64	.2344		5.95
	.2362		6.0
	.2380	B	
	.2402		6.1
	.2420	C	
	.2441		6.2
	.2460	D	
	.2461		6.25
	.2480		6.3
1/4	.2500	E	6.35
	.2520		6.4
	.2559		6.5
	.2570	F	
	.2598		6.6
	.2610	G	
	.2638		6.7
17/64	.2656		6.74
	.2657		6.75
	.2660	H	
	.2677		6.8

Inch	Decimal	Letter	mm
	.2717		6.9
	.2720	I	
	.2756		7.0
	.2770	J	
	.2795		7.1
	.2810	K	
9/32	.2812		7.14
	.2835		7.2
	.2854		7.25
	.2874		7.3
	.2900	L	
	.2913		7.4
	.2950	M	
	.2953		7.5
19/64	.2969		7.54
	.2992		7.6
	.3020	N	
	.3031		7.7
	.3051		7.75
	.3071		7.8
	.3110		7.9
5/16	.3125		7.93
	.3150		8.0
	.3160	O	
	.3189		8.1
	.3228		8.2
	.3230	P	
	.3248		8.25
	.3268		8.3
21/64	.3281		8.33
	.3307		8.4
	.3320	Q	
	.3346		8.5
	.3386		8.6
	.3390	R	
11/32	.3425		8.7
	.3438		8.73
	.3445		8.75
	.3465		8.8
	.3480	S	
	.3504		8.9
	.3543		9.0
	.3580	T	
	.3583		9.1
23/64	.3594		9.12
	.3622		9.2
	.3642		9.25
	.3661		9.3
	.3680	U	
	.3701		9.4
	.3740		9.5
3/8	.3750		9.52
	.3770	V	
	.3780		9.6
	.3819		9.7
	.3839		9.75
	.3858		9.8
	.3860	W	
	.3898		9.9
25/64	.3906		9.92
	.3937		10.0
	.3970	X	
	.4040	Y	
13/32	.4062		10.31
	.4130	Z	
	.4134		10.5
27/64	.4219		10.71

Inch	Decimal	mm
	.4331	11.0
7/16	.4375	11.11
	.4528	11.5
29/64	.4531	11.51
15/32	.4688	11.90
	.4724	12.0
31/64	.4844	12.30
	.4921	12.5
1/2	.5000	12.70
	.5118	13.0
33/64	.5156	13.09
17/32	.5312	13.49
	.5315	13.5
35/64	.5469	13.89
	.5512	14.0
9/16	.5625	14.28
	.5709	14.5
37/64	.5781	14.68
	.5906	15.0
19/32	.5938	15.08
39/64	.6094	15.47
	.6102	15.5
5/8	.6250	15.87
	.6299	16.0
41/64	.6406	16.27
	.6496	16.5
21/32	.6562	16.66
	.6693	17.0
43/64	.6719	17.06
11/16	.6875	17.46
	.6890	17.5
45/64	.7031	17.85
	.7087	18.0
23/32	.7188	18.25
	.7283	18.5
47/64	.7344	18.65
	.7480	19.0
3/4	.7500	19.05
49/64	.7656	19.44
	.7677	19.5
25/32	.7812	19.84
	.7874	20.0
51/64	.7969	20.24
	.8071	20.5
13/16	.8125	20.63
	.8268	21.0
53/64	.8281	21.03
27/32	.8438	21.43
	.8465	21.5
55/64	.8594	21.82
	.8661	22.0
7/8	.8750	22.22
	.8858	22.5
57/64	.8906	22.62
	.9055	23.0
29/32	.9062	23.01
59/64	.9219	23.41
	.9252	23.5
15/16	.9375	23.81
	.9449	24.0
61/64	.9531	24.2
	.9646	24.5
31/32	.9688	24.6
	.9843	25.0
63/64	.9844	25.0
1	1.0000	25.4

GLOSSARY OF TERMS

AIR/FUEL RATIO: The ratio of air to gasoline by weight in the fuel mixture drawn into the engine.

AIR INJECTION: One method of reducing harmful exhaust emissions by injecting air into each of the exhaust ports of an engine. The fresh air entering the hot exhaust manifold causes any remaining fuel to be burned before it can exit the tailpipe.

ALTERNATOR: A device used for converting mechanical energy into electrical energy.

AMMETER: An instrument, calibrated in amperes, used to measure the flow of an electrical current in a circuit. Ammeters are always connected in series with the circuit being tested.

AMPERE: The rate of flow of electrical current present when one volt of electrical pressure is applied against one ohm of electrical resistance.

ANALOG COMPUTER: Any microprocessor that uses similar (analogous) electrical signals to make its calculations.

ARMATURE: A laminated, soft iron core wrapped by a wire that converts electrical energy to mechanical energy as in a motor or relay. When rotated in a magnetic field, it changes mechanical energy into electrical energy as in a generator.

ATMOSPHERIC PRESSURE: The pressure on the Earth's surface caused by the weight of the air in the atmosphere. At sea level, this pressure is 14.7 psi at 32°F (101 kPa at 0°C).

ATOMIZATION: The breaking down of a liquid into a fine mist that can be suspended in air.

AXIAL PLAY: Movement parallel to a shaft or bearing bore.

BACKFIRE: The sudden combustion of gases in the intake or exhaust system that results in a loud explosion.

BACKLASH: The clearance or play between two parts, such as meshed gears.

BACKPRESSURE: Restrictions in the exhaust system that slow the exit of exhaust gases from the combustion chamber.

BAKELITE: A heat resistant, plastic insulator material commonly used in printed circuit boards and transistorized components.

BALL BEARING: A bearing made up of hardened inner and outer races between which hardened steel ball roll.

BALLAST RESISTOR: A resistor in the primary ignition circuit that lowers voltage after the engine is started to reduce wear on ignition components.

BEARING: A friction reducing, supportive device usually located between a stationary part and a moving part.

BIMETAL TEMPERATURE SENSOR: Any sensor or switch made of two dissimilar types of metal that bend when heated or cooled due to the different expansion rates of the alloys. These types of sensors usually function as an on/off switch.

BLOWBY: Combustion gases, composed of water vapor and unburned fuel, that leak past the piston rings into the crankcase during normal engine operation. These gases are removed by the PCV system to prevent the build-up of harmful acids in the crankcase.

BRAKE PAD: A brake shoe and lining assembly used with disc brakes.

BRAKE SHOE: The backing for the brake lining. The term is, however, usually applied to the assembly of the brake backing and lining.

BUSHING: A liner, usually removable, for a bearing; an anti-friction liner used in place of a bearing.

BYPASS: System used to bypass ballast resistor during engine cranking to increase voltage supplied to the coil.

CALIPER: A hydraulically activated device in a disc brake system, which is mounted straddling the brake rotor (disc). The caliper contains at least one piston and two brake pads. Hydraulic pressure on the piston(s) forces the pads against the rotor.

CAMSHAFT: A shaft in the engine on which are the lobes (cams) which operate the valves. The camshaft is driven by the crankshaft, via a belt, chain or gears, at one half the crankshaft speed.

CAPACITOR: A device which stores an electrical charge.

CARBON MONOXIDE (CO): a colorless, odorless gas given off as a normal byproduct of combustion. It is poisonous and extremely dangerous in confined areas, building up slowly to toxic levels without warning if adequate ventilation is not available.

CARBURETOR: A device, usually mounted on the intake manifold of an engine, which mixes the air and fuel in the proper proportion to allow even combustion.

CATALYTIC CONVERTER: A device installed in the exhaust system, like a muffler, that converts harmful byproducts of combustion into carbon dioxide and water vapor by means of a heat-producing chemical reaction.

CENTRIFUGAL ADVANCE: A mechanical method of advancing the spark timing by using flyweights in the distributor that react to centrifugal force generated by the distributor shaft rotation.

CHECK VALVE: Any one-way valve installed to permit the flow of air, fuel or vacuum in one direction only.

CHOKE: A device, usually a moveable valve, placed in the intake path of a carburetor to restrict the flow of air.

CIRCUIT: Any unbroken path through which an electrical current can flow. Also used to describe fuel flow in some instances.

CIRCUIT BREAKER: A switch which protects an electrical circuit from overload by opening the circuit when the current flow exceeds a predetermined level. Some circuit breakers must be reset manually, while other reset automatically

COIL (IGNITION): A transformer in the ignition circuit which steps of the voltage provided to the spark plugs.

COMBINATION MANIFOLD: An assembly which includes both the intake and exhaust manifolds in one casting.

COMBINATION VALVE: A device used in some fuel systems that routes fuel vapors to a charcoal storage canister instead of venting them into the atmosphere. The valve relieves fuel tank pressure and allows fresh air into the tank as fuel level drops to prevent a vapor lock situation.

COMPRESSION RATIO: The comparison of the total volume of the cylinder and combustion chamber with the piston at BDC and the piston at TDC.

CONDENSER: 1. An electrical device which acts to store an electrical charge, preventing voltage surges.
2. A radiator-like device in the air conditioning system in which refrigerant gas condenses into a liquid, giving off heat.

CONDUCTOR: Any material through which an electrical current can be transmitted easily.

CONTINUITY: Continuous or complete circuit. Can be checked with an ohmmeter.

COUNTERSHAFT: An intermediate shaft which is rotated by a mainshaft and transmits, in turn, that rotation to a working part.

CRANKCASE: The lower part of an engine in which the crankshaft and related parts operate.

CRANKSHAFT: The main driving shaft of an engine which receives reciprocating motion from the pistons and converts it to rotary motion.

CYLINDER: In an engine, the round hole in the engine block in which the piston(s) ride.

CYLINDER BLOCK: The main structural member of an engine in which is found the cylinders, crankshaft and other principal parts.

CYLINDER HEAD: The detachable portion of the engine, fastened, usually, to the top of the cylinder block, containing all or most of the combustion chambers. On overhead valve engines, it contains the valves and their operating parts. On overhead cam engines, it contains the camshaft as well.

DEAD CENTER: The extreme top or bottom of the piston stroke.

DETONATION: An unwanted explosion of the air fuel mixture in the combustion chamber caused by excess heat and compression, advanced timing, or an overly lean mixture. Also referred to as "ping".

DIAPHRAGM: A thin, flexible wall separating two cavities, such as in a vacuum advance unit.

DIESELING: A condition in which hot spots in the combustion chamber cause the engine to run on after the key is turned off.

DIFFERENTIAL: A geared assembly which allows the transmission of motion between drive axles, giving one axle the ability to turn faster than the other.

DIODE: An electrical device that will allow current to flow in one direction only.

DISC BRAKE: A hydraulic braking assembly consisting of a brake disc, or rotor, mounted on an axle, and a caliper assembly containing, usually two brake pads which are activated by hydraulic pressure. The pads are forced against the sides of the disc, creating friction which slows the vehicle.

DISTRIBUTOR: A mechanically driven device on an engine which is responsible for electrically firing the spark plug at a predetermined point of the piston stroke.

DOWEL PIN: A pin, inserted in mating holes in two different parts allowing those parts to maintain a fixed relationship.

DRUM BRAKE: A braking system which consists of two brake shoes and one or two wheel cylinders, mounted on a fixed backing plate, and a brake drum, mounted on an axle, which revolves around the assembly. Hydraulic action applied to the wheel cylinders forces the shoes outward against the drum, creating friction and slowing the vehicle.

DWELL: The rate, measured in degrees of shaft rotation, at which an electrical circuit cycles on and off.

ELECTRONIC CONTROL UNIT (ECU): Ignition module, module, amplifier or igniter. See Module for definition.

ELECTRONIC IGNITION: A system in which the timing and firing of the spark plugs is controlled by an electronic control unit, usually called a module. These systems have not points or condenser.

ENDPLAY: The measured amount of axial movement in a shaft.

ENGINE: A device that converts heat into mechanical energy.

EXHAUST MANIFOLD: A set of cast passages or pipes which conduct exhaust gases from the engine.

FEELER GAUGE: A blade, usually metal, of precisely predetermined thickness, used to measure the clearance between two parts. These blades usually are available in sets of assorted thicknesses.

F-Head: An engine configuration in which the intake valves are in the cylinder head, while the camshaft and exhaust valves are located in the cylinder block. The camshaft operates the intake valves via lifters and pushrods, while it operates the exhaust valves directly.

FIRING ORDER: The order in which combustion occurs in the cylinders of an engine. Also the order in which spark is distributed to the plugs by the distributor.

FLATHEAD: An engine configuration in which the camshaft and all the valves are located in the cylinder block.

FLOODING: The presence of too much fuel in the intake manifold and combustion chamber which prevents the air/fuel mixture from firing, thereby causing a no-start situation.

FLYWHEEL: A disc shaped part bolted to the rear end of the crankshaft. Around the outer perimeter is affixed the ring gear. The starter drive engages the ring gear, turning the flywheel, which rotates the crankshaft, imparting the initial starting motion to the engine.

FOOT POUND (ft.lb. or sometimes, ft. lbs.): The amount of energy or work needed to raise an item weighing one pound, a distance of one foot.

FUSE: A protective device in a circuit which prevents circuit overload by breaking the circuit when a specific amperage is present. The device is constructed around a strip or wire of a lower amperage rating than the circuit it is designed to protect. When an amperage higher than that stamped on the fuse is present in the circuit, the strip or wire melts, opening the circuit.

GEAR RATIO: The ratio between the number of teeth on meshing gears.

GENERATOR: A device which converts mechanical energy into electrical energy.

HEAT RANGE: The measure of a spark plug's ability to dissipate heat from its firing end. The higher the heat range, the hotter the plug fires.

HUB: The center part of a wheel or gear.

HYDROCARBON (HC): Any chemical compound made up of hydrogen and carbon. A major pollutant formed by the engine as a byproduct of combustion.

HYDROMETER: An instrument used to measure the specific gravity of a solution.

INCH POUND (in.lb. or sometimes, in. lbs.): One twelfth of a foot pound.

INDUCTION: A means of transferring electrical energy in the form of a magnetic field. Principle used in the ignition coil to increase voltage.

INJECTION PUMP: A device, usually mechanically operated, which meters and delivers fuel under pressure to the fuel injector.

INJECTOR: A device which receives metered fuel under relatively low pressure and is activated to inject the fuel into the engine under relatively high pressure at a predetermined time.

INPUT SHAFT: The shaft to which torque is applied, usually carrying the driving gear or gears.

INTAKE MANIFOLD: A casting of passages or pipes used to conduct air or a fuel/air mixture to the cylinders.

JOURNAL: The bearing surface within which a shaft operates.

KEY: A small block usually fitted in a notch between a shaft and a hub to prevent slippage of the two parts.

MANIFOLD: A casting of passages or set of pipes which connect the cylinders to an inlet or outlet source.

MANIFOLD VACUUM: Low pressure in an engine intake manifold formed just below the throttle plates. Manifold vacuum is highest at idle and drops under acceleration.

MASTER CYLINDER: The primary fluid pressurizing device in a hydraulic system. In automotive use, it is found in brake and hydraulic clutch systems and is pedal activated, either directly or, in a power brake system, through the power booster.

MODULE: Electronic control unit, amplifier or igniter of solid state or integrated design which controls the current flow in the ignition primary circuit based on input from the pickup coil. When the module opens the primary circuit, the high secondary voltage is induced in the coil.

NEEDLE BEARING: A bearing which consists of a number (usually a large number) of long, thin rollers.

OHM: (Ω) The unit used to measure the resistance of conductor to electrical flow. One ohm is the amount of resistance that limits current flow to one ampere in a circuit with one volt of pressure.

OHMMETER: An instrument used for measuring the resistance, in ohms, in an electrical circuit.

OUTPUT SHAFT: The shaft which transmits torque from a device, such as a transmission.

OVERDRIVE: A gear assembly which produces more shaft revolutions than that transmitted to it.

OVERHEAD CAMSHAFT (OHC): An engine configuration in which the camshaft is mounted on top of the cylinder head and operates the valve either directly or by means of rocker arms.

OVERHEAD VALVE (OHV): An engine configuration in which all of the valves are located in the cylinder head and the camshaft is located in the cylinder block. The camshaft operates the valves via lifters and pushrods.

OXIDES OF NITROGEN (NOx): Chemical compounds of nitrogen produced as a byproduct of combustion. They combine with hydrocarbons to produce smog.

OXYGEN SENSOR: Used with the feedback system to sense the presence of oxygen in the exhaust gas and signal the computer which can reference the voltage signal to an air/fuel ratio.

PINION: The smaller of two meshing gears.

PISTON RING: An open ended ring which fits into a groove on the outer diameter of the piston. Its chief function is to form a seal between the piston and cylinder wall. Most automotive pistons have three rings: two for compression sealing; one for oil sealing.

PRELOAD: A predetermined load placed on a bearing during assembly or by adjustment.

PRIMARY CIRCUIT: Is the low voltage side of the ignition system which consists of the ignition switch, ballast resistor or resistance wire, bypass, coil, electronic control unit and pick-up coil as well as the connecting wires and harnesses.

PRESS FIT: The mating of two parts under pressure, due to the inner diameter of one being smaller than the outer diameter of the other, or vice versa; an interference fit.

RACE: The surface on the inner or outer ring of a bearing on which the balls, needles or rollers move.

REGULATOR: A device which maintains the amperage and/or voltage levels of a circuit at predetermined values.

RELAY: A switch which automatically opens and/or closes a circuit.

RESISTANCE: The opposition to the flow of current through a circuit or electrical device, and is measured in ohms. Resistance is equal to the voltage divided by the amperage.

RESISTOR: A device, usually made of wire, which offers a preset amount of resistance in an electrical circuit.

RING GEAR: The name given to a ring-shaped gear attached to a differential case, or affixed to a flywheel or as part a planetary gear set.

ROLLER BEARING: A bearing made up of hardened inner and outer races between which hardened steel rollers move.

ROTOR: 1. The disc-shaped part of a disc brake assembly, upon which the brake pads bear; also called, brake disc.
2. The device mounted atop the distributor shaft, which passes current to the distributor cap tower contacts.

SECONDARY CIRCUIT: The high voltage side of the ignition system, usually above 20,000 volts. The secondary includes the ignition coil, coil wire, distributor cap and rotor, spark plug wires and spark plugs.

SENDING UNIT: A mechanical, electrical, hydraulic or electromagnetic device which transmits information to a gauge.

SENSOR: Any device designed to measure engine operating conditions or ambient pressures and temperatures. Usually electronic in nature and designed to send a voltage signal to an on-board computer, some sensors may operate as a simple on/off switch or they may provide a variable voltage signal (like a potentiometer) as conditions or measured parameters change.

SHIM: Spacers of precise, predetermined thickness used between parts to establish a proper working relationship.

SLAVE CYLINDER: In automotive use, a device in the hydraulic clutch system which is activated by hydraulic force, disengaging the clutch.

SOLENOID: A coil used to produce a magnetic field, the effect of which is produce work.

SPARK PLUG: A device screwed into the combustion chamber of a spark ignition engine. The basic construction is a conductive core inside of a ceramic insulator, mounted in an outer conductive base. An electrical charge from the spark plug wire travels along the conductive core and jumps a preset air gap to a grounding point or points at the end of the conductive base. The resultant spark ignites the fuel/air mixture in the combustion chamber.

SPLINES: Ridges machined or cast onto the outer diameter of a shaft or inner diameter of a bore to enable parts to mate without rotation.

TACHOMETER: A device used to measure the rotary speed of an engine, shaft, gear, etc., usually in rotations per minute.

THERMOSTAT: A valve, located in the cooling system of an engine, which is closed when cold and opens gradually in response to engine heating, controlling the temperature of the coolant and rate of coolant flow.

TOP DEAD CENTER (TDC): The point at which the piston reaches the top of its travel on the compression stroke.

TORQUE: The twisting force applied to an object.

TORQUE CONVERTER: A turbine used to transmit power from a driving member to a driven member via hydraulic action, providing changes in drive ratio and torque. In automotive use, it links the driveplate at the rear of the engine to the automatic transmission.

TRANSDUCER: A device used to change a force into an electrical signal.

TRANSISTOR: A semi-conductor component which can be actuated by a small voltage to perform an electrical switching function.

TUNE-UP: A regular maintenance function, usually associated with the replacement and adjustment of parts and components in the electrical and fuel systems of a vehicle for the purpose of attaining optimum performance.

TURBOCHARGER: An exhaust driven pump which compresses intake air and forces it into the combustion chambers at higher than atmospheric pressures. The increased air pressure allows more fuel to be burned and results in increased horsepower being produced.

VACUUM ADVANCE: A device which advances the ignition timing in response to increased engine vacuum.

VACUUM GAUGE: An instrument used to measure the presence of vacuum in a chamber.

VALVE: A device which control the pressure, direction of flow or rate of flow of a liquid or gas.

VALVE CLEARANCE: The measured gap between the end of the valve stem and the rocker arm, cam lobe or follower that activates the valve.

VISCOSITY: The rating of a liquid's internal resistance to flow.

VOLTMETER: An instrument used for measuring electrical force in units called volts. Voltmeters are always connected parallel with the circuit being tested.

WHEEL CYLINDER: Found in the automotive drum brake assembly, it is a device, actuated by hydraulic pressure, which, through internal pistons, pushes the brake shoes outward against the drums.

ABBREVIATIONS AND SYMBOLS

A: Ampere

AC: Alternating current

A/C: Air conditioning

A-h: Ampere hour

AT: Automatic transmission

ATDC: After top dead center

µA: Microampere

bbl: Barrel

BDC: Bottom dead center

bhp: Brake horsepower

BTDC: Before top dead center

BTU: British thermal unit

C: Celsius (Centigrade)

CCA: Cold cranking amps

cd: Candela

cm^2: Square centimeter

cm^3, cc: Cubic centimeter

CO: Carbon monoxide

CO$_2$: Carbon dioxide

cu.in., in^3: Cubic inch

CV: Constant velocity

Cyl.: Cylinder

DC: Direct current

ECM: Electronic control module

EFE: Early fuel evaporation

EFI: Electronic fuel injection

EGR: Exhaust gas recirculation

Exh.: Exhaust

F: Fahrenheit

F: Farad

pF: Picofarad

µF: Microfarad

FI: Fuel injection

ft.lb., ft. lb., ft. lbs.: foot pound(s)

gal: Gallon

g: Gram

HC: Hydrocarbon

HEI: High energy ignition

HO: High output

hp: Horsepower

Hyd.: Hydraulic

Hz: Hertz

ID: Inside diameter

in.lb.; in. lb.; in. lbs: inch pound(s)

Int.: Intake

K: Kelvin

kg: Kilogram

kHz: Kilohertz

km: Kilometer

km/h: Kilometers per hour

kΩ: Kilohm

kPa: Kilopascal

kV: Kilovolt

kW: Kilowatt

l: Liter

l/s: Liters per second

m: Meter

mA: Milliampere

mg: Milligram

mHz: Megahertz

mm: Millimeter

mm^2: Square millimeter

m^3: Cubic meter

$M\Omega$: Megohm

m/s: Meters per second

MT: Manual transmission

mV: Millivolt

μm: Micrometer

N: Newton

N-m: Newton meter

NOx: Nitrous oxide

OD: Outside diameter

OHC: Over head camshaft

OHV: Over head valve

Ω: Ohm

PCV: Positive crankcase ventilation

psi: Pounds per square inch

pts: Pints

qts: Quarts

rpm: Rotations per minute

rps: Rotations per second

R-12: A refrigerant gas (Freon)

SAE: Society of Automotive Engineers

SO_2: Sulfur dioxide

T: Ton

t: Megagram

TBI: Throttle Body Injection

TPS: Throttle Position Sensor

V: 1. Volt; 2. Venturi

μV: Microvolt

W: Watt

∞: Infinity

<: Less than

>: Greater than

Index

CHILTON'S REPAIR MANUAL MODEL INDEX
Car and truck model names are listed in alphabetical and numerical order

Part No.	Model	Repair Manual Title
6980	Accord	Honda 1973-88
7747	Aerostar	Ford Aerostar 1986-90
7165	Alliance	Renault 1975-85
7199	AMX	AMC 1975-86
7163	Aries	Chrysler Front Wheel Drive 1981-88
7041	Arrow	Champ/Arrow/Sapporo 1978-83
7032	Arrow Pick-Ups	D-50/Arrow Pick-Up 1979-81
6637	Aspen	Aspen/Volare 1976-80
6935	Astre	GM Subcompact 1971-80
7750	Astro	Chevrolet Astro/GMC Safari 1985-90
6934	A100, 200, 300	Dodge/Plymouth Vans 1967-88
5807	Barracuda	Barracuda/Challenger 1965-72
6844	Bavaria	BMW 1970-88
5796	Beetle	Volkswagen 1949-71
6837	Beetle	Volkswagen 1970-81
7135	Bel Air	Chevrolet 1968-88
5821	Belvedere	Roadrunner/Satellite/Belvedere/GTX 1968-73
7849	Beretta	Chevrolet Corsica and Beretta 1988
7317	Berlinetta	Camaro 1982-88
7135	Biscayne	Chevrolet 1968-88
6931	Blazer	Blazer/Jimmy 1969-82
7383	Blazer	Chevy S-10 Blazer/GMC S-15 Jimmy 1982-87
7027	Bobcat	Pinto/Bobcat 1971-80
7308	Bonneville	Buick/Olds/Pontiac 1975-87
6982	BRAT	Subaru 1970-88
7042	Brava	Fiat 1969-81
7140	Bronco	Ford Bronco 1966-86
7829	Bronco	Ford Pick-Ups and Bronco 1987-88
7408	Bronco II	Ford Ranger/Bronco II 1983-88
7135	Brookwood	Chevrolet 1968-88
6326	Brougham 1975-75	Valiant/Duster 1968-76
6934	B100, 150, 200, 250, 300, 350	Dodge/Plymouth Vans 1967-88
7197	B210	Datsun 1200/210/Nissan Sentra 1973-88
7659	B1600, 1800, 2000, 2200, 2600	Mazda Trucks 1971-89
6840	Caballero	Chevrolet Mid-Size 1964-88
7657	Calais	Calais, Grand Am, Skylark, Somerset 1985-86
6735	Camaro	Camaro 1967-81
7317	Camaro	Camaro 1982-88
7740	Camry	Toyota Camry 1983-88
6695	Capri, Capri II	Capri 1970-77
6963	Capri	Mustang/Capri/Merkur 1979-88
7135	Caprice	Chevrolet 1968-88
7482	Caravan	Dodge Caravan/Plymouth Voyager 1984-89
7163	Caravelle	Chrysler Front Wheel Drive 1981-88
7036	Carina	Toyota Corolla/Carina/Tercel/Starlet 1970-87
7308	Catalina	Buick/Olds/Pontiac 1975-90
7059	Cavalier	Cavalier, Skyhawk, Cimarron, 2000 1982-88
7309	Celebrity	Celebrity, Century, Ciera, 6000 1982-88
7043	Celica	Toyota Celica/Supra 1971-87
8058	Celica	Toyota Celica/Supra 1986-90
7309	Century FWD	Celebrity, Century, Ciera, 6000 1982-88
7307	Century RWD	Century/Regal 1975-87
5807	Challenger 1965-72	Barracuda/Challenger 1965-72
7037	Challenger 1977-83	Colt/Challenger/Vista/Conquest 1971-88
7041	Champ	Champ/Arrow/Sapporo 1978-83
6486	Charger	Dodge Charger 1967-70
6845	Charger 2.2	Omni/Horizon/Rampage 1978-88
6739	Cherokee 1974-83	Jeep Wagoneer, Commando, Cherokee, Truck 1957-86
7939	Cherokee 1984-89	Jeep Wagoneer, Comanche, Cherokee 1984-89
6840	Chevelle	Chevrolet Mid-Size 1964-88
6836	Chevette	Chevette/T-1000 1976-88
6841	Chevy II	Chevy II/Nova 1962-79
7309	Ciera	Celebrity, Century, Ciera, 6000 1982-88
7059	Cimarron	Cavalier, Skyhawk, Cimarron, 2000 1982-88
7049	Citation	GM X-Body 1980-85
6980	Civic	Honda 1973-88
6817	CJ-2A, 3A, 3B, 5, 6, 7	Jeep 1945-87
8034	CJ-5, 6, 7	Jeep 1971-90
6842	Colony Park	Ford/Mercury/Lincoln 1968-88
7037	Colt	Colt/Challenger/Vista/Conquest 1971-88
6634	Comet	Maverick/Comet 1971-77
7939	Comanche	Jeep Wagoneer, Comanche, Cherokee 1984-89
6739	Commando	Jeep Wagoneer, Commando, Cherokee, Truck 1957-86
6842	Commuter	Ford/Mercury/Lincoln 1968-88
7199	Concord	AMC 1975-86
7037	Conquest	Colt/Challenger/Vista/Conquest 1971-88
6696	Continental 1982-85	Ford/Mercury/Lincoln Mid-Size 1971-85
7814	Continental 1982-87	Thunderbird, Cougar, Continental 1980-87
7830	Continental 1988-89	Taurus/Sable/Continental 1986-89
7583	Cordia	Mitsubishi 1983-89
5795	Corolla 1968-70	Toyota 1966-70
7036	Corolla	Toyota Corolla/Carina/Tercel/Starlet 1970-87
5795	Corona	Toyota 1966-70
7004	Corona	Toyota Corona/Crown/Cressida/Mk.II/Van 1970-87
6962	Corrado	VW Front Wheel Drive 1974-90
7849	Corsica	Chevrolet Corsica and Beretta 1988
6576	Corvette	Corvette 1953-62
6843	Corvette	Corvette 1963-86
6542	Cougar	Mustang/Cougar 1965-73
6696	Cougar	Ford/Mercury/Lincoln Mid-Size 1971-85
7814	Cougar	Thunderbird, Cougar, Continental 1980-87
6842	Country Sedan	Ford/Mercury/Lincoln 1968-88
6842	Country Squire	Ford/Mercury/Lincoln 1968-88
6983	Courier	Ford Courier 1972-82
7004	Cressida	Toyota Corona/Crown/Cressida/Mk.II/Van 1970-87
5795	Crown	Toyota 1966-70
7004	Crown	Toyota Corona/Crown/Cressida/Mk.II/Van 1970-87
6842	Crown Victoria	Ford/Mercury/Lincoln 1968-88
6980	CRX	Honda 1973-88
6842	Custom	Ford/Mercury/Lincoln 1968-88
6326	Custom	Valiant/Duster 1968-76
6842	Custom 500	Ford/Mercury/Lincoln 1968-88
7950	Cutlass FWD	Lumina/Grand Prix/Cutlass/Regal 1988-90
6933	Cutlass RWD	Cutlass 1970-87
7309	Cutlass Ciera	Celebrity, Century, Ciera, 6000 1982-88
6936	C-10, 20, 30	Chevrolet/GMC Pick-Ups & Suburban 1970-87

Chilton's Repair Manuals are available at your local retailer or by mailing a check or money order for **$15.95** per book plus **$3.50** for 1st book and **$.50** for each additional book to cover postage and handling to:

Chilton Book Company
Dept. DM
Radnor, PA 19089

NOTE: When ordering be sure to include your name & address, book part No. & title.

CHILTON'S REPAIR MANUAL MODEL INDEX
Car and truck model names are listed in alphabetical and numerical order

Part No.	Model	Repair Manual Title	Part No.	Model	Repair Manual Title
8055	C-15, 25, 35	Chevrolet/GMC Pick-Ups & Suburban 1988-90	7593	Golf	VW Front Wheel Drive 1974-90
6324	Dart	Dart/Demon 1968-76	7165	Gordini	Renault 1975-85
6962	Dasher	VW Front Wheel Drive 1974-90	6937	Granada	Granada/Monarch 1975-82
5790	Datsun Pickups	Datsun 1961-72	6552	Gran Coupe	Plymouth 1968-76
6816	Datsun Pickups	Datsun Pick-Ups and Pathfinder 1970-89	6552	Gran Fury	Plymouth 1968-76
7163	Daytona	Chrysler Front Wheel Drive 1981-88	6842	Gran Marquis	Ford/Mercury/Lincoln 1968-88
6486	Daytona Charger	Dodge Charger 1967-70	6552	Gran Sedan	Plymouth 1968-76
6324	Demon	Dart/Demon 1968-76	6696	Gran Torino 1972-76	Ford/Mercury/Lincoln Mid-Size 1971-85
7462	deVille	Cadillac 1967-89	7346	Grand Am	Pontiac Mid-Size 1974-83
7587	deVille	GM C-Body 1985	7657	Grand Am	Calais, Grand Am, Skylark, Somerset 1985-86
6817	DJ-3B	Jeep 1945-87			
7040	DL	Volvo 1970-88	7346	Grand LeMans	Pontiac Mid-Size 1974-83
6326	Duster	Valiant/Duster 1968-76	7346	Grand Prix	Pontiac Mid-Size 1974-83
7032	D-50	D-50/Arrow Pick-Ups 1979-81	7950	Grand Prix FWD	Lumina/Grand Prix/Cutlass/Regal 1988-90
7459	D100, 150, 200, 250, 300, 350	Dodge/Plymouth Trucks 1967-88	7308	Grand Safari	Buick/Olds/Pontiac 1975-87
7199	Eagle	AMC 1975-86	7308	Grand Ville	Buick/Olds/Pontiac 1975-87
7163	E-Class	Chrysler Front Wheel Drive 1981-88	6739	Grand Wagoneer	Jeep Wagoneer, Commando, Cherokee, Truck 1957-86
6840	El Camino	Chevrolet Mid-Size 1964-88			
7462	Eldorado	Cadillac 1967-89	7199	Gremlin	AMC 1975-86
7308	Electra	Buick/Olds/Pontiac 1975-90	6575	GT	Opel 1971-75
7587	Electra	GM C-Body 1985	7593	GTI	VW Front Wheel Drive 1974-90
6696	Elite	Ford/Mercury/Lincoln Mid-Size 1971-85	5905	GTO 1968-73	Tempest/GTO/LeMans 1968-73
			7346	GTO 1974	Pontiac Mid-Size 1974-83
7165	Encore	Renault 1975-85	5821	GTX	Roadrunner/Satellite/Belvedere/GTX 1968-73
7055	Escort	Ford/Mercury Front Wheel Drive 1981-87			
7059	Eurosport	Cavalier, Skyhawk, Cimarron, 2000 1982-88	5910	GT6	Triumph 1969-73
			6542	G.T.350, 500	Mustang/Cougar 1965-73
7760	Excel	Hyundai 1986-90	6930	G-10, 20, 30	Chevy/GMC Vans 1967-86
7163	Executive Sedan	Chrysler Front Wheel Drive 1981-88	6930	G-1500, 2500, 3500	Chevy/GMC Vans 1967-86
7055	EXP	Ford/Mercury Front Wheel Drive 1981-87	8040	G-10, 20, 30	Chevy/GMC Vans 1987-90
			8040	G-1500, 2500, 3500	Chevy/GMC Vans 1987-90
6849	E-100, 150, 200, 250, 300, 350	Ford Vans 1961-88	5795	Hi-Lux	Toyota 1966-70
			6845	Horizon	Omni/Horizon/Rampage 1978-88
6320	Fairlane	Fairlane/Torino 1962-75	7199	Hornet	AMC 1975-86
6965	Fairmont	Fairmont/Zephyr 1978-83	7135	Impala	Chevrolet 1968-88
5796	Fastback	Volkswagen 1949-71	7317	IROC-Z	Camaro 1982-88
6837	Fastback	Volkswagen 1970-81	6739	Jeepster	Jeep Wagoneer, Commando, Cherokee, Truck 1957-86
6739	FC-150, 170	Jeep Wagoneer, Commando, Cherokee, Truck 1957-86			
			7593	Jetta	VW Front Wheel Drive 1974-90
6982	FF-1	Subaru 1970-88	6931	Jimmy	Blazer/Jimmy 1969-82
7571	Fiero	Pontiac Fiero 1984-88	7383	Jimmy	Chevy S-10 Blazer/GMC S-15 Jimmy 1982-87
6846	Fiesta	Fiesta 1978-80			
5996	Firebird	Firebird 1967-81	6739	J-10, 20	Jeep Wagoneer, Commando, Cherokee, Truck 1957-86
7345	Firebird	Firebird 1982-90			
7059	Firenza	Cavalier, Skyhawk, Cimarron, 2000 1982-88	6739	J-100, 200, 300	Jeep Wagoneer, Commando, Cherokee, Truck 1957-86
7462	Fleetwood	Cadillac 1967-89	6575	Kadett	Opel 1971-75
7587	Fleetwood	GM C-Body 1985	7199	Kammback	AMC 1975-86
7829	F-Super Duty	Ford Pick-Ups and Bronco 1987-88	5796	Karmann Ghia	Volkswagen 1949-71
7165	Fuego	Renault 1975-85	6837	Karmann Ghia	Volkswagen 1970-81
6552	Fury	Plymouth 1968-76	7135	Kingswood	Chevrolet 1968-88
7196	F-10	Datsun/Nissan F-10, 310, Stanza, Pulsar 1976-88	6931	K-5	Blazer/Jimmy 1969-82
			6936	K-10, 20, 30	Chevy/GMC Pick-Ups & Suburban 1970-87
6933	F-85	Cutlass 1970-87			
6913	F-100, 150, 200, 250, 300, 350	Ford Pick-Ups 1965-86	6936	K-1500, 2500, 3500	Chevy/GMC Pick-Ups & Suburban 1970-87
			8055	K-10, 20, 30	Chevy/GMC Pick-Ups & Suburban 1988-90
7829	F-150, 250, 350	Ford Pick-Ups and Bronco 1987-88			
7583	Galant	Mitsubishi 1983-89	8055	K-1500, 2500, 3500	Chevy/GMC Pick-Ups & Suburban 1988-90
6842	Galaxie	Ford/Mercury/Lincoln 1968-88			
7040	GL	Volvo 1970-88	6840	Laguna	Chevrolet Mid-Size 1964-88
6739	Gladiator	Jeep Wagoneer, Commando, Cherokee, Truck 1962-86	7041	Lancer	Champ/Arrow/Sapporo 1977-83
			5795	Land Cruiser	Toyota 1966-70
6981	GLC	Mazda 1978-89	7035	Land Cruiser	Toyota Trucks 1970-88
7040	GLE	Volvo 1970-88	7163	Laser	Chrysler Front Wheel Drive 1981-88
7040	GLT	Volvo 1970-88	7163	LeBaron	Chrysler Front Wheel Drive 1981-88
			7165	LeCar	Renault 1975-85

Chilton's Repair Manuals are available at your local retailer or by mailing a check or money order for **$15.95** per book plus **$3.50** for 1st book and **$.50** for each additional book to cover postage and handling to:

Chilton Book Company
Dept. DM
Radnor, PA 19089

NOTE: When ordering be sure to include your name & address, book part No. & title.

CHILTON'S REPAIR MANUAL MODEL INDEX
Car and truck model names are listed in alphabetical and numerical order

Part No.	Model	Repair Manual Title
5905	LeMans	Tempest/GTO/LeMans 1968-73
7346	LeMans	Pontiac Mid-Size 1974-83
7308	LeSabre	Buick/Olds/Pontiac 1975-87
6842	Lincoln	Ford/Mercury/Lincoln 1968-88
7055	LN-7	Ford/Mercury Front Wheel Drive 1981-87
6842	LTD	Ford/Mercury/Lincoln 1968-88
6696	LTD II	Ford/Mercury/Lincoln Mid-Size 1971-85
7950	Lumina	Lumina/Grand Prix/Cutlass/Regal 1988-90
6815	LUV	Chevrolet LUV 1972-81
6575	Luxus	Opel 1971-75
7055	Lynx	Ford/Mercury Front Wheel Drive 1981-87
6844	L6	BMW 1970-88
6344	L7	BMW 1970-88
6542	Mach I	Mustang/Cougar 1965-73
6812	Mach I Ghia	Mustang II 1974-78
6840	Malibu	Chevrolet Mid-Size 1964-88
6575	Manta	Opel 1971-75
6696	Mark IV, V, VI, VII	Ford/Mercury/Lincoln Mid-Size 1971-85
7814	Mark VII	Thunderbird, Cougar, Continental 1980-87
6842	Marquis	Ford/Mercury/Lincoln 1968-88
6696	Marquis	Ford/Mercury/Lincoln Mid-Size 1971-85
7199	Matador	AMC 1975-86
6634	Maverick	Maverick/Comet 1970-77
6817	Maverick	Jeep 1945-87
7170	Maxima	Nissan 200SX, 240SX, 510, 610, 710, 810, Maxima 1973-88
6842	Mercury	Ford/Mercury/Lincoln 1968-88
6963	Merkur	Mustang/Capri/Merkur 1979-88
6780	MGB, MGB-GT, MGC-GT	MG 1961-81
6780	Midget	MG 1961-81
7583	Mighty Max	Mitsubishi 1983-89
7583	Mirage	Mitsubishi 1983-89
5795	Mk.II 1969-70	Toyota 1966-70
7004	Mk.II 1970-76	Toyota Corona/Crown/Cressida/Mk.II/Van 1970-87
6554	Monaco	Dodge 1968-77
6937	Monarch	Granada/Monarch 1975-82
6840	Monte Carlo	Chevrolet Mid-Size 1964-88
6696	Montego	Ford/Mercury/Lincoln Mid-Size 1971-85
6842	Monterey	Ford/Mercury/Lincoln 1968-88
7583	Montero	Mitsubishi 1983-89
6935	Monza 1975-80	GM Subcompact 1971-80
6981	MPV	Mazda 1978-89
6542	Mustang	Mustang/Cougar 1965-73
6963	Mustang	Mustang/Capri/Merkur 1979-88
6812	Mustang II	Mustang II 1974-78
6981	MX6	Mazda 1978-89
6844	M3, M6	BMW 1970-88
7163	New Yorker	Chrysler Front Wheel Drive 1981-88
6841	Nova	Chevy II/Nova 1962-79
7658	Nova	Chevrolet Nova/GEO Prizm 1985-89
7049	Omega	GM X-Body 1980-85
6845	Omni	Omni/Horizon/Rampage 1978-88
6575	Opel	Opel 1971-75
7199	Pacer	AMC 1975-86
7587	Park Avenue	GM C-Body 1985
6842	Park Lane	Ford/Mercury/Lincoln 1968-88
6962	Passat	VW Front Wheel Drive 1974-90
6816	Pathfinder	Datsun/Nissan Pick-Ups and Pathfinder 1970-89
5790	Patrol	Datsun 1961-72
6934	PB100, 150, 200, 250, 300, 350	Dodge/Plymouth Vans 1967-88
5982	Peugeot	Peugeot 1970-74
7049	Phoenix	GM X-Body 1980-85
7027	Pinto	Pinto/Bobcat 1971-80
6554	Polara	Dodge 1968-77
7583	Precis	Mitsubishi 1983-89
6980	Prelude	Honda 1973-88
7658	Prizm	Chevrolet Nova/GEO Prizm 1985-89
8012	Probe	Ford Probe 1989
7660	Pulsar	Datsun/Nissan F-10, 310, Stanza, Pulsar 1976-88
6529	PV-444	Volvo 1956-69
6529	PV-544	Volvo 1956-69
6529	P-1800	Volvo 1956-69
7593	Quantum	VW Front Wheel Drive 1974-87
7593	Rabbit	VW Front Wheel Drive 1974-87
7593	Rabbit Pickup	VW Front Wheel Drive 1974-87
6575	Rallye	Opel 1971-75
7459	Ramcharger	Dodge/Plymouth Trucks 1967-88
6845	Rampage	Omni/Horizon/Rampage 1978-88
6320	Ranchero	Fairlane/Torino 1962-70
6696	Ranchero	Ford/Mercury/Lincoln Mid-Size 1971-85
6842	Ranch Wagon	Ford/Mercury/Lincoln 1968-88
7338	Ranger Pickup	Ford Ranger/Bronco II 1983-88
7307	Regal RWD	Century/Regal 1975-87
7950	Regal FWD 1988-90	Lumina/Grand Prix/Cutlass/Regal 1988-90
7163	Reliant	Chrysler Front Wheel Drive 1981-88
5821	Roadrunner	Roadrunner/Satellite/Belvedere/GTX 1968-73
7659	Rotary Pick-Up	Mazda Trucks 1971-89
6981	RX-7	Mazda 1978-89
7165	R-12, 15, 17, 18, 18i	Renault 1975-85
7830	Sable	Taurus/Sable/Continental 1986-89
7750	Safari	Chevrolet Astro/GMC Safari 1985-90
7041	Sapporo	Champ/Arrow/Sapporo 1978-83
5821	Satellite	Roadrunner/Satellite/Belvedere/GTX 1968-73
6326	Scamp	Valiant/Duster 1968-76
6845	Scamp	Omni/Horizon/Rampage 1978-88
6962	Scirocco	VW Front Wheel Drive 1974-90
6936	Scottsdale	Chevrolet/GMC Pick-Ups & Suburban 1970-87
8055	Scottsdale	Chevrolet/GMC Pick-Ups & Suburban 1988-90
5912	Scout	International Scout 1967-73
8034	Scrambler	Jeep 1971-90
7197	Sentra	Datsun 1200, 210, Nissan Sentra 1973-88
7462	Seville	Cadillac 1967-89
7163	Shadow	Chrysler Front Wheel Drive 1981-88
6936	Siera	Chevrolet/GMC Pick-Ups & Suburban 1970-87
8055	Siera	Chevrolet/GMC Pick-Ups & Suburban 1988-90
7583	Sigma	Mitsubishi 1983-89
6326	Signet	Valiant/Duster 1968-76
6936	Silverado	Chevrolet/GMC Pick-Ups & Suburban 1970-87
8055	Silverado	Chevrolet/GMC Pick-Ups & Suburban 1988-90
6935	Skyhawk	GM Subcompact 1971-80
7059	Skyhawk	Cavalier, Skyhawk, Cimarron, 2000 1982-88
7049	Skylark	GM X-Body 1980-85

Chilton's Repair Manuals are available at your local retailer or by mailing a check or money order for **$15.95** per book plus **$3.50** for 1st book and **$.50** for each additional book to cover postage and handling to:

Chilton Book Company
Dept. DM
Radnor, PA 19089

NOTE: When ordering be sure to include your name & address, book part No. & title.

CHILTON'S REPAIR MANUAL MODEL INDEX
Car and truck model names are listed in alphabetical and numerical order

Part No.	Model	Repair Manual Title	Part No.	Model	Repair Manual Title
7675	Skylark	Calais, Grand Am, Skylark, Somerset 1985-86	7040	Turbo	Volvo 1970-88
7657	Somerset	Calais, Grand Am, Skylark, Somerset 1985-86	5796	Type 1 Sedan 1949-71	Volkswagen 1949-71
7042	Spider 2000	Fiat 1969-81	6837	Type 1 Sedan 1970-80	Volkswagen 1970-81
7199	Spirit	AMC 1975-86	5796	Type 1 Karmann Ghia 1960-71	Volkswagen 1949-71
6552	Sport Fury	Plymouth 1968-76	6837	Type 1 Karmann Ghia 1970-74	Volkswagen 1970-81
7165	Sport Wagon	Renault 1975-85	5796	Type 1 Convertible 1964-71	Volkswagen 1949-71
5796	Squareback	Volkswagen 1949-71	6837	Type 1 Convertible 1970-80	Volkswagen 1970-81
6837	Squareback	Volkswagen 1970-81			
7196	Stanza	Datsun/Nissan F-10, 310, Stanza, Pulsar 1976-88	5796	Type 1 Super Beetle 1971	Volkswagen 1949-71
6935	Starfire	GM Subcompact 1971-80	6837	Type 1 Super Beetle 1971-75	Volkswagen 1970-81
7583	Starion	Mitsubishi 1983-89	5796	Type 2 Bus 1953-71	Volkswagen 1949-71
7036	Starlet	Toyota Corolla/Carina/Tercel/Starlet 1970-87	6837	Type 2 Bus 1970-80	Volkswagen 1970-81
7059	STE	Cavalier, Skyhawk, Cimarron, 2000 1982-88	5796	Type 2 Kombi 1954-71	Volkswagen 1949-71
5795	Stout	Toyota 1966-70	6837	Type 2 Kombi 1970-73	Volkswagen 1970-81
7042	Strada	Fiat 1969-81			
6552	Suburban	Plymouth 1968-76	6837	Type 2 Vanagon 1981	Volkswagen 1970-81
6936	Suburban	Chevy/GMC Pick-Ups & Suburban 1970-87	5796	Type 3 Fastback & Squareback 1961-71	Volkswagen 1949-71
8055	Suburban	Chevy/GMC Pick-Ups & Suburban 1988-90	7081	Type 3 Fastback & Squareback 1970-73	Volkswagen 1970-70
6935	Sunbird	GM Subcompact 1971-80	5796	Type 4 411 1971	Volkswagen 1949-71
7059	Sunbird	Cavalier, Skyhawk, Cimarron, 2000, 1982-88	6837	Type 4 411 1971-72	Volkswagen 1970-81
7163	Sundance	Chrysler Front Wheel Drive 1981-88	5796	Type 4 412 1971	Volkswagen 1949-71
7043	Supra	Toyota Celica/Supra 1971-87	6845	Turismo	Omni/Horizon/Rampage 1978-88
8058	Supra	Toyota Celica/Supra 1986-90	5905	T-37	Tempest/GTO/LeMans 1968-73
6837	Super Beetle	Volkswagen 1970-81	6836	T-1000	Chevette/T-1000 1976-88
7199	SX-4	AMC 1975-86	6935	Vega	GM Subcompact 1971-80
7383	S-10 Blazer	Chevy S-10 Blazer/GMC S-15 Jimmy 1982-87	7346	Ventura	Pontiac Mid-Size 1974-83
7310	S-10 Pick-Up	Chevy S-10/GMC S-15 Pick-Ups 1982-87	6696	Versailles	Ford/Mercury/Lincoln Mid-Size 1971-85
7383	S-15 Jimmy	Chevy S-10 Blazer/GMC S-15 Jimmy 1982-87	6552	VIP	Plymouth 1968-76
7310	S-15 Pick-Up	Chevy S-10/GMC S-15 Pick-Ups 1982-87	7037	Vista	Colt/Challenger/Vista/Conquest 1971-88
7830	Taurus	Taurus/Sable/Continental 1986-89	6933	Vista Cruiser	Cutlass 1970-87
6845	TC-3	Omni/Horizon/Rampage 1978-88	6637	Volare	Aspen/Volare 1976-80
5905	Tempest	Tempest/GTO/LeMans 1968-73	7482	Voyager	Dodge Caravan/Plymouth Voyager 1984-88
7055	Tempo	Ford/Mercury Front Wheel Drive 1981-87	6326	V-100	Valiant/Duster 1968-76
7036	Tercel	Toyota Corolla/Carina/Tercel/Starlet 1970-87	6739	Wagoneer 1962-83	Jeep Wagoneer, Commando, Cherokee, Truck 1957-86
7081	Thing	Volkswagen 1970-81	7939	Wagoneer 1984-89	Jeep Wagoneer, Comanche, Cherokee 1984-89
6696	Thunderbird	Ford/Mercury/Lincoln Mid-Size 1971-85	8034	Wrangler	Jeep 1971-90
7814	Thunderbird	Thunderbird, Cougar, Continental 1980-87	7459	W100, 150, 200, 250, 300, 350	Dodge/Plymouth Trucks 1967-88
7055	Topaz	Ford/Mercury Front Wheel Drive 1981-87	7459	WM300	Dodge/Plymouth Trucks 1967-88
6320	Torino	Fairlane/Torino 1962-75	6842	XL	Ford/Mercury/Lincoln 1968-88
6696	Torino	Ford/Mercury/Lincoln Mid-Size 1971-85	6963	XR4Ti	Mustang/Capri/Merkur 1979-88
			6696	XR-7	Ford/Mercury/Lincoln Mid-Size 1971-85
7163	Town & Country	Chrysler Front Wheel Drive 1981-88	6982	XT Coupe	Subaru 1970-88
6842	Town Car	Ford/Mercury/Lincoln 1968-88	7042	X1/9	Fiat 1969-81
7135	Townsman	Chevrolet 1968-88	6965	Zephyr	Fairmont/Zephyr 1978-83
5795	Toyota Pickups	Toyota 1966-70	7059	Z-24	Cavalier, Skyhawk, Cimarron, 2000 1982-88
7035	Toyota Pickups	Toyota Trucks 1970-88			
7004	Toyota Van	Toyota Corona/Crown/Cressida/Mk.II/Van 1970-87	6735	Z-28	Camaro 1967-81
7459	Trail Duster	Dodge/Plymouth Trucks 1967-88	7318	Z-28	Camaro 1982-88
7046	Trans Am	Firebird 1967-81	6845	024	Omni/Horizon/Rampage 1978-88
7345	Trans Am	Firebird 1982-90	6844	3.0S, 3.0Si, 3.0CS	BMW 1970-88
7583	Tredia	Mitsubishi 1983-89	6817	4-63	Jeep 1981-87

Chilton's Repair Manuals are available at your local retailer or by mailing a check or money order for **$15.95** per book plus **$3.50** for 1st book and **$.50** for each additional book to cover postage and handling to:

**Chilton Book Company
Dept. DM
Radnor, PA 19089**

NOTE: When ordering be sure to include your name & address, book part No. & title.

CHILTON'S REPAIR MANUAL MODEL INDEX

Car and truck model names are listed in alphabetical and numerical order

Chilton's Repair Manuals are available at your local retailer or by mailing a check or money order for **$15.95** per book plus **$3.50** for 1st book and **$.50** for each additional book to cover postage and handling to:

Chilton Book Company
Dept. DM
Radnor, PA 19089

NOTE: When ordering be sure to include your name & address, book part No. & title.

CHILTON'S REPAIR MANUAL MODEL INDEX
Car and truck model names are listed in alphabetical and numerical order

Part No.	Model	Repair Manual Title	Part No.	Model	Repair Manual Title
6844	1500	DMW 1970-88	6844	2000	BMW 1970-88
6936	1500	Chevy/GMC Pick-Ups & Suburban 1970-87	6844	2002, 2002Ti, 2002Tii	BMW 1970-88
8055	1500	Chevy/GMC Pick-Ups & Suburban 1988-90	6936	2500	Chevy/GMC Pick-Ups & Suburban 1970-87
6844	1600	BMW 1970-88	8055	2500	Chevy/GMC Pick-Ups & Suburban 1988-90
5790	1600	Datsun 1961-72			
6982	1600DL, 1600GL, 1600GLF	Subaru 1970-88	6844	2500	BMW 1970-88
6844	1600-2	BMW 1970-88	6844	2800	BMW 1970-88
6844	1800	BMW 1970-88	6936	3500	Chevy/GMC Pick-Ups & Suburban 1970-87
6982	1800DL, 1800GL, 1800GLF	Subaru 1970-88	8055	3500	Chevy/GMC Pick-Ups & Suburban 1988-90
6529	1800, 1800S	Volvo 1956-69	7028	4000	Audi 4000/5000 1978-81
7040	1800E, 1800ES	Volvo 1970-88	7028	5000	Audi 4000/5000 1978-81
5790	2000	Datsun 1961-72	7309	6000	Celebrity, Century, Ciera, 6000 1982-88
7059	2000	Cavalier, Skyhawk, Cimarron, 2000 1982-88			